Voces del
Pueblo

Contextos Series

RAY HERNÁNDEZ-DURÁN, RICHARD SANTOS, MICHAEL TRUJILLO, and **IRENE VÁSQUEZ,** Series Editors

In keeping with the transdisciplinary mission of the Southwest Hispanic Research Institute (SHRI) at the University of New Mexico, the Contextos Series publishes books that deepen our understanding of the historical, social, political, and cultural issues that impact Latinas and Latinos. Topics may span regional, national, and transnational contexts. We invite scholarship in Chicana and Chicano Studies, the social sciences, public policy, the humanities, health and natural science, and other professional fields.

Also available in the Contextos Series:

Borderland Brutalities: Violence and Resistance along the US-Mexico Borderlands in Literature, Film, and Culture by Laura Elena Belmonte

Joaquín Ortega: Forging Pan-Americanism at the University of New Mexico by Russ Davidson

Making Aztlán: Ideology and Culture of the Chicana and Chicano Movement, 1966–1977 by Irene Vásquez and Juan Gómez-Quiñones

Voces del Pueblo

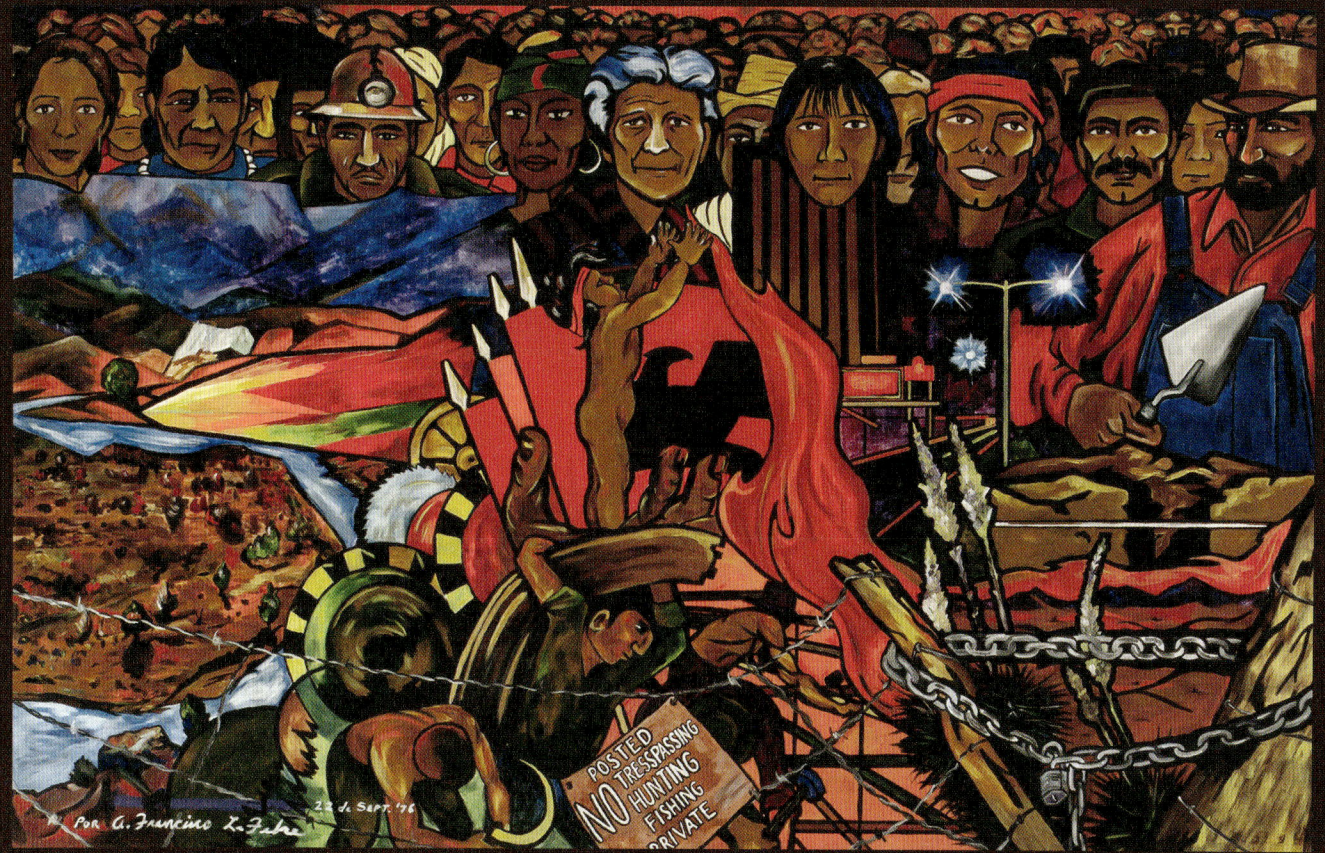

ARTISTS OF THE LEVANTAMIENTO CHICANO IN NEW MEXICO

Ray Hernández-Durán and Irene Vásquez

university of new mexico press
albuquerque

ISBN 978-0-8263-6873-7 (paper)
ISBN 978-0-8263-6874-4 (ePub)

Library of Congress Control Number: 2025006775

Founded in 1889, the University of New Mexico sits on the traditional homelands of the Pueblo of Sandia. The original peoples of New Mexico—Pueblo, Navajo, and Apache—since time immemorial have deep connections to the land and have made significant contributions to the broader community statewide. We honor the land itself and those who remain stewards of this land throughout the generations and also acknowledge our committed relationship to Indigenous peoples. We gratefully recognize our history.

Cover image and frontispiece by Francisco Lefebre,
    Realidades de Nuevo México, 1976.
Designed by Isaac Morris
Composed in Bembo 10 | 13.25,
    Display: BC Monument, BC Parlament, and Broadwinsor,.

Contents

Acknowledgments

The production of this exhibition and catalog would not have been possible without broad community support. The curators would thus like to express their gratitude to the following individuals, units, and institutions.

The curators extend heartfelt thanks to the City of Albuquerque and the Albuquerque City Council members for the enthusiasm expressed for this exhibition and for the generous funding they provided. Councilperson Ken Sanchez as an early supporter championed the City's resources allocation. We acknowledge the integral support of four community leaders who have been committed to this project: Senator Antoinette Sedillo López, Representative Art De La Cruz, Senator Antonio "Moe" Maestas, and Representative Patricia Roybal Caballero. Regarding financial and administrative assistance throughout the planning process, the Department of Chicana and Chicano Studies and the Southwest Hispanic Research Institute at the University of New Mexico have been of central importance in conceptualizing and realizing the exhibition and the accompanying catalog. The curators wish to recognize the specific contributions of Jacqueline Alderete, Unit Administrator I; Antoinette Rael, Department Administrator I; and Rebecca Martínez-Baca, Operations Specialist. Additionally, CCS students Vivian Felipe, Howard Griego, and Ashley Martinez provided research support for the project.

Sincere thanks to Jadira Gurulé, art museum manager and head curator; Emily Hanawalt, head registrar; Jacob Gutiérrez and Adri De La Cruz, set and exhibit designers; and the National Hispanic Cultural Center for agreeing to host the exhibition, for their guidance through the exhibition planning process, and for the labor that went into preparing the galleries and all materials for installation. Much gratitude, also, to Andrew Connors, museum director, and William T. Gassaway, assistant curator, both at the Albuquerque Museum, and to Arif Khan, director, and Angel Jiang, curator of collections and study room initiatives, both at the University of New Mexico Art Museum, for providing venues for related events, as well as for providing invaluable assistance with object loans and image reproduction permission requests.

The curators are indebted to Elise McHugh, senior acquisitions editor; Anna Pohlod, editor; Patricia Kot, copyeditor; James Ayers, assistant director and editorial, design, and production manager; and the University of New Mexico Press for believing in the project and approving the catalog's publication. From meeting with the curators to discuss the project to receiving the manuscript and sending it to reviewers to helping get the revised draft into production, the publication of the catalog would not have been possible without the encouragement, guidance, and efforts of the University of New Mexico Press staff, which included designing the book cover, promoting the book, and preparing the manuscript for publication.

The curators thank photographer Stefan Jennings Batista, who lent his time and skills to documenting the artworks featured in the exhibition. This job entailed long road trips to artists' homes, shooting selected works, sometimes in less-than-ideal conditions, and providing the images included in this catalog. Stefan has been consistently accommodating and willing to offer any assistance needed. The result of his efforts are the striking photographs in the catalog that beautifully capture the featured artworks. Also, thanks to Aaron Anthony Anaya, who photographed several murals in Santa Fe.

A special thanks must go to Sonja Elena Gandert, Phillip B. (Felipe) Gonzales, and Howard Griego for accepting the curators' invitation to write for the catalog. Their respective essays, which are well researched, insightful, and informative, will be significant contributions to the study of New Mexican Chicana and Chicano art moving forward.

The curators express their deepest gratitude to the private collectors for graciously lending artworks and, in particular, to David Montoya and Susan Seymour for sharing invaluable documentary photographs.

Most of all, we are indebted to the participating artists—Ignacio "Nacho" Jaramillo, Juanita J. Lavadie, Francisco Lefebre, Noel Márquez, Roberta Márquez, and Adelita M. Medina—for their lifelong activism, for sharing their work with the community, and for agreeing to be a part of this groundbreaking exhibition. None of this would have been accomplished without their interest and investment in the project, and most importantly, their work. The artists form the heart of this exhibition, and their creative output is shaped by and embodies the wisdom and power that emanate from *familia*, *comunidad*, and *tradición*, all things worth fighting for. The curators hope that those values and sources of inspiration, which have shaped the artists' creative practice and the production of this exhibit and catalog, come through.

The curators wish to dedicate this publication to the memory of Noel Márquez (1953–2020), a *nuevomexicano* Chicano activist and artist, whose stunning work is included in this exhibition. An accomplished and prolific master, Noel was incredibly excited to be a part of this project and wholeheartedly supported it until his death. Sincere thanks to Noel's widow, Madelene Aguinaldo, who was extremely accommodating, despite her loss and busy schedule. Madelene worked with the curators to ensure that her late husband's work was accessible and properly represented in the exhibition and catalog. With Noel's legacy in mind, we conclude with a statement he made in spring 2019 that captures not just the impetus behind these artists' work but the point of this exhibition: "Does activism have a place in our state? You're damn right! We need to start making avenues and talking to people to change this whole culture so that we're more than just quaint and folkloric. We have a strong culture behind us. That's what I'd like to put in everyone's mind, that there's a lot more to do."[1]

Note

1. Ray Hernández-Durán and Irene Vásquez (moderators), "*Artistas del Pueblo*: In Conversation with the History of New Mexican Chicanx Art," *Hemisphere: Visual Cultures of the Americas*, Mandolen Sánchez (ed.), Vol. XII (Department of Art, University of New Mexico, 2019), 94.

Preface

About the Exhibition

The idea for this exhibit originated in spring 2018 during planning discussions to commemorate the fiftieth anniversary of the establishment of Chicana and Chicano Studies (CCS) at the University of New Mexico. Numerous activities and events were scheduled, including programming highlighting *movimiento* activists in New Mexico. CCS faculty and staff had also been invited to serve on the hosting committee for the National Association of Chicana and Chicano Studies (NACCS) conference, which had been scheduled to be held in Albuquerque in April 2019. Leading up to the conference, CCS decided to feature the work of Chicana and Chicano Movement (CCM) artists to explore the rich dynamic between art advocacy and social and political organizing; consequently, CCS proposed an exhibit showcasing the work of a group of artists who were part of the early movement in the state. This exhibit was also meant to underscore how many local Chicana and Chicano artists had gone unrecognized, even though New Mexico had long been the site for Chicana and Chicano activism and of rich artistic traditions.

Francisco Lefebre, an artist and educator with over fifty years of experience as a muralist in New Mexico, was a significant inspiration for the exhibit. As part of the fiftieth anniversary planning, Francisco developed the early concept for the exhibit. He shared it with Dr. Irene Vásquez, chair of the Department of Chicana and Chicano Studies at UNM. At the time, Francisco was restoring the *Nuestra Juventud* mural at Albuquerque High School, where CCS had implemented dual enrollment classes. Irene, as a scholar of the CCM, had previously written about the movement and its art with Chicano historian Dr. Juan Gómez-Quiñones in the book they coauthored, titled, *Making Aztlán: Ideology and Culture of the Chicana and Chicano Movement, 1966–1977* (2014).[1] After preliminary discussions, Irene and Francisco agreed to approach Dr. Ray Hernández-Durán, a professor of art history and museum studies in the Department of Art at UNM, about collaborating on an exhibit featuring *nuevomexicano* artists of the early Chicana and Chicano Movement period.

After discussing the concept of the proposed show in spring 2018, Ray agreed to work with Irene on the exhibition. Shortly after, they started drafting a formal exhibition proposal to present to local museums to confirm an exhibition venue and dates. Since Irene and Ray are faculty members at the University of New Mexico, they decided to hold the exhibition and related programs in Albuquerque; the exhibition venues they considered were thus local and included the University of New Mexico Art Museum, the Albuquerque Museum, and the National Hispanic Cultural Center. Irene and Ray first approached the NHCC, given the history that several of the featured artists had with this institution and the center's record of exhibitions and programming highlighting local New Mexican art and artists. The NHCC staff reviewed the exhibition proposal and agreed to host the show.

To promote the exhibition, in fall 2018, Irene and Ray submitted session proposals to the National Association of Chicana and Chicano Studies (NACCS) and Imagining America conferences, both of which were scheduled to take place in Albuquerque in spring 2019. Accepted to both events, they co-moderated panel discussions on New Mexican Chicana and Chicano art with four of the six participating artists. Concurrently, Ray, as faculty advisor to the Art Department's graduate student journal, *Hemisphere: Visual Cultures of the Americas*, and the chief editor of the journal that year, MA student Mandolen Sánchez, decided to dedicate the issue to US Latinx art. Along with articles on Pepón Osorio, Guillermo Gómez-Peña, Josué Rojas, and Patssi Váldez, including an artist spotlight on queer Latinx artist Martín Wannam, and a transcription of a panel discussion on *Tejana* zines moderated by Claudia Zapata—originally presented at the *Latino Art Now* conference in Houston—the volume included an edited transcription of the panel discussion that Ray and Irene co-moderated at the NACCS conference.

Inspired by these developments, in fall 2019, Ray taught a new course on US Latinx art, which included a section on New Mexican Chicana and Chicano artists. That semester, he was also awarded funding to organize the Gale Memorial Lecture Series, which he organized around Latinx artists. As part of the speaker series, Ray moderated a panel discussion with four of the six New Mexican Chicana and Chicano artists to be featured in the exhibition. Participating venues for the speaker series included the UNM Art Museum, the National Hispanic Cultural Center, and the Albuquerque Museum; the events were well attended and generated much interest. With the course, the speaker series, the conference sessions, the journal, and social media posts, the exhibition was widely promoted and began to generate interest, support, and traction among the local community, as well as among Latinx art historians around the country. Exemplifying the local support generated for this project was a $30,000 grant Ray and Irene received from the City Council of Albuquerque in spring 2020. Community consensus was that the focus on New Mexican Chicana and Chicano artists was overdue, timely, and needed.

As part of the early proposal, Irene and Francisco had generated a working list of New Mexican Chicana and Chicano artists who were active during the early period, ca. 1970; they contacted the people on the list and informed them about the exhibition. A few people had died, others had moved away, some had not held on to any artwork or had sold or given work without keeping a record, and a few were uninterested in participating or didn't respond. When the planning for the exhibition began, it became immediately apparent that strict parameters had to be put in place to guide the exhibition focus and selection process. With this objective in mind, Ray and Irene chose to concentrate on a small group of artists who were affiliated with New Mexico Highlands University in Las Vegas, New Mexico, one of the main sites for activism during the early Chicano Movement in the state. The final criteria for participation included the following: 1) the exhibition would feature living New Mexican artists (an exception would have to be made, sadly, following the death of Noel Márquez not long after he accepted the invitation to participate and the exhibition planning began); 2) participating artists had to be living in New Mexico; 3) participating artists had to be affiliated with New Mexico Highlands University in Las Vegas or somehow be connected to that community; 4) participating artists had to self-identify as Chicana or Chicano; 5) participating artists had to have been involved in the early Chicano Movement in New Mexico ca. 1970; 6) participating artists would need to have work made between 1970 and the present; 7) participating artists had to have work that could be exhibited; 8) preference would be shown to artists who were lesser known nationally; and 9) artists had to express interest in the project and be willing to participate. With these nine criteria in place, a group of six artists was selected as the focus of the exhibition, three men and three women, among them: Ignacio "Nacho" Jaramillo, Juanita J. Lavadie, Francisco Lefebre, Noel Márquez, Roberta Márquez, and Adelita M. Medina. Given that the exhibit would feature material that had not been previously documented, published, and/or exhibited, the exhibition planning presented a series of challenges that inevitably informed the parameters of the show, the criteria for inclusion, and the works selected for exhibition.

Since most artworks were in the possession of the artists, with a few in private or museum collections, Irene and Ray had to conduct studio visits, which meant driving across the state to cities, including Albuquerque, Las Vegas, Santa Fe, Taos, and Artesia. In summer 2019, Ray and Irene visited these various locations with Francisco Lefebre's assistance and met with the artists, discussed their work, and selected material for the exhibition. Follow-up studio visits were then conducted in 2023 and 2024 to complete the remaining photography and finalize the object checklist. A preliminary checklist was generated after initial studio visits, which Ray and Irene reviewed. They then chose works from that longer list for the final checklist of approximately 148 works by these 6 artists; among the media represented were panel painting, drawing, prints, photography, textiles, and sculpture. Given the significance of murals to the Chicano art movement, it was decided to include murals via a video documentary and a catalog essay on Chicana and Chicano murals in New Mexico.

The project, focusing on New Mexican Chicana and Chicano artists of the first generation, consists of four parts: the exhibition; an exhibition catalog with scholarly essays; programming (i.e., lectures, panel discussions, tours, poetry readings, and music events); and a digital archive to support future research (the development of the archive, which will be housed at the Center for Southwest Research at Zimmerman Library at UNM, will be an ongoing project). The exhibition catalog includes five scholarly essays: the first essay by Ray Hernández-Durán examines the historical development of New Mexico's art institutions and its tricultural identity to begin exploring reasons for the general disregard Chicana and Chicano artists have faced; the second essay, also by Hernández-Durán, features the six artists in the show and provides biographical information and an introduction to a selection of each artist's work; the third essay, coauthored by Irene Vásquez and Howard Griego, PhD candidate in CCS, looks at the production of Chicana and Chicano murals in New Mexico; the fourth essay by Sonja Elena Gandert, PhD candidate in Latinx art history at CUNY Graduate Center in New York (also, daughter of New Mexican photographer Miguel Gandert), considers the unique materials and processes characterizing New Mexican Chicana and Chicano arts traditions; and finally, the fifth essay by Phillip B. (Felipe) Gonzales, professor emeritus in sociology at UNM, traces the history of the Chicano Movement in New Mexico during its early years.

Although the exhibition and the accompanying catalog focus on a small group of artists who were connected to New Mexico Highlands University at the beginning of the Chicano Movement in New Mexico, the curators are aware that many other artists were active during the early years of the movement and in the decades that followed. This exhibition is not intended to be comprehensive or the final word on the subject; rather, it is meant to serve as a first step in the study and documentation of this critical period in the history of art in New Mexico and the broader Chicano art movement. In terms of New Mexican Chicana and Chicano art, there is still a need to look at those artists who worked elsewhere in New Mexico, such as Albuquerque, Santa Fe, and Las Cruces, among other cities, not just in the 1970s but throughout the 1980s and 1990s. Future projects could focus on works by New Mexican Chicana artists, works by contemporary New Mexican Chicana and Chicano artists, or works by New Mexican LGBTQ+ Chicanx artists. Possible exhibitions could also be medium specific and focus on New Mexican Chicana and Chicano photography, printmaking, textile work, performance, and so on; the list of potential projects is long. As stated, the hope is that this exhibition, the catalog, and the attendant programming will bring these gifted artists to a broader public, locally and nationally, and inspire further research in an area deserving more attention than it has received until now.

About the Curators

Dr. Irene Vásquez was born in El Paso, Texas, and grew up in California. She received her PhD in Latin American history from the Department of History at the University of California, Los Angeles, and began her teaching career at East Los Angeles College. She then went on to chair the Department of Chicana and Chicano Studies at California State University, Dominguez Hills. She began her position as director of what was then known as Chicano/Hispano/Mexicano Studies at UNM in the fall semester of 2011. In 2014, she transitioned from director to chair of the Department of Chicana and Chicano Studies, which she helped found. Over the years, she has taught Introduction to Chicana and Chicano Studies and The Chicana and Chicano Movement to undergraduates and currently teaches the Practicum in Chicana and Chicano Studies at the graduate level. In addition to serving as chair of CCS, Irene is the director of the Southwest Hispanic Research Institute, where she relaunched the University of New Mexico Press series *Contextos* and coestablished the journal *Chamisa: A Journal of Literary, Performance, and Visual Arts of the Greater Southwest* with Dr. Ray Hernández-Durán and Dr. Leila Flores-Dueñas. In 2015, Irene served as co-curator for the exhibition *Mexico at the Hour of Combat* with Dr. Devorah Romanek, former curator of exhibits at the Maxwell Museum of Anthropology at UNM.

Dr. Ray Hernández-Durán was born and raised in San Antonio, Texas. He received his PhD in Prehispanic and colonial Latin American art history at the University of Chicago. As a graduate student, he taught at Chicago-area schools, including the University of Illinois-Chicago, DePaul University, and Columbia College. Ray's first tenure-track job offer was at UNM, where he has been a faculty member in the Department of Art since fall 2003. At UNM, he is affiliated with Latin American Studies, the Latin American and Iberian Institute, the Department of Chicana and Chicano Studies, the Department of Africana Studies, Museum Studies, and the Southwest Hispanic Research Institute. Although he is the professor of Spanish colonial art and architecture in the Department of Art, he also teaches Arts of Nineteenth-Century Mexico, Arts of Spain (1500–1850), Baroque Art and Architecture, Arts of Africa and the African Diaspora, Chicano and Latinx Art, and Museum Studies. Outside of teaching, Ray has acquired extensive curatorial experience at various museums nationally, including the Art Institute of Chicago, the Smithsonian in Washington, DC, the Smart Museum at the University of Chicago, the Huntington Gallery at UT Austin, and the UNM Art Museum. He serves as chief coeditor with Dr. Irene Vásquez and Dr. Leila Flores-Dueñas of *Chamisa: A Journal of Literary, Performance, and Visual Arts of the Greater Southwest*, which they cofounded and is sponsored by the Southwest Hispanic Research Institute.

Irene and Ray recognize this project's potential significance not only to the history of art in New Mexico or to Chicana and Chicano art history, but also to Latinx art history and US American art history, more broadly. After meeting and getting to know the artists, studying their work, and researching the movement's history in New Mexico, this exhibition became a labor of love for the curators. They hope that their investment, effort, and care are evident in the material presented in this publication, whose primary aim is to document and honor the lives and work of New Mexican artists who helped shape the Chicano Movement at its inception and whose creativity and activism remain vibrant and relevant today.

Note

1. See Juan Gómez-Quiñones and Irene Vásquez, *Making Aztlán: Ideology and Culture of the Chicana and Chicano Movement, 1966–1977* (Albuquerque, NM: *Contextos* Series, University of New Mexico Press, 2014).

One

El pueblo y su arte

Locating Chicana and Chicano Artists

in the Arts Culture of New Mexico

RAY HERNÁNDEZ-DURÁN

"A borderland is a vague and undetermined place created by the emotional residue of an unnatural boundary. It is in a constant state of transition. The prohibited and forbidden are its inhabitants."[1]

—

Introduction

When considering the Chicano art movement in New Mexico and the work done by native-born New Mexican Chicana and Chicano artists who have lived and worked in the state, the noticeable absence of significant scholarship on the subject is not just apparent but striking. What makes this neglect most surprising is the presence of an academic institution like the University of New Mexico, where Chicana and Chicano Studies has been an established program for the last fifty years, and Chicano Art History was taught for two decades as part of the Art of the Americas concentration in the Department of Art. Motivated by an interest in examining the reasons for this disregard, I propose that the marginal attention New Mexican Chicana and Chicano artists have received can be explained in part by looking at the official arts culture in the state of New Mexico, as it has been carefully cultivated and promoted for the past century by various state institutions focused on the visual arts. In this essay, I consider how the arts in New Mexico have been shaped by the institutions and cultural practices that were introduced in the early twentieth century and that have since then selectively documented certain local artistic traditions and promoted them as representative of New Mexican art.

Since the region's absorption by the United States, first as a territory and later as a state, academic, museological, and commercial conversations on the arts in New Mexico have tended to focus on one of three bodies of work associated with a generalized reading of what has been seen as the state's primary demographics: Native art of the Pueblos; "traditional" Spanish, *Hispano*, and/or Spanish colonial arts; and modern art, specifically that produced by white non-Hispanic artists who settled in New Mexico or spent time there in the early twentieth century. I suggest that this tripartite cultural framework has yielded exclusionary structural effects in terms of what bodies of work are typically highlighted, studied, and promoted as New Mexican, while effectively marginalizing—if not erasing, from institutional conversations and programs—other communities and artistic practices in the state, including the arts produced by self-identified Chicana and Chicano artists.[2] This historical discussion is not intended to address the full complexity of issues that a more thoroughly developed study would offer, but rather to initiate a thoughtful consideration of the New Mexican Chicana and Chicano artists featured in this exhibition; a topic in need of further exploration. In the end, what I propose is that a study aimed at analyzing the Chicana and Chicano art movement in New Mexico must be approached with a deeper historical perspective, going back to at least the mid-nineteenth century, if not earlier, given both the state's unique place in the history not just of the United States but of the Americas, and that the legacies of colonialism (Spanish/Hispano/Mexican and Anglo American) continue to shape New Mexico's institutional practices, cultural identity, and social life.

US Imperialism and Anglo-American Colonialism: Setting the Stage for the Official Arts Culture in the State of New Mexico

"Now the Mexicans are no better than Indians, and I see no reason why we should not go on in the same course now and take their land."[3]
—

The history of the Indo-Hispano populations in the Americas, as is widely known, began with Christopher Columbus's fateful voyage across the Atlantic in 1492 in search of a trade route with Asia per the instructions of the Catholic monarchs in Spain, Ferdinand and Isabella. That event eventually led to Spanish and European awareness of the Americas as a continent; a new territory that Spain was quick to claim. The first Spanish city in the Western Hemisphere was Santo Domingo, founded in 1496 on the island of Hispaniola, today known as Haiti and the Dominican Republic. By 1519, Hernan Cortés would arrive on the gulf coast of what today is Mexico, two years before the culmination of the so-called Conquest of Mexico in 1521.[4] With settlements established in the Caribbean, the Spanish sent expeditions to explore the coastal and mainland regions of the Americas. One such expedition, which embarked on a mission to explore Florida, led to the first non-natives known to have entered the US Southwest. Those individuals were the survivors of the expedition led by Panfilo de Narváez, which shipwrecked off the coast of Texas in 1527. The survivors wandered for nine years, crossing what today is Texas and proceeding into New Mexico, where they reached Acoma, before eventually finding their way back down to Mexico City in 1536.

During that time, the viceroyalty of New Spain had been founded and the first Hapsburg Spanish viceroy, Antonio de Mendoza, had taken his place as the king's representative in the imperial capital of these distant American territories. Upon hearing the Narváez expedition survivors' reports, Mendoza sent the governor of Nueva Galicia, Francisco Vásquez de Coronado, who had accompanied Mendoza from Spain in 1535, to explore these unknown regions. Coronado made it as far north as Kansas; however, his mission was ultimately a failure, and he returned to Mexico City in 1542, after which he resumed his governorship of Nueva Galicia. The next major excursion northward did not happen until 1598 when the Novohispanic viceroy Luis de Velasco approved an expedition to be led by Juan de Oñate. Oñate's expedition produced more fruitful results since it led to the foundation of Santa Fe in the newly christened kingdom of *Nuevo México*, of which Oñate served as governor from 1598 through 1610. The larger region, generally considered a part of the northern provinces of New Spain or *tierra adentro*, remained a frontier of the larger viceroyalty across various geopolitical shifts that unfolded throughout the three-century period of Spanish viceregal rule until 1821 when Mexico declared its independence from Spain.[5]

The history of what today is recognized as the state of New Mexico is deep and complicated. It begins with the longstanding Indigenous presence in the region through the Spanish colonial and Mexican periods, and then US intervention, largely defined by the region's transition to American territory in the mid-nineteenth century, followed by statehood in the early twentieth century.[6] The area comprising New Mexico became US territory following the so-called Mexican-American War of 1846–1848, when Mexico lost the northern half of its national territory to the US, which included the annexation of Texas in 1845, the Mexican Cession of 1848, and finally, the Gadsden Purchase in 1853.[7] New Mexico was a US territory from 1853 until 1912, when it officially became a US state; however, Anglos or non-Hispanic whites began arriving from east of the Mississippi, first in Texas and soon after in New Mexico, starting in 1821, the same year that Mexico declared its independence from Spain.[8]

The transition to US territory, however, was not a smooth or peaceful process. Natives and Mexicans throughout the Southwest formed alliances and resisted the invasive US presence, exemplified by the uprising that occurred in Taos, New Mexico, in 1847, which was followed by ongoing conflicts with local communities. As Lawrence R. Murphy notes,

> That the permanent settlement of the Southwest could not be accomplished peacefully became clear during the early months of 1847 when word reached Santa Fe of a bloody anti-American revolt in Taos. Nationalistic Mexican forces there, allied with Indians from the nearby Pueblo, had marched through the streets, massacring and mutilating all who had joined sides with the United States. New Mexico Governor Charles Bent, Taos Sheriff Stephen Luis Lee, and attorney James W. Leal were among the dead. The bloodshed spread rapidly to the nearby towns of Mora, Río Colorado, and Arroyo Hondo.[9]

Conflicts notwithstanding, Anglo incursion increased from 1846 through the end of the US Civil War in 1865, and particularly, after the construction of the railroad ca. 1869–1880; however, it wasn't until the 1920s that the first "colonies" of white writers and artists began to form in Taos and Santa Fe.[10] Attracted to the region's temperate climate, the natural landscape, and the "exotic" Native and *Mexicano* communities that had long inhabited the area, Anglos flocked to New Mexico in search of better health, affordable living conditions, and new cultural experiences, which included a desire to satiate their curiosity about these new populations who, for better or worse, would in time become fellow American citizens. Given the recent conflict with their southern neighbor, US Americans generally held virulently racist anti-Native and anti-Mexican (also anti-Catholic) views. In a presidential debate held in 1858, Abraham Lincoln stated, "I understand that the people of Mexico are most decidedly a race of mongrels," a declaration that captures the derisive anti-Mexican attitudes common to the era.[11] Such biases were fully expressed by Anglos upon their arrival in the recently expropriated Mexican territories, where they came to inform the treatment of local populations.

The larger territory, now identified as the US Southwest, had been part of an older, parallel, colonial settler system, first, as a northern province of the viceroyalty of New Spain beginning in the sixteenth century, and later (albeit briefly), as national territory of independent Mexico from 1821 through 1835 and 1848, respectively. As such, the region and the communities inhabiting it had developed along quite different political, economic, and cultural lines than those areas along the US East Coast associated with British New England and the Anglo-dominated US, a territory that up until then was primarily delimited by the Atlantic coast to the east and the Mississippi River to the west. When the much larger, primarily Native and Mexican western region was subsumed into the Anglo-American union, it was integrated into a different Eurocentric cultural framework—a specifically Anglocentric one—whose perspectives and value system came to dominate and reshape the values and practices the Anglo visitors and settlers came into contact with in these "new" American regions. As Wayne Moquin and Charles Van Doren describe, "The Mexicans were overwhelmed by the newcomers. Almost at once, they became outsiders in their own homeland, as the Anglos poured in by the thousands with new ideas and ways."[12] Joseph Traugott, discussing this process of invasion and assimilation, took a broader historical perspective when he added, "Because the imposition on Native and Hispanic communities of US laws, economic relationships, religious rituals, and profiteering is reminiscent of Spain's dictates over the Pueblos during the *entrada*, I have described this as the American Colonial period in New Mexico."[13]

In New Mexico, after centuries of varying degrees of Spanish viceregal control and the concomitant presence of an increasingly rooted Novohispanic settler population, new and old communities adapted. Although early encounters between Hispano settlers and Natives were often violent, over time, the Indigenous Pueblos and Hispano villages adjusted to and became familiar with one another ("*se acomodaron*") and generally coexisted in a tenuous peace amid periodic tensions.[14] The most significant conflict in the region was the Pueblo Revolt of 1680, organized in part by the Indigenous leader from Ohkay Owingeh, Popay, followed by the Spanish reconquest of the area twelve years later in 1692 under the leadership of Diego de Vargas.[15] Native and Hispano communities not only coexisted, whether by force or circumstance, but came to embrace cultural exchange as a form of adaptation and survival; they traded, interacted socially, and formed relationships, such as those based on *compadrazgo*, or what can be seen as a form of diplomatic cohabitation with familial ties strengthening community relations.[16] The majority of settlers, who came primarily from central New Spain and included creoles and mestizos, central Mexican Natives, and others of mixed-race and Black heritage, settled in areas where they had access to water and could build *acequias* and farm. These settlements were often based in proximity to Indigenous communities. Over time, these populations came to recognize one another's boundaries as they went about their daily lives, but boundaries were often porous, meaning that the communities wound up borrowing cultural elements from one another; members of various communities also intermarried or mixed, a long process that effectively blurred lines and troubles any purist interest in maintaining discreet Hispano and Native identities.[17] These relationships took shape over several centuries and contributed to the development of distinct New Mexican communities and cultural practices—that is, until US Anglos began to arrive.

It is important to note that the New Mexican Indo-Hispano population should not be regarded as a monolithic whole. Despite the predominantly rural nature of life in the region, given its status as a frontier or province of New Spain, social hierarchies existed with castes defined not just by perceived racial identity but also by distinctions between Hispano families who owned the largest tracts of land versus those who lived on and worked that land. As historian Ramón A. Gutiérrez noted,

The land on which Hispanos toiled was inequitably distributed. The *ricos*, as the "rich" or large landholders were called, enjoyed the life of a comfortable regional gentry, engaged in mercantile activity, and lived by exploiting their retainers, their poorer kin, and their share-croppers (*partidarios*). The majority of New Mexico's *pobres*, or land "poor" farmers, eked out a living by working their small private plots and by grazing their livestock on land held in common by their communities as Mercedes, or land grants.[18]

As has historically been the case in most every colonial context, a segment of the local population, normally social elites or those desiring elite status, seeing the writing on the wall and interested in preserving rights and privileges (or gaining them), works with the new establishment, and as such, becomes complicit in the continued or intensified oppression of their less fortunate, lowly placed compatriots; New Mexico was not an exception to this established pattern. Gloria Anzaldúa, discussing her experience growing up in the Southwest, referred to this very phenomenon, not as a historical fact but as evident in the present, when she wrote, "The only 'legitimate' inhabitants [in the borderlands] are those in power, the whites and those who align themselves with whites."[19]

New Anglo arrivals, who were typically well educated and affluent, wielded considerable socioeconomic and political power within the new system being introduced into the region. Local communities were exposed to the alien cultural and social dynamics being introduced. The most insidious of these dynamics were Anglo forms of racism and classism, both of which, in terms of the arts and other kinds of cultural production, fed a sense of cultural and racial superiority among recent arrivals that resulted in a form of cultural paternalism, as far as perceptions of local cultural ways and traditional art production were concerned. The concomitant introduction of capitalistic practices and the redistribution of land restructured local economic systems and arts cultures across all communities. Indigenous and Hispano art forms were reframed as craft, folk, popular, decorative, or utilitarian arts, all categories that were situated lower on the Eurocentric cultural hierarchy that fetishized and overvalued European art forms regarded as fine art, such as painting, sculpture, printmaking, photography, and so on. This form of cultural Darwinism inevitably shaped ideas about a community's degree of advancement and intellectual development, justifying outside intervention and the perceived need to document and preserve what was seen, in certain cases, as "traditional" and an index of a given culture's essential nature and development; in other cases, new interests aimed to erase what was deemed primitive, backward, and contrary to modernization. In all cases, there was a fetishization of various local communities' living artforms that disrupted established, meaningful practices. There was a clear appreciation for the technical quality and esthetics of Native and *Mexicano* arts, but Anglo interest in and patronage of local art forms were informed by this new value system, which manifested in the early collecting practices of the late nineteenth- and early twentieth centuries.

Early Anglo interest in the historical cultures of New Mexico initially focused on Indigenous arts. This interest reflected broader ideas that were academic and political in nature, among them, the anthropological concern over the disappearing "Indian" and US national interest in identifying and claiming its own ancient "classical" cultures. As Erin Shalev observed, "Citizens of the early Republic were not the first to identify the similarities of Natives and classical ancients: from the early days of the Encounter, Europeans had commented on this supposed resemblance . . . The motives, function and context of the representation of indigenous Americans as classical ancients in the declining years of the eighteenth century carried distinct political overtones."[20] Just as Europe had Greece and Rome, the US could now lay claim to an ancient Indigenous heritage of its own, leading to the study and preservation of Native cultural practices and the selective collecting of certain examples of Indigenous material cultures; however, the intrusion of outside influences into the area and the imposition of non-Native esthetics and practices in art production began to inevitably alter so-called traditional art forms. Where Indigenous and Hispano art forms had coexisted, moved across communities, and fed one another, these interpolated artistic traditions were severed and defined as distinct in the new cultural system taking hold.

In line with prominent ideas of the time, US President Theodore Roosevelt himself promoted the idea that white Americans, as members of a more advanced and moral society, were obliged to "civilize" non-white, non-European cultures; in this case, tribal or Native communities, but, interestingly, also the rural Catholic Mexican or Hispanic populations in the region. Such an objective was striking but not surprising coming from representatives of a Protestant-identified nation whose cultural perspective tended to view Catholicism as a religion that promoted ignorance and superstition and was corrupt, backward, and anti-progress; such anti-Catholic sentiments could be traced back centuries to conflicts originating in sixteenth-century Europe and later brought by European settlers to the Americas.[21]

An additional factor motivating the interest in Native arts, in line with developments in the broader art world of the time, was the expectation that they might revitalize non-Hispanic Euro-American art, not unlike what was happening concurrently in Western Europe where modern artists like Pablo Picasso and others were looking outside of Europe to Africa and the Americas, as well as to Europe's prehistory, for new formal models as an antidote to what was perceived as an exhausted arts tradition.[22] Driven in part by such ideas, US imperialism extended west of the Mississippi, leading to a recolonization of the Southwest and West Coast, including a wave of Anglo-led colonialist practices in New Mexico. This phenomenon was not unlike what had transpired in central New Spain 350 years earlier under the direction of the Spanish Crown and Catholic Church.[23]

By the late nineteenth century, Indigenous children began receiving Eurocentric art instruction at mission schools in New Mexico, not under the authority of the Spanish viceregal government or the Catholic Church, as had happened before, but now in response to the Anglo-American presence, which included the religious, scholars, artists, settlers, and tourists. The artwork produced by these Native Pueblo students, formally European but Native in terms of subject matter, was initially sold to white members of various field schools working in New Mexico, including scientists—some of whom were gathering "Indian" artifacts for their home institutions out east—and artists, intending to use this Native student production as a model for their own work. In 1900, for example, Smithsonian anthropologist Jesse Walter Fewkes commissioned what are believed to have been the first paper drawings by Hopi artists.[24] According to Native art historian J. J. Brody, Fewkes's interest was purely ethnographic and motivated by a desire to document local traditional practices in a quest to capture an Indigenous authenticity unblemished by European influence. However, the mere fact that the commissioned works were on paper already signaled contamination of whatever "pure" cultural forms Fewkes sought to preserve.

In terms of the commercial viability and commodification of Native art works, in 1899, Bert Phillips, cofounder of the Taos art colony, and artist Ernest Blumenschein together established the Taos Indian Curio Shop, where Native artworks were sold to primarily white artists in the area.[25] The Spanish and Indian Trading Post, which supplied Native works that were purchased by the Indian Arts Fund for the Museum of New Mexico, was opened in 1926 by John Evans, son of famed (and controversial) arts patron Mabel Dodge Luhan, who we will return to later in this essay. Before the mid-1920s, the Museum of New Mexico had served as the principal outlet for the sale of "Indian" artworks. The first commercial art galleries in Santa Fe were established in 1919 and then later, in 1930. From the late nineteenth century through the mid-twentieth century, the main sites for the sale and purchase of "Indian" art(ifacts) included the Museum of New Mexico, the Palace of the Governors, and these newly opened art galleries, developments that would set the stage for what would become the Santa Fe Indian Market.

US Settler Capitalism and the Commodification of "Traditional" Arts in New Mexico: The Art Markets

"We rapidly grew interested in all the old and almost dishabilitated arts of New Mexico, touched with a profound regret for their disappearance . . . we began to discuss the possibility of reviving [them]."[26]
—

In 1922, the Pueblo Pottery Fund (later, the Indian Arts Fund or IAF) was established in response to the fear that traditional Pueblo arts were disappearing. The stated purpose of the IAF was "to revive the arts and crafts of the Indians by giving them free access to the choicest specimens of their tribal art."[27] The phrasing of this statement exemplifies the dominant ethnocentric paternalistic attitudes of the time. In this brief quote, there are two points of interest. First, the objective to "revive" Indian arts and crafts suggests that "traditional" Native arts were disappearing, which, if true, was due to the intrusive presence of outsiders in the region. Renato Rosaldo refers to this process as "imperialist nostalgia" and describes it in the following manner:

> Curiously enough, agents of colonialism—officials, constabulary officers, missionaries, and other figures from whom anthropologists ritually dissociate themselves—often display nostalgia for the colonized culture as it was "traditionally" (that is, when they first encountered it). The peculiarity of their yearning, of course, is that agents of colonialism long for the very forms of life they intentionally altered or destroyed. Therefore, my concern resides with a particular kind of nostalgia, often found under imperialism, where people mourn the passing of what they themselves have transformed.[28]

Next, the idea of "giving 'them' access" (i.e., Natives) to those Indigenous art forms that Anglos (presumably with some input from Native artists) judged to be exemplary works epitomizes Anglo American gatekeeping when it comes to which art forms were deemed to have value and were thus worth preserving, studying, writing about, or collecting. IAF members were able to gather a sizable collection of Pueblo art objects, which were initially kept in members' homes; however, in 1925, the works were relocated to the basement of the Museum of Fine Arts in Santa Fe before being transferred to the Laboratory of Anthropology, but it wasn't until 1972 that the entire collection of 4,280 works was moved to the School of American Research.[29]

In 1925, Edgar Lee Hewett, director of the School of American Research and New Mexico's state museum system, along with other Indian Arts Fund members, held the first Southwest Indian Fair, the forerunner to the Santa Fe Indian Market. Two central concerns of IAF members were preserving the "best" examples of Indian art and establishing markets for the sale of Pueblo artwork. The collecting of work that—to Anglo eyes—represented artwork of the past and was of greatest value, followed by the intent to use that body of work to instruct contemporary Native artists so they could maintain those traditions, although commendable at first glance, is troubling, given what appears to be a desire to freeze Indigenous art making, preventing it from evolving organically in a way that did not suit the tastes and values of these new outside interests; the same happened with Hispano artists. The preservation of certain Native art forms based in large part on foreign ideas that privileged form, style, technique, and proficiency, as defined by the principles of European art, inevitably interrupted the natural development of Native communities and their art production, resulting in the invention of a new kind of "American" cultural production, one whose significance was tied to collectors, here primarily represented at the institutional level by the museums and at the socioeconomic level by galleries, markets, and collectors. Native artists no longer solely produced works for their own communities but rather produced works in line with buyers' tastes; in the process, irrevocably transforming what had originally determined the form and significance of such objects.

The world Native artists inhabited changed drastically during this early period; they faced new demands, responded to new pressures, and adapted to survive. It is difficult to parse good intentions (preserving significant cultural forms, finding ways for local artists to make a living, and so on) from essentializing colonial practices (cultural intervention and disruption, objectification, commodification, and so on). However, these challenging complexities should not be an obstacle to acknowledging and questioning the more troubling colonial elements of the political and cultural processes that shaped a cultural environment in which the authority and freedom of longstanding communities were limited. Such processes, in large part, continue to shape the official arts culture of New Mexico, a region where historical tensions between communities persist, even if they are not always visible or publicly acknowledged.[30]

Not surprisingly, the founders of the Indian Arts Fund were also involved in the founding of the Spanish Colonial Arts Society.[31] There appears to have been, if not equal interest, at least evident interest in also preserving and protecting what were initially referred to as *Mexicano* artistic and cultural traditions in New Mexico. The combination of the primarily Catholic subject matter and utilitarian function of most Hispano arts, the rural agrarian lifestyles of Hispano communities in the area, the perceived naïvete or self-taught quality of painted and sculpted forms, and their identification with medieval European art traditions resulted in the perception of New Mexican *santos* and *bultos* as corresponding to an earlier stage in the accepted scheme of European cultural development.[32] As Stephanie Lewthwaite observed regarding Anglo attitudes toward Hispanos and their art forms,

In the primitivist mindset of Anglo newcomers, Hispano art was the product of tradition and the preindustrial village landscape . . . that had become suspended in time and isolated geographically and culturally from external influences. Anglo efforts to preserve and revive Spanish Colonial art forms in woodcarving, tinwork, and textiles during the 1920s and 1930s exacerbated this trend. In the primitivist narrative, Hispanos were craftspeople and, at best, folk or "primitive" artists, and when Hispanos engaged with alternative media or modernist techniques, their art was either inauthentic or imitative. Meanwhile, for Anglos, Hispano art forms served as inspiration for the creation of new "modern" literary and artistic forms, and as an emotional salve for their insecurities about modern urban America. Rarely, however, were Hispano art or artists regarded as "modern" or innovative.[33]

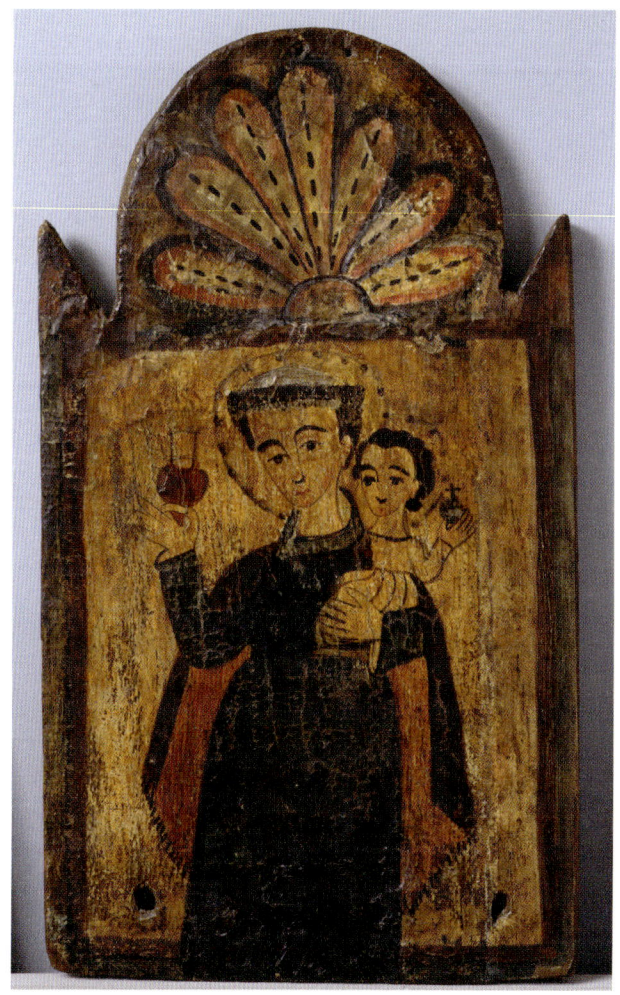

FIGURE 1.1. José Rafael Aragón, *San Antonio de Padua*, ca. 1820. Gesso and water-based paints on wood. Purchased with funds from the Friends of Art, University of New Mexico Art Museum, Albuquerque (94.20.2).

Objects regarded as "traditional" arts in the region included a wide range of material forms, starting with what are normally considered to be utilitarian or decorative arts, such as furniture, ceramics, and textiles; artforms made for daily use and whose manufacture required distinct skill sets and differing technical proficiencies. It also included art that could be considered visual or figurative: works consisting mainly of painted *retablos* and sculpted *bultos*: artforms depicting devotional subjects and thus categorized as religious art (figs. 1.1 and 1.2).[34] Such painted images are described as possessing strong graphic qualities, while sculpted forms have been characterized as stylized, elongated, and intensely expressive.

New Mexican artists used local natural materials just as Native artists had long been doing. Such materials included a variety of woods (distinguished between soft versus

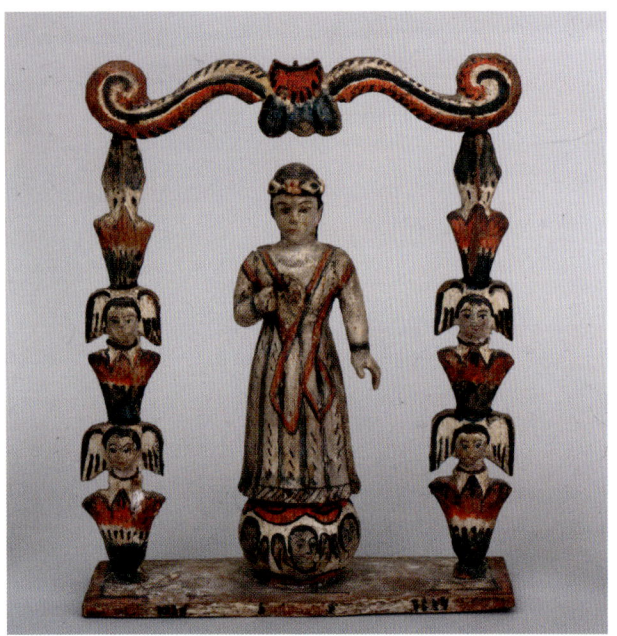

FIGURE 1.2. José Rafael Aragón, *Our Lady of the Immaculate Conception*, ca. 1820–1835. Wood, gesso, water-based paints. The Mary Lester Field and Neill B. Field Collection, University of New Mexico Art Museum, Albuquerque (XO.192).

hard woods, such as cottonwood or pine) and natural pigments (vegetal and mineral), in combination with sacred iconographies or subjects that had mainly originated in Europe and circulated globally, usually in the form of prints. The religious images that were produced reflected not only their makers' inherent skills, but most importantly, their local values, cultural traditions, and social needs. These factors in combination gave shape to unique New Mexican visual and material languages whose esthetics became a selling point to recent Anglo arrivals and collectors.

Ironically, the interest in local Hispano arts and crafts was also often accompanied by a desire to alter "traditional" art forms and practices in order to increase their appeal to Anglo tastes.[35] Not only were new media and technologies introduced into the local artistic ecology (e.g., lithographs, chromolithographs, and mass-produced religious figures) or new object types added to the repertoire of local artistic production (e.g., Lazy Susans, record racks), but requests for changes in practice also yielded new forms and traditions (e.g., as seen in the production of smaller, mobile pieces for tourists and unpainted carved figures).[36] In certain cases, older traditional approaches to art making were modified, if not eradicated, as they were adapted to new demands; for example, the traditional use of bright paints to decorate wood furnishings was considered "too gaudy" for Anglo consumers, leading to the alteration of traditional Hispano furnishing surface treatments to fit Anglo tastes; the very forms of traditional furnishings were also physically transformed to correspond to Anglo ideas of domestic space.[37]

Both Indigenous and Hispano/Mexicano arts were of interest in terms of their "exotic" or anachronistic qualities and their potential utility as subject matter in Euro-American art forms. But Native and Mexicano/Hispano esthetics—the underlying principles of those traditions—were typically rejected since they were not in line with the artistic values of the white Americans who brought with them cultural capital, institutional affiliations, and money. Simultaneously, Hispano artists who were interested in experimenting with new media, as they always had, or adopting modernist idioms were discouraged from doing so, to maintain what was seen as an authentic colonial tradition; tensions often developed between new patrons and local artists. As Stephanie Lewthwaite again noted when writing about Hispano artist Eliseo Rodríguez, whose experimental practice was questioned, "Rodríguez, who worked with various media and stylistic genres, did not follow one aesthetic pathway determined by the Spanish colonial tradition of Anglo patrons . . . [concurrently] . . . folklore scholar Arthur León Campa . . . urged Hispanos to liberate themselves from the shackles of Anglo patronage and forge individualistic forms of artistic expression beyond the confines of the Spanish colonial tradition."[38]

The kind of experimentation noted here was not new; it can be traced back centuries among Indigenous communities—and also to the beginning of Spanish colonialism. Although from a contemporary perspective, perhaps even from an elite Novohispanic point of view, New Mexican artists may have been perceived as limited by a lack of training compared to what was available in larger cities and perhaps, to some extent, by the kinds of resources they had at their disposal, these creators were observant, skilled, and made conscious choices, drawing inspiration from a range of artistic vocabularies including Indigenous, Novohispanic, and Spanish, as well as Asian and European, more broadly. Art historian Donna Pierce identified this historical practice when examining a body of New Mexican *santo* images and tracing "stylistic elements originating in Europe, Asia, and Mexico as they were used in New Mexico, to see how some were adopted, others eschewed, and some manipulated by local artists in the process of developing the region's dynamic artistic identity."[39] One thing that stands out when looking at the colonial arts produced starting in the sixteenth century in the Spanish Americas from New Mexico to Mexico City to the Caribbean down to South America, including the Philippines, is that all colonial art was a product of adaptation, reinterpretation, and transculturation; in other words, colonial art is an art of innovation in its entirety and was continuously evolving and adapting to changing circumstances, contrary to the general views held by Anglo outsiders, based as they were on Eurocentric biases projected onto what they encountered in New Mexico. Regarding such essentializing readings of both local demographics and local art traditions, Stephanie Lewthwaite pointed out their limitations by observing that, "In elevating a pure and authentic form of colonial art, the Spanish Colonial paradigm obscured the long history of intercultural exchange that shaped New Mexico and its artistic production . . . [furthermore] many of the pieces that Anglo patrons identified as authentic 'Spanish' colonial art were created after 1821 and were technically 'Mexican' in origin."[40]

Following New Mexico's transition to a US territory, followed by an increase in the influx of Anglos, traditional and historical ways of life were transformed as local communities were forced to adapt to new political, cultural, and socioeconomic pressures. Hispano settler communities had long been predominantly rural and agricultural in nature; however, new, more powerful interests in the region contributed to a significant loss of land among local families. Where once most Hispanos had supported themselves primarily through subsistence farming and herding, most Mexicanos lost control of the lands that had sustained them, and as a result, their ways of life were disrupted; for the arts, such disruptions also meant a lack of access to traditional materials like wood. As with Native communities, New Mexican Hispanos had to find new ways to support themselves and their families in the new system. Those who had demonstrable artistic skills or interests turned to art and furniture making, but to earn a living in the new economic system, they needed buyers, namely Anglos, who provided a potentially profitable avenue for local traditional arts and crafts.

The history of Spanish Market begins in 1924 with the founding of the Spanish Colonial Arts Society by Mary Austin and Frank Applegate, followed one year later in 1925 by the founding of the market itself, ten years before the Works Progress Administration (the WPA was formed in 1935).[41] The motivations for founding the Spanish Colonial Arts Society and Spanish Market, similar to those motivating the Indian Market, included an interest in keeping Hispano artists in the state; providing an avenue for Hispano artists to sell their work and earn a living; and documenting, preserving, and cultivating an appreciation of historical Hispano art traditions in New Mexico.[42] In a pamphlet she wrote soliciting members for the Spanish Colonial Arts Society, E. Boyd wrote,

> By the purchase of unique examples which might otherwise have been removed from this region, or simply destroyed in the path of progress, the Society has saved, and is now saving, many rare items which can never be duplicated. The revival of the Spanish Colonial Arts Society is a movement of importance, not only in the history of folk art in New Mexico, but in the entire United States. The Southwest, whose history antedates that of our eastern coast, might be called the birthplace of American Colonial Art. The Society is the only active, private organization still engaged in collecting material for preservation and exhibition in the State of New Mexico. Much of the material has already gone out of the State into the hands of Museums or private collectors.[43]

Over the years, Spanish Market has become a central driver of tourism revenue and thus important to the local economy. Additionally, and perhaps more importantly to local communities, Spanish Market has become a marker of local identity; it's been a source of pride and a mechanism through which a selective version of local New Mexican Hispano culture is promoted to visitors and anyone wishing to learn more about this important part of the state's cultural history. Both Indian Market and Traditional Spanish Market have developed into important tourist draws and revenue-generating events for the city and local artist communities, as well as serving as sources of ethnic pride for Pueblo artists and for New Mexicans who identify as Spanish or Hispano. The arts produced by these artist communities are perceived as valuable, in large part, because they are considered markers of living traditions with historical regional significance; however, the markets have introduced new esthetics, idioms, and practices, and motivated the invention of new forms along the way, as well as cultivating inaccurate ethnocentric ideas about purity and authenticity (e.g., the line distinguishing what is Spanish from what is not is blurred in many cases although maintained).

Both events continue to focus on the maintenance and reproduction of historical art forms tied to older preexisting cultures considered foundational in the state. The markets are highly promoted and regarded as representative of New Mexican history and culture. Since collectors and curators purchase works from market artists, we must recognize the role that museums play in reinforcing these ideas of New Mexican cultural production. Scholars contribute to the maintenance and proliferation of these ideas by studying these artistic traditions and exhibiting, publishing, and teaching about them, further reifying the cultural narratives that have taken shape around the organizations and markets; narratives that have been instrumental in determining the arts conversation both within New Mexico and about New Mexico since the early twentieth century. As will be discussed in the next section, in addition to the interest in preserving longstanding local art traditions, foreign art forms and practices would be introduced by new arrivals, which would further alter local cultural production and reshape New Mexican identity.

Modern Primitives in the Southwest:
Race, Modernity, and the Tricultural Myth in New Mexico

"As to the Spanish stock of our Southwest, it is certain to me that we do not begin to appreciate the splendor and sterling value of its race element. Who knows but that element, like the course of some subterranean river, dipping invisibly for a hundred or two years, is now to emerge in broadest flow and permanent action."[44]
—

Indigenous and Mexican or Hispano art forms were of great interest to Anglo outsiders from the very beginning of the Southwestern region's history as a US territory. It may seem odd that one could value an art form while simultaneously devaluing—even despising—its maker, but that is a common phenomenon in many cases of cultural encounter, especially those that have involved European colonialism around the world. In the late nineteenth century, anthropologists and ethnographers from northeastern US institutions documented what they came across and collected works to take back, and missionaries began teaching Native communities how to produce European-style artworks. In the early twentieth century, the first groups of Anglo artists, primarily men, began to form in

Santa Fe and Taos. These recent arrivals, struck by the beauty and perceived isolation of the local landscape, as well as by the wide range of art production of local communities, started to create art presumably inspired by these new experiences and the forms, both man-made and natural, they were encountering. One of the earliest groups of Anglo artists was the Taos Society of Artists, which was founded in Taos in 1915, followed by *Los Cinco Pintores*, formed in Santa Fe in 1921. Eight male artists—B. J. O. Nordfeldt, Frank Applegate, Jozef Bakos, Gustave Baumann, William P. Henderson, Ernest L. Blumenschein, Victor Higgins, and Walter Ufer—some of whom had belonged to the earlier societies, gathered at Nordfeldt's studio one day in 1923 and christened themselves the New Mexico Painters.[45] That same year, they exhibited in New York City and were met with positive reviews. The last recorded exhibitions of the New Mexico Painters were held at the Art Institute of Chicago and at the Denver Art Museum, both in 1927. Some of these artists worked to preserve what they saw as Indian and Spanish artistic traditions they feared would be lost in the face of, as earlier noted, an irreversible change that was, in actuality, detrimental to those very cultural practices; for example, Frank Applegate helped start the Indian Arts Fund and the Spanish Colonial Arts Society to support such a project.[46] Much of the work produced by these men was representational in nature and focused on capturing the beauty of the natural landscape of New Mexico or drawing inspiration from the region's older Pueblo and Hispano communities. There appear to have been tensions among these artists regarding the significance of modernist principles in their own practice, such as the employment of abstraction in painting, which most of them rejected.[47]

Over time, many white artists, originally from the northeast coast but also eventually from other regions of the country, gravitated to New Mexico to satiate their curiosity, search for inspiration, meet and work with some of the more established artists in the area, or settle down for an extended period and produce new work. This voluminous list includes such figures as Marsden Hartley, who, interested in developing an American modern art independent of European art influences, spent one year in Taos and Santa Fe in 1918–1919; Raymond Jonson, who relocated to Santa Fe in 1924, then moved to Albuquerque in 1950 and taught at the University of New Mexico from 1934 to 1954; Mark Rothko, who, according to Noah Hoffman, first visited New Mexico in 1938 then again in 1949 and 1951, and produced new work inspired by his visit; Richard Diebenkorn, who studied with Jonson at the University of New Mexico in 1950–1952; Agnes Martin, who also taught at the University of New Mexico in 1957–1962; Georgia O'Keeffe, Bruce Nauman, Judy Chicago, and Harmony Hammond, all of whom permanently settled in New Mexico; and many others, who, like Hartley, visited New Mexico for varying periods of time and left, including Arthur Dove, John Sloan, Robert Henri, George Bellows, Edward Hopper, Milton Avery, Agnes Pelton, and Josef Albers, to name a few of the more notable visitors during this period.[48] Today, the presence of the Tamarind Institute at the University of

New Mexico in Albuquerque, a world-renowned lithography workshop founded in 1960, continues to draw many artists to the state.[49]

In addition to the artists who were migrating westward and gathering in places like Taos and Santa Fe, we must include those figures who were acting as brokers, such as the patrons, dealers, and collectors. One of the more prominent individuals who worked in this capacity was Mabel Dodge Luhan. Understandably, the scholarship produced on the life and work of Luhan aims to recover lost histories of the women who were involved in the development of modernism in the US—an area of study that has normally highlighted male actors. Considered a radical intellectual who rewrote gender norms of the time and navigated a complex social network that included numerous politically active, creative men and women, Mabel Dodge Luhan is seen as an important figure in the story of the introduction of modern art in New Mexico.[50] Born into an affluent and influential family in Buffalo, New York, she is described as someone who resisted convention and the expectations of women of her class. She spent time traveling between New York and Florence, Italy, hosting salons with artists, writers, and activists, and eventually landed in New Mexico, as was the trend of the period, where she bought a property in Taos. In addition to her intellectual gatherings and philanthropic work, she was an art collector, initially of modern art, and later, Native and Hispano arts; in New Mexico, it is noted that she also fought for Indigenous land rights. She produced memoirs that detailed her social life and that paint a portrait of her time in New Mexico, and she is generally credited with making Taos a destination site for those interested in the Native, Hispano, and Anglo artistic communities in the region.[51] Shortly after buying her home in Taos, she hired Tony Lujan, a local Native man, to make repairs; according to biographers, after Lujan's repeated attempts to seduce her, she wound up having an affair with him, resulting in her divorcing her first husband, Elsie Clews Parsons, and marrying Lujan.[52]

Although most accounts of Luhan's presence in New Mexico focus on her agency as a mover and shaker, Native and Hispano locals who remember Luhan have different stories to share. A recurring theme in such testimonies is how affluent Anglos like Luhan, although fascinated by and invested in preserving local cultural production, fetishized and romanticized Native people while marginalizing, even denigrating, Hispanos; anti-Mexican sentiment among Anglos and other recent arrivals should not be a surprise but make sense when viewing such figures in relation to the larger historical context in question.[53] Such fractures in the older celebratory narratives surrounding Luhan and others like her have gradually come to light. As Lois P. Rudnick wrote, when referring to an essay by anthropologist Ruth Miller,

> We can tell the story of the modern encounter with the 'primitive,' which
> was so fundamental to both European and North American Modernisms,
> in multiple ways. We can tell it as a story of cultural imperialism and

appropriation on the part of European and American artists and patrons, by which indigenous, colonized, and marginalized peoples of color became the fodder for the revitalization of European and Euro-American artists and national cultures. We can also tell it as a story of 'dialogic exchange,' in which indigenous artists found Euro-Americans' 'interest and appreciation a valuable counter to long-standing history of oppression and exclusion.'[54]

I find three things striking about Rudnick's comment. First, the use of the term "primitive," a historicized referent that is a descriptor for the Indigenous and also Hispano cultures in New Mexico; second, the idea of a "dialogic exchange" between Anglos and locals, as if local communities had much choice in the matter; and third, the focus toward the end of the quote on Indigenous artists and not Indigenous and Hispano artists, a reflection of earlier observations of differences in how Anglos perceived and treated various local communities. In addition to any anti-Mexican attitudes that may have been pervasive at that time, there may have also been the perception of Hispanos as descendants of another settler colonial presence, invalidating these communities in the eyes of certain Anglos in terms of Hispano land claims and rights over that of natives.

A review of early- to mid-twentieth-century discourses about the US Southwest and West reveals a pattern where the larger region is characterized, if not as empty and isolated, then as primitive and backward; in either case, strategic representations that justified the perceived need for settlement, civilization, and modernization. Such ethnocentric and paternalistic attitudes inevitably echo the notion of the "white man's burden," as coined by Rudyard Kipling in his poem of the same name in which he frames the Euro-American colonial project in the Philippines (but also, European colonialism, generally), as the moral duty or obligation of the white man (and woman) to help and care for colonized (non-white) subjects, given their need to be educated and civilized. The poem was a paean to imperialism not as an end for the accumulation of wealth or attainment of power but as a service to non-European peoples; the outwardly beneficent but profoundly arrogant sentiment is striking from a contemporary perspective. In the end, the poem by Kipling, a recognized white supremacist, stands as a self-serving, racist justification for expansionist politics that reframed the colonial project as a positive, benevolent, even compassionate activity instead of as one that is oppressive and destructive to the very people it aims to serve.[55] It is important to recognize that this kind of imag(in)ing of the Americas is part of a longer history of European conceptualizations and representations of the Western Hemisphere intended to validate conquest and settlement while simultaneously reinforcing European superiority and authority.

An image that succinctly captures this stance is the well-known drawing by Jan van der Straet (called Stradanus), titled *Allegory of America*, also known as *Amerigo Vespucci Discovers America* (1587–1589) (fig. 1.3).

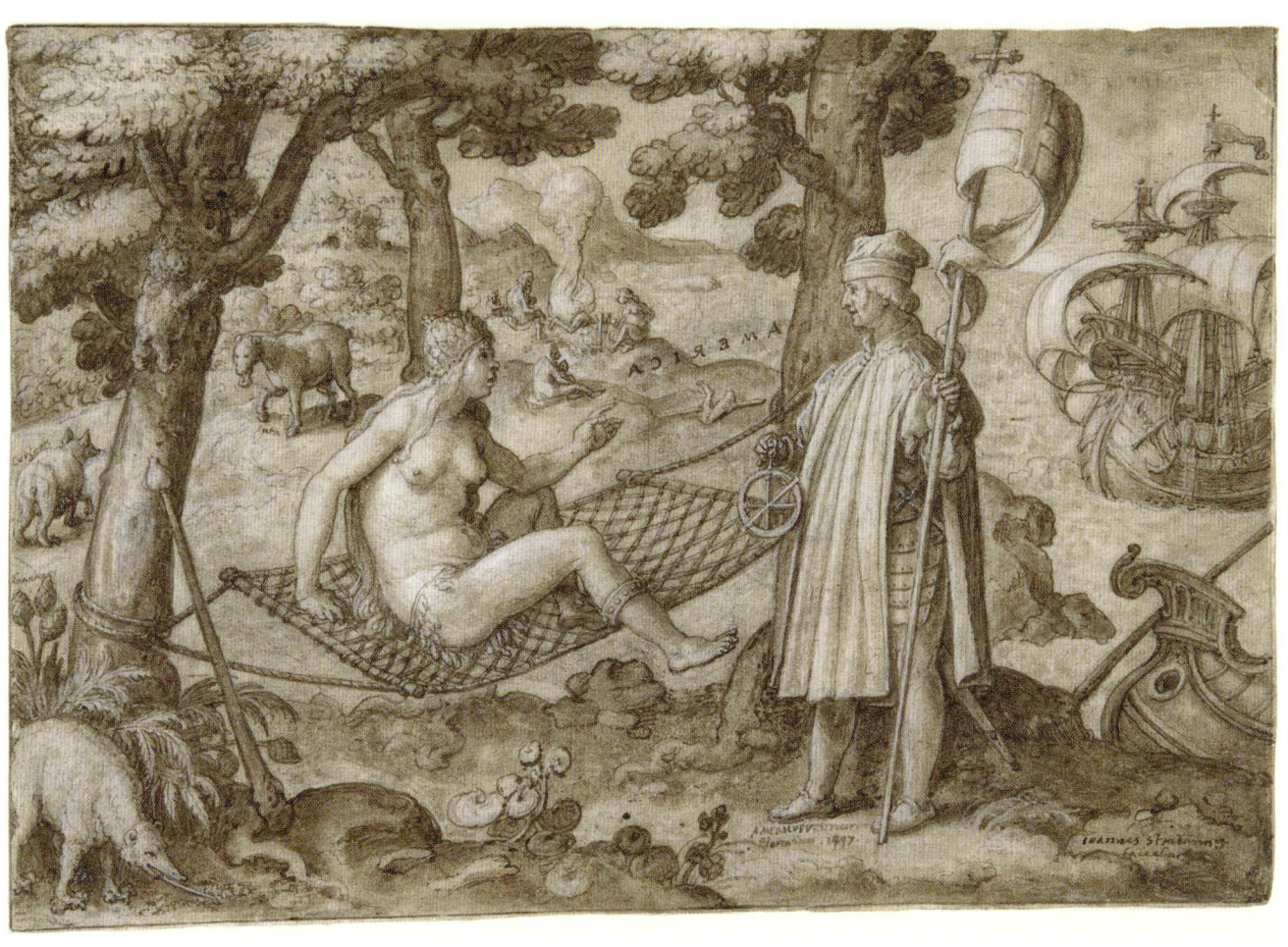

FIGURE 13. Jan van der Straet, called Stradanus, *Allegory of America*, ca. 1587–1589.
Pen and brown ink, brown wash, heightened with white, over black chalk.
Incised, 7 1/2″ × 10 9/16″. Metropolitan Museum of Art, New York. Gift
of Estate of James Hazen Hyde, 1959.

In the drawing, Amerigo Vespucci stands to the right of center in the composition and faces an anonymous nude female figure who is reclining on a woven hammock suspended between two trees; the female figure appears to have been lying down and is sitting up in response to Vespucci's presence. Both the depiction of nudity and the act of cannibalism seen in the background are old European tropes referring to barbarity, here meant to characterize the Indigenous Americas as savage and uncivilized. The symbolism that distinguishes male/female and civilized/uncivilized is further reinforced by the suggestion that before European intervention, the Americas were asleep, or in other words, unproductive and underdeveloped, and existing in an ahistorical, primitive state; it is the European who awakens America from her slumber and activates her.[56] The gendering employed in this allegorical image conveys the idea of victor versus vanquished with the inevitable allusions to rape and ownership that comes to define settlement practices and the large-scale resource extraction that has been part of various European colonial projects across the Western Hemisphere for the past five hundred years. Although such ideas can be traced back to the sixteenth century, if not earlier, the absorption by the US of Mexico's northern territories in the nineteenth century and the Anglo incursions that followed in the twentieth century repeat historical patterns of conquest, colonization, and assimilation with the inevitable upheavals in traditional lifeways, including the destruction of the very practices and forms Anglos found interesting and worth preserving.

The white artists who visited or settled in New Mexico from the 1920s onward can be seen as complicit with this larger colonial project, consciously or not, not only by introducing but also by imposing foreign European and Euro-American esthetic principles and artistic practices, by demanding compliance to new rules and expectations, and by objectifying local peoples and appropriating their cultural traditions; their very presence disrupted longstanding communities and lifeways. That these new ideas are enfolded into a capitalist economic system, itself propelled by an imperialist nationalist engine, inevitably positions local Indigenous and Hispano cultures and art practices as primitive or folkloric foils that can't help but reify (within this new cultural framework) the superiority of the Anglocentric whiteness and modernity seen as defining US culture. In the literature on white artists working in the Southwest, what is normally ignored in the mythologized narratives formed around these allegedly intrepid creatives, their lives, and their work, is their participation in and benefitting from the more destructive side of US imperialist practices and settler colonialism. As noted earlier, the list of white artists who visited, spent time in, or settled in New Mexico is long; however, one artist who stands out as an ideal representative of the Anglo presence in New Mexico and the cultural tensions her presence fomented is Georgia O'Keeffe.[57]

Georgia O'Keeffe first visited New Mexico in 1917 shortly after it became a state and then began visiting regularly in 1929 before permanently settling in Abiquiú in 1949 after deciding to distance herself from the New York art world. Her image as a historical figure and her work have inspired a cult following that has motivated others to study the region and visit or move to New Mexico. Considered one of the more significant American modernists of the early twentieth century, her impressive body of work has been featured in countless publications and exhibits and is found in collections around the world. According to the website for the Georgia O'Keeffe Museum, which was founded in Santa Fe in 1997 (eleven years after the artist's death), the museum holds over 3,000 works, including 140 oil paintings, 700 drawings, and hundreds of other works she produced between 1901 and 1984; the museum is also the appointed custodian of O'Keeffe's home and studio in Abiquiú, as well as housing a research center and library. In the website bio for O'Keeffe, New Mexico is recognized in the following manner:

> In the summer of 1929, O'Keeffe made the first of many trips to northern New Mexico. The stark landscape and Native American and Hispanic cultures of the region inspired a new direction in O'Keeffe's art. For the next two decades she spent most summers living and working in New Mexico. She made the state her permanent residence in 1949, three years after Stieglitz's death.[58]

Much of the scholarship focused on Georgia O'Keeffe and her New Mexican period normally approaches her work biographically and from a modernist formal or esthetic perspective. It also often includes a discussion focused on gender with little critical engagement in terms of the historical or cultural contexts in which she worked. If there is any context, it tends to replicate a hegemonic institutional disciplinary perspective, established canonical narratives, and other often-romanticized tropes associated with the white artist braving the frontier in search of inspiration from the natural landscape and its provincial inhabitants.[59]

Noting how typical writing about O'Keeffe dismisses historical, cultural, and racialized themes in her images, Metropolitan Museum of Art associate curator of Native American art, Patricia Marroquin Norby, states, "The use of visual aesthetics as political and racial analgesic becomes evident once Georgia O'Keeffe's Southwest skull and landscape paintings are recontextualized according to moments of American Indian and Hispano resistance to twentieth-century US colonization in northern New Mexico."[60] In other words, our understanding of O'Keeffe and her work changes when told from the perspective of local Native and Hispano residents with whom she interacted and who were affected by the changes her presence and activities engendered. According to Marroquin Norby, the esthetic and formal emphases found in the scholarship on O'Keeffe's work naturalizes "Eurocentric entitlement and specific acts of land appropriation within the ancient Indian Pueblo *Avéshu* (Abiquiú), New Mexico."[61] Her discussion subtly points to how O'Keeffe's activities in the Southwest developed alongside US colonization and adds that by referring to this region as "O'Keeffe Country," the history and presence of local communities is erased, presenting the land as empty with the individual artist as the main inhabitant or actor worth noting. Natives and Hispanos are relegated to the background and become supplementary to the main story. It appears that early on, O'Keeffe had no awareness or understanding of the communal approach to life in the region, which led to racial, cultural, and territorial conflicts with local *Abiqueños*, Natives, and Hispanos. Over time, she became familiar with local traditions and values but her attempts to contribute to the community can be seen as self-serving, given how she depended on the support and assistance of *Abiqueños* to do her work and to live as she did.

An example of O'Keeffe's practice as an artist that Marroquin Norby identifies as in need of further consideration is the artist's use of animal skeletal remains as subject matter in some of her best known works.[62] O'Keeffe was known to walk the land and collect copious amounts of cow skulls and other bones, which she referred to as "trash," and then use them as models to create some of her most iconic paintings.[63] The esthetic rendition of such remains occludes the fact of Anglo disruption of local lifeways, in this case, as a result of land grant violations, whereby Anglos swindled local Native and Hispano landowners out of their properties or outright stole land—acts that were accompanied by the wholesale executions of livestock on which locals depended for their livelihoods. The animal remains that O'Keeffe collected are material evidence of the effects of such brutal land appropriation tactics by Anglos and the forced disruption of local subsistence practices that adversely affected local communities, a historical reality that is erased by the artist's work and the formalist manners in which it has been discussed. Similarly, O'Keeffe's comments in interviews and in letters claiming the New Mexican land as hers, or those who referred to the area around Abiquiú, an ancient region significant to Indigenous communities and where numerous historical events of import to Native and Hispano populations took place, as "O'Keeffe Country," echo colonialist attitudes.[64] As Marroquin Norby observes, beyond such complicity in the more destructive practice of land appropriation and displacements is how the narratives that were formed around figures like O'Keeffe and others like her center Anglo artists, patrons, and benefactors while omitting the Native and Hispano peoples and their contributions not only to Anglo activities in the area, but also to the development of American modern art itself.[65]

Given the history of New Mexico as one defined by waves of migration and colonization, one of the more enduring myths about New Mexico that emerges during this period is the idea of the state's "tricultural" (Native/Hispano/Anglo) heritage, a simplified cultural representation of New Mexico's varied inhabitants promoted in the early twentieth century by members of the new Anglo establishment and its cultural institutions. Despite this idea's continuing popularity, the essentializing nature of its suppositions need to be recognized and reconsidered. The original Indigenous inhabitants of the region were varied and diverse, including the different native communities collectively termed *Pueblos* by the

Spanish, as well as the Diné or Navajo, the Comanche, the Apache, and others. Earlier Iberian and Ibero-American settlers were ethnically and racially distinct as well, contrary to the singular mythologized figure of the conquistador, which still holds power among many New Mexican Hispanos and others. Estevan Rael–Gálvez, former New Mexico state historian, describes the diversity of colonial settlers as follows:

> Just as Indigenous peoples were distinct by culture and history, so "Spaniards" constituted people born in Aragón, Galicia, Andalusia, Castile, and Extremadura, some of them with Moorish and Jewish lineages, even if converted and quietly held. Distinct regions of Mexico also defined the early settlers' identities as they arrived from various Indigenous and Euro-Mestizo communities, including Zacatecas, Durango, Puebla, and Mexico City itself—a stream of people that has flowed even until the present. As was true of the colonial state elsewhere, New Mexico's colonial records also reveal people originating in many other places throughout the world, including Greece, France, Portugal, and even Angola, Africa.[66]

Arriving in the Americas, Iberians, regardless of ethnicity, were absorbed into the Peninsular category and their descendants were either *criollo* or *mestizo*, some *negro* or *mulatto*, among other mixtures that reflected the caste nomenclature resulting from the miscegenation and pluralism of the viceroyalty's population, especially in the larger cities to the south, such as the viceregal capital, Mexico City. Early Hispano, mestizo, Indigenous, and Black settlers from central New Spain arrived in waves over a three-century period, establishing or adding to a range of diverse communities; further processes of mixing among the various populations in New Mexico unfolded, adding to the demographic complexity of the region. The Anglos or recent white arrivals were not a monolithic group either.[67] A problem with the tricultural framework is that it effectively erases differences among each branch's constituent populations and creates homogenizing umbrella categories that also positions each branch as separate and distinct from the others. The suggestion of three distinct branches in this new framework ignores the historical fact of diversity, miscegenation, and the persistent transculturation that had been occurring for centuries across various Native groups, initially, and then later among colonial settlers and the Native peoples. How did the tricultural myth start?

An early mention of this tricultural concept is found in the exhibition catalog to the 1923 New Mexico Painters' exhibit in New York City, which presents an explanation of the group's name and refers to this idea. The relevant excerpt states: "The name New Mexican Painters may suggest that the object is to represent New Mexican landscape, Mexicans, Indians. While this is true in a way, subjects are only an accidental urge to the creative artist. The name has been chosen in that wider sense of the Province of *Nueva Mexico*, which originally embraced most of the Southwest, and which to these Painters means the blended elements of three civilizations."[68] The suggestion of three foundational cultures in the region increasingly appears in a range of media, from tourist campaigns and brochures to exhibition catalogs to publications on the history and art of the state. In an article on noted scholar of colonial New Mexican art, E. Boyd, who moved to Santa Fe in 1929, the author mentions that during a three-month visit to Santa Fe with her husband, the Chamber of Commerce advertised the city as holding evidence of "three distinct cultures"; again, an essentialized reading of local demographics that served as a simplified and digestible marketing tool to describe the local population and attract potential tourists.[69] The appeal of the tricultural idea is also found in the manner it subtly neutralizes and sidesteps violent histories in the region and any hint of internal conflicts among its constituent groups, implying, instead, equal status and peaceful cohabitation; the idea survives because it is romanticized and thus palatable by those wishing for a sanitized view of history that does not upset the status quo. Slowly but surely, through its dissemination and repetition, even locals from historical communities in the state started to adopt and apply this framework in defining their own identities and cultural production. Anthropologist Sylvia Rodríguez, recognizing the complicated effects of this idea in practice, adds that, "the tri-ethnic trap is a situation in which Hispanos, unable to advance beyond clearcut secondary economic status and faced with the steady and irrevocable loss of their traditional land base, must abide by a tourism-engendered Anglo glorification of Indian culture, as well as the federal protection and even restoration of Indian lands, sometimes at the expense of Hispano ownership."[70]

Considering the historical period in question, we must take into account the new racial dynamics introduced by non-Hispanic whites in the region, particularly in terms of how they motivated a segment of the local New Mexican Hispano population to cultivate an emphasis on a Spanish identity in contradistinction to both the Native and the Mexican populations of which they had been a part since the sixteenth century. As Sylvia Rodríguez again observed, "the 'Spanish' or 'Spanish American' myth was originally perpetuated by the Mexican (and mestizo) or recently Mexican American elite and middle classes as a self-protective measure against the progressive institutionalization of Anglo American racism. That this measure simultaneously served their class interests and reflected Spanish racism against the Indians is also apparent."[71] This Iberophilic tendency appears to be unique to New Mexico, primarily among certain Hispanos or Indo-Hispanos of northern New Mexico and southern Colorado since this emphasis on Spanish descent is not found to the same degree if at all in the neighboring states of Texas, Arizona, or California, despite similar histories and longstanding Hispano presences in those areas. What we find in New Mexico, in part a response to the unique communities that formed in the region, is a concerted attempt at distancing the local Hispano-identified populations from Natives and from Mexico and Mexicans via the cultivation and promotion of a European Spanish identity.

This emphasis on Iberian identification appears to emerge in the early twentieth century shortly after the construction of the transcontinental railroad that made travel to the Southwest easier and brought Anglos from east of the Mississippi into the area along with their racial politics and anti-Mexican attitudes.[72] New Mexican Hispanos, many of who, after centuries of coexistence, were mixed with Natives and/or whose cultures were a result of these exchanges, responded in this manner as a survival strategy. European identification was expected to allow New Mexican Hispanos the opportunity to carve out a space for themselves in the rapidly changing landscape that offered them some degree of agency and a way to construct new identities as US citizens, unlike the larger view of Natives and Mexicans as alien and incapable of being assimilated into the modern Anglocentric culture of white Americans. Spanish identification served to whiten the local Hispano population in the region, and this process of re-inscription was pushed by the new US leadership. For example, L. Bradford Prince, a lawyer and politician from New York who served as governor of the New Mexico Territory from 1889 to 1893, founded the Spanish American Normal School in Española. At the school, New Mexican students were encouraged to promote their Spanish identity as a counter to the discrimination that Natives and Mexicans were experiencing.[73] Sylvia Rodríguez noted how geographer Richard Nostrand continued to promote in his work the idea that Spanish Americans from southern Colorado and northern New Mexico were ethnically distinct from Mexicans and other Mexican Americans; she writes, "Nostrand's homeland . . . is by definition exclusively Hispano or northern New Mexican. He sees the homeland as a pre-American phenomenon progressively diminished by Mexican infiltration as well as Anglo encroachment and assimilation."[74]

Non-Hispanic whites, perhaps oblivious to the distinctions among and across members of these communities, initially perceived two general populations in New Mexico: Natives and *Mexicanos*, which appears to have contributed to the reification of this Spanish emphasis among locals. Most importantly, the tricultural framework provided an avenue through which Anglos could insert themselves into the historical and cultural fabric of the region, not just as the latest arrivals but as a new dominant presence. Over time, the tricultural myth became an accessible and easily disseminated type of shorthand for the demographic and cultural makeup of the state that could be promoted to outsiders to attract not only tourism but also investment, occupation, and development; that many New Mexicans embraced this idea cemented its status as one of the primary signifiers of New Mexico's population demographics.

The tricultural myth of New Mexico's cultural foundations has continued to inform both the wider perception of cultural traditions and arts in the state, as well as approaches to how collections, markets, and exhibitions continue to be handled, including how New Mexico is promoted, to the present day. Two examples of artworks that illustrate the influence of the tricultural idea in representations of New Mexican identity include a painting from a group of panels painted by artist Kenneth Adams at Zimmerman Library at the University of New Mexico, and a sculpture of the "three foundational cultures" located at the *Santuario de Chimayó* in Chimayó, New Mexico.

An excerpt from the UNM Campus Histories website discussing Kenneth Adams's murals mentions the following: "President James F. Zimmerman's stated purpose for the murals was so that they would 'represent each of the three major cultures in New Mexico and their contributions to civilization.'"[75] The mural, one of four panels, titled "The Union of All Three in the Life of the Southwest," was commissioned and painted in 1939 as part of the Public Works of Art Project, an extension of the New Deal initiatives implemented by US President Franklin D. Roosevelt between 1933 and 1939, intended to provide employment to artists nationwide (fig. 1.4).[76] Adams had previously been a member of the Taos Society of Artists and was brought to the University of New Mexico as an artist-in-residence, funded in part by the Carnegie Corporation. The mural panels have been controversial since they were first installed; complaints and protests have been happening with some regularity since the 1970s and continue to this day.[77] The panel that is of interest to this discussion depicts three male figures who are holding hands and standing outside in a natural landscape. The figures and the landscape are described as using flat graphic forms and abstract geometric motifs, suggestive of Indigenous visual esthetics.

Some of the registered complaints refer to the Anglo figure (depicted with light skin and blond hair; he is also the only figure with discernible facial features, which include blue eyes) who is placed in the center of the triad and faces the viewer. The other two figures, representing a Native man and a Hispano, have clearly marked darker skin tones, lack facial features, and are depicted in profile, thus not engaging with the viewer; rather, they both focus on the central white figure. The figures, as suggested by the title, are meant to represent the three foundational cultures of New Mexico; however, the decision to privilege the white figure by his placement and posture was ill received and criticized for marginalizing the two figures associated with the earlier, non-white inhabitants of the region, in particular the Native figure, representing the original inhabitants of the region who survived two major waves of conquest and colonization. The image is seen as echoing the outdated paternalistic belief that equate the Anglo with civilization, having led the way by introducing the Native and the Hispano populations in the region to modernity; here, old colonial tropes are evident.[78]

The second example is a sculpture called *The Three Cultures Monument*, which is located at the Santuario de Chimayó in northern New Mexico (fig. 1.5). The sculpture consists of five elements: a figure of a white man, a figure of a Hispanic man, a figure of an Indigenous man, the cylindrical pedestal upon which all three figures are placed, and a shrine-like backdrop containing an elevated niche with a sculpture of the Virgin of Guadalupe.

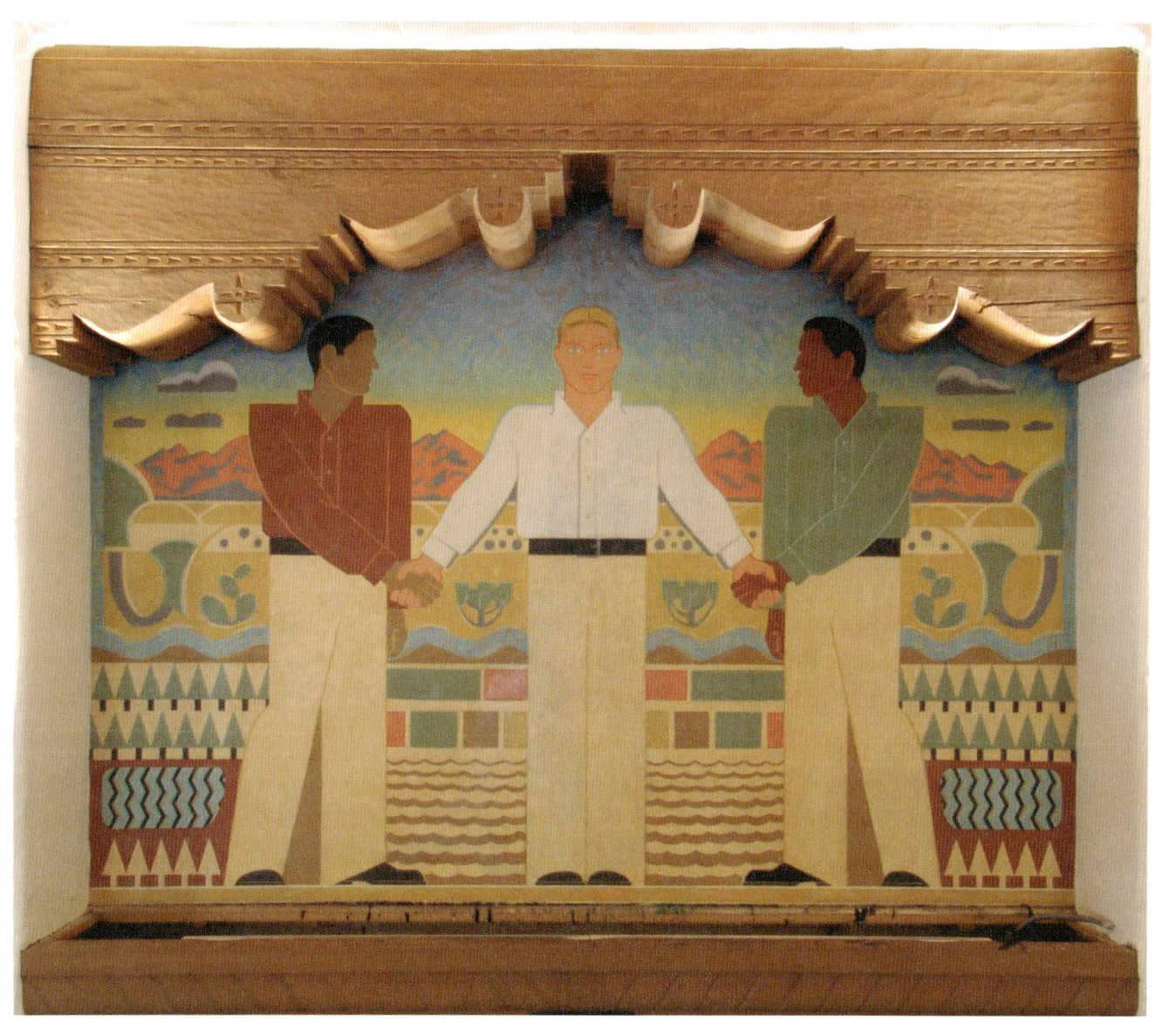

FIGURE 1.4. Kenneth M. Adams, *The Union of All Three in the Life of the Southwest*, 1939. Mural, Zimmerman Library, Center for Southwest Research, University of New Mexico.

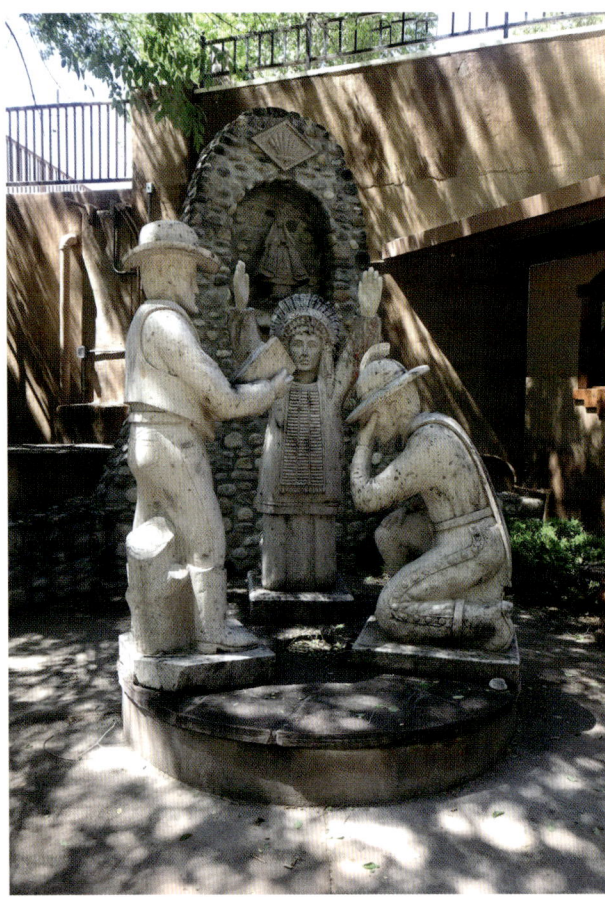

FIGURE 1.5. Gil Martínez, *The Three Cultures Monument, Santuario de Chimayó,* Chimayó, New Mexico, 2007. Stone sculpture. Image courtesy of Ray Hernández-Durán.

Gil Martínez is associated with the sculptural group and is described as having designed the monument at the bequest of Father Julio González in 2007; another name that is mentioned in conjunction with Martínez is Nidia Corral Gómez.[79] The three figures seem to be depicted in prayer and are in varying orant poses. The Native man kneels with both arms outstretched towards the sky; the Hispanic man is down on one knee with his left hand covering his closed eyes; and the white man is standing and holds what is presumably a bible, which he is reading to the other two men. In this case, besides the reference to the tricultural myth is the fact that it is the white man who possesses literacy and holds the Holy Book as the Hispano contemplates inwardly and the Native prays outwardly.

The desire to recognize and give expression to what are considered three distinct communities, whether intentionally or not, reinforces the questionable essentializing symbolism of this culturally inflected framework, which completely ignores the interpolated historical realities of historical communities and the transcultural processes that resulted in numerous cultural exchanges, adaptations, and transformations.[80] Furthermore, other groups with historical ties to New Mexico but that are not aligned with these three populations—for example, African American/Black, Asian American, Jewish, Muslim, including later Mexican and other Latin American immigrants, have tended to be invisibilized and left out of the conversation. Although contemporary art exhibitions in places like Taos, Santa Fe, and Albuquerque have been increasingly more inclusive, there is still the issue that New Mexico has historically been more diverse and culturally entangled than implied by the tricultural idea. This concept continues to hold power because it has been useful in marketing New Mexico and shaping its cultural identity, in addition to how it plays into the innate human tendency toward tribal thinking; however, could it be time to see the tricultural myth as a relic of the past and an obstacle to historical veracity and demographic inclusivity?

In the face of this dominant, institutionalized framework, which is a legacy of US intervention in the region, where do self-identified Chicanas and Chicanos fit? What about Chicano art? Within this triumvirate of art traditions, which, not coincidentally both mirrors the mythologized tricultural foundation of the state and reflects its high-profile art markets and trademark museum collections, Chicana and Chicano art does not register and is thus excluded. In terms of institutional inclusion and representation, Chicana and Chicano artists have been relegated to the periphery, if not erased. Unlike what are considered traditional Hispano or Spanish arts, which have been produced for the last four hundred years, Chicano art, specifically material associated with the civil rights movements of the mid- to late twentieth century, is not historical or traditional in the same sense, nor was it generally made with a market or collectors in mind in contrast to the arts promoted by the art institutions in the state. Furthermore, in terms of contemporary art—what could be considered a fourth branch of New Mexican art production—established museums and galleries would not have recognized Chicano art or included it in their exhibition programming in the 1970s and 1980s since Chicano art forms, given their origin, forms, and functions, were not considered high art nor were they generally made by artists with valued pedigrees or ties to the institutional art world of the period. In response to this neglect, Chicana and Chicano artists created their own spaces for the display of and engagement with art and they disseminated their work among members of their communities.

Early Chicano art, as a cultural production associated with community, labor, land, activism, and the fight for equal rights, is generally not regarded as historical in the same way that Indigenous/Pueblo or Hispano/Spanish arts have been, a perspective that has been critiqued given that the land grant movement in New Mexico, considered to be one of the starting points for the Chicano rights movement, is tied in part to the area's colonial legacies. Neglecting Chicano art denies the movement's cultural significance in New Mexico and in the Americas, more broadly, as one in a long series of anticolonial and/or anti-imperial protests, revolts, and struggles going back centuries, not to mention negating the identity of many New Mexicans, given that New Mexican Chicanas and Chicanos came from the local Hispano/ Indo-Hispano/Mexicano population. Referring to the politicized conscience of Chicano identity in an editorial published in the *Los Angeles Times* (1970), Chicano journalist Ruben Salazar stated, "A Chicano is a Mexican-American with a non-Anglo image of himself."[81] This statement, presumably, could be extended to include non-European or non-Spanish identification, more broadly, as well, given the focus on reclaiming and promoting with pride the Indigenous heritage of Chicano communities. This form of identification presents an interesting case in New Mexico. New Mexican Chicana and Chicano art reflects the ideals and politics of the *movimiento* and serves to communicate, educate, organize, and inspire; simultaneously, as heirs to New Mexican Hispano traditions, New Mexican Chicana and Chicano artists freely draw from local practices and forms creating a Chicano art inflected by local New Mexican experience and esthetics.

New Mexican Chicana and Chicano artists have faced various obstacles in terms of gaining any kind of significant local institutional recognition. First, although Chicana and Chicano identity is anchored to indigeneity and the Indigenous homeland of the South-west, many in the state's Native American communities are troubled by that identification and do not recognize Chicanos as Indigenous. María Eugenia Cotera and María Josefina Saldaña-Portillo, discussing the convening of the international symposium, *Indigenous Peoples of the Americas: Conflict, Resistance, and Peace-Making*, held at the University of New Mexico in 2005, note that a boycott of the event organized by the Tricentennial Truth Alliance (made up of local Indigenous Pueblo representatives) was aimed at pointing out illegitimate claims to indigeneity, a criticism targeting Chicanos. They write, "These questions had been accumulating since at least the late 1960s, when the Chicana/o movement placed indigeneity at the center of its political imaginary and Aztlán (the Southwest) as that imaginary's homeland. The contradictory nature of Mexican *mestizo* identity in the borderlands (Were they "settlers" or "Indians," "enemies" or "allies"?) also undermined the potential for productive collaboration between Chicana/os and Natives at the symposium."[82] On the other hand, because Chicanos align themselves with indigeneity, critique Eurocentric values, and promote anticolonial ideas and actions, they resist sole identification with the Spanish or European colonial presence, conflicting with New Mexican Hispanos who claim Spanish identity. The other side of this positionality is that many Hispanos in New Mexico who identify as Spanish and/or hold anti-Mexican sentiments do not identify with or recognize Chicanos as part of their communities; their responses may range from simple disregard to an extreme vilification that borders on racism, colorism, and/or classism. Then there is the troubling racist history the Chicano community, primarily comprised of people of Mexican descent, has faced by being marginalized, exploited, and in certain cases, violently attacked by Anglo settlers (and others), especially once New Mexico became a US territory. With this history behind the current arts culture of the state, how does Chicana and Chicano art fit into the history of New Mexican art? Conversely, how does Chicana and Chicano New Mexican art correspond to the history of the Chicano art movement? We can also ask how it all relates to the broader fields of Latinx Art History and American Art History. Although the production of Chicano art in New Mexico from the 1970s through the present allows us to technically approach this broad body of work as a branch of contemporary US art, Chicano art has not been easily embraced as such by most (primarily white) curators, academics, and artists in the United States due to questions of quality, esthetics, and reservations about the role of identity politics in Chicano art production, among other things.

Ultimately, due to the logic of the tripartite model of New Mexican cultural identity, Chicanas and Chicanos have rarely been offered an official or institutional space that ties them to the region, allows their experiences to be recognized, or documents and promotes their work as in the case of other New Mexican art cultures. The investment in this tripartite representation by local communities, including artists and collectors, and local institutions, such as museums and archives, further reinforces this marginalization. The art markets that were established in the early twentieth century to bring attention to those cultural traditions seen as historical and tied to New Mexico strictly delineate and regulate what can and can't be included in the cultural forms they display and sell as "authentic" New Mexican art. Museum collections and exhibitions, likewise, primarily focus on artwork that corresponds to these accepted ethno-historical categories with the addition of what has been growing interest in contemporary art over the last fifty years or so. Chicano art, typically regarded as lowbrow, activist, or insignificant to the New Mexican experience, is thus disregarded and left out of the larger cultural conversation; in the best of cases, it becomes a footnote in the art history of the state, if acknowledged at all.

In Joseph Traugott's time-spanning survey of the arts of New Mexico, he reifies the tricultural concept in the bodies of work he selects for inclusion. In the last chapter, the Chicano art movement goes unnamed but is indirectly referenced via the inclusion of a drawing—a preliminary study of a sculpture by the Chicano artist Luis Jiménez. The term "Chicano" is never mentioned, although Traugott writes, "Some artists responded to political movements in American society by directly addressing issues of gender, identity, and racism through their art."[83] Traugott's focus is Native, Hispanic, and modern art (predominantly by white artists) up to contemporary art, which becomes a bit more diverse. To what extent this erasure has been intentional or simply a result of the state's official focus on its regional historical traditions is difficult to ascertain; however, what must be taken into consideration is how these areas of emphasis, their promotion, and the institutions that have developed around them have calcified around certain essentialized narratives about the state's cultural and historic legacies. Such practices must be seen as symptoms or conditions of larger systemic racist, classist, and ethnocentric attitudes that were introduced during the territorial and early state periods of New Mexico and that, sadly, in spite of some change, continue to inform the political and cultural environment today, not just in the state, but also nationally.

"Towards Liberation with One Heart and One Mind": The Chicano Movement, Its Artists, and Their Art

"Brotherhood unites us, and love for our brothers makes us a people whose time has come and who struggle against the foreigner 'gabacho' who exploits our riches and destroys our culture."[84]

—

Although Chicanas and Chicanos, as part of the Mexican American and Hispano communities in the Southwest, can trace their history in the Americas back centuries thus pre-dating the existence of the United States, the Chicano Movement proper is generally seen as emerging and taking shape in the mid- to late twentieth century, during the height of the Civil Rights Movement, which had earlier formed under the able leadership and effective organization of the Black community, initially in the southern US states going back to at least the 1950s, if not earlier.[85] Inspired by the Black Civil Rights Movement and fueled in part by criticism of the Vietnam War and the concurrent loss of life, mostly among youths from communities of color, the Chicano Movement aimed to address the poverty, racism, exclusion, displacement, and exploitation faced by longstanding working-class Mexican communities in the Southwest as a result of the racialized class system enabled and sustained by Anglos. Chicana and Chicano activists, too, responded to the call of other disenfranchised populations and formed alliances with Black Civil Rights groups, Native American groups, Puerto Ricans, Filipinos, and other working-class communities.[86] Central to the movement was a focus on addressing inequities in education, health, land rights, and workers' rights, all concerns resulting from the changes introduced in the region over the previous 150 years; the Chicano movement, like other civil rights movements in the country, was thus anticolonial and anticapitalist and at odds with the dominant American social, cultural, and institutional status quo. As Rodolfo Acuña stated in his seminal publication, *Occupied America: A History of Chicanos* (First Edition, 1972),

> The 1960s were a time of discovery, a decade when presidential candidates and the media suddenly discovered that poor folk lived in "America." This revelation affected Mexican Americans, who had largely been unknown outside of the Southwest. Chicanos, for a time, hoped that awareness of their plight would lead to a reform of the political structure, resulting in the removal of the barriers to their full participation in society. No such changes occurred, and, by the end of the decade, the poor remained poor.[87]

The socioeconomic, political, and cultural gaps between Mexican Americans and Anglo Americans had been widening, and Mexican American poverty was central in most conversations among activists and community organizers of the time. Early studies of the Chicano community during this period were often centered on the family unit and approached the Chicano family in terms of deficiency or pathology instead of addressing the historical systemic marginalization that Chicanos were subjected to and had to contend with on a daily basis.[88] The national debate over the culture of poverty that was of concern took shape, in large part, as a result of Chicano-led research and its dissemination via community-based publications, such as *El Grito: A Journal of Contemporary Mexican American Thought*, which was founded in 1967 and ran until 1974. Although based in Berkeley, California, scholarly and creative work produced by Mexican Americans from around the country was featured in the periodical. In spite of its short run, *El Grito* inspired similar publications in Chicana and Chicano communities throughout the Southwest and around the country, including New Mexico; such periodicals played a central role in communicating a range of information to its readers, as did theater, a tool through which to reach various segments of the community, specifically those comprising the labor force in the agricultural industries.[89]

In addition to the groundbreaking activism and organizing work done in the name of civil rights, members of the community also explored what it meant to be Chicana or Chicano. Chicana and Chicano writers published editorials, articles, and books examining the community's history; the Chicano experience; and Chicana and Chicano identity. Many who came of age during this period of activism, such as Sergio Troncoso, who went from living in poverty near the Texas-Mexico border to attending Ivy League universities in the US northeast, employed their biographies as case studies to convey to broader audiences what life was like in the Southwest borderlands as a US citizen of Mexican descent. A quote from Troncoso's published biography that captures one of the recurring tropes about life as a Chicana or Chicano states,

> I am in between. Trying to write to be understood by those who matter
> to me, yet also trying to push my mind with ideas beyond the everyday.
> It is another borderland I inhabit. Not quite here nor there. On good
> days I feel I am a bridge. On bad days I just feel alone.[90]

The experience of being from or of the Borderlands, what some scholars, using Indigenous Nahua or Aztec concepts and terminology, have termed *nepantla*, an existential state of being "in-between," in this case, caught between Mexico and the US—not quite Mexican for one side nor quite American for the other—has been a thread connecting stories about the Chicana and Chicano experience across the Southwest that appears in various productions, from scholarly publications to the visual arts to literary works to popular culture.[91]

As American Studies scholar Arlene Dávila has observed regarding the experiences of artists of color, "At the same time, African American and Latinx artists occupy different places in the contemporary art world that underlie the challenges of achieving a similar level of recognition for Latinx art. African American artists in the US have been historically marginalized, yet the dominant US Black/white racial binary nevertheless anchors African American artists as undeniably 'American,' recognition often denied to Latinxs. Instead, Latinxs have been historically racialized as unbelonging and forever foreigners, despite their historical presence in the United States prior to its establishment (as with Mexican Americans), or despite their citizenship status (as with Puerto Ricans)."[92] Although generally misunderstood and vilified on both sides of the border, as in the case with Chicanos, it is necessary to recognize that the birth of the Mexican American community was a direct result not just of US belligerence, imperialist designs, and territorial expansion but also of Mexico's disorganization, debilitated state, and inability to defend its national territory and protect its own citizens.

A central idea that served as a geographic anchor to the movement was identifying the US Southwest as Aztlán, the mythical home of the Mexica or Aztec people, now the Chicana and Chicano homeland.[93] In *El Plan Espiritual de Aztlán*, presented in 1969 at the national Chicano Youth Liberation Conference held in Denver, Colorado, Chicano activist Alurista declares the right of Chicanos to the US Southwest, i.e., Aztlán, as a "bronze people" on a "bronze continent."[94] Rejecting the dominant Anglocentric and/or Eurocentric notions of national origin and ethnic identification promoted in the US and searching for an alternate narrative that reflected the community's history and experience, the Chicano movement embraced the Mexican and Indigenous heritage of the people. Instead of it being a source of shame, as had historically been the case in the context of European and Euro-American colonialism, Native identity became a source of pride that came to define the cultural production that emerged from the movement. Renewed interest in Mexican history and culture, particularly that tied to Indigenous cultures and specifically the Aztec, became a focal point for the representations, whether written, visual, or performed, around which Chicana and Chicano identity was tied. As has been noted by various Chicana and Chicano scholars, *El Plan Espiritual de Aztlán* recognized the visual arts as an essential tool or vehicle for the revolutionary movement to educate, organize, and inspire by reflecting the diverse community's history, culture, values, experiences, and identity.[95] Many also looked to Mexico, the Mexican Revolution, and other Latin American political movements of the early twentieth century and their heroes, such as the leader of the Mexican agrarian movement, Emiliano Zapata, and the Argentine guerrilla and leading figure of the Cuban Revolution Che Guevara.[96]

The focus on Aztlán centered the Southwest as an Indigenous homeland to which Chicanas and Chicanos laid claim; a declaration in part intended to counter popular views by US Americans of Mexicans as aliens or outsiders and that recognized how Indigenous and Mexicano communities located west of the Mississippi pre-dated the existence of the nation itself and had legitimate claims to living on and regaining control over their homeland. This focus on rights to territory in the Southwest was tied to claims of violations of the Treaty of Guadalupe Hidalgo following the Mexican American War of 1846–1848, which resulted in the expropriation of Mexican and Hispano land grants, thus motivating a renewed interest in restoring lost land rights. The question of which region was privileged in the rhetoric of the Chicano movement was complex and generated criticism, as did Native identification.[97] Although stemming from historical precedent, as well as political interest, the focus on the Southwest eventually came to be questioned, given the presence of Mexican Americans or Chicanos in other parts of the country. Pointing out the need to consider Chicano communities and artists in the Midwest, for instance, art historian Dylan Miner noted the need for a broader, more encompassing Chicano art history; Miner writes, "The existence of a Chicana/o artistic canon is still very much in question. Although certain artists have achieved mainstream recognition, a Chicana/o art history has yet to be fully written."[98] My question at this point is, Has there been any substantial progress made in this regard since he penned these words fifteen years ago?

In the context of the Southwest, an issue in need of remediation is that California has, to a great extent, been centered in the scholarship on the history of Chicano art. The focus on this region has yielded an ample literature on the subject that is canonical in the field and serves as a model for the study of Chicana and Chicano art more generally, although it is focused specifically on the Chicano experience in places like Los Angeles. For example, art historians Holly Barnet-Sánchez and Tim Drescher, writing about the Chicano murals in East Los Angeles, state, "The murals painted in the eastern part of Los Angeles in the 1970s helped create Chicanismo, the idea of what it meant to be Chicano . . . This point is essential: the murals in this study do not merely represent or celebrate Chicanismo, they helped create it."[99] A question that comes to mind is, Can the LA Chicano experience speak for or represent the broader range of Chicano experiences across the Southwest and elsewhere? Most would agree that the answer to this question is a firm no. California's importance in both the movement and its art history is understood and is indisputable for evident reasons, including the focus on labor and workers' rights tied to the agricultural industries in the southern parts of the state, exemplified by Cesar Chávez and his organizing work, for instance, and also, given the presence of large urban centers with dense Mexican populations, such as seen in Los Angeles, San Diego, and other cities in the area. Given the large urban environments in the state, there was and continues to be a concentration of Chicanos and other Latino communities, as well as various communal and institutional infrastructures that facilitated organizing, supported cultural production, and provided media coverage unlike the more rural regions of New Mexico.

The earliest Chicano artist groups, cultural centers, and art exhibitions from the late 1960s on primarily originated in places like Los Angeles, San Diego, Sacramento, San Francisco, and Oakland; as is evident, the vast majority of Chicano art-based projects were centered on the West Coast.[100] New Mexican Chicana artist Roberta Márquez recalled that shortly before Pedro Rodríguez, professor of Chicano studies at New Mexico Highlands University, was summarily dismissed, he had proposed the founding of a Chicano art center, ca. 1971, in Las Vegas, New Mexico, but he received no support; Rodríguez not only faced challenges from the Anglo university administrators but also from New Mexican Hispanos, who were anti-Chicano.[101] Regarding California's status as a center for the Chicano art movement, Karen Mary Davalos noted that, in spite of Southern California having the largest Mexican American community, a venerated history of Chicano activism and art production, and recent exhibitions of Chicano art supported by such entities as the Getty, institutions in the state continue to marginalize Chicano artists and Chicano art where it matters, such as in long-term support, preservation, and study; she writes,

> None of the major museums in the region have a permanent collection policy for preserving Chicano art. None permanently display the artwork, and none of them have employed a full-time expert on Chicano art. Following the national trend, you will only find Chicano art specialists in the education or public programs departments, and not in curatorial positions, where they might shape the interpretation and presentation of these museum collections. Without systematic stewardship, what will happen to the masterpieces created by Chicano artists?[102]

If this, indeed, is the case for Chicano art in California, what could be happening in other states? California's status as perhaps the most important center for the Chicano art movement is well established; however, the question remains, Why isn't there a more developed literature on those figures, events, works, etc., that were important and contributed to the larger movement in other states in the region and across the country?[103]

Although on a smaller scale than in places like Los Angeles, Chicana and Chicano artists in New Mexico were active in cities with universities and significant communities, such as Albuquerque, Santa Fe, Las Vegas, Las Cruces, and others. Although Chicanos in New Mexico did not have access to the kinds of art museums and galleries found in larger urban centers, artists formed their own associations, painted murals throughout the state, produced work for the community, and organized their own events; much of that activity was unfortunately not documented sufficiently, or if it was, that documentation has been lost and has not been recovered. That said, testimonies from artists and others who were active in the 1970s provide an idea of the work that was done. Besides its geographical distance from California and its mostly rural status, New Mexico presents certain challenges that are unique to the region, which questions the idea of a monolithic Chicano population, identity, or movement. It is important to recognize that among the larger Chicano population in the country, there are regional variations, distinct histories, competing interests, and varied access to resources—differences that have often engendered tribalism and internal tensions among certain groups, such as those defined by state, for example, *Californios* versus *Nuevo Mexicanos* versus *Tejanos*, and so on; for example, an ongoing debate asks which region has the most "authentic" or the "best" Mexican food.[104] The need to bring other voices that were part of the movement to light, such as that of Chicanas or LGBTQ Chicanxs, has also been recognized; there is a need to continue approaching the movement not as singular but as constituted by multiple more localized movements, each responding to the larger movement's principles, as well as to broader social politics but in tune with the peculiarities of their respective communities and locations.[105] Already by the mid-1980s, when the fervor of the early Civil Rights Movement began dying down, the various demographic subgroups of the Chicana and Chicano population began expressing diverse, sometimes conflicting, interests and priorities; as happens with all communities and movements, identity evolves and shifts in tune with the times. As Shifra Goldman observed when writing during that period, "Rifts have been opening in the alliance between students, urban workers, farmworkers (whose unionizing of the mid-sixties galvanized what has been called the 'Chicano renaissance') and the newly-augmented professional/business middle class."[106]

In addition to questions of geographical disparities, there is the inconsistency between the history of the Chicano movement and Chicano art history. Chicana and Chicano activists and organizers from throughout the Southwest are recognized in the literature; however, the same cannot be said for New Mexican Chicana and Chicano artists, specifically those who remained in New Mexico to work. Although the early beginnings of the movement have been tied to New Mexico with figures like Reies López Tijerina (originally from Texas) and Dolores Huerta, who figures prominently in Chicano art history, the New Mexican Chicana and Chicano artists who remained in New Mexico have been understudied and are less familiar, despite the central role the arts played in the region during the early period of the movement.[107] New Mexican Chicana and Chicano artists and their art have had to contend with not only what can be seen as exclusionary cultural politics in New Mexico, but also what can be seen as a selective focus in Chicano art history. How can we begin to address this neglect? A step in redressing this omission might be to look at Chicana and Chicano art in New Mexico not just on its own terms but in relation to Chicano art in places like California, Texas, or the Midwest; what elements do these movements share? How are they different, and why? Shifra Goldman and Tomás Ybarra-Frausto, describing the early Chicano art movement, organized it into two phases: one, from 1968–1975, and two, from 1975–1981. They wrote,

> The first period was marked by the noncommercial community-oriented
> attitudes and expectations of the art groups, the purposes they served,
> the audiences they addressed, the facilities established to promote their
> arts, and the collectives that flourished. The second period witnessed
> changes in the dynamics of an art movement subject to the fluctuations
> of the political movement and the imperatives of the dominant society
> to which that art was opposed. Crucial to this second period was the
> changing perception of the Chicano . . . in the United States and in the

international arena, a perception that brought an end to separatism for most Chicanos and a closer alignment with . . . Third World, especially Latin American, struggles.[108]

Would New Mexican Chicano art from this period fit into this chronological framework? Similarly, Chicana and Chicano scholars and artists, such as Tomás Ybarra-Frausto and Amalia Mesa-Bains, have contributed, along with others, to defining a Chicana and/or Chicano esthetic sensibility manifested in Chicana and Chicano art production; here, I refer to the now-familiar concepts of *rasquachismo* and *domesticana*.[109] Again, does New Mexican Chicano art correspond to or reflect the esthetics and concepts here outlined, or are there differences? If the latter, what factors could explain those discrepancies, and what would that tell us about the New Mexican context of Chicana and Chicano art production?

One thing that stands out when reviewing the arts made by Chicana and Chicano artists living and working in New Mexico is the use of traditional Hispano artistic idioms and materials tied to this region; as noted, the location inflects the arts that are made. Given that Chicanos in New Mexico came out of the local Hispano/Mexicano population, there may be cases where artists embrace multiple identities and fluidly move between them. For instance, there may be Hispana and Hispano artists who participate in Spanish Market but who may support the principles of the movement and even identify as Chicana or Chicano without any sense of conflict, given the interpolated nature of community histories; unlike California where Mexico is centered in Chicano identity in light of ongoing waves of Mexican immigrants over time, in New Mexico, identity even among Chicanos is tied to communities that have lived in the region for centuries, an experience that has fostered a strong, rooted, local consciousness and identity. Reflecting this dynamic, there are Chicana and Chicano artists who work with materials and forms associated more closely with New Mexican Hispano art traditions, exemplified, for instance, in the use of wool, adobe, local woods, and natural pigments, and in the production of forms inspired by historical weaving practices or retablo formats. These artists freely draw from European, Mexican, Indigenous, New Mexican, and Chicano expressive idioms to make work that visually conveys the principles of the movement but from a uniquely New Mexican point of view.

Although there has been some interest in Chicano art in the state, continuing challenges in New Mexico include unfamiliarity with the Chicano movement, especially among affluent Anglos, and/or a pervasive view by many who are a part of the official arts establishment, Anglo and Hispano, that questions both the term "Chicano" as a desirable identifier and the quality of Chicano art, the latter question regarding quality being a recurrent concern. Reviewing the history of the groundbreaking *Chicano Art: Resistance and Affirmation, 1965–1985* (CARA) 1991 exhibition, which was scheduled to travel from California to New Mexico and Texas, Alicia Gaspar de Alba noted that in places like Albuquerque and El Paso, cities with large Mexican-American populations, sponsoring venues expressed concern over the use of "Chicano" in the exhibition's title and promotional materials for reasons that included racial, ethnic, and class-based criticism of the term's meaning; for instance, one individual characterized the word Chicano as potentially offensive to middle-class Mexican Americans while another expressed concern that the term would alienate people who identified as Spanish or Hispano.[110] Similarly, referring to art critic Lucy Lippard's statement that quality is only identifiable by those in power, Gaspar de Alba added that "Quality is an exclusionary tactic, a password meant to keep out those whose race, ethnicity, gender, and/or sexual orientation reflect a conflict of interests with white patriarchy; in short, Quality functions as a euphemism for racism, sexism, heterosexism, and ethnocentrism."[111]

With the Chicano movement's original intent tied to addressing the concerns and needs of working-class Mexican Americans, Chicana and Chicano artists addressed themes relevant to such interests in their art; however, a concern that emerged following the CARA exhibition and the increasing institutional recognition of Chicana and Chicano artists and their work was the possibility that the original motive of the movement would be radically transformed from liberation to validation as Chicano art became more mainstream and Chicana and Chicano artists gained access to elitist arts institutions. How does that apply to New Mexican artists? Although a handful of Chicana and Chicano New Mexican artists were included in the CARA exhibition, as well as in other exhibitions and collections nationally, the productivity, exhibition, and reception of these artists has varied over time, as a result not just of an individual artist's productivity but also a general lack of awareness or interest on behalf of local arts institutions. As a traveling survey of Chicano art, CARA was exhibited at the Albuquerque Museum; however, since then and in the past thirty years, there has not been a similar large-scale exhibition on Chicana and Chicano art, whether New Mexican or national, organized by or at any of the larger art museums in the state, although there have been a handful of smaller shows in local galleries, such as *Chicana Badgirls: Las Hociconas*, cocurated by Chicana artist Delilah Montoya and Chicanx/Latinx Studies scholar Laura Pérez at 516 Arts in downtown Albuquerque in 2009. That members of the Hispano/Chicano community have been the primary supporters of and writers on Chicano art in New Mexico may reflect the general disregard of this material by outsiders in terms of questions of quality, the political or activist content of some of the work, or the perception of the work as out of sync with contemporary artistic trends; the latter may explain why Chicano art seems to be disregarded as an expression of contemporary US art, although exhibitions, such as *Phantom Sightings: Art after the Chicano Movement*, cocurated by Rita González, Howard Fox, and Chon Noriega at the Los Angeles County Museum of Art in 2008, have attempted to bring this material into conversation with current developments, though not without criticism. In New Mexico, the Chicano movement is not as present in the cultural discourses or the communal imaginary of the region as in California or even Texas. There, too, seems to be a widely held perception of the movement as a relic of the past with no currency today. We can add these variables to the long list of challenges facing anyone wanting to study New Mexican Chicana and Chicano artists and their art, especially that of the first generation of activists.

The topic of Chicana and Chicano artists working in New Mexico over the past fifty years is wide-ranging and exceeds the parameters of the current project. With a more focused scope in mind, the artists here featured were affiliated with New Mexico Highlands University in Las Vegas, as students at the university, as activists, and as community members when the Chicano movement began to take shape in the state. In some ways, New Mexico Highlands University can be seen as one of the first centers for Chicano student activism in the state due to the influence of the aforementioned Chicano Studies scholar Pedro Rodríguez, who was originally from San Antonio, Texas and briefly served on the New Mexico Highlands University (NMHU) faculty as inaugural director of the new Chicano Studies program from 1971 to 1973 before departing for the University of Washington in Pullman.[112] During his short-lived tenure at NMHU, Pedro taught courses in Chicano Studies and classes on Chicano and Mexican art. He mentored students and sent them to study in Mexico where they, for the first time, learned about the history of Mexican art from the Prehispanic through modern periods. In Mexico City, Pedro's students learned about the muralist tradition from the painter Ramiro Romo Estrada. Most of Rodríguez's students, primarily local young men and women from Las Vegas and other small towns and villages in northern New Mexico, had not traveled out of state, much less out of the country, and they had not been exposed to anything outside of European art history; consequently, they were stunned upon arriving in Mexico City and immediately inspired when they were introduced to the rich history of Mexican art, as well as recognizing the relevance of Mexican traditions to their own back home. The fact that much of the history they were learning about in Mexico was evidently shaped by Mexico's Indigenous peoples also heightened these students' awareness of their home communities' relationships to the native populations in New Mexico and to their own Indigenous connections.

In Las Vegas, New Mexico, in addition to making art, the students organized, demonstrated, produced a student newsletter and paper, and went on to become educators, journalists, and community organizers, as well as continuing to work as artists and as public art advocates. The students with creative tendencies who were interested in the arts and who had worked with Pedro, after returning from Mexico, began producing artwork that reflected a developing Chicana and Chicano political consciousness and sensibility, one that drew visually from Latin American and Mexican history, including murals that represented well-known and respected political or revolutionary figures.[113] Pedro, who became popular with the students as a teacher and mentor, recalled promoting activism through art. Relating the unceremonious manner in which he was let go, he mentioned that he and those he was associating with were perceived as agitators by the administration. Pedro added that the murals painted at NMHU during the administration of then-president, Frank Ángel (1971–1975), were whitewashed at the bequest of Gilbert Sánchez (a faculty member who would later serve as president in 1985–1995); one of the artists who was a student at that time mentioned having heard that the New Mexico Speaker of the House, Les Houston (R) told Sánchez that if he expected to receive university funding, he would have to remove the murals, which he did to gain favor with the Republican Governor Bruce King.[114] Frank Ángel's position and that of other university administrators was made clear at a public meeting when Ángel, a New Mexican Hispano, stated that not only were murals not art but that Mexico had nothing to do with New Mexico, an argument supported by the Spanish-identified Hispanos in the administration and allegedly some Chicanos seeking to gain favor with institutional leaders.[115] Apparently, it wasn't just the Anglo administrators who were bothered by the Chicano activism spreading throughout their campus. In a letter written by Ángel in 1973, he describes the Chicano protesters in the following manner: "There is, on the campus and the community, a very small (50–60) group of extremist Chicanos, who

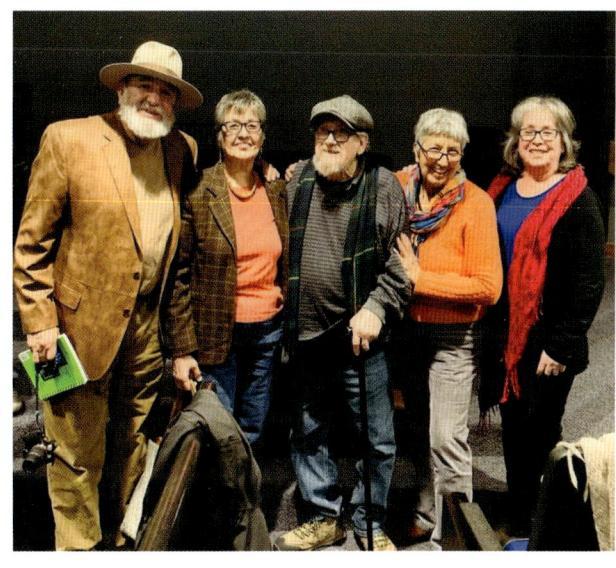

FIGURE 1.6. Pedro Rodríguez (1936–2022) (center) with four of his NMHU students: (left to right) Francisco Lefebre, Adelita M. Medina, Juanita J. Lavadie, and Roberta Márquez, Albuquerque Museum, October 24, 2019. Photograph courtesy of Ray Hernández-Durán.

have a narrow, self-serving, concept of Chicanismo. They have the idea that this institution should become entirely Chicano and that I, because I am a Chicano, should yield to their demands."[116] In another memo, also from 1973, Ángel accuses Pedro and a fellow Chicano Studies faculty member William R. Lux of being the masterminds behind the student unrest; he wrote, "Two professors, Pedro Rodriguez and Bill Lux, are probably the real behind-the-scenes leaders. Pedro especially is a behind-the-scenes manipulator. He never openly shows his claws."[117] Pedro's experience was not anomalous at NMHU during this tumultuous period in its history based on court documents implicating Frank Ángel and his successor, John Aragón (1975–1985) in the illegal firing of Pedro's colleague, William R. Lux, who had been hired to teach Southwestern History in 1971, the same year that Pedro was hired.[118]

Each of the Chicana and Chicano artists who were students at NMHU during this period acknowledge Pedro Rodríguez's role in educating and mentoring them and awakening them politically (fig. 1.6). It was this work promoting Chicano activism through art, deemed unacceptable and disruptive to the status quo, that led to Rodríguez's abrupt and unexpected dismissal less than two years after his hire. As Pedro himself stated, "There was no explanation other than that we were troublemakers."[119] Based on various accounts, Pedro was the catalyst that ignited Chicana and Chicano youth activism at NMHU, ca. 1971, a movement that only continued to grow after his departure in 1973 and that motivated Chicano activism and art production beyond NMHU and Las Vegas up through the present.

Concluding Remarks

Despite successful markets and growing scholarship on the arts in New Mexico, the Anglo-dominated institutional arts culture in New Mexico has been a point of contention for various segments of Natives and Hispanos for decades. New Mexican Hispana and Hispano artists, perhaps inspired by the growing Chicano resistance of the late 1960s, reacted against this power imbalance in 1970 by establishing *La Cofradía de Artes y Artesanos Hispanos*, in opposition to and/or as an alternate to the Traditional Spanish Market, which, founded in 1925 by the Spanish Colonial Arts Society, occupies a central place in the promotion of Spanish arts in Santa Fe, northern New Mexico, and southern Colorado.[120] It is clear that in an art market where the commodification of certain local art traditions is central to the socioeconomic interests of both the elites running cultural institutions and the Hispana and Hispano artists who participate and espouse a distinctly Spanish identity in their work, the kind of art production associated with the early Chicano Movement in New Mexico would not have access to the same kinds of inclusion and promotion, given its more overt political and activist nature and its centering of Indigenous and Mexican cultural forms and historical figures; for example, when I served on the Spanish Market Standards Committee, I was surprised to learn that *Día de muertos* imagery was not allowed in the art sold at Spanish Market since it was considered Mexican and not New Mexican. The fact that the Chicano movement's critical stance against racism and injustice, and its aim to undo the damaging effects of settler colonialism and Eurocentric institutions, both Anglo and Hispano, while emphasizing and monumentalizing the histories, values, experiences, and practices associated with historically marginalized communities—i.e., non-white, disenfranchised, and poor—meant that the arts produced in tandem with the Chicano movement would often stand in opposition to and/or contradict the politics and priorities that structure the official arts culture in the state. In doing so, such critical postures wound up alienating many of the Anglo and Hispano gatekeepers in places like Santa Fe and Taos. In other words, the systemic racism, elitism, and institutional politics normally targeted and critiqued by Chicanas and Chicanos inevitably implicate the very cultural institutions and agents that regulate the official arts culture in New Mexico.

A recent incident that exemplifies these continuing tensions involves the destruction of a community mural painted on a wall of the Haplin Building in Santa Fe in 1980 by artist Gilberto Guzmán along with other members of the local community, including students at the Institute of American Indian Arts. The mural depicted a brown Indigenous woman with outstretched arms surrounded by images referencing the local landscape, local history, and New Mexico's diverse communities. The New Mexico Department of Cultural Affairs had approved the mural's removal in preparation for the remodeling of the building into the new Vladem Contemporary Art Museum, a satellite of the New Mexico Museum of

Art. Funded by private and public monies, the project's main donors are Bob and Ellen Vladem, whose name brands the new site. Originally from Chicago, the Vladems, identified as Santa Fe philanthropists, gave a $4 million gift to support the construction and also to pay for in-perpetuity naming rights.[121] The expansion was motivated by several concerns most people would agree are valid, including the need for additional storage space, a desire for more art spaces dedicated to contemporary art, an interest in developing curatorial and educational programming, and plans to house an artist-in-residence program, all noble motives—but at what or whose cost? The mural, a familiar and valued part of the local cultural environment in Santa Fe, reflected the histories of Chicano and Indigenous communities in the region and reinforced a sense of belonging and pride. When the mural's destruction was announced, Guzmán filed a lawsuit, and a series of protests followed. According to court documents, as noted by the local press, the case was settled in September 2021 and a compromise was reached where Guzmán would create a condensed digital version of the mural that would then be temporarily displayed in the lobby of the new museum.[122]

State Senator Gerald Ortiz y Pino, a political figure from a longstanding Hispano New Mexican family, had earmarked money for the mural's restoration but was told the mural could not be preserved since the supporting wall was going to be torn down. Although he didn't feel the mural's preservation should block the museum's construction, he added, "I'm not in Santa Fe anymore; I left because I thought the culture war had been lost back in the 70s . . . I just don't see much in the way of the Santa Fe that I knew growing up left in town . . . I'm afraid the changes are irreversible."[123] It wasn't just members of the Santa Fe or local Chicano community who were disturbed by the politics at play. Taylor Spence, a postdoctoral fellow in the Department of History at the University of New Mexico and a muralist himself, was interviewed about this controversy and stated, "I think it's disturbing that an elite institution that frankly is probably largely funded by white, wealthy, privileged people, seems so willing to just get rid of a piece of art like this with impunity."[124] He notes the value judgments being made; judgments that involve deciding which or whose art has value and is thus worth preserving.

Looking back at this extended conflict, it became clear that the local community's voice and interests don't hold much weight in such decision-making processes and were only acknowledged, in this case, in response to the lawsuit and ensuing protests. In the face of conflicting interests, the message that is loud and clear is that this community's art is worth sacrificing in the name of progress and in the attaining of goals held by those who hold the cultural capital and promote fine art in line with the priorities of local arts institutions and the contemporary art world they represent. In an unpublished interview conducted in October 2020 by New Mexican journalist Alicia Inez Guzmán with Bob Vladem, when addressing the protests motivated by the destruction of the community mural, Vladem declared, "There seems to be a lot of thoughts, and obviously you're interviewing me because somehow everybody thinks I'm the one who got rid of this mural. Never . . .

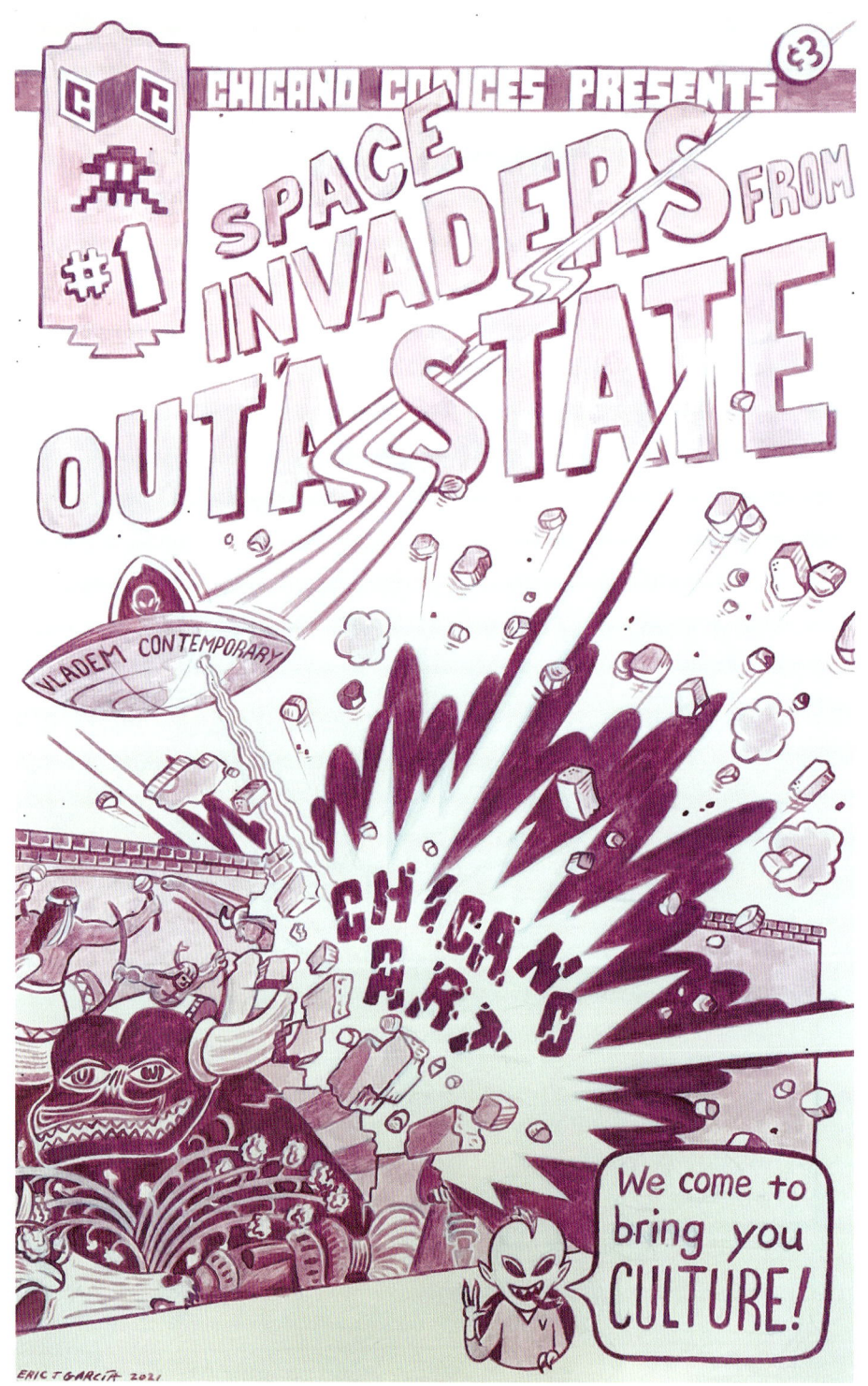

FIGURE 1.7. Eric J. García, *Space Invaders from Out'a State*, 2023. Drawing on paper with prickly pear ink. Image courtesy of Eric J. García.

it wasn't important enough to get rid of. It was already gone. It wasn't even part of the conversation."[125] Alicia added that the general attitude seemed to be that "they" should be grateful; here, echoes of Kipling's "white man's burden," as discussed earlier, ring loudly. To be clear, the problem is not responding to a need for museum facility expansion or even with supporting development or progress but rather with the pursuit and actualization of such goals at the expense of the longstanding local community, its valued cultural production, and its stated concerns. Sadly, as is often the case, the people who hold the purse strings are not members of the historic community but more recent arrivals, and in some cases, complete outsiders who do not share the same histories, values, or interests as longstanding locals, echoing Marroquin Norby's observations regarding Georgia O'Keeffe's conflicts with local Abiquiú residents. This question of outsiders intruding and colonizing local communities, as a historical reality in the region and as it relates to this recent controversy in Santa Fe, motivated much debate among community members. Contemporary New Mexican Chicano artist Eric J. García addressed the subject in a drawing he produced in his signature "comic" style while an artist-in-residence in Roswell in 2023 (fig. 1.7).

Cases such as this recent one must be seen not only in relation to Santa Fe's cultural politics but also to the deeper history in the region. These institutional practices and cultural priorities that disenfranchise local longstanding communities of color and relegate their interests and needs to the margins are exactly what the Chicano movement targeted and aimed to change. That we continue to encounter the same classist, racist obstacles; paternalistic attitudes; and "progressive" capitalist justifications today may seem, at first, outrageous to some; however, it's business as usual in New Mexico, at least, as it has been for the past century and as it has been in the rest of the country since 1848.[126] In spite of evident progress in certain sectors, the current state of affairs suggests that the original concerns motivating the Chicano movement fifty years ago continue to be relevant today and that the work of politically and socially conscious artists may be more important than ever.

Notes

1. Gloria Anzaldúa, *Borderlands / La Frontera: The New Mestiza* (Spinsters / Aunt Lute Book Company, 1987), 3.

2. I wish to express my gratitude to my colleague in the Department of Art, Native American Art historian, Aaron Fry, for his help as I worked on this essay. His profound knowledge of the arts in New Mexico proved indispensable to me as I began to research this history.

3. Quote taken from a speech Senator Sam Houston gave at Tammany Hall in New York City on February 22, 1848, following the Mexican American War of 1846–1848; see, Amelia W. Williams and Eugene C. Barker (eds), *The Writings of Sam Houston, 1813–1863* (The University of Texas Press, 1938).

4. There exists an ample body of literature on Columbus and the Conquest of Mexico. A few

select readings would include Hans Koning, *Columbus: His Enterprise, Exploding the Myth* (Monthly Review Press, 1976); Tzvetan Todorov, *The Conquest of America* (Harper and Rowe, 1984); and Matthew Restall, *Seven Myths of the Spanish Conquest* (Oxford University Press, 2003).

5. For more on the Spanish incursion into the Americas, see Cabeza de Vaca, *Adventures in the Unknown Interior of America*, translated and edited by Cyclone Covey (University of New Mexico Press, 1961); Bernard L. Fontana, *Entrada: The Legacy of Spain and Mexico in the United States* (University of New Mexico Press, 1994); Albert Marrin, *Empires Lost and Won: The Spanish Heritage in the Southwest* (Simon and Schuster, 1997); and Rolena Adorno and Patrick Charles Pautz, *Alvar Núñez Cabeza de Vaca: His Account, His Life, and the Expedition of Pánfilo de Narváez* (University of Nebraska Press, 1999).

6. There is no shortage of publications on New Mexico and its history; for example, see: Joseph P. Sánchez, Robert L. Spude, and Art Gómez, *New Mexico: A History* (University of Oklahoma Press, 2013); Martha Weigle, Frances Levine, and Louise Stiver, eds., *Telling New Mexico: A New History* (Museum of New Mexico Press, 2009); Thomas E. Chavez, *An Illustrated History of New Mexico* (University of New Mexico Press, 2002); and Susan A. Roberts and Calvin A. Roberts, *A History of New Mexico* (University of New Mexico Press, 1986).

7. For more on the Mexican-American War, see Ray John de Aragón, *New Mexico in the Mexican-American War* (The History Press, 2019); Ruth Tenzer Feldman, *The Mexican-American War* (Lerner Publications Co., 2004); Ron Field, *Mexican-American War, 1846–48* (Brassey, 1997); and Norman E. Tutorow, ed., *The Mexican-American War: An Annotated Bibliography* (Greenwood Press, 1981).

8. For the purposes of this essay, the term "Anglo," although technically referring to someone of British or English descent, will be used to identify all white individuals, that is, individuals of primarily northern European descent associated

with white racial status, who spent time in or settled in New Mexico. The use of the term Anglo as an umbrella racial identifier for whiteness follows common practice throughout the Southwest.

9. See Lawrence R. Murphy, "The United States Army in Taos, 1847–1852," *New Mexico Historical Review* 47, no. 1 (2021): 1; https://digitalrepository.unm.edu/nmhr/vol47/iss1/3.

10. See Charles L. Briggs, "The Role of Mexicano Artists and the Anglo Elite in the Emergence of Contemporary Folk Art," *Folk Art and Art Worlds*, John Michael Vlach and Simon J. Bronner, eds., Utah State University Press, 1986, 195–224.

11. Abraham Lincoln, "Speech of Hon. Abraham Lincoln at Springfield, June 17, 1858," *Debates of Lincoln and Douglas: Carefully Prepared by the Reporters of Each Party at the times of their Delivery* (1858).

12. Wayne Moquin and Charles Van Doren, eds., *A Documentary History of the Mexican Americans* (Bantam Books, 1971), 251.

13. Joseph Traugott, *New Mexico Art through Time: Prehistory to the Present* (Museum of New Mexico Press, 2012), 226; see also Bernard L. Fontana, *Entrada: The Legacy of Spain and Mexico in the United States* (The University of New Mexico Press, 1994); and James Early, *Presidio, Mission, and Pueblo: Spanish Architecture and Urbanism in the United States* (Southern Methodist University Press, 2004)

14. Estevan Rael-Gálvez, "Coyote Convergence: Introduction through Interrogation," in *Converging Streams: Art of the Hispanic and Native American Southwest*, William Wroth and Robin Farwell Gavin, eds., (Museum of New Mexico Press, 2010), 18.

15. For more information on the Pueblo Revolt, please see the following: Matthew Liebmann, *Revolt: An Archaeological History of Pueblo Resistance and Revitalization in 17th Century New Mexico* (University of Arizona Press, 2012); Michael V. Wilcox, *The Pueblo Revolt and the Mythology of Conquest: An Indigenous Archaeology of Contact* (University of California Press, 2009); David Roberts, *The Pueblo*

Revolt: The Secret Rebellion that Drove the Spaniards out of the Southwest (Simon and Shuster, 2004); and Andrew L. Knaut, *The Pueblo Revolt of 1680: Conquest and Resistance in Seventeenth-Century New Mexico* (University of Oklahoma Press, 1995).

16. For more on the *Genízaro* phenomenon in New Mexico, see Moises Gonzales and Enrique R. Lamadrid, eds., *Nación Genízara: Ethnogenesis, Place, and Identity in New Mexico* (University of New Mexico Press, 2019); Samuel Sisneros, "Los Genizaros and the Colonial Mission Pueblo of Belen, New Mexico," *New Mexico Historical Review* 92, no. 4 (October 2017): 453–94; Bernardo P. Gallegos, "Education and Indigenous Slavery in New Mexico," *American Educational History Journal* 43, Issues 1–2 (2016); Moises Gonzales, "The Genizaro Land Grant Settlement of New Mexico," *Journal of the Southwest* 56, no. 4 (Winter 2014), 583–602; and Doris Swann Avery, "Into the Den of Evils: The *Genizaros* in Colonial New Mexico" (2008), Graduate Student Theses, Dissertations, and Professional Papers, 592; https://scholarworks.umt.edu/etd/592. Exciting new work on the question of Indigenous slavery is being conducted by Estevan Rael-Gálvez via *Native Bound-Unbound*, a Mellon Foundation funded digital humanities project he directs; see, https://fromthepage.com/nativeboundunbound.

17. See Enrique R. Lamadrid, "*Entre Cíbolos Criado*: Images of Native Americans in the Popular Culture of Colonial New Mexico," in *Reconstructing A Chicano/a Literary Heritage: Hispanic Colonial Literature of the Southwest*, ed. María Herrera-Sobek (University of Arizona Press, 1993), 158–200.

18. Ramón A. Gutiérrez, "Aztlán, Montezuma, and New Mexico: The Political Uses of American Indian Mythology," in *Aztlán: Essays on the Chicano Homeland*, Rudolfo A. Anaya and Francisco Lomeli, eds., (University of New Mexico Press, 1989), 175.

19. Anzaldúa, *Borderlands*, 3–4.

20. Erin Shalev, "'This Natural Defect of Apprehension': Native Americans and the Politics of Time in the Young United States," *European Journal of American Studies* 16, no. 2 (Summer 2021),

https://journals.openedition.org/ejas/16983; see also Caroline Winterer, *The Culture of Classicism: Ancient Greece and Rome in American Intellectual Life, 1780–1910* (Johns Hopkins University Press, 2001); Carl J. Richard, *The Founders and the Classics: Greece, Rome, and the American Enlightenment* (Harvard University Press, 1994); David Lupher, *Romans in a New World: Classical Models in Sixteenth-Century Spanish America* (University of Michigan Press, 2006); and John M.D. Pohl and Claire L. Lyons, eds., *Altera Roma: Art and Empire from Mérida to Mexico* (UCLA Cotsen Institute of Archaeology Press, 2016).

21. Benjamin Keen, "The Black Legend Revisited: Assumptions and Realities," *Hispanic American Historical Review*, 49 (4) (1969): 703–19; María de Guzmán, *Spain's Long Shadow: he Black Legend, Off-Whiteness, and Anglo-American Empire* (Minneapolis, 2005); Madeleine Gray, *The Protestant Reformation: Belief, Practice, and Tradition* (Sussex Academic Press, 2003); A. D. Wright, *The Counter Reformation: Catholic Europe and the Non-Christian World* (St. Martin's Press, 1982); and Gregg Allison and Chris Castaldo, *The Unfinished Reformation: What Unites and Divides Catholics and Protestants after 500 Years* (Zondervan, 2016).

22. One of the canonical subject areas in art history, modern art scholarship is extensive. A selection of publications here referenced on the relationship between so-called primitive art and modern art would include, James Robinson Sweeney, "Picasso and Iberian Sculpture," *The Art Bulletin* 23, no. 3 (September 1941): 191–98; Robert Goldwater, *Primitivism in Modern Art* (Belknap Press, 1986); Frances S. Connelly, *The Sleep of Reason: Primitivism in Modern European Art and Aesthetics, 1725–1907* (Pennsylvania State University Press, 1995); Simon Gikandi, "Picasso, Africa, and the Schemata of Difference," *Modernism/Modernity* 10, no. 3 (September 2003), 455–80; Elizabeth Hutchinson, *The Indian Craze: Primitivism, Modernism, and Transculturation in American Art, 1890–1915* (Duke University Press, 2009); Aneta Pawlowska, "Avant-Gardists and Primitivism," *Art Inquiry* 19 (2017), 153–69; and John Warne Monroe,

Metropolitan Fetish: African Sculpture and the Imperial French Invention of Primitive Art (Cornell University Press, 2019).

23. Here, I am referring to the missions established by the Franciscans and other religious orders in the areas around Mexico City in the early to mid-sixteenth century to convert Indigenous populations, and also to the schools and workshops aimed at re-educating the sons of Indigenous nobility and training native artists to produce artwork following European and Spanish models. See James Early, The Colonial Architecture of Mexico (University of New Mexico Press, 1994); Jeanette Favrot Peterson, "Synthesis and Survival: The Native Presence in Sixteenth-Century Murals of New Spain," in Native Artists and Patrons in Colonial Latin America: Phœbus—A Journal of Art History, Emily Umberger and Tom Cummins, eds., vol. 7 (Arizona State University, 1995), 14–35; Ellen Baird, "Adaptation and Accommodation: The Transformation of the Pictorial Text in Sahagún's Manuscripts," in Native Artists and Patrons in Colonial Latin America: Phœbus—A Journal of Art History, Emily Umberger and Tom Cummins, eds., vol. 7 (Arizona State University, 1995), 36–51; Samuel Y. Edgerton, Theaters of Conversion: Religious Architecture and Indian Artisans in Colonial Mexico (University of New Mexico Press, 2001); and Jaime Lara, Christian Texts for Aztecs: Art and Liturgy in Colonial Mexico (Notre Dame Press, 2008).

24. J. J. Brody, "A Tradition is Born," in Pueblo Indian Painting (School for American Research, 1997), 36.

25. For more on early Anglo artists in New Mexico, see Dana Sullivant and Robert R. White, Artists of Territorial New Mexico, 1846–1912: Dr. Robert R. White (Grekel Film/Video/Animation, 1995)

26. Mary Austin, 1932b, 214; see, Marta Weigle, "The First Twenty-Five Years of the Spanish Colonial Arts Society," in Hispanic Arts and Ethnohistory in the Southwest: New Papers Inspired by the Work of E. Boyd, Marta Weigle, Claudia Larcombe, and Samuel Larcombe, eds., (Ancient City Press, 1983), 183.

27. Duane Anderson, "The History of the Indian Arts Fund," in Legacy: Southwest Indian Art at the School of American Research, ed. Duane Anderson (School of American Research, 1999), 4.

28. See Renato Rosaldo, Culture and Truth: The Remaking of Social Analysis (Beacon Press, 1989), 69.

29. Anderson, "The History of the Indian Arts Fund," 5

30. Anita O. Rodríguez, "How La Raza Became Invisible," Chamisa: A Journal of Literary, Performance, and Visual Arts of the Greater Southwest 1 (2021): 23–29.

31. Brody, "A Tradition is Born."

32. See E. Boyd, Saints and Saint Makers (Laboratory of Anthropology/Rydal Press, 1946); E. Boyd, Popular Arts of Colonial New Mexico (Museum of International Folk Art, 1959); and E. Boyd, Popular Arts of Spanish New Mexico (Museum of New Mexico Press, 1974).

33. Stephanie Lewthwaite, A Contested Art: Modernism and Mestizaje in New Mexico (University of Oklahoma Press, 2015), 5.

34. See E. Boyd Hall, Portfolio of Spanish Colonial Design in New Mexico (LPD Press, 2001; originally published in 1938 by the Works Progress Administration); George Kubler, Santos: An Exhibition of the Religious Folk Art of New Mexico (Amon Carter Museum of Western Art, 1964), 1–9; Thomas J. Steele, S.J., Santos and Saints: The Religious Folk Art of Hispanic New Mexico (Ancient City Press, 1974); and Claire Farago, "Introduction: Locating New Mexican Santos in-between Worlds," in Transforming Images: New Mexican Santos In-Between Worlds, Claire Farago and Donna Pierce, eds., (The Pennsylvania State University Press, 2006), 1–11.

35. Briggs (1992), 217–219.

36. Briggs, 208–211.

37. Briggs.

38. Lewthwaite, A Contested Art, 52–3.

39. Donna Pierce, "The Active Reception of International Artistic Sources in New Mexico," Transforming Images: New Mexican Santos In-Between Worlds, Claire Farago and Donna Pierce, eds., (The

Pennsylvania State University Press, 2006), 44; see also, Carmella Padilla and Donna Pierce, *Conexiones: Connections in Spanish Colonial Art* (Museum of New Mexico Press, 2002).

40. Lewthwaite, *A Contested Art*, 53. Certain media and forms, such as tinwork, likewise, were introduced during the US territorial period and were not colonial or traditionally Hispano while other forms, such as seen in furniture ornamentation, date from the mid-twentieth century. In cases such as this, what exactly is traditional?

41. Although established in 1925, Spanish Market has only been an annual event in Santa Fe since 1967. Traditional Spanish Market, as it is known and normally held in July, is considered one of the oldest arts and crafts festivals in the United States. In 2002, the Museum of Spanish Colonial Art was founded, also, in Santa Fe. The museum, located in a Pueblo-Spanish Revival style residence designed by architect, John Gaw Meem in 1930, houses 4,000 devotional, decorative, and utilitarian art objects representing traditional Hispano traditions from New Mexico and southern Colorado. In 2015, Winter Spanish Market was held in Albuquerque in late November. In 2024, the Museum of Spanish Colonial Art was rebranded as the Nuevo Mexicano Heritage Arts Museum to better align with its mission, collections, and exhibitions as the institution adapts to the changing arts culture in the region.

42. See Paulette Beete, "Grounded in the Old: Santa Fe's Spanish Market," *National Endowment for the Arts*, no. 3 (2011); https://www.arts.gov/stories/magazine/2011/3/celebration-look-art-festival/grounded-old.

43. E. Boyd, *Leaflet soliciting memberships*, n.d.; see Ann Vedder, "History of the Spanish Colonial Arts Society, Inc., 1951–1981," *Hispanic Arts and Ethnohistory in the Southwest: New Papers Inspired by the Work of E. Boyd*, Marta Weigle, Claudia Larcombe, and Samuel Larcombe, eds., (Ancient City Press, 1983), 205.

44. Walt Whitman, *The Spanish Element in Our Nationality* (1883); the quote is taken from a letter Whitman wrote to commemorate the 333rd anniversary of the founding of Santa Fe, New Mexico. See also, M. Elizabeth Boone, *The Spanish Element in Our Nationality: Spain and America at the World's Fairs and Centennial Celebrations, 1876–1915* (The Pennsylvania State University Press, 2019).

45. Robert R. White, "The New Mexico Painters, 1923–1927," *The New Mexico Painters* (Gerald Peters Gallery, 1999), 7.

46. White, "The New Mexico Painters," 15–17.

47. White, "The New Mexico Painters," 36.

48. See Ed Garman, *The Art of Raymond Jonson Painter* (University of New Mexico Press, 1976); Timothy Robert Rodgers, *In Pursuit of Perfection: The Art of Agnes Martin, Maria Martinez, and Florence Pierce* (Museum of New Mexico Press and Museum of Fine Arts, 2004); Gerard Nordland, Mark Lavatelli, et. al., *Richard Diebenkorn in New Mexico* (Harwood Museum of Art, 2007); Heather Hole, *Marsden Hartley and the West: The Search for an American Modernism* (Yale University Press, 2008); Gilbert Vicario, ed., *Agnes Pelton: Desert Transcendentalist* (Hirmer Verlag, 2019); and Noah Hoffman, "SFR Talk: Revising Rothko," *Santa Fe Reporter*, May 12, 2010; https://www.sfreporter.com/news/interviews/2010/05/12/sfr-talk-revising-rothko/

49. See Marjorie Devon, *Tamarind Touchstones: Fabulous at Fifty: Celebrating Excellence in Fine Art Lithography* (University of New Mexico Press, 2010).

50. The first scholar to write about Mabel Dodge Luhan, according to Wanda M. Corn, was Christopher Lasch in his book, *The New Radicalism in America, 1889–1963* (Chatto and Windus, 1965). Other significant studies include Patricia R. Everett, *Mabel Dodge: The Salon Years, 1912–1917* (Barbara Mathes Gallery/AbeBooks, 1985); Lois Palken Rudnick, *Mabel Dodge Luhan: New Woman, New Worlds* (University of New Mexico Press, 1987); and Lois P. Rudnick and MaLin Wilson-Powell, eds., *Mabel Dodge Luhan and Company: American Modernisms and the West* (Museum of New Mexico Press/Harwood Museum of Art, Taos, 2016).

51. Rudnick and Wilson-Powell, *Mabel Dodge Luhan and Company*, 15.

52. Christine Stansell, *American Moderns: Bohemian New York and the Creation of a New Century* (Metropolitan Books, Henry Holt and Company, 2000).

53. See Laura E. Gómez, *Manifest Destinies: The Invention of the Mexican American Race* (New York University Press, 2008). Note: The individuals I interviewed who remembered Luhan or whose family members knew her asked to remain anonymous.

54. Lois P. Rudnick, "'A Real Creator of Creators': How Mabel Dodge Luhan Catalyzed American Modernism," *Mabel Dodge Luhan and Company: American Modernisms and the West*, Lois P. Rudnick and MaLin Wilson-Powell, eds., (Museum of New Mexico Press/Harwood Museum of Art, Taos, 2016), 24.

55. Rudyard Kipling, "The White Man's Burden: The United States and the Philippine Islands, 1899," *Rudyard Kipling's Verse: Definitive Edition* (Doubleday, 1929). See also, William Easterly, *The White Man's Burden: Why the West's Efforts to Aid the Rest Have Done So Much Ill and So Little Good* (Penguin Books, 2007)

56. An insightful analysis that offers a new perspective on this image and related ideas can be found in Maria Cristina Fumagalli, *Caribbean Perspectives on Modernity: Returning Medusa's Gaze* (University of Virginia Press, 2009); see also, Marguerite Deslauriers, "Sexual Difference in Aristotle's Politics and his Biology," *The Classical World* 102, no. 3 (Spring 2009), 215–231.

57. There is an ample bibliography on Georgia O'Keeffe for anyone interested in learning more about her life and work. In this essay, I chose to examine her as a case study in this discussion about the arts that illustrates the settler colonial processes, which violently disrupted and reshaped longstanding cultural practices in the region.

58. See, "About Georgia O'Keeffe: Biography," Georgia O'Keeffe Museum; https://www.okeeffemuseum.org/about-georgia-okeeffe/

59. David G. Turner, *Georgia O'Keeffe: Paintings* (Museum of Fine Arts/Museum of New Mexico, 1987); Charles C. Eldredge, *Georgia O'Keeffe: American and Modern* (Yale University Press, 1993); Emily Rose Kucharczyk, *Georgia O'Keeffe: Desert Painter* (Blackbirch Press, 2002); Wanda Corn, *Georgia O'Keeffe: Living Modern* (DelMonico Books/Prestel, 2017); and Isadora A. Helfgott, "Art in 'Life': Fashioning Political Ideology through Visual Culture in Mid-Century America," *American Periodicals* 20, no. 2 (2010), 269–94.

60. Patricia Marroquin Norby, *Visual Violence in the Land of Enchantment* (unpublished dissertation: University of Minnesota, 2013), 87.

61. Patricia Marroquin Norby, *Visual Violence*, 87.

62. "Georgia O'Keeffe Turns Dead Bones to Live Art," *Life Magazine*, February 14, 1938, 28–31.

63. "Georgia O'Keeffe Turns Dead Bones to Live Art," 100, footnote 154; see also, Sarah Greenough, *My Faraway One: Selected Letters of Georgia O'Keeffe and Alfred Stieglitz* (New Haven, 2011), letters dated: July 10, 1931, and October 20, 1931.

64. Patricia Marroquin Norby, *Visual Violence*, 95, 102–105.

65. Patricia Marroquin Norby, *Visual Violence*, 89; see also, Aaron Fry, "Local Knowledge and Art Historical Methodology: A New Perspective on Awa Tsireh and the San Ildefonso Easel Painting Movement," *Hemisphere: Visual Cultures of the Americas* 1 (2008), 46–61.

66. For a more nuanced and elegantly written discussion of New Mexico's colonial demographics, see, Rael-Gálvez, "Coyote Convergence," 16.

67. See Claire Farago, "Mediating Ethnicity and Culture: Framing New Mexico as a Case Study," in *Transforming Images: New Mexican Santos In-Between Worlds*, Claire Farago and Donna Pierce, eds., (The Pennsylvania State University Press, 2006), 16–17.

68. Claire Farago, "Mediating Ethnicity," 9. See *The New Mexico Painters* exhibition catalogue, Montross Gallery, New York, October 1–27, 1923,

Library of the Museum of Fine Arts, Santa Fe, New Mexico; see also Chris Wilson, *The Myth of Santa Fe: Creating a Modern Regional Tradition* (University of New Mexico Press, 1997).

69. See, Claudia Larcombe, "E. Boyd: A Biographical Sketch," *Hispanic Arts and Ethnohistory in the Southwest: New Papers Inspired by the Work of E. Boyd*, Marta Weigle, et al., eds., (Ancient City Press, 1983), 4.

70. Sylvia Rodríguez, "The Hispano Homeland Debate," *Working Paper Series No. 17*. Stanford Center for Chicano Research, October 1986, 18.

71. Rodríguez, "The Hispano Homeland Debate," 6.

72. Gómez, *Manifest Destinies*.

73. See Deborah Jackson Taffa, "Race and Class in New Mexico," *Searchlight New Mexico: Independent Investigative Journalism* (November 9, 2023); https://searchlightnm.org/race-and-class-in-new-mexico/?fbclid=IwAR02z-rZHz2Ga7KkrcJ1QWb6jekAFA0NQJUHVcje29_ay_TLv7C8HHZSiQJo.

74. Rodríguez, "The Hispano Homeland Debate," 9.

75. UNM Campus Histories, Zimmerman Library, Art: https://unm-campus-histories.github.io/spaces/essays/zimmerman.html.

76. For more on the New Deal Era and the experiences of Hispano artists working during this period, see Tey Marianna Nunn, *Sin Nombre: Hispana and Hispano Artists of the New Deal Era* (University of New Mexico Press, 2001).

77. For more on the protests, see Sameer Rao, "University of New Mexico May Remove Murals that Ignore Indigenous POV," *Colorlines*, October 9, 2019; https://colorlines.com/article/university-new-mexico-may-remove-murals-ignore-indigenous-pov/.

78. Earlier examples of this subject include depictions of the betrothal of Mary and Joseph, where we see the rabbi in a frontal pose standing between the Virgin and Joseph depicted in profile or in 3/4 stance; typically, the rabbi holds their hands as Joseph places a ring on Mary's finger, solidifying their commitment and uniting the two families. Later artists, such as Diego Rivera drew from this colonial visual language in their representations of the Conquest of Mexico, specifically, the episode where Cortés and Moctezuma meet with Doña Marina functioning as interlocutor. In a grisaille mural by Rivera at the Palacio de Cortés in Cuernavaca, Mexico, she stands between the profiled figures of Cortés and Moctezuma, yielding a composition that is undeniably inspired by the older betrothal images. The painting suggests reading the encounter as a union of the Spanish and the Aztec, and thus, as the origin of Mexico as a mestizo nation. See Ray Hernández-Durán, "*El Encuentro de Cortés y Moctezuma*: The Betrothal of Two Worlds in Eighteenth-Century New Spain," in *Woman and Art in Early Modern Latin America* (Brill Press, 2007), 181–206; see also, Jaime Cuadriello, "*El encuentro de Cortés y Moctezuma como escena de Concordia,*" in *El amor y desamor en las artes*, ed. A. Herrera, (Instituto de Investigaciones Estéticas/UNAM, 2001), 263–92.

79. Gustavo Arellano, "The Transformation of a Centuries-Old Refuge in New Mexico," *High Country News*, May 13, 2019; https://www.hcn.org/issues/51.8/communities-the-transformation-of-a-centuries-old-refuge-in-new-mexico.

80. See, William Wroth and Robin Farwell Gavin, eds., Introduction by Estevan Rael-Gálvez, *Converging Streams: Art of the Hispanic and Native American Southwest* (Museum of Spanish Colonial Art/Museum of New Mexico Press, 2010).

81. Ruben Salazar, "Who is a Chicano? And What is it the Chicanos Want?" *Los Angeles Times* (February 6, 1970).

82. See, María Eugenia Cotera and María Josefina Saldaña-Portillo, "Indigenous but not Indian? Chicana/os and the Politics of Indigeneity," in *The World of Indigenous North America*, ed. Robert Warrior (Routledge, 2015), 550; see also, Laura Pulido, "Geographies of Race and Ethnicity III: Settler Colonialism and Non-Native People of Color," *Progress in Human Geography* 42, no. 2 (2018), 309–18.

83. Traugott, *New Mexico Art through Time*, 183.

84. Excerpt taken from *El Plan Espiritual de Aztlán*, written during the first Chicano Youth National Conference, Denver, Colorado, 1969; see, Antonio Camejo, ed., *Documents of the Chicano Struggle* (Pathfinder Press, 1971). For a discussion focused on the history of the Chicano movement in New Mexico, see the chapter by Philip (Felipe) B. Gonzales.

85. See Rodolfo Acuña, *Occupied America: A History of Chicanos*, Third Edition (New York: HarperCollins Publishers, 1988); also, Carlos C. Vélez-Ibáñez, *Border Visions: Mexican Cultures of the Southwest United States* (University of Arizona Press, 1996); and Moquin and Van Doren, *A Documentary History*.

86. See Martha M. Argüello, "We Joined Others Who Were Poor: The Young Lords, the Black Freedom Struggle, and the 'Original' Rainbow Coalition," *Journal of African American Studies* 23, no. 4 (December 2019), 435–54; also, Ray Santisteban, "The First Rainbow Coalition," *PBS: Independent Lens* (January 27, 2020), https://www.pbs.org/independentlens/documentaries/the-first-rainbow-coalition/.

87. Acuña, *Occupied America*, 307.

88. See Miguel Montiel, "The Chicano Family: A Review of Research," *Social Work* 18, no. 2 (March 1973), 22–31.

89. See Francisco Jiménez, "Dramatic Principles of the Teatro Campesino," *Bilingual Review/La Revista Bilingüe* 2, nos. 1 and 2 (January–August 1975), 99–111; Arturo C. Flores, *El Teatro Campesino de Luis Valdez* (Editorial Pliegos, 1990); and also, *El Teatro Campesino* at: https://elteatrocampesino.com.

90. Sergio Troncoso, *Crossing Borders: Personal Essays* (Arte Público Press, 2011); other sources examining the Chicano/a experience via biography and short fiction include, Richard Rodríguez, *Brown: The Last Discovery of America* (Penguin Books, 2003); Carlos Aceves, "The Xinachtli Project: Transforming Whiteness through Mythic Pedagogy," *Counterpoints* 273 (2004), 257–77; Tiffany Ana López, ed., *Growing Up Chicana/o: An Anthology* (Bill Adler Books, 1993); and Edward Simmen, ed., *The Chicano: From Caricature to Self-Portrait* (New American Library, 1971).

91. For discussions on the concept of *nepantla*, see, Gloria Anzaldua, "Chicana Artists: Exploring Nepantla, el lugar de la frontera," *NACLA Report on the Americas* 27, Issue 1 (1993), 37–45; Gabriele Pisarz-Ramírez, "From Nepantla to Amerindia: Transnationality in Mexican American Literature and Art," *Iberoamericana: Nueva Época* 7, no. 25 (Marzo de 2007), 155–172; and Charlene Villaseñor Black, "Thoughts from Nepantla," *Latin American and Latinx Visual Culture* 1, Issue 2 (April 2019), 3–7. In the film *Selena* (1997), a biopic directed by Gregory Nava on the life of the late *Tejana* singer, Selena Quintanilla, starring Jennifer López, the actor Edward James Olmos, playing Selena's father, in one of the more memorable scenes, articulates this idea. In the scene, the father is driving with Selena and her brother as they express excitement at having received their first invitation to perform in Mexico. Olmos expresses reservations given Selena's limited Spanish-speaking ability. He states, "We are Mexican American and they don't like Mexican Americans . . . Being Mexican American is tough. Anglos jump all over you if you don't speak English perfectly. Mexicans jump all over you if you don't speak Spanish perfectly. We have to be twice as perfect as anybody else . . . Our family has been here for centuries and yet they treat us as if we just swam across the Río Grande." One can see the clip in question via YouTube at: https://youtu.be/HIBYaeYQFok

92. Arlene Dávila, *Latinx Art: Artists, Markets, Politics* (Duke University Press, 2020), 7.

93. See Jack D. Forbes, *Aztecas del Norte: The Chicanos of Aztlán* (Fawcett Publications, Inc., 1973); Rudolfo A. Anaya and Francisco A. Lomelí, eds., *Aztlán: Essays on the Chicano Homeland* (University of New Mexico Press/El Norte Publications, 1991); Virginia M. Fields and Victor Zamudio-Taylor, eds., *The Road to Aztlan: Art from a Mythic Homeland* (Los Angeles County Museum of Art and the University of New Mexico Press, 2001); and Dylan

Miner, *Creating Aztlán: Chicano Art, Indigenous Sovereignty, and Lowriding Across Turtle Island* (University of Arizona Press, 2014)

94. See Camejo, *Documents of the Chicano Struggle*; and Anaya and Lomeli, *Aztlán: Essays on the Chicano Homeland*.

95. Victor Zamudio-Taylor, "Inventing Tradition, Negotiating Modernism: Chicano/a Art and the Pre-Columbian Past," *The Road to Aztlan: Art from a Mythic Homeland*, curated by Virginia M. Fields and Victor Zamudio-Taylor (Los Angeles County Museum of Art, 2001), 348.

96. For more detailed discussions of these revolutions, figures, and the role of the arts, see David Craven, *Art and Revolution in Latin America, 1910–1990* (Yale University Press, 2002); Theresa Avila, "Laborious Arts: *El Taller de Gráfica Popular* and the Meaning of Labor in *Las estampas de la revolución Mexicana*," *Hemisphere: Visual Cultures of the Americas* 1 (Spring 2008), 62–82; and David Kunzle, *Che Guevara: Icon, Myth, and Message* (UCLA Fowler Museum of Cultural History/Center for the Study of Political Graphics, 1997).

97. Cotera and S`aldaña-Portillo, "Indigenous but not Indian?" and Pulido, "Geographies of Race."

98. See Dylan Miner, "Straddling la otra frontera: Revisioning Chicana/o Art History through Michicana/o Visual Culture," *Aztlán: The Journal of Chicano Studies* (Spring 2008), 89–122.

99. Holly Barnet-Sanchez and Tim Drescher, *Give Me Life: Iconography and Identity in East L.A. Murals* (University of New Mexico Press, 2016), 3.

100. Jacinto Quirarte, "Exhibitions of Chicano Art, 1965 to the Present," *Chicano Art: Resistance and Affirmation, 1965–1985*, Richard Griswold del Castillo, Teresa McKenna, and Yvonne Yarbro-Bejarano, eds., (Wight Art Gallery/University of California, Los Angeles, 1991), 163–79.

101. Personal Communication with Roberta Márquez on Tuesday, July 11, 2023.

102. Karen Mary Davalos, "Champions of Chicano Art Need to Face Reality: A Response to Cheech Marin's New Art Center," *Artnet* (May 8, 2017); https://news.artnet.com/opinion/champions-chicano-art-need-face-reality-948758/amp-page

103. Miner, "Straddling la otra frontera,"; an example of new work addressing this issue includes the dissertation by Ph.D. candidate in Art History at City University of New York, Sonja Elena Gandert, who has been researching and writing about Chicana and Chicano artists in New Mexico and Texas; her dissertation is titled, "*La resolana*: Chicano Artistic Imaginaries of Place, Race, and Activism in New Mexico and Texas, 1969–1985" (CUNY, 2025).

104. A controversial response lauded by conservatives questioning claims of discrimination by activists was by Linda Chavez in her book, *Out of the Barrio: Toward a New Politics of Hispanic Assimilation* (BasicBooks/HarperCollins Publishers, 1991).

105. For a selection of publications on Chicana artists, see Amalia Mesa-Bains, "*Domesticana: The Sensibility of Chicana Rasquache*," *Aztlán: A Journal of Chicano Studies* 24, no. 2 (Fall 1999), 157–67; Holly Barnet-Sánchez, "Where are the Chicana Printmakers? Presence and Absence in the Work of Chicana Artists of the Movimiento = Dónde están las grabadistas Chicanas: Presencia y ausencia de la obra de las artistas Chicanas en el movimiento Chicano," in *Just Another Poster? Chicano Graphic Arts in California*, ed. Chon A. Noriega (University of Washington Press, 2001), 117–49; and Laura Pérez, *Chicana Art: The Politics of Spiritual and Aesthetic Altarities* (Duke University Press, 2007).

106. Shifra M. Goldman, "Chicano Art of the Southwest in the Eighties," *Imagine: International Chicano Poetry Journal, Arte Chicano Issue* III, nos. 1 & 2 (Summer/Winter 1986), 42.

107. For new work on Reies López Tijerina, see Ramón A. Gutiérrez, *New Mexico's Moses: Reies López Tijerina and the Religious Origins of the Mexican American Civil Rights Movement* (University of New Mexico Press, 2022)

108. Shifra M. Goldman and Tomás Ybarra-Frausto, "The Political and Social Contexts of

Chicano Art," *Chicano Studies: Survey and Analysis*, Dennis J. Bixler-Márquez, Carlos F. Ortega, et. al., eds., (Kendall/Hunt Publishing Company, 1997), 303.

109. See Tomás Ybarra-Frausto, "*Rasquachismo*: A Chicano Sensibility," *Chicano Aesthetics: Rasquachismo* (MARS *Movimiento Artístico del Río Salado*, 1989), 5–8; reprinted in *Chicano Art: Resistance and Affirmation* (1991). See also Mesa-Bains, "*Domesticana*," 157–67; and Ramón García, "Against *Rasquache*: Chicano Identity and the Politics of Popular Culture in Los Angeles," *Critica: A Journal of Critical Essays*, (Spring 1998), 1–26.

110. Gaspar de Alba, *Chicano Art*, 191; see also, Shifra M. Goldman and Tomas Ybarra-Frausto, "The Political and Social Contexts of Chicano Art," *Chicano Art: Resistance and Affirmation, 1965–1985*, Richard Griswold del Castillo, Teresa McKenna, and Yvonne Yarbro-Bejarano, eds., (Wight Art Gallery/University of California, Los Angeles, 1991), 83–93.

111. Alicia Gaspar de Alba, *Chicano Art Inside Outside the Master's House: Cultural Politics and the CARA Exhibition* (University of Texas Press, 1998), 169; also, Lucy Lippard, *Mixed Blessings: New Art in a Multicultural America* (The New Press, 1990); and Quirarte, "Exhibitions of Chicano Art,", 163–79.

112. The most developed study of the early Chicano movement at New Mexico Highlands University is found in Julianna C. Wiggins, *Written and Oral Histories of the Chicano Movement at New Mexico Highlands University, 1968–1970*. Unpublished thesis, University of New Mexico, 2019; for more on Pedro Rodriguez, please see "Guide to the Pedro Rodriguez Oral History 2013," *Washington State University Libraries, Manuscripts, Archives, and Special Collections,* Cage 5065, http://ntserver1. wsulibs.wsu.edu/masc/finders/cg5065.htm; Linda Fregoso, "Chicano Art: History and Politics," *Onda Latina,* October 19, 1981, https://www.laits.utexas. edu/onda_latina/program?sernum=MAE_81_48_ mp3&theme=Art; Pedro Rodríguez, "Toward the Future: Chicano Art, A Voice for Tomorrow (1991)," *International Center for the Arts of the Americas at the Museum of Fine Arts, Houston*, https://icaa.mfah. org/s/en/item/803413; also, *Mexican American Art Since 1848 (MAAS1848)*, https://maas1848. umn.edu/s/mexican-american-art-since-1848/ item/135583.

113. Interview with Pedro Rodríguez, Department of Chicana and Chicano Studies, University of New Mexico, Albuquerque, October 25, 2019.

114. Personal communication with Roberta Márquez, July 7, 2023.

115. Personal communication with Roberta Márquez, July 7, 2023.

116. See *Lux v. Board of Regents of New Mexico Highlands University;* https://casetext.com/case/ lux-v-bd-of-regents-of-nm-highlands

117. See *Lux v. Board of Regents of New Mexico Highlands University*.

118. According to the court document, Lux was granted tenure the following year and was then appointed to serve as assistant academic dean of the Title III Programs; however, student dissatisfaction with the programs led to the student takeover of the administrative offices in September 1973. That following October, Lux gave a speech that was highly critical of the university administration, leading to a disagreement between Lux and Ángel and Lux's removal from the Title III programs. After Lux penned a letter to the Regents criticizing Ángel and the administration, Lux was dismissed in 1975. Interestingly, the jury returned a verdict in support of Lux. See *Lux vs Board of Regents of New Mexico Highlands University*, 95 N.M. 361, 622 P.2d 266 (1980), https://cite.case.law/ nm/95/361/

119. Interview with Pedro Rodríguez, October 25, 2019.

120. Reflecting ongoing tensions between members of the local Hispanic arts community and the longstanding Anglo-dominated art markets, in fall 2021, a group of local New Mexican Hispana and Hispano artists decided to hold their own Winter Spanish Market in Santa Fe, independently of the Spanish Colonial

Arts Society–sponsored Winter Market that has been held for several years in Albuquerque. See Robert Nott, "Santa Fe-Area Artists Plan Their Own Winter Spanish Market," *Santa Fe New Mexican* (Saturday, October 16, 2021). Interviewed on Thursday, October 14, 2021; https://www.santafenewmexican.com/news/local_news/santa-fe-area-artists-plan-their-own-winter-spanish-market/article_595b2ad0-2a24-11ec-ac65-777502da6a3e.html

121. See, Steve Jansen, "Santa Fe Gets a New Home for Art in the Vladem Contemporary," *Southwest Contemporary: Curated and Critical Perspectives on Arts and Culture*, May 27, 2022; https://southwestcontemporary.com/santa-fe-new-home-for-art-vladem-contemporary/

122. See Steve Jansen, "Sante Fe Gets a New Home."

123. See Isabella Alves, "Multicultural Mural Not Dead Yet," *Albuquerque Journal*, April 11, 2021; https://www.abqjournal.com/2378699/multicultural-mural-not-dead-yet-ex-theres-still-hope-the-embattled-artwork-can-be-saved.html.

124. See Isabella Alves, "Multicultural Mural Not Dead Yet."

125. Personal communication with Alicia Inez Guzmán, October 30, 2024.

126. Sadly, one sees similar forms of systemic racism, elitism, and marginalization in New Mexican institutions, such as the University of New Mexico, the state's flagship university. At UNM, ethnic studies departments, including Chicana and Chicano Studies, Africana Studies, and Native American Studies are not considered along with other academic programs in annual budget funding decisions but are expected to apply for funding on their own and in competition with one another. CCS has grown in recent years with the addition of a successful Ph.D. program and various community-based programs; enrollments in CCS classes have also skyrocketed yet the department's working budget continues to be miniscule and their facilities inadequate compared to equivalent programs. There has been an ongoing conflict between CCS and UNM given the administration's interest in moving Chicana and Chicano Studies from their current location, i.e. *La casita*, and relocating them to an alternate space (again) without any input from the department or consideration of the program's needs. Similarly, in the Department of Art at UNM, long recognized nationally and internationally for its Art of the Americas concentration, the loss of the Chicano Art History line following the retirement of Associate Professor of Chicano Art Holly Barnet-Sánchez in 2015 was unexpected and damaging to the program, especially given the growth of interest in the US in Latinx Art over the last decade; attempts to regain the line have been unsuccessful. That such actions and attitudes persist in the Southwest, in New Mexico, in Albuquerque, and at a university like UNM, a federally recognized "Hispanic Serving Institution," given the majority Hispanic demographic they serve, is untenable but reflective of priorities that do not adequately take into consideration the local Hispano/Chicano community, its interests, and its needs as has been the case for the past century.

Bibliography

"About Georgia O'Keeffe: Biography," Georgia O'Keeffe Museum; https://www.okeeffe-museum.org/about-georgia-okeeffe/

Aceves, Carlos. "The Xinachtli Project: Transforming Whiteness through Mythic Pedagogy." *Counterpoints* 273 (2004), 257–77.

Acuña, Rodolfo. *Occupied America: A History of Chicanos*. 3rd Ed. HarperCollins Publishers, 1988.

Adorno, Rolena, and Patrick Charles Pautz. *Alvar Núñez Cabeza de Vaca: His Account, His Life, and the Expedition of Pánfilo de Narváez*. University of Nebraska Press, 1999.

Allison, Gregg, and Chris Castaldo. *The Unfinished Reformation: What Unites and Divides Catholics and Protestants after 500 Years*. Zondervan, 2016.

Alves, Isabella. "Multicultural Mural Not Dead Yet." *Albuquerque Journal*, April 11, 2021. https://www.abqjournal.com/2378699/multicultural-mural-not-dead-yet-ex-theres-still-hope-the-embattled-artwork-can-be-saved.html.

Anaya, Rudolfo A., and Francisco A. Lomelí, eds. *Aztlán: Essays on the Chicano Homeland*. University of New Mexico Press/El Norte Publications, 1991.

Anderson, Duane. "The History of the Indian Arts Fund." In *Legacy: Southwest Indian Art at the School of American Research*, edited by Duane Anderson. School of American Research, 1999.

Anzaldúa, Gloria. "Chicana Artists: Exploring Nepantla, el lugar de la frontera." *NACLA Report on the Americas* 27, issue 1 (1993), 37–45.

Anzaldúa, Gloria. *Borderlands/La Frontera: The New Mestiza*. Spinsters/Aunt Lute Book Company, 1987.

Aragón, Ray John de. *New Mexico in the Mexican-American War*. The History Press, 2019.

Arellano, Gustavo. "The Transformation of a Centuries-Old Refuge in New Mexico," *High Country News*, May 13, 2019, https://www.hcn.org/issues/51.8/communities-the-transformation-of-a-centuries-old-refuge-in-new-mexico.

Argüello, Martha M. "We Joined Others Who Were Poor: The Young Lords, the Black Freedom Struggle, and the 'Original' Rainbow Coalition," *Journal of African American Studies* 23, no. 4 (December 2019): 435–54.

Avery, Doris Swann. "Into the Den of Evils: The *Genizaros* in Colonial New Mexico," Graduate Student Theses, Dissertations, and Professional Papers, 2008, https://scholarworks.umt.edu/etd/592.

Avila, Theresa. "Laborious Arts: *El Taller de Gráfica Popular* and the Meaning of Labor in *Las estampas de la revolución Mexicana*." *Hemisphere: Visual Cultures of the Americas*, 1 (Spring 2008), 62–82.

Baird, Ellen. "Adaptation and Accommodation: The Transformation of the Pictorial Text in Sahagún's Manuscripts." In *Native Artists and Patrons in Colonial Latin America: Phoebus—A Journal of Art History*, edited by Emily Umberger and Tom Cummins, Vol. 7. Arizona State University, 1995.

Barnet-Sánchez, Holly. "Where are the Chicana Printmakers? Presence and Absence in the Work of Chicana Artists of the Movimiento = Dónde están las grabadistas Chicanas: Presencia y ausencia de la obra de las artistas Chicanas en el movimiento Chicano." In *Just Another Poster? Chicano Graphic Arts in California*, edited by Chon A. Noriega. University of Washington Press, 2001.

Barnet-Sanchez, Holly, and Tim Drescher. *Give Me Life: Iconography and Identity in East L.A. Murals*. University of New Mexico Press, 2016.

Beete, Paulette. "Grounded in the Old: Santa Fe's Spanish Market," *National Endowment for the Arts*, no. 3 (2011), https://www.arts.gov/stories/magazine/2011/3/celebration-look-art-festival/grounded-old.

Benson, Nancy C. *New Mexico Colcha Club: Spanish Colonial Embroidery and the Women who Saved It.* Museum of New Mexico Press, 2008.

Boone, M. Elizabeth. *The Spanish Element in Our Nationality: Spain and America at the World's Fairs and Centennial Celebrations, 1876–1915.* The Pennsylvania State University Press, 2019.

Boyd, E. *Popular Arts of Spanish New Mexico.* Museum of New Mexico Press, 1974.

Boyd Hall, E. *Portfolio of Spanish Colonial Design in New Mexico.* LPD Press, 2001; originally published in 1938 by the Works Progress Administration.

Briggs, Charles L. "The Role of Mexicano Artists and the Anglo Elite in the Emergence of Contemporary Folk Art." *Folk Art and Art Worlds*, edited by John Michael Vlach and Simon J. Bronner. Utah State University Press, 1986.

Brody, J. J. "A Tradition is Born." *Pueblo Indian Painting.* School for American Research, 1997.

Cabeza de Vaca. *Adventures in the Unknown Interior of America*, translated and edited by Cyclone Covey. University of New Mexico Press, 1961.

Camejo, Antonio, ed. *Documents of the Chicano Struggle.* Pathfinder Press, 1971.

Carrillo, Charles, and Thomas J. Steele. *A Century of Retablos: The Dennis and Janis Lyon Collection of New Mexican Santos, 1780–1880.* Hudson Hills Press, 2007.

Chavez, Linda. *Out of the Barrio: Toward a New Politics of Hispanic Assimilation.* BasicBooks/HarperCollins Publishers, 1991.

Chavez, Thomas E. *An Illustrated History of New Mexico.* University of New Mexico Press, 2002.

Connelly, Frances S. *The Sleep of Reason: Primitivism in Modern European Art and Aesthetics, 1725–1907.* Pennsylvania State University Press, 1995.

Corn, Wanda, *Georgia O'Keeffe: Living Modern.* DelMonico Books/Prestel, 2017.

Cotera, María Eugenia, and María Josefina Saldaña-Portillo. "Indigenous but not Indian? Chicana/os and the Politics of Indigeneity." In *The World of Indigenous North America*, edited by Robert Warrior. Routledge, 2015.

Craven, David. *Art and Revolution in Latin America, 1910–1990.* Yale University Press, 2002.

Cuadriello, Jaime. "*El encuentro de Cortés y Moctezuma como escena de Concordia.*" In *El amor y desamor en las artes.* Edited by A. Herrera. Mexico City: Instituto de Investigaciones Estéticas/UNAM, 2001.

Davalos, Karen Mary. "Champions of Chicano Art Need to Face Reality: A Response to Cheech Marin's New Art Center," *Artnet* (May 8, 2017), https://news.artnet.com/opinion/champions-chicano-art-need-face-reality-948758/amp-page.

Davalos, Karen Mary. *Exhibiting Mestizaje: Mexican (American) Museums in the Diaspora.* University of New Mexico Press, 2001.

Dávila, Arlene. *Latinx Art: Artists, Markets, Politics.* Duke University Press, 2020.

Deslauriers, Marguerite. "Sexual Difference in Aristotle's Politics and His Biology." *The Classical World* 102, no. 3 (Spring 2009), 215–231.

Devon, Marjorie. *Tamarind Touchstones: Fabulous at Fifty: Celebrating Excellence in Fine Art Lithography.* University of New Mexico Press, 2010.

Dixon, Maurice M. *The Artistic Odyssey of Higinio V. Gonzáles: A Tinsmith and Poet in Territorial New Mexico.* University of Oklahoma Press, 2015.

Early, James. *Presidio, Mission, and Pueblo: Spanish Architecture and Urbanism in the United States.* Southern Methodist University Press, 2004.

Early, James. *The Colonial Architecture of Mexico.* University of New Mexico Press, 1994.

Easterly, William. *The White Man's Burden: Why the West's Efforts to Aid the Rest Have Done So Much Ill and So Little Good.* Penguin Books, 2007.

Edgerton, Samuel Y. *Theaters of Conversion: Religious Architecture and Indian Artisans in Colonial Mexico.* University of New Mexico Press, 2001.

El Plan Espiritual de Aztlán. First Chicano National Conference, Denver, Colorado, 1969.

El Teatro Campesino. https://elteatrocampesino.com.

Eldredge, Charles C. *Georgia O'Keeffe: American and Modern.* Yale University Press, 1993.

Everett, Patricia R. *Mabel Dodge: The Salon Years, 1912–1917.* Barbara Mathes Gallery/Abe-Books, 1985.

Farago, Claire. "Introduction: Locating New Mexican Santos in-between Worlds." In *Transforming Images: New Mexican Santos In-Between Worlds.* Edited by Claire Farago and Donna Pierce. The Pennsylvania State University Press, 2006.

Farago, Claire. "Mediating Ethnicity and Culture: Framing New Mexico as a Case Study." In *Transforming Images: New Mexican Santos In-Between Worlds*, edited by Claire Farago and Donna Pierce. The Pennsylvania State University Press, 2006.

Farago, Claire, and Donna Pierce, eds. *Transforming Images: New Mexican Santos In-Between Worlds.* The Pennsylvania State University Press, 2006.

Field, Ron. *Mexican-American War, 1846–48.* Brassey, 1997.

Fields, Virginia M., and Victor Zamudio-Taylor, eds. *The Road to Aztlan: Art from a Mythic Homeland.* Los Angeles County Museum of Art and the University of New Mexico Press, 2001.

Fontana, Bernard L. *Entrada: The Legacy of Spain and Mexico in the United States.* The University of New Mexico Press, 1994.

Flores, Arturo C. *El Teatro Campesino de Luis Valdez.* Editorial Pliegos, 1990.

Forbes, Jack D. *Aztecas del Norte: The Chicanos of Aztlán.* Fawcett Publications, Inc., 1973.

Fregoso, Linda "Chicano Art: History and Politics with Amado Peña and Pedro Rodríguez." *Onda Latina*, October 19, 1981, https://www.laits.utexas.edu/onda_latina/program?sernum=-MAE_81_48_mp3&theme=Art.

Fry, Aaron. "Local Knowledge and Art Historical Methodology: A New Perspective on Awa Tsireh and the San Ildefonso Easel Painting Movement." *Hemisphere: Visual Cultures of the Americas* 1 (2008): 46–61.

Fumagalli, Maria Cristina. *Caribbean Perspectives on Modernity: Returning Medusa's Gaze.* University of Virginia Press, 2009.

Gallegos, Bernardo P. "Education and Indigenous Slavery in New Mexico." *American Educational History Journal*, 43, issues 1–2 (2016).

Gandert, Sonja Elena. "*La resolana*: Chicano Artistic Imaginaries of Place, Race, and Activism in New Mexico and Texas, 1969–1985." Unpublished dissertation, CUNY, 2025.

García, Ramón. "Against *Rasquache*: Chicano Identity and the Politics of Popular Culture in Los Angeles." *Critica: A Journal of Critical Essays* (Spring 1998): 1–26.

Garman, Ed. *The Art of Raymond Jonson Painter.* University of New Mexico Press, 1976.

Gaspar de Alba, Alicia. *Chicano Art Inside Outside the Master's House: Cultural Politics and the CARA Exhibition.* University of Texas Press, 1998.

Gavin, Robin Farwell. *Traditional Arts of Spanish New Mexico: The Hispanic Heritage Wing at the Museum of International Folk Art.* Museum of New Mexico Press, 1994.

"Georgia O'Keeffe Turns Dead Bones to Live Art," *Life Magazine*, February 14, 1938.

Gikandi, Simon. "Picasso, Africa, and the Schemata of Difference," *Modernism/Modernity* 10, no. 3 (September 2003): 455–480.

Goldman, Shifra M. "Chicano Art of the Southwest in the Eighties." *Imagine: International Chicano Poetry Journal, Arte Chicano Issue* III, nos. 1 & 2 (Summer/Winter 1986): 42–50.

Goldman, Shifra M., and Tomás Ybarra-Frausto. "The Political and Social Contexts of Chicano Art." In *Chicano Studies: Survey and Analysis*, edited by Dennis J. Bixler-Márquez, Carlos F. Ortega, and Rosaliá Solórzano Torres. Kendall/Hunt Publishing Company, 1997.

Goldman, Shifra M., and Tomás Ybarra-Frausto. "The Political and Social Contexts of Chicano Art." In *Chicano Art: Resistance and Affirmation, 1965–1985*, edited by Richard Griswold del Castillo, Teresa McKenna, and Yvonne Yarbro-Bejarano. Wight Art Gallery/University of California, Los Angeles, 1991.

Goldwater, Robert. *Primitivism in Modern Art*. Belknap Press, 1986.

Gómez, Laura E. *Manifest Destinies: The Invention of the Mexican American Race*. New York University Press, 2008.

González, Jennifer A., C. Ondine Chavoya, Chon Noriega, and Terezita Romo, eds. *Chicano and Chicana Art: A Critical Anthology*. Duke University Press, 2019.

Gonzales, Moises. "The Genizaro Land Grant Settlement of New Mexico." *Journal of the Southwest* 56, no. 4 (Winter 2014): 583–602.

González, Moises, and Enrique R. Lamadrid, eds. *Nación Genízara: Ethnogenesis, Place, and Identity in New Mexico*. University of New Mexico Press, 2019.

Gray, Madeleine. *The Protestant Reformation: Belief, Practice, and Tradition*. Sussex Academic Press, 2003.

Greenough, Sarah. *My Faraway One: Selected Letters of Georgia O'Keeffe and Alfred Stieglitz*. Yale University Press, 2011.

Griswold del Castillo, Richard, Teresa McKenna, and Yvonne Yarbro-Bejarano, eds. *Chicano Art: Resistance and Affirmation, 1965–1985*. Wight Art Gallery/University of California, Los Angeles, 1991.

"Guide to the Pedro Rodriguez Oral History 2013," *Washington State University Libraries, Manuscripts, Archives, and Special Collections*, Cage 5065, http://ntserver1.wsulibs.wsu.edu/masc/finders/cg5065.htm.

Gutiérrez, Ramón A. *New Mexico's Moses: Reies López Tijerina and the Religious Origins of the Mexican American Civil Rights Movement*. University of New Mexico Press, 2022.

Gutiérrez, Ramón A. "Aztlán, Montezuma, and New Mexico: The Political Uses of American Indian Mythology." In *Aztlán: Essays on the Chicano Homeland*, edited by Rudolfo A. Anaya and Francisco Lomeli. University of New Mexico Press, 1989.

Guzman, Alicia Inez. Unpublished Interview with Bob Vladem. Santa Fe, New Mexico, October 2020; Personal communication with Guzman, October 30, 2024.

Guzmán, María de. *Spain's Long Shadow: The Black Legend, Off-Whiteness, and Anglo-American Empire*. University of Minnesota Press, 2005.

Helfgott, Isadora A. "Art in 'Life': Fashioning Political Ideology through Visual Culture in Mid Century America," *American Periodicals* 20, no. 2 (2010): 269–294.

Hernández-Durán, Ray. "*El Encuentro de Cortés y Moctezuma*: The Betrothal of Two Worlds in Eighteenth-Century New Spain." *Woman and Art in Early Modern Latin America*, edited by Kellen Kee McIntyre and Richard E. Phillips. Brill Press, 2007.

Hernández-Durán, Ray. *Interview with Pedro Rodríguez*. Department of Chicana and Chicano

Studies, University of New Mexico in Albuquerque, October 25, 2019.

Hernández-Durán, Ray, and Irene Vásquez. "'*Artistas del Pueblo*': In Conversation with the History of New Mexican Chicanx Art." *Hemisphere: Visual Cultures of the Americas*, edited by Mandolen Sánchez. Vol. XII (Department of Art, University of New Mexico, 2019): 80–97.

Hoffman, Noah. "SFR Talk: Revising Rothko," *Santa Fe Reporter*, May 12, 2010: https://www.sfreporter.com/news/interviews/2010/05/12/sfr-talk-revising-rothko/.

Hole, Heather. *Marsden Hartley and the West: The Search for an American Modernism.* Yale University Press, 2008.

Hutchinson, Elizabeth. *The Indian Craze: Primitivism, Modernism, and Transculturation in American Art, 1890–1915.* Duke University Press, 2009.

Jackson Taffa, Deborah. "Race and Class in New Mexico," *Searchlight New Mexico: Independent Investigative Journalism* (November 9, 2023); https://searchlightnm.org/race-and-class-in-new-mexico/?fbclid=I-wAR02zrZHz2Ga7KkrcJ1QWb6jekAF-A0NQJUHVcje29_ay_TLv7C8HHZSiQJo.

Jansen, Steve. "Santa Fe Gets a New Home for Art in the Vladem Contemporary," *Southwest Contemporary: Curated and Critical Perspectives on Arts and Culture*, May 27, 2022; https://southwestcontemporary.com/santa-fe-new-home-for-art-vladem-contemporary/.

Jiménez, Francisco. "Dramatic Principles of the Teatro Campesino." *Bilingual Review/La Revista Bilingüe* 2, nos. 1 and 2 (January–August 1975): 99–111.

Keen, Benjamin. "The Black Legend Revisited: Assumptions and Realities." *Hispanic American Historical Review* 49, no. 4 (1969): 703–71.

Kipling, Rudyard. "The White Man's Burden: The United States and the Philippine Islands, 1899." In *Rudyard Kipling's Verse: Definitive Edition.* Doubleday, 1929.

Knaut, Andrew L. *The Pueblo Revolt of 1680: Conquest and Resistance in Seventeenth-Century New Mexico.* University of Oklahoma Press, 1995.

Koning, Hans. *Columbus: His Enterprise, Exploding the Myth.* Monthly Review Press, 1976.

Kubler, George. *Santos: An Exhibition of the Religious Folk Art of New Mexico.* Amon Carter Museum of Western Art, 1964.

Kucharczyk, Emily Rose. *Georgia O'Keeffe: Desert Painter.* Blackbirch Press, 2002.

Kunzle, David. *Che Guevara: Icon, Myth, and Message.* UCLA Fowler Museum of Cultural History/Center for the Study of Political Graphics, 1997.

Lamadrid, Enrique R. "*Entre Cíbolos Criado*: Images of Native Americans in the Popular Culture of Colonial New Mexico." In *Reconstructing A Chicano/a Literary Heritage: Hispanic Colonial Literature of the Southwest*, edited by María Herrera-Sobek. University of Arizona Press, 1993.

Lara, Jaime. *Christian Texts for Aztecs: Art and Liturgy in Colonial Mexico.* Notre Dame Press, 2008.

Larcombe, Claudia. "E. Boyd: A Biographical Sketch." In *Hispanic Arts and Ethnohistory in the Southwest: New Papers Inspired by the Work of E. Boyd*, edited by Marta Weigle, Claudia Larcombe, and Samuel Larcombe. Ancient City Press, 1983.

Lasch, Christopher. *The New Radicalism in America, 1889–1963: The Intellectual as Social Type.* Chatto and Windus, 1965.

Lewthwaite, Stephanie. *A Contested Art: Modernism and Mestizaje in New Mexico.* University of Oklahoma Press, 2015.

Liebmann, Matthew. *Revolt: An Archaeological History of Pueblo Resistance and Revitalization in 17th Century New Mexico.* University of Arizona Press, 2012.

Lincoln, Abraham. "Speech of Hon. Abraham Lincoln at Springfield, June 17, 1858." In *Debates* of Lincoln and Douglas: Carefully Prepared by the Reporters of Each Party at the times of their Delivery (1858).

Lippard, Lucy. *Mixed Blessings: New Art in a Multicultural America*. The New Press, 1990.

López, Tiffany Ana, ed. *Growing Up Chicana/o: An Anthology*. Bill Adler Books, 1993.

Lupher, David. *Romans in a New World: Classical Models in Sixteenth-Century Spanish America*. University of Michigan Press, 2006.

Lux vs. Board of Regents of New Mexico Highlands University, 95 N.M. 361, 622 P.2d 266 (1980), https://cite.case.law/nm/95/361/.

Márquez, Roberta. Personal communication, Albuquerque, New Mexico, July 7, 2023.

Marrin, Albert. *Empires Lost and Won: The Spanish Heritage in the Southwest*. Simon and Schuster, 1997.

Mendoza, Valerie, review of *Chicano! History of the Mexican American Civil Rights Movement*, by NLCC Educational Media (1996), *The Journal for Multimedia History*, Vol. 3 (2000), https://www.albany.edu/jmmh/vol3/chicano/chicano.html.

Mesa-Bains, Amalia. "*Domesticana*: The Sensibility of Chicana *Rasquache*." *Aztlán: A Journal of Chicano Studies* 24, no. 2 (Fall 1999): 157–167.

Miner, Dylan. *Creating Aztlán: Chicano Art, Indigenous Sovereignty, and Lowriding Across Turtle Island*. University of Arizona Press, 2014.

Miner, Dylan. "Straddling *la otra frontera*: Revisioning Chicana/o Art History through Michicana/o Visual Culture." *Aztlán: The Journal of Chicano Studies* (Spring 2008): 89–122.

Monroe, John Warne. *Metropolitan Fetish: African Sculpture and the Imperial French Invention of Primitive Art*. Cornell University Press, 2019.

Montiel, Miuel. "The Chicano Family: A Review of Research." *Social Work* 18, no. 2 (March 1973): 22–31.

Moquin, Wayne, and Charles Van Doren, eds. *A Documentary History of the Mexican Americans*. Bantam Books, 1971.

Nava, Gregory, dir. *Selena* (1997), Q-Productions, Warner Bros.

New Mexico Art Museum. https://www.nmartmuseum.org/exhitions/poetic-justice-judith-f-baca-mildred-howard-and-jaune-quick-to-see-smith/

NLCC Educational Media. *Chicano! History of the Mexican American Civil Rights Movement*, Video Documentary, 1996.

Norby, Patricia Marroquin. *Visual Violence in the Land of Enchantment*. Unpublished dissertation: University of Minnesota, 2013.

Nordland, Gerard. *Richard Diebenkorn in New Mexico*. Harwood Museum of Art, 2007.

Nott, Robert. "Santa Fe-Area Artists Plan Their Own Winter Spanish Market," *Santa Fe New Mexican* (Saturday, October 16, 2021). Interviewed on Thursday, October 14, 2021. https://www.santafenewmexican.com/news/local_news/santa-fe-area-artists-plan-their-own-winter-spanish-market/article_595b2ad0-2a24-11ec-ac65-777502da6a3e.html.

Nunn, Tey Marianna. *Sin Nombre: Hispana and Hispano Artists of the New Deal Era*. University of New Mexico Press, 2001.

Padilla, Carmella, and Donna Pierce. *Conexiones: Connections in Spanish Colonial art*. Museum of New Mexico Press, 2002.

Pawlowska, Aneta. "Avant-Gardists and Primitivism." *Art Inquiry* 19 (2017): 153–169.

Peterson, Jeanette Favrot. "Synthesis and Survival: The Native Presence in Sixteenth-Century Murals of New Spain." In *Native Artists and Patrons in Colonial Latin America: Phœbus—A Journal of Art History*, edited by Emily Umberger and Tom Cummins, 7 (Arizona State University, 1995), 14–35.

Pérez, Laura. *Chicana Art: The Politics of Spiritual and Aesthetic Altarities*. Duke University Press, 2007.

Pierce, Donna. "The Active Reception of International Artistic Sources in New Mexico." In *Transforming Images: New Mexican Santos*

In-Between Worlds, edited by Claire Farago and Donna Pierce. The Pennsylvania State University Press, 2006: 44–61.

Pisarz-Ramírez, Gabriele. "From Nepantla to Amerindia: Transnationality in Mexican American Literature and Art." *Iberoamericana: Nueva Época*, 7, no. 25 (Marzo de 2007): 155–72.

Pohl, John M.D., and Claire L. Lyons, eds. *Altera Roma: Art and Empire from Mérida to Mexico*. UCLA Cotsen Institute of Archaeology Press, 2016.

Pulido, Laura. "Geographies of Race and Ethnicity III: Settler Colonialism and Non-Native People of Color." In *Progress in Human Geography*, 42, no. 2 (2018): 309–18.

Quirarte, Jacinto. "Exhibitions of Chicano Art, 1965 to the Present." In *Chicano Art: Resistance and Affirmation, 1965–1985*, edited by Richard Griswold del Castillo, Teresa McKenna, and Yvonne Yarbro-Bejarano. Wight Art Gallery/University of California, Los Angeles, 1991.

Rael-Gálvez, Estevan. "Coyote Convergence: Introduction through Interrogation." *Converging Streams: Art of the Hispanic and Native American Southwest*, edited by William Wroth and Robin Farwell Gavin. Museum of New Mexico Press, 2010.

Rael-Gálvez, Estevan (dir.), *Native Bound-Unbound*; https://fromthepage.com/nativeboundunbound.

Restall, Matthew. *Seven Myths of the Spanish Conquest*. Oxford University Press, 2003.

Richard, Carl J. *The Founders and the Classics: Greece, Rome, and the American Enlightenment*. Harvard University Press, 1994.

Roberts, David. *The Pueblo Revolt: The Secret Rebellion that Drove the Spaniards out of the Southwest*. Simon and Shuster, 2004.

Roberts, Susan A., and Calvin A. Roberts. *A History of New Mexico*. University of New Mexico Press, 1986.

Rodgers, Timothy Robert. *In Pursuit of Perfection: The Art of Agnes Martin, Maria Martinez, and Florence Pierce*. Museum of New Mexico Press and Museum of Fine Arts, 2004.

Rodríguez, Anita O. "How *La Raza* Became Invisible." *Chamisa: A Journal of Literary, Performance, and Visual Arts of the Greater Southwest*, 1 (2021): 23–9.

Rodríguez, Anita O. *Coyota in the Kitchen: A Memoir of New and Old Mexico*. New Mexico: University of New Mexico Press, 2016.

Rodríguez, Pedro. "Toward the Future: Chicano Art, A Voice for Tomorrow (1991)," *International Center for the Arts of the Americas at the Museum of Fine Arts, Houston*, https://icaa.mfah.org/s/en/item/803413.

Rodríguez, Richard. *Brown: The Last Discovery of America*. Penguin Books, 2003.

Rodríguez, Sylvia. "The Hispano Homeland Debate," *Working Paper Series No. 17*. Stanford Center for Chicano Research, October 1986: 1–22.

Rosaldo, Renato. *Culture and Truth: The Remaking of Social Analysis*. Beacon Press, 1989.

Rudnick, Lois P., and MaLin Wilson-Powell, eds. *Mabel Dodge Luhan and Company: American Moderns and the West*. Museum of New Mexico Press, 2016.

Rudnick, Lois Palken. *Mabel Dodge Luhan: New Woman, New Worlds*. University of New Mexico Press, 1987.

Salazar, Ruben. "Who is a Chicano? And What is it the Chicanos Want?" *Los Angeles Times* (February 6, 1970).

Sánchez, Joseph P., Robert L. Spude, and Art Gómez. *New Mexico: A History*. University of Oklahoma Press, 2013.

Santisteban, Ray. "The First Rainbow Coalition," *PBS: Independent Lens* (January 27, 2020), https://www.pbs.org/independentlens/documentaries/the-first-rainbow-coalition/

Shalev, Erin. "'This Natural Defect of Apprehension': Native Americans and the Politics of Time in the Young United States." *European Journal of American Studies* 16, no. 2 (Summer 2021), https://journals.openedition.org/ejas/16983.

Simmen, Edward, ed. *The Chicano: From Caricature to Self-Portrait.* New American Library, 1971.

Sisneros, Samuel. "Los Genizaros and the Colonial Mission Pueblo of Belen, New Mexico." *New Mexico Historical Review* 92, no. 4 (October 2017): 453–94.

Stansell, Christine. *American Moderns: Bohemian New York and the Creation of a New Century.* Metropolitan Books, Henry Holt and Company, 2000.

Steele, Thomas J., S. J.. *Santos and Saints: The Religious Folk Art of Hispanic New Mexico.* Ancient City Press, 1974.

Sullivant, Dana, and Robert R. White. *Artists of Territorial New Mexico, 1846–1912: Dr. Robert R. White.* Grekel Film/Video/Animation, 1995.

Sweeney, James Robinson. "Picasso and Iberian Sculpture." *The Art Bulletin* 23, no. 3 (September 1941): 191–98.

Tenzer Feldman, Ruth. *The Mexican-American War.* Lerner Publications Co., 2004.

Todorov, Tzvetan. *The Conquest of America.* Harper and Rowe, 1984.

Troncoso, Sergio. *Crossing Borders: Personal Essays.* Arte Público Press, 2011.

Traugott, Joseph. *New Mexico Art through Time: Prehistory to the Present.* Museum of New Mexico Press, 2012.

Turner, David G. *Georgia O'Keeffe: Paintings.* Museum of Fine Arts/Museum of New Mexico, 1987.

Tutorow, Norman E., ed. *The Mexican-American War: An Annotated Bibliography.* Greenwood Press, 1981.

Vedder, Ann. "History of the Spanish Colonial Arts Society, Inc., 1951–1981." In *Hispanic Arts and Ethnohistory in the Southwest: New Papers Inspired by the Work of E. Boyd,* edited by Marta Weigle, Claudia Larcombe, and Samuel Larcombe. Ancient City Press, 1983.

Vélez-Ibáñez, Carlos C., *Border Visions: Mexican Cultures of the Southwest United States.* University of Arizona Press, 1996.

Vicario, Gilbert, ed. *Agnes Pelton: Desert Transcendentalist.* Hirmer Verlag, 2019.

Villaseñor Black, Charlene. "Thoughts from Nepantla." *Latin American and Latinx Visual Culture* 1, Issue 2 (April 2019), 3–7.

Weigle, Marta. "The First Twenty-Five Years of the Spanish Colonial Arts Society." In *Hispanic Arts and Ethnohistory in the Southwest: New Papers Inspired by the Work of E. Boyd,* edited by Marta Weigle, Claudia Larcombe, and Samuel Larcombe. Ancient City Press, 1983.

Weigle, Martha, Frances Levine, and Louise Stiver, eds. *Telling New Mexico: A New History.* Museum of New Mexico Press, 2009.

Whitman, Walt. *The Spanish Element in Our Nationality,* 1883.

Wiggins, Julianna C. *Written and Oral Histories of the Chicano Movement at New Mexico Highlands University, 1968–1970.* Unpublished thesis, University of New Mexico, 2019.

Wilcox, Michael V. *The Pueblo Revolt and the Mythology of Conquest: An Indigenous Archaeology of Contact.* University of California Press, 2009.

Williams, Amelia W., and Eugene C. Barker, eds. *The Writings of Sam Houston, 1813–1863.* The University of Texas Press, 1938.

Wilson, Chris. *The Myth of Santa Fe: Creating a Modern Regional Tradition.* University of New Mexico Press, 1997.

Winterer, Caroline. *The Culture of Classicism: Ancient Greece and Rome in American Intellectual Life, 1780–1910.* Johns Hopkins University Press, 2001.

Wright, A. D. *The Counter Reformation: Catholic Europe and the Non-Christian World.* St. Martin's Press, 1982.

Wroth, William, and Robin Farwell Gavin, eds. Introduction by Estevan Rael-Gálvez, *Converging Streams: Art of the Hispanic and*

Native American Southwest. Museum of Spanish Colonial Art/Museum of New Mexico Press, 2010.

Ybarra-Frausto, Tomás. "*Rasquachismo*: A Chicano Sensibility," *Chicano Aesthetics: Rasquachismo*. Exhibition catalog. MARS *Movimiento Artístico del Río Salado*, 1989: 5–8.

Yzaguirre, Raul, and Mari Carmen Aponte. *Willful Neglect: The Smithsonian Institution and U.S. Latinos, Report of the Smithsonian Institution Task Force on Latino Issues*. The Smithsonian Institution, 1994.

Zamudio-Taylor, Victor. "Inventing Tradition, Negotiating Modernism: Chicano/a Art and the Pre-Columbian Past." In *The Road to Aztlan: Art from a Mythic Homeland*, curated by Virginia M. Fields and Victor Zamudio-Taylor. Los Angeles County Museum of Art and University of New Mexico Press, 2001.

El oro del barrio

Two

First-Generation New Mexican

Chicana and Chicano Activists and Their Art

RAY HERNÁNDEZ-DURÁN

"We're community artists, we're activists, and we're going to use art to
activate and inspire, and to connect to our community."[1]
—

*T*he decade framed by the years 1970 and 1980 marks a decisive period in the
Chicano Movement in New Mexico. Commonly known as the *movimiento*,
this moment represents a formative development in the local history of the
movement through forms of community empowerment that brought about social change
throughout the state. From community leaders inspired by the activism and organization
in places like Southern California and Texas to local university and high school students
demonstrating and demanding the hiring of more Chicano faculty, Chicana and Chicano
activism in New Mexico took root and spread throughout the state very quickly. Students
at universities played an important role in shaping the movement that unfolded starting
in the late 1960s through the 1970s, first at the University of New Mexico through the
founding of United Mexican American Students (UMAS) in 1968, followed by the formation
of the Spanish American Student Organization, soon renamed the Chicano Associated
Student Organization at New Mexico Highlands University in Las Vegas, New Mexico.
Students involved in these early organizations fought for inclusion and representation in
the administration and in the curriculum, and they formed alliances with other groups,
including Black and Native American students.

Nuevomexicana and *nuevomexicano* artists were central to the early Chicano Movement in the region through their activism and art production. Artists from Albuquerque,
Santa Fe, Las Vegas, Taos, Tucumcari, Artesia, and other regions of the state, many of them
students, played a seminal role in giving visual form to the developing political discourse.
They organized actions that both shaped the tone of the *movimiento* in the state and tied
it to larger national developments. A group of early artists, most of who were inspired

by *Tejano* Chicano scholar, Pedro Rodríguez (1936–2022), helped galvanize Chicana and Chicano students at New Mexico Highlands University in Las Vegas, New Mexico. Phillip B. (Felipe) Gonzales describes the student activism at NMHU as militant—perhaps the most militant of all the student groups in New Mexico.[2] These young artists, including Francisco Lefebre, who describes the movement as an uprising or *levantamiento*, proceeded to create diverse and vibrant forms of art that spoke to both regional and global conditions of the times while promoting activism, social protest, and civil disobedience in concert with local and national events.

As noted, although Chicana and Chicano activists, such as Reies López Tijerina and Dolores Huerta are salient presences in the history of the larger Chicano Movement and known for the work they did (and in Huerta's case, are still doing) around issues involving land grants and farmworkers' and/or workers' rights, in the case of Chicano art history, artists and art-related events in New Mexico have generally been underplayed, if not overlooked, with few exceptions.[3] New Mexican Chicana and Chicano artists who moved away from New Mexico to places like California, Texas, or elsewhere have received varying levels of recognition, with a handful of artists, such as Malaquías Montoya, included in the Chicano art historical canon that is taught. In contrast, artists who remained in the state have generally been rendered peripheral, if not absent, from the art historical conversation with few exceptions. Certain New Mexican artists, a few of whom we are including in this exhibition, such as Juanita J. Lavadie and Francisco Lefebre, along with Samuel Leyba, Gilberto Guzmán, Gerónimo Garduño, and Miguel Gandert, were mentioned in the groundbreaking exhibition, *CARA: Chicano Art: Resistance and Affirmation* (1991) but have received differing degrees of attention since then. There are also Chicana and Chicano artists, who, although born elsewhere, such as in California and Texas, settled in New Mexico and have been exhibited and studied, including the late Luis Jiménez (1940–2006) and Delilah Montoya (who is scheduled to have a retrospective at the Albuquerque Museum in 2026). Most of the artists who were born in New Mexico and who chose to remain in the state, especially those who began working during the early years of the movement, have generally been neglected in the broader scholarship that features Chicana and Chicano artists, not only nationally but also locally by the institutional art scene in the larger cities of New Mexico, such as Taos, Santa Fe, and Albuquerque (although things may be changing).

In terms of understanding this lack of—or inconsistent—recognition, I suggest that we consider at least three variables, in addition to the structural influence of the tricultural myth. One variable is to recognize that New Mexico is a state with a small population, much of which is rural, and with no comparable metropolitan urban centers with large Mexican/Mexican American communities, such as Los Angeles, Houston, or Chicago; given the circumstances, outside of community interest there has been no significant institutional infrastructure to support or cultivate Chicano art production as happened in Southern California. Next, when reviewing the career trajectories and productivity of the featured artists over the last fifty years, we note that a few artists have been working consistently and thus have substantial bodies of work, while others either didn't pursue a career in the arts or halted their art practice for a variety of reasons and then started up again later, yielding bodies of work with gaps or that are inconsistent over the span of five decades. What this means is that even for those artists who have been producing art consistently, their activity has tended to be more regional and localized, although a few have exhibited work nationally, even if sporadically. Finally, we should acknowledge how Chicano art history has developed, including which artists and which areas of the country have received the most attention, and why.

A review of the Chicano art historical literature reveals that artists from or working in California have been largely centered in the arts conversation, given the centrality of that region in the history of the movement, especially in the fight for farmworker rights and in the concentration of artistic productivity in cities like Los Angeles and San Diego. Conversely, Chicana and Chicano artists in other regions of the Southwest, including New Mexico and Texas, as well as other areas of the country such as the Midwest, have, until recently, received little attention.[4] Given that we are focusing on artists living and working in New Mexico, I have proposed that we consider the cultural and political environment that has shaped the production, promotion, and recognition of an arts culture in the state, as a way of beginning to understand what can be seen as a form of *olvido*, or forgetting, resulting from a disregard if not a willful neglect of the New Mexican Chicana and Chicano artists who have been active since the first decade of the movement. This general lack of attention is not a unique occurrence; it must be seen as part of a larger ongoing dismissal or erasure of Chicano/a/x communities, and more broadly, Latinx communities, their histories, and contributions in the master narrative of this country.[5] For those who are not only members of these communities but who have also dedicated their lives to the study, documentation, dissemination, and promotion of these peoples, their histories, and their lives, there is no greater task than the one aimed at documenting these communities' cultural production and demonstrating its significance not just to Chicano or Latinx art history but as an expression of the American experience and thus, its relevance to US American art history.

Un compadrazgo de artistas:
Six Chicana and Chicano Artists to Know

"You know, you should study a little bit about your own culture, where you come from."[6]
—

The artists included in this exhibit have contributed to social and political advocacy both in New Mexico and nationally through their work with community-based organizations, art spaces, and educational centers. Although the activist work of most of these artists began with Pedro Rodríguez at NMHU, over time, some became part of extensive transborder networks that fostered dialogues, exchanges, and collaborative creative expressions with artists from California, Texas, Mexico, and Cuba, including the forming of alliances with the Puerto Rican movement in New York and Chicago. In the 1970s, as was generally the case with Chicana and Chicano activists who made art, when the students were starting their art practices, they made art not to display in art galleries or to sell, but rather to distribute within their own communities to educate, promote, organize, and inspire; they gave work away or traded it. Much work was done on paper (prints, drawings, photography), a medium that is at the same time affordable and accessible but is also characterized by its fragility and loss unless great care is taken to preserve it; there was also painting on canvas, panel, and mural, which has better stood the test of time. Given the nature of the movement and the activist intent of the artists, the archival aspect of their art was not something they prioritized as part of their practice or work commitments; consequently, much of the early art production of this group was not documented or preserved. This is most clearly illustrated by the destruction of murals these artists created when they were students.

Each of the featured artists, all of whom come from multigeneration Nuevomexicano families, was a member of the early generation of New Mexican Chicana and Chicano activists; however, for the reasons noted the selected body of work for each artist varies. Some artists have work that spans the entirety of the last fifty years, others have gaps in their production, and others may have access to only more recent work. This exhibition features art produced by these six New Mexican Chicana and Chicano artists from approximately 1970 through the present. The exhibition presents a body of work that, although inconsistent and with gaps, should provide a cohesive view of the visual languages, forms, materials, and subjects or themes employed by artists who were living and working in New Mexico but responding to the principles and objectives of the larger national Chicano movement of the time.

An overview of the subjects represented in the artwork reveals distinctive regional foci while engaging with the broader themes associated with the kind of canonical

Chicano art that came out of the movement in the 1970s in places like California and Texas. While there are references to Prehispanic Mexican cultures, Catholic icons, and Mexican/Latin American historical figures, we also note subjects, materials, and forms that appear to be particular to New Mexico, thus distinguishing the Chicana and Chicano art produced in the state from that produced elsewhere. What we see is a particularly New Mexican expression of the Chicano Movement, one shaped by the primarily rural, communal, land-based way of life seen in communities across the state; similarly, some of the artists draw from historical artistic traditions, which may go back four hundred years. Writing in 1986, art historian Shifra Goldman had already noted this phenomenon when discussing the work of artist Juanita J. Lavadie, here identified as Juanita Jaramillo, her maiden name. Goldman wrote:

> The case of Juanita Jaramillo is particularly interesting in tying the new Chicano tradition to the Mexican American and Spanish arts that go back several centuries. Born in Taos, New Mexico from a family of traditional weavers, Jaramillo studied muralism in Mexico and has done murals in New Mexico, Chicago, and Wisconsin. She subsequently returned to New Mexico which, with southern Colorado, has long been known for "Hispanic folk arts"—the crafts that provided household necessities and luxuries and religious images from the 16th to the 19th centuries when these territories were within the frontier settlements of the Spanish empire, and then a peripheral part of the new Mexican nation. Jaramillo undertook to bridge the gap between those realities and the present by producing modern blankets within this centuries-old tradition. She is one of a generation of craftspeople in New Mexico using the old skills to create new forms.[7]

When the featured works are viewed as a group, the subject that stands out is landscape: the land in New Mexico, the land one lives and works on, the land that is central to one's communal and individual identity. There is a sacred bond between local communities and the land they inhabit and that sustains them. This relationship, which is logical when looking at the mostly agrarian-based communities in the region, expresses itself in New Mexican culture as a connection to or love of place identified locally as *querencia*, a term derived from the Spanish word meaning "desire" but that also refers to the ties one feels to one's homeland. Juan Estevan Arellano, referring to this idea in relation to New Mexico, explains that *querencia* is "that which gives us a sense of place, that which anchors us to the land, that which makes us a unique people, for it implies a deeply rooted knowledge of place, and for that reason we respect it as our home."[8] This consciousness is something that normally only develops among populations that have inhabited a place for a long time. Because most, if not all, of historical or traditional New Mexican *Hispano* arts consisted of either religious imagery or utilitarian objects, New Mexican Chicana and Chicano artists, responding to contemporary interests and reflecting their experiences in Mexico, focused much of their attention on capturing or documenting their homeland, their communities' cultural traditions, and the people around them, in addition to the kinds of subjects seen in works by Chicano artists living and working elsewhere.

The group of artists whose works form the core of this exhibition include three New Mexican men and three New Mexican women: Ignacio "Nacho" Jaramillo, Juanita J. Lavadie, Francisco Lefebre, Noel Márquez, Roberta Márquez, and Adelita M. Medina.[9] When studying New Mexican Chicana and Chicano art and especially when talking to these artists about their work, the community's oral traditions of remembering and passing on the wisdom of those who came before by telling *cuentos* and *dichos*, passing down family *historias*, sharing *chisme*, and partaking in *pláticas*, all come to the fore and resonate with the New Mexican idea of *la resolana* (a sunny spot or place where members of the community gather to talk). Each of these artists has a story to tell, and their stories, like their bodies of work, professional activities, and life choices, differ, despite them having come together to participate in shaping the early *movimiento* in New Mexico. To understand their work, it is essential that one become familiar with each artist's life and experiences, each artist's perspective of and involvement in the Chicano movement, and each artist's artistic production over the past five decades. What has been the most fulfilling and enlightening part of this project has been hearing the artists speak and share their experiences, ideas, concerns, and hopes. With this objective in mind, let us meet each of these artists and learn about their lives and their work.

Ignacio "Nacho" Jaramillo

"I'm a Chicano, a village Chicano. I grew up speaking Spanish and my first portraits were of the *santos* I grew up around."[10]
—

Ignacio "Nacho" Jaramillo was born in 1943 in La Plaza de Arriba, a small village just north of Anton Chico, a town where he spent most of his childhood. He currently resides in Las Vegas, New Mexico, which is located east of Santa Fe in northern New Mexico. Nacho states that he expressed an interest in art early on—an interest in part fueled by a great-uncle he grew up with who was a weaver, leatherworker, and a painter. He doesn't know how or when his uncle started painting but he remembers his oil paintings and adds that on the occasions he'd visit, he'd watch his uncle work and would help him weave. Nacho would spend time sketching animals he'd see, such as horses, and would also sketch the images of saints surrounding him. He mentions being fascinated by the sculpted and painted faces of these santos, which he would study and draw. He studied art when he could and enjoyed looking at art, especially on trips to Santa Fe. He recalls being in Santa Fe in the 1960s and notes the drastic changes he saw taking place due to rapid gentrification. He recalls what Canyon Road was like before commercial galleries took it over and describes the artist studios that could be found in that area. Due to the changing social and cultural environment brought on by outside interests and rising costs, local artists were pushed out, many of them moving out into the country.

A bright, studious kid, Nacho finished high school at the age of sixteen in 1960 and was awarded funding to attend New Mexico Highlands University in Las Vegas; however, he admits not being ready for college at that time, so he dropped out and hitchhiked to San Francisco in 1962. After arriving in the Bay Area, he was homeless for several months but always found places to stay. Having grown up in a conservative community in a rural area, Nacho was very careful with his newfound freedom, unlike so many youths back then. While living in San Francisco, he befriended a Puerto Rican who told Nacho that he reminded him of his grandparents. The man's father was from the island; however, it turned out that his mother was Hispanic and from a New Mexican family. Nacho met his friend's grandparents and was surprised to learn that they were originally from Belen and Socorro in New Mexico. The couple had married young, and as many New Mexican Hispanos had done in the 1930s and 1940s, they moved to San Francisco looking for work in the canneries. Nacho mentioned finding a club in Oakland that was frequented by New Mexicans, and to his surprise, he met relatives from Anton Chico there.

He then moved to Berkeley in 1963, where he found work with a ceramicist who he helped by building kilns and firing ceramics. He worked there for three years, and in 1966, he moved to Los Angeles. Nacho states that he didn't like Los Angeles because he felt it was too big. He also encountered anti-Mexican racism and decided to move back home. Back in Las Vegas, he re-entered NMHU but quit, again, and moved to Albuquerque, where he continued his studies at the University of New Mexico (UNM); he remembers taking art history classes at UNM with famed photo historian Bainbridge Bunting. He describes himself as not a serious student; he didn't follow any academic program and simply took the courses he wanted to take. He remembers moving around a lot during that time; he also briefly attended College of the Sequoias in Visalia, California, before returning to New Mexico again. He eventually wound up back in Las Vegas. Although he had originally majored in biology, he got his BA in art education at New Mexico Highlands University in 1971. In 1972, he started teaching for the Head Start program in Las Vegas, where he was the first male teacher, and later, he moved to the Head Start program in Denver. He quit teaching after deciding to pursue an MA degree, which he never finished. He then taught at the technical school in Luna and at Santa Rosa High School.

Nacho got involved in the Chicano movement while at New Mexico Highlands University (NMHU), where Vietnam veterans were helping organize, but he adds that he was more involved in community activism than in the student movement at the school. He supported a walkout organized at Robertson High School in east Las Vegas, which was held in opposition to the hiring of an outsider to be principal of the school; according to him, this protest was the first walkout at a local high school. He also took part in another movement led by David Montoya at the Padre Antonio José Martínez School at the Montezuma Castle. At NMHU, he participated in the takeover of the administration building by Chicana and Chicano students who demanded that the school hire John Aragón as university president following the retirement of Frank Ángel; the regents proceeded to hire Gilbert Sánchez. As this was unfolding, the athletes at NMHU counterprotested in defense of the university; what was interesting to Nacho was that most of the athletes, Hispanic Tejanos from Texas, were siding with the predominantly white administration. He remembers the athletes waving US flags and, ironically, telling the Chicano protesters to go back to Mexico.

It was at NMHU that Nacho met other student activists, including artists, such as Francisco Lefebre and Noel Márquez. At the time, these students, who were studying with Chicano Studies scholar Pedro Rodríguez, were painting a mural at the student union building; Nacho would help them out by obtaining paint and other supplies for them. According to Nacho, the Chicano students, along with Rodríguez, were accused of being radicals and troublemakers; not long after, the newly hired university president, Gilbert Sánchez, declared that he would not set foot on the campus until the mural produced by Chicana and Chicano students was painted over, leading to lawsuits and the university paying millions of dollars to settle. Nacho adds that some of his problems at school included being made to feel as if he was always on the outside regardless of what he did. In 1961, he joined the Chicano fraternity at NMHU but was hassled by the older Chicanos running it; they claimed that he wouldn't vote in the student senate how they wanted him to and used that as a pretense to expel him. He explains that their decision to expel him was in response to the fact that he hung out with whomever he wanted to, which included the Black students on campus, which they didn't like. Nacho adds that while he supported Chicano ideals, he had to be his own person.

Nacho states that he identifies as a Chicano but not as a Chicano artist; he simply identifies as an artist. He believes one must be real and not try to be something else or like anyone else, and he sees his art as an extension of these principles. He primarily produces portraits and landscapes. In terms of medium, his work consists of painting and printmaking. He paints the people around him, people he knows, and people he meets; as he stated, "My portraits are of Chicanos."[11] He has always been interested in faces and has been making portraits since he was quite young. He started painting images of the *santos*, the saint figures that are such a fundamental part of his culture and a ubiquitous presence in older New Mexican communities, not by copying them but interpreting them in his own style.[12] He then proceeded to paint portraits of his family members, including paintings based on photographs of uncles who had been soldiers in World War II. His preferred medium is tempera applied with a dry brush; he credits his study and love of watercolor for this approach. He explains that he prefers a dry brush because he learned to draw with a brush and this method, which is fast, gestural, and expressive, helps capture a certain feeling. He works from black to white and sometimes scratches the picture surface to create the effects he desires. Many of his portraits are painted cutouts, where the figure is excised from the painting surface and brought out into our space. Nacho feels that by cutting out the figure in his portraits, they become more real and develop a personality.

Nacho recalls, as many older New Mexican Hispanos have noted, that many nuevomexicano families began trading their traditional religious images for the newer, shiny, gaudy ones introduced by Anglos after New Mexico became part of the US. He adds that when French archbishop Jean-Baptiste Lamy arrived in New Mexico in 1851, he attempted to suppress local religious organizations, such as the Hermanos de Nuestro Padre Jesús, of which Nacho's father was a member, leaving many *moradas* (private meeting places for the Penitente Brotherhood in New Mexico) and *capillas* (chapels) abandoned. This led to the ransacking and sale of traditional ceremonial objects to Anglo collectors. Precious older images, some of them presumably dating back to the colonial period, would be removed from their original sites of display, where they held privileged positions, and were sold to museums and collectors; new labels would be applied to them, such as folk art, crafts, and colonial art, along with the attachment of monetary value—the basis for such forms of cultural resignification. Nacho knew several established Santa Fe artists and writers who had old santos in their collections. When he would ask them how they came to acquire such objects, they'd reply that they'd obtained them "off the street" but couldn't remember from whom. Nacho's mother, critical of such practices, would say, "You do not sell *santos*, not once they are blessed!"[13] The commercialized system into which these objects were inserted went against fundamental Hispano beliefs and values, contributing to tensions between local communities and the new Anglo presence. This perception of images as sacred, as alive, and as possessing a presence is shared throughout the Spanish Catholic world, prompting the question, Does this belief in the power and presence of the image translate into the reading of portraits?

With this idea in mind, we can look at the three-dimensional sculptural quality of Nacho's cutouts, which are reminiscent of *fotoescultura*, a type of portrait studio photography that was popular from the 1920s through the 1980s, especially among Mexican and Mexican American communities[14] (Fig. 2.1). Normally sold by traveling salesman, these photographic works would consist of a hand-colored photograph, where the human figure would be cut out and adhered to a wooden panel cut into the silhouette of the image; the entire cutout would then be mounted

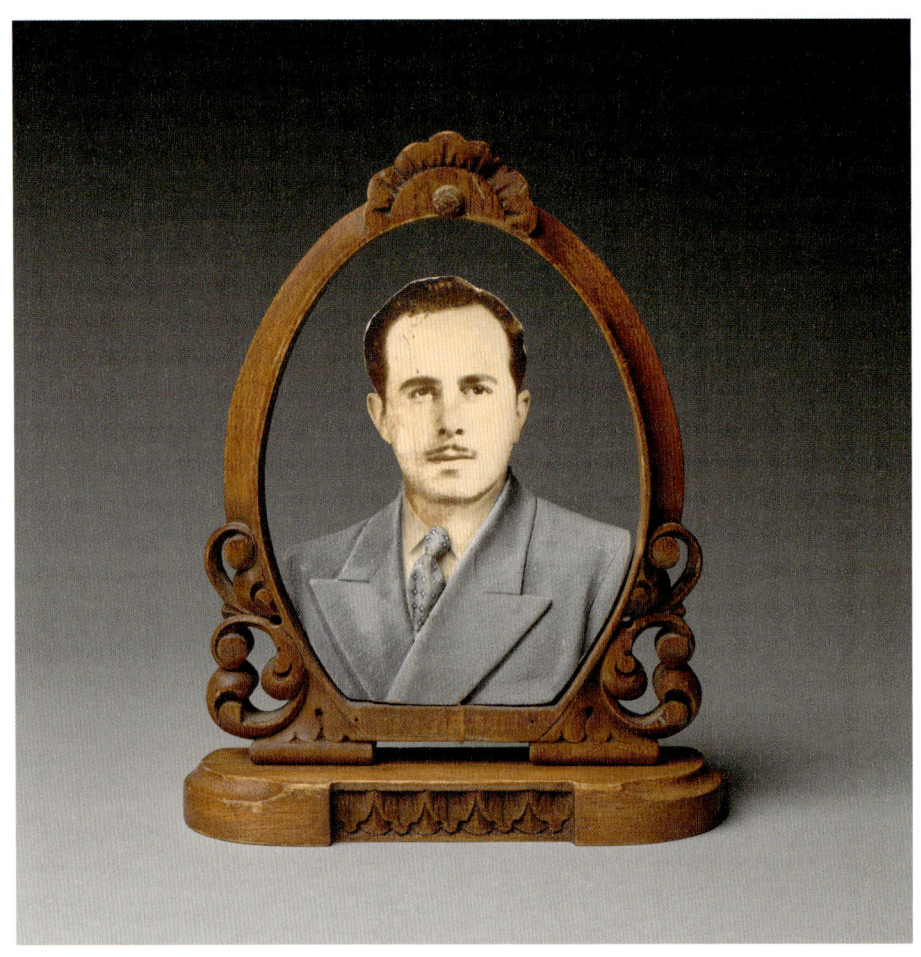

FIGURE 2.1. Artist unknown, *Fotoescultura*, ca. 1930. Gelatin silver print with applied color, mounted to wood, 11″ × 9″ × 2 1/4″. Museum of Fine Arts, Houston. Barbara Levine and Paige Ramey Collection. Museum purchase funded by the Caroline Wiess Law Accessions Endowment Fund.

on a stand within an elaborately carved wooden frame and often encased in a convex glass shell. This object's form and function recall relics and monstrances. The photographs would also often have surface areas in relief to enhance their three-dimensional quality. Reaching the height of popularity around World War II, the pictured subjects would mostly include absent family members, sometimes deceased individuals, converting such objects into memorials to loved ones. The three-dimensional nature of the photograph seemed to animate the subject, which aided in the cathartic expression of grief and in keeping the subject's memory alive. Jaramillo's cutouts, although not necessarily memorials, function similarly, given how they appear to bring the painted subjects to life by releasing them from a painted two-dimensional surface and projecting them into our space; as he states, by cutting out the figures, they seem "more real."

An example of his cutout portraits would be *Hijo de la luna* (2018), a painting done in tempera and acrylic on board (Plate 15). The image is of a man depicted from his shoulders up as is typical in all of Nacho's portraits. The figure wears a blue shirt over a purple t-shirt, a cream-colored newsboy cap, and a small earring in his left ear; he could be someone you see walking down the street or reading at the café. The man, set against a nocturnal sky filled with stars and a full moon, faces forward but he turns to his right and seems to be gazing at something beyond the picture frame and past the viewer. The cutout figure is not flush with the back panel but is placed in front of it and is slightly elevated. The expressive features of the man's face, his pose, and his projection into our space animate the subject. Surrounding the main figure are three diaphanous images placed against the night sky where they resemble constellations. The three images are of a fish, an owl, and the Virgin of Guadalupe. Nacho explains that the three images are drawn from the classic novel, *Bless Me, Ultima* by famed New Mexican Chicano author, Rudolfo Anaya; Jaramillo shared that the title for the work was inspired by Anaya's birthplace, Puerto de Luna, New Mexico.[15] The novel, published in 1972, is described as a coming-of-age story and centers on a young boy named Antonio Márez y Luna and his life growing up in rural 1940s New Mexico. A central theme in the narrative is Antonio's relationship with an older woman named Última (which is Spanish for "last one"), who is a curandera (a traditional healer) regarded respectfully as La Grande (Spanish for "the great one") but who is suspected by various community members of being a witch. As we get to know Última and witness her mentoring of Antonio, we see how Indigenous beliefs and customs are woven into the Indo-Hispano cultural practices in the region, such as the gathering of medicinal plants, about which Última teaches Antonio. As the story unfolds, we see the repeated appearance of an owl believed to belong to Última, and we hear the story of a magical golden carp. As Antonio learns, he begins to question things, including the faith he was brought up with, focused as it is on the Virgin and God. The world that Anaya lovingly crafts in this story captures life among Indo-Hispano communities in New Mexico at mid-century, its people, and their culture, shaped as it was and, in many cases, continues to be by religion, folk traditions, and a belief in the mystical. Threaded throughout the story is the idea of a world in transition as old ways give way to new ones and the tensions such developments inevitably engender. We witness Antonio becoming increasingly aware of these changes and the conflicts they reveal, and how he reconciles and embraces these disjunctive beliefs and lifeways, which are part of his cultural heritage and identity. Nacho describes the portrait in the following manner: "A take on *Bless Me, Ultima* with love and respect for a wonderful book by Rudolfo Anaya. Antonio becomes a man. He is still being nurtured by Ultima's owl, the Golden Carp, and Our Lady of Guadalupe."[16]

Another portrait that presents a range of thematic associations is *Raza cósmica* (made some time between 1970 and 1980), also acrylic and tempera on board (Plate 1). The anonymous portrait represents a young man, possibly Native or mestizo. The figure, also a cutout, is placed before a painted panel depicting the starry night sky with a full moon to the upper left and glyph-like constellations, as we saw in the last portrait. The man, depicted from the shoulders up, is bare chested and wears a bandanna on his head. Clean shaven, he has what appears to be one long stripe across his face running under his eyes and over the bridge of his nose. Placed underneath his left and right shoulders are two images of a human hand with an eye. The forms, possibly read as tattoos here, resemble what is known as the *hamsa* or *Khamsa*. Also known as the Hand of Fátima, the hamsa is an ancient symbol, whose origin may date back to Mesopotamia and is found in Jewish and Muslim cultures in the Middle East and North Africa, and throughout the world today. The symbol, often found in amulet form, is believed to ward off evil or the evil eye, suggesting that its presence on the young man may perhaps signal protection. As for the title of the portrait, it may be a reference to the book by Mexican intellectual, José Vasconcelos, titled *La raza cósmica*, published in 1925 on the heels of the Mexican Revolution and in line with the tenets of the Mexican *Indigenismo* movement. The book presents a vindicatory ethnography of sorts that, starting with ancient cultures in Mesopotamia, the Andes, and the Americas, including Spain, Portugal, and other world regions, argues for *mestizaje*, racial mixing, as the moral path for humankind.[17] Although Vasconcelo's propositions in this text have been critiqued as racist, among other things, many Chicanos involved in the early movement were familiar with this work and quoted from it given its recognition of Mexican indigeneity and its emphasis on mestizaje as the promise of a utopic future. Looking at the image with the title in mind, the viewer thus reads the young man as the product of such racial mixtures, a historical reality for most New Mexicans, the demographics of which this subject can be seen as representing. The nocturnal setting and the presence of the hamsa symbols on the unclothed, vulnerable figure possess an almost mystical quality imbuing the image with a talismanic power.

In addition to his striking cutout portraits, Nacho's landscapes are equally notable. One of these works is *San Francisco de Asis* (2002), created in tempera, acrylic, and watercolor on panel (Plate 6). Often focusing on local buildings, his landscapes feature the unique traits of New Mexican architectural vernaculars. In this example, we see a church centered and occupying most of the picture space; we are positioned outside behind the church and our view is of the church apse. Set against a cloud-filled blue sky, the building's earthen color and irregular contours anchor it to the landscape it, both, occupies and from which its material was derived. The monumental structure is pared down with little detail besides variations in the surface texture of the adobe structure. This minimalist rendition allows the hand-built forms of the church to stand out with their undulating corners and organic silhouette. The shading of the forms enhances the building's three-dimensional quality and sensual sculptural presence. There is an atmospheric softness and lightness in the image that is pleasing to the eye and might even be considered seductive. This type of construction with its amalgamation of local materials that speak to both Native and Spanish design and building techniques has come to symbolize the unique historical character and cultural landscape of New Mexico.[18]

One can sense in Nacho's carefully executed images—both portraits and landscapes—a tenderness for and connection with the subjects he is capturing and representing. These people and locations are more than just subjects to the artist; they're part of his community, his life, and his identity as a nuevomexicano, subjects most of which are normally absent in most American art. Aware of but consciously eschewing current trends, he follows his vision and makes the art he feels like making. Such an expression of sincerity in terms of his art practice, as that of many of these artists, ironically, could be characterized as metamodern.[19] If we were to examine this material using such contemporary analytical frameworks, we could interpret this body of work as an intellectual and philosophical reflection of its time and place, rather than as an uncritical anachronistic repetition that nostalgically or uncritically echoes past politics or esthetics. The work is alive, and its power lies in its tenderness, its accessibility, and its continued relevance.

Juanita J. Lavadie

"You know what, historical trauma is a real thing and we're still suffering from it."[20]
—

Juanita J. Lavadie, who currently resides in Taos, comes from an old family with deep roots in that area of northern New Mexico. Her mother's side includes five generations of teachers and six generations of weavers. In addition to her artwork, she has been an educator for twenty-two years. Juanita describes her work, which consists primarily of woven textiles and painting, as "a testimony to my land-based culture."[21] She credits her father, an educator and a storyteller, with being her first teacher and the person who cultivated in her an interest in the arts. She remembers meeting what she terms her *compradazgo de artistas* at New Mexico Highlands University at the beginning of the Chicano Movement, thanks to Pedro Rodríguez, who introduced her to muralism and sent her to study in Mexico City with Ramiro Romo Estrada. She states that learning about muralism is what helped develop an interest in and recognition of the significance of visual literacy. As a teacher, she worked primarily with third graders and adds that her involvement in the Chicano Movement was tied to early childhood education. Another important project for her was collecting oral histories, which, although a digression from Chicano graphic art, as she states, was significant given the need to document voices that were not heard. She interviewed community elders, such as her Tía Romancita, who was in her nineties at the time, and shared their stories with younger generations; stories that Chicano sociologist Tomás Atencio called "*el oro del barrio*" (the gold or treasure of the neighborhood or community). Juanita asserts the central importance of these stories and of the arts—not just visual arts, but also music, theater, dance, and so on, in fostering self-awareness and community among children. She believes that when knowledge of and appreciation for the arts is not part of early childhood education, society stagnates. Since the arts permeate everything, as she states, here we see one of the rationales for promoting the arts within the Chicano Movement; the arts become invaluable tools for documenting, educating, and self-expression. The arts thus play an essential role, particularly in relation to communities whose histories, cultural practices, values, and very existence have been intentionally marginalized, if not willfully erased, as is evident with Mexican American/Chicano communities throughout the Southwest and the rest of the Anglophone US.

Juanita's activism and involvement in various civil rights movements increased after college. After graduating from NMHU, Juanita moved to Chicago, where she continued her activist work with such organizations as Casa Aztlán; Movimiento Artístico Chicano; the Association of Latino Brotherhood of Artists, which included Chicano, Puerto Rican,

Latino, and Latin American artists; and Anishinaabe Waki Aztlán, a collaboration between Chicano and Native American activists. After leaving Chicago, she returned to New Mexico and became involved with La Cofradía de Arte y Artesanía in Santa Fe, where she worked alongside figures like Frederico Vigil, Luis Tapia, Wilfredo Miera, Teresa Archuleta-Sagel (now Spires), and Benjamin and Irene López; she also worked with Tomás Atencio, Esteban Arellano, Alejandro López, and others at La Academia de la Nueva Raza (1965–1988), and helped produce various publications and organize events.[22] Other organizations that Juanita became involved with include the Río Grande Institute—a collaboration between Native Americans and Chicanos from northern New Mexico and the Río Grande Valley—and Hembras de Colores, a women's organization that included artists and activists, such as Enriqueta Vásquez, Tania Ocanas, Victoria Plata, and Estrella Apolonia Delgado. Juanita's late husband, Eduardo Lavadie, was cofounder of the Taos Valley Acequia Association; it was through him that she became active in the *acequia* movement, which focuses on subsistence farming and water rights.

Juanita recalls the sketches she made when she first went to Mexico to study. Among these sketches were landscape studies of the volcanoes, and she observes how that experience made her and her peers more aware of their Indigenous *raíces* or roots, which she admits were always present but not openly discussed. Of central interest is what she refers to as a "conspiracy of silence" that dominated the community in northern New Mexico. Looking back at history, she talks about the period when New Mexico became a US territory, what was a significantly disruptive event for local communities, both Native and Hispano. The US military aggressively intervened, and locals responded in self-defense.[23] There was an uprising against the Anglo-American presence and many lives were lost in both Pueblo and nuevomexicano communities in Taos, Mora, and Santa Cruz. After the uprising was quelled, Juanita adds that anyone suspected of subversive, anti-US activity would be identified, captured, and lynched, a brutal response that resulted in the loss of many young men, especially those viewed as capable of bearing arms. Given the terror that local communities were subjected to by US agents, people kept silent to avoid any reprisals that might bring harm to their families and communities. She notes that a form of *vergüenza* or shame developed out of this experience, which caused communities to repress or silence these traumatic memories, resulting in a form of denial.[24] One of the most important effects of the Chicano movement, Juanita adds, was the manner in which it reacted against and advocated for the open recognition of multigenerational trauma, where this violent past was not simply seen as historical but as continuing to shape the present. As Juanita stated, "It was . . . opening up like a dam, just coming out and saying, 'Hey, you know what, historical trauma is a real thing and we're still suffering from it.'"[25]

Given her background, activities, and concerns, and guided in part by this history, Juanita's artwork can be seen as driven by an investment in preserving local tradition while working toward a more positive future. Much of the work she has produced, which is reflected in this exhibition, has been textile work with a focus on traditional or historical local materials, weaving techniques, and forms, including some experimentation with the same. Juanita's work with wool and weaving allows us to talk about media and materials that appear to speak directly to the New Mexican landscape and the cultural practices that developed in the region—in this case, sheep herding and the rich, complex textile tradition seen in local woven forms; forms that evince Native and Mexican influences.

Juanita's painting, *Tejiendo el Río Grande* (ca. 1990) depicts a pair of hands weaving the New Mexican landscape (Plate 24). The two hands, located in the lower third of the picture space, are placed before a loom. Working from the top down, the fingers skillfully draw the weft yarns through the warp, producing a landscape of sky, clouds, mountains, hills, and waterways. This image resonates on multiple levels. It engages with local textile traditions and strongly speaks to the relationship between weaving and the land when thinking of the use of handspun dyed wool gathered from the churro sheep that have been herded in this region for centuries. The land sustains the sheep, who then produce the wool that becomes the material in the production of a wide range of textiles. There is also the idea of human stewardship of the natural environment, of people's duty to care for the land so that it keeps providing sustenance and shelter to the community. The image evokes a bond with and respect for the land that brings to mind the concept of *querencia*, the love of place, of community, and of home that is characteristic of New Mexican culture. Juanita's textile work is just as rich as her paintings and murals. She has mostly produced weavings that are traditional in style and form, but she has also made others that employ traditional materials yet are experimental in form, such as her circular weavings, illustrated by her *Round Tapestry* (1974), what could be considered a contemporary interpretation of a traditional medium, as referenced by Shifra Goldman when discussing Lavadie's work (Plate 19).

A stellar example of a traditional textile would be the *Cibolero Shirt, Jerga Cuadrada (Buffalo Plaid Work Shirt Prototype)* (2016) (Plate 30). Made of handspun brown and white wool, the work shirt is the type of garment that would've been worn by sheep herders, ranchers, and mountain men to protect them from the elements. There would be no need for additional layers; the thick wool was lined and could withstand rainstorms and blizzard temperatures. Juanita noted the popularity of long-sleeved plaid button-down shirts among Chicanas and Chicanos—in particular, *cholos* and *cholas*—not just in LA but throughout the Southwest, and she wonders if there might be a connection between historical *jergas* and this plaid esthetic.

Another painting, titled *Nuestra Señora Guadalupe Norteña* (ca. 1980) is striking due to the scale and the subject matter (Plate 22). Measuring thirty inches by eighty inches, the image depicts a nocturnal desert landscape. Dominating the lower half of the landscape is a large *arroyo* that runs from the upper left to the lower right. To the lower left, in the corner, we see a lone sheep herder sitting next to a fire alongside two sheep. In the distance, we can make out a shadowy horizon dotted by snowcapped mountains. The upper half of the picture space is filled with a star-studded night sky containing a gibbous moon, a scene whose tranquility is punctuated by the miraculous appearance of the Virgin Mary. The holy figure appears ethereal, dressed in a white tunic with a blue cloak. She gently floats across the heavens and extends her right hand in which she holds a rose as if an offering. The apparition's divine radiance illuminates the land below like a spotlight. The seated figure, hunched over the fire, appears unaware of her, suggesting the Virgin's protective presence in the desolate landscape; upon closer study, one notes how the rose held by Our Lady of Guadalupe is reflected in the campfire. According to Juanita, the shepherd was inspired by Father Luis Jaramillo, a good friend, patron, and supporter of her work. Here, he appears lost in thought; however, one of the sheep gazes upward as if it is aware of the apparition. This type of image has a long history in the arts of the Indo-Hispanic Americas; there are numerous paintings and prints from the colonial period depicting the Virgin in various guises appearing in the heavens above the land or the city to mark certain events. These scenes imply her blessing or protection. Add text and you'd have an ex-voto, another example of a traditional image making use of similar formal elements. As with many of these paintings, the land is central, given human dependence on it for survival and as a foundation for tradition and community, all of which recall the *querencia* that is such a fundamental part of New Mexican identity. In Juanita's work, whether textile or painting, we see a collapsing or accumulation of time. The past is not forgotten or relegated to the margin; it is acknowledged, integrated, and centered. History and tradition continue to be the basis of nuevomexicano life today and thus of the Chicana and Chicano artists who capture this quality in their work.

Francisco Lefebre

"As an artist, I want to speak out against poverty and injustice, and that's what I'm all about."[26]
—

Francisco Lefebre is one of the members of this group who has been consistently working as an artist and advocating for the arts for the past fifty years. Originally from Wagon Mound, he currently lives and works in Albuquerque, although he describes himself as half *Sierreño* (from the Sangre de Cristo Mountains) and half *Llanero* (from El Cañon del Río Colorado). His father, from the Ocate Valley, worked in the logging camps as a *cuartonero* while his mother was from El Cañon del Río Colorado. Francisco recalls growing up in Wagon Mound, which he describes as a village composed mainly of *Raza* and a handful of white people. He mentions the reality of the segregation that shaped life in the village; he remembers that white people had their own churches, their own cemeteries, their own gatherings, and also sent their kids to schools outside of the village with little intermingling between groups except for the annual festival known as "Bean Day," when everyone would gather to watch the parade, attend the rodeo, and participate in street events. He adds that his awareness of the racism that was present when he was growing up did not develop until much later. Unlike the other artists, Francisco was drafted into the US Army, a development that took him abroad and introduced him to foreign cultures and peoples, and to white American racism. It was this experience that began sensitizing him to various forms of prejudice, and thus to questioning assumptions and values he held. He openly shares that he had never been around Black people until his stint in the Army. It was then that he came to know African American men and witnessed white racism at work. He recalls hearing white soldiers referring to Blacks using the N-word and to Mexican Americans as "wetbacks." While in Vietnam, he then heard US soldiers refer to locals with similar offensive racist terms and he laments how the Americans mistreated the Vietnamese. These experiences made him wonder about the Americans' purpose and to question what they were doing there, but the virulent anti-Communist attitudes he encountered initially led him to believe that their presence and actions in Vietnam were justified. After completing his tour of duty and being released from the military, he decided to attend New Mexico Highlands University in search of, as he states, "education and enlightenment," in a way to understand and make sense of what he had seen while in the military.[27]

Once at NMHU, he started taking art classes with studio art faculty members, including Elmer Schooley, Frank Walker, and others. At that time, modern art, and conceptual and abstract art were being promoted. Not feeling a connection to that material, he dropped out and moved to Los Angeles, California, for a while. It was following his return to New Mexico that he was first introduced to Pedro Rodríguez, who, after seeing his work, told him that he had a gift and convinced him to go back to college. While studying with Pedro at NMHU, Francisco traveled to Mexico City to study muralism for a semester with Mexican muralist Ramiro Romo Estrada. Although he initially didn't feel moved by Prehispanic art, he states that learning about modern Mexican muralism was life changing. Prior to studying in Mexico, the highest artforms in his opinion had been works by the canonical Renaissance masters, such as Michelangelo; he also had special admiration for the Impressionists and for European artists, generally. However, his time in Mexico and then studying with Pedro in Las Vegas introduced him to a completely different world of art and artists that, at that time, were undervalued, misunderstood, and disregarded. But as he noted, the Mexican artists and their artworks were more relevant to him and to his community back home. It was while learning about this material that he found his voice. As he states about that period, "It finally hit me. I don't think I slept for a couple of days, just thinking about all that he [Pedro] was saying. Eventually, I became a part of the Chicano movement."[28]

Francisco shares that he became an artist at that point because he wanted to contribute something and make a name for himself. He feels that art and social activism are interdependent and relevant not only to the Chicano movement but also to other similar movements with which he also associated. Francisco's work is diverse in terms of media and genre, and includes painting, both canvas and mural, printmaking, and drawing. Inspired by the time he spent in Mexico as a student, in addition to his later travels, his subject matter includes genre scenes, many of them of Mexican subjects, as well as portraits, landscape, architecture, political posters, and even painted objects. He shared that when he returned to New Mexico after studying in Mexico, the response to his genre scenes was negative and seen as alien to New Mexican traditions by many in his community, since the images depicted people and the world around them rather than religious icons, which is what locals were accustomed to seeing and how they understood the function of painting—in the service of faith and cult practice.[29]

An example of the kind of image Francisco made after his study in Mexico is a painting titled *Trabajadores* (1974), or laborers (Plate 43). The colorful image depicts two men with their backs to the viewer. They stand in front of a cart and face the vendor, who is preparing food for them. The bright green, blue, and gold reflect the vibrant colors of Mexican culture. He states that such scenes of daily life were unknown in the historical arts of New Mexico. This painting corresponds to the kinds of genre subjects that were popular in Mexico, starting in the eighteenth century, and followed an older European tradition dating back to the sixteenth century. Lefebre's exposure to these artistic languages and practices opened new avenues he had not previously considered as a way to document the world around him instead of replicating formulaic devotional images as had been done for centuries in the region. Upon returning to New Mexico, Francisco, armed with these new ideas and practices, began to draw and paint scenes of life drawn from the world he knew.

A spectacular drawing, titled, *Santuario* (1976) illustrates this new vision or interest inspired not by Anglo traditions but by Mexican ones (Plate 48). The pencil drawing captures the facade of a New Mexican church. The upper half of the picture space is dominated by heavier, thicker lines that firmly render the bell towers and roof structure, while the lower half of the image, containing the major body of the building, is defined by shading and softer surface textures referencing the adobe construction. The architecture that developed in the region following colonial intervention and that evinces both Indigenous and Spanish influences yielded an architectural vernacular that speaks to local history, local materials, and local culture. This elegantly rendered drawing captures those elements that are characteristic of construction in the area and that make New Mexican architecture so unique.

A large-scale painting that captures what can be considered his mature style as a painter is *Realidades de Nuevo México* (1976) (Plate 46). The canvas, painted in mostly warm hues of red, orange, yellow, and brown, depicts a crowd of people in the upper register of the composition that Francisco describes as "the diversity of people of New Mexico."[30] The lower half of the painting is filled with New Mexico landscape scenes, both natural and urban, and depictions of laborers. In the lower foreground of the image, we see barbed wire and chains along with a sign that states, "Posted NO Trespassing Hunting Fishing Private." Historically, in Native and Hispano communities, land was often communal and shared, a practice that changed with the arrival of Anglo-American settlers. Francisco describes the painting as telling a story of a community's struggle for survival in a changing world. The work itself has an interesting history. When asked how this painting came about, he mentioned that he painted it to serve as a backdrop for a local TV program on Channel 7 called *Realidades de Nuevo México*, from which the work derives its title. At the time, Eduardo Díaz, former deputy director of the National Museum of the American Latino at the Smithsonian in Washington DC, had just received his law degree from the University of California at Davis and relocated to Albuquerque where he hosted the TV show, focusing on the local community and local events. When the program ended, Eduardo gave back the painting to Francisco; eventually, the work was acquired by the Albuquerque Museum. In this painting, we can see how he took the lessons he learned in Mexico and combined them with local subject matter, in line with the principles of the larger Chicano art movement. This monumental canvas is characteristic not just of his painting style but of his larger mural production.

Francisco is accomplished in the tradition of the Mexican muralists he studied in Mexico as a college student in the early 1970s.[31] For the past fifty years, he has been painting murals consistently throughout the state. Regarding his work as a muralist, he stated,

> Painting on a wall is so satisfying—much more than painting on canvas. You get a real feeling of conquest when you create something as spacious as a mural. But it's also a lonely feeling. Every time you start a mural, there's a point where you think there's no way you can do it. And a mural is so public; you know that people are going to see it if it's awful and they're going to see it if it's wonderful. If you're painting a canvas in your studio, the investment isn't quite the same because you can just hide it until it's ready. You can never show it at all. A mural is right out there."[32]

Recent mural projects he was commissioned to paint include a large-scale mural in the cafeteria of Highlands High School and another at Robert F. Kennedy High School, both in Albuquerque; the mural project at Robert F. Kennedy was a collaborative project with high school students and students enrolled in the course, CCS 1110: Introduction to Comparative Ethnic Studies (The Social Science of Mural Making in New Mexico), taught by Irene Vásquez, PhD, through the Department of Chicana and Chicano Studies at the University of New Mexico. Because, as Francisco states, murals are public communal works, the content must be relevant to the people who will be living with and working beside it; consequently, reflecting his principles as a Chicano artist, an essential practice continues to be involving the local community in the conceptualization, creation, and maintenance of the work.

Noel Márquez

"There's always gotta be a little controversy when you get people thinking and wanting to activate."[33]
—

Noel Márquez (1953–2020) was born in Artesia, New Mexico, which is located in the southeast quadrant of the state, and is, as he noted, quite different from the communities to the north, where all of the other artists originated.[34] In spite of those differences, as was generally the case with most kids born and raised in New Mexico, he knew very little about Mexican culture. He had a natural affinity for art, so he taught himself to paint. Although he was not exposed to art museums growing up, he recalled going to Juárez, Mexico, and noticing the velveteen paintings that were for sale in the markets. His knowledge of European art came from a set of encyclopedias his mother had bought for the family. It was through reading the encyclopedias that he first saw and learned about European art—specifically, Renaissance art and the Impressionists, who he identified as his first heroes; that all changed when he enrolled at New Mexico Highlands University. Noel remarked that after graduating from high school, he was arrested for getting involved in a fight. After being released from jail, his father told him, "You're going to school or you are going to be the local bum."[35] Noel decided that he'd attend New Mexico Highlands University in Las Vegas and had intended to work with studio art professor Elmer Schooley; however, he adds that he wound up never meeting Schooley due to having been intercepted by Chicano Studies via the figure of Pedro Rodríguez.

When Noel met Pedro, and Pedro learned of his interests in Renaissance and Impressionist arts, Pedro suggested that he learn a bit about his own culture and where he came from. As happened with Francisco Lefebre and others, Noel found himself in Mexico City; while there, he visited the sites of Teotihuacan, Palenque, and Veracruz, and he learned about the Toltecs, Olmecs, Zapotecs, and Maya. Learning about these root cultures in those sacred spaces was inspiring and gave him a purpose for making art—an art that reflected the culture and land he grew up around. Upon his return from Mexico in 1972, he and others painted a mural at Highlands High School, which became the first of several murals he helped paint. As they worked collaboratively on the mural, Noel felt reawakened and realized that he and the others were community artists and activists, and would use art to activate and inspire, to connect with their community. Part of this newfound awareness was a renewed investment in the land and the desire for a safe environment, an urgent call to action given the US government's historical use of land in this region for nuclear testing and as a radioactive material dumping site. From this point forward, Noel became an environmental activist focused on caring for the land, recycling, etc., to ensure that future generations would be able to flourish. He saw his mural work as a way to address cultural and environmental issues by educating and bringing together people from all walks of life but with the same objectives. Noel noted the work he had been doing with anti-nuclear activist Janet Greenwald and the Navajo Nation to fight the powers that be and to safeguard the Earth. To him, political activism is a working-class struggle but one that is dependent on education. He supported education and promoted learning to children when visiting and speaking at local schools. He looked at his own educational trajectory as proof of the importance of formal study.

Noel credited Pedro Rodríguez with getting the ball rolling and presenting him with learning opportunities. In addition to teaching his students about Mexican and Chicano art, or sending them to Mexico to study, Rodríguez invited tortilla artists from California to talk about their work.[36] He also brought the Teatro Campesino to Las Vegas and invited Chicano activist Reies López Tijerina to campus. Noel went to hear López Tijerina speak, met and talked with him, and had him sign his draft card. Eventually, Noel went to the University of California in San Diego to continue his studies, and while at UCSD, he met figures, such as Mario Torrero, Victor Ochoa, and Jorge Huerta, who was connected to playwright Luis Valdez. Later, he would meet famed Chicano artist Luis Jiménez, who would become a mentor, teacher, and big brother to Noel. When referring to the teachers he'd had and the historical figures he'd met who inspired him, he speaks of "passing the baton" between generations and the duty one has to continue the good fight. Part of that fight to him included being informed and critical of history and certain historical figures who have been celebrated. He noted how in Mexico, Cortés was not celebrated as a hero, and he suggested a similar critical awareness of local New Mexican figures, like Juan de Oñate, who was celebrated and commemorated with monuments, such as those found in Española and El Paso.[37] Noel wondered why the University of New Mexico did not have a mural that questioned this history, such as the Orozco mural at Dartmouth, instead of having, as he put it, "that controversial mural that limits our dreams."[38] Noel's stance as an activist and artist is best summarized when he asks, "Does activism have a place in our state?"[39] His response is, "You're damn right! We need to start making avenues and talking to people to change this whole culture so that we're more than quaint and folkloric. We have a strong culture behind us."[40]

Noel's work includes a broad range of media and genres, from painting, both, canvas and mural, printmaking, drawing, and sculpture. A monumental canvas he painted, titled *La tierra* (1997), captures Noel's impressive skills as a draftsman and painter, and also conveys his activist tendencies (Plate 76). The large-scale canvas, painted in a naturalistic mural style, is composed of four major figural groups. The upper left register is filled with a vigorously rendered desert landscape overlaid with dancing Indigenous figures representing Mescalero Apache Crown or Mountain Spirit dancers known as *Gaan* from south-central New Mexico. The upper right register depicts Hispano farmers working the land with a church in the background. The entire bottom register is populated with images of technology and industry, including an eighteen-wheeler, factory smokestacks, a tank, cars, and a Spanish galleon; a lone cow stands next to the ship and the cars in the far lower right. At the center of the large composition is a nude female figure with brown skin and long black hair posed in a crouched position; she is enveloped by an embryo-like sphere from which maguey or agave *pencas* radiate out like rays. One thing that is striking about this painting is how it builds upon the tricultural idea; in other words, the Indigenous associated with the natural landscape and Native cultural traditions via the dancers in full ritual regalia; the Hispano depicted as farmers cultivating the soil and identified with Catholicism; and finally, the Anglo, here associated with industry or progress; this reference to the tricultural myth is not done uncritically but quite consciously and strategically. The lower section associated with the Anglo "modernizing" presence is where we find technological and industrial developments, but developments presented as destructive to the environment through allusions to contamination via radiation (the eighteen-wheeler glows and the truck driver appears skeletal and death-like) and pollution, the military, cars, and so on. Even the Spanish settlers are implicated through the presence of the galleon and the cow. Cows, first brought to the Americas by the Spanish, are known to be detrimental in large numbers to the environment; they are estimated to produce 40 percent of the methane in our atmosphere, thus contributing to greenhouse gases, in addition to the degradation of plant life and erosion of soil due to grazing.[41] As a whole, the work can be read as representing the main roots of nuevomexicano identity, the Indigenous and the Hispano, with the Anglo representing the most destructive element in this triumvirate. Meanwhile, the central figure, like an embryo isolated in its cocoon, is protected by the maguey, a plant native to the Americas and that was cultivated by Prehispanic Indigenous peoples, as she gestates and waits to be born.

The effects of various forms of contamination have long been felt by local communities; in New Mexico, there is a long history of state-sanctioned military, technological, and industrial activities that have resulted in different kinds of environmental destruction and pollution, from nuclear experiments to the production of industrial waste, all of which have poisoned water supplies, affected soil arability, and resulted in illnesses, such as cancer and the deaths among many members of rural, mostly brown, New Mexican communities.[42] Noel grew up in the area around Artesia and was exposed to the oil refineries in the region. He had long been living with an illness that was slowly deteriorating his physical health; his condition was never firmly diagnosed but he was convinced it was due to exposure to local contamination from the nearby refineries. As such, he had for years been a strident activist lobbying against the local oil industry and fighting for environmental justice and communal protections. That activist part of his practice as a Chicano-identified New Mexican artist is clearly conveyed in this painting through these myriad references.

Another work that represents Noel's range and is notable for its quality and subject is a graphite drawing on paper of a portrait of neighbors; the drawing, a study for a painting, is titled *Jorge y Martina Hernández* (2003) (Plate 77). The figures and background details are delicately rendered in pencil. In this drawing, one can clearly see Noel's mastery as a draftsman in his delicate varied linework and shading. The couple, dressed in what appears to be their daily work clothes, stands outside next to the mailbox in front of their humble home; we can see their names inscribed on the side of the box. To our right, we can see past the house and note a rural landscape with another home in the distant background. The man wears a cowboy or cattleman's hat with top crown creases and curled brim, and a long-sleeved shirt that is buttoned up to the neck; he also holds a pair of gloves in his right hand, although it's unclear if they are winter gloves or work gloves. The woman, with hair pulled back, wears a coat over her patterned blouse, suggesting cooler weather. Their faces are caringly rendered and capture the lines, wrinkles, and wear that come with age and experience. Although their expressions appear neutral, the couple gazes directly at the viewer and seems to be greeting you. Despite their reserve, the couple exudes a warmth that is typical of longstanding community members whose lives, tied to the land, family, and tradition, have weathered all manner of challenges.

Noel's preservation of his numerous studies for murals, paintings, etc., provides an idea of his process, something we do not have for any of the other artists in the show. In his practice, one can see the influence of his early art historical education and his emulation of both the Old Masters and the Mexican muralists; his methodical process, attention to detail, figuration, and overall approach to composition recall the Renaissance artists he learned about as a college student and who also were studied by Mexican artists whose work he saw on his trip to Mexico City.

Another example of his wide-ranging practice and mastery of diverse media and techniques is the print *El Taller* (1989), a lithograph with color pencil (Plate 63). The image depicts a printing press on which rests a lithographer's stone with an image drawn on it; in a surrealist move, part of the image seems to extend beyond the flat surface of the stone and extend into the air. The image resembles clouds of smoke, above which we see what resembles a military aircraft, possibly suggesting bombardment or perhaps alluding to the nuclear bomb tests that were conducted in New Mexico. Given Noel's activist work and his fight against environmental contamination, this reading is plausible. The press itself is rendered with almost photographic precision; we can see every part of the equipment, including bolts and screws. Beyond the lithographic subject and any political references, Noel operated a printing workshop called Marquez Arts/Taller Sin Fronteras: Public Art Murals in Artesia, New Mexico. The image of his printing press appears to be a reflection not just on the art of printmaking but specifically on his work as a New Mexican printmaker.

Noel, like Francisco Lefebre and a few of the other artists, was also a muralist and had been working consistently over the past fifty years since his student days. He was quite prolific and left behind a sizable body of work. Not including the murals that he was commissioned to paint across the state, his home studio is filled with hundreds of artworks, including, paintings, drawings, prints, maquettes, etc., at various stages of completion. He also left an ample archive consisting of newspaper and magazine clippings documenting his work and exhibitions and numerous journals or notebooks that his wife, Madelene Aguinaldo, said he obsessively kept. Reflecting his thoughtful and ordered practice, his studio is incredibly well-organized, but effort will be required to gather and document everything. The material that survives is copious and rich and will undoubtedly provide any future students and/or researchers much to do to properly study and write about this important prolific New Mexican artist.

Roberta Márquez

"Pedro talked about Chicano art, and I was like, 'We have art? What does that look like?' Painting murals gave us one way to think about it."[43]
—

Roberta Márquez was born in 1949 in Tucumcari, New Mexico, and currently resides in Albuquerque. She is the second-eldest of five children born to Abraham Márquez and Guadalupe Romero. Her father's parents were from El Rito and Anton Chico, and her mother's parents were from Las Tusas in northern New Mexico. Her ancestry can be traced back twenty generations of nuevomexicanos, not counting the Indigenous people who are part of her ancestry. She describes Tucumcari during her childhood as a racially divided community: Mexicans on one side, Anglos on the other. She describes her parents as strong people who experienced racial injustice and racial division. After completing high school, her mother attended New Mexico Highlands University and majored in education. With her teaching degree in hand, she then taught local children in one-room schoolhouses in the towns of Mora and Montoya. Her father was a dry land farmer and rancher with an eighth-grade education, who had served in the military during World War II. Her grandparents on both sides of the family only spoke Spanish. Roberta's mother would admonish her and her siblings, telling them to feel proud of being Mexican and being bilingual; however, Roberta states that she was too dumb to understand what it all meant at the time. Her parents sent their children to a Catholic elementary school where most of the students were Chicano and sheltered from racism, but they went to a public high school, where racial divisions were evident in how the students grouped themselves and were treated. She recalls that among the Mexican students, *pachucos* (members of a counter-cultural movement that first appeared among youth in the late 1930s in El Paso, Texas, and was characterized by zoot suit fashion) were popular; therefore, all the boys wore their hair slicked back and dressed accordingly. She graduated from high school in 1968, a tumultuous period in US history, but she admits that she was very naïve and uninformed about the Vietnam War and civil rights.

Like her mother, Roberta chose to go to New Mexico Highlands University instead of Eastern New Mexico University, which she considered to be too conservative and redneck. She mentioned that back then, women could either become secretaries or nurses, so like her mother, she chose to focus on education. She worked with professors Cecilio Orozco and Henry Pasqual, who were instrumental in establishing bilingual and multicultural education at NMHU. After graduating, she worked for Head Start and taught bilingual education, which she saw as an opportunity to teach the children about their community and their language. The Chicano Movement had just started to take hold on campus when she started college; she states that she was in the bilingual education program and didn't quite understand what was happening. She remembers the Vietnam veterans were the most vocal and fearless when it came to fighting for civil rights. Her ex-husband, whom she describes as the only gringo (white man) who got involved, chaired the protest committee. She adds that many New Mexican Hispanos had negative perceptions about the Chicano students and parents were alarmed by the protests. It was around that time that Pedro Rodríguez arrived at NMHU. She describes having Pedro around as exciting. As others have noted, he sent students down to Mexico to study art, and he taught students about Chicano art; they also began to paint murals on campus with his guidance, which was how Roberta was introduced to the movement, and to Chicano art and the mural tradition. Under Pedro's tutelage, she learned about Spanish artists, including Picasso and Goya, as well as Latin American and Mexican painters, such as Siqueiros. She recalls how learning these art histories got her excited. However, it was her college roommate, Marcia García, who got her into drawing and painting. As a student in education, she started taking art and art education classes, which included drawing, painting, and weaving. She laments not joining her fellow students to Mexico as part of a travel abroad program Pedro had arranged, although she eventually went as an MA student in bilingual education. She excitedly remembers learning about history and culture in Mexico, and how it helped her see who Chicanos and Mexicans were; the experience informed her art and she mentions how the trips to Mexico made her cohort aware and "set everyone on fire." They were learning about subjects no one back home had taught them. This new knowledge activated them, and upon their return to New Mexico, they all began to create. Roberta says that when she started painting, she was thinking, "This is so much better than writing!"[44]

After graduating with her BA in education, she was accepted into the MA program at NMHU. However, during the summer before she started her MA in education, Pedro offered a course on mural painting, so she enrolled in the class. The students wound up painting a large mural under Pedro's supervision in the Student Union Building at NMHU. Roberta recalls that the focus of the mural was Chicano/Mexican history and culture; her contribution to the mural was adding the female figures—images of goddesses and historical women. The mural was political and critical of the university administration, specifically university president Frank Ángel. She states that she became involved in the Chicano Movement when students organized protests to oust Ángel. Initially, Roberta describes being on the fringes and feeling intimidated, especially with her parents demanding that she not get involved, but she eventually began attending protests and Chicano Associated Student Organization meetings. As others who were present at the time have stated, NMHU was at the forefront of political activism during that time. Leading movement figures, such as Reies López Tijerina, spoke on campus several times and promoted bilingual and multicultural education so that community members would learn and take pride in who they were. It was around that time that the new university president, Gilbert Sánchez, had all Chicano murals on campus destroyed. Roberta states that she and Juanita J. Lavadie went to the student senate and talked to Sánchez after the murals had been whitewashed. Francisco Lefebre also organized a meeting with the artists who had worked on the mural to discuss what had happened. Chicano students were facing pushback, not just from the white and Hispano faculty and students on campus, but also from members of the larger community in Las Vegas. She recalls hearing that white people were leaving Las Vegas because of the Chicano presence and because they felt intimidated by the murals. One of the things Pedro repeatedly told his students who were learning to paint murals was, "Don't expect for your work to last forever."[45] Chicano art was political in those days and Roberta adds that luckily, the murals that were destroyed were documented by fellow community members Mary Lou and Chris Griego, who have photographs of the works.

One thing that stands out to Roberta when remembering her student years was the prominence of women leaders, such as Adelita M. Medina and Linda Martínez. These women stood up and spoke their minds. A couple of them were journalism students and went on to become journalists and work on behalf of civil rights movements. Roberta was seeing women take on leadership roles, something she had never seen before or considered coming from her traditional community. Roberta is also open about the colorism in the Chicano community and admits that due to her light-skinned appearance, she was privileged and more easily accepted by the Anglo students at school. The white students at her high school elected her to be class secretary, and she mentioned being called a "nice Spanish girl," something the meaning of which she wouldn't come to understand until later. She married in 1972, shortly before completing her MA, and got pregnant not long after starting her work as a bilingual teacher in Tucumcari; however, her work in Tucamari didn't last long. Her husband got a job in Santa Fe, so they moved to the New Mexican capital where she got a job as a resource teacher with the Chama school district and served the Chama, Tierra Amarilla, and Canjilón villages. Two years later, they then moved to Taos, where she had her second daughter; in Taos, she taught bilingual education for the Taos School District, applied for grants to fund programs, and taught local children about their history and culture. She then worked for the University of New Mexico and took more classes in painting, printmaking, and art education. She did a lot of plein-air work and mostly produced drawings and watercolors that she describes as figural and/or representational.

One of the classes she took was with a Korean artist named Yung Sook Park. Park owned an art gallery in Old Town in Albuquerque that sold contemporary Asian art; Park hired Roberta and took her to Korea and Germany, where Roberta was able to show some of her work. Working with Park, Roberta realized she preferred to paint and to produce large-scale paintings, which she attributes to her early training in mural painting with Pedro. Today, she describes her work as mostly being about the Chicano community and featuring "our stories." She is clear that her painting is about "us." She never saw that represented growing up; she notes seeing *santos* and beautiful craftwork but not anything related to the community's experiences or those of her own life. For the past ten years, family, community, history, land, and ranch life have been the focus of her work. She identifies with the writings of New Mexican Chicano author Rudolfo Anaya and regards her work as painted interpretations of his writing focused as it is on New Mexico. She also centers women in her work. She characterizes herself as a figurative painter who also does landscape and primarily works in oils but also does watercolor. She refers to her painting style as a stylized naturalism, a bit impressionistic and minimal, since she doesn't duplicate what she sees but rather renders an interpretation of it. When speaking of her painting, she states, "It's not overtly political, but I suppose by featuring people, places, and events that have been missing or erased, what I do can be seen as political."[46]

Thinking about featuring the local community and the life experience of fellow nuevomexicanos, we can look at Roberta's painting, *El entierro* (2017) (Plate 105). The large painting depicts a lone male figure wearing black pants, a white long-sleeved button-down shirt, and dress shoes; he also sports a hat and sunglasses. He stands in slight quarter turn, faces to our right, and seems to be engaged by something beyond the frame, presumably the burial. The day is sunny with blue skies and clouds hanging in the distant background.

The man holds a red and white umbrella to protect himself from the bright, hot sun, and we see his shadow projected on the grass in front of him. Most of the picture space is filled by the grass, which is painted in varying shades of green. In the distance, the high horizon line is marked by trees. Roberta states that this image was from a photograph she took at a family member's burial. The deceased was Zeke, Roberta's sister-in-law's brother. Zeke came from a large family and was a Vietnam vet; he was a laborer and was well-respected in the community. Interestingly, we don't see the actual grave site or the burial in the image; we only see the lone figure, whose name was Rudy. Rudy is someone Roberta describes as a *camarado*, someone she knew from her hometown of Tucumcari; she adds that growing up, he was also known as Ramada, since he worked in one of the hotels.

Roberta added that what caught her attention that day was that she had never seen Rudy dressed up; he was a laborer and was normally seen wearing jeans and a t-shirt. That day, he was standing under the umbrella, talking to Roberta's sister. She was struck by the image and asked him if she could take a photograph, and he agreed. She notes that two details in the photo captured her eye: the gestures of his hands and the dark shadow on the ground in front of him. Roberta informed Rudy that she was going to paint a portrait of him and had promised to give him a print of the painting. Sadly, Rudy died the very next year. In the end, the painting wound up becoming a memorial of sorts to her old friend, although she states that the figure doesn't entirely resemble the subject. In line with her practice as a painter, Roberta states that she avoids painting exactly what she sees and prefers to capture an impression of the moment. The final painting lacks fine details, is simplified, and is focused more on the overall composition, the areas of color, and the interplay of form and light. As a painter, she states that local subject matter aside, her interests are formal and compositional; as such, although the painting is legible as a figure in a landscape, she describes the resulting image as abstract. Roberta's painting with its lone figure in a landscape and its flat, simplified yet keen composition can be seen in the same vein as in notable works by canonical American artists, such as Edward Hopper, Grant Wood, and Alex Katz.

In Roberta's practice, each painting has a story attached to it—in some ways, perhaps reflecting the storytelling that is a central part of the oral traditions common to Hispano and Chicano communities. Another painting that beautifully exemplifies this idea and her approach to artmaking is a work titled *Senaida and Old Blue* (2016) (Plate 104). The large painting depicts a lone female figure standing in an open field against a blue cloudless sky; she stands slightly right of center and directly behind her to our left is a white horse in the far background. The young woman, standing awkwardly with arms to the side, silently gazes at the viewer; she wears a white dress that is cinched at the waist but loose on her small frame. Roberta said the painting was based on a very old photograph she found of her cousin Senaida. Senaida lived with her family on a small ranch located next door to Roberta's father's family's ranch. Senaida was one of seven children, and her family was very poor; the family had also lived through much heartbreak and loss. Senaida's mother died, and then in the early 1930s, at a funeral gathering, numerous attendees died of accidental food poisoning, including one of Senaida's brothers and two of her sisters. With no access to medical care in the area, people reached out to nearby cities for help getting treatment. An antidote was sent from Amarillo, Texas, but it did not arrive in time, resulting in the death of many community members who were present that day. Senaida's niece, Lucy, who is now in her nineties, remembers those tragic events. Roberta adds that Senaida did well in life, which was welcome given the tragic events of her youth. Senaida went to college at Eastern New Mexico University, where she studied business administration; after graduating, she got a job doing secretarial work, married, and had a son who later went to medical school and worked as a doctor at the University of New Mexico. Senaida also wrote a book in which she described the food poisoning incident; in it, she recalled hearing her father sobbing in the barn every night following the loss of his wife and three of his children, a story that Roberta continues to find compelling. Regarding the horse in the background, known as Old Blue, Roberta mentioned that he was her uncle Ben's workhorse, although she recalls other people in the community using him. She adds that the horse was quite tame and gentle, and that all the children in the area would ride him. The photo had to have been taken a few years after that terrible incident; Lucy might have been the photographer. Roberta describes Senaida as seeming forlorn in the painting. The setting and solitude conveyed in the image brings to mind the work of Edward Hopper and Andrew Wyeth.

Another painting that captures both Roberta's focus on the local community and landscape, as well as the community of New Mexican artists, in particular those who were part of the first generation of Chicana and Chicano activism, is titled *Juanita* (2011) (Plate 96). The portrait, painted in warm reds, oranges, and yellows, complemented by blues and greens, depicts artist Juanita J. Lavadie. Friends since their college days at NMHU, Roberta and Juanita visit one another regularly and have collaborated on artworks; this painting was produced when Roberta was visiting Juanita one day and she asked if she could paint her. In the painting, Juanita dominates the picture space. She is seated and unaware of the viewer; instead, she gazes down and is consumed as she works on a textile; Roberta states that Juanita was tying the fringes on a small weaving she had made. The quiet, contemplative scene is set outdoors. In the background, which was added later, we see a horizon lined with trees at the base of a mountain range, surrounded by a blue sky. Roberta mentioned that she was visiting Juanita in Taos, where she lives. As Juanita worked, Roberta made several sketches, which she then used for the painting. Juanita is a highly regarded activist and artist known for her work in both traditional and contemporary weaving; she also paints, as previously noted. Roberta decided to place Juanita in front of the Taos mountains as a marker of Juanita's identity; Juanita is from an old family with roots in the region that go back generations. Roberta describes Juanita as a *Taoseña* through and through, strong, independent, creative, and self-made; she adds that Juanita is well educated and shares her knowledge with her community. These are all qualities that Roberta aimed to capture in this painting by focusing on Juanita's traditional art practice and her ties to the land in Taos and northern New Mexico.

Roberta is also an accomplished landscape painter, whose eye, conditioned by her familiarity with the New Mexican environment, recognizes and captures the colors, patterns, forms, and the light that surround her. A good example of her landscape painting would be *Mesas and Llanos, Eastern Plains* (2021) (Plate 110). She shares that her approach to landscape consists of both plein-air painting, and painting from photographs she takes on drives around the state, a practice that goes back to at least 1970 when she was a student. As with her portraits, she makes conscious choices as she paints, playing up certain elements while toning down others. Her work can be appreciated on its formal merits but knowing the stories behind the images, especially those with figures, is what brings them to life and puts them into conversation with New Mexican Chicana and Chicano life and the art it inspires.

Adelita M. Medina

"Like I said, we need to use our skills and talents to create a better world."[47]
—

Adelita M. Medina was born in 1950 in Española, New Mexico, a town known for its lowrider culture. She grew up on a small farm owned by her grandfather and her great-aunt in a village called Ranchitos and notes that she was raised in a strict Catholic environment. Growing up, she drew pictures of Jesus Christ, the Virgin Mary, and various saints, which is how she discovered her artistic talent. When she attended New Mexico Highlands University, she double majored in art and English, and studied with studio art professors Elmer Schooley, Harry Leippe, Paul Volckening, and Bob Hill; she adds that she took three years of art history courses and mostly learned about European art. She did not study with Pedro Rodríguez, although she knew the students who had. Her personal encounter with the Chicano Movement thus began differently. She shares an anecdote of how she first became aware of the movement one day while hanging out in her apartment in downtown Las Vegas. She recounts: "One day, I heard a lot of racket outside my window in the park, and I looked out the blinds and saw all of these people marching around Old Town Plaza."[48] Adelita noticed her older brother, Benji, and a friend, Fred Trujillo, in the crowd, so she put on her shoes, went out, and asked them what was happening. When her brother told her they were protesting the discrimination they faced by the gringo administration at the university, she decided to join the struggle then and there.

Adelita describes herself as one of the more radical Chicanas on campus and recalled joining a student group called the Spanish American Student Organization; she adds that, at that time, they had all grown up in northern New Mexico, thinking they were Spanish American. Students who had visited other campuses where student activism was taking place returned to Las Vegas and informed their peers that they were now calling themselves Chicanos, so they changed the name of the group to the Chicano Associated Student Organization. Adelita estimates that there were only three Chicano professors on the faculty at the university, at that time, a campus that was 75 percent to 80 percent Chicano, 13 percent Native, and that included a small community of Black students, all in a state that was, itself, around 80 percent Chicano. Meanwhile, the entire administration was white, with several of them being outright racist and generally dismissive of student concerns. The students were fighting against the exclusion and discrimination that had endured for decades. Adelita, along with other students, including Juanita J. Lavadie's sister, started putting out an underground newsletter, *El Machete*, a small production using a mimeograph machine that "told it like it was" on campus and promoted news and current events related to the movement and student organizing. This was Adelita's introduction to journalism, an interest she would continue to pursue as time went on. It was around that time that she and others were introduced to the widely known and respected Chicano newspaper, *El Grito del Norte*, and to its founder and editor, Betita Martínez, and also to Enriqueta Vásquez, who wrote a column for the newspaper. The two women, who mentored many young Chicanas, became her first mentors.

Although as tended to be case in the early 1970s, the men occupied the prominent leadership positions while relegating the women to secretarial work or to passing out flyers, something Adelita and her friends resisted. However, since Adelita's apartment was next door to the main Democratic headquarters for San Miguel County, she and the other women got to know the local *políticos* (politicians), such as Donaldo "Tiny" Martínez, a district attorney who was a proud Mexicano and had sued the university for discrimination. They all became friends, and the politicians would keep the students informed of secret meetings to which the women would always be invited and included.

One of the organized protests included the students taking over the administrative buildings on the campus and demanding the university hire a Chicano president, which, if accomplished, would have been the first Chicano university president in the country. The students' candidate was a man named John Aragón, an educator from Albuquerque. The university instead hired a man from Wisconsin named Charles Graham, which ignited a violent backlash from the students and the local community; the protests resulted in Graham's resignation not long after he took office. The university, in a kind of compromise, hired Frank Ángel, who became the first Chicano university president in the history of the US. However, the Chicano students and some of the newly hired Chicano faculty found him ineffectual and not supportive of the Chicano student movement.

After graduating from NMHU, Adelita began a master's program in anthropology at SUNY Albany, but after auditing two journalism classes at City College in Manhattan, she decided to study journalism instead. One of her professors, Stu Kampel, then the editor of the Long Island section of *The New York Times*, helped her get into the graduate school of journalism at Columbia University, where she earned a master's degree in journalism. Interestingly, after graduation, she did not pursue a career in journalism but went to work for Boricua College in their office of projects and grants, where she learned about grant proposal writing. She worked in the nonprofit sector for the next thirty years, during which time, she admits not having had any extra time to make art as she had done in college. While in New York City, given her activist background and interests, she got involved with the Puerto Rican independence movement and worked for the Puerto Rican Legal Defense and Education Fund and at the Center for Constitutional Rights, which had been started by Jewish activist lawyers William Kunstler, Morty Stavis, and others.

In 1990, at the start of the Persian Gulf War, Adelita found herself back in New Mexico. Despite her antiwar sentiments, her son joined the military and was immediately shipped off to the Persian Gulf. She went back to New York City where she joined the Military Family Support Network, a national antiwar movement composed of concerned parents and relatives that was supported by peace activists. She became the head of their New York chapter and later, after the short-lived war, she became the executive director at their Washington, DC, office, where she led efforts to support the Persian Gulf War veterans and their families. She began working with a radical newspaper called the *Guardian News Weekly*, which she worked for until 2004. In 2004, she decided she wanted to come back home to her native New Mexico. At the time, she was the executive director of the National Latino Alliance for the Elimination of Domestic Violence, and she convinced her board of directors to let her move the organization's main office to New Mexico, where she continued to lead that organization until 2014, when she retired.

It was at that time that she came back to artmaking, especially, as she notes, after Donald Trump was elected President in 2016. Filled with anxiety, fear, and anger, she decided she should write and publish about what she feared would happen to the country under the Trump administration. She found herself sitting at her computer to write but nothing would come out, so she decided to turn to her art to create the messages she wanted to share; she started making collages that were political in nature and critical of the new administration and the destructive policies they promoted. She started showing her new work to friends and coworkers, who encouraged her to make more and to exhibit them publicly. By late 2017, she had created about a dozen new works and decided to invite other artists she had known at New Mexico Highlands University, including Juanita J.

Lavadie, Francisco Lefebre, Roberta Márquez, Marcia García Medina, and Ignacio "Nacho" Jaramillo to participate in a show. Working with Bianca Encinias, owner of El Chante: Casa de Cultura in downtown Albuquerque, she curated a well-received exhibit, *We the People United for Peace, Justice, and Mother Earth*. More than two hundred people attended the opening on November 10, 2017. After sharing images of her collages on Facebook, she received an invitation to show her work in New York City in a small gallery located in the Manhattan Neighborhood Network Center in East Harlem.

An example of this more recent collage work is titled *We the People—El pueblo unido* (2017) (Plate 114). The foundation of the image is a geographic map of North America, including Canada, the United States, and Mexico. The underlying painting is in yellow (Canada); the red, white, and blue of the American flag (US), green (Mexico), and blue (Atlantic and Pacific oceans). The collaged elements are images excised from books and magazines depicting protestors of various racial and ethnic groups, along with activist slogans, some of them familiar, such as "*El agua es vida*," "If he builds a wall, I'll grow up and tear it down," "They tried to bury us. They didn't know we were seeds," and "Fuck your nationalism, we are all Earthlings." The theme of the work embraces a wide range of current political movements in the US, including immigration reform and border security, environmental sustainability and access to water, military service and veteran healthcare, rights to protest and police brutality, and tax reform. As with all of Adelita's art production during this period, this collage is a response not only to these ongoing crises, but also the threats to our democracy. She states that her interest in restarting an art practice became a way to cathartically process her conflicted emotions and to also comment on the social and political state of the nation.

A striking example of Adelita's painting that captures her woman-centered politics is *Campesinas* (2019) (Plate 120). The painting depicts women migrants working outside in the fields. Seven figures are in the fields picking strawberries and collecting them in box containers. In the lower left corner, we see a table with a white tablecloth on which rests a bottle, presumably of wine, and an assortment of fruit, including strawberries, cherries, pears, apples, mangoes, and grapes, all products we enjoy, which are the result of migrant agricultural labor. In the upper right corner, there is an image of a woman picking apples; her head and face are completely covered. Opposite her, in the upper left corner, we see a close-up of a woman's face; she wears a hat over a bandanna, what appears to be a hoodie, and another bandanna over her mouth and nose. The work brings attention to three realities of migrant fieldwork. First, it is important to note that women comprise a significant portion of the workforce alongside men in the US agricultural industry. Next, migrant agricultural workers have routinely been exposed to toxic pesticides intended to kill insects and other parasites but that have resulted in illness and deaths for workers. Finally, we notice that the women all wear baggy, androgynous clothing and that most of their heads and faces are covered, not just for their comfort as they work or to protect them from pesticide poisoning but to protect themselves from being sexually harassed and/or assaulted by male workers, what is not an uncommon occurrence.[49] The painting, resembling a collage in its composition and combination of forms, focuses our attention on the role and plight of women workers, whose well-being is central to the healthy function of the agricultural industry and our economy.

A painting that is more reflective of Adelita's New Mexican heritage is *Vatos at the Santuario* (2019) (Plate 124). The painting depicts the Santuario de Chimayó, located in northern New Mexico, which is a historical sacred site to Natives and Hispanos, as well as a draw to tourists and other visitors. Placed in front of the sanctuary is an old model blue car and two men, one standing in front of the car, the other squatting beside it. The Santuario de Chimayó, located in the Sangre de Cristo Mountains in Chimayó, New Mexico, is a pilgrimage destination for many Catholics in the region. The shrine, a national historic landmark, is located at a site that has been sacred for centuries among local Indigenous communities and later, during the Spanish colonial period up to the present.[50] The actual shrine, an excellent example of the Spanish Colonial architecture associated with the region, was constructed in 1813 in the small village of El Potrero. Long associated with miraculous healing, the faithful go to the sanctuary to request divine intercession or to give thanks. A striking element at the sanctuary is the presence of what many consider to be holy dirt. Located in a hole in the ground in part of the shrine, the sacred soil is available to visitors to take since it is believed that the dirt possesses miraculous properties. Given its history and cultural significance, the sanctuary is a fundamental part of New Mexican identity, whether one is religious or not, and especially to the Hispano community.

The car and the two figures who occupy the foreground of the picture space in the painting perfectly illustrate New Mexican Hispano/Chicano identity. The blue auto, possibly a 1940s Chevrolet, is associated with Chicano communities across the Southwest and Chicano lowrider culture. Adding an autobiographical detail, she states that she chose to include this model of car because at the age of twelve, she learned to drive in her uncle's 1940 green Chevy. Reflecting the working-class background of Chicanos, the refurbishment and ornamentation of old model automobiles can be understood as an expression of the *rasquache* esthetic as outlined by Tomás Ybarra-Frausto, who states, "Very generally, *rasquachismo* is an underdog perspective—a view from *los de abajo*. [It is] an attitude rooted in resourcefulness and adaptability yet mindful of stance and style."[51] In terms of cultural production, processes of hybridization, juxtaposition, and integration are tied to using what is at hand, often materials regarded as having little economic or reuse value. The process of repairing, embellishing, and customizing old cars, which is traced back to the 1940s, if not earlier, although done out of necessity, was transformed into an artform, whose *rasquache* esthetic has become a source of identification and pride.[52] The two figures standing beside the car, identified as *vatos*, are dressed in traditional Chicano or *cholo* (a reference to a man of Indigenous and/or Mexican American heritage, often associated with gangs) attire, i.e., bandana tied around the head, trimmed mustache, white undershirt tucked into high-waisted baggy pleated pants or a long-sleeved button-down with only the top button buttoned over a white t-shirt and tan or khaki pants with a fedora, sunglasses, and a goatee. These forms of dress can also be traced to the 1940s, if not earlier, when the zoot suit look originated in the African American community and was adopted by youth from other communities, such as the Chicano and the Filipino.[53] Taking into consideration these various visual elements, we can see how the painting places New Mexico's Hispano heritage in conversation with contemporary Chicano culture, again collapsing history into the present as we've seen in the work of other artists. From a nuevomexicana perspective, history and place continue to shape the present just as it did the Chicano movement in the 1970s.

Concluding Remarks

Since the turn of the millennium, we have seen exciting new exhibitions and scholarship on Chicana and Chicano art; a few of the more notable exhibitions would include *Just Another Poster? Chicano Graphic Arts in California* (2000–2003), which opened at the Blanton Museum of Art at the University of Texas at Austin and traveled; *Chicano Art for Our Millennium: Collected Works from the Arizona State University Community* (2004), which was held at the Mesa Southwest Museum (today the Arizona Museum of Natural History) in Mesa, Arizona; *Phantom Sightings: Art after the Chicano Movement* (2008), which opened at the Los Angeles County Museum of Art and traveled; *Asco: Elite of the Obscure: A Retrospective, 1972–1987* (2011), which was held at the Los Angeles County Museum of Art; *Axis Mundo: Queer Networks in Chicano L.A.* (2017–2022), which opened at the Museum of Contemporary Art, Los Angeles and traveled; and *Printing the Revolution! The Rise and Impact of Chicano Graphics, 1965 to Now* (2020–2024), which opened at the Smithsonian American Art Museum and is currently traveling. There have also been monographs, edited volumes, and journal articles published on the subject, too numerous to list here. Although many continue to see Chicano art as a practice tied to the civil rights movements of the mid- to late twentieth century, Chicana and Chicano artists have been creating art across generations up to the present. The increase in exhibitions and publications suggests the continuing viability and importance of this material, which, in part, may be due to the explosion of interest in and growing recognition of Latinx art, especially in the last decade, and the development of Latinx art history as a formally recognized institutionalized area of study in the field.

As has been noted, although Chicana and Chicano art of the past fifty years is chronologically commensurate with contemporary American art, it has generally been overlooked, if not entirely excluded, due to questions of quality, esthetics, timeliness, and political content; I would venture to propose that we could add to this list a general or systemic disregard of these communities and their cultural production by Anglophone American institutions and its representatives due to racism, classism, and perhaps even anti-immigrant attitudes, among other things. American Studies scholar Arlene Dávila addressed this troubling reception when she noted,

> . . . the possessive investment in whiteness is also evident in the most intimate spaces, such as in the ways in which artists choose to identify or are identified by others. Racist and Eurocentric ideas of universality in the arts still impact these identifications, fostering a continuous tiptoeing around identifying or embracing any identity that is nonwhite. Hence the disinvestment in "Latinx" identities, because they are seen to compromise artists' quality and artistry; "universality" becomes a key indication of the whiteness of the market, and any artists that cannot come across as "unmarked" (i.e., white) are immediately devalued.[54]

At this point, it seems worthwhile to resurrect a question posed in 2010 by Ken Johnson in his *New York Times* review of *Phantom Sightings: Art after the Chicano Movement*, in which he asked, "Is it time to retire the identity-based group show?"[55] He described the exhibition, which opened at El Museo del Barrio in New York City, as confused and confusing due to a lack of unity, and proceeded to add that few works possessed the ideologically charged quality of the art produced during the height of the Chicano movement of the 1960s and 1970s. He notes that the curators' stated intent was to demonstrate how Mexican American artists have adapted mainstream conceptual strategies to more local concerns; here, I can't help but think of the concerns expressed by first-generation Chicano art scholars, such as Shifra Goldman, after the CARA exhibition opened that Chicano art might shift from one focused on liberation to one seeking validation, as Chicano artists became more mainstream. This echoes of the ways in which artists from historically marginalized communities, primarily communities of color, have been compelled to either produce art that somehow references or draws from their racial or ethnic identity versus producing art that is in conversation with larger esthetic and conceptual trends, in other words, not tied to identity; here, we run into a "damned if you do, damned if you don't" scenario. A question that has been asked before but makes sense to ask again in this context is, Are Chicana and Chicano artists Chicanos first, or are they artists first? Can we even separate the two? Johnson viewed the *Phantom Sightings* curators' intentions and the works they selected as opposed to the historical Chicano movement in terms of one of its most significant contributions, as he understood it, that is, elevating popular cultural conventions to the level of high art; a bit tongue-in-cheek, he blamed MFA programs for this loss of direction.

More recently, and presenting an alternate perspective, former Smithsonian American Art Museum Curator of Latino Art, E. Carmen Ramos, currently chief curatorial and conservation officer at the National Gallery of Art in Washington DC, speaking about her exhibition, *Printing the Revolution: The Rise and Impact of Chicano Graphics, 1965 to Now*, commented that "A common misconception of Chicano graphics is that it is a fossilized aspect of the historic civil rights era of the 1960s and 1970s. What we saw when we dug deeper into this field is that Chicanx graphics artists continue to thrive and produce exciting, relevant work. In part this has to do with the ongoing struggles of our world and the ways in which graphics is still an especially productive medium to engage contemporary society. People in this country, especially BIPOC people, are still fighting the same battles."[56] I propose that we can extend this reading to other Chicano art forms and media beyond the graphic arts and ask, is Chicana and Chicano art still relevant? And couldn't Chicana and Chicano artists do both—that is, reflect their experience as racial/ethnic minorities while being in dialogue with and/or responding to contemporary art developments? The answer that immediately comes to mind is, yes! Beyond questions about the role of subjectivity in determining how one moves through the world, perhaps if racism, classism, and other exclusionary politics were indeed things of the past, as many seem to believe, artists could simply make work without the need to factor in identity politics but, sadly, that's not the case, as we have been witnessing in this country since at least 2016, if not throughout the last two-hundred-plus years. Such a historical awareness of systemic injustice and inequality suggests that there still is a need for the kind of activist liberatory art we saw in the 1970s, especially given the current political climate. Perhaps this may be an opportune moment to add New Mexico's Chicana/o/x voices into the conversation given the state's deep history in this region of the Americas and the anticolonial resistance that has been a part of the cultural fabric in the region for the last four-hundred years.

Notes

1. Quote taken from a panel discussion at the National Association for Chicana and Chicano Studies (NACCS) conference held in Albuquerque, New Mexico in April 2019. Four New Mexican Chicana and Chicano artists (two men and two women) who were involved in the early Chicano Movement in the 1970s, were invited to serve as panelists. The panel was comoderated by UNM professors Ray Hernández-Durán, PhD, and Irene Vásquez, PhD, who posed three questions. The first question was, Can you tell us about your background, where you grew up, and how you became an artist? This excerpt was taken from the response by the late artist Noel Márquez (1953–2020). The panel discussion was recorded, transcribed, and published. Please see Ray Hernández-Durán and Irene Vásquez (moderators), "'*Artistas del Pueblo*': In Conversation with the History of New Mexican Chicanx Art," *Hemisphere: Visual Cultures of the Americas*, ed. Mandolen Sánchez, Vol. XII (Department of Art, University of New Mexico, 2019), 80–97.

2. See Chapter Five: *Coyuntura in the Land of Enchantment: Knowing of the Chicana and Chicano Movement in New Mexico* by Phillip Gonzales.

3. A recent study of Reies López Tijerina is the book by historian Ramón A. Gutiérrez, *New Mexico's Moses: Reies López Tijerina and the Religious Origins of the Mexican American Civil Rights Movement* (University of New Mexico Press, 2022).

4. A larger conversation regarding the status of Chicano/a/x art in Chicano art history and in US art history, more generally, although significant and ongoing among US Latinx Art specialists, extends beyond the scope of this catalogue essay; however, Constance Cortez's essay in this volume contributes to that conversation. See also, Jacinto Quirarte, "Exhibitions of Chicano Art, 1965 to the Present," *Chicano Art: Resistance and Affirmation,*

1965–1985, ed. Richard Griswold del Castillo, Teresa McKenna, and Yvonne Yarbro-Bejarano, Wight Art Gallery/University of California, Los Angeles, 1991), 163–179.

5. An example or index of this kind of cultural and institutional erasure is found in a report produced in 1994 by the Smithsonian Institution Task Force on Latino Issues. The exhaustive study documents the institution's lack of inclusion and representation of Latinos and their histories in its programming, collections, and staff. An excerpt from the report's conclusion states the following: "The Smithsonian Institution, the largest museum complex in the world, displays a pattern of willful neglect towards the estimated 25 million Latinos in the United States. Because of both Indigenous roots and Spanish heritage, Latinos pre-date the British in the Americas. They [Latinos] have contributed significantly to every phase and aspect of American history and culture. Yet the institution almost entirely excludes and ignores Latinos in nearly every aspect of its operations . . . Many Smithsonian officials project the impression that Latino history and culture are somehow not a legitimate part of the American experience. It is difficult for the Task Force to understand how such a consistent pattern of Latino exclusion from the work of the Smithsonian could have occurred by chance." See Raul Yzaguirre and Mari Carmen Aponte, *Willful Neglect: The Smithsonian Institution and U.S. Latinos, Report of the Smithsonian Institution Task Force on Latino Issues* (The Smithsonian Institution, 1994).

6. Comment made by Chicano studies professor Pedro Rodríguez to Noel Márquez in 1971 when Márquez was a freshman at New Mexico Highlands University in Las Vegas, New Mexico; see Hernández-Durán and Vásquez, "In Conversation with the History of New Mexican Chicanx Art," 84.

7. Goldman, Shifra M. "Chicano Art of the Southwest in the Eighties," *Imagine: International Chicano Poetry Journal, Arte Chicano Issue*, nos. 1 & 2 (Summer/Winter 1986), 50.

8. An edited volume that explores this concept would be Vanessa Fonseca-Chávez, Levi Romero, and Spencer R. Herrera, eds., *Querencia: Reflections on the New Mexico Homeland* (University of New Mexico Press, 2020). See also Harrison Candelaria Fletcher, *Finding Querencia: Essays from In-Between* (The Ohio State University Press, 2022); and Judith Dianne Duff et al., *The Spirit that Wants Me: A New Mexico Anthology* (Duff, 1991).

9. In this essay, I will focus on the six main artists in the exhibition. Chicana and Chicano muralists and murals will be discussed by Irene Vásquez and Howard Griego in their essay on Chicano muralism in New Mexico.

10. Quote taken from an interview with Ignacio Jaramillo, February 19, 2023.

11. Quote taken from an interview with Ignacio Jaramillo, February 19, 2023.

12. For more on New Mexican *santos*, see, E. Boyd Hall, *Portfolio of Spanish Colonial Design in New Mexico* (Federal Art Project of the Works Progress Administration, 1938); George Kubler, *Santos: An Exhibition of the Religious Folk Art of New Mexico* (Amon Carter Museum of Western Art, 1964); Clair Farago and Donna Pierce, eds., *Transforming Images: New Mexican Santos In-Between Worlds* (The Pennsylvania State University Press, 2006); and William Wroth, "The Meaning and Role of Sacred Images in Indigenous and Hispanic Cultures of Mexico and the Southwest," in *Converging Streams: Art of the Hispanic and Native American Southwest*, William Wroth and Robin Farwell Gavin, eds., (Museum of New Mexico Press, 2010), 83–95.

13. Quote taken from an interview with Ignacio Jaramillo, February 19, 2023.

14. See Monica Garza, *Foto-Escultura: A Mexican Photographic Tradition* (University of New Mexico Art Museum, 1998); and Geoffrey Batchen, *Forget Me Not: Photography and Remembrance* (Princeton Architectural Press, 2004).

15. See, Rudolfo Anaya, *Bless Me, Última* (TQS Publications, 1972).

16. Ignacio Jaramillo, Facebook, July 11, 2023.

17. See José Vasconcelos, *La raza cósmica: Misión de la raza iberoamericana: Notas de viajes a la América del Sur* (Agencia Mundial de Librería, 1925); also, Alan Knight, "Racism, Revolution, and Indigenismo: Mexico, 1910–1940," in *The Idea of Race in Latin America, 1870–1940* (University of Texas Press, 1990), 71–113; Tace Hedrick, *Mestizo Modernism: Race, Nation, and Identity in Latin American Culture, 1900–1940* (Rutgers University Press, 2003); Mary Coffey, "The Cosmic Race: José Vasconcelos," in *Modern Art in Africa, Asia, and Latin America: An Introduction to Global Modernisms*, ed. Elaine O'Brien, et. al. (Blackwell Publishing Ltd., 2013), 402–404; and Laura J. Torres-Rodríguez, "Orientalizing Mexico: *Estudios indostánicos* and the Place of India in José Vasconcelos' *La raza cósmica*," *Revista Hispánica Moderna*, no. 1 (June 2015): 77–91.

18. For more on New Mexican architecture, see Alison E. Rautman, *Constructing Community: The Archaeology of Early Villages in Central New Mexico* (The University of Arizona Press, 2014); Kate Wingert-Playdon, *John Gaw Meem at Acoma: The Restoration of San Esteban del Rey Mission* (University of New Mexico Press, 2012); Roland F. Dickey and Tom Faris, "Earth is Lifted: Domestic Architecture in New Mexico," *Southwest Review* 33, no. 1 (Winter 1948), 31–37; and George Kubler, *The Religious Architecture of New Mexico in the Colonial Period and Since the American Occupation* (The Taylor Museum, 1940).

19. There is a growing literature on the topic of metamodern or metamodernism; for more on this subject, see, Jason Ananda Josephson Storm, *Metamodernism: The Future of Theory* (The University of Chicago Press, 2021); and Robin Van Den Akker, Alison Gibbons, and Timotheus Vermeulen, eds., *Metamodernism: Historicity, Affect, and Depth after Postmodernism* (Rowman and Littlefield, 2017). For a more accessible explanation of metamodernism, see Gregg Henriques, "What is Metamodernism: Metamodernism is the Cultural Code that Comes after Postmodernism," *Psychology*

Today (April 17, 2020), https://www.psychology-today.com/us/blog/theory-knowledge/202004/what-is-metamodernism.

20. Hernández-Durán and Vásquez, "In Conversation with the History of New Mexican Chicanx Art," 88.

21. Hernández-Durán and Vásquez, "In Conversation with the History of New Mexican Chicanx Art," 81.

22. For more on La Academia de la Nueva Raza, see, "Academia de la Nueva Raza," SNAC, https://snaccooperative.org/ark:/99166/w6tj5b0t; and "Tomás Atencio Papers and Academia de la Nueva Raza/Río Grande Institute Records," *New Mexico Archives Online*, https://nmarchives-dev.unm.edu/repositories/22/resources/2290.

23. See, Lawrence R. Murphy, "The United States Army in Taos, 1847–1852," *New Mexico Historical Review* 47, no. 1 (2021); https://digitalrepository.unm.edu/nmhr/vol47/iss1/3.

24. Juanita credits social work professor at NMHU and founder of La Academia de la Nueva Raza in Dixon, New Mexico, Facundo Valdez, as the first to openly comment on this phenomenon and recognize it as a form of shame or embarrassment. Hernández-Durán and Vásquez, "In Conversation with the History of New Mexican Chicanx Art," 88 and 96.

25. Hernández-Durán and Vásquez, "In Conversation with the History of New Mexican Chicanx Art," 88.

26. Hernández-Durán and Vásquez, "In Conversation with the History of New Mexican Chicanx Art," 89.

27. Hernández-Durán and Vásquez, "In Conversation with the History of New Mexican Chicanx Art," 83.

28. Hernández-Durán and Vásquez, "In Conversation with the History of New Mexican Chicanx Art," 83.

29. Information drawn from a guest lecture that Francisco Lefebre gave in fall 2019. See, Francisco Lefebre, "My Life and Work as a Chicano Artist," Guest Lecture: ARTH 429: *U.S. Latinx Art*, Department of Art, University of New Mexico in Albuquerque, October 3, 2019

30. Personal communication with the artist, November 7, 2024.

31. The essay in this catalog by Irene Vázquez and Howard Griego, which examine Chicano murals in New Mexico, will address the mural work done by several artists in the show, including Francisco, as well as Noel Márquez, Samuel Leyba, Juanita J. Lavadie, and others.

32. Tino Villanueva, *Imagine: International Chicano Poetry Journal*, *Arte Chicano Issue* III, nos. 1 & 2 (Summer/Winter 1986), 125.

33. Hernández-Durán and Vásquez, "In Conversation with the History of New Mexican Chicanx Art," 90.

34. Sadly, Noel Márquez died in December 2020 as this exhibition was being prepared.

35. Hernández-Durán and Vásquez, "In Conversation with the History of New Mexican Chicanx Art," 84.

36. Tortilla artists were artists who printed and painted on tortillas. They were affiliated with The Great Tortilla Conspiracy, a group based in San Francisco, California. The use of tortillas as the canvas for their work reflected the cultural roots of the group members and the cultural significance of the food. An additional element worth noting is how the ephemeral nature of the tortilla-based artwork complicated the commodification of the art object, what could be considered a critique of the contemporary art world and art market. For more on this subject, please see: "Tortilla Art," Joe Bravo at: http://joebravo.net/sample-page/tortilla-art/.

37. See Jami Seymore, "City of Albuquerque Removes Status of Juan de Oñate in Old Town," *KRQE Albuquerque News* (June 16, 2020), https://www.krqe.com/news/albuquerque-metro/city-of-albuquerque-to-remove-statue-of-juan-de-onate/; and John Burnett, "Statues of Conquistador Juan de Oñate Come Down as New Mexico Wrestles with History," *NPR* (July 13, 2020), https://www.npr.org/2020/07/13/890122729/statues-of-conquistador-juan-de-o-ate-come-down-as-new-mexico-wrestles-with-hist. For broader discussions of the politics of public monuments, see, Erin L. Thompson, *Smashing Statues:*

The Rise and Fall of America's Public Monuments (W.W. Norton, 2022); Benjamin Cohen Rossi, "False Exemplars: Admiration and Ethics of Public Monuments," *Journal of Ethics and Social Philosophy* 18, Issue 1 (July 2020): 49–84; Sanford Levinson, "Written in Stone: The Meaning of Public Monuments and Whether They Remain or Go," *Kentucky Law Journal* 108, Issue 4 (20119–2020): 641–664; and Sergiusz Michalski, *Public Monuments: Art in Political Bondage, 1870–1997* (Reaktion Books, 1998)

38. Here, Noel was referring to the 1939 mural by Kenneth Adams at Zimmerman Library, which I discuss in chapter one.

39. Hernández-Durán and Vásquez, "In Conversation with the History of New Mexican Chicanx Art," 94.

40. Hernández-Durán and Vásquez, "In Conversation with the History of New Mexican Chicanx Art," 94.

41. See, Amy Quinton, "Cows and Climate Change: Making Cattle More Sustainable," *In Focus: Feeding a Growing Population Series*, (UC Davis, June 27, 2019), https://www.ucdavis.edu/food/news/making-cattle-more-sustainable; Center for Biological Diversity, "Public Lands: Grazing," https://www.biologicaldiversity.org/programs/public_lands/grazing/.

42. For a recent outstanding study of this history, see Myrriah Gómez, *Nuclear Nuevo México: Colonialism and the Effects of the Nuclear Industrial Complex on Nuevomexicanos* (University of Arizona Press, 2022).

43. Quote taken from an interview with Roberta Márquez, February 21, 2023.

44. Quote taken from an interview with Roberta Márquez, February 21, 2023.

45. Quote taken from an interview with Roberta Márquez, February 21, 2023.

46. Interview with Roberta Márquez, February 21, 2023

47. Hernández-Durán and Vásquez, "In Conversation with the History of New Mexican Chicanx Art," 95.

48. Hernández-Durán and Vásquez, "In Conversation with the History of New Mexican Chicanx Art," 90.

49. See Charlene Galarneau, "Farm Labor, Reproductive Justice: Migrant Women Farmworkers in the U.S.," *Health and Human Rights Journal* 15, no. 1 (October 24, 2013), https://www.hhrjournal.org/2013/10/farm-labor-reproductive-justice-migrant-women-farmworkers-in-the-us/; Thomas A. Arcury and Sara A. Quandt, "Pesticides at Work and at Home: Exposure of Migrant Farmworkers," *The Lancet: Health and Human Rights* 362, no. 9400 (December 13, 2003), https://www.thelancet.com/journals/lancet/article/PIIS0140-6736(03)15027-1/fulltext; Rupali Das, Andrea Steege, et al., "Pesticide-Related Illness among Migrant Farm Workers in the United States," *International Journal of Occupational and Environmental Health* 7, no. 4 (October/December 2001), 303–312; and Victoria Arena, "Migrant Women Face Greater Risk of Violence and Assault," *Latinas in Business Inc.* (July 21, 2022), https://latinasinbusiness.us/2022/07/21/migrant-women-face-greater-risk-of-violence-and-sexual-assault/.

50. See Brett Hendrickson, *The Healing Power of the Santuario de Chimayó: America's Miraculous Church (Religion, Race, and Ethnicity)* (NYU Press, 2017); and *El Santuario de Chimayo* New Mexico, National Park Service, U.S. Department of the Interior, https://www.nps.gov/nr/travel/american_latino_heritage/el_santuario_de_chimayo.html.

51. Ybarra-Frausto, Tomás, "*Rasquachismo*: A Chicano Sensibility," *Chicano Aesthetics: Rasquachismo* (Phoenix, AZ: MARS *Movimiento Artístico del Río Salado*, 1989), 5.

52. For more on lowriders, see, Charles M. Tatum, *Lowriders in Chicano Culture: From Low to Slow to Show* (Greenwood Publishing Group, 2011); Michael Juan Chávez, *The Performance of Chicano Masculinity in Lowrider Car Culture: The Erotic Triangle, Visual Sovereignty, and Rasquachismo*

(Unpublished dissertation, UC Riverside, 2012); and Dylan Miner, *Creating Aztlán: Chicano Art, Indigenous Sovereignty, and Lowriding Across Turtle Island* (University of Arizona Press, 2014).

53. See Kathy Lee Peiss, *Zoot Suit: The Enigmatic Career of an Extreme Style* (University of Pennsylvania Press, 2011); Ashley Lucas, "Reinventing the 'Pachuco': The Radical Transformation from the Criminalized to the Heroic in Luis Valdez's Play 'Zoot Suit,'" *Journal for the Study of Radicalism* 3, no. 1 (Spring 2009), 61–87; Catherine S. Ramírez, *The Woman in the Zoot Suit: Gender, Nationalism, and the Cultural Politics of Memory* (Duke University Press, 2009); and Matthew Wills, "The Zoot Suit Riots were Race Riots," *JSTOR Daily* (October 13, 2021), https://daily.jstor.org/the-zoot-suit-riots-were-race-riots/.

54. Arlene Dávila, *Latinx Art: Artists, Markets, Politics* (Duke University Press, 2020), 3–4.

55. Ken Johnson, "They're Chicanos and Artists. But Is Their Art Chicano?" *New York Times* (April 9, 2010); https://www.nytimes.com/2010/04/10/arts/design/10chicano.html.

56. Claudia Zapata and E. Carmen Ramos, "Chicano Graphic Arts and the Making of the Landmark Exhibition 'Printing the Revolution!'," *Smithsonian Voices: From the Smithsonian Museums* (January 26, 2021); https://www.smithsonianmag.com/blogs/smithsonian-american-art-museum/2021/01/26/chicano-graphic-arts-and-making-landmark-exhibition-printing-revolution/.

Bibliography

"Academia de la Nueva Raza," SNAC, https://snaccooperative.org/ark:/99166/w6tj5bot.

Ahlborn, Richard E., *The Penitente Moradas of Abiquiú*. Smithsonian Institution Press, 1968.

Akker, Robin Van Den, Alison Gibbons, and Timotheus Vermeulen, eds. *Metamodernism: Historicity, Affect, and Depth after Postmodernism*. Rowman and Littlefield, 2017.

Aldea, Eva. *Magical Realism and Deleuze: The Indiscernibilty of Difference in Postcolonial Literature*. Bloomsbury Publishing Plc., 2013.

Anaya, Rudolfo. *Bless Me, Ultima*. TQS Publications, 1972.

Arcury, Thomas A., and Sara A. Quandt. "Pesticides at Work and at Home: Exposure of Migrant Farmworkers." *The Lancet: Health and Human Rights* 362, no. 9400 (December 13, 2003), https://www.thelancet.com/journals/lancet/article/PIIS0140–6736(03)15027–1/fulltext.

Arena, Victoria. "Migrant Women Face Greater Risk of Violence and Assault," *Latinas in Business Inc.* (July 21, 2022), https://latinasinbusiness.us/2022/07/21/migrant-women-face-greater-risk-of-violence-and-sexual-assault/.

Barajas, Rafael. *Posada: Mito y Mitote: La caricatura política de José Guadalupe Posada y Manuel Alfonso Manila*. Fondo de Cultura Económica, 2009.

Batchen, Geoffrey. *Forget Me Not: Photography and Remembrance*. Princeton Architectural Press, 2004.

Boyd Hall, E. *Portfolio of Spanish Colonial Design in New Mexico*. Federal Art Project of the Works Progress Administration, 1938.

Bravo, Joe. "Tortilla Art"; http://joebravo.net/sample-page/tortilla-art/.

Burnett, John. "Statues of Conquistador Juan de Oñate Come Down as New

Mexico Wrestles with History." *NPR* (July 13, 2020), https://www.npr.org/2020/07/13/890122729/statues-of-conquistador-juan-de-o-ate-come-down-as-new-mexico-wrestles-with-hist.

Candelaria Fletcher, Harrison. *Finding Querencia: Essays from In-Between.* The Ohio State University Press, 2022.

Cardoza y Aragón, Luis, "Las calaveras de José Guadalupe Posada," *Artes de México,* no. 67 (2011), 36–41.

Center for Biological Diversity, "Public Lands: Grazing," https://www.biologicaldiversity.org/programs/public_lands/grazing/

Chávez, Michael Juan. *The Performance of Chicano Masculinity in Lowrider Car Culture: The Erotic Triangle, Visual Sovereignty, and Rasquachismo.* Unpublished dissertation, UC Riverside, 2012.

Coffey, Mary. "The Cosmic Race: José Vasconcelos," *Modern Art in Africa, Asia, and Latin America: An Introduction to Global Modernisms.* Edited by Elaine O'Brien, Everlyn Nicodemus, et al. Blackwell Publishing Ltd., 2013, 402–404.

Das, Rupali, Andrea Steege, et al., "Pesticide-Related Illness among Migrant Farm Workers in the United States." *International Journal of Occupational and Environmental Health* 7, no. 4 (October/December 2001): 303–12.

Dávila, Arlene. *Latinx Art: Artists, Markets, Politics.* Duke University Press, 2020.

Dickey, Roland F., and Tom Faris. "Earth is Lifted: Domestic Architecture in New Mexico." *Southwest Review* 33, no. 1 (Winter 1948): 31–37.

Duff, Judith Dianne, Jill Kiefer, and Michele Miller, eds. *The Spirit that Wants Me: A New Mexico Anthology.* Duff, 1991.

El Santuario de Chimayo New Mexico, National Park Service, U.S. Department of the Interior, https://www.nps.gov/nr/travel/american_latino_heritage/el_santuario_de_chimayo.html.

Farago, Claire, and Donna Pierce, eds. *Transforming Images: New Mexican Santos In-Between Worlds.* The Pennsylvania State University Press, 2006.

Fonseca-Chávez, Vanessa, Levi Romero, and Spencer R. Herrera, eds. *Querencia: Reflections on the New Mexico Homeland.* University of New Mexico Press, 2020; https://www.unmpress.com/9780826361608/querencia/.

Galarneau, Charlene. "Farm Labor, Reproductive Justice: Migrant Women Farmworkers in the U.S." *Health and Human Rights Journal* 15, no. 1 (October 24, 2013), https://www.hhrjournal.org/2013/10/farm-labor-reproductive-justice-migrant-women-farmworkers-in-the-us/.

Garza, Monica. *Foto-Escultura: A Mexican Photographic Tradition.* University of New Mexico Art Museum, 1998.

Gómez, Myrriah. *Nuclear Nuevo México: Colonialism and the Effects of the Nuclear Industrial Complex on Nuevomexicanos.* University of Arizona Press, 2022.

Goldman, Shifra M. "Chicano Art of the Southwest in the Eighties" *Imagine: International Chicano Poetry Journal, Arte Chicano Issue* III, nos. 1 & 2 (Summer/Winter 1986): 42–50.

Gretton, Thomas. "Posada and the 'Popular': Commodities and Social Constructs in Mexico before the Revolution," *Oxford Art Journal* 17. no. 2 (1994), 32–47.

Gutiérrez, Ramón A. *New Mexico's Moses: Reies López Tijerina and the Religious Origins of the Mexican American Civil Rights Movement.* University of New Mexico Press, 2022.

Hart, Steven M., and Wen-Chin Ouyang, eds. *A Companion to Magical Realism.* Tamesis, 2005.

Hedrick, Tace. *Mestizo Modernism: Race, Nation, and Identity in Latin American Culture, 1900–1940.* Rutgers University Press, 2003.

Hendrickson, Brett. *The Healing Power of the Santuario de Chimayó: America's Miraculous Church (Religion, Race, and Ethnicity).* NYU Press, 2017.

Henriques, Gregg. "What is Metamodernism: Metamodernism is the Cultural Code that Comes after Postmodernism," *Psychology Today* (April 17, 2020), https://www.psychologytoday.com/us/blog/theory-knowledge/202004/what-is-metamodernism.

Interview with Roberta Márquez, interviewed by Ray Hernández-Durán, February 21, 2023.

Interview with Ignacio Jaramillo, interviewed by Ray Hernández-Durán, February 19, 2023.

Hernández-Durán, Ray, and Irene Vásquez (moderators). "'*Artistas del Pueblo*': In Conversation with the History of New Mexican Chicanx Art." *Hemisphere: Visual Cultures of the Americas*. Mandolen Sánchez, ed. Vol. XII (Department of Art, University of New Mexico, 2019), 80–97.

Jaramillo, Ignacio. Facebook Post, July 11, 2023.

Johnson, Ken. "They're Chicanos and Artists. But Is Their Art Chicano?" *New York Times* (April 9, 2010); https://www.nytimes.com/2010/04/10/arts/design/10chicano.html.

Josephson Storm, Jason Ananda. *Metamodernism: The Future of Theory*. The University of Chicago Press, 2021.

Knight, Alan. "Racism, Revolution, and Indigenismo: Mexico, 1910–1940." In *The Idea of Race in Latin America, 1870–1940*, edited by Richard Graham. University of Texas Press, 1990.

Kubler, George. *Santos: An Exhibition of the Religious Folk Art of New Mexico*. Amon Carter Museum of Western Art, 1964.

Kubler, George. *The Religious Architecture of New Mexico in the Colonial Period and Since the American Occupation*. The Taylor Museum, 1940.

Lefebre, Francisco. "My Life and Work as a Chicano Artist," Guest Lecture: ARTH 429: *U.S. Latinx Art*, Department of Art, University of New Mexico in Albuquerque, October 3, 2019.

Levinson, Sanford. "Written in Stone: The Meaning of Public Monuments and Whether They Remain or Go." *Kentucky Law Journal* 108, Issue 4 (2019–2020): 641–64.

Lucas, Ashley. "Reinventing the 'Pachuco': The Radical Transformation from the Criminalized to the Heroic in Luis Valdez's Play 'Zoot Suit.'" *Journal for the Study of Radicalism* 3, No. 1 (Spring 2009): 61–87.

Michalski, Sergiusz. *Public Monuments: Art in Political Bondage, 1870–1997*. Reaktion Books, 1998.

Miner, Dylan. *Creating Aztlán: Chicano Art, Indigenous Sovereignty, and Lowriding Across Turtle Island*. University of Arizona Press, 2014.

Peiss, Kathy Lee. *Zoot Suit: The Enigmatic Career of an Extreme Style*. University of Pennsylvania Press, 2011.

Quinton, Amy. "Cows and Climate Change: Making Cattle More Sustainable." *In Focus: Feeding a Growing Population Series*. (UC Davis, June 27, 2019), https://www.ucdavis.edu/food/news/making-cattle-more-sustainable.

Quirarte, Jacinto. "Exhibitions of Chicano Art, 1965 to the Present." In *Chicano Art: Resistance and Affirmation, 1965–1985*. Richard Griswold del Castillo, Teresa McKenna, and Yvonne Yarbro-Bejarano, eds. Wight Art Gallery/University of California, Los Angeles, 1991.

Ramírez, Catherine S. *The Woman in the Zoot Suit: Gender, Nationalism, and the Cultural Politics of Memory*. Duke University Press, 2009.

Rautman, Alison E. *Constructing Community: The Archaeology of Early Villages in Central New Mexico*. The University of Arizona Press, 2014.

Rodríguez, Anita O. "How *La Raza* Became Invisible," *Chamisa: A Journal of Literary, Performance, and Visual Arts of the Greater Southwest* 1 (2021): 23–29.

Rossi, Benjamin Cohen. "False Exemplars: Admiration and Ethics of Public Monuments." *Journal of Ethics and Social Philosophy* 18, Issue 1 (July 2020): 49–84.

Seymore, Jami. "City of Albuquerque Removes Status of Juan de Oñate in Old Town," *KRQE Albuquerque News* (June 16, 2020), https://www.krqe.com/news/albuquerque-metro/city-of-albuquerque-to-remove-statue-of-juan-de-onate/.

Simms, Norman Toby. *Marranos on the Moradas: Secret Jews and Penitentes in the Southwestern United States.* Academic Studies Press, 2009.

Simpkins, Scott. "Magical Strategies: The Supplement of Realism." *Twentieth Century Literature* 34, no. 2 (Summer 1988): 140–54.

Steele, Thomas J. *Penitente Self-Government: Brotherhoods and Councils, 1797–1947.* Ancient City Press, 1985.

Tatum, Charles M. *Lowriders in Chicano Culture: From Low to Slow to Show.* Greenwood Publishing Group, 2011.

Thompson, Erin L. *Smashing Statues: The Rise and Fall of America's Public Monuments.* W. W. Norton, 2022.

"Tomás Atencio Papers and Academia de la Nueva Raza/Río Grande Institute Records," *New Mexico Archives Online*, https://nmarchives-dev.unm.edu/repositories/22/resources/2290.

Torres-Rodríguez, Laura J. "Orientalizing Mexico: *Estudios indostánicos* and the Place of India in José Vasconcelos' *La raza cósmica*," *Revista Hispánica Moderna* 68, no. 1 (June 2015): 77–91.

Vasconcelos, José. *La raza cósmica: Misión de la raza iberoamericana: Notas de viajes a la América del Sur.* Agencia Mundial de Librería, 1925.

Villanueva, Tino. *Imagine: International Chicano Poetry Journal, Arte Chicano* Issue III, nos. 1 & 2 (Summer/Winter 1986).

Wallis, Michael with photos by Craig Varjabedian. *En divina luz: The Penitente Moradas of New Mexico.* University of New Mexico Press, 1994.

Wills, Matthew. "The Zoot Suit Riots were Race Riots," *JSTOR Daily* (October 13, 2021), https://daily.jstor.org/the-zoot-suit-riots-were-race-riots/.

Wingert-Playdon, Kate. *John Gaw Meem at Acoma: The Restoration of San Esteban del Rey Mission.* University of New Mexico Press, 2012).

Wroth, William. "The Meaning and Role of Sacred Images in Indigenous and Hispanic Cultures of Mexico and the Southwest." In *Converging Streams: Art of the Hispanic and Native American Southwest.* William Wroth and Robin Farwell Gavin, eds. Museum of New Mexico Press, 2010.

Ybarra-Frausto, Tomás. "*Rasquachismo*: A Chicano Sensibility," *Chicano Aesthetics: Rasquachismo.* Exhibition catalog (MARS *Movimiento Artístico del Río Salado*, 1989): 5–8.

Yzaguirre, Raul. and Mari Carmen Aponte. *Willful Neglect: The Smithsonian Institution and U.S. Latinos, Report of the Smithsonian Institution Task Force on Latino Issues.* Washington, DC: The Smithsonian Institution, 1994.

Zamora, Lois Parkinson, and Wendy B. Faris. *Magical Realism: Theory, History, Community.* Duke University Press, 1995.

Zapata, Claudia, and E. Carmen Ramos. "Chicano Graphic Arts and the Making of the Landmark Exhibition 'Printing the Revolution!'," *Smithsonian Voices: From the Smithsonian Museums* (January 26, 2021); https://www.smithsonianmag.com/blogs/smithsonian-american-art-museum/2021/01/26/chicano-graphic-arts-and-making-landmark-exhibition-printing-revolution/.

Chicana and Chicano Muralism in New Mexico, 1970–1990

Three

The Radical Roots of Culturally Relevant
and Community-Responsive Art

IRENE VÁSQUEZ AND HOWARD GRIEGO

During the 1960s and 1970s, discourses on liberation circulated among Chicana and Chicano artists across the US Southwest.[1] Notably, artists in New Mexico participated in a national Chicana/o Mural Movement to propel liberatory visual esthetics that supported people's demands for freedom, justice, and self-determination. Through their art, *nuevomexicana/o* muralists rendered local, national, and global critiques of settler colonialism, racialized capitalism, US Westward expansionism, and post–World War I and II industrialization on prominent public facades. While their art contributed to the national Chicana/o Mural Movement, nuevomexicana/o muralists advanced site-specific critiques about local issues and histories. Often, they referenced images of landscapes and human interaction with the environment and animals because of their histories and the changes to rural-based cultures throughout the twentieth century. Often intended to beautify local neighborhoods, community centers, and schools, murals by Chicana and Chicano artists were also used to uplift and inspire residents. However, their murals went beyond celebrating the nostalgia for local rural or agricultural community life. Artists associated with the Chicana and Chicano Mural Movement developed a critical view of the effects of capitalism and industrialism from a unique vantage point, making their work different and meaningful in the genre of Chicana and Chicano mural art. In effect, murals depicted alternative landscapes that offered a pictorial representation of change based on past grievances and new proclamations for peoplehood, grounded in a New Mexican perspective and context.

This essay analyzes select Chicana and Chicano murals in New Mexico from the 1970s through the 1990s to understand the complex political statements forged during the region's heightened social conflict of the Chicana and Chicano Movement (CCM). It also examines the impact of the CCM discourse and politics on artists and their bodies of work. Not all artists shared the same career trajectory or continued with mural making or what was referenced at the time as an art of the people. Despite the success of murals, art institutions needed to evenly embrace the political work of Chicana and Chicano artists. Nevertheless, all the artists and their works referenced in this essay reflected a deep commitment to community that they also attached to movement politics. Their art activism impacted how they saw themselves as agents of change in the world and the kinds of artwork they produced over their lifetimes. Most of the murals featured in this essay no longer exist. Still, they speak to a critical moment when artists examined social conditions connected to a past where their communities bore the brunt of the ongoing effects of colonialism and imperialism. These artists aspired to produce artwork to help shape a more bountiful future for their community.

Nuevomexicana/o mural art produced in the 1970s and 1980s reflected local, national, and international contexts via social and political commentary. Although the myth of tricultural harmony—a narrative posing a cultural model of separate and coexisting populations—has been used to explore New Mexican heritage and culture, it effectively glosses over the Chicana and Chicano Movement period, revealing ideological cleavages in institutional rhetoric. During the height of this movement, artists explored critical views of coloniality and espoused decoloniality to contest issues of racial and economic discrimination as by-products of colonialism and imperialism. Chicana artists also pressed issues of gender discrimination and established creative avenues where they centered women as complex subjects.[2] Significantly, nuevomexicana/o muralists affirmed solidarity with communities of color, both nationally and globally. Their artwork advocated for more significant equities, opportunities, and dignity for their communities in all aspects of society. They did so through locally informed lenses that centered New Mexican cultural expressions and landscapes.

For over fifty years, art historians have considered the colonial, expansionist, imperial, and postcolonial ramifications on the development of Chicana and Chicano mural art.[3] In the extant literature relevant to Chicana and Chicano murals, scholars and art critics pay scant attention to murals by self-identified Spanish American and New Mexican artists. Several early studies examine the works of mural collectives in the formative period of the Chicana and Chicano Movement in New Mexico; however, attention to the subject faded in the mid-1970s as mural production grew across the state.[4] Murals became a vibrant site for nuevomexicana/o artists to depict their community's struggles and engage in political advocacy. For example, Chicana and Chicano artists painted murals at New Mexico Highlands University (NMHU) as part of their educational, artistic, and political aspirations during a tumultuous period of social activism across the US. Murals appealed to activists because of their visibility and proximity to the locus of protests like schools and universities. One mural at NMHU represents an early example of social protest in an institution of higher education in northern New Mexico (fig. 3.1). Through visual depictions, students documented their grievances with university and state officials, who they critiqued for upholding structures of white supremacy and ignoring the voices and needs of their communities.

Although widely appreciated among their nuevomexicana/o peers for their esthetic power and influence, New Mexican murals are not a focal point in existing scholarship or the work of museum and art institutions, despite the continuous production of murals in the state. New Mexican artists, such as Francisco Lefebre, Samuel Leyba, and Noel Márquez, have remained prolific muralists during and after the CCM up to the present. The chapter on New Mexican muralists still needs to be written, and additional research is necessary to explore the state's prolific and complex history of Chicana and Chicano mural making.

The Advent of Twentieth-Century Muralism and Its Impact on Nuevomexicanas/os

Mural painting in New Mexico pre-dates the Chicana and Chicano Movement period and formed part of a global phenomenon that in the Americas can be traced to ancient Indigenous Prehispanic cultures, such as the Maya and Aztecs, through the period of Spanish colonialism up to modern Mexican nationalism and the work of the Mexican muralists, such as Diego Rivera, José Clemente Orozco, and David Alfaro Siqueiros.[5] During the early twentieth century, a formative influence derived from Mexican muralism, encouraged and sponsored by the Mexican government, and aimed to produce a unifying identity among the masses after more than a decade of civil conflict following the Mexican Revolution. Although artists of the Mexican Mural Movement reflected revolutionary rhetoric, Mexican officials sought to consolidate and institutionalize social concerns through reform efforts. Art offered a forum for addressing popular grievances; however, Mexican artists produced nostalgic views of Indigenous communities and societies in their murals. Other artists were highly critical of the exploitation of the working classes. The Mexican Mural Movement influenced public mural art in Europe and the US. For example, several artists, architects, and designers in France, including Fernand Léger and Le Corbusier, participated in a French mural movement intended to produce large-scale decorative and architectural backdrops.[6] The federal government's Works Progress Administration (WPA), an employment and infrastructure initiative created in 1935 by President Franklin Roosevelt, sponsored public art projects nationwide. In the US, mural paintings were used in public service projects to celebrate aspects of American life as it played out in city streets and landscapes of rural communities.

Nuevomexicanos participated in the WPA mural projects. In the late 1930s and early 1940s, Edward Arcenio Chávez, from Ocate in northern New Mexico, developed

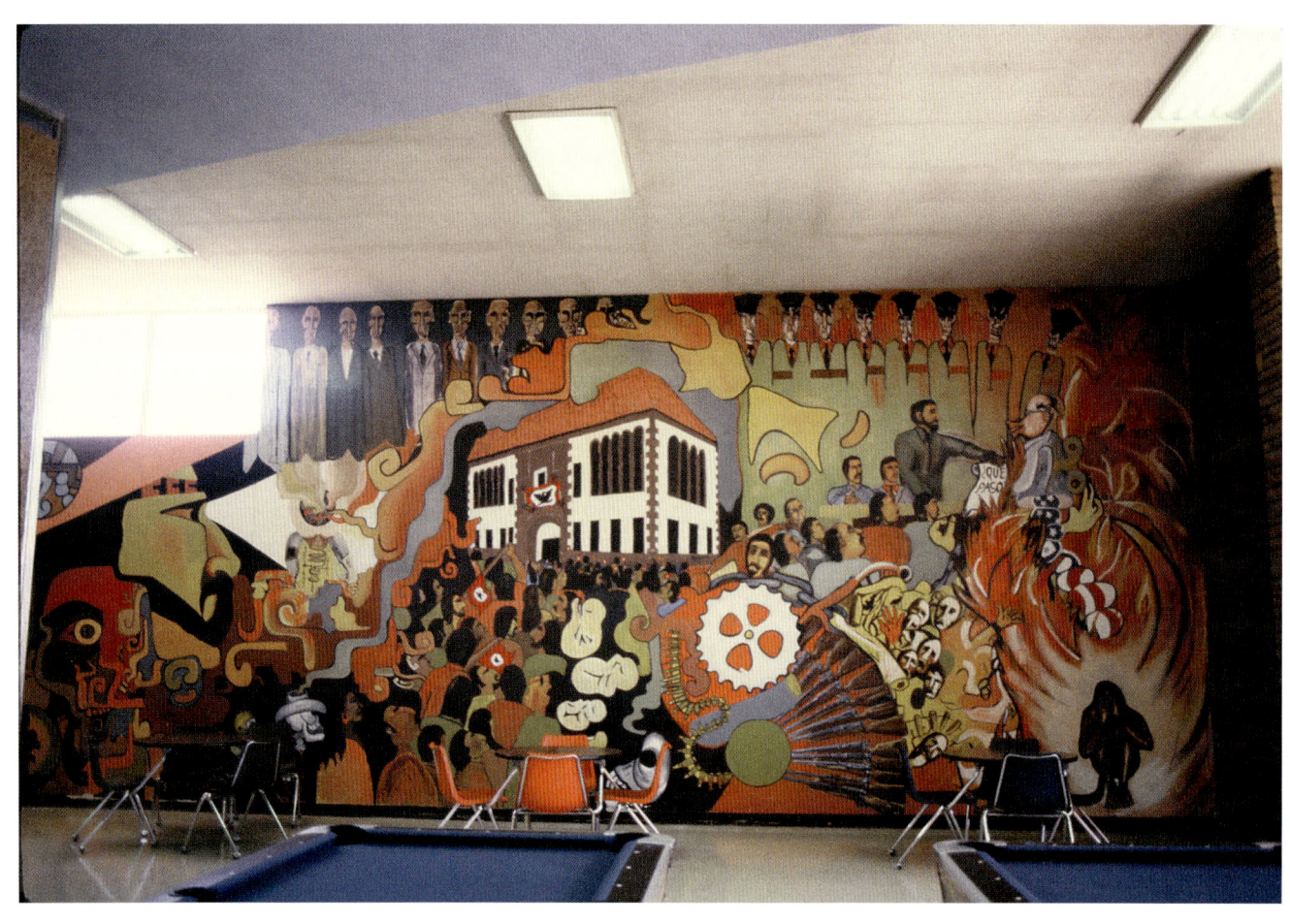

FIGURE 3.1. Unidentified Artists, Untitled Mural, 1972. Acrylic. New Mexico Highlands University, Las Vegas, New Mexico.

art projects for the Treasury Relief Art Project and painted murals in high schools and post offices for the WPA Federal Art Project. Chávez served as a war art correspondent for the Engineering Office of the US War Department. He became known for his landscape painting, lithography, sculptures, and murals. Chávez's work was exhibited in prestigious venues, including the Cleveland Institute, the Los Angeles Museum of Art, the National Academy of Design, and the San Francisco Museum of Modern Art. The display of his work nationwide represented the diffusion of New Mexican Hispanic art across the US. A member of the National Society for Mural Painters, Chávez also taught at several institutions, including as a visiting professor of art at Colorado College from 1959 to 1960, and then as a professor of art at Syracuse University from 1960 to 1962.

As in Mexico, WPA murals, like those painted by Chávez, sought to unify the public by producing nostalgic views of life in the United States. They were displayed in public institutional spaces such as post offices. One such mural depicts Anglo Americans preparing materials for the construction of a sod house (fig. 3.2). The woman and child, placed to the far left and in the shadow, appear to be passive, almost helpless observers. Meanwhile, the men move wood or restrain horses, implying physical strength and endurance. In the background, the image captures the hilly natural landscape of northern New Mexico, a familiar view to Chávez, who had spent his childhood in Ocate and Wagon Mound.

Despite Chávez's renown, it would be another thirty years before New Mexican muralists emerged as a branch of the Chicana/o Mural Movement. The murals produced during the height of the Chicana and Chicano movement were created by a new generation of community artists who offered new interpretations of New Mexican history and culture. Chicana/o muralists incorporated the landscapes of New Mexico, including valleys, mountains, canyons, and rivers. They did so to raise specific social and political critiques related to land dispossession and development.

Unlike the serene imagery of the WPA murals period of the 1940s, Chicana/o mural making in New Mexico displayed bold and critical views of local, national, and global politics. The conditions for expanding mural making by nuevomexicana/o artists corresponded to the widespread national organizing of Mexican and Chicana/o communities. The Chicana and Chicano Mural Movement in New Mexico arose in the socio-historical context of the Chicana and Chicano Movement. Mural content produced during this period reflected an ethos of social justice, community empowerment, and progressive arts advocacy, supporting the artists' ideological and political aims.

The overlap of illustrations, subject matter, patterns, and designs used by artists reflected the ideological and cultural framing of the Chicana and Chicano Movement and also uniquely expressed individual choices tied to community concerns. For instance, Chicana/o murals in New Mexico relate specific community-based issues from those in San Antonio, Texas, or Los Angeles, California. They deal with land, rural life, and the environment because many nuevomexicana/o artists grew up in rural, land-based communities. At the same

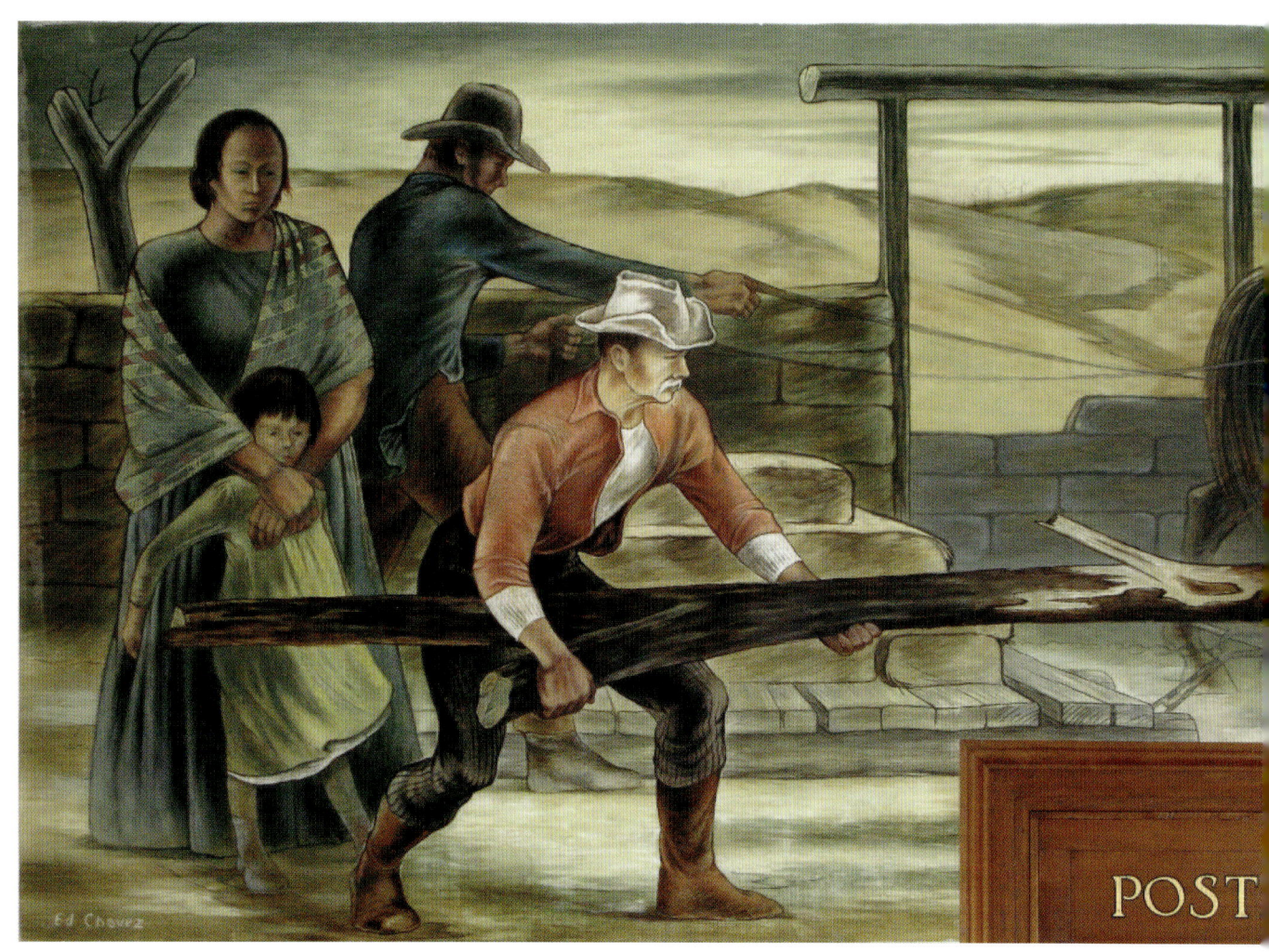

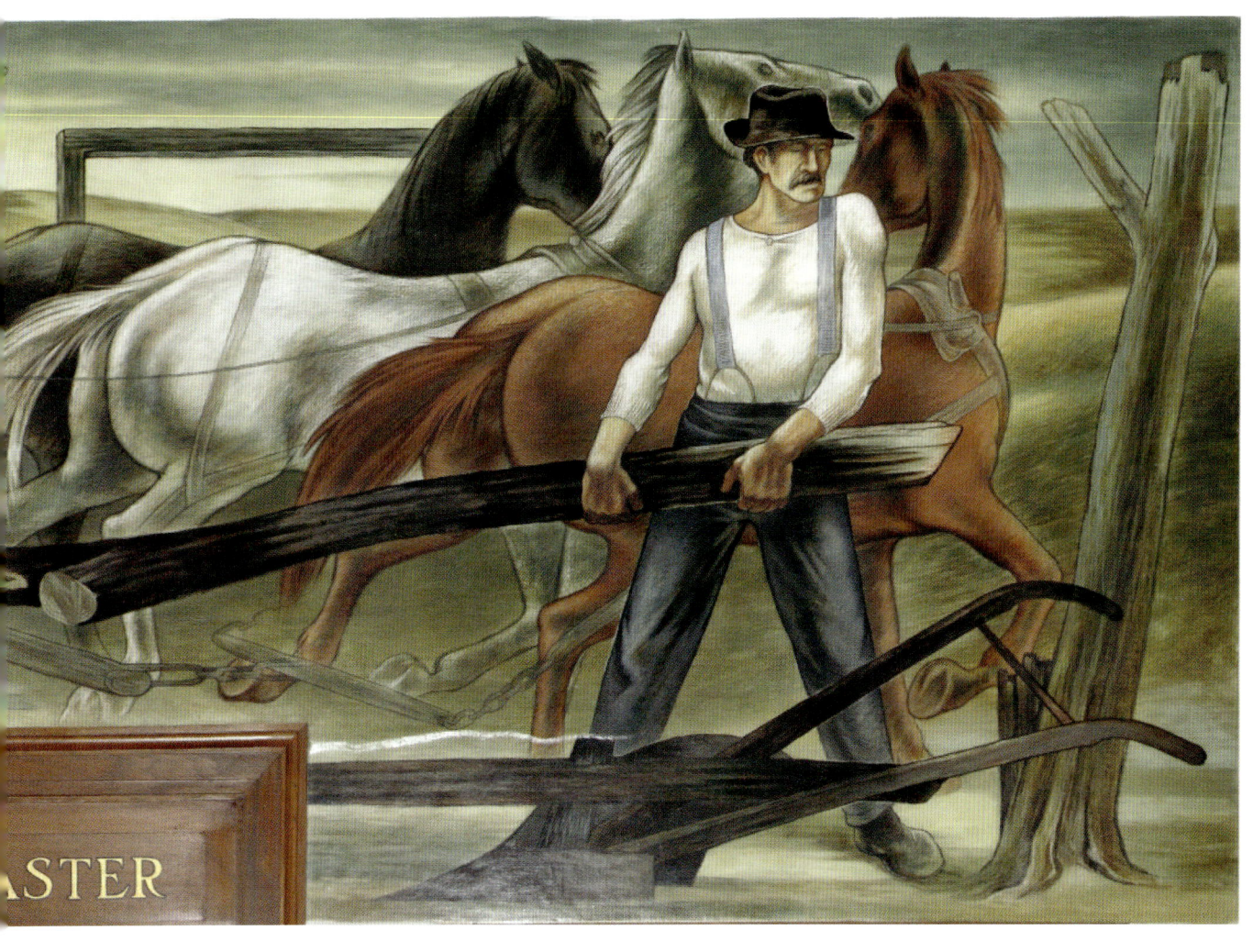

FIGURE 3.2. Edward Arcenio Chávez, *Building a Sod House*, 1941. Geneva Post
Office Lobby.

time, nuevomexicana/o muralists, like other Chicana and Chicano muralists, illustrated cultural integration—combining American, Mexican, and local traditions into distinct understandings of culture and identity. Understanding the heterogeneous expressions of the Chicana and Chicano Mural Movement helps advance knowledge about how muralists expressed and perceived their community's struggles in relation to economic, social, and political dynamics in New Mexico.

The Development of the Chicana/o Mural Movement

The Chicana and Chicano Mural Movement started in the 1960s in Mexican American communities throughout the Southwest. Mural production emerged as part of the political and cultural landscape alongside the Mexican American artistic and literary resurgence in the 1960s and 1970s. Chicana and Chicano art historians of the 1970s documented the early formation of and contributions made by Chicana and Chicano muralists. Shifra M. Goldman, a pioneer in the study of Chicana and Chicano art, offered an early history and thematic analysis of the iconography of Chicana and Chicano muralism. Later scholars, such as Eva Cockcroft and Holly Barnet-Sánchez, built upon Goldman's work, which categorized mural themes into religion, Indigenous motifs, historical events, modern portraits, political and social themes, nonreligious symbols, landscapes, flora and fauna, decorative motifs, family themes, urban culture, and legendary or mythical figures. Cockcroft and Barnet-Sánchez argued that specific categories proposed by Goldman applied specifically to Chicana/o murals in East Los Angeles and asserted that Chicana and Chicano artists used the walls of city buildings, housing projects, schools, and churches to illustrate Mexican American culture and social-political messaging. Their conclusions were drawn from their analysis of material conditions and cultural production in Mexico and Latin America.

The Chicana and Chicano Mural Movement, not unlike the Mexican Mural Movement of the early twentieth century, critiqued the status quo and the governmental neglect of their communities. Chicana and Chicano artists sought to reclaim cultural heritage to develop pride and unity. Murals often transcend individual expressions or visions by enlisting community participation in the design and placement of the murals. Noting this communal practice, Carlos F. Jackson states that Chicana/o visual art is an important cultural expression of the Chicano community and influences the development of Chicano culture. In their studies of mural painting in East Los Angeles, Holly Barnet-Sánchez and Tim Drescher emphasized the impact of the Chicana and Chicano Movement on murals. They argue that oppressed groups drew upon symbolic alternatives that countered the dominant group's stereotypes with celebratory and critical images of their histories and cultural traditions.

They add that murals as social interactive tools not only reflected *Chicanismo* but also helped formulate a sense of what it meant to be a Chicana or Chicano.[7] To this end, Chicana and Chicano artists incorporated Mesoamerican heroes, pyramids, and idols like Quetzalcoatl, Coyoxauhqui, and Coatlicue as part of a cultural spectrum influencing conceptions of Chicana/o identity. These deities signified the spiritual energies worshipped by some of the people's ancestors who later came to be called Mexican Americans or Chicanas or Chicanos. Murals also depicted leaders of the Mexican Independence movement and the Mexican Revolution. Recurrent figures on Chicana and Chicano murals included Miguel Hidalgo y Costilla, José María Morelos, Emiliano Zapata, Pancho Villa, and *soldaderas* (female camp followers). At the turn of the twentieth century, thousands of Mexicans fled their country for the US in response to the Mexican Revolution. Therefore, given the political context of the Chicana and Chicano Movement, the revolution and its leaders provided some interpretive social and historical context for Mexican Americans' political beliefs.

A review of the Chicana and Chicano Movement's principles affirm different aspects and issues prioritized by Chicana and Chicano Movement activists. For example, in their work, Barnet-Sánchez and Drescher emphasize the Vietnam War and its social implications as setting the stage for mass political engagement from 1960 to 1974. Chicano communities staged mass antiwar rallies that often ended in acts of police violence. Activists used various social and civic organizing tactics to combat discrimination and demand social equality. Chicanas identified the disempowering costs of a patriarchal society. Artists contributed significantly to and shaped the civil rights discourse, too. Nuevomexicana/o muralists countered dominant oppressive discourse by sharing critical perspectives of their histories and social conditions.

Murals embodied a visual record of Chicana and Chicano Movement discourse within the United States' dominant culture. Alicia Gaspar de Alba analyzed *Chicano Art: Resistance and Affirmation (CARA)*, the first national art exhibition featuring diverse Chicana and Chicano artists and their artwork. Gaspar de Alba argued that Chicana and Chicano artists contested hegemonic constructs of mainstream America that upheld "melting pot" ideas. Chicana/o artists asserted their multilingual and multicultural heritage, articulated in the concepts of mestizaje and *La Raza*. By rejecting externally imposed classifications, such as Mexican American and Hispanic, and then identifying as Chicana/o, these artists and activists offered a political statement about their lives, a declaration of freedom from homogenizing and subordinating constructs that upheld inequalities enabled in the educational system, represented in mass media, and promoted by the arts industry.

The use of heroic icons is a common occurrence among different muralists in the Chicana and Chicano Movement. Mexican revolutionary icons and civil rights contemporary political figures stood for revolution, activism, and resistance, embodying champions fighting for the people. Chicana and Chicano artists captured individuals and leaders for their courage and ability to mobilize the poor people of Mexico and the US and win struggles against overwhelming odds. By drawing from these sources, Chicana and Chicano muralists aimed to help their communities learn their history and understand their identity and culture within settler colonialism and Western imperialism.

Early Chicana and Chicano Movement New Mexican muralists and artists, some featured in this exhibit, including Marcia García, Ignacio Jaramillo, Juanita J. Lavadie, Francisco Lefebre, Samuel Leyba, Noel Márquez, Roberta Márquez, and Enriqueta Vásquez, were part of student and community collectives, as well as working as individual artists, who engaged in mural making as public educational praxis. Given the lack of attention to nuevomexicana/o history and culture in public institutions, the mural-making phase of the Chicana and Chicano Movement offered striking cultural expressions responsive to local communities and their histories and lived realities. Through their art, they provided critical appraisals of social and economic conditions in New Mexico. Some murals analyzed the transitions in the region from Indigenous to Spanish, then Mexican, and finally, US societies. Their visual depictions recognized New Mexican pastoral and folk traditions but also centered on an economic analysis of globalized capitalism, particularly related to diverse, communal, and subsistence-oriented societies in New Mexico. Artists from land-based cultures emphasized the negative impacts of capitalism as directly impacting their family and community's abilities to sustain themselves in changing economic circumstances. Historical loss of land and degradation of soil and water limited their immediate opportunities to grow food and feed their families. Nuevomexicana/o artists added a unique perspective to the Chicana and Chicano Movement.

Culture Framing:
The Chicana and Chicano Movement Art Era

In the book *Making Aztlan: Ideology and Culture of the Chicana and Chicano Movement, 1966–1977*, Juan Gómez-Quiñones and Irene Vásquez offer a frame for understanding the culturally expressive politics of the Chicana and Chicano Movement. In the 1960s and 1970s, activists and artists responded collectively to juridical and cultural ideologies that positioned Chicanas, Chicanos, and nuevomexicanas/os as second-class citizens. Diverse culturally derived historical memories informed and shaped movement activists' political, artistic, and ideological grievances and demands. Past recollections shared across families and communities sharpened by social and political analysis offered sources of local inspiration and action addressing dynamics of exclusion and belonging. During this period, the visual arts were brought into conversations as a readily accessible and legible vehicle for contestation, community empowerment, and agency. Murals exemplified this instrumentalization of public art forms accessible to many in low-income communities, thus becoming a people's art or pedagogy of the streets.

Murals were not monological articulations; they depicted positive, neutral, and negative associations of Spanish, Mexican, and US historical and contemporary dynamics. By the 1960s, New Mexico had been a US state for only forty-eight years. Before that, the region had been a US territory for sixty-four years, an area of Mexico for twenty-eight years, and a part of the Spanish colonies for over one hundred forty years. Thus, colonial Mexican history, geography, culture, and heritage informed Chicana and Chicano and nuevomexicana/o identities. Through education and art, Chicanas and Chicanos explored decoloniality in relation to the Spanish, Mexican, and US settler colonial processes that informed their consciousness as citizens deprived of their full rights in the United States. Chicana and Chicano murals, therefore, reflected locally specific identities and perspectives, but their politics were part of a national imaginary that constructed Chicana and Chicano peoples as a historically subordinated and exploited population. Although not evenly or universally, Chicana and Chicano muralists nurtured constitutive group-identity formations from various culturally expressive local, national, and global dynamics. Los Artes Guadalupanos de Aztlán from Santa Fe, New Mexico, offered vivid artistic examples reflecting the brewing Chicana/o Mural Movement. Their bold, colorful depictions reverberated throughout northern New Mexico. Chicana and Chicano muralists positioned nuevomexicanas/os in a hemispheric dialogue with other activists and artists in North America, sharpening their understanding of who they were in the context of US society.

Chicana and Chicano artists participated in constitutive group-identity formations that shaped their muralism in New Mexico. Gómez-Quiñones and Vásquez assert that artists of the Chicana and Chicano Movement were influenced in unique cultural and political ways that included the following:

1. Chicanas and Chicanos insisted on their Native American origins or relations to Native American heritage and ancestry and rejected the notion that they were "alien" or "foreign" to North America. The Indian countenance—the Native American physiognomy—was upheld as beautiful and desirable in murals.

2. Mestizaje was acknowledged as an ongoing historical and cultural synthesis of the past and present with the Native American, Spanish, and African influences. Artists conveyed pride in mixed ethnic and racial descent as a negation of the racism they experienced and witnessed in society. The emphasis on not being "White" circulated among Chicanas and Chicanos and in the larger society.

3. Identification with the land infused the recognition of living and historical communities. Many nuevomexicanas/os still lived on the lands of their ancestors or had recent memories of doing so, which made their affinity to the earth more clearly articulated in their art.

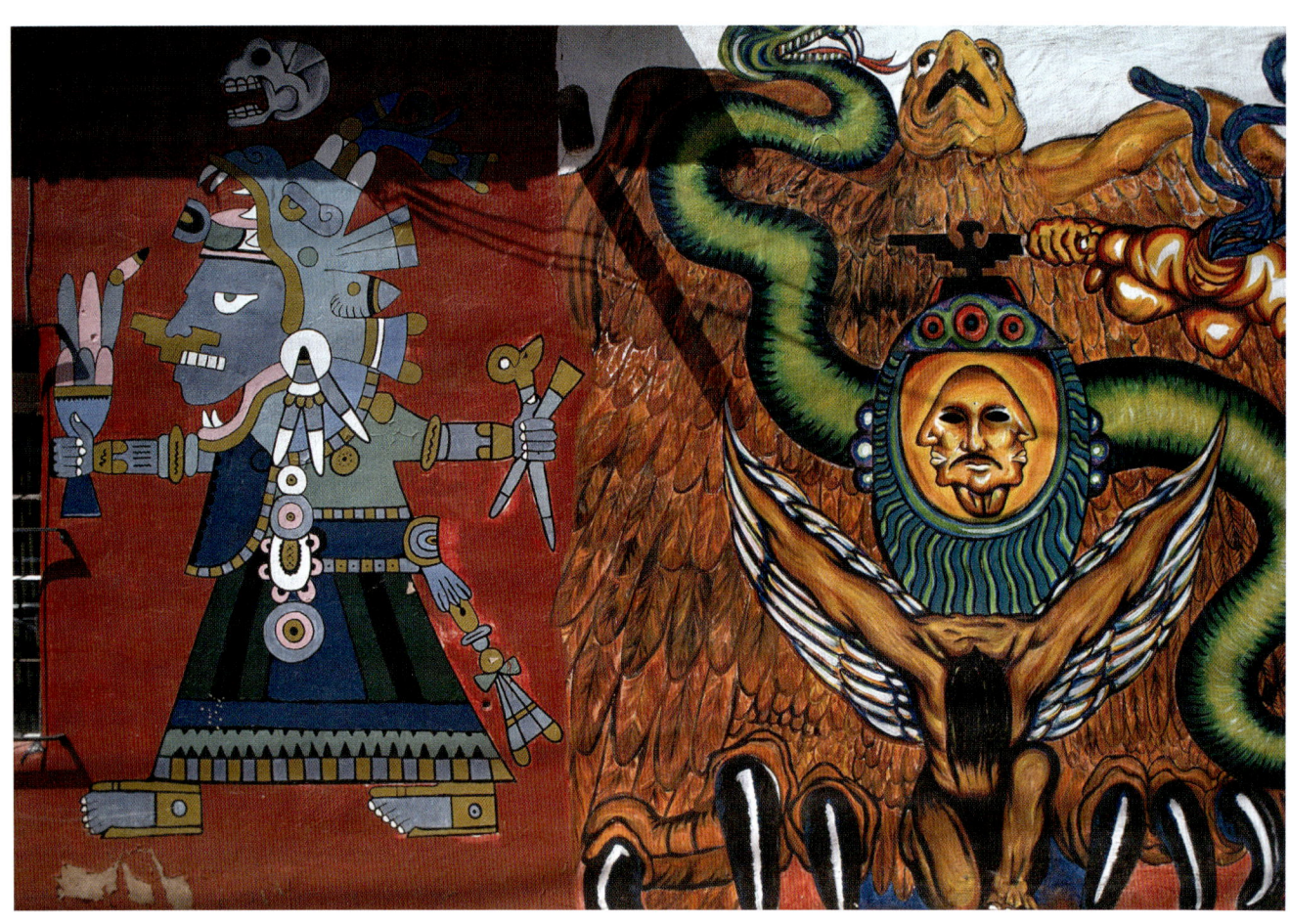

FIGURE 33. Los Artes Guadalupanos de Aztlán, *La Clínica de la Gente*, 1971–1973, Sante Fe, New Mexico, Bob Fitch Photography Archive, Department of Special Collections, Stanford University Library.

4.   Land tied families and communities through a collective effort. Emphasis on the importance of survival and the ethos of daily living practices shaped social priorities and cultural values. Families farmed on their lands, kept livestock, and produced food products for their families.

5.   A growing acknowledgment expanded of the importance of women within the family and society and of everyone's dependence on and responsibility for others. Women seized upon a basic acknowledgment of self-worth and dignity premised on women-centered and women-led social change and depicted this in murals. Beginning in the 1970s, male artists incrementally recognized this in their art.

6.   A basic personal and cultural epistemology evident in art was a claimed "historical narrative" that explained Chicana and Chicano origins and included or assumed triumphs and tragedies. It countered the erasure imposed by the official US historical teleology. Art was a form of decolonial pedagogy, including resistance to colonization, the struggles for independence, the United States–Mexico war, the Mexican Revolution, and all the circumstances that led to self and collective being on the US side of the border. Recognition of the personal importance of history and culture was essential to explaining community, family, and self, and this orientation provided the bases or justifications for claims to uniqueness. There was a formative consciousness among Chicana and Chicano artists that involved a set of cultural practices, a story being acted upon by individuals and communities— the making of community-based history.

7.   A popular saying emphasizing the strength of character and heritage among rural laboring or *barrio*-affiliated Mexican American populations was, "*raíz fuerte que no se arranca*" (a strong root can never be uprooted). In New Mexico, labor was the basis for survival and productivity for land-based families.[8]

The above cultural phenomena derived from colonialist, imperialist, and modernist forces of change and strongly influenced the arts and murals of the people of the US Southwest, including nuevomexicanas/os. Any of these elements can be found in the murals included in this essay. If muralists identified with one or several identities and cultural expressions, it did not diminish the interactive and constitutive processes that influenced identity formations within the larger Chicana and Chicano Movement. As in other regions, Chicana and Chicano identity formation expressed in murals in New Mexico involved complex and dynamic processes and individual choices amid various diverse options. Not all Chicana and Chicano artists drew uniformly or evenly from the above seven cultural identifiers. However, these sociocultural characteristics or cultural discourses of the movement circulated in Chicana and Chicano Movement art spaces. To some extent, all or most of these cultural sentiments informed movement artists' rhetorical testimonials, artistic compositions, and creative energies.

In New Mexico, Chicana and Chicano art conveying action-inspiring tenets occurred in the practices of historically derived cultural preferences that evolved under specific historical and modern circumstances. The cultural life of artists embodied customs, values, attitudes, ideas, behaviors, and arts common to group members. These offered a design for living and a basis for collective action vis-à-vis others during the period of the Chicana and Chicano Movement. Cultural practices and preferences reflected rural land-based communities and working-class relations, and changed over time. In New Mexico, mural making involved contesting forces that minimized nuevomexicana/o lives and communities and the impact of social and historical conditions on their contemporary material conditions. Artists consciously identified or disidentified with cultural expressions and practices available to them within various social contexts. Cultural expressions encompassed innovative possibilities, including the inclusion of diverse ethnic and political art. Interdependence and forms of collectivity advanced social cohesion, group preservation, and cultural expression among artists and art communities.

Artes Guadalupanos de Aztlán, the first known Chicano mural collective, inspired other collectives among nuevomexicana/o artists. Later a second mural collective that included Gilbert Guzman, Frederico Vigil, and Zara Kriegstein emerged in Sante Fe. Through the 1970s, Artes Guadalupanos de Aztlán painted evocative murals in public spaces for the community. Their murals often featured beautiful local landscapes, Mesoamerican iconography, Aztec pyramids and adobe/Pueblo structures, Indigenous and *mestiza/o* women, men and children, maize and flowers, and birds and snakes. In their images, they addressed issues of racism, worker exploitation, environmental racism, warfare, police abuse, and authoritarianism/fascism. Artes Guadalupanos de Aztlán espoused workers' rights, education, literacy, veterans' rights, and the arts to strengthen the community and forge a vision for a better future.[9]

When Artes Guadalupanos de Aztlán began painting murals, the Chicana and Chicano Movement had spread to most major cities and small towns in the Southwest. In the early 1970s, students attending New Mexico Highlands University (NMHU) sparked a renaissance of Chicana and Chicano mural art under the artistic supervision of a Chicano professor, Pedro Rodríguez. Pedro Rodríguez came to NMHU after serving as a director of Chicano Studies at Texas A&I (now Texas A&M) in Kingsville, Texas, in the late 1960s. Pedro was a La Raza Unida Party member and participated in significant demonstrations and boycotts in Texas and nationally. When hired, he became the first director of Chicano Studies at NMHU. In 1981, Rodríguez summarized the political nature of his art mentorship of Chicana and Chicano artists at NMHU in the following manner:

A number of tendencies have run the length of the Chicano art movement. There is, of course, what I consider to be the central, most important tendency, but by no means the only valid one: that which reflects the social, political, and economic reality of our people. This tendency expresses the true aspiration of the Mexican people in the U.S. and responds to the needs of our community. It addresses the issues which related to the class nature of our struggle within the context of national liberation. Our people do not desire assimilation into a system that perpetuates inequities, class differences, and cultural domination. Therefore, it is the art that addresses these issues that attains the highest form of artistic creation and expression among Chicano/Mexican artists.[10]

At NMHU, Rodríguez used art instruction and production as a form of consciousness-raising among students who felt the university privileged "Western" knowledge and White students more than local history or local students. The NMHU administration hired Rodríguez to make changes that better served local populations. He raised funds to offer students scholarships for study abroad opportunities in Mexico. He felt that Mesoamerican art and Mexican muralism offered the budding Chicana and Chicano muralists a different perspective. Several of the NMHU students went to study art in Mexico, including Francisco Lefebre, Marcia García, Juanita J. Lavadie, and Noel Márquez. Rodríguez encouraged New Mexican students to immerse themselves in the art production in Mexico. As he stated,

> Because the students from northern New Mexico, most of them, if not all of them, had never been out of this area, had never been out of the country, had never been to Mexico. To me, the logical step for the art students was to take them where they could see firsthand what everybody missed. . . . the socialistic art of Mexico is not just a matter of ideology or things like that. It has to do a lot with the kind of art they chose to pursue, which was socialistic art as its endeavor and, as a result, the attempt to create public art. Art that focuses on people, primarily poor people, primarily people who are disadvantaged, and rewards it with the knowledge of that. Whereas the art of capitalism, what it was doing was basically teaching people to pursue the usual structures of Western knowledge. It is not the art of the poor, nor is it the art of the disadvantaged. It's art for those who can go to a museum and purchase it; it is art for those who can have somebody commission them a big mural project or something, which is very different. The focus on who it's for is very different and who it's accessible to.[11]

Murals painted by Chicana and Chicano Students at NMHU reflected the esthetics, values, and politics of the growing Chicana and Chicano Movement. Studying Mexican history, art, and culture offered nuevomexicanas/os a broad range of inspiration that came to shape their hemispheric visions. Contrary to a longstanding view of New Mexican *Hispanos* as rejecting Mexico as a cultural or ancestral influence, Chicana and Chicano artists and activists visited Mexico, studied under or with Mexican artists and creative workers, and transmitted Mexican imagery with local New Mexican iconography. They were creating new canvases depicting the multi-faceted histories and lives of Mexican and New Mexican peoples. Murals from this period display the striking historical, political, and social content associated with Chicana and Chicano muralism, as well as bold coloring and iconography.

The *Despertar* mural painted between 1971 and 1972 is attributed to three NMHU students, Marcia García, Juanita J. Lavadie, and Roberta Márquez, who worked under the guidance of Rodríguez (fig. 3.4). Although often glossed over, from an early period, Chicana activists participated in designing and painting murals at the university. *Despertar* pays homage to Indigenous heritage, education, and the racial and ethnic admixture of Chicana/o peoples. Like Artes Guadalupanos de Aztlán, the motifs and iconography in the mural signal both pre-Columbian and contemporary influences. The chained individual points to a history of exploitation and domination. The opened book leans toward the central image, highlighting education, unity, and social movements (symbolized by the UFW Eagle), pointing the way to liberation. The muralists signed the bottom corner of their mural as RCAF ARTISTAS, a pictorial homage to the Royal Chicano Art Force in California. Referencing this community of artists, Juanita J. Lavadie, who participated in a moderated panel held in 2019 that brought together several muralists from NMHU, stated,

> I met my *compadrazco de artistas* at Highlands at the beginning of the Chicano movement with Pedro Rodríguez from San Antonio, Texas. He introduced us to the concept of, not only Chicano art but also, *muralismo*. Pedro provided us with opportunities to study in Mexico City with Ramiro Romo Estrada.[12]

Pedro Rodríguez aimed to inspire students to view their communities and histories as part of the fabric of the Americas. Visiting Mexico gave them a different vantage point to imagine themselves and their lives as firmly established on the continent, given that their ancestors had lived on the American continent for centuries before the arrival of Anglo-American settlers. For some in New Mexico, the imposition of the US-Mexico

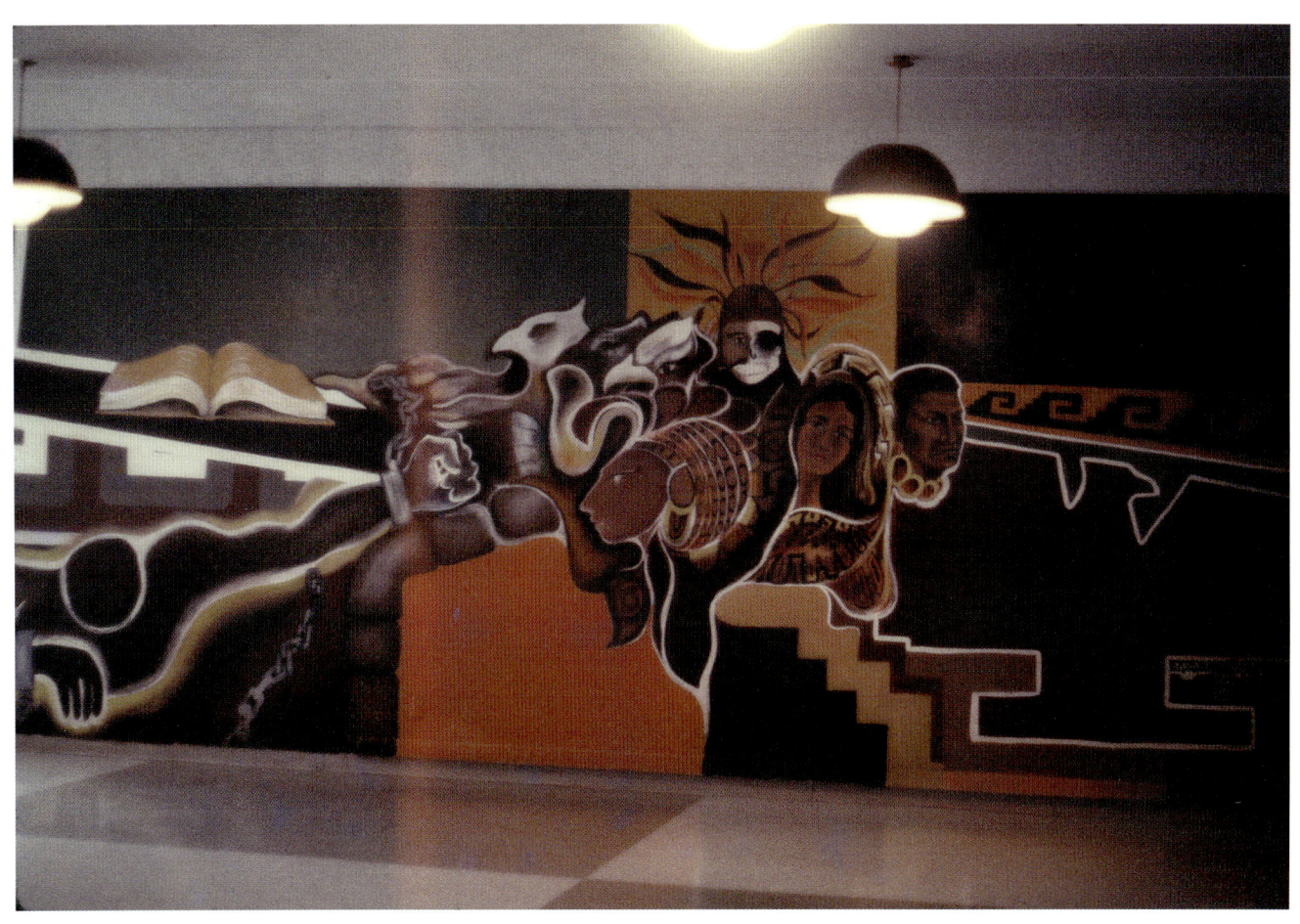

FIGURE 3.4. Pedro Rodríguez, Marcia García, Juanita Jaramillo, and Roberta
Márquez, *Despertar*, 1971–1972. Acrylic. New Mexico Highlands University,
Las Vegas, New Mexico.

border did not abrogate the complex historical connections between New Mexico and Mexico. This political messaging was contrary to the usual depictions of Mexicans and nuevomexicanas/os as the "Other."

When Chicana and Chicano students from NMHU visited Mexico City and viewed the monumental murals produced by José Clemente Orozco, Diego Rivera, and David Alfaro Siqueiros, they noted the faces and images of Aztec and Mayan figures. Like other Chicana and Chicano Movement murals of the period, murals at NMHU emphasized brown bodies and brown skin. They rooted artists in the esthetic influences of the original peoples of the Americas. The murals at NMHU exemplify this new awareness as captured in features of the Aztec calendar from central Mexico (fig. 3.5). The artists signed their mural as a collective, highlighting their identity as *muralistas norteñas*. While nuevomexicano artists depicted Aztec works in their murals, they also incorporated local imagery, such as New Mexican landscapes, corn, and adobe, to situate their cultural perspectives.

Once in Mexico, Chicana and Chicano muralists were exposed to revolutionary thinking espoused by artists and organizers whose ideologies were connected to Third World liberation movements. Artists like Enriqueta Vásquez understood the violence imposed on people of color fighting in US wars abroad.[13] Images of revolutionary figures, such as Che Guevara, the Argentine-born Marxist revolutionary guerrilla leader killed in 1967, were included to underline the message (fig. 3.6). As Rodríguez stated,

> You know that the painting of that image (Che) on that mural never raised much controversy. It's like the students were very accepting of it, that gives you an example of the sophistication of these students. A lot of people don't believe that but it's true . . . They learned. There were very advanced-thinking people; they were radicals.[14]

Artists like Francisco Lefebre and Noel Márquez participated in workshops at Mexico City's Taller de Gráfica Popular (TGP), where they studied the woodcuts and prints of Alberto Beltrán, Juan de la Cabada, Leopoldo Méndez, Pablo O'Higgins, Ignacio Aguirre, and Mariana Yampolsky.[15] After a period of study, nuevomexicana/o students returned from Mexico with a strong sense of muralism as a form of people's art that could communicate their political perspectives on contemporary struggles.

Art as Historical Refraction:
Interpreting the Past as a Vehicle for Change

For New Mexican Chicana and Chicano muralists, the past colored their views of the present and the future. Their murals addressed the historical origins of their communities, social and economic conditions, relationships to land and place, and social justice movements.[16] These compositions offered subjective windows to the past that related New Mexico's history as a colony of Spain, a satellite of the Mexican Republic, and finally, an imperial outpost of the US. History was not an object of the past but a wellspring of knowledge for the future. Contestations of social inequalities, racism, discrimination, and proclamations for self and community empowerment appeared in Chicana and Chicano murals. Throughout history, the development of Hispana/o communities was directly impacted by their relationship with Indigenous peoples, colonialism, land tenure, soil fertility, and access to water and natural resources. These elements also influenced the production of murals into and past the twentieth century. A basic underlying theme of New Mexican murals is their relationship to land once populated by the original peoples.

Indigenous peoples, such as the Pueblo Indians, Navajo, Apache, and Comanche, established productive land-based societies in New Mexico. In New Mexico, nineteen Pueblos, four Apache tribes, and the Navajo Nation had a significant social-cultural influence on all subsequent settler populations. Their innovations provided the basis for later social and economic transformations. Despite facing challenges to sovereignty, economic base, and land stewardship, Native artists represented their communities as vibrant and persistent throughout the twentieth century.

Pueblo Indians and other Indigenous peoples influenced the cultures and societies that developed around them. Moreover, the lifeways of many *Hispanas and Hispanos*, who also had Indigenous ancestors, were more reminiscent of the original peoples than of European and European American settler populations. Although some families descended from Spanish colonists, most of the nuevomexicano population developed from mixed-race populations. Chicana and Chicano artists depicted the enduring presence and impact of Indigenous populations and often represented the presence of Spanish settlers as part of the dynamics that shaped the historical development of nuevomexicana/o communities. Spanish settlers and influences also impacted Indigenous communities in several ways, including language, religion, land-dwelling, and economic transformations. However, the Indigenous presence remained continuous and notable in the lives of later populations of settlers of Spanish and Mexican descent.

Over four hundred years, the relationship established between Indigenous and nuevomexicano communities entailed a shared history of cooperation, conflict, and accommodation. New Mexican parents passed down stories of Indigenous resistance to

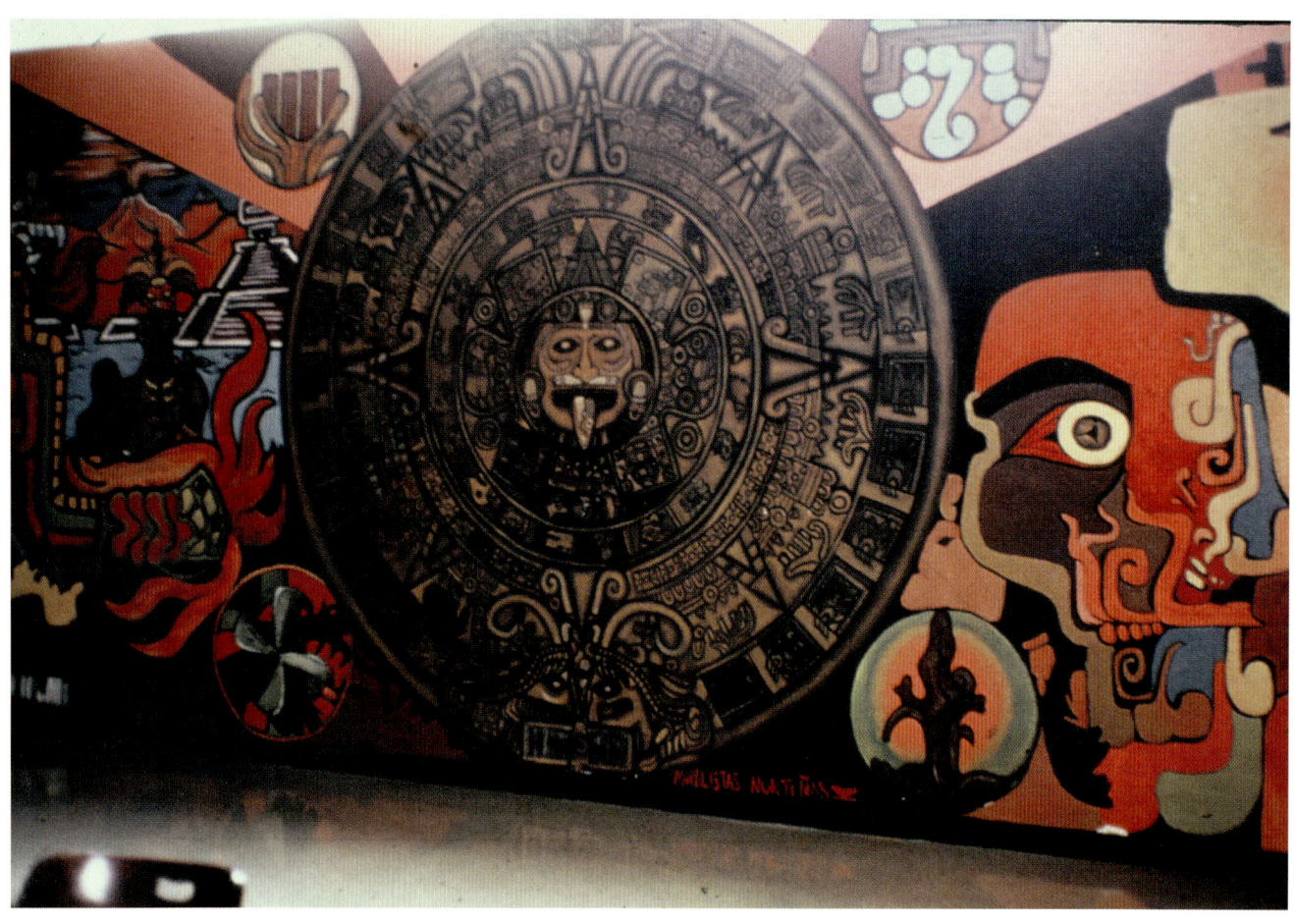

FIGURE 35. Unidentified students, *The Aztec Calendar*, 1972. Acrylic. New Mexico Highlands University, Las Vegas, New Mexico.

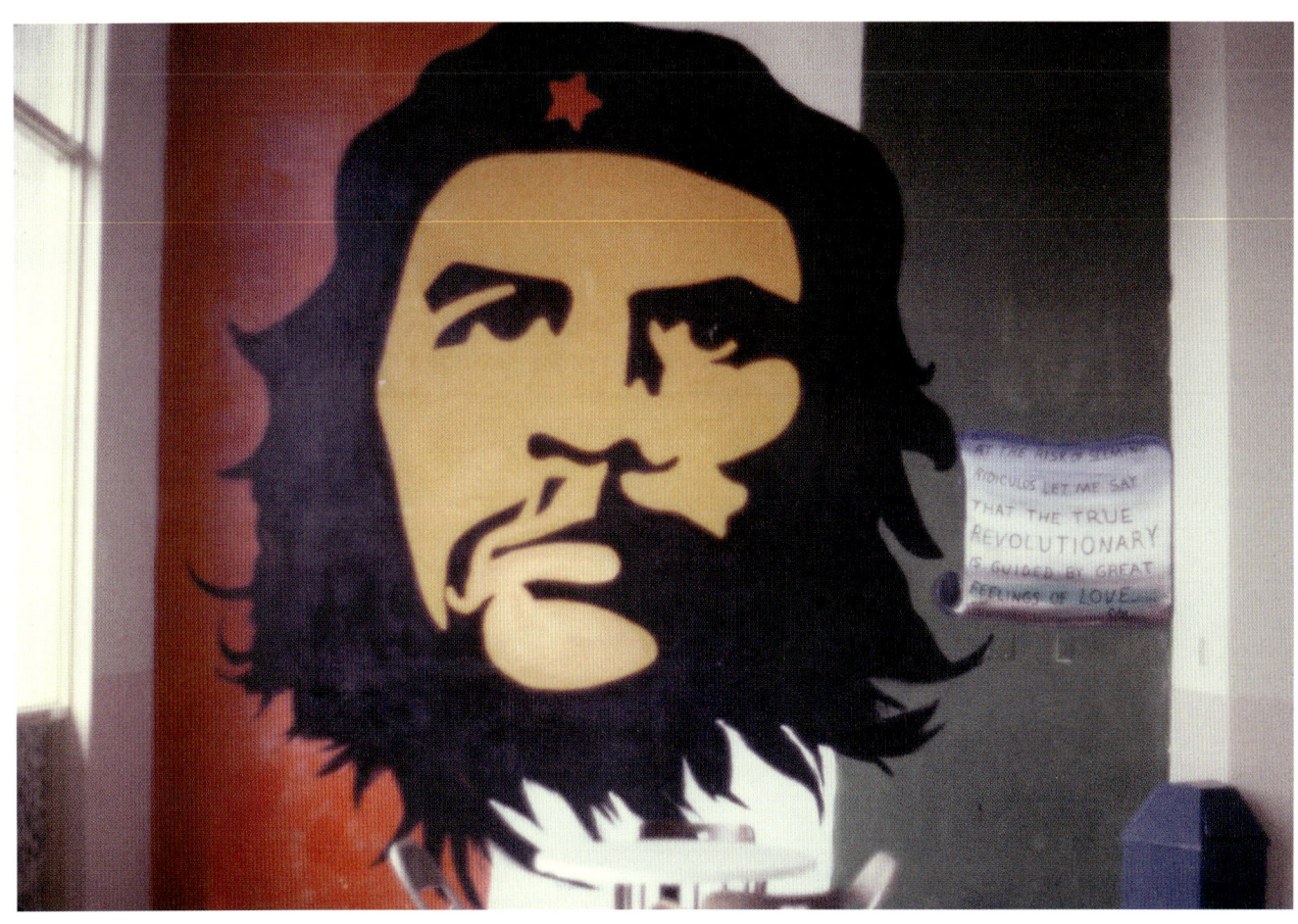

FIGURE 36. Francisco LeFebre, *Che, El Comandante,* 1972. Acrylic. New Mexico
Highlands University, Las Vegas, New Mexico.

Spanish colonial rule to their children. In 1598, Spanish settlers accompanying Juan de Oñate established a settlement on the Río Grande. By 1610, the Spanish outpost of Santa Fe was founded and designated the capital of New Mexico. However, the yoke of colonial rule interfered with the economic, political, and cultural lifestyles and well-being of the Native peoples in the region. The Native population declined substantially from disease and exploitative work conditions, and many were physically punished and persecuted for resisting colonial rule. A major rebellion in 1680 pushed back Spanish settlement for a time. The Pueblo Revolt became a turning point in Pueblo and Spanish-speaking settler relations. The Indigenous peoples maintained their resistance to cultural assimilation. They provided a critical symbolic reference to resistance to colonialism that later influenced New Mexican Chicanas and Chicanos, who were critical of coloniality and imperialism. The exploitation of Native peoples and their forms of resistance surfaced in Chicana and Chicano murals by Artes Guadalupanos de Aztlán, Francisco Lefebre, Noel Márquez, Juanita J. Lavadie, and Enriqueta Vásquez.

Chicana and Chicano muralists often incorporated Indigenous symbols and iconography to shift the colonial paradigm that essentialized the origins of New Mexicans as descending primarily from Spanish origins. This positionality shifted away from the widely accepted tricultural myth tied to New Mexico's demographics. In many Chicana and Chicano murals produced during the Chicana and Chicano Movement, images centered on the Indigenous peoples, including the Aztec and Maya, not to be confused with *Indigenismo*, a Spanish term referring to early and mid-twentieth century trends in Mexico emphasizing romanticized views of Indigenous societies in the arts, texts, or motifs. Instead, Chicana and Chicano artists adopted a form of Indigenism. Guisela Latorre defines Indigenism as "an elastic metaphor or political consciousness that allowed for innovative articulations of cultural and gendered identity."[17] In New Mexico, muralists used images of Aztecs and Mayans but also incorporated references to local Indigenous peoples. They recognized the original presence of the Pueblo, Navajo, Apache, Kiowa, and Comanche peoples and their experiences and survival under colonialism.

New Mexican artists lived close to Native American communities, and some descended from them. Francisco Lefebre marks the brutal assault against the Acoma Pueblo in the mural titled *Nuestra Juventud*, completed in 1978 at Albuquerque High School (fig. 3.7). In the same mural, he renders tribute to the Pueblo Revolt and the liberatory Indigenous movements that coalesced under the leadership of Gerónimo (Chiricahua Apache), Manuelito (Diné), and Cochise (Chiricahua Apache). These images counter existing notions of Native Americans as being prone to violence and cruelty. Their resistance was about survival, dignity, and self-preservation within the context of colonialism and imperialism. Their faces are rendered large-scale and in color. Lefebre's mural, like others produced during the Chicana and Chicano Mural Movement, inverted the discourse of colonialism and the tricultural myth to raise questions about history and the dominant perspective of settler colonialism in New Mexico.

Throughout the eighteenth and nineteenth centuries, miscegenation grew between Native American and Hispanic settlers who themselves were already racially mixed. Still, geographical borders divided Spanish and Native American Pueblos and later reservations and Hispano settlements. Moreover, colonial by-products, including racial/ethnic, gender, and economic inequalities, existed beyond the Spanish period and reinforced social tensions.[18] However, some communities of New Mexico also retained recognizable communities of *Genízaros* that complicated divisive narratives and representations of Indigenous and Hispano peoples and histories. As Moises Gonzales explains, *Genízaro* was the designation given by Fray Angelico Chavez to "North American Indians of mixed tribal derivation living among the Hispanic population in Spanish fashion: that is, having Spanish surnames from their masters, Christian names through baptism, speaking a simple form of Spanish, and living together or sprinkled among the Hispanic towns and ranchos."[19] This specific aspect of mural representation in New Mexico has not been fully explored in nuevomexicana/o murals. These nuanced histories were often suppressed or glossed over by US historical narratives.

Given their long history of living close to Native American sovereign communities and the miscegenation that occurred historically in the state between Spanish-speaking settlers and Indigenous populations, nuevomexicana/o muralists adopted what appears to be Pan-Indian or Indo-Hispano elements. Through their art, they underscored the Indigenous presence and the ancestry of the nuevomexicana/o communities. The mural painted by Juanita J. Lavadie and Enriqueta Vásquez in 1977 titled *Un Puño de Tierra*, at the El Prado liquor store in El Prado, New Mexico, offers a visual portrait of the clash between traditional land-based cultures and industrial and militarized development in New Mexico (fig. 3.8). The mural presents a Native American figure within the larger Taos mountains and valley environs, where Lavadie and Vásquez made their lives. The mural broadcasts a visual dialogue, or cultural assemblage, combining past, present, and future, a characteristic of the Chicano Mural Movement. Although originally completed in 1978, the mural received a touch-up in 2003 and was repainted in 2008 due to damage from a car collision.

Un Puño de Tierra begins from the left with Mesoamerican designs on the perimeter of the mural. The mural's title fades into the Indigenous iconography along the border and is punctuated by circular images of the sun. One in the center has radiating lines representing the left half of a Zia symbol. Indigenous designs border the edges of the mural. The right border has another half-Zia symbol, representing Taos, New Mexico. Taos is one of the state's largest and most continuously inhabited Indigenous Pueblos. The majestic Taos Mountain and its valley cover the broad expanse of the mural.

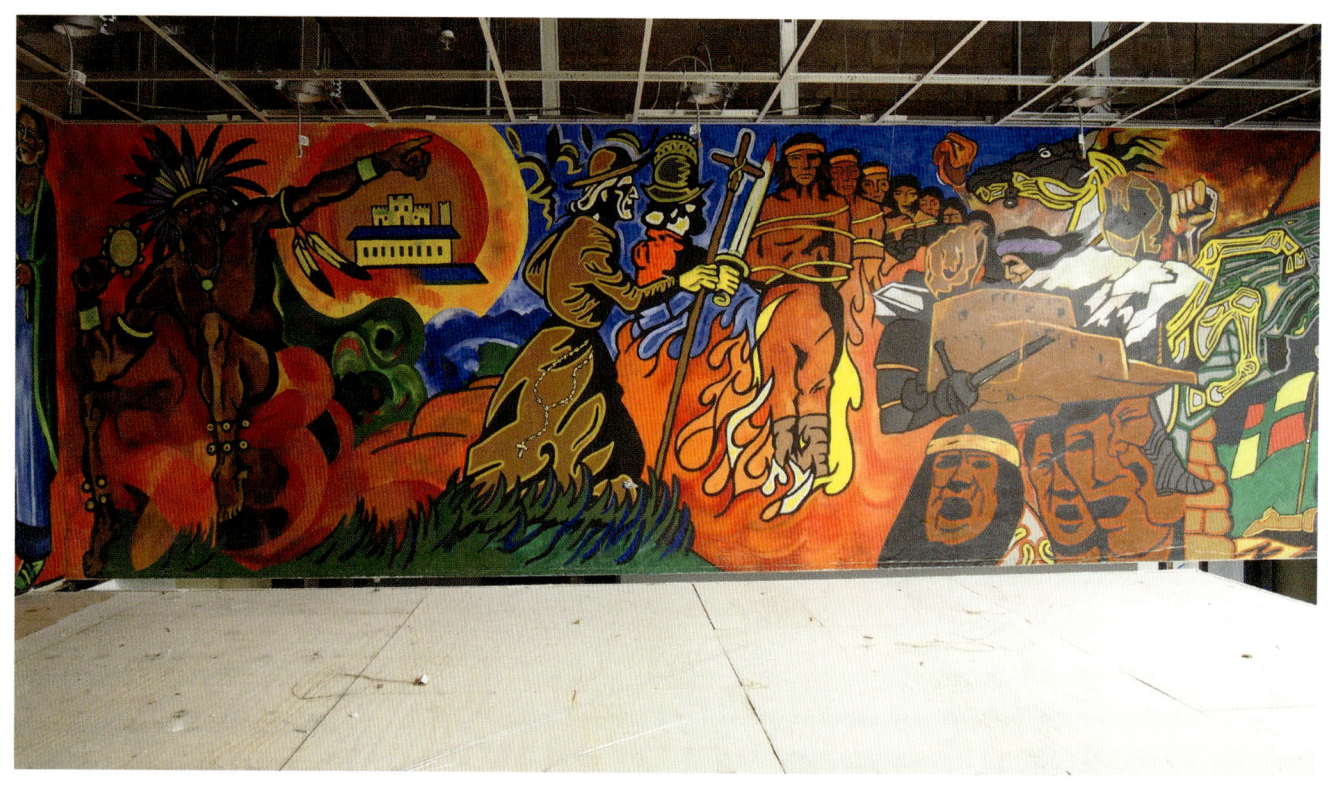

FIGURE 3.7. Francisco LeFebre, *Nuestra Juventud,* 1976–1978. Acrylic. Albuquerque High School.

Un Puño de Tierra

Antonio Aguilar

Life soon ends
La vida pronto se acaba

What happened in this world
Lo que pasó en este mundo

Only the memory remains
Nomás el recuerdo queda

Already dead I'm going to take
Ya muerto voy a llevarme

Just a fist of earth
Nomás un puño de tierra

The day I die
El día que yo me muera

I'm not going to take anything
No voy a llevarme nada[20]

The mural's title parallels Antonio Aguilar's 1960 song of the same name and underscores the connection to the homeland. Originally intended as an homage to Mexican people, Aguilar's song resonated with Mexicans living abroad. In the mural, the apparent reference is to northern New Mexico. The song and the mural celebrate the lasting bond between Taoseños and their homelands. When Vásquez and Lavadie developed and finalized the mural design with community input, they emphasized the need for a spiritual message to resonate with the local community. Gonzales, longtime owner of the family-run liquor store, wanted to use the side of his building for public art. The three agreed that the mural should reflect the region's cultural values and the ties between the people and the land.[21] Although the cultural landscape contrasts with the liquor store's immediate environment, paved streets, and parking spaces, the mural is a community treasure that has tantalized generations of local community members.

In work from the 1970s, nuevomexicana/o muralists often comment on the negative impacts of technological and industrial expansion. In *Un Puño de Tierra*, space is marked by nostalgic rurality and affective emotion. Emerging from a green gas cloud in the top left corner of the mural, a warplane descends, firing machine guns or launching rockets into what appears to be a barren land. Below the plane is an oil or natural gas tower. A flame from the top of an industrial plant underscores a contrast between the natural landscape and environmental contamination. To the right of the plane and the green gas hangs the white moon with the face of a skull, representing *muerte* (death). In the bottom left corner stands a resolute, striking Indigenous figure, enveloped in a buffalo robe with horns. The figure has gray hair and a white feather hanging from his ear. The eyes have two figures inside them: in the left eye, an embryo; in the right eye, a skull. In this image, life and death are part of a continuum. Under the hanging white feather is an image of a heart on fire. This mural section reflects Mexican influences, including the skull and heart. Juanita and Enriqueta traveled separately to Mexico City in the 1970s as part of their educational journeys. Juanita studied art in Mexico City as part of organized trips by Pedro Rodríguez. Enriqueta studied Danza Azteca and education in Mexico City with organizers from Denver as part of the Crusade for Justice to enhance cultural knowledge and experiences among Chicana and Chicano youth.

Notably, the iconography of *Puño de Tierra* takes the viewer through a visual portal that connects Hispano communities to the region's original inhabitants primarily through pan-Indian iconography that blends Indian regalia, references to Taos Pueblo, and Mesoamerican imagery. Although the Native American figure in the mural represents a pan-Indian identity, it does point to the significant Indigenous presence in Taos. Moving to the right of the Indigenous figure, the hand presents what appears to be incense or copal. Faces arise from the smoke sprouting as flowers, pointing to the future and its portended productivity, considering industrial development, war, and pollution. Further to the mural's right is the Río Grande Gorge. A bridge lays across the gorge, connecting the land masses and presumably the past to the future.

Animal life is linked to the earth's fertility and abundance. To the far right of the mural, connected to the border of the mural, is a transparent sphere. At the top left of the sphere, an object appears to be in the shape of an arrowhead, striking the sphere and causing it to shatter at the point of impact. Inside the sphere, we can discern images of the land with water running in the Río Grande trees covering the Taos mountains. Elk feed in the high green grass. The stalk of corn is green, indicating bountiful life, while the roots outside the bottom of the sphere appear dry in the browner landscape. Although this could point to topsoil drying, it may also signal resilience in the face of environmental degradation. Below the sphere, coyotes howl at the moon (muerte). The artists hold the natural landscape and all life forms sacred and integral to nuevomexicano communities. Death is part of a natural cycle emblematized by a circle of life in the mural.

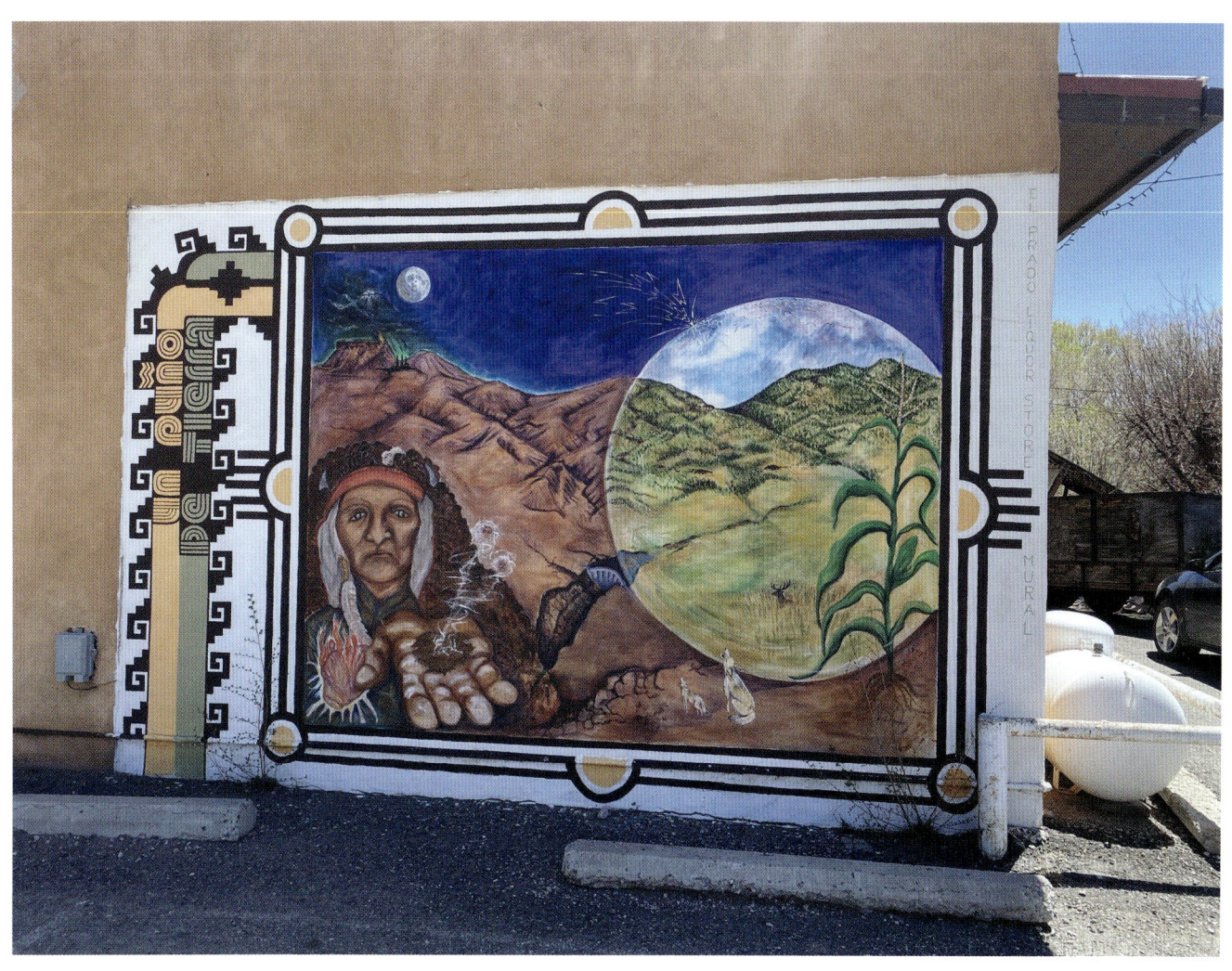

FIGURE 3.8. Enriqueta Vásquez and Juanita Lavadie-Jaramillo, *Un Puño de Tierra*, 1978. Mural, acrylic on stucco. El Prado Liquor Store, El Prado, New Mexico. Photograph by Stefan Jennings Batista.

Due to their understanding of Indigenous communities' closer cultural proximity to environmental stewardship and community cohesion, nuevomexicana/o muralists often positively portrayed close identification with land and nature. They looked back at exploitative colonial practices as aberrations, even while some descended from Spanish-speaking settlers. Having had the opportunity to study in Mexico and being politicized during the Chicana and Chicano Movement, they took issue with colonial and settler appropriations of land and water, which impacted how they portrayed New Mexican history. Nuevomexicana/o artists understood their heritage reflected mixed and, at times, competing claims. They were not ingrained in the myth of tricultural harmony that often sanitized the lasting impacts of settler colonialism.

Artists conveyed settler colonialism as limiting the fullest expression of liberty and freedom for all social sectors except the propertied classes and the wealthiest absentee landlords. Unequal social relations and statuses ultimately led to broad-based assertions for autonomy in the nineteenth century, including free-market economies among investors. Colonial rule and its debilitating effects on Indigenous and mixed-race peoples increasingly came under scrutiny. Chicana and Chicano muralists celebrated the region's independence from Spain while others around them espoused idealized notions of Spanish colonialism. This tension reflected the spirit of independence from Spain that swept through its colonies. By 1821, the Mexican Republic was established, and its authority extended to present-day New Mexico. The Republic held the political reins of the region for twenty-seven years.

Independence from Spain did not lead to greater liberty or security for Native peoples or the mixed-race Spanish-speaking, Spanish-surnamed population of New Mexico. Mexican land grants held by Hispano peoples ensured their economic and cultural well-being. However, once Anglo-American merchants, traders, and ranchers moved into the New Mexico territory, they coveted the most productive lands held by Native Americans and Hispano populations. Land dispossessions further impacted the social and economic well-being of Native and nuevomexicano communities. Chicana and Chicano historians have explored the transition from the hegemony of the Mexican Republic to Anglo-dominated US society. Western imperialism and the commodification of land and labor colored the narrative and rhetoric of the Chicana and Chicano Movement. Neo-Marxist critiques influenced budding scholars and community activists alike. Muralists of the Chicano Movement commented upon the destructive impact of global capitalism and private investment in their mural painting. In *Nuestra Juventud*, Lefebre depicts an oxen-drawn wagon moving from the left of the scene, indicating the westward movement by Anglo settlers into New Mexico (fig. 3.9). Manifest Destiny was a rallying cry for expansionists, including politicians, church leaders, journalists, and settlers. The idea that the Anglo-Saxon government of the US was inevitably destined to expand from coast to coast and spread democracy and free-market capitalism undergirded the actions and discourse of the US government and European American settlers in New Mexico.

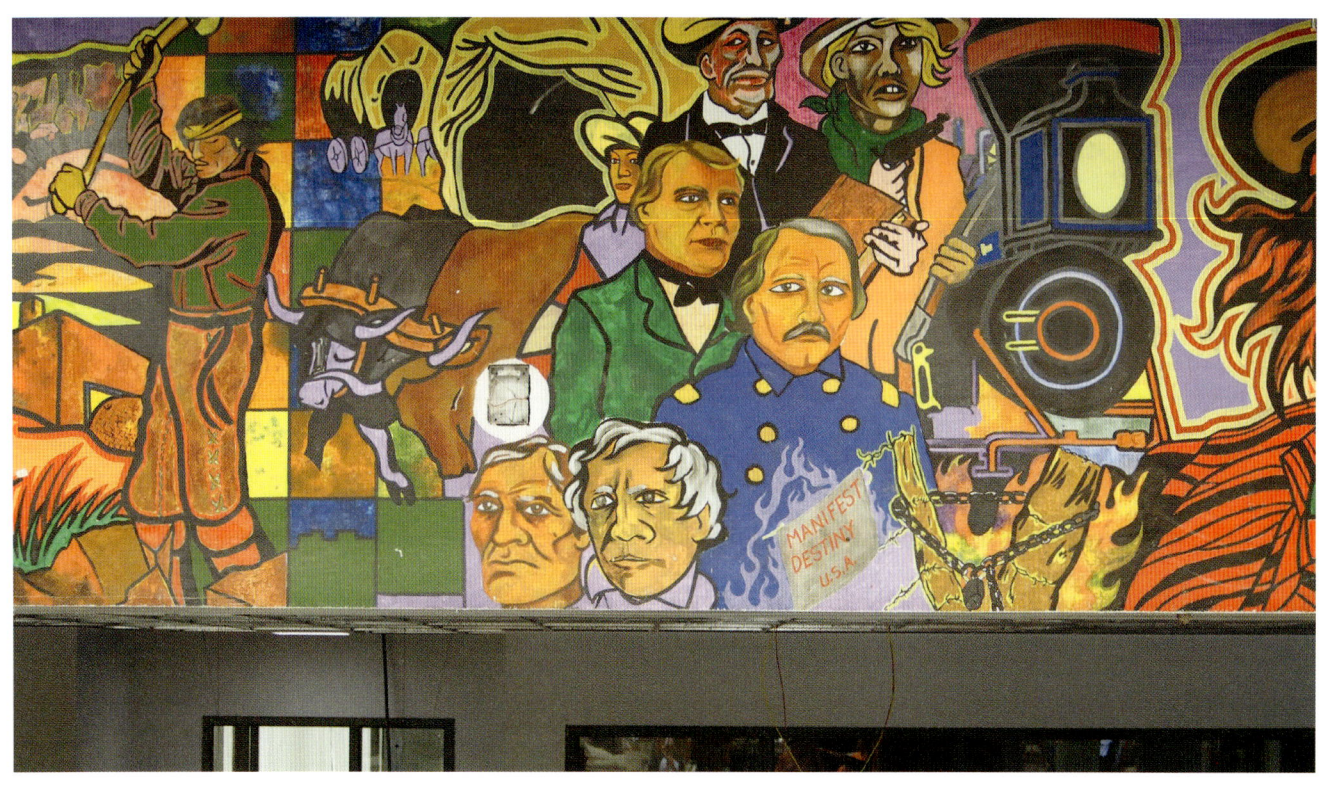

FIGURE 39. Francisco LeFebre, *Nuestra Juventud,* detail, 1976–1978. Acrylic.
Albuquerque High School.

Lefebre depicts several Western imperialist iconic figures that dominated the history of the territory of New Mexico after the Treaty of Guadalupe Hidalgo of 1848. The figures include Thomas B. Catron, Billy the Kid, Governor Bent, Kit Carson, General Stephen W. Kearny, and archbishop Jean-Baptiste Lamy. The image of a steam engine approaching behind a locked fence with a sign reading "Manifest Destiny" represents the advent of US industrial capital and the railroad. Typically, authors and artists in US textbooks depict the westward movement as a positive process that minimizes the violence, trauma, and suffering experienced by communities of color. In the mural, land dispossession of nuevomexicana/os and Indigenous folks weighs heavily on villages and towns. In a previous scene, the intrusion of Anglo-American settlers and US modernism overrides the peaceful, idealized rural life of a nuevomexicano family living off the land. Lefebre's depictions of Anglo intervention reflect a counter-hegemonic perspective, partly because the faces and images of Anglos are distorted. At the same time, those of Native Americans and Hispanos appear stoic and brave.

In their writings, US journalists, historians, and elected officials often portrayed Indigenous and Hispana and Hispano peoples as uncivilized, uneducated, and unproductive.[22] Like prior Spanish and Mexican officials, they viewed Indigenous peoples and mestizo communities as unable to adapt to new governmental norms. Lefebre depicts the westward movement as violent and unsolicited, destructive to the diverse and prosperous communities that inhabited the area. This ideological departure from settler narratives disrupts the idealized versions of US history that present Manifest Destiny as cultural teleology. As Chicano scholar Tomás Ybarra-Frausto writes, "The resistance aspect of the Chicano Movement was both a reaction against these derogatory stereotypes and a counteraction to the assimilating tactics of the dominant society."[23]

US imperialism and the privatization of land grants led to significant negative social and economic changes for Hispano peoples. Roxanne Dunbar-Ortiz writes, "In New Mexico, the capitalist mode of production and development of land as a commodity came with the U.S. conquest. The land had not been a commodity in the Spanish colonial system. Land tenure based on cooperation characterized the poor communities of New Mexico, while individualism and competition for material gain characterized the capitalism mode in the United States."[24] Several Chicana and Chicano muralists depicted this historical transition and its devastating impact on Hispano life and culture. This theme is evident in New Mexican murals from the early 1970s, including those by Artes Guadalupanos de Aztlán and the NMHU student muralists. The 1977 mural titled *Un Puño de Tierra* in Taos, New Mexico, by Juanita J. Lavadie and Enriqueta Vásquez reflected the land-based cultural and spiritual values of Hispano Taoseños. In the mural, a Native American figure oversees the land—its past, present, and future incarnations. The mural also criticizes the effects of industry and development efforts in Taos, bridging the colonial and imperial pasts. Over the next two decades, Francisco Lefebre and Noel Márquez continued to implicate Western development as disruptive and cataclysmic to Hispana/o and Native American lands and communities, and thus to the lives of local peoples.

The themes of land and caretaking are significant in *Un Puño de Tierra*. Water and the Taos Mountain are sacred to the people of Taos Pueblo. The Taos people venerate the Taos Mountain because it is the place of their emergence. In 1903, the US federal government appropriated the Blue Lake as part of natural forestation efforts and cut off the Taos Pueblo from a sacred location. Taos Pueblo sought different avenues to regain the Blue Lake from the US federal government, which was finally returned in 1970 under President Nixon. Lavadie and Vásquez use two lenses to underscore the sacred nature of the Taos Mountain. One lens appears as a barren region with the Río Grande Gorge dried up. The second lens is a version of abundance with tall grass, animals feeding, and water flowing in the gorge with the existing mountains to the south. Although the images of helicopters and towers indicate the negative impact of modern development, these appear small in comparison to the vast landscape of the Taos area. The artists raised concern and respect for land and nature through the mural.

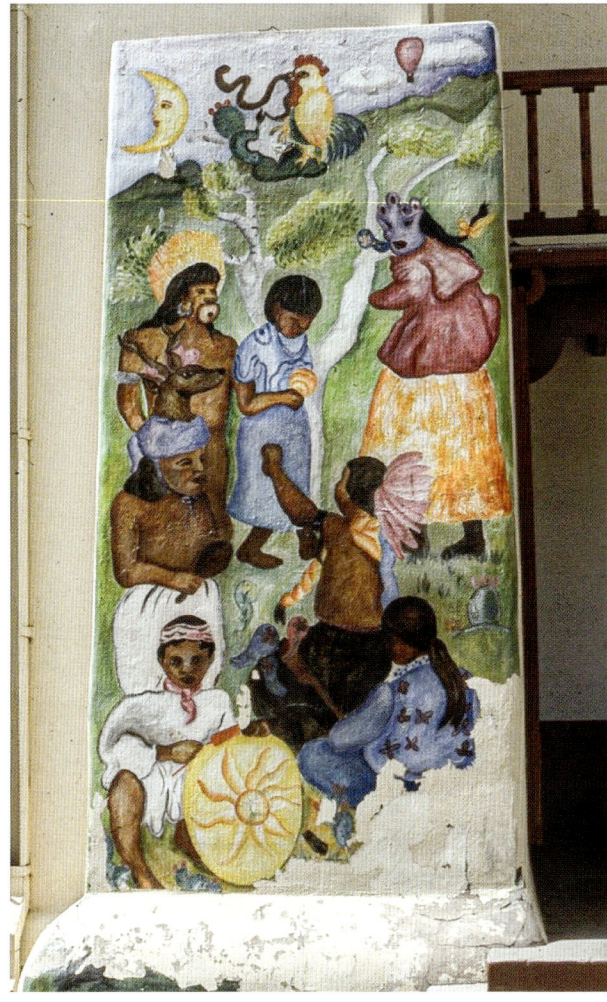

FIGURE 3.10. Graciela Carrillo and Linda Loma Haftewa, *Untitled*, 1978–1979. Acrylic. Institute of American Indian Arts, Santa Fe, New Mexico.

Native American and Hispana/o communities shared some commonalities as land-based cultures. This was recognized when Native American cultural institutions worked with Chicana and Chicano artists. For example, in the late 1970s, the Institute of American Indian Arts (IAIA) in Sante Fe commissioned a Chicana artist, Graciela Carrillo, to design and paint a mural at a prestigious American Indian art institute. Two mural panels painted by Graciela Carrillo and Hopi/Choctaw artist Linda Loma Haftewa (figs. 3.10 and 3.11). The panels contain imagery emphasizing the Indigenous peoples of the Americas. Both panels were later painted over when the Santa Fe Indian School opened on the grounds of IAIA in 1980.[25]

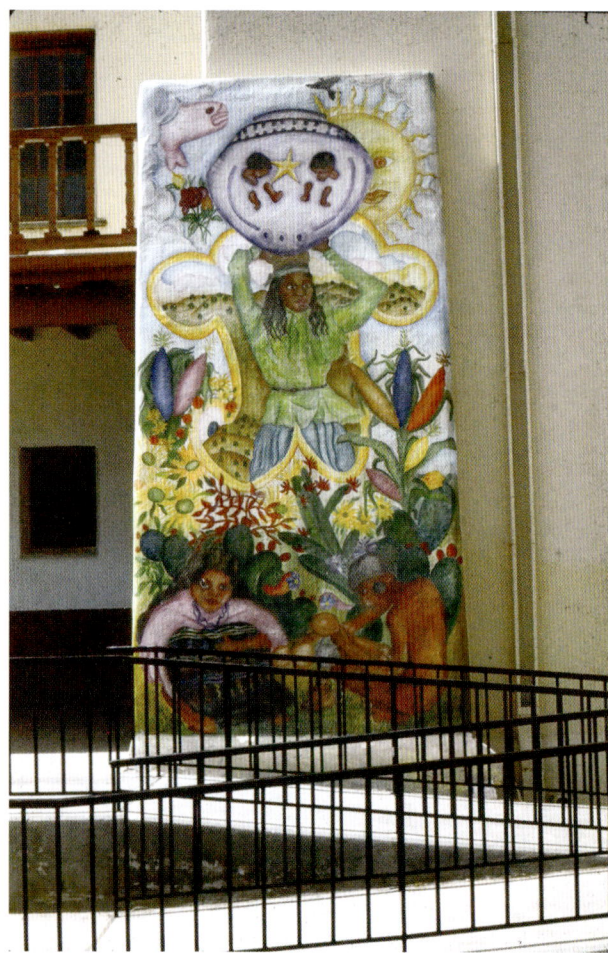

FIGURE 3.11. Graciela Carrillo and Linda Loma Haftewa, *Untitled*, 1978–1979. Acrylic. Institute of American Indian Arts, Santa Fe, New Mexico.

The images show different Indigenous people wearing a variety of regalia. Children and adults are pictured in natural landscapes in close communion with animals, plants, mountains, and trees. Images of the sun, stars, and the moon are present, with multicolored corn growing abundantly. The edges of the images are softened, and the use of pastel and bold colors differs from those murals that underscored rebellion and resistance in the early 1970s.

Murals as Tools for Political Organizing

Mural production accompanied civil rights and Chicana and Chicano Movement activities. Chicana and Chicano political activism in New Mexico during the 1960s and 1970s entailed broad mobilizations to ensure civil and human rights, fair economic opportunities, just political representation, and dynamic cultural expressions. Land grant heirs sought to obtain protection of land and the restoration of land grants. Laborers emphasized better pay and working conditions. Community representatives rallied on behalf of equitable political representation. Chicanas demanded equality and respect from all men in society, including Chicanos. Youth assumed the helm of leadership for educational transformation and cultural determinacy. Activists demanded immigrant and due process rights. These organizing activities created an energetic momentum for economic, social, institutional, and political change and transformation.

Chicana and Chicano muralism and art have often been studied as reflecting a culturally descriptive aesthetic form regarding thematics, iconography, and stylistic elements. As conceptualized by Goldman and Ybarra-Frausto, Barnet-Sanchez and Drescher, Gaspar de Alba, Jackson, Latorre, Gómez-Quiñones and Vasquez, Chicana and Chicano murals conveyed diverse self and community representations, constructed historical genealogies of the Chicanx community, offered revisionist interpretations of the past, and affirmed people's self-determination. Consequently, Chicana/o murals were used to build consciousness and advocate for a change in social conditions. These elements form a system of meaning and purpose that has defined the genre of Chicana and Chicano muralism.

Murals communicated social problems and needs through visual dialogues. Gaspar de Alba writes,

> One form of activism was the Chicano art movement, which, through the popularly accessible forms of murals and posters, represented the community's social problems and injustices while creating a new artistic and politically responsible sensibility.[26]

Chicana and Chicano muralists assumed an emboldened positionality in the world of public art. They were responding to colonial and imperial depictions of Mexican American communities that offered stereotypical representations of Mexican men in sombreros and Mexican women as virgins or harlots. As previously discussed, in the early twentieth century, Mexican and Mexican American artists produced mural works in the US Southwest. The emergence and development of the Chicana and Chicano mural movement in the 1960s and 1970s occurred in tandem with the Chicana and Chicano Movement. Across the US, the mural movement gained traction as part of public expressions tied to social movements. The Civil Rights Movement in the 1960s and 1970s prompted political protests on public streets, roads, and sidewalks. Although the Chicana and Chicano Movement brought about essential gains, subsequent assessments of the movement also impacted how Chicana and Chicano muralism has been conceptualized and what has been identified as worthy of study. New Mexican artists, at times, have been referred to primarily as folk artists as their illustrations often center on rural life and traditions. However, New Mexican muralists also viewed the content of their murals as offering visual educational landscapes intended to convey oral and textual critiques of society.

During the Chicana and Chicano Movement, voices and expressions centering women and women's experiences in history and society grew and changed the politics and tenor of CCM. Chicana artists in the US Southwest identified women's representations as missing from iconic murals celebrating resistance, revolution, and rebellion themes, and they sought out their own spaces on collective murals to depict women as integral to art and society. Chicana artists in New Mexico, like other women artists of the Chicana and Chicano Movement period, often found inspiration in their everyday lives or the environment around them. Some art historians are revising our understanding of different genres of Chicana and Chicano art and finding that the conception of art and its connection to iconographic images of the Chicana and Chicano Movement often masks the complexity and criticality of the body of work produced in the 1970s and 1980s. For example, Constance

Córtez questions the definition of categories applied to Chicana and Chicano artists. She finds the notion of "folk art" simplistic when applied to Carmen Lomas Garza's work. Ybarra-Frausto and Córtez posit that images of everyday life can challenge the dominant social order by reflecting harmony and permanence in the representation of everyday life and culture.[27] Las Mujeres Muralistas in California reflected this ethos of community life. Murals depicted by women increasingly grew in the 1980s and 1990s.

In New Mexico, everyday life was intimately connected to the health and well-being of land and nature. As evident in murals previously discussed by Artes Guadalupanos de Aztlán, Francisco Lefebre, Enriqueta Vasquez, Juanita J. Lavadie, and Graciela and Carrillo Linda Loma Haftewa, Chicana and Chicano artists of New Mexico incorporated land-based communities' visual aesthetics and ethos. In this regard, they were ahead of their time. New Mexicans demonstrated a politics of concern for the environment, further supported by the fact that one of the national organizers for Earth Day was Arturo Sandoval, a Chicano activist from New Mexico. Given that Chicana/o artists of New Mexico grew up in rural communities that often depended upon subsistence activities, they often witnessed the brunt of land dispossession, land development, and environmental degradation because it directly impacted their families' livelihoods. Moreover, New Mexicans also participated in migrant agricultural labor, where they witnessed the effects of agribusiness on land and people.

Working from the southeastern part of New Mexico, the prolific and talented artist Noel Márquez offered compelling aesthetics of nuevomexicana/o mural making. His murals often highlighted the natural landscape, industrial contamination, and environmental degradation. When describing the impetus for his work as an artist, Noel states,

> Mainstream culture is about consuming; it is wasteful. We have to learn to value things and to recycle, just like keeping a friendship, not to throw everything away and not to devalue human life. That's what we can do as muralists by addressing cultural and environmental issues. We are like weavers. We weave all this fabric together of people and a life that share love and concern.[28]

As discussed in Ray Hernández-Durán's essay in this catalog, "*El oro del Barrio*: First-Generation New Mexican Chicana and Chicano Activists and their Art," Noel was inspired by the pre-Columbian art he studied in Mexico City. Like Juanita J. Lavadie and Francisco Lefebre, Noel Márquez traveled to Mexico City with Pedro Rodríguez, an important faculty mentor in his early college education, and studied Mexican art with Mexican masters. His visit to Mexico transformed the way he viewed the role of art. Noel Márquez states,

And so, when we returned from the first trip to Mexico in 1972, we painted a mural at Highlands University, and that was our first mural. And that was powerful; it reawakened our spirit and we just started thinking, "We're community artists, we're activists, and we're going to use art to activate and inspire, and to connect to our community." It is not just about exclusion, inclusion, or racism; it is also about our natural rights to a safe environment.[29]

In several mural designs, Márquez captured the captivating landscape of Southeastern New Mexico. His 2010 restoration of the 1994 *Agave Americana* illustrates his artistic fixation with natural life, land, labor, and development (fig. 3.12). Noel credited the collective efforts of those involved in supporting and producing the mural. Four circular images converge, indicating movement, perhaps cycles of time and life. In the center of the image is a male worker blending into the base and center of an agave. A warm-blooded red color radiates upward to the top center of the mural. The worker stands majestically with a shovel in the left hand. Moving to the right, a cosmic agave bursts through a chain link fence, stretching to the north side of the building's wall, beckoning the viewer to turn the corner. The two agave cover two-thirds of the mural. Márquez was a practitioner of medicinal plants and advised people on homeopathic alternatives to pharmaceuticals. He built his family's home and had a beautiful garden of local plant species. He practiced his living philosophy of environmentalism and was active in environmental efforts to eliminate nuclear energy and uranium mining.

Márquez acknowledges the sacred nature of labor as an act of nourishment and physical sacrifice. This tribute to workers is evident in other artworks (figs. 3.13 and 3.14). On one side of the mural, two women are featured, one stooping in the field rows and the other carrying a basket of garlic. Although agricultural field labor is often done in grueling conditions, this mural offers a dignified space where those who produce food are exalted as life givers. Garlic is a highly consumed plant used globally and has medicinal properties. The timeless convergence of land, plants, people, and glorious skies offers an alternative vision in times of global warming and human and environmental ravages.

Chicana and Chicano Movement murals by nuevomexicana/o artists offer visual portrayals of complex historical subject matter, including indigeneity, mestizaje, colonialism, decolonization, Catholicism, capitalism, imperialism, and racism. Artists used background settings, iconography, style, colors, and thematics to define the esthetic objectives. New Mexican Chicana and Chicano artists shaped the Chicana and Chicano Mural Movement and contributed a compelling vision of their history and identity, reflecting their specific land-based cultural expressions.

In the New Mexican murals included in this catalog, the representation of Indigenous elements equals and, in some examples, outnumbers references to mestizaje. There is also a strong presence of imagery related to mestizaje. Like in other states, New Mexican murals situate their communities within a visual historical timeline beginning with the pre-Columbian era. However, given the long-term and monumental presence of Native Americans in the state, nuevomexicana/o murals incorporated a variety of Indigenous themes referencing Indigenous groups of the region, such as the Apache, Comanche, Navajo, and Pueblo Indians. Murals point to Spanish colonialism, the westward movement of "Manifest Destiny," and the resistance of nuevomexicana/o communities to the destructive impact of the US westward movement on New Mexico and the larger US Southwest. They communicated messages that critiqued war, police violence, industrial development, and environmental degradation. Chicana artists paid homage to women and their centrality in history by carving out spaces in murals or creating their own that celebrated the continuity and balance of women who contributed to New Mexican society. Thus, they offered sweeping views of the past, present, and future to inspire their communities.

During the early twentieth century, New Mexico was the last territory to integrate into the US polity. Chicana and Chicano political activism in New Mexico during the 1960s and 1970s entailed broad mobilizations to ensure civil and human rights, fair economic opportunities, just political representation, and dynamic cultural expressions. Land grant heirs sought to obtain protection of land and the restoration of land grants. Laborers emphasized better pay and working conditions. Community representatives rallied on behalf of equitable political representation. Chicanas demanded equality and respect from all men in society, including Chicanos. Youth assumed the helm of leadership for educational transformation and cultural determinacy. Activists demanded immigrant and due process rights. These organizing activities created an energetic momentum for economic, social, institutional, and political change and transformation.

As Chicana and Chicano muralism increased as part of the Movement, the diversity of expressions and the quantity of artists multiplied in the Southwest. New Mexico's economic development and political evolution from an Indigenous to colonial and then to an imperial-controlled region became illustrated by Chicana and Chicano muralists of New Mexico. As a state of New Mexico characterized by diverse rural and semi-urban settlements, economic developments, and cultural landscapes, the region offered fertile grounds for developing Chicana/o mural making.

Several New Mexican muralists trained in Mexico City in the 1970s, and they understood how their unique cultural landscapes could inspire site-specific imagery. Chicana and Chicano artists used the walls of community centers, local businesses, and educational institutions to offer an alternative understanding of society in the past, the present, and the future (fig. 3.15). Carlos Francisco Jackson writes, "The mural provided Chicano artists and activists with an art form that bypasses mainstream media and institutions."[30] Alicia Gaspar de Alba writes, "We find the foundation of Chicana/o popular culture not at the bottom of the structure, nor in the basement where its invisibility can be perpetuated, but

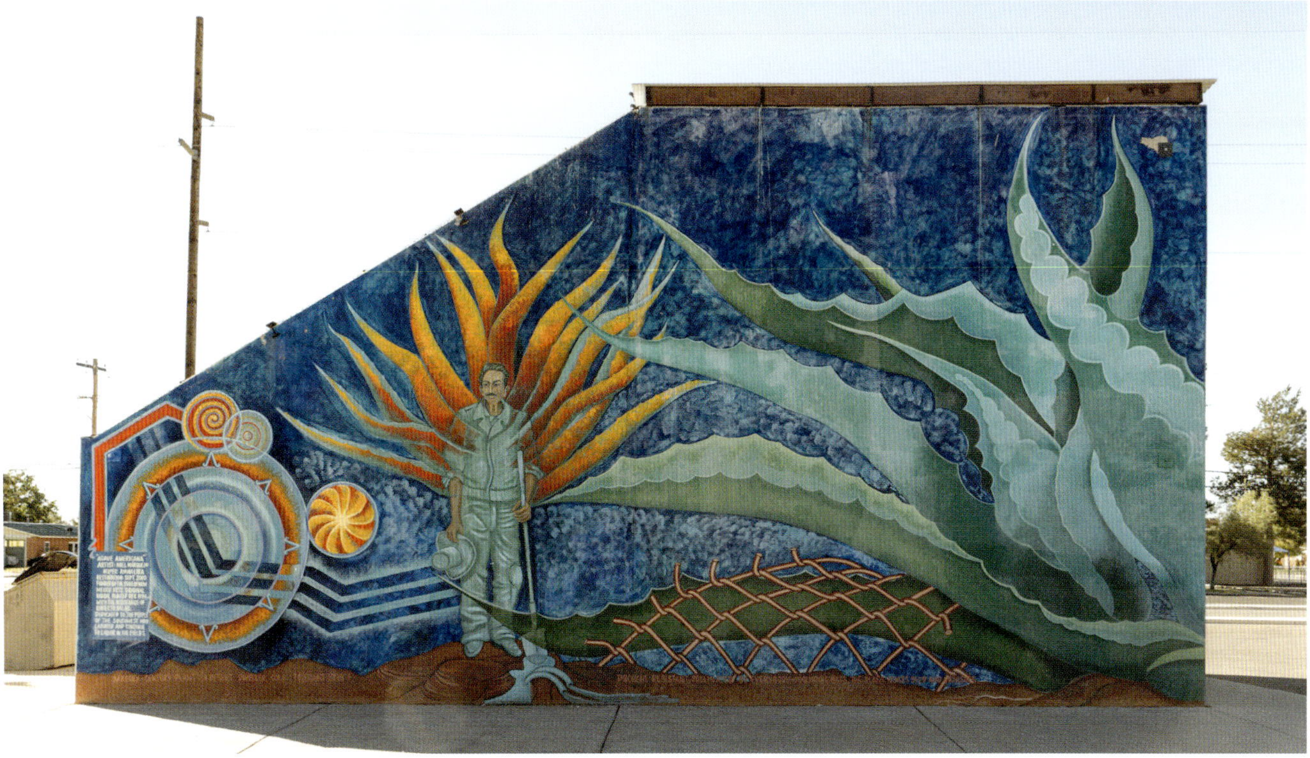

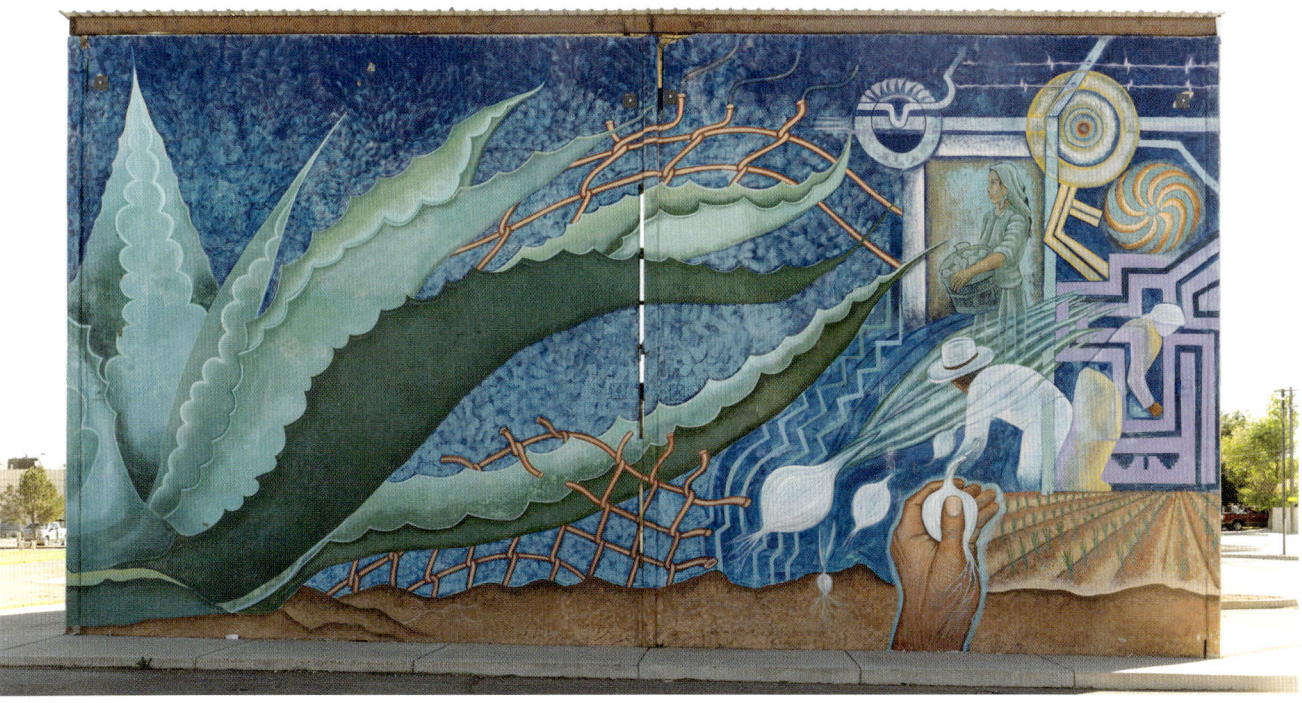

FIGURE 3.12 (*above*) Noel Márquez, Detail: *Agave Americana*, 1994. Acrylic. Mural restored in 2010. Martin Luther King Recreational Park Complex, Artesia, New Mexico. Photograph by Stefan Jennings Batista.

FIGURE 3.13 (*below*) Noel Márquez, *Agave Americana*, detail, 1994. Acrylic. Mural restored in 2010. Martin Luther King Recreational Park Complex, Artesia, New Mexico. Photograph by Stefan Jennings Batista.

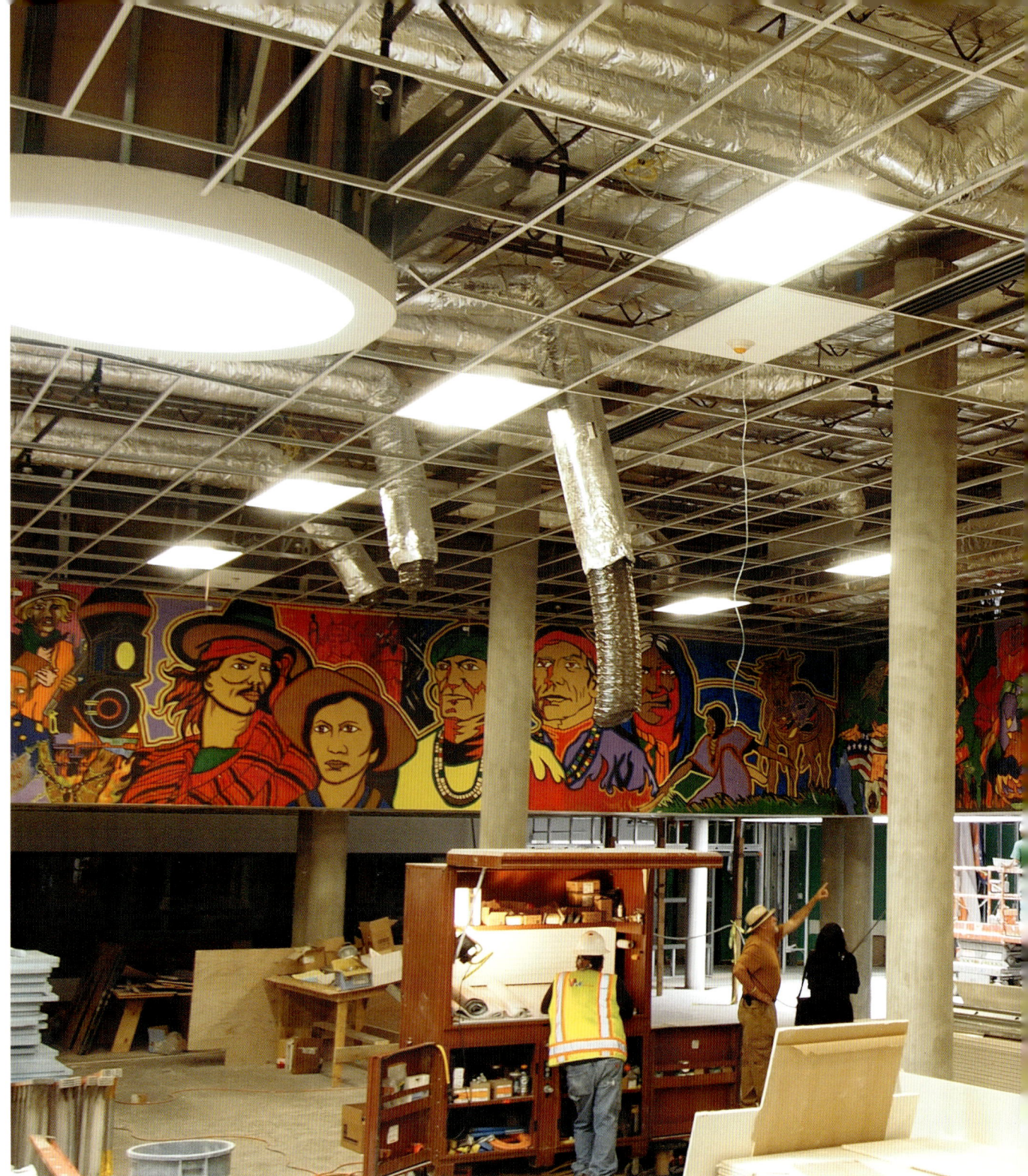

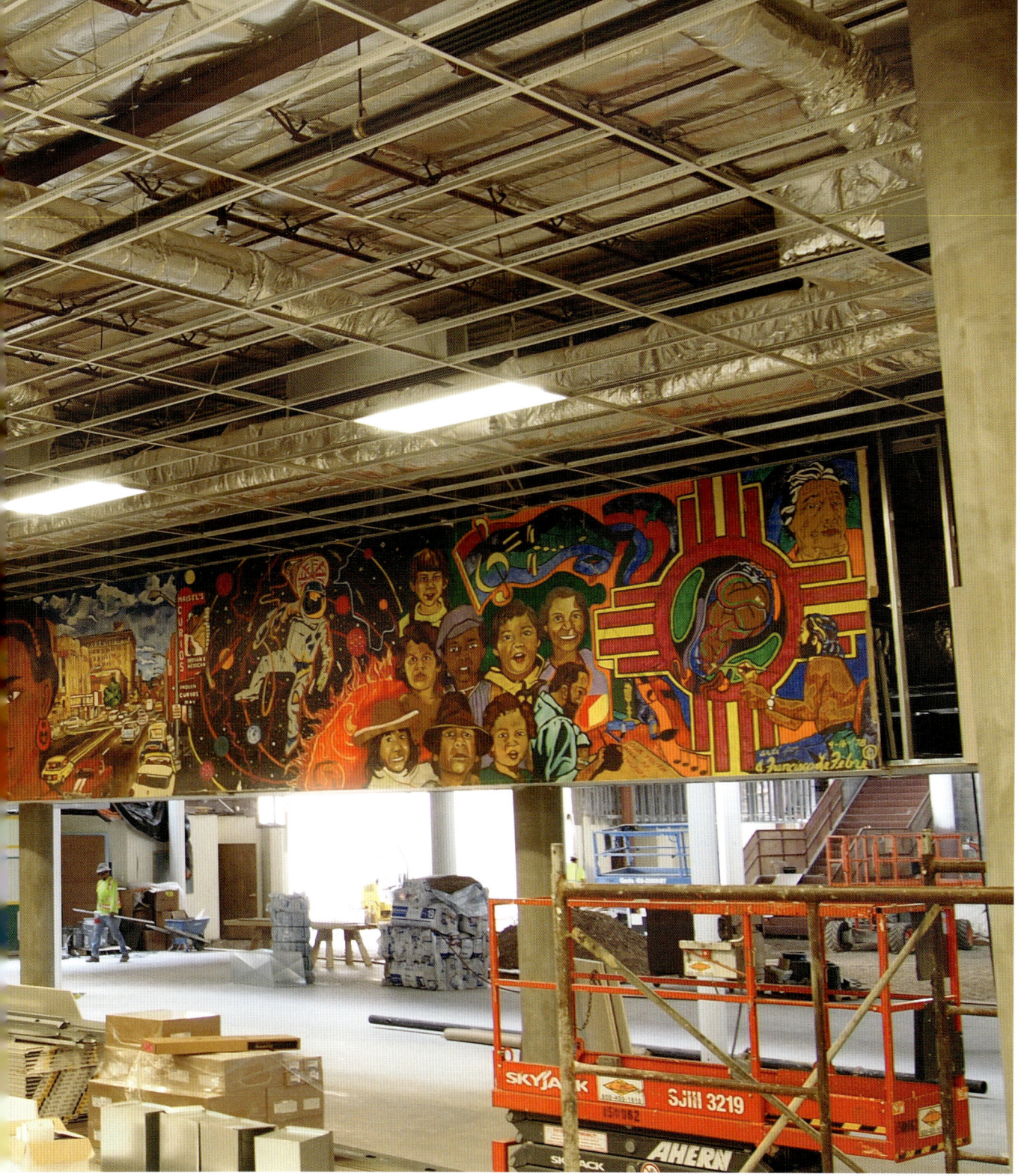

FIGURE 3.14. Francisco LeFebre, *Nuestra Juventud*, partial view, 1976–1978.
Acrylic. Albuquerque High School.

on the inner and outer walls of the building, boldly and lyrically rendered in the most public form of Chicano/a art, *murales*."[31]

The late 1960s and early 1970s served as a sparking point for the production of Chicana and Chicano murals in New Mexico. New Mexican Chicana and Chicano muralists displayed a variety of subjects, thematics, iconographic images, and stylistic influences that reflected local, national, and international influences. Like other muralists of the time, they did so by emphasizing their regional histories and experiences. Although New Mexican artists drew on popular iconography and images illustrated by Chicana and Chicano artists in the 1970s in California and Texas, rather than echoing social and political critiques, they reflected their nuanced and localized understandings of their social and material conditions. While drawing on modernist vernaculars, the Mexican art movement, and Indigenous influences, New Mexican artists contributed their interpretations of the detrimental impact of racialized capitalism, its attendant industrial war complex, and their combined deleterious effects on rural and semi-urban spaces. Additional research on the subject will diversify our understanding of Chicana and Chicano cultural production, which currently overlooks New Mexican artists in the formative and middle periods of the Chicana and Chicano Movement.

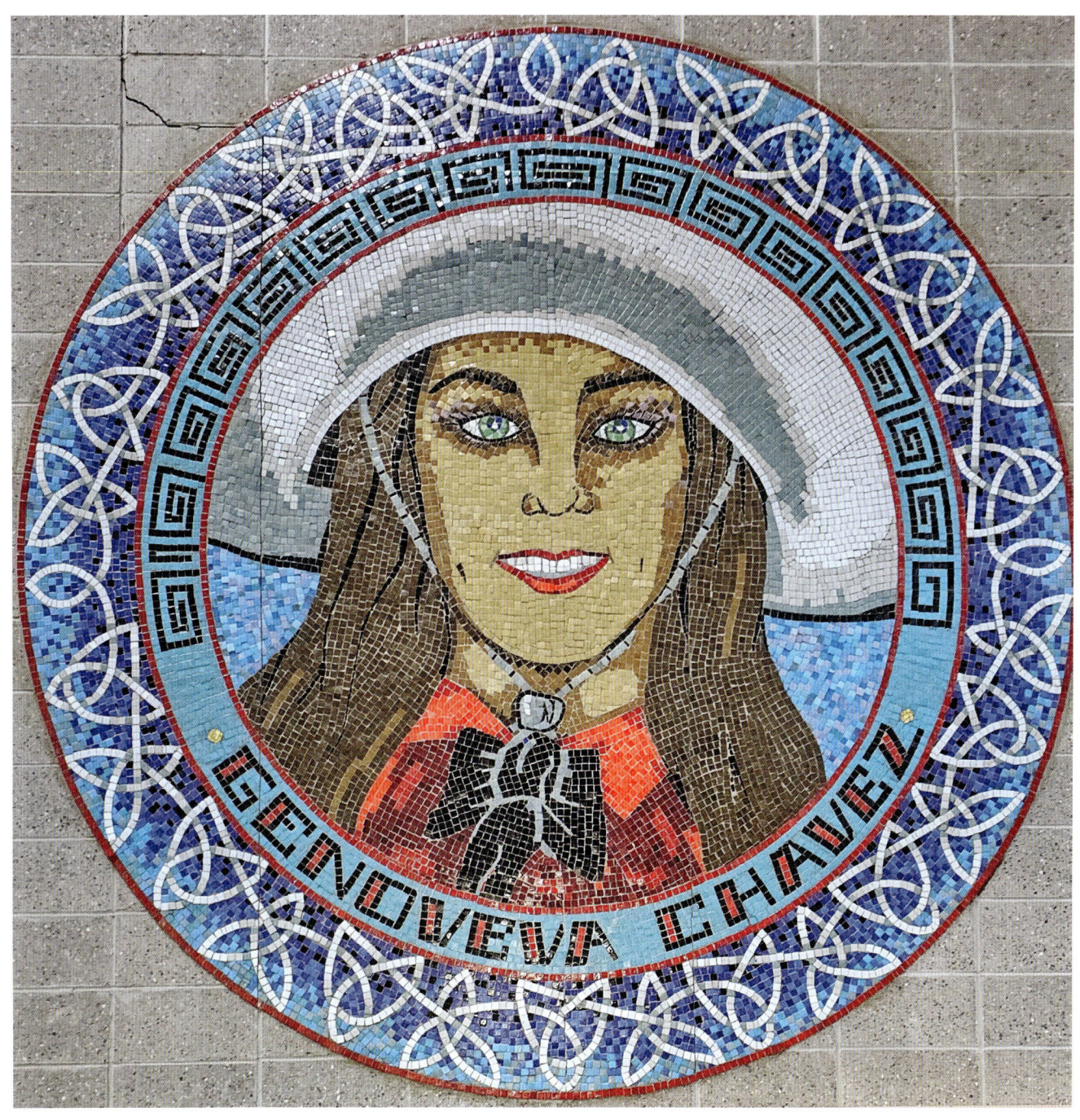

FIGURE 3.15. Sammy Leyba, *Genoveva Chavez*, 1999. Mosaic. Genoveva Chavez
Recreation Complex, Santa Fe, New Mexico. Photograph by Aaron
Anthony Anaya.

Select List of Chicana/o Murals in New Mexico

GRACIELA CARRILLO AND LINDA LOMA HAFTEWA

Panels 1 and 2, Institute of American Indian Arts, Sante Fe, New Mexico, 1978–1979.

EDWARD ARCENIO CHÁVEZ

Building a Sod House, Geneva Post Office Lobby, 1941.

FRANCISCO LEFEBRE

Highlands Murals, Student Union Building, New Mexico Highlands University, Las Vegas, New Mexico, 1971.

Migrant Building, New Mexico Highlands University, Las Vegas, New Mexico, 1973.

Chicano Studies, University of New Mexico, Albuquerque, New Mexico, 1974.

North Valley Multi-Service Center—City of Albuquerque, 1975 (collaboration with youth).

Longfellow Elementary School—Albuquerque Public Schools—Albuquerque, New Mexico, 1977.

Albuquerque High School—Albuquerque Public Schools, Albuquerque, New Mexico, 1978 (collaboration with youth).

Casa Armijo (indoor)—Albuquerque South Valley, Albuquerque, New Mexico, 1979.

Casa Armijo (outdoor)—Albuquerque South Valley, Albuquerque, New Mexico, 1980.

Santa Clara Catholic Church Altar—Wagon Mound, New Mexico, 1981.

East Central Multi-Service Center—City of Albuquerque, Albuquerque, New Mexico, 1982.

Highland Senior Citizen Center, City of Albuquerque, Albuquerque, New Mexico, 1985.

Parking Garage 4th Street and Copper NW—City of Albuquerque, Albuquerque, New Mexico, 1986 (collaboration with youth).

Conocimiento, Student Service Center—UNM—Albuquerque, New Mexico, 1989.

Hawthorn Elementary School—Albuquerque, Public Schools, Albuquerque, New Mexico, 1990.

La Amistad—Martinez Town—Albuquerque, New Mexico, 1991.

Barelas Community Center—Albuquerque, New Mexico, 1991.

Hogares School—Albuquerque, New Mexico, 1991 (collaboration with youth).

Luna Vocational Institute—Las Vegas, New Mexico, 1991.

Nuevo Mexico, Technical Vocational Institute—Albuquerque, New Mexico, 1991.

Piedra Lisa Dam—Albuquerque, New Mexico, 1993 (collaboration with youth).

San Jose Senior Citizen Center—Carlsbad, New Mexico, 1993.

Jaurequi Park Mural—Silver City, New Mexico, 1994.

Our History, Peace and Justice Center—Albuquerque, New Mexico, 2013 (collaboration with youth).

El Corazon, I—4th Street and Pacific SW—Albuquerque, New Mexico, 2015 (collaboration with youth).

La Gente, II—4th Street and Pacific SW—Albuquerque, New Mexico, 2016.

Jaquar, Atrisco Heritage Academy High School—Albuquerque, New Mexico, 2017.

LOS ARTES GUADALUPANOS DE AZTLÁN

Children's Park Mural, 1971.

La Clinica de la Gente Mural, 1971–1973.

St. Francis Drive Mural, Sante Fe, New Mexico, 1972.

Lady of Justice mural, Sante Fe, 1972.

Las Vegas High School Mural, Las Vegas, New Mexico, 1973.

The Studio, Los Artes Guadalupanos de Aztlán headquarters.

Community Law Center.

Crucifixion Mural.

SAMUEL LEYBA

El Museo Mural, Sante Fe, New Mexico.

Learning (restoration), Gonzales Elementary School, Sante Fe, New Mexico, 1995.

Duality and the Fifth Sun, Sante Fe, New Mexico, 1995.

Sign of the Times, Fort Marcy Recreation Complex, Sante Fe, New Mexico, 1996.

La Piedra del Sol, Sante Fe Community College Visual Arts Center, Sante Fe, New Mexico 1998.

Genoveva Chavez, Genoveva Chavez Recreation Complex, Santa Fe, New Mexico, 1999.

NOEL MÁRQUEZ

Lakewood Mural, New Mexico Labor Department, Artesia, New Mexico, 1996.

Agave Americana, Martin Luther King Recreational Park Complex, Artesia, New Mexico, 1994.

Eddy County Fair, Commissioned by the First National Bank of Artesia, New Mexico, 1994.

Bulldogmania, Commissioned by George Meshoto, Country Connection, Artesia, New Mexico, 1994.

Alimentando La Vida, St. Francis Medical Center, Carlsbad, New Mexico, 1996.

Rancher and Drillers, Lea County Event Center, Hobbs, New Mexico, 1996.

Caminos De Tiempo, Town Hall Council Chambers, Lake Arthur, New Mexico, 1996.

Con Cariño, Artesia Head Start School, Artesia, New Mexico, 1997.

La Tierra, collection of the artist, Artesia, New Mexico, 1997.

Tlalticpac, Del Cerro Multi-Purpose Facility, Mesquite, New Mexico, 1998.

Cosmovision, A traveling portable mural, collection of the artist, Artesia, New Mexico, 1999.

Artesian Landscape, Heritage Walkway, Artesia, New Mexico, 2004.

La Otra Voz, Guadalupe Park Archway, Commissioned by the City of Artesia, New Mexico, 2000.

Interstate Corridors, Albuquerque Freeway Corridors Artwork Enhancement Project, Albuquerque, New Mexico, 2001–03.

Señora De Gracia, mural, buon fresco, Commissioned by Our Lady of Grace Catholic Church, Artesia, New Mexico, 2001.

Curandera, Allied Health Center, Luna Community College, Commissioned by the Art in Public Spaces Program of the State of New Mexico, Las Vegas, New Mexico, 2005.

Dream of a Sunday Afternoon in Halagueno Pary, Carlsbad Public Library, Carlsbad, New Mexico, 2006.

Paisaje Petrolero, Riverside, Artesia, New Mexico, 2008.

Bowl of Champions, Bulldog Museum, Bulldog Bowl, New Mexico, 2009.

Agave Americana, Restoration of 1994 mural, Martin Luther King Recreational Park Complex, Artesia, New Mexico, 2010.

Journeys, Heartland Care Nursing Home, Artesia, New Mexico, 2013.

La Mula, 36″ × 50″, 1980, oil painting, Luna County Law Enforcement Complex, Deming, New Mexico, 2015.

Agave #2, Hagerman Joy Center, Hagerman, New Mexico, 2016.

ENRIQUETA VÁSQUEZ AND JUANITA J. LAVADIE

Un de Tierra, color acrylic, El Prado Liquor Store, El Prado, New Mexico 1977.

Notes

1. Throughout this essay, the coauthors use several terms to describe the artist's identity and cultural expressions. Chicana and Chicano are used because the artists featured in this study included these terms as a descriptor of their work. We also use nuevomexicana, nuevomexicano, and *Indo-Hispano* because they are a part of the lexicon used in self-identification to describe the people of New Mexico. When the term Chicanx is applied, it serves as an umbrella term to encapsulate different labels used by those who identify with multiple and sometimes overlapping labels, such as, Chicana/o, Mexicana/o, Latina/o, Hispana/o, Nuevomexicana/o, Hispanic, and Mexican American. As a group referent, Chicanx embodies the masculine form of Chicano, the feminine form of Chicana, and the non-gender-binary form of Chican@.

2. For a description of the emergence of specific Chicana muralism in the US, see "*Mujeres Muralistas*," The San Francisco Digital History Archive, 2011; https://www.foundsf.org/index.php?title=Mujeres_Muralistas.

3. See Shifra M. Goldman and Tomás Ybarro-Frausto, *Arte Chicano: A Comprehensive Annotated Bibliography of Chicano Art, 1965–1981* (Chicano Studies Library, 1985); Richard Griswold del Castillo, Teresa McKenna, and Yvonne Yarbro-Bejarano, eds., *Chicano Art: Resistance and Affirmation* (Wight Art Gallery, University of California, 1991); Alicia Gaspar de Alba, "A Theoretical Introduction: Alter-Native Ethnography," *Chicano Art Inside/ Outside the Master's House: Cultural Politics and the CARA Exhibition* (University of Texas Austin 1998); Laura E. Pérez, *Chicana Art: The Politics of Spiritual and Aesthetic Altarities* (Duke University Press, 2007); Guisela Latorre, *Walls of Empowerment: Chicana/o Indigenist Murals of California* (University of Texas, Press, 2008); and Shifra M. Goldman, *Dimensions of the Americas: Art and Social Change in Latin America and the United States* (University of Chicago Press, 1994).

4. Jackson, Carlos F., "Chicana and Chicano Art: Protest Arte," *Chicana and Chicano Art: Protest Arte* (University of Arizona Press, 2009), 1–24.

5. For Prehispanic Muralism see Celina B. Barrios de Senisterra, *Mesoamerican Open Spaces and Mural Paintings as Statements of Cultural Identity* (Cambridge Scholars Publishing, 2019) and Mary Ellen Miller, *The Art of Mesoamerica: From Olmec to Aztec*. Fifth edition. World of Art. Thames & Hudson, 2012. For modern Mexican muralism see Leonard Folgarait, *Mural Painting and Social Revolution in Mexico, 1920-1940: Art of the New Order* (Cambridge University Press, 1998); Anna Indych-López. *Muralism without Walls: Rivera, Orozco, and Siqueiros in the United States, 1927-1940* (Illuminations. University of Pittsburgh Press, 2009) ; Renato González Mello, et al. *Paint the Revolution: Mexican Modernism, 1910-1950* (Yale University Press, 2016); and Roberto Cantú, *Mexican Mural Art: Critical Essays on a Belligerent Aesthetic* (Cambridge Scholars Publishing, 2021).

6. For scholarship that explores the interactive influence on Mexican, US and French muralism see Margarita Nieto, "Mexican Art and Los Angeles, 1920–1940," Karlstrom, Paul J., ed., *On the Edge of America: California Modernist Art, 1900-1950.* (University of California Press, 1996). http://ark.cdlib.org/ark:/13030/ft5p30070c/; Fernandez-Barkan, Davida. *International Arte Popular: Mexican, American, and French Muralism 1920–1940.* PhD dissertation, Harvard University Graduate School of Arts and Sciences, 2023.

7. Holly Barnet-Sánchez, and Tim Dresher, *Give Me Life: Iconography and Identity in East L.A. Murals* (University of New Mexico Press, 2016).

8. Gómez-Quiñones, Juan, and Irene Vásquez, *Making Aztlán: Ideology and Culture of the Chicana and Chicano Movement, 1966–1977* (University of New Mexico Press, 2014), 44–47.

9. "Sante Fe New Mexico Murals," Bob Fitch Photography Archive, Department of Special Collections and University Archives, Stanford University. Stanford University's Department

of Special Collections and University Archives digitized many of their murals from 1971 to 1973, and they can be viewed on the library website https://exhibits.stanford.edu/fitch/browse/santa-fe-new-mexico-murals.

10. Pedro Rodríguez, "*Arte como expresion de del pueblo,*" *Metamorfosis: Northwest Chicano Magazine of Literature, Art, and Culture,* 3 and 4, no. 1 (Centro de Estudios Chicanos, University of Washington, 1981), 59–62.

11. Ray Hernández-Durán and Irene Vásquez, *Interview with Pedro Rodríguez,* Department of Chicana and Chicano Studies, University of New Mexico in Albuquerque, October 25, 2019.

12. Ray Hernández-Durán and Irene Vásquez, "'*Artistas del Pueblo*': In Conversation with the History of New Mexican Chicanx Art," *Hemisphere: Visual Cultures of the Americas,* Mandolen Sánchez (ed.), Vol. XII (Department of Art, University of New Mexico, 2019), 81–82.

13. See the section titled, "International Politics" in Lorena Oropeza and Dionne Espinoza, eds., *Enriqueta Vásquez and the Chicano Movement: Writings from El Grito del Norte* (Arte Público Press, 2006), 169–204.

14. Ray Hernández-Durán and Irene Vásquez, *Interview with Pedro Rodríguez.*

15. *El Taller de Gráfica Popular: Vida y Arte* (Georgia Museum of Art, University of Georgia, 2015).

16. See the essays titled "International Politics," by Enriqueta Vásquez in Lorena Oropeza and Dionne Espinoza, eds., *Enriqueta Vasquez and the Chicano Movement: Writings from El Grito del Norte* (Arte Público Press, 2006) 169–204.

17. Latorre, *Walls of Empowerment,* 2.

18. For a discussion of the social distinctions between Native Americans, Spaniards, *mestizos,* and *Genízaros* in New Mexico during the colonial period, see Ramón A. Gutiérrez, *When Jesus Came the Corn Mothers Went Away: Marriage, Sexuality, and Power in New Mexico, 1500–1846* (Stanford University Press, 1991), 148–51.

19. Ramón A. Gutiérrez, *When Jesus Came the Corn Mothers Went Away,* 148–51, and Moises Gonzales, "The Genízaro Land Grant Settlements of New Mexico," *Journal of the Southwest* 56, no. 4 (Winter 2014): 583.

20. Antonio Aguilar, "Un Puño De Tierra," Lyrics.com, STANDS4 LLC, 2023; https://www.lyrics.com/lyric/1414766/Antonio+Aguilar/Un+Pu%C3%B1o+De+Tierra.

21. Ariana Kramer, "Visions of Life and Death: Mural on a Liquor Store Wall in El Prado Holds More Significance Than You Think," *Taos News,* Jan 27, 2011; https://www.taosnews.com/news/vision-of-life-and-death-mural-on-a-liquor-store-wall-in-el-prado-holds/article_90926240-6ab0-5da5-989c-d180a388a38a.html.

22. David J. Weber, ed. *Foreigners in their Native Lands: Historical Roots of the Mexican Americans* (University of New Mexico Press, 2003), 132–33.

23. Alicia Gaspar de Alba, *Chicano Art: Inside Outside the Master's House* (University of Texas Press, 1998), 40.

24. Roxanne Dunbar-Ortiz, *Roots of Resistance: A History of Land Tenure in New Mexico* (University of Oklahoma Press, 2007), 5.

25. David Steinberg, Muralists Recall Distress When Their Creations Were Defaced," *Albuquerque Journal,* April 15, 1990.

26. Gaspar de Alba, *Chicano Art,* 39.

27. Tomás Ybarra-Frausto, "*Arte Chicano*: Images of a Community," in *Signs from the Heart: Heart: California Chicano Murals,* ed. Eva Cockcroft and Holly Barnet-Sánchez Cockcroft, (University of New Mexico Press, 1993), 56–7; and Constance Cortez, *Carmen Lomas Garza* (Chicano Studies Research Center, 2010).

28. Ray Hernández-Durán and Irene Vásquez, *Interview with Pedro Rodríguez,* 84.

29. Ray Hernández-Durán and Irene Vásquez, *Interview with Pedro Rodríguez,* 84.

30. Carlos F. Jackson, *Chicana and Chicano Art: ProtestArte* (University of Arizona Press, 2009) 74.

31. Gaspar de Alba, *Chicano Art: Inside Outside the Master's House,* 38.

Bibliography

Acosta, Teresa Palomo. *Handbook of Texas Online*. August 1, 1995. https://www.tshaonline.org/handbook/entries/chicano-mural-movement.

Acuña, Rudolfo. *Occupied America: The Chicano's Struggle Toward Liberation*. New York, New York: Harper and Row, 1972.

Aguilar, Antonio. "Un Puño De Tierra Lyrics," Lyrics.com, STANDS4 LLC, 2023; https://www.lyrics.com/lyric/1414766/Antonio+Aguilar/Un+Pu%C3%B1o+De+Tierra.

Barnet-Sanchez, Holly, and Tim Dresher. *Give Me Life: Iconography and Identity In East LA Murals*. University of New Mexico Press, 2016.

Barnett, Alan W. *Community Murals: The People's Art*. Associated University Presses Inc. Cornwall Books, 1984.

Barrios de Senisterra, Celina B. *Mesoamerican Open Spaces and Mural Paintings as Statements of Cultural Identity*. Cambridge Scholars Publishing, 2019.

Bebout, Lee. *Mythohistorical Interventions: The Chicano Movement and Its Legacies*. University of Minnesota Press, 2011.

Cantú, Roberto. *Mexican Mural Art: Critical Essays on a Belligerent Aesthetic*. Cambridge Scholars Publishing, 2021.

Chavez, John R. "Aliens in Their Native Lands: The Persistence of Internal Colonial Theory," *Journal of World History* 22 (2011): 785–809.

Cockcroft, Eva, and Holly Barnet-Sanchez. *Signs from the Heart: California Chicano Murals*. University of New Mexico Press, 1993.

Cockcroft, Eva, W Jon Pitman, and James Cockcroft. *Toward a People's Art*. E. P. Dutton and Company, 1977.

Cortez, Constance. *Carmen Lomas Garza*. Chicano Studies Research Center, 2010.

de Orellana, Juan Carlos. *Gramsci on Hegemony. Not Even Past*. May 26, 2015. https://notevenpast.org/gramsci-on-hegemony/.

Deverell, William F. *The Return of Blue Lake to the Taos Pueblo. The Princeton University Library Chronicle* 49, no. 1 (Autumn 1987): 57–60.

Dunbar-Ortiz, Roxanne. *Roots of Resistance: A History of Land Tenure in New Mexico*. University of Oklahoma Press, 2007.

Enger, Reed. *Art History Methodologies: Eight Ways to Understand Art*. 1987. https://arthistoryproject.com/essays/art-history-methodologies/.

Fernandez, Justino, and Joshua C. Taylor. *A Guide to Mexican Art*. University of Chicago Press, 1961.

Folgarait, Leonard. *Mural Painting and Social Revolution in Mexico, 1920–1940: Art of the New Order*. Cambridge University Press, 1998.

Garcia, Ignacio M. *Chicanismo: The Forging of a Militant Ethos Among Mexican Americans*. University of Arizona Press, 1997.

Gaspar de Alba, Alicia. *Chicano Art: Inside Outside the Master's House*. University of Texas Press, 1998.

Goldman, Shifra M. *Dimensions of the Americas: Art and Social Change in Latin America and the United States*. University of Chicago Press, 1994.

Goldman, Shifra M. "The Iconography of Chicano Self-Determination: Race, Ethnicity, and Class," *Art Journal*, no. 49 (1990), 167–73.

Goldman, Shifra M. "Mexican Muralism: Its Social-Educative Roles in Latin America and The United States," *International Journal of Chicano Studies Research* (1982): 111–33.

Goldman, Shifra M., and Tomás Ybarro-Frausto. *Arte Chicano: A Comprehensive Annotated Bibliography of Chicano Art, 1965–1981*. Chicano Studies Library, 1985.

Gómez-Quiñones, Juan, and Irene Vásquez. *Making Aztlán: Ideology and Culture of the Chicana and Chicano Movement, 1966–1977.* University of New Mexico Press, 2014.

Gonzales, Phillip B. *Expressing New Mexico: Nuevomexicano Creativity, Ritual, And Memory.* The University of Arizona Press, 2007.

González Mello, Renato et al. *Paint the Revolution: Mexican Modernism, 1910–1950.* Yale University Press, 2016.

Gramsci, Antonio. *Selections from Prison Notebooks: Problems of Marxism.* New York International Publishers, 1973.

Gutiérrez, Ramón A. *When Jesus Came the Corn Mothers Went Away: Marriage, Sexuality, and Power in New Mexico, 1500–1846.* Stanford University Press 1991.

Hernández-Durán, Ray, and Irene Vásquez. "'*Artistas del Pueblo*': In Conversation with the History of New Mexican Chicanx Art," *Hemisphere: Visual Cultures of the Americas,* edited by Mandolen Sánchez, Vol. XII (Department of Art, University of New Mexico, 2019) 80–97.

Hernández-Durán, Ray, and Irene Vásquez. *Interview with Pedro Rodríguez,* Department of Chicana and Chicano Studies, University of New Mexico in Albuquerque, October 25, 2019.

Indych-López, Anna. *Muralism without Walls: Rivera, Orozco, and Siqueiros in the United States, 1927–1940.* Illuminations. University of Pittsburgh Press, 2009. https://search-ebscohostcom.libproxy.unm.edu/login.aspx?direct=true&db=cat05987a&AN=unm.326552736&site=eds-live&scope=site.

Jackson, Carlos F. *Chicana and Chicano Art: ProtestArte.* University of Arizona Press, 2009.

Jameson, Fredric. *Representing Capital.* New York: Verso, 2011.

Jameson, Fredric. *Valences of the Dialectic.* Verso, 2009.

Korb, Katrina, A. *Calculating Descriptive Statistics.* April 15, 2021. http://korbedpsych.com/R17bDescriptive.html.

Korb, Katrina, A. *Conducting Educational Research / Steps in Conducting a Research Study* (2013) http://korbedpsych.com/R17bDescriptive.html.

Kramer, Ariana, "Visions of Life and Death: Mural on a Liquor Store Wall in El Prado Holds More Significance Than You Think," *Taos News,* Jan 27, 2011; https://www.taosnews.com/news/vision-of-life-and-death-mural-on-a-liquor-store-wall-in-el-prado-holds/article_90926240–6ab0–5da5–989c-d180a388a38a.html.

Kroll, Eric. "Murals in New Mexico," *ArtForum* 12, no. 1 (1973): 55–57.

Latorre, Guisela. *Walls of Empowerment: Chicana/o Indigenist Murals of California.* University of Texas Press, 2008.

Lomeli, Francisco A., Victor A. Sorell, and Genaro M. Padilla. *Nuevomexicano: Cultural Legacy Forms, Agencies, and Discourse.* University of New Mexico Press, 2002.

Mercado, Juan P. "Judy Baca, SPARC, and A Chicana Mural Movement: Reconstructing U.S. History Through Public Art," Unpublished Dissertation, University of California, Los Angeles, 2018.

Miller, Mary Ellen. *The Art of Mesoamerica : From Olmec to Aztec.* Fifth edition. World of Art. Thames & Hudson, 2012. https://search-ebscohost-com.libproxy.unm.edu/login.aspx?direct=true&db=cat05987a&AN=unm.792747355&site=eds-live&scope=site.

"*Mujeres Muralistas,*" The San Francisco Digital History Archive, 2011. https://www.foundsf.org/index.php?title=Mujeres_Muralistas.

Nieto-Phillips, John M., *The Language of Blood: The Making of Spanish-American Identity in New Mexico, 1880s–1930s.* University of New Mexico Press, 2004.

Oropeza, Lorena. *The King of Adobe: Reies López Tijerina, Lost Prophet of the Chicano Movement.* The University of North Carolina Press, 2019.

Oropeza, Lorena, and Dionne Espinoza, eds. *Enriqueta Vasquez and the Chicano Movement: Writings from El Grito del Norte*. Arte Público Press, 2006.

Panofsky, Erwin. *Studies in Iconology: Humanistic Themes in The Art of The Renaissance*. Oxford University Press, 1938.

Pérez, Laura E. *Chicana Art: The Politics of Spiritual and Aesthetic Altarities*. Duke University Press, 2007.

Rodríguez, Roberto. "The Origins and History of the Chicano Movement," *Julian Samora Research Institute JSRI Occasional Paper, #7* (1996), 1–7.

Rodríguez, Pedro. "*Arte como expresión del pueblo*," *Metamorfosis: Northwest Chicano Magazine of Literature, Art, and Culture* 3 and 4, no. 1. Centro de Estudios Chicanos, University of Washington, 1981: 59–62.

"Sante Fe New Mexico Murals," Bob Fitch Photography Archive, Department of Special Collections and University Archives, Stanford University; https://exhibits.stanford.edu/fitch/browse/santa-fe-new-mexico-murals.\

Steinberg, David. "Muralists Recall Distress When Their Creations Were Defaced," *Albuquerque Journal*, April 15, 1990.

Stewart, Ron. *Looking Back 500 Years: The Tiguex War, National Park Service* (2017); https://www.nps.gov/coro/learn/historyculture/the-tiguex-war.htm.

Thipphawong, Laura. *Art Theory: Iconography* (2020) https://www.artshelp.net/art-theoryiconography.

Weber, David J., Wd. *Foreigners in their Native Lands: Historical Roots of the Mexican Americans*. University of New Mexico Press, 2003.

Four

Mud, Wool, and Wood

Contested Materiality and Land-Based Activism in Chicano Art of

New Mexico, Late 1960s–Early 1980s

SONJA ELENA GANDERT

"I have modernized *enjarrando*. It is now a living organism, and it will
adapt, like all living organisms must adapt, to the demands of the twentieth
century."[1]

—

By 1976, New Mexico's archetypal adobe architecture was under siege on multiple fronts. At least, that is, according to Taos-born artist Anita O. Rodríguez. Writing in the foreword to *Mud Space & Spirit: Handmade Adobes*, a publication that showcased an array of uniquely idiosyncratic owner-built adobe houses scattered throughout northern New Mexico, Rodríguez warned that the centuries-old earthen building practice ran the risk of "slowly melting back into the earth from which it grew."[2] Her prognosis stemmed from two separate but complementary concerns: on one hand, New Mexico's *enjarradoras* (adobe plasterers), who had for generations served as the keepers of this ancestral knowledge, were growing old, placing their practices at risk of disappearance. On the other, a more recent vogue in domestic architecture of using a waterproof cement stucco coating to cover old adobe walls, ostensibly obviating the need for annual replastering, was producing unexpected consequences. As Rodríguez wrote, "Cement and earth are incompatible, they expand and contract at different rates. The inside of cement plaster sweats. Adobe not only expands and contracts—it settles. Rigid cement cannot respond to the movement of adobe and eventually the cement must crack. Water seeps in, freezing, thawing, and deteriorating the walls. All this happens behind an innocent looking exterior until the day of reckoning."[3]

Best known for her handmade custom *fogones* (fireplaces), Rodríguez's timely description of the incommensurability of adobe and stucco walls serves as an apt metaphor for a particular set of contradictions faced by Chicano artists active in northern New

Mexico from the late 1960s to early 1980s: the desire to make art that was both informed by longstanding tradition and responsive to contemporary sociopolitical concerns (fig. 4.1). Rodríguez was a formidable presence in Taos's artistic and cultural sphere during the 1970s and 1980s, performing roles as both a professional enjarradora and licensed contractor and as an artist-activist, community educator, and writer, leading workshops for adults and children on the historical and technical tenets of *enjarrando* and spearheading the preservation of historic adobe buildings. Working against the fertile backdrop of politically charged activist mobilization aligned with the local and national Chicano civil rights movement to address issues such as the struggles for land, water, and environmental justice and against gentrification, artists participated in an ecosystem of interlocking and coactive artist-activist collectives and organizations. Amid this dynamic and impassioned surge of activity, they found their footing at the threshold of cultural revindication and preservation, but on terms that resisted the homogenizing strictures that dominated the tourist apparatus in cities such as Santa Fe and Taos. Invested in a particular vision of New Mexican culture, the

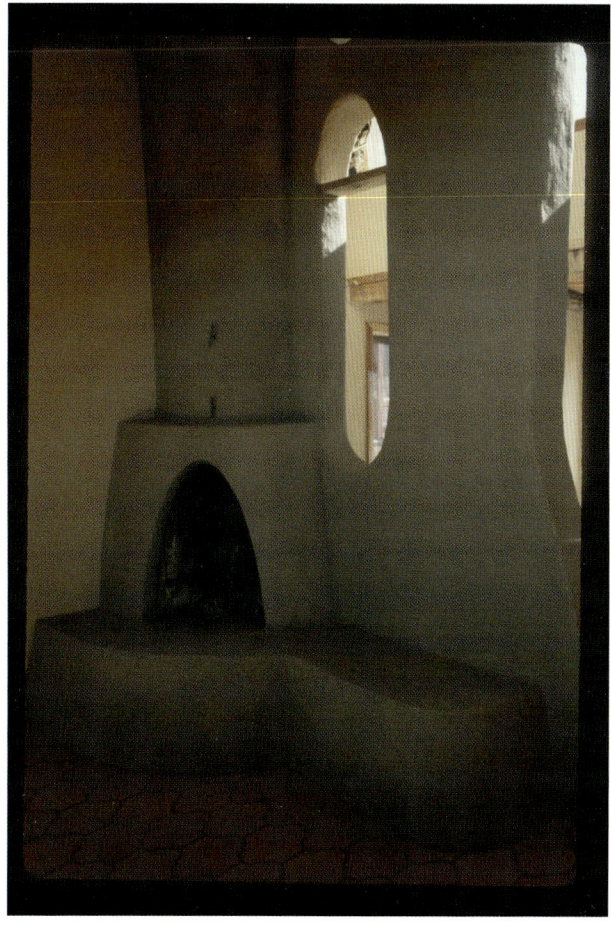

FIGURE 4.1. Anita O. Rodríguez, *Fireplace in Toby Varos's Residence*, 1980. Courtesy of Anita O. Rodríguez, Taos, New Mexico.

mainstream institutions in these cities, particularly those that promoted so-called Spanish Colonial art, imposed a regimented set of guidelines of putative authenticity in order to participate. These guidelines left little space for the experimentation and politically charged interventions that many artists involved in the Chicano movement endeavored to undertake. The creation of infrastructures operated by and for them thus laid the foundation for the renewed Chicano artistic practices discussed here.

Beginning in the late 1960s, Chicano artists of all stripes converged throughout the state under the aegis of grassroots organizations, artist collectives, and other local initiatives established to resist the discrimination, erasure, and paternalistic art world and market dictates frequently imposed on *nuevomexicanos*. Among the groups that emerged were La Academia de la Nueva Raza and its later incarnation as the Río Grande Institute (Dixon), La Escuelita

(Española), and La Cofradía de Artes y Artesanos Hispánicos (Santa Fe), as well as the muralist group Los Artes Guadalupanos de Aztlán (Santa Fe). These organizations complemented the work of local publications such as *El Grito del Norte* (Española), a newspaper first founded as the official mouthpiece of Reies López Tijerina's Alianza Federal de las Mercedes that later expanded its coverage to connect Native American and Chicano social issues in New Mexico to parallel Chicano, Black, and Indigenous civil rights struggles throughout the US, as well as Third World liberation movements internationally.[4] Bolstered by this dynamic climate, artists working in both conventional fine arts media and those artisanal practices often referred to as folk art, craft, or traditional arts benefited from previously unheard of opportunities to showcase their work. Of note were contemporary artists' efforts to revive practices hitherto in decline among nuevomexicano populations: *santero* woodcarving, Río Grande and Chimayó style weaving, *colcha* embroidery, inlaid straw marquetry, and punched tinwork, to name a few. Thus, Rodríguez's renewed engagement with adobe techniques mirrors the work of numerous other artists invested in the preservation and reclamation of practices that had been at best co-opted and at worst rendered nearly obsolete. These 1970s artistic reclamations echoed, yet also diverged significantly from, New Deal–era revivals of these so-called traditional practices, the driving forces of which had often been outsiders.

I examine here an array of New Mexican Chicano artists whose work, like Rodríguez's, makes use of or otherwise engages directly with "living" materials (to use her term)—in this case, mud, wool, and wood. Though not constituting a wholly unified group, the artists under discussion exhibited under the banner of both the Chicano art movement and as contemporary "Hispanic" artists. They also participated in the abovementioned organizations and artist collectives, and aligned themselves with the land-based, environmental, and anti-development activist mobilizations that were occurring in their communities.

Rodríguez's theorization of adobe as "living architecture" elucidates the real and conceptual analogues between New Mexico's ubiquitous earthen buildings, the land, and the body. In her words, "Although as smooth as human skin, the walls are not mechanically flat and evoke a sense of living earth—'*Madre Tierra*' to the *enjarradora*.'"[5] In a later interview, she added, "Mud is the flesh of the earth. Stones are the bones."[6] Rodríguez's cousin and fellow artist Juanita J. Lavadie, also of Taos, describes the similarly responsive capacities of the wool that she, an accomplished weaver, learned to spin into yarn to create her signature Río Grande–style textiles: "Wool is a natural insulator. The wool fibers breathe. Wool retains the body heat, and in some cases, can keep the body cool in excessively hot climates. Wool also has more resistance than cotton and most other fibers to flame, which makes an excellent blanket for working outdoors near the campfire."[7] Similarly integral to nuevomexicanos' daily life in both secular and spiritual ways is what Chicano studies scholars Devon G. Peña and Rubén O. Martínez have characterized as a "rich material culture based on the careful use of wood," citing both furniture making and saint-carving as evidence.[8] Alongside this emphasis on care in craftsmanship emerges a corresponding resistance to capitalist consumption among the earlier generations whose legacies the Chicano artists endeavored to preserve. In an oral history conducted in the early 1970s by Robert Coles, Dolores García, an elder from the woodcarving hub of Córdova, New Mexico, corroborates this view after appreciatively gesturing to a suite of wooden furniture—a table, twelve chairs, beds, a bureau—all built by hand by her husband. As she states, "This is what I would like to say about Domingo: he plants, builds, and harvests, he tries to keep us alive and sleep on what he has put together. We have never had a spring on our bed, but I have to admit, we bought our mattress. Buying, that is the sickness. I have gone to the city and watched people. They are hungry, but nothing satisfies their hunger. They come to stores like flies to sticky paper; they are caught."[9] In his 1973 publication *Abiquiu y Don Cacahuate: A Folk History of a New Mexican Village*, G. Benito Córdova recounts an example of community resourcefulness and a move from sacred to secular in the 1937 construction of the new church of Santo Tomás in Abiquiú, wherein the *vigas* (wooden beams) from the old sanctuary were repurposed to construct the floor of a new dance hall.[10] Like wool and mud, wood possesses an innate porosity, mutability, and responsiveness to elements. Particularly during a period in which modernization and rampant environmental overreach by the government and corporations rendered access to natural resources ever more complicated, a new generation of New Mexican Chicano artists embraced the tensions of "living" materiality at risk of decline as a counter to the forces that sought to commodify and erase it in equal measure.[11]

Chicano Art in New Mexico: A Material Paradox

It would not be a stretch to suggest that New Mexican Chicano artists have been sidelined in discussions of the Chicano art movement. Indeed, I have heard the false claim made on more than one occasion that there were no Chicano artists in New Mexico during the early years of the *movimiento*. Such misconceptions may stem in part from the oversimplified assumption that all nuevomexicanos uniformly identify as Spanish, placing them at odds with the Chicano movement's emphasis on Mexican and Indigenous cultural roots.[12] Yet in a place whose significance to the Chicano movement is so well documented—Reies López Tijerina's land grant activism in northern New Mexico being the most prominent example—it would be unusual not to find a parallel efflorescence in artistic production. Though often given more prominence than Chicano artists in New Mexico working in more conventional fine arts media, I argue that Chicano artists working in "traditional" modes are either overlooked or treated as exceptional in dominant narratives on Chicano art.[13] This framing—wittingly or not—creates the false impression that in its recurrence to tradition, their work contains a less explicitly political message than more overt statements communicated through muralism, the graphic arts, and other art forms more commonly associated with the movement.

The tension between the apparently depoliticized "traditional" arts and the Chicano movement's activist impetus becomes particularly marked in the ways that curators and scholars during the period under study have presented the work of Chicano artists working in so-called traditional modes. On one hand, it has often been presumed to be self-evident, given the prevalence of Spanish Colonial art in the visual inventory of New Mexico's cultural heritage, that artists would continue to adhere to the artistic precedents set by previous generations. Yet limiting our understanding of their production to the continuation of historical legacies denies them creative agency and fails to acknowledge impulses to innovate and diverge from convention. Moreover, New Mexico Chicano artists' works are seldom explicitly linked to the activism that was flourishing in their communities and in which they were frequently personally involved. This essay aims to reinscribe the lines between Chicano artists in New Mexico and the land-based mobilizations that surrounded them, thereby complicating our understanding of New Mexican artists as exceptional, as less activated by political imperatives, than practitioners of Chicano art elsewhere in the US. Instead, I posit that the primacy of land-based activism to their work and lives has itself played a role in propelling investment in what I conceive of as an embodied materiality of land and place that pays tribute to an ancestral past while simultaneously contending with the demands of the present.

The incorporation of New Mexican artists into survey exhibitions of Chicano art has been spotty at best.[14] One notable exception occurred in 1983, when the Los Angeles–based art historian Shifra M. Goldman curated a National Endowment for the Arts–funded exhibition at the Social and Public Arts Research Center (SPARC), an organization co-founded by Chicana artist Judith F. Baca, located in Venice, California. A recognized specialist in both Mexican and Chicano art history, Goldman was one of the earliest chroniclers of the movement. However, given her location, her knowledge of Chicano contexts outside of California came somewhat belatedly, as she expanded her repertoire to incorporate Texan and later New Mexican artists during the 1970s.[15] Her heightened engagement with the full geographic breadth of Chicano art can be observed in her participation in the 1979 Conferencia Plástica Chicana in Austin, Texas, organized by artists from the feminist collective Mujeres Artistas del Suroeste, as well as the ongoing research she was conducting to prepare for the publication of the magisterial 1985 compilation *Arte Chicano: A Comprehensive Annotated Bibliography of Chicano Art, 1965–1981*, coedited with Tomás Ybarra-Frausto.[16] During the early 1980s, Goldman came into contact with Rodríguez, Lavadie, and fellow weaver and collaborator Teresa Archuleta-Sagel, an Española-born artist who at the time was married to novelist Jim Sagel.[17] Goldman also met Tomás Atencio, cofounder of La Academia de la Nueva Raza, who along with the aforementioned artists, was instrumental in bolstering her knowledge of art and politics in the state. During a 1983 recorded conversation with Atencio, plainly intended to further her research, she demonstrated a still incipient knowledge of New Mexico's history and geography, as well as of internecine conflicts and divergences between northern and southern populations in the state.[18] Her emerging expertise aside, these connections led Goldman to include a handful of nuevomexicana artists in the SPARC exhibition. Similarly, and with some overlap, including Archuleta-Sagel and Lavadie, several New Mexican artists were included in *A través de la frontera*, an exhibition of Mexican American artists organized by the Centro de Estudios Económicos y Sociales del Tercer Mundo and the Instituto de Investigaciones Estéticas at Universidad Nacional Autónoma de México, for which Goldman contributed a catalog essay and substantial curatorial input, including selecting and gathering many of the artworks for shipment to Mexico. The exhibition opened in August 1983 at the Museo Universitario del Chopo in Mexico City. Later that year, in December 1983, Goldman's exhibition at SPARC, *Chicana Voices and Visions: A National Exhibit of Women Artists*, opened as well.

Goldman's curatorial choices in *Chicana Voices and Visions* reify the perception that artists from New Mexico (in this case all women) favor so-called traditional arts over more conventional fine arts media. The show featured twenty-seven Chicana artists hailing from California, Texas, Arizona, Colorado, and New Mexico, as well as Michigan. Somewhat surprisingly, the Midwest Mexican American hub of Chicago was not represented. Of the artists in the exhibition, the largest number (twelve) were from California, including recognized artists such as Ester Hernández and Yolanda López. Texas had six artists represented, Arizona and Colorado had only one artist each, and one Texas-born, Michigan-based artist, Nora Mendoza, was included as well. The rest of the artists—six in total—hailed from New Mexico. Given Goldman's expertise and background, the robust presence of New Mexican artists is surprising.

The works in the exhibition ran the gamut in terms of medium—including drawing, painting, printmaking, sculpture (including both fiber and cast ceramic), book arts, and Diane Gamboa's leopard-spotted "paper fashion." However, with only one exception the New Mexican artists showed work that would typically be classified as "traditional," by which I mean aligning with a circumscribed array of craft practices (woodcarving, weaving, ceramics, and adobe) that have been codified as part of a New Mexico's Hispano historical legacy.[19]

Lavadie and Archuleta-Sagel both exhibited weavings. Archuleta-Sagel's *Electric Ikat* (1981) is a vegetal-dyed wool textile composed of thick bands of deep red weave punctuated by segmented white forms (fig. 4.2). Alternating beige and white stripes surround the larger bands. Ikat, a word of Malay origin meaning "to tie" or "to bind," is a resist-dyeing method found throughout Asia and Latin America in which the yarn is wrapped or twisted before the dye is applied, producing patterns that only emerge once the weaving is finished. Believed to have arrived in New Mexico via Mexico in the early 1800s, only a few extant

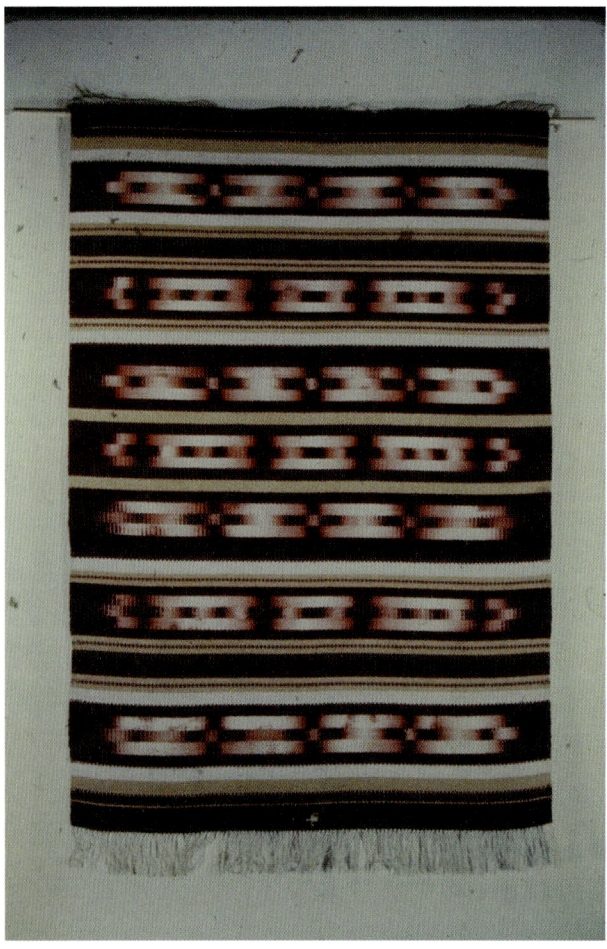

FIGURE 4.2. Teresa Archuleta-Sagel, *Electric Ikat*, 1981. Wool yarn and vegetal dye, 56 ½″ × 30″. Collection of the Albuquerque Museum. Shifra M. Goldman Papers, CEMA 119. Department of Special Research Collections, UC Santa Barbara Library.

examples of historical weft ikat survive.[20] In Archuleta-Sagel's rendition, the patterns produced by the preordained designs of the wrapped and dyed fibers create a dizzying, gradient blur effect. Though less flashy, in Lavadie's *Adivinanza (Prophecy)* (1982), pared-down bands of dark and bright red, blue, white, and black are interspersed with larger fields of heather gray to showcase the vibrancy of natural dyes (fig. 4.3). As she wrote in her artist statement, "This work evolves out of change, working towards the finer yarns I have been spinning. The title points at the innuendos in communication and in changes, because it's never just a black and white story."[21]

Linda Martínez de Pedro, a Chimayó-based *santera* (saint carver) also known for her disability activism and advocacy, exhibited two retablos in *Chicana Voices and Visions*, one titled *Anunciación (Virgen de las Rosas)* (1981), and the other *Nuestro Señor de los Trabajos* (1982).[22] Camilla Trujillo exhibited two ceramic pieces, *The Gift* and *Bailadora* (Dancer), both from 1983. According to the artist's statement, *Bailadora* was finished with golden and beige micaceous clay slip gathered from Taos, Picuris, and Abiquiú, and *The Gift* with white slip from Kha-'Po Owingeh (Santa Clara Pueblo).[23] The practice of using naturally occurring micaceous (mica-infused) clay to create glittery surfaced decorative vessels and objects has a long history in Pueblo pottery, particularly in P'ɴwweltha (Picuris Pueblo) and t'óynemɴ (Taos Pueblo), and experienced a major revival in the 1980s.[24] Micaceous clay is also used as an *alís*, or slip finish, on adobe walls to impart a shimmery gleaming effect, indirectly creating a visual parallel between the clay vessels and an adobe kitchen in which they might have been stored. Trujillo's statement in the exhibition catalog echoes Rodríguez's understanding of earthen materials: "I don't consider the clay to be an inanimate object. I approach it with the same respect that I would any living thing."[25]

The exhibition likewise positioned Rodríguez's adobe creations as artworks in their own right. While no mud nor architectural elements made their way into the gallery, Rodríguez's practice was presented in the form of a didactic display consisting of two matted photographs showing an interior view of an ornate, hand-sculpted fireplace with a Río Grande–style weaving hanging alongside it (the two photographs appear to show the same fireplace and interior setting) (fig. 4.4). The two smaller photographs flank a larger architectural drawing with cross-sectional and exterior drawings and accompanying text detailing the construction process of an adobe fireplace. Below the drawing, Rodríguez assembled an assortment of images (in correspondence with Goldman, she referred to it as a "photomural") showing several of her completed fireplaces, an adobe brickyard, and process photographs of the construction of the firebox, of the plastering (enjarrando), and of the gathering of colored clays to prepare the alís.[26] Other images show iconic landmarks of New Mexico, including both ancient Indigenous architectural sites and more recent constructions as the San Francisco de Asís church in Ranchos de Taos, built in the early 1800s. Rodríguez draws a clear visual analogue between the sinuous rounded forms of the church, whose silhouette and volumes have long elicited modernist fascination, and one of her fireplaces by superimposing the image of the fireplace onto the corner of the image of the church. A text at the center of the photomural reads, "The ancient earth-building people converged here and gave birth to certain unique architectural forms and traditions. One of these is the adobe fireplace." Each of the images is numbered and referenced in captions on a sheet of paper to the left of the installation.

The final New Mexican artist included in *Chicana Voices and Visions*, Pola López, was the only painter in the group. Her exhibited painting nonetheless thematizes land and the body in ways that suggest kinship to the work of the other New Mexican Chicanas and

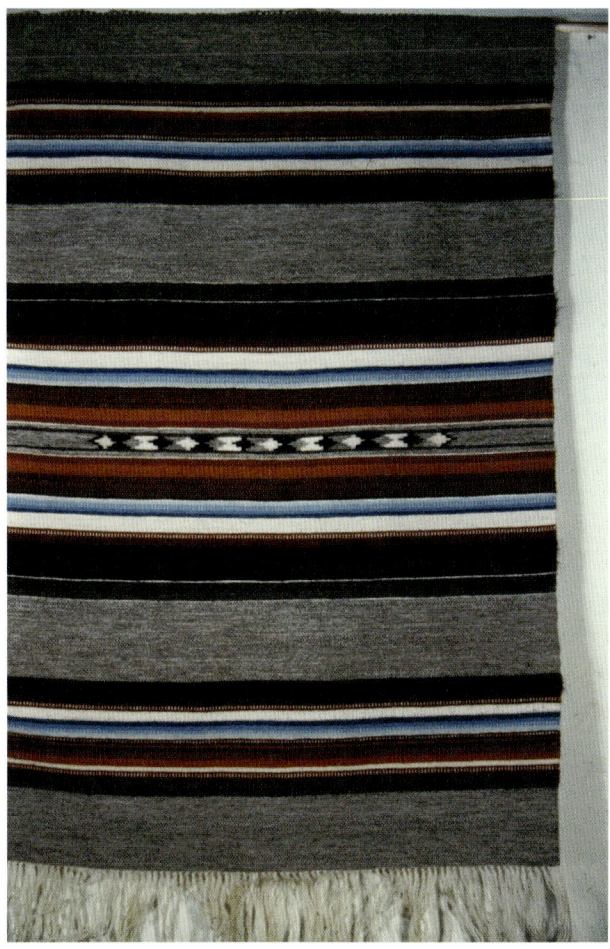

FIGURE 43. Juanita Jaramillo Lavadie, *Adivinanza (Prophecy)*, 1982. Vegetal dye, commercial wool, homespun wool, and homespun alpaca. Shifra M. Goldman Papers, CEMA 119. Department of Special Research Collections, UC Santa Barbara Library.

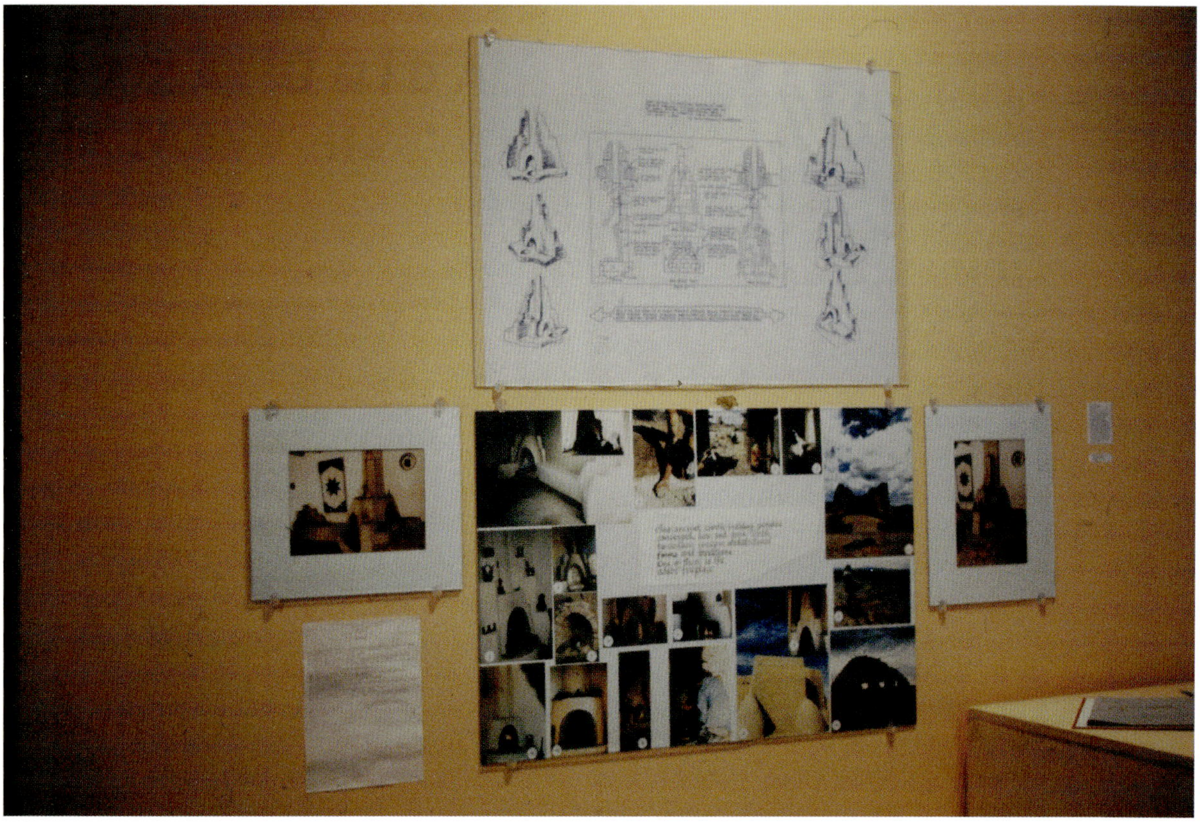

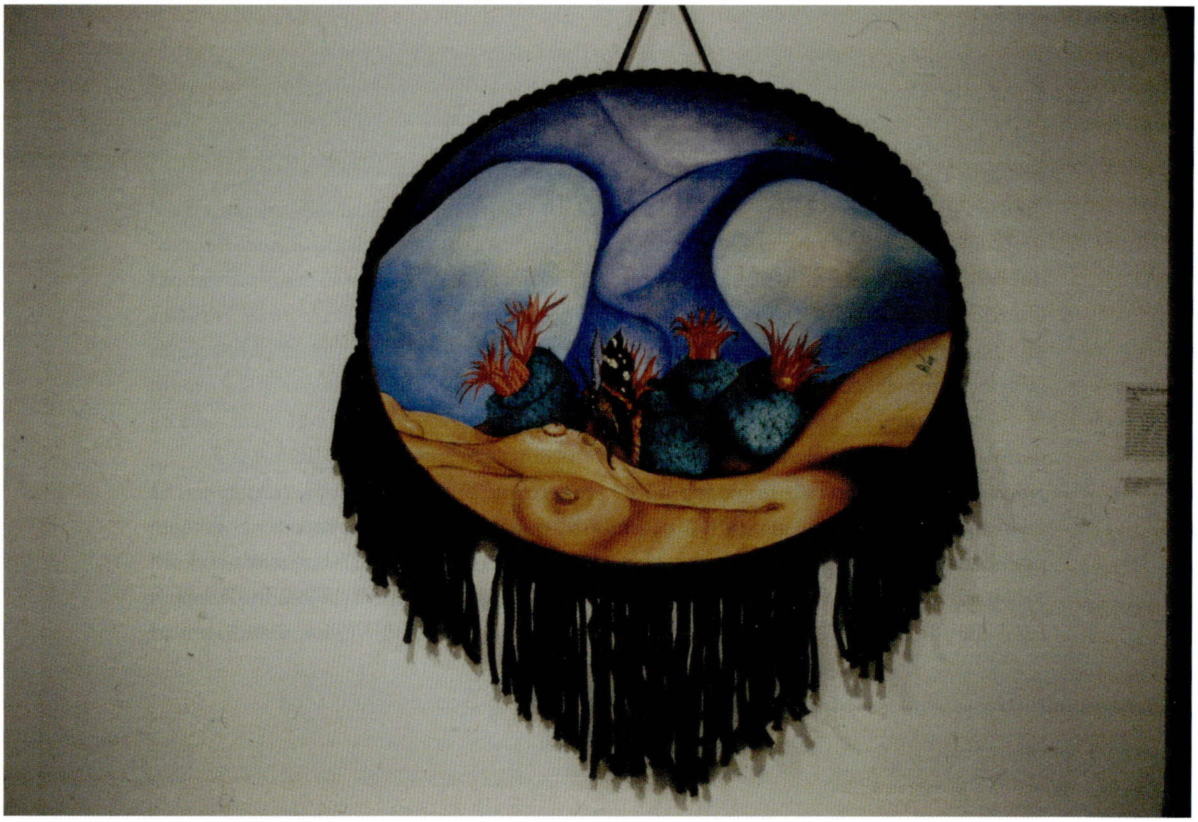

underscore connections to the embodied forms of knowing and making that each one expresses. In *Las picoteadas* (Many little points), an oil on canvas composition from 1980, López presents a landscape in roundel form with a custom frame adorned with a fringe of dark-colored yarn tassels tapering to a point at the bottom (fig. 4.5).[27] The painting depicts four bristling cacti with anemone-like flowery tendrils emerging from their blue-green forms. They nestle alongside what at first glance appears to be an expanse of desert landscape but upon further inspection is revealed to be a human torso, rendered in warm shades of brown, with breasts and nipples gently rising above a flat belly and darkened groin area. A winged insect hovers above the body/land, and the view is completed by abstracted icy blue and cobalt forms which read as either rocks or sky. Even as López's landscape revels in the bountiful and life-giving, equating the flowering plants with an abundant earth, the prickly antagonism of their thorns bespeaks the harshness and hostility of the land.[28] As we will see elsewhere in the essay, López's landscapes strayed even farther from an idyllic representation, instead reflecting the horrors of environmental catastrophe.

In the exhibition catalog essay for *Chicana Voices and Visions*, Goldman undertakes the daunting task of summarizing the social factors undergirding the Chicano art movement, while simultaneously attending to the specific challenges at play for Chicana artists working at the intersection of feminist and Chicano mobilization, both strains that on their own tended to exclude their specific concerns, histories, and cultural expressions. Germane to the New Mexican discussion, in a section of the essay with the heading "The Many Facets of Chicana Art: New Needs, New Themes," on several occasions, Goldman underscores the longevity and relatively (to her mind) unchanged nature of artisanal production in New Mexico's Hispano communities. Beginning with the Spanish Colonial period and focusing on the Río Grande Valley region, she highlights women's participation in the area's rural economy. Speaking to a more contemporary era, she writes,

> In more recent years, the artisanship that formerly supplied internally needed domestic and religious articles for the isolated colonizers of northern New Spain/Mexico, has been transformed into production for collectors, tourists, and the new Chicano middle class. In northern New Mexico, women are engaged in work as artisans, alone or with husbands and families, in making more or less traditional painted and carved religious images, silver jewelry, ornamental tinwork, straw inlay, rawhide work, embroidery, and quilting—as well as weaving and plastering adobe structures.[29]

FIGURE 4.4. (*opposite above*) Anita O. Rodríguez, installation in the exhibition *Chicana Voices and Visions*, 1983. Shifra M. Goldman Papers, CEMA 119. Department of Special Research Collections, UC Santa Barbara Library.

FIGURE 4.5. (*opposite below*) Pola López, *Las picoteadas (Many Little Points)*, 1980. Oil on canvas, 16″ × 20″ Shifra M. Goldman Papers, CEMA 119. Department of Special Research Collections, UC Santa Barbara Library. Courtesy of Pola López, Santa Fe, New Mexico.

Goldman goes on to make the case that very little documented artwork by Mexican American women in the early twentieth century survives, which, by extension, makes early examples of artisanal practice particularly valuable as records of artistic production. Yet the turn of phrase "more or less traditional" invites more questions than it answers, and only serves to reinforce the vexed and binary construction of "traditional" versus—what? What does it mean to be "more or less" traditional? Goldman's characterization flattens the temporal and historical distinctions between the colonial period, which was belatedly studied and codified by outsiders during the New Deal era; the contemporaneous revival period of the 1920s and 1930s when those same Anglo cultural brokers established codes of authenticity and tradition and imposed them upon Hispano makers; and the later Chicano movement–inflected period during the 1970s, when artists such as Archuleta-Sagel, Lavadie, Rodríguez, and a host of others working in woodcarving, weaving, and other "traditional" crafts pushed up against the bounds of such codified norms.[30]

At a later point in the essay, Goldman does acknowledge the private and federal patronage sustaining New Deal artists and gestures to the "impetus of the Chicano movement and the land grant struggle" that helped inspire the 1970s-era revivals, but the implication is that the latter work is created principally as a form of "tribute to their ancestors of several generations back who have passed on these skills."[31] Goldman's language suggests a narrative of stasis and the persistence of unchanging traditions over one of innovation or experimentation. In point of fact, the majority of the Chicano artists practicing crafts such as woodcarving, weaving, and adobe architecture during the 1970s and 1980s had *not* automatically been guaranteed access to their familial legacies and were often forced to seek out training through their own means, as the forthcoming sections of this essay will show.

Nonetheless, *Chicana Voices and Visions* was forward-thinking in its act of bringing together artists working in more conventional artistic media in dialogue with the weavings of Archuleta-Sagel and Lavadie, the adobe sculptural creations of Rodríguez, the retablos of Martínez de Pedro, and the ceramics of Trujillo. Goldman's summary of the exhibit's diverse expressions speaks to this point and is worth quoting at length.

> This is by no means a complete list of the concerns which occupy
> Chicana artists; it is intended merely as an indicator. By the same token,
> Chicana artists employ a range of styles and techniques, from the most
> traditional of *retablos* (religious works painted on wood) to the most
> avant-garde methods of manipulated photography, xerography, and book
> art. If there are unifying characteristics in this exhibit, they include the
> overwhelming concern with images of women, their condition, and their
> environment. Many works are directly or indirectly autobiographical;
> a certain number deal with sexuality. Another common denominator
> that has emerged is the tendency to use organic rather than geometric

form: the rounded corner, the flowing line; the pot-like shape shared by clay vessels, the pregnant body [referring to a body cast work by Arizona-based artist Liz Lerma Bowerman], and the adobe fireplace.[32]

Refreshing in its heterogeneity, the show (and Goldman's assessment thereof) cannot wholly be disentangled from the binaries of such modernist throwbacks as "avant-garde" and "traditional," a framing that refuses the possibility that retablos, textiles, and indeed, an idiosyncratically sculpted earthen fireplace might in fact operate on more conceptual registers even as they reference, honor, and extract meaning from the past. Indeed, Rodríguez's combination of historical images, documentation, diagrams, and text echo artistic strategies prevalent in contemporaneous feminist, conceptual, post-minimalist, process, and land art practices. Even so, the exhibition is a rare example of positioning Rodríguez's work within the framework of the Chicano art movement, at least in part due to the fact that in situ fireplaces, *hornos* (outdoor ovens), and custom hand-laid mud floors for which she was renowned in the community are challenging to translate into a gallery setting. Goldman is to be commended for acknowledging the connections between artists working in "traditional" arts and the Chicano movement, albeit in passing. I argue here, however, that as objects that scuttle the boundaries of architecture, design, and painting and sculpture, Rodríguez's works evade categorization, and the same can be said of her compatriots working in other "traditional" mediums. Earlier presentations of contemporary nuevomexicano artists that preceded *Chicana Voices and Visions* throughout New Mexico and Colorado took varying tacks on how to reckon with their elusive status.

One of the first institutional, non-Chicano organized showcases that included several of the aforementioned artists took place in 1977 at the Taylor Museum of the Colorado Fine Arts Center (now the Fine Arts Center) located on the campus of Colorado College in Colorado Springs. Titled *Hispanic Crafts of the Southwest*, the exhibition featured predominantly northern New Mexican artists and aimed to showcase the continuity between historical and contemporary forms prominent in the region. The brainchild of Taylor Museum chief curator William Wroth, a longstanding proponent of both Native American and Hispano arts in New Mexico, the exhibition featured both nineteenth-century and contemporary examples of Río Grande weavings, including work by Lavadie, María Vergara Wilson, Gilbert Fernández, and members of the renowned Ortega and Trujillo families of weavers.[33] Other genres included hand-carved wooden furniture, including a number of pieces by Luis Tapia; historical and contemporary *colcha* embroidery; and *santos* and other woodcarvings by members of the Córdova school, whose patriarch, José Dolores López, had garnered renown in the 1930s; works by López's contemporary Patrocinio Barela, known for his sinuous, organic wood sculptures; as well as more contemporary carved works by Felipe Archuleta, Horacio Valdez, Felix López, Benjamin Ortega, Federico Armijo, Leo Salazar, Ramón Rochas, and three retablos by Linda Martínez de Pedro. It is likely through this exhibition that Goldman first encountered Martínez de Pedro and elected to include her, as one of only a couple of female carvers in the Taylor Museum exhibition, in *Chicana Voices and Visions*.[34] Tapia, who had been amply represented in the furniture section, also had several vividly polychromed sculptures in the exhibition, including *San Miguel* (1975), *Noah's Ark* (1977), and *The Last Supper* (1976). The exhibition also included jewelry, tinwork, and straw appliqué.

Hispanic Crafts of the Southwest was a remarkable early attempt to place the 1970s revival, itself quite incipient, in the broader historical context of earlier precedents. The museum was well-positioned to undertake the exhibition, as it held a substantial collection of Spanish Colonial and Native American objects from New Mexico that had been acquired by the museum's namesake and primary benefactor, philanthropist Alice Bemis Taylor. Designed by John Gaw Meem, the Fine Arts Center opened in 1936, and Bemis Taylor's collections inaugurated the visual arts arm of the museum. Notorious among these collections were an altar screen by José Rafael Aragón, arguably the colonial period's most renowned *santero*, and an accompanying collection of santos that had been removed whole cloth from the Chapel of Our Lady of Talpa, also known as the Durán Family Chapel. In 1977, in conjunction with *Hispanic Crafts of the Southwest*, the museum constructed a full-scale replica of Our Lady of Talpa's interior in which to display the santos, complete with adobe architectural elements, which Rodríguez was commissioned to realize (fig. 4.6).[35] Introductory didactics to the installation (the chapel is no longer extant, though the museum still holds the santos in its collection) included a photograph of her plastering.

The widespread vogue for individuals to amass personal collections of colonial santos from the 1920s onward has meant that there are few such sets that represent the complete contents of any single church or chapel, rendering the Taylor Museum's holdings both exceptional and fraught. Made for expressly devotional purposes, many of these objects were unlawfully looted or otherwise removed from their original siting, raising ethical questions regarding objects made for expressly devotional purposes. Hispano artists are not covered by the 1990 Native American Graves Protection and Repatriation Act (NAGPRA), a federal law that, despite flaws and limitations, has enabled the return of sacred materials to Indigenous communities throughout the United States. Some have suggested that living practitioners associated with the religious confraternity Los Hermanos de la Fraternidad Piadosa de Nuestro Padre Jesús Nazareno, colloquially known as Los Hermanos Penitentes or just Penitentes, many of whom continue to practice in churches, chapels, and *moradas* (meeting houses) throughout the state, may have some claim to them.[36] The Taylor Museum's holdings had already played a critical role in the exhibition of Spanish Colonial religious sculpture during its early years, and well before Wroth took the curatorial helm in 1976, the Museum of Modern Art in New York held an exhibition of what they called "Religious Folk Art in the Southwest," drawn from the Taylor Museum's collection. The exhibition also included a few 1930s woodcarvings by José Dolores López and Patrocinio

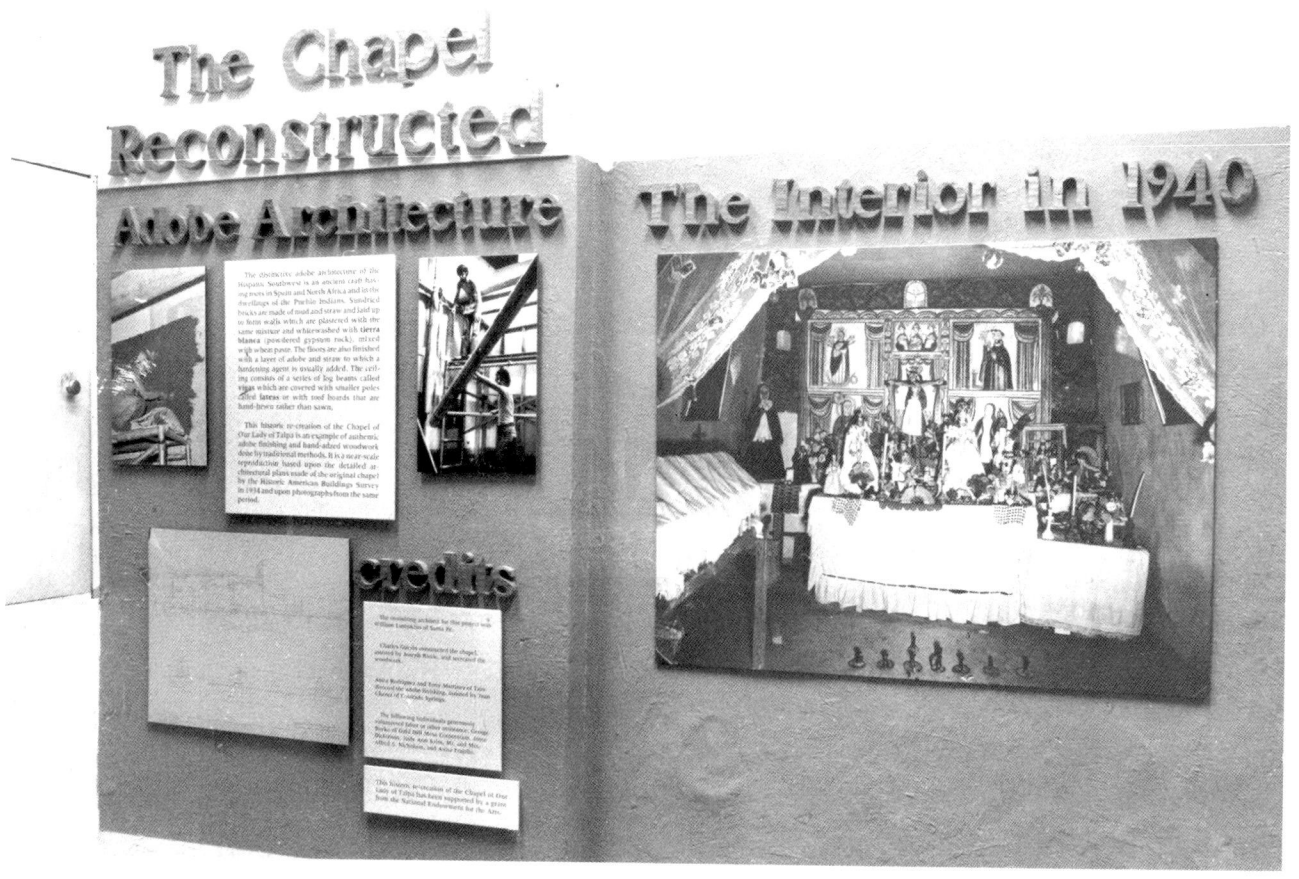

FIGURE 46. Introductory panels on the exterior of the reconstructed Chapel of
Our Lady of Talpa. Taylor Museum of the Colorado Fine Arts Center,
Colorado Springs, 1977. Courtesy of the Colorado Springs Fine Arts Center
at Colorado College.

Barela, and shortly after the exhibition, MoMA acquired *Adam and Eve and the Serpent* (1930), an unpainted wood sculpture by López.[37]

Thirty-four years after the MoMA exhibition, *Hispanic Crafts of the Southwest* represented a laudable early spotlighting of contemporary practitioners alongside nineteenth- and early twentieth-century antecedents. However, the exhibition omitted any mention of the connection between some (though decidedly not all) of the contemporary artists and the Chicano movement. In tracing the multigenerational history, Wroth links the "vibrant regional tradition" of works made under both Spanish and Mexican jurisdiction, which he claims "thrived with little direct influence from the outside world (other than Mexico)" until the period of US territorial occupation beginning in 1846.[38] Pivoting to the case of the 1970s-era contemporary artists, he links their work to a broader global phenomenon of artists revisiting autochthonous local and regional art forms, writing, "There is little ethnic art and craft work anywhere in this age which is made solely to fulfill the needs and criteria of the makers. Indigenous people all over the world have adapted their traditional art forms (sometimes minimally, often radically) to the technology and to the economies and tastes of the industrial Western World."[39] This shift in socioeconomic and societal conditions, he suggests, occasions an altered role whereby there is a move from "art forms which were once an integral, necessary part of daily life to forms which are now on the one hand a luxury, and on the other hand, a vital, powerful affirmation of cultural identity and a significant means of economic survival."[40] Other contributors to the catalog make passing mention of the term Chicano to reference the artists of the present moment—Juanita J. Lavadie in an essay on Río Grande weaving, and Charles L. Briggs in one on Santa Fe Anglo patronage of Hispano woodcarvers during the first half of the twentieth century—but neither highlights the potent intersection between movement activism and the artistic production of many contemporary nuevomexicano artists.[41]

In 1979 the Albuquerque Museum took a slightly different curatorial approach. The museum, which had historically disregarded contemporary nuevomexicano artists, organized a group exhibition focused on recent craft practice called *One Space/Three Visions*. Organized by guest curator Dextra Frankel, the exhibition celebrated the paradigmatic "three New Mexican cultures"—Native American, Hispanic, and Contemporary—into which the artists were subdivided. The catalog features black and white photographs of each of the included works, as well as portraits of many of the artists by photographer Meridel Rubenstein. Fifty-one artists in total participated; like *Hispanic Crafts of the Southwest*, it constitutes an admirable survey of the state's myriad practitioners of work in a variety of mediums, techniques, and styles, and evinces considerable engagement with artists from Native and Hispano communities alike. Yet the exhibition circumscribes artists from the former two categories into the role of heirs to a tradition (in the case of Pueblo artists, some two thousand years' worth) while affording the majority Anglo/white artists in the Contemporary category more explicit access to the here and now. The exhibition's differentiation on the basis of ethnicity for Hispano and Native artist versus contemporaneity on the part of the rest relegates artists from the former two categories to a place where they are viewed as merely adherents to an inevitable legacy, even as their mastery is celebrated. For it is undeniable that the Pueblo and Hispano artists featured in the exhibition were themselves *also* contemporary artists, given that the vast majority of the works in the exhibition were created from the 1960s onward, with a few outliers going back only as far as the 1950s. One cannot help but wonder what would happen if the exhibition had instead been grouped by medium, blurring at least temporarily the putative divisions of culture, which in their own way map too cleanly onto what Chris Wilson has called New Mexico's "rhetoric of tricultural harmony" that "overstates the purity and separateness of Indian, Hispano, and Anglo" while also ignoring racial and ethnic groups that fall outside of those three.[42]

The Native American section includes pottery, weavings, and silver jewelry, with care taken to include representatives from the northern and southern Pueblos, as well as Diné (Navajo) and Apache artists. The catalog features a blurb about each one of the groups and an overview of language groups, geography, and other contextual information, and extensive interviews were conducted with artists in preparation for the exhibition. The Hispanic section shares much of the scope of *Hispanic Crafts of the Southwest* both in terms of the categories of works (woodcarving, weaving, furniture, embroidery, and jewelry) and many of the artists whose work is included. In her catalog essay, Suzanne de Borhegyi-Forrest does acknowledge the 1960s as a vital moment of consciousness-raising and cites the activism of the Chicano movement as a catalyst for self-affirmation. Describing the 1960s and 1970s generation of nuevomexicanos as a "rootless and restless generation of young people [who] had grown up after World War II, alienated from their culture and frequently unable even to speak their native Spanish," she suggests that for many of them folk traditions served as an alternative to the ancient Mesoamerican cultural touchstones that inspired Chicano artists in other corners of the movement. Strikingly, since the essays for each of the three sections were written by different authors and do not follow a prescribed format, there is no parallel reference to the American Indian Movement or other Native activist currents in the essay on Native arts, which appears to foreclose the possibility of any similar political revindication on the part of any of the Native artists and reaffirms an artificial separation between enduring tradition and responsiveness to present-day political and social currents.

The final, "Contemporary" section of *One Space / Three Visions* showcased artists who, in their vast majority, had lived in New Mexico for no more than six years; according to the essay, their testimonies often alluded to the sense of space, openness, and unfettered creativity that New Mexico afforded them as a destination and haven. Pueblo ceramics, Diné and Río Grande weavings, and other regional art forms were cited as direct sources of inspiration for many of the artists, who, as mentioned before, were with a few exceptions neither Indigenous nor Hispano.[43] Furthermore, gallerist Arthur Adair, who wrote the text for the section, uses the term "artist-craftsmen" to characterize the artists, many of whom, he notes, originally trained in painting or graphic arts. Though it is true that some "traditional" artists attended art school (Juanita J. Lavadie, a prolific painter and printmaker as well as weaver, is one such example), the book's segmentation of work that formally bears considerable kinship misses opportunities to skirt artistic categories and open new and productive dialogues. And though there are a few apparently Hispanic and/or nuevo-mexicano artists in the Contemporary section, their placement there can seem somewhat arbitrary, particularly given that both Tapia and Archuleta-Sagel, both of whom actively advocated for asserting observably "contemporary" adaptations to traditional forms, are both included in the Hispanic section. Overall, as these three exhibitions indicate, the problematics of framing artistic practices such as weaving, adobe, and woodcarving as "traditional," "Chicano," and "contemporary" raise apparently intractable categorical paradoxes and at times serve to reinscribe a sense of New Mexican exceptionalism that refuses to reconcile generationally transmitted practices with political militancy. Yet Chicano artists in New Mexico—whether working in so-called fine arts, folk art, or some intersection of the two, responded to the loaded cultural imaginary of the state, one that fetishizes land, people, and cultural practices alike. Animated by the threats to land and livelihood, they produced work that, through adaptation and innovation, reclaimed that imaginary to affirm the ineffable and essential but also imperiled nature of place. The section that follows outlines the historical and visual antecedents that were instrumental in establishing this imaginary, which creates a springboard for the subsequent discussions of art, activism and Chicano artists' activation of mud, wool, and wood that constitutes these vital yet underappreciated modes of socially engaged art practice.

Mythologies and Imaginaries of Place: Adobe, Art, and Land in New Mexico

As an adobe art practitioner, Rodríguez's work builds upon a rich, variegated, yet often fraught visual and material legacy in New Mexico. Her compatriots working in other mediums likewise have contended with a range of legacies of creation and commodification alike. Accordingly, this section provides background on the art historical legacy of New Mexico from the early twentieth century to the post–Chicana and Chicano movement moment, emphasizing the construction of romanticized narratives around adobe, as well as the unbridled fascination with landscape, sky, and the land.

The Spanish word *adobe* derives from the Arabic word for brick.[44] Remarkably simple in its fundamentals, in adobe building, clay-rich mud is mixed with sand, straw, and water to create a compound (known in New Mexico as *zoquete* or *soquete*, a derivation of the Nahuatl word *zoquitl*), formed into a brick shape, and allowed to dry in the sun.[45] Bricks (known individually as *adobes*) are joined using a mortar of the same materials, and the whole surface is blanketed in layers of hand-applied mud *enjarre* (plaster). Once dry, adobe walls shelter the dweller from the elements, resisting rain and snow and keeping heat in during the winter and heat out during the searingly hot high desert summer months. As architectural historian and artist Ronald Rael and others have noted, mud buildings can be found on every continent and across the globe and lend themselves to a range of climates.[46] Yet there is almost nowhere where adobe is more tethered to the popular imaginary of place than New Mexico. Its stacked hive-like arrangement of multilevel earthen structures has made Taos Pueblo world famous as one of the oldest extant adobe architectural compounds. Elsewhere in the state, historical churches, *moradas*, *ranchos*, *haciendas*, and more modest houses have remained intact thanks to familial and community upkeep and preservation efforts. Yet as Rodríguez's trajectory demonstrates, the impetus to preserve adobe structures was not always a priority, despite the environmental advantages earth building proffered. Among architectural historians, the 1960s efforts of Bainbridge Bunting constituted an important effort to chronicle many of the state's most iconic adobe buildings. His comprehensive publication *Early Architecture in New Mexico* came out in 1976, the same year that Rodríguez's essay on the history of enjarradoras was published in *Mud, Space & Spirit*.[47] These two publications highlight a contradictory juncture of the moment: on one hand, Bunting's impulse to historize those buildings that had withstood the postwar modernization kick, and on the other, *Mud, Space & Spirit*'s emphasis on unique and whimsical homes built by amateurs, which evoked a sense of the fantastical rather than the everyday. Rodríguez's work, which pays tribute to history, generational memory, and practical know-how but introduces idiosyncratic elements, operates at the vexed crossroads of the two.

Before the arrival of the Spanish, earthen construction was in use among the Pueblo people (Taos Pueblo was reportedly built between 1000 and 1450 CE). Prior to colonization, walls were typically constructed using a technique known as puddling, where successive layers of wet mud are piled upon one another and then left to dry, with more layers added until the proper height was achieved. When friars came to Pueblo communities to proselytize, they quickly erected mission churches of both adobe and stone, drawing on Gothic, Renaissance, and Mudéjar architectural idioms; the vestiges of some of the stone architecture can be seen in the southern New Mexican mission sites of Abó, Quarai, and others. Church architecture flourished with the arrival of the Spanish settlers, though during the Pueblo Revolt of 1680, many of them were destroyed.[48]

Homes followed a codified formula as well, with Pueblo builders opting for triangular-shaped room layouts while Spanish houses followed a "defensive" I-, L-, or U-shaped arrangement with interior courtyards, according to Bunting's observations.[49] Whether large *haciendas* or more humble structures, domestic architecture adhered to roughly the following formula: adobe bricks, pintle hinges on doors and windows, a *fogón* (fireplace), ceilings constructed using *vigas* (large wooden ceiling beams) and *latillas* (smaller sticks placed in between the *vigas*) and filled in with straw and mud, small windows, wooden drainage channels (*canales*), and short doors with low entryways.[50]

The development of the architectural style variously known as Santa Fe style, Pueblo style, or New Mexico Mission style, instructively illustrates how the once-humble adobe came to simultaneously operate as a tourist draw and, as folklore scholar Enrique Lamadrid has suggested, "a sort of protest against this new world of technocracy, individualisms, specialties, and alienation" brought on by US occupation.[51] The architectural vogue emerged in the immediate aftermath of New Mexico's statehood in 1912. In an effort spearheaded by the Museum of New Mexico in Santa Fe, constructions inspired by the spare massing, dramatic facades, and gently rounded walls of Pueblo and Spanish Colonial architecture cropped up throughout the city. Against an earlier push toward neoclassicism as the burgeoning city's official architectural style, the decision to turn to local source material aligned with the tenets of the Arts and Crafts movement, which favored drawing on local histories, materials, and climate to invoke a homey, preindustrial, and artisanal feel. Chris Wilson describes the phenomenon of "pseudopueblos," faux adobe replicas of Pueblo villages and adobe mission architecture that were displayed at world's fairs and were instrumental in drumming up support for municipal architecture that mimicked adobe. More ambitious projects such as the buildings on the University of New Mexico's Albuquerque campus began to crop up, as well as hotels and commercial buildings.[52] Today, faux adobe is used for everything from hotels to banks to fast food restaurants throughout New Mexico.

The architectural identity of Santa Fe was further solidified when mayor Arthur Seligman convened the Santa Fe City Planning Board, which in 1912 produced a "City Beautiful"-esque plan for modernization and economic growth that called for the use of locally inspired buildings over the more habitual Beaux-Arts style. According to Wilson, "If nineteenth-century Anglo-Americans had judged Santa Fe's people and architecture to be uncivilized, this generation of newcomers found them picturesque, even noble. Winding lanes, which the leading citizens would once have widened and straightened if only they could, became quaint, even essential to the city's progress as a tourist center." It was this embrace and codification of the unusual (for non-native-New Mexicans) that earned Santa Fe its moniker the "City Different."[53] Meanwhile, photographer Jesse Nusbaum, who had earlier conducted an extensive photographic survey of ancient, colonial, vernacular architecture, oversaw a 1909–1912 renovation of the Palace of the Governors that Wilson calls a "speculative or interpretive recreation" in that it was only loosely based on a 1766 Spanish map. As he notes, its reconstructed facade "stands not as an example of Spanish architecture, but as a key monument in the development and popularization of a regional revival."[54] Between 1915 and 1918, city boosters including the Fine Arts Museum's director

Edgar Lee Hewett, painter Carlos Vierra, and architect William Templeton Johnson pushed to bolster tourism by reactivating aspects of the city's colonial-era appearance, emphasizing the main plaza's covered *portales*. Pueblo- and Spanish-derived architectural forms were freely intermingled, and interiors were frequently adorned with Pueblo pottery and Diné weavings.[55]

At the same time that the Fine Arts Museum (now the New Mexico Museum of Art) was inaugurated and the state's tourism campaign was in full swing, artists began to arrive in droves from elsewhere in the country, coalescing around artist fraternities or other groups, some loosely organized, others more exclusive. The Taos Society of Artists is perhaps the most renowned. The Society, whose original members were Joseph Henry Sharp, Ernest L. Blumenschein, E. Irving Couse, Oscar Berninghaus, Herbert "Buck" Dunton, and Bert Geer Phillips, later expanded to include numerous other non-Native, non-Hispano artists living in Taos. Though varied in their stylistic preoccupations and academic versus modernist bent, their subject matter was uniformly dominated by regional genre scenes: romanticized portrayals of Pueblo sitters surrounded by pottery and textiles, adobe architectural scenes, and in some cases, possibly unsanctioned representations of Native American and Hispano religious celebrations and rituals, such as the Antelope Dance and the Holy Week procession of the Hermanos Penitentes.[56]

Adobe, the New Mexican landscape, and the material culture of nuevomexicanos likewise proved irresistible for modernist arrivals who followed in the wake of the Taos Society of Artists beginning in the late 1920s and early 1930s. Some only visited, but many chose to make a permanent home in the state, in so doing contributing to the visual repertoire of an idealized New Mexico that Taos-born anthropologist Sylvia Rodríguez (Anita's sister) has denominated a "site of modernist utopian longing."[57] Beginning in 1918, the Buffalo-born, New York City–based socialite Mabel Dodge Luhan purchased the land for and began to construct Los Gallos, a sprawling adobe compound consisting of five guest houses, a gatehouse, and a three-story "Big House" on twelve acres of land directly adjacent to Taos Pueblo. Under her auspices, Los Gallos attracted a steady stream of visitors that read like a veritable who's-who of the artistic, musical, literary, and philosophical intelligentsia of the time, including Willa Cather, D. H. Lawrence, and Aldous Huxley alongside the era's most prominent painters and photographers. Her fourth husband Antonio "Tony" Lujan was Native Tiwa from Taos Pueblo, affording her a certain privileged access and to some degree a more insightful viewpoint into the adjacent Pueblo community. However, as Lois Palken Rudnick points out, the presence of Dodge Luhan and her Taos coterie, who felt free to "adapt certain native aesthetics to their own modes of self-expression in order to make their art and theory more than just a matter of personal vision" frequently clashed with harsh economic and social realities faced by Hispano and Native peoples, raising ethical questions about race, power, patronage, and resources.[58] Subsequently, the house was acquired by the actor Dennis Hopper, where it took on a second life as a hub of 1960s hippie counterculture.

Tensions around contested land in and around Taos continued throughout the decades. In a potent exploration of the social and spatial conjuncture between Taos Pueblo, the Hermanos Penitentes, and the bohemian artist community cultivated by Dodge Luhan, Sylvia Rodríguez analyzes a territorial dispute that arose in 1979 when the Kit Carson Memorial Foundation attempted to open a morada chapel it had purchased two years earlier to the public, which, as it turned out, was allegedly located on land belonging to Taos Pueblo. Members of the Penitente Brotherhood protested in Taos, and the matter was tabled for a later date. The morada, as well as an imposing wooden cross located behind it, had earlier provided visual fodder for artists like Georgia O'Keeffe, Paul Strand, and Dodge Luhan, whose friends at times treated it as almost an extension of her property; in time it came to be known as "Mabel's morada."[59]

Sylvia Rodríguez places the morada, the Pueblo, and Dodge Luhan's house into dialogue with yet another phenomenon: the network of *acequias* (irrigation ditches), a system of communal water supply and management crucial to the upkeep of communities throughout the state. According to Rodríguez, the *Acequia madre*, or mother ditch from which the offshoots of the system originate, transported water over an arroyo where Dodge Luhan and her friends used to hide to observe the secretive Good Friday celebrations held by the Penitentes. Like the land on which the morada was sited, water rights in Taos and other northern communities were likewise frequently subject to dispute.[60] Drawing on the concept of "Thirdspace" coined by Henri Lefebvre and later theorized by Edward Soja, she concludes,

> The Las Cruces arroyo is such a "third" space: a geographical, physical place that is and has been perceived, conceived, and lived very differently by different people at different times, as well as at the same time. But unlike the town plaza, for example, or Mabel's house, the morada, Taos Pueblo, or some other architectural structure or site, it is not bounded, mapped, owned, or previously conceptualized or visualized as a single entity. Instead, it is more like an open force field where multiple overlapping, interpenetrating, and conflicting spaces and places are constantly being produced, transformed, and eradicated. It is a real but also imagined topos that surrounds, makes possible, and yet contradicts, utopian space."[61]

By triangulating these architectural, agricultural, artistic, and contested cross-cultural phenomena, Rodríguez reminds us of the impossibility of divorcing the potency of land from its artistic representations.

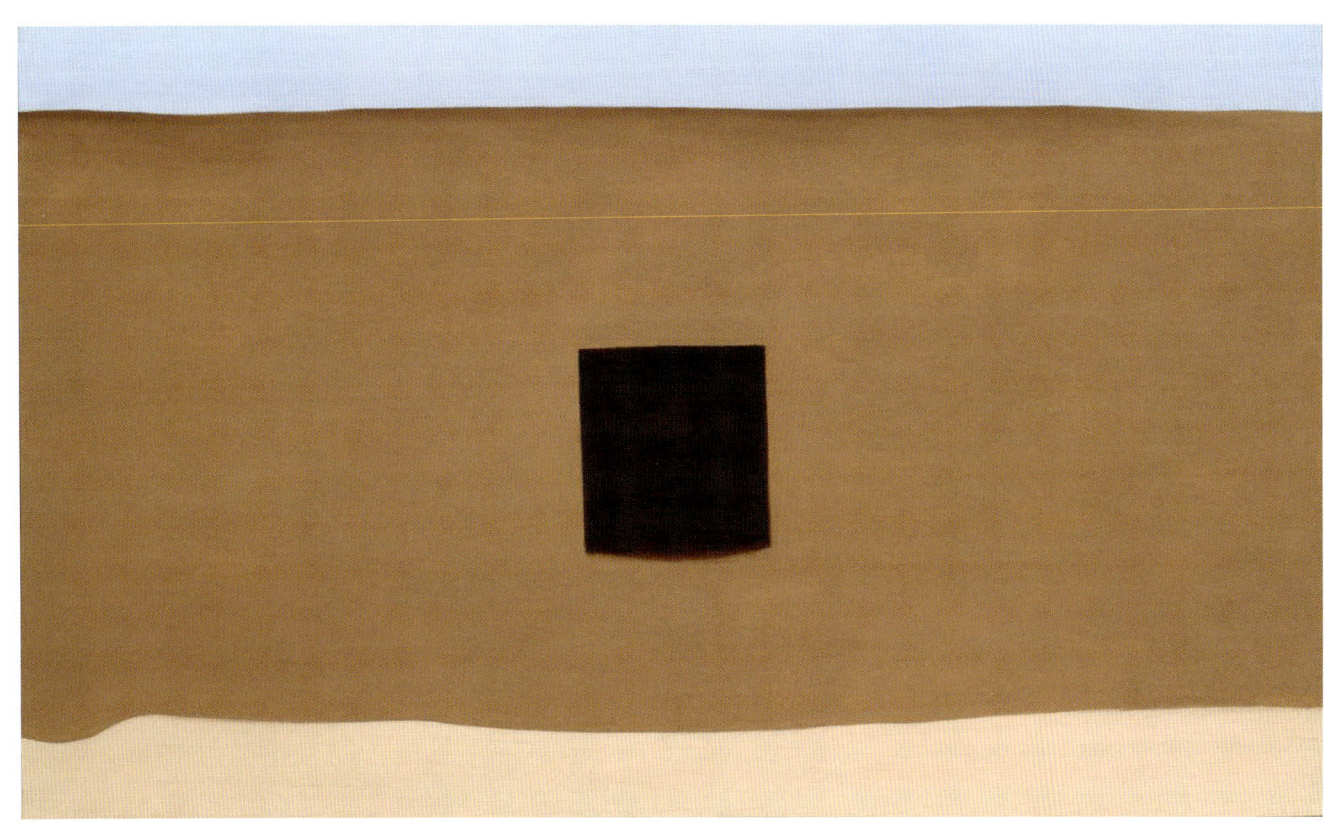

FIGURE 4.7. Georgia O'Keeffe, *In the Patio, II*, 1948. Oil on linen, 17 3/4" × 29 3/4".
(support). New Mexico Museum of Art, Bequest of Helen Miller Jones, 1986,
© New Mexico Museum of Art / Artists Rights Society (ARS), New York.

It would be impossible to survey the sheer quantity of artists that chose adobe, the New Mexican landscape, or some combination thereof as subject matter. Many of the artists that flocked to Mabel Dodge Luhan's, including Andrew Dasburg, Marsden Hartley, Paul Strand, John Marin, Ansel Adams, and of course Georgia O'Keeffe, sought inspiration in the land, people, and artistic production they encountered in Taos and other parts of northern New Mexico. Among the most popular architectural sites to represent were Taos Pueblo; the Santuario de Chimayó, a popular pilgrimage site; and the San Francisco de Asís church in Ranchos de Taos, included in Anita O. Rodríguez's 1983 photomural for *Chicana Voices and Visions*.

Arguably the state's most famous transplant artist, O'Keeffe arrived in May 1929 at Dodge Luhan's invitation and spent extended stretches there during the 1930s, before ultimately settling permanently in the state in 1949. In 1940, she purchased a property at Ghost Ranch, north of Abiquiú, and in 1945, she acquired an additional property—an eighteen-room hacienda in Abiquiú, which she restored with the assistance of a friend, Marie Chabot. Though O'Keeffe is but one of many who partook in the artistic mythologization of northern New Mexico through engagement with the visual terrain of the desert landscape, flora, and vernacular architectural tradition, her singular impact on its enduring idealization cannot be overlooked. New Mexico's tourist apparatus has long embraced the moniker of "O'Keeffe country" to promote the romanticized vision that O'Keeffe herself fostered through her artwork, lifestyle, and the sense of personal investment and possessive ownership that she harbored for the land that surrounded her. O'Keeffe's relentless painting of dozens of variations on the landscape of Cerro Pedernal (Tsiping in Tewa), a flat mesa located just south of Abiquiú, evinces her obsession with the prominent landmark, which she famously called her "private mountain," obscuring its significance to Pueblo and Genízaro inhabitants of the area. Using her signature abstracted visual vocabulary, O'Keeffe rendered mountains, desert flatlands, and adobe forms like San Francisco de Asís, as well as her own properties, into iterative expressions of the warm shades of earthy brown that constitute the dominant color palette of the Southwest. A particularly striking example is *In the Patio, II* (1948), which reduces the already spare volumes of an adobe wall to a flattened, monochromatic swatch of deep earthy tan with subtly darker shading at its upper edge (fig. 4.7). A narrow band of sky blue above and another of creamy beige below articulate floor and sky, but the composition remains sparely abstract and devoid of spatial depth. A darker brown square at the center recalls a window but offers no illusionistic view of what lies inside, outside, or through.

Patricia Marroquin Norby describes the complex legal machinations required to obtain title for La Tapia, O'Keeffe's Abiquiú hacienda, which was located on an eighteenth-century Genízaro land grant. Though the property had been unoccupied for a time, local residents had communally maintained its water rights and general upkeep, and the property was intended to be converted into a new school. O'Keeffe's purchasing of the property officially set it outside the bounds of the Abiquiú land grant, a fiercely circumscribed area of importance to community leaders and residents. The negotiations for O'Keeffe's purchase, which were aided by a donation to the local Roman Catholic diocese, served both to sever her land from the grant and release Abiquiú residents from communal rights to the land and responsibility for its upkeep. However, Abiquiú's leaders likewise ostensibly controlled her access to the acequia, leading to additional conflict. The loss of this important property only heightened tensions between O'Keeffe and the Abiquiú community, which was enduring a period of economic and environmental hardship, largely due to federal government intervention on their traditional agricultural methods and other lifeways. For her entire life, O'Keeffe's relationship to her Abiquiú neighbors would remain fraught.[62] Both Dodge Luhan and O'Keeffe serve as limit cases in terms of the cultural capital that they wielded, but represent only a fraction of innumerable examples of artists whose presence willfully or not intensified the widespread racism, inequities, and frictions that have occurred between artist communities and the lifelong Native and Hispano residents, despite the mythology of harmonious coexistence that the state tourist apparatus promoted.[63] O'Keeffe's persona, which became inextricable from her paintings, her artfully decorated homes, and the landscape that she embraced as her own, played an immense role in shaping northern New Mexico's image for years to come, even as more recent scholarship and public debate have implicated the colonizing nature of her legacy.[64]

The modernist impulse to represent land and adobe alike complemented a parallel movement, beginning in the 1920s and 1930s, to preserve Hispano crafts that were perceived to be under threat of disappearance and bolster the tourist market. The Atchison, Topeka, and Santa Fe Railroad's arrival in 1880 ushered in a period of increased commerce. In tandem with the codification of Santa Fe's architecture, an interest in both Native American and Hispano art forms grew steadily, though the vogue for Pueblo art and design objects pre-dates the later investment in their Hispano counterparts.[65] Mabel Dodge Luhan was an avid collector of santos and led the charge on a renewed focus on Spanish Colonial material, which was also incorporated into artworks by artists such as Marsden Hartley and Cady Wells. In 1925, Mary Hunter Austin and Frank Applegate founded the Spanish Colonial Arts Society (SCAS), which promoted the study and collection of santos. Applegate also was instrumental in promoting the persistence of woodcarving and other techniques among contemporary makers. SCAS set up relationships with local trade schools and promoted vocational training. They also established Spanish Market, part of the annual Santa Fe Fiesta, and when Applegate and Austin died, it was renamed Native Market and operated by SCAS member Leonora Curtin. Relations were likewise maintained with museums such as the Harwood Museum in Taos and the Fine Arts Museum in Santa Fe to exhibit and provide studio space for artists. Native Market featured open-air demonstrations of artists working in woodcarving and weaving.[66]

In her pioneering study of Hispano artists and the New Deal, Tey Marianna Nunn highlights the understudied contributions of nuevomexicanos to the federal government's Public Works of Art Project (PWAP), Federal Art Project (FAP), and other initiatives associated with the Works Progress Administration (WPA) and President Franklin Delano Roosevelt's Depression-era New Deal program of the 1930s. Nunn's detailed study examines the intertwined nature of WPA-era work and the revival movements outlined above.[67] In addition to the promotion of local handicrafts, nuevomexicano painters engaged with the local landscape and autochthonous architecture in ways that both aligned with and differed from their better-known modernist transplant peers. According to Nunn, Hispano painters supported by the "*Diablo a pie*" (literally the "devil on foot," a tongue-in-cheek play on words for how "WPA" sounds when said out loud by Spanish-dominant speakers) received far less attention than Anglo artists. This is ironic, she suggests, given the popularity of Diego Rivera and other Mexican muralists in the United States at the time, which might have elicited parallel interest in their Mexican American counterparts.[68] Nonetheless, a handful of FSA artists, including Pedro Cervántez and Edward Chávez, were able to make names for themselves and achieve recognition outside the state. Both artists frequently represented both the desert landscape and New Mexican built environment. An early painting by Chávez, *Colt* (1939) features a mother and baby horse amid a dreamlike mountainous environment (fig. 4.8). The frenzied brushstrokes and limited palette seem to fuse the animals directly to the land around them. Chávez was born in Ocate, New Mexico, to a Taoseña mother and Texan sheep rancher father. After studying with Frank Mechau and Boardman Robinson at the Colorado Springs Fine Arts Center, he began painting for the FAP. After WWII, he moved to Woodstock, New York, though he frequently returned to the Southwest. In Woodstock, his style, perhaps reflecting his proximity to the postwar New York City art world milieu, underwent a radical shift toward experiments in abstraction.[69]

In a statement, Cervántez, who was born in Wilcox, Arizona, to mestizo and Spanish descended Mexican parents and came to New Mexico when his father began working for the railroad, affirmed, "My favorite subject is landscapes, direct from nature, because I feel that all this beauty and color should have a place in every home."[70] Cervántez trained in painting with Russell Vernon Hunter, the director of the New Mexico WPA. He was recognized outside the state as well, showing in several exhibitions at the Museum of Modern Art in New York, including *New Horizons of American Art* (1936), *Masters of Modern Painting: Modern Primitives of Europe and America* (1938), *Modern Primitives: Artists of the People* (1944), and *America Seen: Between the Wars* (1961). The framing of Hispano artists as "modern primitives" is consistent with MoMA's dichotomous separation of apparently avant-garde or modernist artists from their regional, self-taught, or otherwise unconventional counterparts (who were, in many cases, artists of color) even as MoMA curators emphasized these latter artists' work's formal similarities to modern art; other New Mexicans, such as woodcarvers Patrocinio Barela and José Dolores López were also promoted by the museum

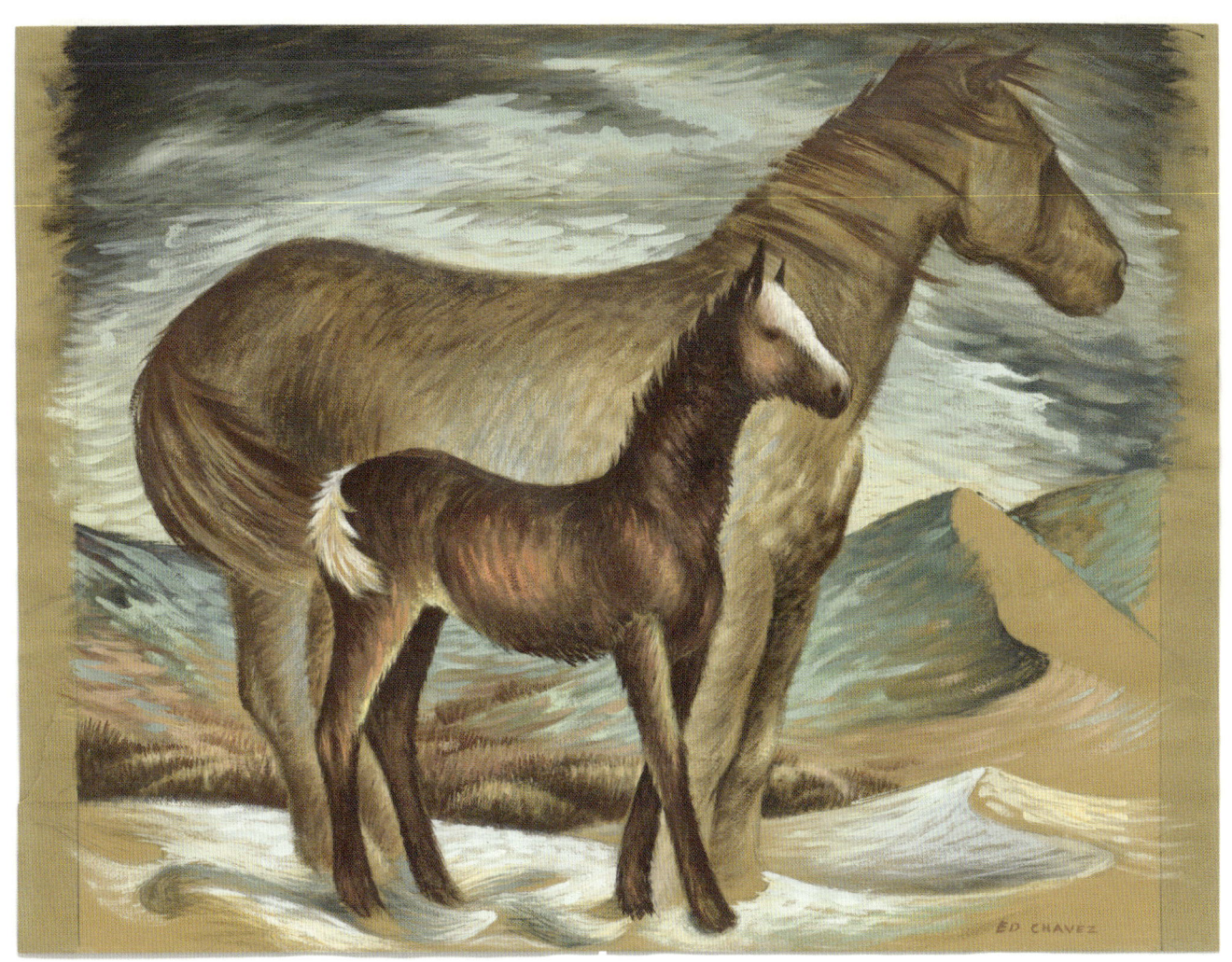

FIGURE 4.8. Edward Chávez, *Colt*, ca. 1939. Gouache on board, 17 ⅞" × 21 ½".
The Museum of Modern Art, New York. Abby Aldrich Rockefeller Fund.
Digital Image © The Museum of Modern Art/Licensed by SCALA / Art
Resource, New York.

under this rubric.[71] Though Cervántez was fond of landscapes, his inclusion of industrial or less romantic-looking structures distinguishes him from others for whom rendering landscapes that were picturesque, unspoiled, or devoid of human presence constituted the ideal form of paying tribute to a place. Working in a more ambiguous vein, in *Los privados* (The Privies) (1937), Cervántez depicts a humble wood-beam structure with a pitched roof (fig. 4.9). Two twin doors with exposed open space at the top identify their function—the painting has alternatively been titled *Los cuates privados* (The Twin Privies).[72] The doors are echoed in the landscape, with two nearly identical hills rising the background. Clothing in pink and white tones dangles from a clothesline and is reflected on the ground below, as if a saturated ray of sunlight was casting light from above. This emphasis on the strangely disembodied elements of the clothing and the apparently empty privies imparts a surreal and slightly uncanny cast to the painting, dispelling any assumption of a wholly idealized landscape and rendering the banal extraordinary.

Earthen Imaginaries Reclaimed: La Academia de la Nueva Raza and *Resolana*

Not merely the purview of modernists, New Deal artists, and the subsequent wave of hippie arrivals, building with earth, working with clay, and creating using land-based materials held profound symbolic and even spiritual significance for Hispano, Pueblo, and Genízaro communities.[73] In her 1976 MA thesis in architecture, the architect and artist Rina Swentzell (Santa Clara Pueblo/Kha-'Po Owingeh describes the ways that Pueblo philosophy was inscribed into each component of the built environment (plazas, kivas, habitation structures, and the *nansipu*, or earth center): "These elements created directional forces inward—into the earth. The structures were ground-connected, and the focus of the Pueblo form, given the entrance into the ground through the nansipu, was into the earth, revealing the desire to be inseparable from nature. The building materials were of the earth, and handled so that continuity of wall and ground were not lost."[74] Anita O. Rodríguez's ruminations on adobe corroborate this viewpoint, albeit from a more pragmatic standpoint. On the environmental benefits of adobe architecture, in a 1978 interview Rodríguez observed: "A house can be made to really belong to the land from which it was raised," adding that once it has run its logical life course it can return organically to the land below it without leaving traces of 'technological garbage.'"[75]

One of Rodríguez's earliest forays into adobe plastering occurred when she assisted Tomás Atencio with the replastering of a *torreón* (fortified tower) on his family property in Dixon, a small town located in northern New Mexico's Río Arriba County, located

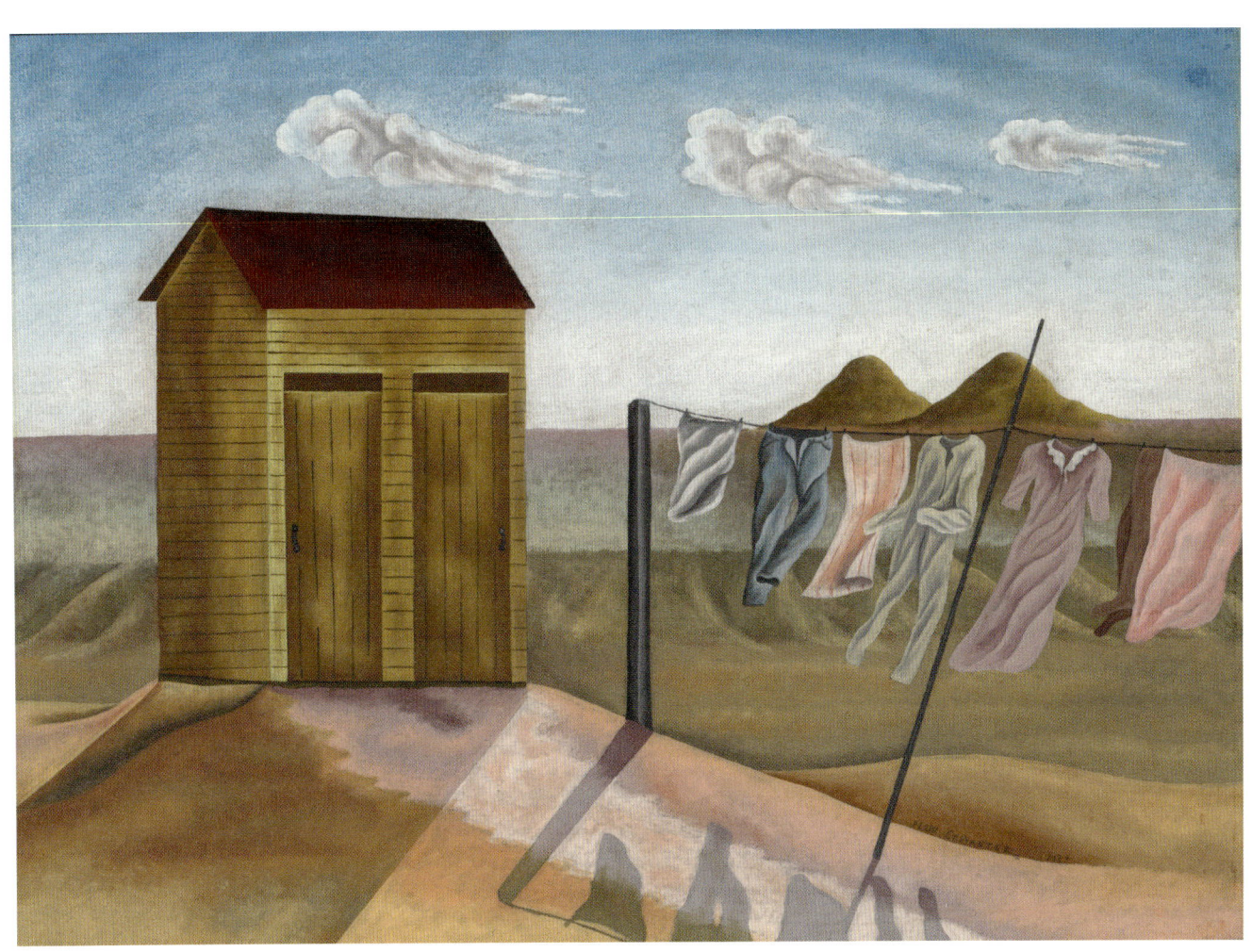

FIGURE 49. Pedro Cervántez, *Los Privados*, 1937. Oil on fiberboard, 14 ¾" × 19 ¾". Smithsonian American Art Museum, transfer from the General Services Administration.

between Española and Taos, and the site of encounter for La Academia de Nueva Raza, an activist collective focused on Chicano consciousness building, dialogical pedagogy, and community engagement.[76] Atencio, the group's cofounder, was the son of a Presbyterian minister whose familial property constituted the spatial core of a group that was actually more of an abstract collective of practitioners than a physical "Academy."[77]

Atencio, a trained social worker, helped establish La Academia in the late 1960s in an attempt to marshal ancestral knowledge to combat the struggles facing beleaguered northern New Mexico communities fraught with poverty, rampant drug use, and social stagnation as well as dispossession and other threats to land and livelihood.[78] Adobe held pride of place in his thinking. In a 2009 text describing one of the rooms in the group's Dixon headquarters, he reflected extensively on the physical properties of the gathering place:

> The walls were nearly two feet thick and had no windows. A crude door at one time had opened to the road. It was so well secured that we left it closed and patched it over with adobe while leaving the frame exposed. A year or so later Guillermo Chávez Rosete, a Chicano/Indio roving activist and artist from El Centro Cultural de la Raza in San Diego, stopped by, stayed a few nights, and painted the Virgen de Guadalupe, the patron saint of Mexico and a widely recognized movement icon, within the old door frame. On the west wall hung a large crucifix carved by Cleofes Vigil, a famous folklorist, story-teller, and woodcarver. On the floor in front of the crucifix was *la carreta de la Muerte*, a cart carrying a sculpted skeleton with a bow and arrow carved by Horacio Valdez, the famed *santero*. On one corner was an Alberto Baros *santo*; opposite was an abstract piece by Estevan Arellano. Only two of the carvers were or had been Penitente brothers, but we decided with all due respect to call that room *la morada*, the brothers' spiritual home and chapel. It had a small adobe fireplace in the corner and adobe *banquitos* [benches] to sit on. It was a place for meditation, reflection, and relaxation, and it also became a home for our growing production of woodcarvings.[79]

As Atencio's exegesis demonstrates, the physical and symbolic space generated by and around adobe walls, fireplace, and bancos, and amplified by spontaneous artistic interventions, particularly those in wood, was emblematic of the group's overarching ethos.

Originally from Dixon, Atencio drew on experiences working in California and Texas to help formalize the philosophical and pedagogical bent of La Academia. Along with Consuelo Pacheco, a nurse from Albuquerque whom he eventually married, he advocated for culturally informed health clinics—particularly emphasizing mental health—in rural communities, which were systematically underserved by hospitals in the larger cities of

Santa Fe, Taos, and Española. Atencio and compatriots such as Pacheco, Estevan Arellano, Elena (Ellen) Arellano, Facundo Valdez, E. A. "Tony" Mares, Alejandro "Jerry" López, Vicente Martínez, Dorotea Martínez, Cleofes Vigil, and others, began to gather regularly in Dixon from about 1969 on, eventually establishing a nonprofit organization centered on preserving the linguistic, cultural, and artistic heritage of the earlier generations of northern New Mexico Chicano communities, which they accomplished through workshops, publications, and exhibitions. Among their earliest endeavors, La Academia sponsored an exhibition around 1971 in Ranchitos (near Española) at the Artes del Norte Arts and Crafts Centro, a venue founded by Alberto Baros and Lorenzo Valdez.[80] Baros, a santero, was also responsible for the pen and ink illustrations found in La Academia's 1972 signal publication *Entre verde y seco* ("between the green and the dry," an expression that speaks to the cyclical nature of good and bad, the mutability and seasonality of time, and so forth). *Entre verde y seco* compiled interviews, *dichos* and *refranes* (sayings and proverbs), and social commentary primarily drawn from the older generations alongside photographs of the northern New Mexico landscape, vernacular architecture, and the woodcarvings of Cleofes Vigil, as well as Baros's drawings.[81]

Loosely imagined as a Chicano rethinking of Plato's Academy in Athens, the group's name was initially conceived as La Academia de Aztlán, referencing the mythical homeland of the Mexica (Aztec) people whose territorial and spiritual claims to the region that we now know as the US Southwest were frequently adopted by Chicano activists. In 1970, the group changed its name to La Academia de la Nueva Raza, which they translated as "the new humanity" rather than the more literal version of *raza* (race). According to Estevan Arellano, with this shift the group rejected a stridently Chicano nationalistic position to favor a more humanistic one.[82] It is likewise possible that the invocation of Aztlán, a frequently deployed trope among Chicano artist and activist circles throughout the country, held less discursive currency in a New Mexican context. Given the aforementioned factors of both the state's overdetermined and constructed myth of tricultural harmony (Native, Hispano/Spanish, Anglo), as well as the lived adjacency between Hispano, Pueblo, and Genízaro communities, it makes sense that the more strident Mexican indigenist rhetoric prevalent in other places would find less traction in northern New Mexico. Though not explicitly named, Indo-Hispano and Genízaro consciousness as a counter to Spanish identity may have found a better foothold, perhaps explaining the relatively rapid excision of Aztlán from La Academia's identity.[83]

Sun-baked adobe walls are obliquely invoked in one of La Academia's core theoretical tenets, *la resolana*. Literally a sunny spot or glare, in New Mexico parlance, the word "resolana" is used to refer to a sunny, wind-protected side of a building where community members gather to exchange knowledge, stories, and the latest news and gossip. Despite the generative valence suggested by both the word (which directly speaks to sun, comfort, and community) and its colloquial usage, at various points the notion of resolana had historically been viewed pejoratively and with racist undertones. As David Floyd García has documented, late nineteenth- and early twentieth-century print media were known to critique the supposed vices of Puerto Rican and nuevomexicano populations, citing wine and *jaranas* (a type of stringed instrument) in the case of the former, and cigarettes and resolanas in the case of the latter. Another source referred to nuevomexicano*s* as a "*populacho resolanero y vagabundo*" (a resolana-enjoying and vagabond populace), suggesting laziness and lawlessness.[84]

Much like the embrace of the similarly ambivalent term "Chicano," activists in 1960s northern New Mexico reclaimed and theorized resolana anew, transforming it into a guiding principle and cornerstone of La Academia's ethos and praxis. In a 1988 lecture delivered at Stanford University, Atencio stated, "The term resolana derives from a real place—a space of sunny tamped earth on the south side of a building or plaza."[85] In an earlier essay, Atencio and Consuelo Pacheco further elaborate on the practices of so-called *resolaneros*: "Protected from the wind and spurred on by the sun they talked about many things. At times they engaged in idle gossip or made sharp satirical comments about some event or occurrence of village interest. They related *cuentos*, *chistes*, *dichos*, and they joked and laughed about the tragicomedy of life's paradoxes. They lamented the death of a *compañero* or made wry observations about villagers who passed by. And in the sun-filled area of *la resolana*, they reached into their memories and found ways to sustain and strengthen life and realize a sense of plenitude."[86]

The mission and methodology employed by La Academia can be productively compared to the concept of *conscientização* (critical consciousness-raising) expounded on by the Brazilian educator Paulo Freire, whose influential text *Pedagogy of the Oppressed* was written between 1967 and 1968; it was first published in Spanish in 1968, followed by an English translation in 1970. Freire paid a visit to northern New Mexico over the period of January 14 to 17, 1973, delivering a closed-door lecture for La Academia members and invited guests at the Ghost Ranch conference center in Abiquiú. He also visited La Academia's headquarters in Dixon.[87] In conducting interviews and studies, Freire favored an approach that was both collaborative and dialogical: "To investigate the generative theme is to investigate people's thinking about reality and people's action upon reality, which is their praxis. For precisely this reason, the methodology proposed requires that the investigators and the people (who would normally be considered objects of that investigation) should act as co-investigators. The more active an attitude men and women take in regard to the exploration of their thematics, the more they deepen their critical awareness of reality and, in spelling out those thematics, take possession of that reality."[88] This echoes a complaint regarding the extractive nature of scholarly research made by Atencio in *Entre verde y seco*: that outsider scholars, both English and Spanish speaking, had "combed our villages, taking the gold from our people, and they have not reciprocated nor contributed toward a popular education using what they have accumulated."[89]

Comparing La Academia's approach to Freire's conscientização, Atencio explains, "The uncovering and understanding of information with a contributor is facilitated and enhanced in dialogue by the knowledge and skill of the interviewer. In this interaction both parties reach a mutual understanding and learn from each other through the exchange of information. It was clear at the outset of our documentation program that some of the material being documented had already been critically analyzed by the contributors, and the dialogue facilitated reflection." To prove his point, he argues that phrases such as the *refrán* or *dicho* (proverb or saying) have already undergone critical reflection, and that therefore a community already possesses the tools to understand its own reality without the help of added interpretation.[90] Just as Atencio and his collaborators at La Academia undertook the task of gathering oral histories, recipes, proverbs, and anecdotes from northern New Mexico community members for *Entre verde y seco*, so too was the collection and documentation of ancestral practices central to the practices of Rodríguez in adobe, Archuleta-Sagel and Lavadie in weaving, and Tapia and other woodcarvers in santero iconography and carving technique. This drive to gather and foment community knowledge-building, to preserve the histories and practices of past generations with an eye to the future, and to resist stereotypical perceptions imposed by art markets and the tourist industry was exemplary of a practice and artistic ethos grounded in the notion of resolana.[91] Animated by the activist militancy of land and water-based activism happening simultaneously, New Mexican artists associated with the Chicano movement found themselves ideally positioned to revive and re-present ancestral traditions on their own terms.

Adobe, Activism, and the Land

During the 1960s and 1970s, the broader sociopolitical panorama of northern New Mexico surrounding housing, land, and resource management, as well as what we might characterize as an incipient "adobe industry" that itself contributed to ongoing gentrification, was laden with tensions, often with racially and ethnically motivated conflict at its core. Sylvia Rodríguez has written extensively about the politics of land, water, and the crosscurrents of race, class, and ethnicity in the region. As she describes, between 1968 and 1971, Taos was hit by the "Great Hippie Invasion," an influx of Anglo transplants whose arrival echoed the earlier wave of Mabel Dodge Luhan, Georgia O'Keeffe, and their ilk under a new guise. Though some came to New Mexico for the possibly more innocent pursuit of spiritual enlightenment and a "back-to-the-earth" ethos, others embarked on exploitative land acquisition and speculation practices. After purchasing cheap parcels of land from Hispanos, many new arrivals resold their land for a profit in a moment that coincided with the rise of the skiing industry and a renewed tourism boom in Taos.[92] Though Reies López Tijerina's land grant movement is easily the most publicized instance of land-based activism among Chicano communities in northern New Mexico, it was hardly the only instance mobilization of protest.[93] Sylvia Rodríguez undertakes an in-depth analysis of the Indian Camp Dam case, a divisive conflict involving the construction of a dam and reservoir southeast of Taos. The dam, which was never built, served as the inspiration for Taos-based writer John Nichols's acclaimed novel *The Milagro Beanfield War* (1974), which was adapted into a major motion picture directed by Robert Redford in 1988.[94] As a real estate boom sprung up during the 1970s, grassroots coalitions, often of a multiethnic character, protested the construction of the Taos Ski Valley resort. Lower-profile fights against other zoning plans that favored new constructions targeted at attracting transplants despite housing shortages among lower- and middle-income households were likewise commonplace.[95]

In Valdez, a small Hispano-dominant land grant community downriver from the ski resort, a series of protests precipitated by Taos businessman Jeffrey Cottam's proposal to develop thirty-nine condominiums in the middle of the town erupted in full force. Activists, townspeople, and the mayordomo of the village's *acequia* were concerned (with reason) about the condos' excessive water use, already impacted by the ski resort, and a broad-based resistance effort known as the "Condo Wars" took shape.[96] Argentine feminist philosopher María Lugones, who maintained part-time residence in Valdez, was a key organizer in the actions, as was Sylvia Rodríguez herself. A group of activists disrupted the Taos Fiesta, carrying with them a banner made of a white sheet onto which Valdez residents had signed their names and ages next to blood pricked from their own fingers to protest yet another prospective condo builder, Pete Crandall. Signs read "The blood of Valdez is on your hands."[97] According to Lugones, "Of course, our marching behind that sign had a carnate intentionality, like blood brothers and sisters, made anew out of love and anger."[98] Others in the artist and activist community were involved in these efforts—an advertisement in *The Taos News* announced a September 26, 1982, protest in Valdez, with featured speakers including musician and poet Cleofes Vigil, santera and disability activist Linda Martínez de Pedro, social worker and La Academia cofounder Facundo Valdez, and land grant activists Pedro Archuleta and Reies López Tijerina.[99] Though ultimately successful in running out the prospective developers, the condo wars were emblematic of the ongoing threat to land and livelihood that continue to impact Chicano and Native groups due to widespread development and profiteering.

Artists took up environmental concerns in their artworks as well. Pola López's painting *El veneno está encima de nosotros* (The Poison Is Upon Us) from 1980 offers a visceral commentary on the proposed Waste Isolation Pilot Plant (WIPP) in Carlsbad, in southern New Mexico, the world's first geologic military waste repository (fig. 4.10). WIPP was, according to Jack Kutz, among the most controversial environmental disputes to unfold in the state.[100] In response to rapidly increasing quantities of transuranic waste (a category of high-level radioactive waste established by the Atomic Energy Commission to encompass waste that consisted of all atomic numbers higher than uranium's), in the wake of the Manhattan Project and other developments in nuclear technology, the U.S. Department of Energy took steps to begin building a site to dispose of the waste in a former potash mine site. Potash mining had been the main economic driver in Carlsbad, and the mayor enthusiastically supported the new prospect of housing this massive high-level radioactive waste storage facility. An earlier proposed site, the salt mines of Lyons, Kansas, had fallen through, but in 1971 the Atomic Energy Commission began to lay the groundwork to build the facility in Carlsbad instead, with construction beginning in 1981.[101] However, a summer 1983 issue of *Nuclear Waste News* indicated that the project was still awaiting public comment due to a number of grave safety concerns from both the state government and the general public, including regarding whether the site was suitable for high-level waste at all. The DOE countered, but doubt remained among safety advocates about the project.[102] After numerous false starts, the plant began operations in 1999.

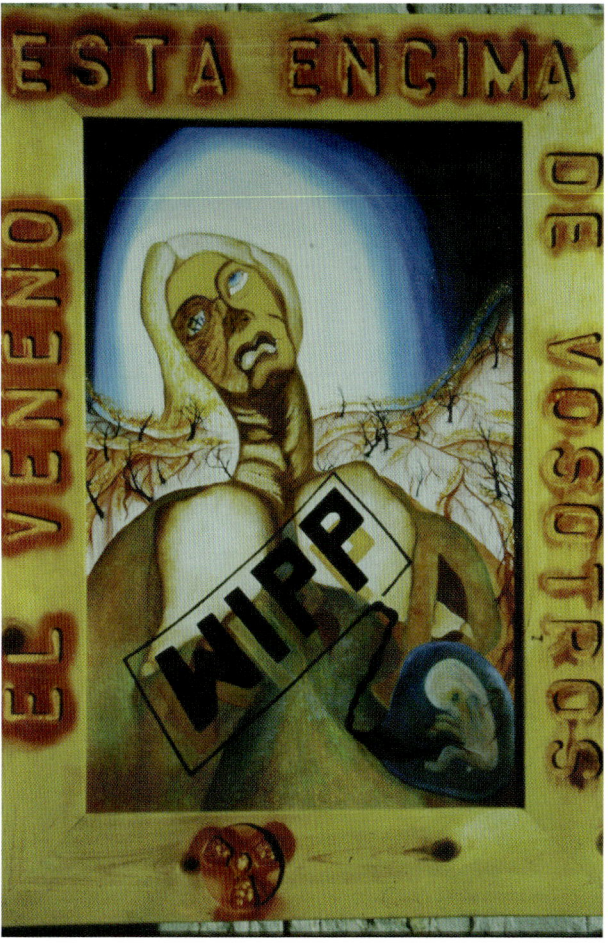

FIGURE 4.10. Pola López, *El veneno está encima de nosotros* (The poison is upon us), 1980. Mixed media. Shifra M. Goldman Papers, CEMA 119. Department of Special Research Collections, UC Santa Barbara Library.

López's painting, dated before the beginning of the plant's construction, visualizes the concern felt by many over the environmental damage, contamination, and other consequences that would be occasioned by the WIPP's construction. As in *Las picoteadas*, discussed earlier, the land is visualized as an unclothed figure, in this case a woman whose flowing hair dissolves into the desert landscape and whose bare breasts mimic the hills behind her. The land is spare, with bare trees punctuating the otherwise open ground. The woman's face is illuminated by a radioactive burst of white light haloed in darker blue, as if the sky was exploding, recalling the enduring visual memory of Trinity, the first atomic bomb detonation, which took place also in the southern part of the state in 1945. A fetus attached to an umbilical cord appears to emerge from her belly to float nearby, foreshadowing the project's impacts on future generations. The painting is housed in a custom wooden frame built by the artist's then-husband Luis Jaramillo, on which the title is written in relief along with a radioactive sign. The letters WIPP appear over the body-land as if stamped, signaling bureaucratic inevitability despite the numerous voices of dissent.[103]

Though less overt than the destructive environmental policies of the WIPP case, developments around adobe, the environment, and government policy escalated considerably during the 1970s, resulting in a contested terrain ripe for activism. Albert Narath's study of earth architecture and ecologies in postwar New Mexico tackles a complex array of critical issues emerging from the seemingly humble material, including the boom in environmentally friendly "solar-adobe" construction, increased regulation in building codes, the politics of Indigenous sovereignty in adobe construction, and links between government research and adobe experimentation.[104] During this same period, Anita O. Rodríguez was launching her construction career and found herself confronting a local adobe landscape at a paradoxical crossroads. On the one hand, as Anglo settlement began to outstrip Native and Hispano populations and real estate boomed, adobe construction, which had been a largely communal and familial enterprise, saw a marked uptick in professionalization. On the other, both the land grabs and building code modifications had the effect of limiting its access to those Native and Hispano communities that had practiced earthen construction for generations.

Nowhere was the trend toward professionalization more evident than in the rise of adobe aficionado publications, such as *Adobe News*, whose first issue was published in 1974 (its name was later changed to *Adobe Today* in 1978 and *Earthbuilder* in 1983). The publication covered developments related to the rise in so-called solar-adobe construction, which capitalized on adobe's potential to produce solar power for low energy, environmentally responsive housing. The publication also included numerous do-it-yourself tips, book reviews, write-ups on notable owner-built properties, and profiles of contractors and businesspeople working in the field. Rodríguez herself wrote a piece on the history of enjarradoras, the women who had historically taken charge of the upkeep of mud-plastered walls, for a 1977 issue of the magazine.[105] As Orlando Romero and David Larkin have argued, the term "adobe industry" would have been a "contradiction in terms" before the 1970s, but riding the wave of interest, the publications' editors were also active in the creation of the Southwest Adobe Association (SAA).[106] As a practicing contractor in the adobe construction field, Rodríguez had an ambivalent relationship to the largely Anglo, boys' club–type leadership of the publication (and presumably by extension the SAA). Nevertheless, she spoke positively about organizing with the SAA as a strategy to help dispel misconceptions about the suitability of adobe as a material fit for adoption on a municipal rather than individual scale. According to members of the organization, adobe was habitually "slandered" by officials.[107] Indeed, in a widely publicized case in 1976, the U.S. Department of Housing and Urban Development (HUD)'s Office of Indian Programs called into question the energy efficiency of adobe for use in affordable public housing on the Pueblos. The Office required the addition of what most experts deemed to be unnecessary insulation, which in turn led them to conclude that adobe housing would be too costly for HUD to finance. HUD measured adobe's resistance to temperature change, an isolated and inaccurate metric that failed to holistically consider its ability to self-regulate.[108] The SAA supported the Eight Northern Pueblos Indian Council in its bid to allow adobe building on Pueblo land, as well as New Mexico Senator Pete Domenici's 1980 challenge to the HUD ruling, but changes to the building code and adobe regulations moved at a glacial pace, a fact that flew in the face of the rise in adobe's popularity among wealthy residents, not to mention a spike of interest in adobe among the environmentally conscious precisely for its energy efficient and minimally damaging ecological footprint.

As these examples have shown, artists seamlessly oscillated between art making and land-based activism. While artistic institutions might have disregarded their contributions and denied them access, their so-called traditional practices served as a form and method of political advocacy and praxis in their own right.

Mud, Wool, and Wood: Reclaiming Materiality in Chicano Art and Exhibition Practice

The paradigmatic exhibitions that circumscribed a set of prescriptions and contradictions around Chicano artists, contemporaneity, and so-called traditional arts analyzed at the start of this essay were the product of non-Chicano curators and were held in spaces where the binary strictures were largely upheld. La Cofradía de Artes y Artesanos Hispánicos, an artist collective founded in 1978 and active until 1982, represents an alternative model. Initially convened by a small group of artists including woodcarver Luis Tapia, as more artists were recruited, the collective expanded to comprise a large assortment of nuevo-mexicano artists working across mediums. Laurie Beth Kalb has suggested that group leaders' decision to call themselves a *cofradía*, or brotherhood (in a religious sense) was due to the word's association with "defiance and struggle" given the Hispano cofradías' resistance to the religious hegemony of the Anglo Catholic Church.[109] But there must also have been something tongue-in-cheek about the decision, which both pays tribute to the lay religious traditions of New Mexico and their relationship to the production of religious sculpture and affirms the possibility of a departure from tradition that many of the artists espoused. Indeed, Tapia has claimed as of thirty or forty years ago, he no longer identifies as a santero due to the secular character of more recent work. Even in the 1970s and 1980s, his work flouted convention.

Born in Agua Fría, near Santa Fe, Tapia was given access early in his career to the historical collections of Hispano art now housed at the Museum of International Folk Art, which inspired him to begin painting santos and building and restoring furniture. In the *bulto* (three-dimensional santo, meant to be viewed in the round, as opposed to a two-dimensional *retablo*) of *San Miguel Arcángel* (1970s), Tapia depicts Saint Michael, the angel of judgment tasked with preparing for the second coming of Christ. Tapia's version follows Saint Michael's traditional iconography, including a set of scales to determine who enters the Kingdom of Heaven (fig. 4.11).[110] Clad in a red and yellow tunic, white leggings, and black boots, he stands upright with one foot perched on a black-horned devil figure, representing Satan, whom he has speared with the unpainted sharpened wood stake he holds in his right hand. Pointed teeth and a gleaming red tongue contrast sharply with devil's inky body. Saint Michael's face and hands are also rendered in bright white, accentuating the contrast further.

In his own work, Tapia habitually worked in acrylic paint, though as someone who was frequently commissioned by museums and churches to restore colonial furniture, santos, and altarpieces, he was deeply familiar with traditional pigments. The use of commercial pigments gave his work a brilliant gleaming sheen and pops of saturated color that distinguished it from the work of some other artists working in the santero tradition, who tended to create either unpainted santos or work in more muted color palettes. In particular, his work deviated strongly from the Córdova tradition of unpainted santos, begun by José Dolores López, who was famously encouraged by Frank Applegate to stop painting his sculptures as a way to appeal to tourists.[111] Tapia has, however, argued that when the colonial-era carvings were freshly painted, their colors would have likewise been brilliant.[112] In this way, the conventional view of them as faded and worn is an inaccurate perception that plays into their allure, and also to the ways that early collectors of santos valued them as simpler, more humble objects in comparison to religious paintings from Spain and Latin America's colonial centers. James Córdova has argued that the colonial New Mexican santos produced from the seventeenth century onward exhibit "artistic bricolage" that fuse Roman Catholic imagery with motifs found in Pueblo pottery, rock art, and other cultural forms. However, as he writes, "Despite these similarities, cross-cultural bricolage in New Mexico's santos does not indicate fusion of Hispano and Pueblo symbols and their meanings, but rather it points to a shared graphic system and aesthetic borne of centuries of Hispano-Pueblo relations. This allowed for a range of understandings and uses of santos that depended on the viewer's cultural frame of reference."[113] In a similar vein, Tapia has stated that he enjoys the hidden political allegories and social commentary that can be gleaned from biblical stories: in the case of Saint Michael, whom he has jokingly referred to as the "bouncer," one might analogize the archangel's quest in the fight of good against evil to the Hispano artist's plight to "make it" in an art market ecosystem in which their work is marginalized, instrumentalized, or ignored entirely.[114] By using non-"traditional"

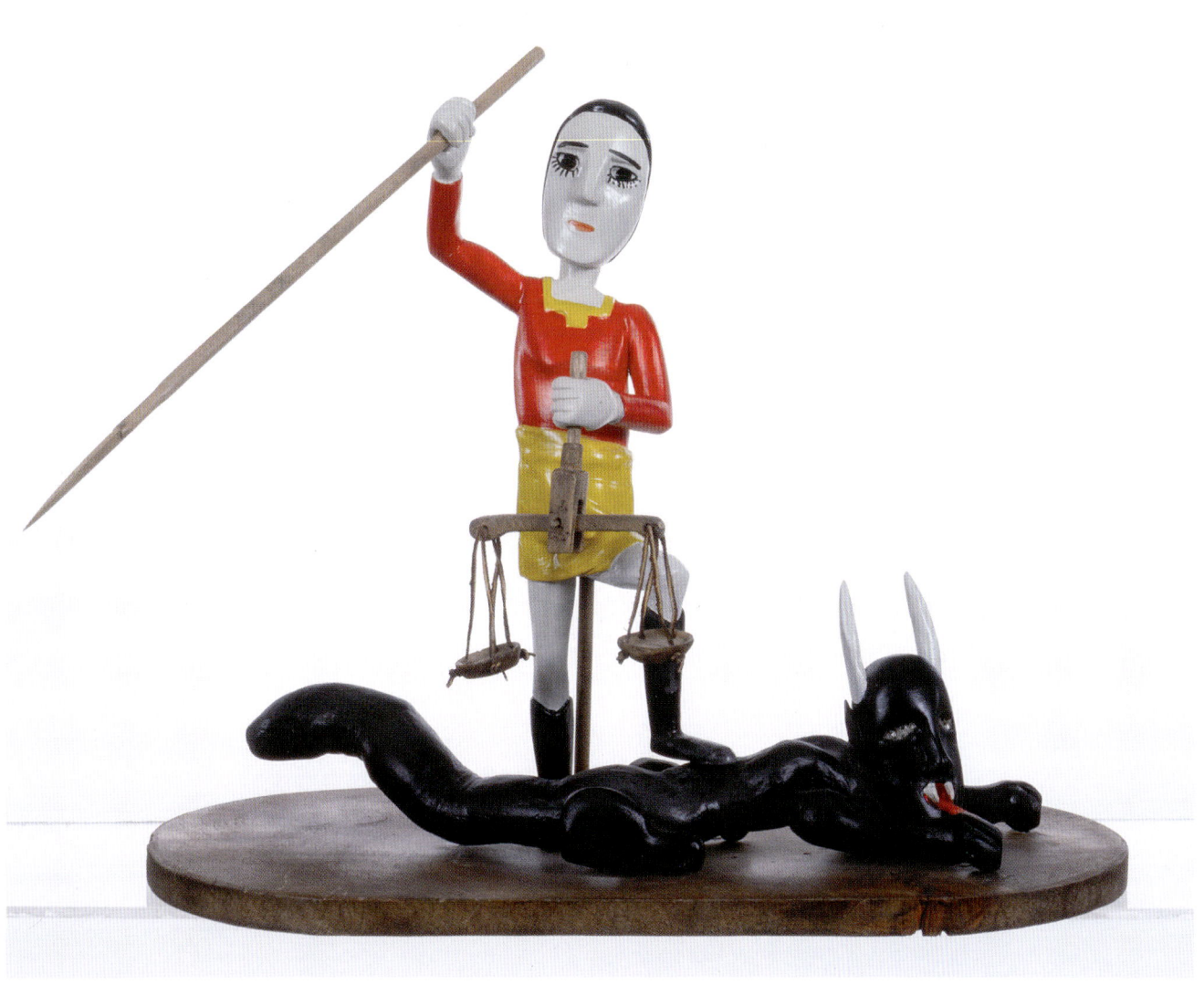

FIGURE 4.11. Luis Tapia, *Bulto of San Miguel Arcángel*, 1975. Pigment on wood.
Collection of the Nuevo Mexicano Heritage Museum. Courtesy Luis E.
Tapia, Santa Fe, New Mexico.

pigments to allude to an overlooked historical past as well as the semi-obscured meanings embedded in the iconography, Tapia straddles temporalities, updating the santo for the contemporary moment while paying tribute to longstanding practices.

Tapia was instrumental to the organization of Cofradía's series of increasingly ambitious exhibitions organized during the group's relatively short duration. Initially comprising Tapia (the group's first president), Frederico Vigil, Star Sánchez, Wilfredo Miera, María Luisa Delgado, Rolando de Leon, and Raphael Lovato, for the group's organizers, a major impetus was the restrictions placed on artists to exhibit in Spanish Market and other spaces sanctioned by the Santa Fe art market intelligentsia, including curators, collectors, and folk-art galleries. As the artist-curators of a 1991 Cofradía retrospective characterize it, "The combination of the Spanish Market and the patron not only defined what New Mexico Hispanic art was to be, it played a vital role in forcing the Hispanic artist to remain working in traditional and approved art forms."[115] Tapia himself had the experience of having to drop out of Spanish Market when his work did not conform to their requirements.[116]

Cofradía's first exhibition was entitled *Cultura '79* and was held at the Santuario de Guadalupe church in Santa Fe. The installation included work by Tapia (who contributed several death-themed sculptures, including a *carreta de la muerte* (death cart) featuring Doña Sebastiana, the angel of death), a large crucifixion by José Benjamin López, and organic, semi-abstract works in carved wood by Estevan Arellano, as well as work by other carvers (fig. 4.12). The wood sculptures, which were favorably received by reviewers of the exhibition, were freely interspersed with weavings, retablos, paintings, and work in other sculptural media.[117] Exhibiting a harmonious visual synergy with the church's architecture, the preponderance of natural material stands out. Subsequently, the group exhibited at Santa Fe's Armory for the Arts as part of their Festival Hispánico, which featured adobe demonstrations by Anita O. Rodríguez.[118] Due to the immense toll the volunteer-run organization took on its members, the group did not curate any exhibitions in 1980, but returned in 1981 with the exhibition *Native American–Hispanic Festival: Contemporary and Historic Visions*, organized in conjunction with the Institute of American Indian Arts (IAIA). This exhibition ran parallel to another Hispano-Native collaboration, the 1981 Academia/Tri-Centennial Commission of the All-Indian Pueblo Council publication *Ceremony of Brotherhood*, edited by Rudolfo A. Anaya and Simon J. Ortiz, which featured artworks and poetry by Chicano and Indigenous artists and was published to commemorate the tricentennial of the 1680 Pueblo Revolt.[119] Cofradía's final exhibition was called *Tiempos* and was held in 1982 at the Santuario de Guadalupe, where their first exhibition had taken place. Despite the group's relatively short lifespan, it was an important springboard for many of the artists to further expand their careers.

An exhibition that spotlighted Cofradía artists was *Hebras de vision/Threads of Vision*, an exhibition of women weavers held at the Millicent Rogers Museum in Taos in 1982. Teresa Archuleta-Sagel, Juanita Jaramillo Lavadie, María Vergara Wilson, Dorotea Martínez, and

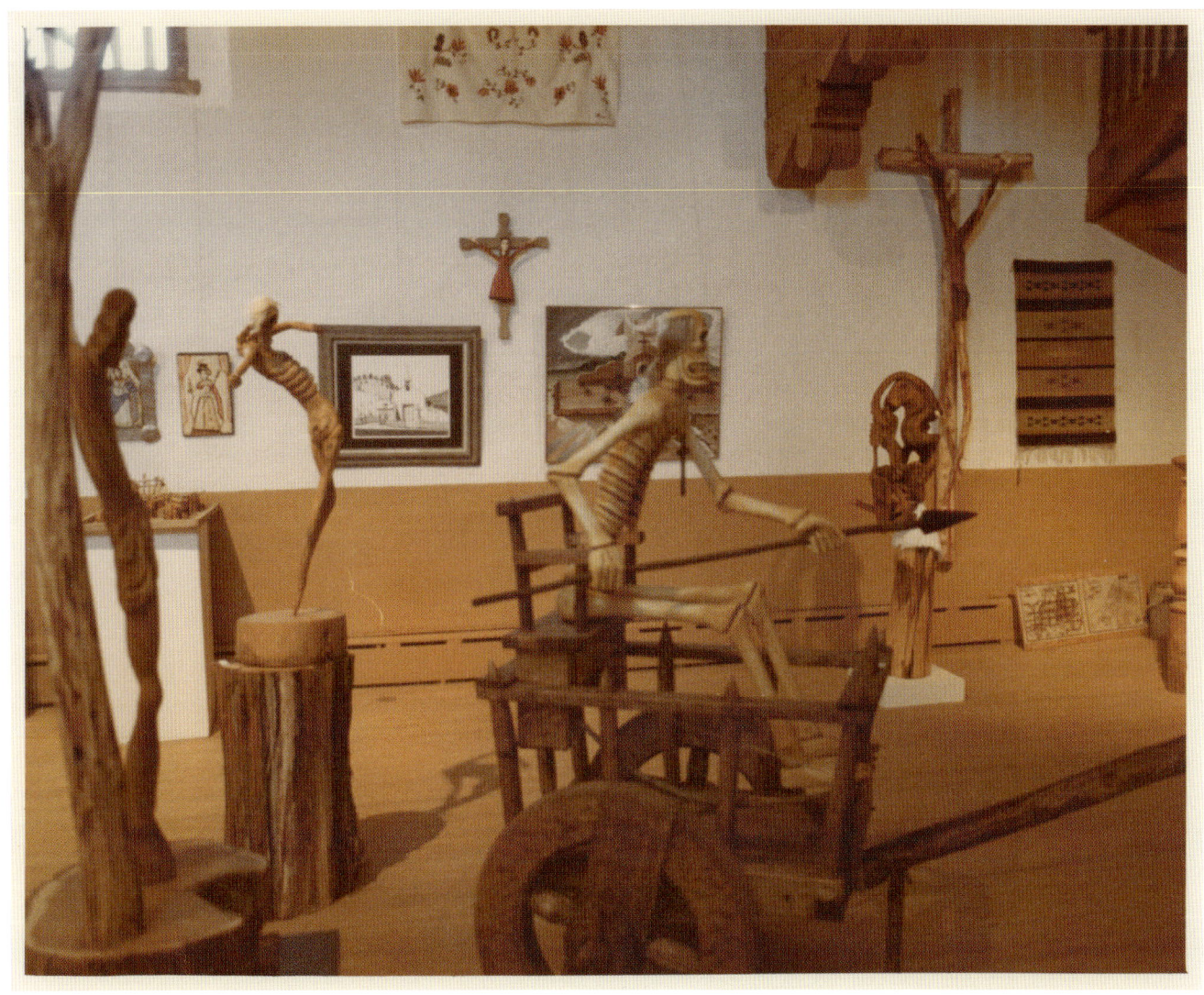

FIGURE 4.12. Installation view of *Cultura '79* exhibition, Santuario de Guadalupe, Santa Fe, 1979. Courtesy of the National Hispanic Cultural Center Archives and Special Collections, La Cofradia Archive collection.

Norma Maestas all exhibited textiles inspired to varying degrees by the Río Grande and Chimayó weaving traditions. One of the weavings by Jaramillo Lavadie, *Vallero/Reconociendo raíces*, paid tribute to the El Valle style of weaving. A native of Taos descended from six generations of weavers, including the Montoya family of El Valle, she did not benefit from the direct familial inheritance of weaving traditions as did members of the Trujillo family. Rather, she was first exposed to weaving through a professor of ceramics, Paul Volkening, while studying art at New Mexico Highlands University. Volkening encouraged students to experiment with making their own pigments in his ceramics classes, which Jaramillo Lavadie carried forward into her own trial-and-error approach to carding and spinning different varieties of wool and working with natural and synthetic dyes alike.[120]

Her engagement with Chicano art began at NMHU with another professor, the San Antonio–born muralist Pedro Rodríguez, who instilled the militancy and social consciousness of the Chicano movement in his New Mexican students.[121] After college, Jaramillo Lavadie left New Mexico for Chicago, where she worked with Casa Aztlán (founded 1970), in Chicago's Pilsen neighborhood, as well as related organizations and events, such as the Association of Latino Brotherhood of Artists (ALBA), a collective that included Chicano, Puerto Rican, and other Latin American and Latino artists; and Anishinaabewaki Aztlán, a collaborative exhibition venture merging the efforts of the collectives Movimiento Artístico Chicano (MARCH) and the Chicago Indian Artists' Guild.[122] While attending the Midwest Canto al Pueblo, a 1977 Chicano convening that ran from April 29 to May 8, 1977, in cities across Wisconsin, she felt unexpectedly compelled to return to Taos. As she recalls, "I had a dream. . . . I was at the edge of this precipice, facing the sunset, and there were warblers, birds, that were flying around, and. . . . I realized I was describing home."[123] Upon her return, she entered the interlocking realms of La Academia, Cofradía, and into collaboration with Archuleta-Sagel, who had studied with Águeda Martínez and Ruth Vigil, and who in 1978 participated in Spanish Market despite some of the deviations from tradition found in many of her textiles.[124]

A flurry of activity around Río Grande–style weaving, sheepherding, wool production, and the resuscitation of related cultural knowledge occurred during the 1970s and '80s, much of it spearheaded by individuals active in the Chicano movement. Lavadie and Archuleta-Sagel traveled to villages throughout northern New Mexico to interview elders, examine textiles, and gather wool and dye samples. In 1977, the Los Angeles–based Chicano filmmaker Moctesuma Esparza, who would later go on to produce *The Milagro Beanfield War* and *Selena*, worked with director Esperanza Vásquez to produce the Academy Award–winning documentary, *Águeda Martínez: Our People, Our Country*, about Martínez, a veteran weaver from Medernales, New Mexico. In 1979, the Museum of International Folk Art in Santa Fe organized the exhibition *Spanish Textile Tradition of New Mexico and Colorado*, which showcased historical and contemporary Río Grande–style weavings. Jaramillo Lavadie did not wholly abandon her muralist training; in 1977 she and Chicana artist and activist Enriqueta Vásquez painted *Un Puño de Tierra*, which thematizes life, death, and land, on the wall of the El Prado liquor store in Taos. The mural was originally going to picture the proposed Indian Camp Dam. Though the controversial and divisive case had by that point reached a resolution and the dam was never realized, it was still a loaded topic, and under community pressure the artists modified the mural to depict a bridge.[125]

Another weaving initiative was Ganados del Valle, a nonprofit founded in Los Ojos, Río Arriba County, by Chicana photographer and community organizer María Varela, rancher Antonio Manzanares, and shepherd Gumercindo Salazar, who began raising *churro* sheep. Under its auspices, a weaving collaborative, Tierra Wools, was also established. According to Kristina Gray Fisher, investment in human capital development was key to the organization's ability to foster real economic benefits where President Lyndon B. Johnson's War on Poverty had floundered.[126]

Though best known for her weaving, Jaramillo Lavadie's painting practice illustrates her understanding of the generational links between the weaver's labor, land, and place. In *Señora Guadalupe Norteña* (Our Northern Lady of Guadalupe) (Plate 22) from 1980, commissioned by Padre Luis Jaramillo, a Catholic priest and Chicano activist, she locates the Virgin of Guadalupe, the patron saint of Mexico, within a specific northern New Mexico geography: the canyon in Arroyo Hondo, near Taos, though she takes liberties in orientation (imagining the viewer facing the mountains from the west rather than the east). Below the expansive, constellation-filled sky (the artist is an avid stargazer), which echoes the patterns and coloring of the virgin's mantle, a zigzagging downhill trail leads the eye toward the rocky Río Hondo tributary coursing through the valley and bordered on all sides by local trees and brush.[127] Seated on a rocky outcropping at the bottom left of the painting, a shepherd in a red cloak hunches over a roaring fire whose form mirrors the rose, symbolizing prayer, in the virgin's outstretched hand.[128] Two sheep linger nearby, one inquisitively peering up at the virgin while the other reclines placidly. The shepherd can be variously read as the fabled Juan Diego of the original Mexican narrative or as Padre Luis himself. Though the near obsessive fervor of modernist artists to document the southwestern landscape while ignoring its inhabitants and the harm that their presence has wrought haunts any artistic representation of land, Jaramillo Lavadie's rendering of autochthonous flora and geological elements attest to her generations-long ties to place. Painted during a time in which she was conducting extensive research on the weaving practices in local communities, the presence of sheep as well as plants used make dyes, medicine, and foodstuffs underscores the potent connections between land, sustenance, and spirituality.[129]

An even more explicit link between weaving, landscape, and the body can be seen in another painting by Jaramillo Lavadie. *Tejiendo el Río Grande* (Weaving the Rio Grande) (Plate 24), a 1990 acrylic on canvas painting based on a 1984–1985 panel that she created as part of a *buon fresco* workshop taught by Lucienne Bloch, who had worked in New

York and Detroit with Diego Rivera, and Stephen Pope Dimitroff. The 1990 painting was painted for the Taos Valley Acequia Association (TVAA), cofounded by her husband Eduardo Lavadie.[130]

In *Tejiendo el Río Grande*, two hands hover delicately over a taut matrix of white warp threads overlaying a brown-hued topographical map of an aquifer, viewed from above. The hands expertly maneuver the sky-blue yarn—despite the static image, the steady rhythm of undulating yarn seems palpable. Individual weft threads dissolve into a coherent landscape (though still maintaining the painterly translation of the nubby weave texture), the color shifting from blue to green to yellow to a warm ochre to delineate rolling flatlands. Yet the woven texture does not fully dissolve into a naturalistic landscape, even as the composition depicts a mesa and other mountainous elements punctuated by a high horizon line and a narrow expanse of sky. Instead, the blue thread that extends from the weaver's hands coalesces into a jagged blue zigzag that simultaneously articulates a river and references *culebrías* (zigzags) and *calabrotes* (enchained diamonds), traditional patterns ubiquitous in Río Grande–style weaving.[131] In this synthesis of her various artistic materials and philosophies, Jaramillo Lavadie powerfully thematizes the parallels between cultivation and care of the ever changing land and waterways of her ancestral homeland and the embodied act of weaving as both a tradition to be conserved and an innovation to bring forward to the present day.

Like Jaramillo Lavadie and Archuleta-Sagel, Anita O. Rodríguez's career was characterized by the cultivation of skills and knowledge of the older generation, only to then adapt her techniques freely to the demands of the present. Born and raised in Taos, Rodríguez was a preschool teacher in the Head Start program on Taos Pueblo in the late 1960s, where she began learning to build *hornos* (outdoor ovens) and to replaster adobe walls. In 1971, a series of challenges befell her: her father died, her marriage ended in divorce, and the adobe house she had inherited as part of the settlement burned partially to the ground.[132] Forced to sell her house in order to support her daughter and herself, she took a job on a salmon boat before returning to Taos to embark on a full-time career as a construction professional.[133]

From the outset, Rodríguez was attentive to learning from and preserving the voices of older generations of enjarradoras. Early in her career, she toured villages in northern New Mexico in a pickup truck, milling around local post offices, small rural shops, and ranchos in search of enjarradoras whose skills she hoped to both document for posterity and incorporate into her own self-taught practice. As she wrote in her 2016 autobiography-cum-cookbook, "Besides learning actual how-to earth-building techniques I could use professionally, I saw how collective, cooperative building had been woven into Native and Hispanic culture."[134]

In exchange for the kernels of wisdom borne of a lifetime of embodied knowledge that she garnered from her informants, Rodríguez assisted with ongoing plastering, performed household and outdoor chores, and ran errands. Meanwhile, she experimented with techniques on her own before beginning to bring them to bear on a construction industry with an increasingly regulated set of standards and building codes.[135]

Amid a competitive field saturated with professional contractors and do-it-yourself amateur practitioners alike, Rodríguez's path to success in the adobe construction industry, particularly as a Chicana and as a woman, was far from straightforward. Ultimately, her notoriety grew through word-of-mouth testimonies, the cultivation of several specific areas of specialization for which she became particularly renowned—custom fireplaces, hand-laid mud floors, and the exquisite mineral alís used to finish interior walls chief among them. A veritable force of nature, her dynamic and outspoken persona emerged in her public demonstrations, lectures, and writing.

In her letter of nomination of Rodríguez for the 1983 Wonder Woman Foundation Awards, awarded to accomplished women over the age of forty, Enriqueta Vásquez succinctly outlined Rodríguez's trajectory from single mother to one of region's most sought-after consultants. Highlighting Rodríguez's innovations and artistic prowess in fireplace design and construction, asphalt-infused waterproof plaster, and durable hand-laid mud floors, Vásquez's narrative spoke to the challenges she faced, as well as the opportunities she sought out to deepen her technical knowledge through travel. Vásquez underscored how Rodríguez had gone to Guatemala in 1975 and China in 1976. Following the arrival of Hassan Fathy, Egyptian architect and author of the influential treatise on mud architecture, *Architecture for the Poor: An Experiment in Rural Egypt* (1973) to Abiquiú, where in 1980 he built the highly anticipated Dar al Islam mosque, Rodríguez also traveled to Egypt with him and a group of architects. In drawing attention to Rodríguez's accomplishments, Vásquez wrote,

> It was difficult to decide which category of nomination in which to place Anita. In one way or another, she qualifies for all of them. Going into business in a traditional and forgotten craft in the indisputably masculine field of construction was certainly a risk-taking venture. She is a strong feminist, and her aspirations and work have certainly been inspirational to women. But basically, Anita is an artist. Her major achievements, and those from which she draws the greatest satisfaction, are monumental sculptures.[136]

Rodríguez's fireplaces blur the line between functional objects and autonomous works of art. Like notable enjarradora forebears, such as Marie Mondragón of Taos Pueblo and Carmen Velarde of Taos, Rodríguez received numerous commissions to realize custom fireplaces, particularly as the vogue for adobe intensified. With no two exactly alike, her fireplaces boast sinuous, curving yet precise lines and gently rounded volumes. Echoing adobe architecture's simultaneously minimal and organic formal qualities, her fireplaces and the environments created by the enclosing mud walls and floors that her practice encompasses invite comparisons to the postminimalist and land arts practices that emerged in the wake of minimalism and rebelled against its geometric volumes and grids.[137] Though less well-publicized than monumental scale artworks such as Walter De Maria's *Lightning Field* (1977) built near Quemado, in western New Mexico in 1982 the artist couple Ana Mendieta and Carl Andre came to Albuquerque, where both created artworks using organic earth in dialogue with both the natural environment and the region's adobe built environment. Andre created a sculpture comprising a linear arrangement of adobe bricks for an exhibition at University of New Mexico Art Museum. He titled the work *Palanca* (Spanish for lever), a nod to his eponymous firebrick sculpture included in the 1966 Jewish Museum exhibition Primary Structures. His Albuquerque iteration thus riffed on his habitual engagement with factory-produced, modular, and serial forms that eschewed individuality while evincing an understanding of New Mexico's sunbaked mud bricks and their connection to Hispano (Spanish-speaking) culture through the use of Spanish in the title. For her part, Mendieta chiseled ephemeral earthworks in the form of a female body along the banks of the Río Grande, thematizing corporeality, landscape, ritual, and the cyclical and permeable nature of time.[138] As with land art more broadly, I am reticent to read too deeply into historically unsubstantiated affinities between Rodríguez's adobe practice and that of either Andre or Mendieta's works made in Albuquerque. Nevertheless, their respective engagements with earthen materials echo Rodríguez's plays with the tensions between industrial innovations and adaptations and her celebration and frequent invocation of the primordial nature of adobe's literal grounding in the land. Her fireplaces and other adobe creations meld the tenets of both sides of this apparently irreconcilable dichotomy, suggesting that Andre and Mendieta were, if nothing else, in their own ways responsive to the potent land-based imaginaries of culture and place that animated Rodríguez's own practice. The history of the New Mexican corner fireplace combines the innovation of moving the heat source to the corner, a trait first found in Zuni Pueblo, with the mud brick construction technologies used to create the fireplace hood (as well as the outdoor *horno*) that came to New Mexico from North Africa via Spain.[139] Fireplace adobes are small and slender, enabling the sculpting of a more precise curve. During the colonial period, a consistent internal structure was developed: a straight-backed firebox and chimney without a smokeshelf or flue.

Due to tightening building codes, as well as to ensure maximum longevity of her creations, Rodríguez developed adaptations to earlier fireplaces, some of which were based on investigations into heat distribution developed by the US-born British physicist Sir Benjamin Thompson, Count Rumford, whose writings on fireplace design were influential in Europe and the US during the early nineteenth century. For Rodríguez, the Count Rumford–inspired tenets used in her fireplaces included adding a smokeshelf, a four-inch protruding lip accompanied by a set-back flue, to eliminate what had formerly been a straight trajectory from chimney to hearth. The purpose of the smokeshelf was twofold: on one hand, it prevented cold air from outside from entering the house through the chimney and flue. On the other, it helped expel smoke by trapping it above the shelf, after which point the warm air inside the firebox would push it outside along with the cold air. Another modification was to make the fireplace's form more compact yet also more open, widening and lengthening the overall shape ("less like a horseshoe, more like an open parenthesis") to ensure that the heat would radiate outward rather than in.[140]

An in-progress fireplace made for the Beardsley residence illustrates the Rumford-inspired tenets (fig. 4.13). Its open back, Roman arched opening, slender chimney, recessed hearth, and stepped decorative wing walls all serve to capture and contain heat while occupying minimal floor space. Also visible in the interior of the hearth and the firebox are ceramic fire bricks, an adjustment Rodríguez began adding to her formula not long after building her earliest fireplaces, which were made exclusively with structural adobes. Despite her predilection for natural materials and her disdain for faux adobe cement coating, Rodríguez found that fire bricks were more durable and easier to maintain. Building code requirements

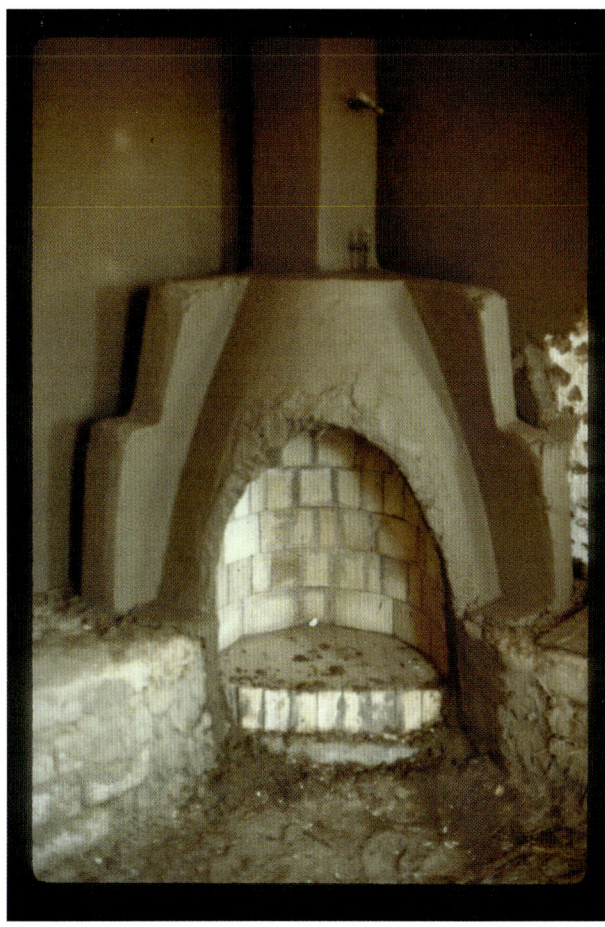

FIGURE 4.13. Anita O. Rodríguez, fireplace in Beardsley residence, process image, ca. 1970s–80s. Courtesy of Anita O. Rodríguez, Taos, New Mexico.

likewise mandated an eight-by-eight-inch standard ceramic flue, which she customized with double-dampers, two welded steel plates inserted between pieces of flue using notches carved in the edges of the flue that could be opened or closed at will using attached metal handles, which when finished would protrude outside the plaster on the flue (fig. 4.14).

When two rather than one damper was used, it was possible to exercise more control over trapping hot air and releasing smoke, resulting in greater energy efficiency.[141] Outside the frame, adobe bancos integrated directly into the design were akin to pair of arms, reaching out in an embrace of the enclosed interior space; in addition to creating an organically integrated seating area, they absorbed heat from the fireplace, which radiated outward to create a warm and inviting space.

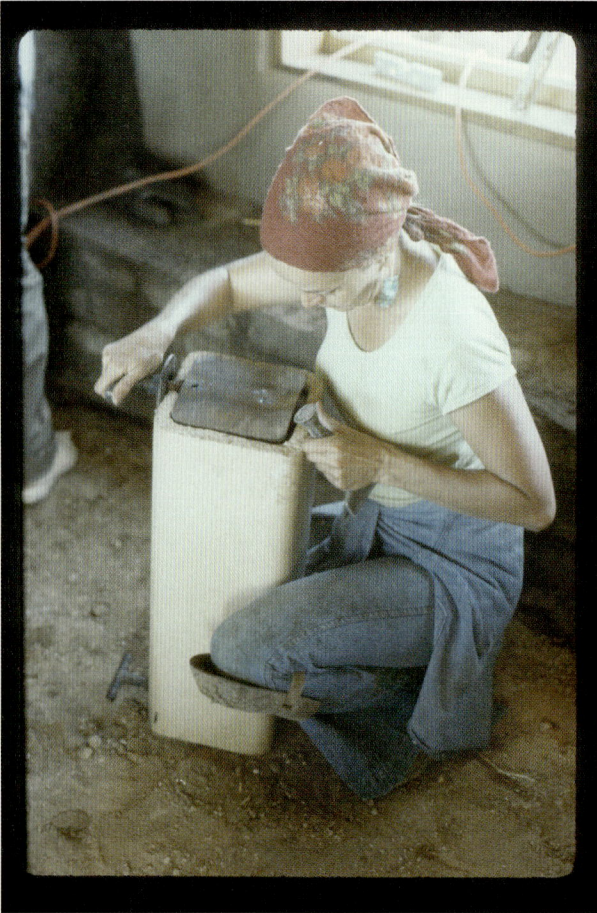

FIGURE 4.14. Anita O. Rodríguez demonstrating double damper technique. Photograph by Alejandro López. Courtesy of Anita O. Rodríguez, Taos, New Mexico.

Where Rodríguez's artistry was most evident was in the idiosyncratic sculptural flourishes that made each fireplace unique and integrated them into their individual environments, affording singularity and personality to each one. One example, located in the Boyle residence in El Salto, comprises an asymmetrical arrangement of softly angled and stepped volumes, their harmonious undulating play between solids and voids of varying depths guiding the eye in a circular motion (fig. 4.15). The fireplace's silky beige surface suggests the use of *tierra vallita*, a pale, tan-colored clay that enjoyed great popularity in Taos as an alís. The final step in the plastering process, *alisando* constituted a brilliantly simple overlay of dirt on dirt, allowing one to "paint" earthen plastered surfaces without introducing a foreign element. Minerals were highly prized, and the location of the colored clays were closely guarded secrets. Their shades were varied: *tierra colorada* (iron-red), *tierra amarilla* (yellow), micaceous *tierra blanca*, (bright white), and even green blue *tierra azul*. Alís is applied by first wetting the plastered surface of a wall, then using sheepskin or other soft material to gently dab the pigment onto it. According to Rodríguez, alís's advantages were manifold:

> Alisando seals the adobe surface, giving it greater resistance to erosion if it is exterior plaster, and hardening it against chipping and bruising if it is inside the house. Unlike commercial paints or plastic, [with alís] silicone sprays, glues, and some other materials can be used successfully in conjunction with traditional methods to produce a practical and inexpensive wall surface and a wall with a "look" no other material can give. Freshly slipped clays, especially those that contain mica, have a luminous quality that seems to make the wall glow from within. There are no adequate imitations of authentic adobe finished in the old way—the difference is striking—and heartwarming."[142]

Private yet inviting, each one of Rodríguez's fireplaces adapts to its spatial situation to create a protected yet warm and sunlit space of refugee, warmth, and gathering—a potential resolana. Fireplaces and other adobe structures represented only one facet of her practice: she led community workshops, gave lectures, and wrote prolifically on the adobe's history and future potential. She was also an active leader in the ongoing effort to restore and maintain historic buildings that adobe's innate properties necessitate, enabling her to extend her advocacy beyond private commissions. Her consistent engagement with the long arc of adobe's history provided a springboard to diverge formally, technologically, and materially, innovating even as she strove to revive the voices of the past to whom she was indebted.

Conclusion

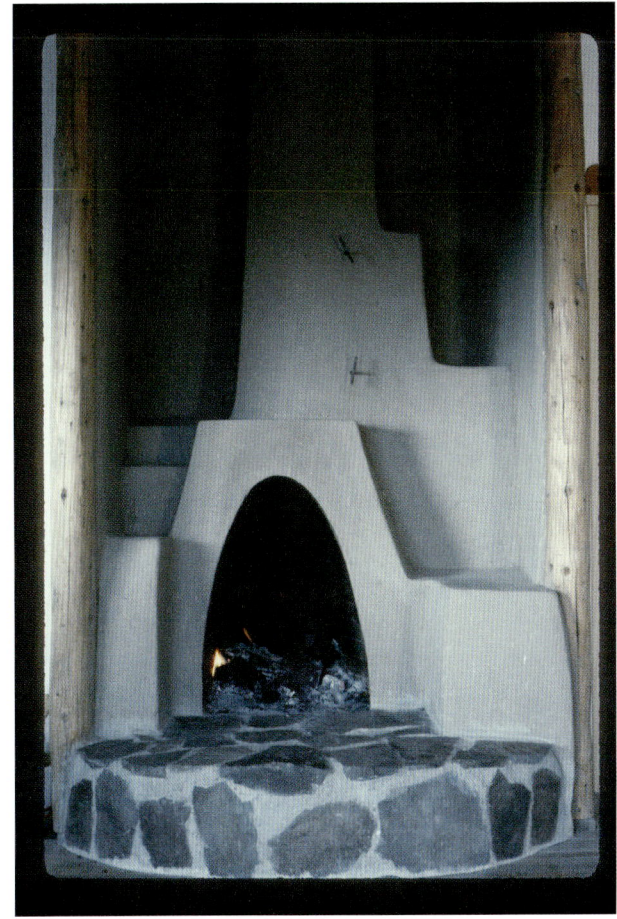

FIGURE 4.15. Anita O. Rodríguez, fireplace in Boyle residence, El Salto, New Mexico, ca. 1970s–80s. Courtesy of Anita O. Rodríguez, Taos, New Mexico.

In the 1976 short documentary *Águeda Martínez: Our People, Our Country*, the elderly weaver demonstrates the commingling of foodways, weaving, and architecture in the upkeep of her rancho. In the film, which comprises footage of her working with a voiceover of her ruminations on life, cultivation, and remaining close to the land, she concludes, "*La tierra es la única que da la vida. Y cuando ya uno se va a . . . a la tierra, la tierra se lo come*" ("The land is the only thing that gives life. And when one goes back to the land, the land swallows you up"). This awareness of the cyclical vicissitudes of a life wholly in harmony with the land operates as both a vestige of the past and a provocation for those artists who aim to both honor and update the legacy of Martínez and others of her generation. For nuevomexicano artists working in the years following the Chicano movement, the intimate entanglement of materials derived from the land and activist practice is undeniable yet reveals the contradictory position that making art in a place shaped by tourism, racism, and environmental degradation can engender.

Navigating the paradigms of exclusion that have made their work at times less palatable in Chicano and contemporary art circles alike, these artists persevered, speaking to both a reverence to the past and its politics of memory and a forward-thinking drive to bring artistic, environmental, and cultural resolanas into the next generation.

Notes

1. Anita O. Rodríguez, quoted in Ron Franscell, "A Woman's Place is in the Home: Rebuilding a Dying Tradition." *The New Mexican*, December 18, 1983. D-1. Anita O. Rodríguez personal archive.

2. Anita O. Rodríguez, "The Vanishing *Enjarradora*," in *Mud Space & Spirit: Handmade Adobes*, eds. Virginia Gray and Alan Macrae. (Capra Press, 1976), 11.

3. Rodríguez, "The Vanishing *Enjarradora*," in *Mud Space & Spirit*, 13.

4. Dennis Lópe,. "*El Grito del Norte*, Chicana/o Print Culture, and the Politics of Anti-Imperialism," *Science and Society* 79, no. 4 (2015). 538–9.

5. Rodríguez, "The Vanishing *Enjarradora*" in *Mud Space & Spirit*, 12.

6. Rodríguez, quoted in Becky Lovato. "Anita Rodríguez—Enjarradora," *Fly Taos – Taos Profile*. October 1983, 19. Anita O. Rodríguez personal archive.

7. Juanita J. Lavadie, "Río Grande Weaving: A Continuing Tradition," in *Hispanic Crafts of the Southwest*, exh. cat. ed William Wroth. (Taylor Museum of the Colorado Fine Arts Center, 1977), 10.

8. Devon G. Peña and Rubén O. Martínez, "The Capitalist Tool, the Lawless, the Violent," in *Chicano Culture, Ecology, Politics: Subversive Kin*, ed. Devon G. Peña. (University of Arizona Press, 1999), 160.

9. Robert Coles, *The Old Ones of New Mexico*. (University of New Mexico Press, 1973), 21.

10. G. Benito Córdova, *Abiquiu y Don Cacahuate: A Folk History of a New Mexican Village*. (San Marcos Press, 1973), 56.

11. A succinct overview of many of the most prominent instances of grassroots mobilization against environmental threat can be found in Jack Kutz, *Grassroots New Mexico: A History of Citizen Activism* (The Inter-Hemispheric Education Resource Center, 1989).

12. Though it is true that a constructed notion of "Spanish" identity was mobilized by both Anglo outsiders and by nuevomexicanos themselves, particularly in asserting a proximity to whiteness and Europeanness that would aid them in garnering US statehood, the claim to Spanish American identity was not uniformly held and indeed, was being actively questioned and contested by Chicano activists in New Mexico. See David R. Maciel and Juan José Peña, "La Reconquista: The Chicano Movement in New Mexico" in *The Contested Homeland: A Chicano History of New Mexico*, eds. Erlinda Gonzales-Berry and David R. Maciel. (University of New Mexico Press, 2000), 269–301. Though not widespread, the term *Genízaro* circulated, particularly among academic circles. Reies López Tijerina's land grant movement likewise helped to popularize the term "Indo-Hispano." Many nuevomexicanos identify as simply Hispano (rather than Hispanic—the two are not necessarily synonymous) or have been known to refer to themselves as *Mexicanos* when speaking Spanish but Spanish or Hispanic when speaking English. The term *manita/o* (short for "*hermanita/o*" or brother/sister) is also preferred by some. On the history of self-identification in New Mexico, see John M. Nieto-Phillips, *The Language of Blood: The Making of Spanish-American Identity in New Mexico, 1880s–1930s*. (University of New Mexico

Press, 2004). On constructed Spanish identity and its reverberations on the architectural and cultural sphere, see also Chris Wilson, *The Myth of Santa Fe: Creating a Modern Regional Tradition*. (University of New Mexico Press, 1997.

13. The treatment of New Mexico as exceptional is not limited to art and is likewise observable in narratives of Mexican American history. See Laura E. Gómez, *Manifest Destinies, Second Edition: The Making of the Mexican American Race*. (NYU Press, 2018).

14. During the period under study, exhibitions of Chicano art generally focused on local or regional artists (e.g., Texas, Bay Area, Los Angeles, etc.). The first major survey of Chicano art, *Chicano Art: Resistance and Affirmation, 1965–1985* (1990) a touring exhibition organized by the Wight Art Gallery, UCLA, that subsequently traveled to venues throughout the country between 1990 and 1993, had minimal New Mexico representation. To date, the overwhelming majority of scholarship on Chicano art continues to center the work of California artists.

15. Research in Texas conducted by Goldman is summarized in two 1981 publications. See Goldman, "Women artists of Texas: MAS = More Artists Women = MAS." Chismearte no. 7 (January 1981): 21–2 and "Chicano art alive and well in Texas: a 1981 Update." *Revista Chicano-Riqueña* IX (Fall 1981), 34–40.

16. Shifra M. Goldman and Tomás Ybarra-Frausto. *Arte Chicano: A Comprehensive Annotated Bibliography of Chicano Art, 1965–1981*. (Chicano Studies Library Publications Unit, University of California, Berkeley, 1985).

17. The artist remarried and now goes by Teresa Archuleta-Spires. As Archuleta-Sagel was the name that she used professionally during the period under study, at her request I use that name to refer to her throughout this essay.

18. Shifra M. Goldman. Interview with Tomás Atencio, 1983. Shifra M. Goldman Papers, CEMA 119. Department of Special Research Collections, UC Santa Barbara Library.

19. Checklist and artist list can be found in Shifra M. Goldman. *Chicana Voices and Visions: A National Exhibit of Women Artists*, exh. cat. ed. Shifra M. Goldman (Social and Public Art Resource Center, 1983).

20. Mary Montaño. *Tradiciones Nuevomexicanas: Hispano Arts and Culture of New Mexico*. (The University of New Mexico Press, 2001), 124–5.

21. Statement in *Chicana Voices and Visions: A National Exhibit of Women Artists*, exh. cat. ed. Shifra M. Goldman (Social and Public Art Resource Center, 1983), n.p.

22. Charlene E. Neel. "Surviving Our Society with Its Limitations." *Off Our Backs* 11, no. 5 Women With Disabilities (1981), 12–13. In 1966 Martínez de Pedro was involved in an automobile accident, suffering a spinal injury that left her paralyzed. In 1978, a lawsuit she filed to get an attendant in order not to lose custody of her child was successful. She developed her art practice, training in the art of retablo-painting, concurrently to her activism as a disabled single mother.

23. Artist statement in *Chicana Voices and Visions* exhibition records, Shifra M. Goldman Papers, CEMA 119. Department of Special Research Collections, UC Santa Barbara Library.

24. See Duane Anderson, *All That Glitters: The Emergence of Native American Micaceous Art Pottery in Northern New Mexico*. (School of American Research Press, 1999).

25. Statement in *Chicana Voices and Visions: A National Exhibit of Women Artists*, exh. cat. ed. Shifra M. Goldman (Social and Public Art Resource Center, 1983), n.p.

26. Letter from Anita O. Rodríguez to Shifra M. Goldman, September 18, 1983. Shifra M. Goldman Papers, CEMA 119. Department of Special Research Collections, UC Santa Barbara Library.

27. *Picotear* means "to peck"; the English translation "Many Little Points" reflects its listing in the exhibition catalog.

28. Pola López, conversation with the author, April 20, 2024.

29. Shifra M. Goldman. "Chicana Voices & Visions," in *Chicana Voices and Visions: A National Exhibit of Women Artists*, exh. cat. ed. Shifra M. Goldman (Social and Public Art Resource Center, 1983), n.p.

30. The literature on New Deal Hispano art and the Spanish Colonial legacy is extensive. Some starting points include Tey Marianna Nunn. *Sin Nombre: Hispana and Hispano Artists of the New Deal Era* (University of New Mexico Press, 2001); Mary Montaño, *Tradiciones Nuevomexicanas: Hispano Arts and Culture of New Mexico* (The University of New Mexico Press, 2001); Stephanie Lewthwaite, *A Contested Art: Modernism and Mestizaje in New Mexico.* (University of Oklahoma Press, 2015).

31. Goldman, "Chicana Voices & Visions" in *Chicana Voices and Visions*, n.p.

32. Goldman, "Chicana Voices & Visions," n.p

33. For an in-depth profile of the Ortega, Trujillo, and Martínez families of weavers, see Helen Lucero and Suzanne Baizerman, *Chimayó Weaving: The Transformation of a Tradition.* (University of New Mexico Press, 1999), 131–57.

34. A note in Goldman's exhibition file makes reference to the entry on Martínez de Pedro in *Hispanic Crafts of the Southwest* and there is no additional record of correspondence between the two to indicate prior connections. Shifra M. Goldman Papers, CEMA 119. Department of Special Research Collections, UC Santa Barbara Library.

35. Documentation of Rodríguez's commission and correspondence between her and William Wroth can be found in Wroth's curatorial files at the Fine Arts Center at Colorado College, Colorado Springs, CO.

36. In September of 2020, the Fine Arts Center (FAC) at Colorado College, formerly the Taylor Museum, held a virtual panel discussion that aimed to spark conversation around envisioning an ethical future fate of collections of Hispano Catholic devotional objects such as those held at the FAC. The panel was hosted by former FAC curator Polly Nordstrand (Hopi) and featured panelists Anita O. Rodríguez, Jessica Kahkoska, and Miguel A. Gandert, accessed December 11, 2023, https://fac. coloradocollege.edu/connect/healing-reconciliation-and-the-taylor-collection-santos-story/.

37. See *Religious Folk Art of the Southwest.* exh. cat. ed. Dorothy C. Miller. (The Museum of Modern Art, 1943). Catalogue, checklist, and other documentation available on MoMA's website, accessed December 11, 2023, https://www.moma. org/calendar/exhibitions/3131 Subsequently, Meredith Hale, who had lent the sculpture to exhibition, donated it to the museum in 1943.

38. William Wroth, "Introduction: Hispanic Southwestern Craft Traditions in the 20th Century" in *Hispanic Crafts of the Southwest*, exh. cat. ed William Wroth. (Taylor Museum of the Colorado Fine Arts Center, 1977), 2–3.

39. Wroth, "Introduction: Hispanic Southwestern Craft Traditions in the 20th Century" in *Hispanic Crafts of the Southwest*, 3.

40. Wroth, "Introduction: Hispanic Southwestern Craft Traditions in the 20th Century" in *Hispanic Crafts of the Southwest*, 3.

41. Lavadie, "Río Grande Weaving: A Continuing Tradition," and Briggs, "To Talk in Different Tongues: The "Discovery" and "Encouragement" of Hispano Woodcarvers by Santa Fe Patrons, 1919–1945" in *Hispanic Crafts of the Southwest*, exh. cat. ed. William Wroth, 9 and 49. (Colorado Springs, CO: Taylor Museum of the Colorado Fine Arts Center, 1977). Lavadie addresses possible accusations of self-stereotyping among artists of color who work in traditional modes, while Briggs optimistically signals an "intracultural intertwining of Hispano past and Chicano present," which gestures to a shift in political orientation but does not explicitly name it.

42. Wilson, *The Myth of Santa Fe*, 170.

43. Arthur Adair, "Contemporary Crafts of New Mexico," In *One Space/Three Visions*. exh. cat. ed. Dextra Frankel. (Albuquerque: The Albuquerque Museum, 1979), 273–74.

44. "Adobe." Merriam-Webster.com Dictionary, Merriam-Webster, https://www. merriam-webster.com/dictionary/adobe. Accessed November 6, 2024.

45. Enrique Lamadrid, "'Platicando del adobe': zoquete, pan, carne y las dimensiones del discurso de enjarradoras y zoqueteros," *Revista de dialectología y tradiciones populares* 42 (1987): 264.

46. Ronald Rael, *Earth Architecture*. (Princeton Architectural Press, 2009), 9. See also Jean-Louis Bourgeois, *Spectacular Vernacular: The Adobe Tradition*. (Aperture Foundation, 1996) and Orlando Romero and David Larkin, *Adobe: Building and Living with Earth*. (Houghton Mifflin, 1994).

47. Bainbridge Bunting, *Early Architecture of New Mexico*. (University of New Mexico Press, 1976).

48. Mary Montaño, *Tradiciones Nuevomexicanas*, 90–92.

49. Bainbridge's observation summarized in Montaño, *Tradiciones Nuevomexicanas*, 95.

50. Mary Montaño, *Tradiciones Nuevomexicanas*, 95.

51. Lamadrid, "'Platicando del adobe': zoquete, pan, carne y las dimensiones del discurso de enjarradoras y zoqueteros," 263. "Una especie de protesta antes este nuevo mundo de tecnocracia, individualismos, especialismos y enajenación." All translations are by the author unless otherwise noted.

52. Wilson, *The Myth of Santa Fe*, 115–16.

53. Wilson, *The Myth of Santa Fe*, 122–23.

54. Wilson, *The Myth of Santa Fe*, 127.

55. Wilson, *The Myth of Santa Fe*, 135–39.

56. Joseph Traugott, *New Mexico Art Through Time: Prehistory to the Present* (Museum of New Mexico Press, 2012), 105–18.

57. Sylvia Rodríguez, "Over Behind Mabel's on Indian Land: Utopia and Thirdspace in Taos." *Journal of the Southwest* 53, nos. 3 and 4 (2011): 380.

58. Lois Palken Rudnick, *Utopian Vistas: The Mabel Dodge Luhan House and the American Counterculture*. (University of New Mexico Press, 1996), 9.

59. Rodríguez, "Over Behind Mabel's on Indian Land: Utopia and Thirdspace in Taos," 382–84.

60. Rodríguez, "Over Behind Mabel's on Indian Land: Utopia and Thirdspace in Taos," 391.

61. Rodríguez, "Over Behind Mabel's on Indian Land: Utopia and Thirdspace in Taos," 397.

62. See Patricia Marroquin Norby, "Visual Violence in the Land of Enchantment." PhD diss., University of Minnesota, 2013, 105–14. See also Marroquin Norby, "The Abiqueños and the Artist." *American Historical Review* 129, No. 1 (March 2024). 114–132.

63. Sylvia Rodríguez. "Tourism, Difference, and Power in the Borderlands" in *The Culture of Tourism, the Tourism of Culture*. ed. Hal Rothman. (University of New Mexico Press, 2003). 185–205.

64. In 2020, the Georgia O'Keeffe Museum held a panel discussion moderated by Alicia Inez Guzmán that addressed the need rethink the problematics of the "O'Keeffe country" framing in the state's cultural sector to acknowledge its inherent erasure of Native and Hispano culture. Accessed December 13, 2023. https://www.youtube.com/live/rJiNhBMPK7Q. Nonetheless, the New Mexico Tourism Department faced immediate backlash the following year when its New Mexico True campaign debuted an "O'Keeffe country" spot, drawing condemnation from many local community members, particularly Indigenous groups. The O'Keeffe Museum likewise condemned the ad. See Alex de Vore, "New Mexico True Campaign Refresh Draws Ire," *Santa Fe Reporter* April 16, 2023. Accessed December 13, 2023. https://www.sfreporter.com/news/2021/04/16/new-mexico-true-campaign-refresh-draws-ire/.

65. Stephanie Lewthwaite, *A Contested Art: Modernism and Mestizaje in New Mexico* (University of Oklahoma Press, 2015, 31–32).

66. Lewthwaite, *A Contested Art*, 35–38.

67. Tey Marianna Nunn. *Sin Nombre: Hispana and Hispano Artists of the New Deal Era*. (University of New Mexico Press, 2001), 4–5.

68. Nunn, *Sin Nombre*, 43.

69. Nunn, *Sin Nombre*, 47–60. For more on Chávez's later career, see Lewthwaite, *A Contested Art*, 155–81.

70. From an unpublished manuscript found in the collection of MoMA curator Dorothy C. Miller. Francis V. O'Conner Papers, Archives of American Art, Smithsonian Institution. Quoted in Nunn, *Sin Nombre*, 55. As Nunn points out, this quote by Cervántez was slated for inclusion in the

1973 compilation *Art for the Millions: Essays from the 1930s by Artists and Administrators of the WPA Feredal Art Projects*, edited by O'Conner, but was ultimately edited out, leaving the volume without a single Hispano artist's first-person voice.

71. This phenomenon is treated extensively in catalog essays written in conjunction with the traveling exhibition *Outliers and American Vanguard Art*, exh. cat. ed. Lynne Cooke (National Gallery of Art / University of Chicago Press, 2018). See especially Richard Meyer, "How to Make a Modern Primitive." 42–51. On the New Mexican examples, see Lynne Cooke, "Boundary Trouble: Navigating Margin and Mainstream." 8; and Jennifer Jane Marshall, "Find-and-Seek: Discovery Narratives, Americanization, and Other Tales of Genius in Modern American Folk Art." 53–54.

72. See catalogue for the 1938 MoMA exhibition *Masters of Modern Painting: Modern Primitives of Europe and America*: https://www.moma.org/calendar/exhibitions/2090.

73. Though the term *Genízaro* did not circulate as widely during the 1960s and 1970s as it does now, it was not unknown to many of the scholars and activists associated with the Chicano art milieu of northern New Mexico. For instance, G. Benito Córdova's doctoral dissertation, "Missionization and Hispanicization of Santo Tomás de Apóstol de Abiquiú, 1750–1770" (University of New Mexico, 1979) is an example of early scholarship on New Mexico's *Genízaro* (detribalized Native American, often enslaved or adopted into domestic servitude by Spanish settler families) communities, indicating that among *norteños* an awareness of many New Mexico Chicanos' unacknowledged Indigenous histories was growing. Genízaros are also mentioned by William Wroth in the essay he wrote for the 1977 traveling exhibition *Hispanic Crafts of the Southwest* (Taylor Museum of the Colorado Fine Arts Center). For a fuller historiographic reckoning of the term, see Enrique R. Lamadrid, "*Sueños del Coyote*: The Emergence of *Genízaros* in the *Nuevomexicano* Literary Imagination," *Latin American Literature Today* 9 (2019), accessed December 13, 2023. https://latinamericanliteraturetoday.org/2019/02/suenos-del-coyote-emergence-genizaros-nuevo-mexicano-literary-imagination-enrique-r/. See also the edited volume: Moises Gonzales and Enrique R. Lamadrid, eds. *Nación Genízara: Ethnogenesis, Place, and Identity in New Mexico* (The University of New Mexico Press, 2019).

74. Rina Swentzell, "An Architectural History of Santa Clara Pueblo," MA thesis, University of New Mexico, 1976, 4.

75. Rodríguez quoted in Pat Walsh. "Woman's hands vital part of her adobe work, words." *The Camp Verde Bugle* 31, no. 52 (The Independent, Cottonwood, Arizona), 33.

76. Anita O. Rodríguez, conversation with the author October 12, 2019. Rodríguez regularly participated in La Academia's meetings.

77. The group held physical meetings in Dixon and at Ghost Ranch, but as the Michigan-born Chicana artist, educator, and actress Victoria Plata has told me on multiple occasions, she initially came to northern New Mexico in the early 1970s under the impression that La Academia was a formally incorporated school and was surprised to learn of its relatively informal nature. Nonetheless, La Academia operated a publishing arm and organized events and symposia along with its outreach campaigns.

78. According to Consuelo Pacheco, Atencio's widow and a healthcare worker, Academia board member, and collaborator, heroin use was a pervasive problem in northern New Mexico at the time, and the couple's work in substance abuse clinics and more broadly with local communities at times made them targets of drug-related threats. Conversation with the author, December 6, 2023.

79. Tomás Atencio, "El Oro del Barrio in the Cyber Age: Leapfrogging the Industrial Revolution," in *Resolana: Emerging Chicano Dialogues on Community and Globalization*. (The University of Arizona Press, 2009), 55.

80. Information about the exhibition in Esteban [sic] Arellano. "Art showing at Chicano

center," *The Santa Fe New Mexican*, n.d. (ca. 1971). Tomás Atencio Papers and Academia de la Nueva Raza / Río Grande Institute Records, Center for Southwest Research and Special Collections, University of New Mexico.

81. See Estevan Arellano (ed.) and Tomás Atencio, *Entre Verde y Seco* (Academia de la Nueva Raza, 1972).

82. Estevan Arellano, "Chicano Values Studied at La Academia," *Albuquerque Journal*, Feb 13, 1971. Tomás Atencio Papers and Academia de la Nueva Raza / Río Grande Institute Records, Center for Southwest Research and Special Collections, University of New Mexico.

83. On the vexed Chicano relationship to indigeneity surrounding the land grant disputes, see Simón Ventura Trujillo, *Land Uprising: Native Story Power and the Insurgent Horizons of Latinx Indigeneity* (The University of Arizona Press, 2020).

84. David Floyd García, "La Resolana: Tracing the Communicative Cartographies of Gathering Spaces in North Central New Mexico." PhD diss., The University of Texas at Austin, 2015, 57–60.

85. Tomás Atencio, "Resolana: A Chicano Pathway to Knowledge" (Ernesto Galarza Commemorative Lecture). (Stanford Center for Chicano Research, Stanford University), 1.

86. Tomás Atencio and Consuelo Pacheco, "The Concept of resolana," *Agenda* (1981). Quoted in Atencio, "Resolana: A Chicano Pathway to Knowledge," 2.

87. Recording was not allowed during Freire's lecture; E. A. "Tony" Mares wrote a reflection on the visit after the fact, which was published in La Academia's journal *El cuaderno (de vez en cuando)* 3, no. 1 (winter 1973). Alejandro "Jerry" López also sketched a portrait of Freire, published in the same issue.

88. Paulo Freire, *Pedagogy of the Oppressed* (1970), trans. Myra Bergman Ramos. (New York and London: Continuum, 2008), 106.

89. Tomás Atencio, "Introducción" in *Entre verde y seco*. (La Academia de la Nueva Raza, 1972). 6. "Universitarios ambos de habla español e inglés

han peinado nuestras aldeas sacando el oro de nuestra gente, y no han reciprocado y contribuído para una educación popular con lo que han acumulado."

90. Atencio, "Resolana: A Chicano Pathway to Knowledge," 9.

91. I elaborate in greater depth on artistic strategies of resolana among Chicana/o artists in New Mexico and Texas in my doctoral dissertation, "*La resolana*: Chicano Artistic Imaginaries of Place, Race, and Activism in New Mexico and Texas, 1969–1985" (The Graduate Center, City University of New York, 2025).

92. Sylvia Rodríguez, "Land, Water, and Ethnic Identity in Taos," in *Land, Water, and Culture: New Perspectives on Hispanic Land Grants*. eds. Charles L. Briggs and John R. Van Ness (University of New Mexico Press, 1987), 349–50.

93. For background on Tijerina, see Lorena Oropeza. *The King of Adobe: Reies López Tijerina, Lost Prophet of the Chicano Movement*. (University of North Carolina Press, 2019); Juan Gómez-Quiñones and Irene Vásquez, *Making Aztlán: Ideology and Culture of the Chicana and Chicano Movement, 1966–1977*. (University of New Mexico Press, 2014); Ramón A. Gutiérrez, *New Mexico's Moses: Reies López Tijerina and the Religious Origins of the Mexican American Civil Rights Movement*. (University of New Mexico Press, 2022); Simon Ventura Trujillo, *Land Uprising: Native Story Power and the Insurgent Horizons of Latinx Indigeneity* (The University of Arizona Press, 2020).

94. Rodríguez, "Land, Water, and Ethnic Identity in Taos," 353.

95. Rodríguez, "Land, Water, and Ethnic Identity in Taos." 357–61.

96. Leah Leach, "Condo Wars Heat Up." *Albuquerque Journal*, n.d. (ca. 1982). Anita O. Rodríguez personal archive.

97. Rodríguez, "Land, Water, and Ethnic Identity in Taos," 367–75.

98. María Lugones, *Pilgrimages / Peregrinajes: Theorizing Coalition Against Multiple Oppressions* (Rowman & Littlefield, 2003), 2.

99. "Rally por Valdez" advertisement, *The Taos News*, September 23, 1982. B8. Tomás Atencio Papers and Academia de la Nueva Raza / Río Grande Institute Records, Center for Southwest Research and Special Collections, University of New Mexico.

100. Kutz, *Grassroots New Mexico*, 20.

101. A summary of the process can be found on the U.S. Department of Energy's website accessed December 14, 2023: https://www.wipp.energy.gov/library/pioneering/LongRoad1.pdf.

102. "DOE Says Go to WIPP, but New Mexico Says Not Yet" *Nuclear Waste News* (Newsletter of the National Campaign for Radioactive Safety) No. 7 (early summer 1983), n.p. Shifra M. Goldman Papers, CEMA 119. Department of Special Research Collections, UC Santa Barbara Library.

103. Pola López, conversation with the author, April 20, 2024.

104. See Albert Narath, *Solar Adobe: Energy, Ecology, and Earthen Architecture* (University of Minnesota Press, 2024).

105. Anita Rodríguez, "Tradiciones de adobe en Nuevo Méjico norteño / Adobe Traditions in Northern New Mexico," *Adobe News* 15 (1977), 20–22.

106. Romero and Larkin, *Adobe: Building and Living with Earth*, 166.

107. Anita Rodríguez, "Adobe workers attack myths," *The Taos News*, January 24, 1980. Anita O. Rodríguez personal archive. Rodríguez shared her ambivalence toward *Adobe News*'s editors and the adobe industry writ large in a Zoom conversation with the author, January 4, 2022.

108. Steve Frazier, "Adobe is Adorable, But Today's Pueblos Can't Build with It," *The Wall Street Journal*, February 4, 1980. Anita O. Rodríguez personal archive. See also Romero and Larkin, *Adobe: Building and Living with Earth*. 166–68.

109. Laurie Beth Kalb. *Crafting Devotions: Tradition in Contemporary New Mexico Santos*. Albuquerque: University of New Mexico Press, 1994, 52.

110. See the glossary of saints in William Wroth. *Christian Images in Hispanic New Mexico*. (Taylor Museum of the Colorado Fine Arts Center, 1977), 205.

111. For a thorough discussion of López, Applegate, and the Santa Fe art market, see Charles L. Briggs. *The Wood Carvers of Córdova, New Mexico: Social Dimensions of an Artistic "Revival"* rev. ed. (The University of Tennessee Press, 1980).

112. Kalb, *Crafting Devotions*, 55.

113. James Córdova, "New Mexico's Unmistakable Santos: Artistic Bricolage and the Formation of Style," in *Appropriation & Invention: Three Centuries of Art in Spanish America*. exh. cat. ed. Jorge F. Rivas Pérez. (Denver Art Museum, 2022). 225.

114. Tapia made the "bouncer" comment amid a broader discussion of the hidden facets of social commentary embedded in Catholic iconography in a telephone conversation with the author, October 21, 2022. Extending that metaphor to the art market is my own extrapolation.

115. Text accompanying the commemorative exhibition "Encuentros: Recordando La Cofradía" held from May 5 to September 1, 1991, at the Millicent Rogers Museum in Taos. The exhibition was curated by Tapia, Archuleta-Sagel, Jaramillo Lavadie, Wilberto Miera, and Frederico Vigil, all former Cofradía members. National Hispanic Cultural Center Archives and Special Collections, La Cofradia Archive collection.

116. Luis Tapia, telephone conversation with the author, October 21, 2022. See also Tey Marianna Nunn, "¡Órale!" in *Borderless: The Art of Luis Tapia* exh. cat. ed. Carmella Padilla. (Museum of Latin American Art / University of Oklahoma Press, 2017). 37–83.

117. Press included Walter Loniak, "New Visions for Muertos and Santos" *The Santa Fe Reporter*, January 25, 1979, 15; Allan Pearson, "Santa Fe Hispanic Exhibition 'Cultura '79' Exciting," *The Albuquerque Journal*, n.d., n.p.; Janice Daigh, "Hispanic Artists Unite for Exhibit," *The Taos News*, January 18, 1979, B1; Janice Daigh, "Old

Church Alive with Art," *The Taos News*, January 25, 1979, B1; Don Fabricant, "Art Show has a New Awareness," *The New Mexican*, n.d., n.p.; Rosanna Hall, "Bold, New Forms for Hispanic Art Show," *The New Mexican*, n.d., p. 3. National Hispanic Cultural Center Archives and Special Collections, La Cofradia Archive collection.

118. Per a flyer announcement of the program. Anita O. Rodríguez personal archive.

119. Rudolfo A. Anaya and Simon J. Ortiz, eds. *Ceremony of Brotherhood*. (Academia, 1981).

120. Juanita J. Lavadie, Zoom interview with the author, June 29, 2021.

121. "Artistas del Pueblo: In Conversation with the History of New Mexican Chicanx Art," *Hemisphere: Visual Cultures of the Americas* 12, 1 (2019), 81.

122. Juanita J. Lavadie, Zoom interview with the author, June 29, 2021. On the Chicano art movement in Chicago, see Victor Sorrell, "The Enduring Presence of the Chicano-Mexicano Mural in Chicago" in *The Barrio Murals—Murales del Barrio*. Exh. cat. ed. René Arceo. (Mexican Fine Arts Center – Museum, 1987), 3–7.

123. Juanita J. Lavadie, Zoom interview with the author, June 29, 2021.

124. *Chispas: Cultural Warriors of New Mexico*. exh. cat. ed. Diana Pardue. (Phoenix: The Heard Museum, 1992).

125. On the mural's iconography, damage, and subsequent restoration, see Ariana Kramer, "Vision of Life and Death: Mural on a Liquor Store Wall in El Prado Holds More Significance than You'd Think." *Taos News*, January 27, 2011, accessed November 3, 2024, https://www.taosnews.com/news/vision-of-life-and-death-mural-on-a-liquor-store-wall-in-el-prado-holds/article_90926240-6ab0-5da5-989c-d180a388a38a.html.

126. Kristina Gray Fisher, "Reclaiming Querencia: The Quest for Culturally Appropriate, Environmentally Sustainable Economic Development Northern New Mexico." *Natural Resources Journal* 48, no. 2 (2008): 495–96. See also Laura

Pulido, "Sustainable Development in Ganados del Valle" in *Confronting Environmental Racism: Voices from the Grassroots*, ed. Robert D. Bullard (South End Press, 1993), 123–39; and Devon Peña, "The 'Brown' and the 'Green': Chicanos and Environmental Politics in the Upper Rio Grande," *Capitalism, Nature, Socialism* 3, no. 1 (1992): 79–103. For more on weaving operations, see Helen Lucero and Suzanne Baizerman, *Chimayó Weaving: The Transformation of a Tradition*. (University of New Mexico Press, 1999).

127. Juanita J. Lavadie, Zoom interview with the author, July 29, 2021. She also included constellations in cover image she illustrated for *Ceremony of Brotherhood* (ed. Rudolfo Anaya and Simon J. Ortiz). The constellation she depicted was Leo, which matches the precise time of year (August 1680) that the Revolt took place.

128. Juanita J. Lavadie, Zoom interview with the author, June 29, 2021.

129. Lavadie received a 1980–1981 National Endowment for the Arts grant to study traditional Hispano textiles. Grant report available in Helen Lucero Papers, Museum of International Folk Art Library.

130. Juanita J. Lavadie, Zoom interview with the author, June 29, 2021.

131. Discussed in Juanita J. Lavadie, "Rio Grande Weaving: A Continuing Tradition," in *Hispanic Crafts of the Southwest*, 15.

132. Tricia Hurst, "The Good Earth: For Anita Rodríguez, the Future is as Clear as Mud," *Empire Magazine, The Denver Post*, January 13, 1985, 8. See also Anita Rodríguez, *Coyota in the Kitchen: A Memoir of New and Old Mexico* (University of New Mexico Press, 2016), 73–74.

133. Marlou Quintana, "Anita Rodríguez preserves adobe architecture." *The Taos News*, November 2, 1978.

134. Rodríguez, *Coyota in the Kitchen*, 78.

135. Rodríguez, *Coyota in the Kitchen*, 79.

136. Enriqueta Vásquez. The Wonder Woman Foundation Awards 1983 Nomination Form: Anita Otilia Rodríguez, stamped May 19, 1983, n.p., Anita O. Rodríguez personal archives.

137. On the problematics of land art in New Mexico and the Southwest, see Alicia Inez Guzmán, "Connected in Isolation: Land and Landscape in New Mexico and the Greater Southwest." PhD diss., University of Rochester, 2016.

138. See "Carl Andre's Adobe Strip" *Adobe Today* 38 (1983), 33. See also Laura Roulet, "Ana Mendieta and Carl Andre: Duet of Leaf and Stone," *Art Journal* 63, no. 3 (2004): 86.

139. Ruth H. Morgenson, "Warming with Wood," *New Mexico Magazine* 58, no. 2 (February 1980): 28. Rodríguez is quoted in the article and wrote a companion piece about enjarradoras and fireplaces in the same issue.

140. Anita Rodríguez, Zoom conversation with the author, January 4, 2022.

141. Anita Rodríguez, Zoom conversation with the author, January 4, 2022.

142. Anita Rodríguez. "Las enjarradoras— Women of the Earth." *New Mexico Magazine* 58, no. 2 (February 1980): 58.

Bibliography

Anaya, Rudolfo A. and Simon J. Ortiz, eds., *Ceremony of Brotherhood*. Academia, 1981.

Anderson, Duane. *All That Glitters: The Emergence of Native American Micaceous Art Pottery in Northern New Mexico.* School of American Research Press, 1999.

Arellano, Estevan, ed., and Tomás Atencio, *Entre Verde y Seco.* Academia de la Nueva Raza, 1972.

Atencio, Tomás. *Resolana: A Chicano Pathway to Knowledge* (Stanford Center for Chicano Research, Stanford University, 1988).

Baca, Damián. "Rural Literacies, Postindustrial Countrysides: Resolana, Entre Seco y Verde, and the Shadow of the Atomic Age." In *Reclaiming the Rural: Essays on Literacy, Rhetoric, and Pedagogy*, edited by Kim Donehower and Eileen E Schell. Southern Illinois University Press, 2012.

Bourgeois, Jean-Louis. *Spectacular Vernacular: The Adobe Tradition.* Aperture Foundation, 1996.

Briggs, Charles L. *The Wood Carvers of Córdova, New Mexico: Social Dimensions of an Artistic "Revival,"* rev. ed. The University of Tennessee Press, 1980.

Coles, Robert. *The Old Ones of New Mexico.* University of New Mexico Press, 1973.

Cooke, Lynne, ed. *Outliers and American Vanguard Art.* Exhibition catalog, National Gallery of Art / University of Chicago Press, 2018.

Córdova, G. Benito. *Abiquiu y Don Cacahuate.* San Marcos Press, 1973.

Córdova, G. Benito. "Missionization and Hispanicization of Santo Thomas Apostol de Abiquiu, 1750–1770" PhD diss., University of New Mexico, 1979.

Córdova, James. "New Mexico's Unmistakable Santos: Artistic Bricolage and the Formation of Style." In *Appropriation and Invention: Three Centuries of Art in Spanish America.* Exhibition catalog edited by Jorge F. Rivas Pérez. Denver Art Museum, 2022.

Fisher, Nora, ed. *Spanish Textile Tradition of New Mexico and Colorado.* Museum of International Folk Art, 1979.

Frankel, Dextra, *One Space / Three Visions.* The Albuquerque Museum, 1979. Exhibition catalog.

Freire, Paulo, *Pedagogy of the Oppressed.* Translated by Myra Bergman Ramos. Continuum, 2008.

Garcia, David Floyd, "La Resolana: Tracing the Communicative Cartographies of Gathering Spaces in North Central New Mexico." PhD diss., The University of Texas at Austin, 2015.

Garrison, James W. and Elizabeth F. Ruffner, eds. *Adobe: Practical & Technical Aspects of Adobe Preservation*. Heritage Foundation of Arizona, 1983.

Goldman, Shifra M., *Chicana Voices and Visions: A National Exhibit of Women Artists*. Social and Public Art Resource Center, 1983. Exhibition catalog.

Goldman, Shifra M., and Tomás Ybarra-Frausto, *Arte Chicano: A Comprehensive Annotated Bibliography of Chicano Art, 1965–1981*. Chicano Studies Library Publications Unit, University of California, Berkeley, 1985.

Gonzales, Moises, and Enrique R. Lamadrid, eds. *Nación Genízara: Ethnogenesis, Place, and Identity in New Mexico*. The University of New Mexico Press, 2019.

Gonzales-Berry, Erlinda, and David R. Maciel. *The Contested Homeland: A Chicano History of New Mexico*. University of New Mexico Press, 2000.

Gray, Virginia, and Alan Macrae, eds., *Mud Space & Spirit: Handmade Adobes*. Capra Press, 1976.

Gómez, Laura E. *Manifest Destinies, Second Edition: The Making of the Mexican American Race*. NYU Press, 2018.

Gómez-Quiñones, Juan, and Irene Vásquez. *Making Aztlán: Ideology and Culture of the Chicana and Chicano Movement, 1966–1977*. University of New Mexico Press, 2014.

Guthrie, Thomas H. *Recognizing Heritage: The Politics of Multiculturalism in New Mexico*. University of Nebraska Press, 2013.

Gutiérrez, Ramón A. *New Mexico's Moses: Reies López Tijerina and the Religious Origins of the Mexican American Civil Rights Movement*. University of New Mexico Press, 2022.

Guzmán, Alicia Inez. "Connected in Isolation: Land and Landscape in New Mexico and the Greater Southwest." PhD diss., University of Rochester, 2016.

Kalb, Laurie Beth. *Crafting Devotions: Tradition in Contemporary New Mexico Santos*. University of New Mexico Press, 1994.

Kutz, Jack. *Grassroots New Mexico: A History of Citizen Activism*. The Inter-Hemispheric Education Resource Center, 1989.

Lamadrid, Enrique R., "'Platicando del adobe': zoquete, pan, carne y las dimensiones del discurso de enjarradoras y zoqueteros," *Revista de dialectología y tradiciones populares* 42 (1987), 261–69.

Lamadrid, Enrique R. "*Sueños del Coyote*: The Emergence of *Genízaros* in the *Nuevomexicano* Literary Imagination," *Latin American Literature Today* 9 (2019); https://latinamericanliteraturetoday.org/2019/02/suenos-del-coyote-emergence-genizaros-nuevomexicano-literary-imagination-enrique-r/.

Lewthwaite, Stephanie, "Remaking the Spanish Colonial Paradigm: Mestizaje and Spirituality in Contemporary New Mexican Art." In *Journal of American Studies* 47 (2013), 339–62.

Lewthwaite, Stephanie. *A Contested Art: Modernism and Mestizaje in New Mexico*. University of Oklahoma Press, 2015.

Loeffler, Jack, ed. *Voices of Counterculture in the Southwest*. Museum of New Mexico Press, 2017.

López, Dennis. "*El Grito del Norte*, Chicana/o Print Culture, and the Politics of Anti-Imperialism." *Science and Society*, 79, no. 4 (2015), 527–54.

Lucero, Helen, and Suzanne Baizerman. *Chimayó Weaving: The Transformation of a Tradition*. University of New Mexico Press, 1999.

Lugones, Maria. *Pilgrimages/Peregrinajes: Theorizing Coalition Against Multiple Oppressions*. Rowman and Littlefield, 2003.

Marroquin Norby, Patricia. "The Abiqueños and the Artist." *American Historical Review* 129, no. 1 (March 2024). 114–32.

Marroquin Norby, Patricia. "Visual Violence in the Land of Enchantment," PhD diss., University of Minnesota, 2013.

McHenry, Paul Graham Jr. *Adobe and Rammed Earth Buildings: Design and Construction*. University of Arizona Press, 1984.

Miller, Dorothy C., ed. *Religious Folk Art of the Southwest.* The Museum of Modern Art, 1943. Exhibition catalog.

Montaño, Mary, *Tradiciones Nuevomexicanas: Hispano Arts and Culture of New Mexico.* The University of New Mexico Press, 2001.

Narath, Albert. *Solar Adobe: Energy, Ecology, and Earthen Architecture.* University of Minnesota Press, 2024.

Neel, Charlene E. "Surviving Our Society with Its Limitations." *Off Our Backs* 11, no. 5 Women with Disabilities (1981), 12–13.

Nieto-Phillips, John M. *The Language of Blood: The Making of Spanish-American Identity in New Mexico, 1880s–1930s.* University of New Mexico Press, 2004.

Nugent, Carlos Alonso. "Lost Archives, Lost Lands: Rereading New Mexico's Imagined Environments." *American Literature* 92, no. 2 (2020): 309–41.

Nunn, Tey Marianna. *Sin Nombre: Hispana and Hispano Artists of the New Deal Era.* University of New Mexico Press, 2001.

Oropeza, Lorena. *The King of Adobe: Reies López Tijerina, Lost Prophet of the Chicano Movement.* University of North Carolina Press, 2019.

Padilla, Carmella, ed. *Borderless: The Art of Luis Tapia.* Museum of Latin American Art, 2017. Exhibition catalog.

Pardue, Diana, ed. *Chispas: Cultural Warriors of New Mexico.* The Heard Museum, 1992. Exhibition catalog.

Peña, Devon G., ed. *Chicano Culture, Ecology, Politics: Subversive Kin.* University of Arizona Press, 1999.

Pulido, Laura. "Geographies of Race and Ethnicity III: Settler Colonialism and Nonnative People of Color." *Progress in Human Geography*, 42, no. 2 (2018): 309–18.

Rael, Ronald. *Earth Architecture.* Princeton Architectural Press, 2010.

Rodríguez, Anita O. *Coyota in the Kitchen: A Memoir of New and Old Mexico.* University of New Mexico Press, 2016.

Rodriguez, Anita, and Katherine Pettus, "The Importance of Vernacular Traditions." *APT Bulletin* 22, no. 3 (1990): 2–4.

Rodríguez, Sylvia. "Land, Water, and Ethnic Identity in Taos." *Land, Water, and Culture: New Perspectives on Hispanic Land Grants*, edited by Charles L. Briggs and John R. Van Ness. University of New Mexico Press, 1987.

Rodríguez, Sylvia. "Fiesta Time and Plaza Space: Resistance and Accommodation in a Tourist Town," *The Journal of American Folklore*, 111, no. 439 (1998): 39–56.

Rodríguez, Sylvia. "Tourism, Difference, and Power in the Borderlands," *The Culture of Tourism, the Tourism of Culture*, edited by Hal Rothman. University of New Mexico Press, 2003.

Rodríguez, Sylvia. "Over Behind Mabel's on Indian Land: Utopia and Thirdspace in Taos." *Journal of the Southwest,* 53, nos. 3 and 4 (2011): 379–402.

Romero, Orlando, and David Larkin. *Adobe: Building and Living with Earth.* Houghton Mifflin, 1994.

Rosenak, Chuck, and Rosenak, Jan. *The Saint Makers: Contemporary Santeras y Santeros.* Northland Publishing, 1998.

Roulet, Laura. "Ana Mendieta and Carl Andre: Duet of Leaf and Stone." *Art Journal* 63, no. 3 (2004): 80–101.

Rudnick, Lois Palken. *Utopian Vistas: The Mabel Dodge Luhan House and the American Counterculture.* University of New Mexico Press, 1996.

Saldaña-Portillo, María. *Indian Given: Racial Geographies across Mexico and the United States.* Duke University Press, 2016.

Salvador, Mari Lyn C. *Cuando hablan los santos: Contemporary Santero Traditions from Northern New Mexico.* Maxwell Museum of Anthropology, 1995.

Santistevan, Corina A., and Julia Moore, *Taos: A Topical History.* Taos Historical Society/ Museum of New Mexico Press, 2013.

Solís Ybarra, Priscilla. *Writing the Goodlife: Mexican American Literature and the Environment.* University of Arizona Press, 2016.

Swentzell, Rina. "An Architectural History of Santa Clara Pueblo," MA thesis, University of New Mexico, 1976.

Templeton, Rini. *El arte de / The Art of Rini Templeton: Donde hay vida y lucha / Where there is life and struggle.* Centro de Documentación Gráfica Rini Templeton and The Real Comet Press, 1988.

Trujillo, Michael. *Land of Disenchantment: Latina/o Identities and Transformations in Northern New Mexico.* University of New Mexico Press, 2009.

Trujillo, Simón Ventura. *Land Uprising: Native Story Power and the Insurgent Horizons of Latinx Indigeneity.* The University of Arizona Press, 2020.

Traugott, Joseph. *The Art of New Mexico: How the West is One.* Museum of New Mexico Press, 2007.

Wilson, Chris. *The Myth of Santa Fe: Creating a Modern Regional Tradition.* University of New Mexico Press, 1997.

Wolf, Arthur, ed. *Hebras de visión / Threads of Vision.* Millicent Rogers Museum, 1982. Exhibition catalog.

Wroth, William. *Hispanic Crafts of the Southwest,* edited by William Wroth. Taylor Museum of the Colorado Fine Arts Center, 1977. Exhibition catalog.

Wroth, William. *The Chapel of Our Lady of Talpa.* Taylor Museum of the Colorado Fine Arts Center, 1979.

Wroth, William. *Christian Images of Hispanic New Mexico.* Taylor Museum of the Colorado Fine Arts Center, 1982.

Wroth, William. *Images of Penance, Images of Mercy: Southwestern Santos in the Nineteenth Century.* Taylor Museum of the Colorado Fine Arts Center, 1991.

Coyuntura in the Land of Enchantment

Knowing of the Chicana and Chicano Movement in New Mexico

PHILLIP B. (FELIPE) GONZALES

Five

The artists and artistry featured in the *Voces del Pueblo* exhibition and catalog chapters took their places in New Mexico history through the power of the Chicano and Chicana Movement (CCM). Accordingly, it enhances our appreciation of their contributions to have a sense of what the CCM looked like as it hit and established itself in New Mexico, which it did full force. This chapter samples from the range of Chicano and Chicana organizational efforts that arose in the state in the decade of the 1970s. In doing so, it provides a resource for this occasion of remembrance of the creative energies of the CCM in New Mexico.

The United Farmworker Movement in New Mexico

As the initial wave of the CCM crashed into New Mexico, experienced activists and those who were primed for politicization readily identified with the issues it raised, the polemics it expressed, and the forceful rhetorics that it emitted. It was a process that Juan Gómez-Quiñones and Irene Vásquez called *coyuntura*—the spontaneous uprising, conjoining, and convergence into a "certain identifiable ethos" for the cause of justice and the "liberation" of their people.[1]

It is well known that the CCM sprung out of the massive support that was given to the United Farmworker Movement (UFW) in the Central Valley of California.[2] In 1965, after years of organizing in the fields, the United Farm Workers Organizing Committee sponsored a grape picker strike. Unprecedented for a labor union, what became the UFW went beyond issues of salary, work conditions, and benefits on to the realm of human justice. The farmworker cause drew volunteers from areas of civil rights, Mexican American organizations, organized workers in other industries, and the social service professions.[3] Displaying symbols drawn from Mexican heritage, such as *La Virgen de Guadalupe*, the farmworker movement appealed to the Catholic Church.[4] The potential for collective empowerment was demonstrated in the UFW's providential 280-mile march from Delano in central California north to the state capitol in Sacramento. Led by the charismatic leaders Cesar Chávez and Dolores Huerta, news of the march brought political and public attention to the plight of farm workers such that by the time it reached its destination, the Delano March had drawn a crowd of five thousand participants.[5] Followers of the UFW innovated highly charged protest methods, such as Luis Valdez's El Teatro Campesino, a street theater modeled on the San Francisco Mime Troupe that made heroes of the *huelgistas* (strikers) while villainizing rich, cigar-smoking growers, goons, and scabs.[6]

The UFW boycott of non-union grapes went impressively national. Farm worker organizing spread beyond California.[7] In southeastern New Mexico, UFW strikes hit large agricultural fields.[8] Students at New Mexico universities flew the UFW banner and supported the boycott of grocery stores that sold union grapes and vegetables. At Eastern New Mexico University in Portales, Chicana and Chicano students boycotted dining halls for not serving union lettuce.[9]

UFW support groups came together in the state's cities. In Santa Fe, they staged demonstrations, picketed the local Safeway grocery store, and handed out leaflets urging customers to boycott non-union vegetable merchants.[10] The Albuquerque Lettuce Boycott Committee conducted research on local food stores and wholesalers on the amount of union lettuce they were selling. Finding "very little," it organized to inform consumers, urging them to assist the union efforts of migrant farmworkers.[11]

To many participants, the UFW struggle became the heart of the Chicana and Chicano Movement. Still, as one researcher observes, "Not necessarily related to the strike, but no doubt influenced by it, the movement of Mexican Americans became known as the Chicano movement in the course of the strike."[12] As such, the UFW embodied the struggles to rectify the problems of poverty, racism, and worker exploitation more generally.

Cesar Chávez was clearly aware of the political uses of strategic images. As he famously stated, "A symbol is an important thing. That is why we chose an Aztec eagle. It gives pride. When people see it, they know it means dignity." Chávez himself designed the squared-off eagle symbol that would come to be used in so much CCM organizing besides the farm worker movement. The eagle conveyed a powerful legacy for Mexican American remembrance and imaginaries. The Albuquerque painter, sculptor, and curator Augustine (Gus) Romero recalled the UFW eagle from the time of his youth during the CCM.[13] Not least from his experiences of discrimination in the arts field, Romero matured into a CCM artist.[14] The UFW eagle helped Romero claim a sense of place where he came from, which in the movement went by Aztlán, the Aztec name for the Mexican territories to the far north (fig. 5.1). To Romero, it also signified Cuauhtémoc, the Aztec emperor whose name meant "Descending Eagle," and who fought to stave off the Spanish conquest of Tenochtitlan (the precursor of Mexico City), a parallel to the Chicano Movement to fight off the US conquest of Aztlán (fig. 5.2).

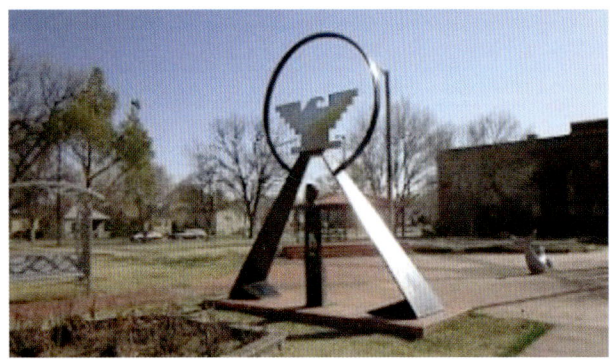

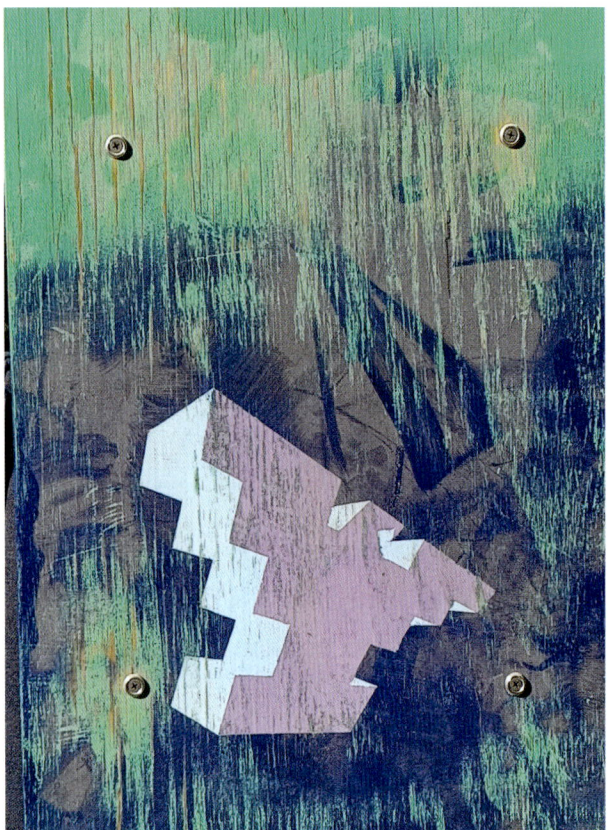

FIGURE 5.1. (*above*) Augustine (Gus) Romero, *Cesar Chavez Memorial*, 1993. Stainless steel. 4″ × 4 ft. base; 14 ft. length; 4″ × 17 ft. eagle crown. Unveiled September 17, 1996. El Centro De Quinto Sol, Pueblo, Colorado. Courtesy of *Romero Sculpture*, vol. 23, March 26, 2013, https://romerosculpture.blogspot.com/. Used by permission of the artist.

FIGURE 5.2. (*below*) Augustine (Gus) Romero, *Cuauhtémoc,* 2006. Spray paint on plywood, 24″ × 26″. Photographed by the author, courtesy of the author.

In Defense of Chicano Lands

While New Mexico's CCM contributed to national causes like the UFW, there were also issues more specific to New Mexico history, some of which were braided into the fabric of the greater CCM. Such was the case with respect to the traditional Spanish and Mexican land grants.

After the US annexation of New Mexico in 1848, land-hungry Anglo settlers eyed the *mercedes*, that is, the communal lands that the governments of New Spain and Mexico granted to *nuevomexicano* families.[15] By the time American speculators, corporate interests (especially the railroads), and the US Forest Service were done, nuevomexicano heirs lost not all but certainly millions of acres of their ancestral patrimony.[16]

A nuevomexicano movement to take back or save given land grants began in the 1890s, some of it violent in nature.[17] The goal of securing mercedes was still active in the early 1960s when Reies López Tijerina arrived from Texas and established *La Alianza Federal de Pueblos Libres*, Alliance of Free City States (hereafter, La Alianza). La Alianza brought the heirs of various grants into a unified movement and quickly developed a large membership base.[18] In 1966, La Alianza replicated the UFW's peaceful Delano March, with Tijerina leading hundreds of participants on a two-day, sixty-two-mile walk from Albuquerque, where La Alianza had its headquarters, to the state capital of Santa Fe. The event effectively led to a "respectful conference" between Tijerina and Governor Jack Campbell.[19]

The land grant issue became a pillar of Chicano-Chicana coyuntura in New Mexico. Alianza meetings and rallies attracted impressive audiences. Tijerina's fire-eating speeches caught the attention of land grant heirs throughout northern New Mexico. Roque García became an important aide to Tijerina at the 1968 Poor People's Campaign in Washington, DC, where the Tijerina contingent participated in Chicano/Chicana protests at the Supreme Court and established contacts with Native American warriors and Black Civil Rights leaders.[20] Los Comancheros, a northern New Mexico youth group in Tierra Amarilla, carried out street rallies to highlight the issue of nuevomexicano land displacement.[21] New Mexico college students across the state rallied in support of La Alianza.[22]

In greater measure, the CCM quickly identified with La Alianza's focus on lost Mexican lands. Outside of New Mexico, Tijerina was hailed as an example of a strong Chicano leader.[23] In Denver, the rising *movimiento* leader Rodolfo "Corky" Gonzales hitched his organization, the Crusade for Justice, to Tijerina's Alianza. Gonzales attended Tijerina's 1966 convention in New Mexico, and in turn, Gonzales in Denver called on "dedicated and concerned members" of Southwest communities to aid La Alianza's "just and honorable cause."[24] Cesar Chávez himself, while in New Mexico for a fundraising event, attended an Alianza meeting. Embracing Tijerina, Chávez linked the fight for farmworkers with the struggle for land grant heirs. In his address, he said he would have joined La Alianza if he lived in New Mexico "because the issue of the land is crucial to rural *Mexicanos* and reflects the cruel injustices to which they have been subjected."[25]

The notion of La Alianza as a nonviolent organization was upended in 1967 when armed members attempted a citizens' arrest of Río Arriba County district attorney Alfonso Sánchez at the Tierra Amarilla Courthouse. Alianzistas charged Sánchez with violating their rights when he declared it unlawful for Alianzistas to assemble on forest property that they claimed was part of the autonomous merced San Joaquín del Río Chama. Sánchez was not at the courthouse that day. Alianzistas and police officers exchanged gunfire. After a jailor and a state policeman were wounded, Alianza members took individuals hostage and fled into the national forest. The hostages were released, but a National Guard manhunt, replete with tanks, drew national media attention. Alianzistas were eventually arrested, including Tijerina. In the meantime, the so-called TA Raid charged up the CCM, as it was the "first militant armed action taken by Mexican Americans anywhere in the Southwest for over a hundred years."[26] The Crusade for Justice's widely circulating newspaper, *El Gallo*, published full-page photos of Tijerina being escorted to court. Gonzales remained in New Mexico to assist La Alianza's struggle.[27]

As Tijerina's fame mounted, Chicano students in California invited him to speak alongside Cesar Chávez and Corky Gonzales, making him an instant public figure. School activist Sal Castro remembered Tijerina's "fiery, evangelistic, and charismatic image."[28] Both the Mexican American Political Association in California and the Mexican American Youth Organization in Texas endorsed Tijerina and La Alianza.[29]

La Alianza fired up the Chicano historical imaginary. The "brutal 'Gringo' invasion of our territories" in the Mexican American War of 1846–1848 became a principal grievance of the "Chicano people's" origin story.[30] The imperialist intrusion of Anglo Americans on Mexican soil reinforced the image of Mexican origin people in the United States as a colonized people, and it informed, for example, the very title of Rodolfo Acuña's classic history, *Occupied America*. Published in 1972, *Occupied America* became "a central part of the discourse that [was] in quest of defining and maintaining the new Chicano reality."[31]

Beret Chicanismo

In 1967 Mexican American youth in Los Angeles left the moderate Mexican American Youth Leadership Conference and launched the Brown Berets. Modeled on the paramilitary Black Panther Party, the Brown Berets decked themselves out in a martial-brown uniform and beret. Parallel to the Black Panther Party's focus on ghetto conditions, the Brown Berets recruited barrio youth and former gang members, molding them into an agency for "protecting" the community, addressing police brutality and drug use among street Chicanos, and agitating for neighborhood improvement. Collaborating with other grassroots efforts, they also responded to emerging issues in "the hood."[32]

The California Berets organized a car caravan, *La Caravana de la Reconquista*, to tour the Southwest and Midwest to spread the news of the CCM. By conveying a vision of Mexican American oppression they believed that Chicano communities would recognize the need to affirm their rights and contest the misleading memories of the American conquest of their lands.[33]

Passing out of Arizona, the California Berets visited Silver City in southwestern New Mexico. At a rally in a city park they denounced racism and demanded that a monument be constructed to commemorate CCM heroes. The optic of boots militantly marching through town shook up residents. The United Veterans Hall denied the subversive-appearing group permission to show a film in their building. Union leaders, teachers, and the League of United Latin American Citizens took out an ad in the Silver City *Daily Press* denouncing "self-appointed Saviors" who came to "add to our problems by agitating imagined or real social problems."[34] Yet young local Chicanos, some who were already socially active, drew inspiration from the Berets and the force with which they represented *el pueblo*. In a spirit of pride in being part of Mexican Portales, the Chicano Youth Association now sported wore berets and imitated Beret militancy. The organization created a Beret chapter. On the Black Panther model, it included an officer corps of "ministers" of education, justice, and information. Seventeen of its members learned Beret rules of discipline and respect in the presence of the community. The group participated in demonstrations against a grocery store owner accused of wrongly accusing Mexican American customers of being shoplifters.[35]

In Albuquerque, barrio activist Gilbert Ballejos returned from the Poor People's March, where he met California Brown Berets.[36] Back home, Carlos Cansino, Wilfredo Sedillo, and Roger Anderson joined Ballejos in forming an independent Brown Beret organization. Their community newsletter, *El Papel*, informed the people of critical issues affecting their community but not covered by mainstream media. They spotlighted a range of issues: a judicial system that harassed La Alianza; the high casualty rate of Chicanos in Vietnam; Anglo domination of state politics; and the extreme poverty in Chicano neighborhoods. The Berets called for stronger state minimum-wage laws, community control public school boards, effective bilingual education, respectful welfare regulations, and reform of state corporation tax laws.[37]

Ballejos attacked the Ford Foundation for donating $500,000 to start a program to train new leadership as an alternative to Tijerina's radicalism. The initiative, he argued, attempted to create "*Vendido* [sellout] Power," that is, to create "leaders" the system could use as tools, and in this way, bring Vietnam to New Mexico. "But it hasn't worked with the Vietnamese," Ballejos charged, "and it's not going to work with Raza here in the United States."[38]

In Santa Fe, the Brown Berets supported Tijerina's land movement, struggled with police-community tensions, and established a community school in a building owned by the Catholic Church in a westside barrio. In a tragic incident, Santa Fe police raided the school under the mistaken impression that there were armed individuals inside. Claiming that they encountered gunshots (which was never proven), officers launched an all-out attack on the building. With state officers providing reinforcement, they wounded escaping individuals, arrested eleven, and destroyed the building. At trial members of the so-called Santa Fe Seven were acquitted on charges of carrying illegal weapons, rioting, and attempted murder.[39]

The most impactful Beret Chicanismo in New Mexico took form in the Black Berets, founded in Albuquerque in 1969. Former VISTA (Volunteers in Service to America) member Richard Moore, former Brown Beret Joaquín Luján, college student Plácido Salazar, Father Luis Jaramillo, Marvin García, and Richard Sawtelle formed the initial nucleus of the Black Berets.[40] Their choice of organizational nomenclature evoked the Latin American revolutionary Che Guevara. At the same time, its structure resembled the Black Panther Party with "ministers" of defense, justice, politics, and education. Important early initiatives included a free breakfast program for low-income children, a clothing distribution project for the poor, a wood carving cooperative, a "liberation school" for preschool age children, a free dental clinic, and free health care services.[41] Black Beret politics expanded, as a journalist noted, to "virtually every issue that cropped up in New Mexico—labor strikes, student struggles, prisoner rights, protests against a noxious sewer plant in [Albuquerque], the Chicano Moratorium against the War in Vietnam, and opposition to gentrification, including a landmark fight over urban renewal."[42] Alliances were forged with the American Indian Movement, Navajo resistance against racism in Gallup, the National Organization for Women, and the Black Power Movement.[43]

Ideologically, the Black Berets' "12-Point Program and Platform" stressed "self-determination and liberation" for *la Chicanidad* and for "all Latinos and Third World Peoples" as well as community control of institutions and land and "true" education for "our mestizo culture and Spanish language." The social reform agenda called for "freedom for all political prisoners" and Chicano "freedom fighters"; opposition to the US's "unjust wars of oppression"; equality for women and the end of conservative machismo; an end to police brutality; full employment for "our people"; a struggle against capitalism and its "treacherous" Chicano allies; and armed self-defense and armed struggle as "the only means to liberation."[44] The Black Berets crashed the inauguration of New Mexico's governor-elect to present him with their twelve-point program, and it disrupted a meeting of the City of Albuquerque Commission to demand that it take immediate steps to redress its alleged discriminations against minority groups.[45]

A virtual war between law enforcement and the Black Berets erupted (as it did with Tijerina and La Alianza). In the background FBI Director J. Edgar Hoover's COINTELPRO campaign disrupted and often neutralized Black liberation, Chicano, Native American, Puerto Rican, and antiwar movements. It became common knowledge that police at all levels infiltrated resistance movements, including the Chicana and Chicano Movement, the Black Berets, and activist students, creating dossiers on individuals.[46] Police repression resulted in violence. In 1972, Beret members Antonio Córdova and Rito Canales were ambushed and killed at a construction site by the Albuquerque Police Department, New Mexico State Police, and the Bernalillo County Sheriff's Office. Police charged that the pair attempted to steal dynamite and resisted arrest when confronted. The Berets countered that the assault on Córdova and Canales was meant to stop exposure of corruption at the state penitentiary. Years later, Tim Chapa admitted that he was a police informant who helped set up Córdova and Canales for assassination.[47]

Black Beret militancy faced fierce backlash. On a poster-like circular, the Black Berets explained why they armed themselves. In one corner the message they received from the right-wing Minutemen bore crosshairs and a warning of possible assassination. Another section alluded to random threats they had incurred on the streets. Police harassment of an ally was suggested in the caption of a photograph. Chicanos were advised to arm themselves.[48]

Chicano Press Power: *El Grito del Norte*

The advent of the Delano Grape Strike and the organization of the National Farm Workers Union agitated Chicano political consciousness and awareness through their movement newspaper, *El Malcriado* (1964).[49] *El Malcriado* touched off an industry of Chicano journalism and newspaper production throughout the Southwest and beyond. Raza newspapers provided information on movement events and reported on national and local issues. Key aspects of Chicano history were publicized. Writers filled columns with political and cultural polemics. The networks associated with the Chicano Press Association and La Raza Latina Press Association formed solidarities of resistance. Major articles were distributed and copies disseminated at meetings and protest crowds.[50] Columns provided platforms for contributors to generate propaganda, programs, principles of struggle, demands to lodge against the establishment, and strategies for achieving national liberation.[51]

Three types of newspapers emerged. One was an organization's journal as in the UFW's *El Malcriado*, the Crusade for Justice's *El Gallo*, the California Brown Beret's *La Causa*, and the Mexican American Youth Organization's *El Deguello*, *El Azteca*, *Hoy*, and *La Revolución*. Student publications were another type. College papers reported on matters of general interest to the movement while informing on higher education concerns such as academic freedom, Chicano studies, and student politics. *El Chile* at Texas A&I Kingsville and *El Chingazo* at San Diego State University were examples. The third variety was the independent organ meant as a resource for the greater community. Such outlets circulated widely, for example, Los Angeles' *La Raza* and San Antonio's *El Caracol*.[52]

All three appeared in New Mexico. Regarding the first, Albuquerque's Brown Berets had *El Papel*, the Black Berets put out *La Revolución de Albuquerque*, La Academia de la Nueva Raza printed *El Cuaderno de Vez en Cuando* (1969), and *La Voz de la Alianza* (1967) came out in Albuquerque. College student papers included *Plumas de UMAS* from the United Mexican American Students at the University of New Mexico; *El Grito del Sur*, *La Raza Habla*, and *La Verdad de Las Cruces* by Los Chicanos at New Mexico State University; and *El Renacimiento*, representing AHORA at Eastern New Mexico University.[53]

Among community outlets, José Armas edited *El Cuaderno* (1973) in Albuquerque.[54] However, *El Grito del Norte* (*El Grito*) became the most influential newspaper in the New Mexico theater of the Chicano Chicana Movement. *El Grito* started in 1968 in the town of Española north of Santa Fe as the project of two newly arrived civil rights veterans, attorney Beverly Axelrod and former Southern Christian Leadership Conference activist and writer Elizabeth (Betita) Martínez.[55] Axelrod would soon drop away and Martínez went on to helm the monthly *El Grito*.

El Grito won the support of La Alianza, and it continued reporting on the land grant struggle. It soon expanded its CCM coverage to include issues in urban neighborhoods, with the interests of industrial workers and Latino political prisoners, in support of Black liberation, white radicalism, student protest in Mexico, and the "course of justice of poor people."[56] *El Grito* surged to the point that, as one researcher comments, it was "one of the most distinctive and wide-ranging publications of the Chicano Movement."[57] With a crew of nineteen "spirited workers," it operated as an effective social movement organization unto itself.[58] Under Martínez's guidance, *El Grito* became a major left internationalist publication.[59] Its columnists were among the members of the Chicano Press Association who were invited to the 1969 celebration of the tenth anniversary of the Cuban Revolution. In attendance as well were representatives of North American magazines and newspapers, including *Seventeen Magazine*, *Monthly Review*, the *Wall Street Journal*, *Look*, and foreign news services.[60]

Significantly, it was a collective of women that operated *El Grito*. Editorial policy was formulated from the standpoint of Chicana feminism and feminism in general. Enriqueta Longeaux y Vásquez, who became *El Grito*'s permanent editorial writer and most committed reporter, engaged in a conversation with the greater CCM over women's roles, gender equality, the family, and women's communities.[61] Longeaux y Vásquez sought to reconcile women's liberation and Chicano cultural nationalism. Promoting Chicana *coyuntura*, Martínez mentored young women with interests in journalism, one of whom established her own paper in Las Vegas, New Mexico.[62] Based on a commission, Valentina Valdes wrote a series of articles on Vietnam, a project Martínez later called one of the most important successes in the paper's goal of encouraging and training young Chicanas in creating and running a newspaper.[63]

El Grito's female prominence reflected the significant participation of women in the CCM: Dolores Huerta and others in the United Farmworkers Union; a women's auxiliary of the Brown Berets; scores of women in the Crusade for Justice; and thousands of women in student ranks. In New Mexico, Rosa Tijerina and other women participated in La Alianza. In the incident that led to the imprisonment and conviction of Reies López Tijerina for destruction of federal property, Patricia "Patsy" Tijerina hurled the firebomb and burned a U.S. Forest Service sign.[64] At New Mexico Highlands University, women students were said to be "particularly active."[65]

El Grito managed an image-making print shop. The choices in photos and graphics represented the paper's key themes, subjects, and political interests. The front page of the August 29, 1970, issue demonstrates its international frame of reference, conjoining the people of Vietnam with the people of northern New Mexico in a common revolutionary cause (fig. 5.3).

The staff at *El Grito* began looking for what Martínez called "a new strategy and tactics" within the CCM. The paper ceased publishing in 1973, and some participants moved to Albuquerque where they launched the Chicano Communications Center, a multimedia, educational barrio project. The Chicano Communications Center formed

FIGURE 5.3. (*opposite*) Front page, *El Grito del Norte*, August 29, 1970.

SPECIAL ISSUE: RAZA REPORT FROM NORTH VIETNAM

EL GRITO
DEL NORTE

Vol. III. No 30. Española, N.M. Aug. 29, 1970

15¢

CHICANO MORATORIUM · AGAINST THE WAR IN S.E. ASIA
¡RAZA SI! ¡GUERRA NO!

VIETNAM WAR- WHY?

Their People...   Our People...

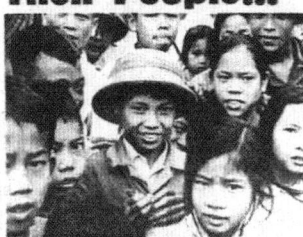

Children of North Vietnam

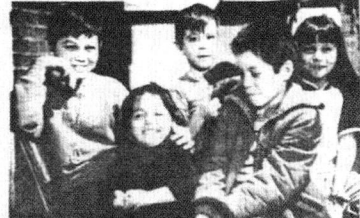

Children of Northern New Mexico

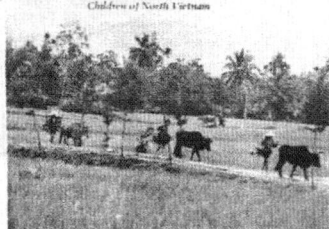

Campesinos of North Vietnam

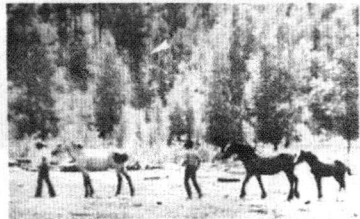

Campesinos of Northern New Mexico

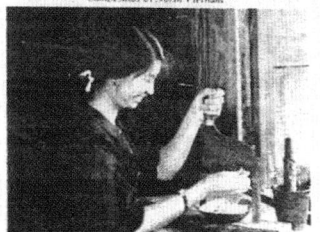

A North Vietnamese Woman

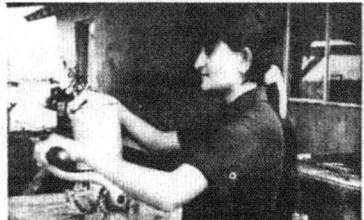

La Chicana

the Chicano League Against Racism and Oppression (CLARO), forging alliances with the Bobby Garcia Memorial Clinic and a land grant organization based outside of Albuquerque, the Cañoncito Wood Cooperative.[66] In 1976 it published *450 Years of Chicano History in Pictures*. Widely used in schools,[67] it graphically promoted wide-ranging historical and contemporary critical discourse.[68] (In 2008 Martínez published *500 Years of Chicana Women's History / 500 Años de la Mujer Chicana*).

La Academia de la Nueva Raza

Like other regions in the pre-American Southwest, northern New Mexico is associated with a distinctive Mexicano culture with its characteristic dialect and folk traditions. Social worker Tomás Atencio based his organization, La Academia de la Nueva Raza (La Academia) on this subculture. Atencio steeped himself in a philosophy of everyday life among northern New Mexico villagers. In his political theory (for Atencio's contribution to Chicano/Chicana art, see Sonja Elena Gandert's chapter above), the potential for liberation lay firmly in their systems of folk knowledge. In collaboration with Facundo Valdez, Father Luis Jaramillo, and Consuelo Pacheco, Atencio invited friends and colleagues in 1969 to his ancestral village of Embudo to discursively bathe in *el oro del barrio* ("the golden wisdom of the people"), a concept he borrowed from Mariano Aguilar, director of the American Unity Council in San Antonio, Texas. El oro del barrio held the key for the people to lift themselves from poverty and achieve empowerment. "When released," the thesis maintained, "this wisdom would lead to a new awareness and understanding of our lives, plenitude, and ultimately to a New Humanity—La Nueva Raza."[69]

A set of community organizers, educators, writers, poets, and artists in the Española Valley (north of Santa Fe), Taos County, Mora County, San Miguel County, Albuquerque, and Las Cruces formed Los Asociados de La Academia.[70] This community of interest strategized to capture el oro del barrio based on Socratic dialogues and *testimonios* of life experience.[71] The forces that impinged on life were addressed through "a vehicle to build a body of knowledge . . . thus providing oppressed people alternatives to learning, acting, and styles of living." In this version of cultural nationalism, the teacher was also a learner.[72]

La Academia formed a nonprofit corporation and received financial support from churches and logistical assistance from the New Mexico Home Education Livelihood program.[73] With these resources it developed the metaphorical concept of *la resolana*.[74] For generations, Atencio explained, village folk gathered against sun-drenched walls, conversing, gossiping, and sharing folk tales and bits of common wisdom. *Cuentos* (stories), *chistes* (jests), and *dichos* (folk sayings) animated the talk about the "tragic comedy of life's paradoxes."[75] To render la resolana into a CCM instrument for consciousness building, Asociados convened village dialogical sessions in which issues, problems, and solutions were explored.[76]

As it was supposed to happen, the people of el oro del barrio would naturally come to a "new awareness and a respond-ability," the capacity to confront the conditions of their subjugation "with commitment, courage, and fortitude," and through the truth and realities of life as captured in their folk knowledge.[77] Oral interviews were transcribed and published in Academia journals and booklets such as *El Cuaderno de Vez en Cuando*, *La Resolana*, *La Madrugada*, and *Entre Verde y Seco*. These little journals presented artistic caricatures of village scenes and spiritual figures. *Entre Verde y Seco* carried poetry, art prints, *adivinanzas* (popular riddles), photographs, and classic Iberian and Latin American folklore as in the story of the rogue archetype Pedro Ordemalas, whose exploits suggested pieces of wisdom from lived experience.[78]

La Academia's alternative education project based on Paulo Freire's "praxis learning" and "circles of culture" gained a following.[79] (For a brief description of Freire's visit to La Academica de la Raza's facility, see Sonja Elena Gandert's chapter above.) La Academia-modeled programs, using el oro del barrio and resolana methods in Mexican immigrant neighborhoods, were replicated in Las Cruces, New Mexico; El Paso and San Antonio, Texas; Brawley, California; and Phoenix, Arizona.[80]

Estudiantes Moviendo: The College Student Movement

The CCM swept onto the campuses of colleges and universities.[81] A first order of business was for students to form their own organizations. In 1967, the United Mexican American Students (UMAS) rose to prominence in Southern California. UCLA UMAS showed the way by facing the administration over low Chicano and Chicana enrollments and organizing a conference to discuss the issue. UMAS chapters proliferated. East Los Angeles Community College, Loyola Marymount, University of Southern California, California State College Los Angeles, and California State College San Fernando Valley formed a coordinating structure. The UMAS momentum spread rapidly in California and outward to institutions like the University of Colorado and Notre Dame University.[82]

At the University of New Mexico (UNM) in Albuquerque, UMAS was formed in the spring of 1969 by Arturo Sandoval, Juan Abeyta, Antonio Gómez, Ricardo Barros, Ezequiel López, Luis Torrez, Dickie Gallegos, Proceso Montoya, and others. Open UMAS meetings quickly drew new members. UMAS fanned out in support of a range of CCM activity, some helping to bring the UFW boycott and a UFW support group to the campus and the city,[83] others adding to Tijerina's Alianza force.[84] A large group of UMAS students attended the Crusade for Justice's first national Chicano Youth Liberation Conference in Denver.[85]

UMAS majorly focused on campus issues. For example, it urged Chicano workers at the campus physical plant to confront the administration around salary disparities, inadequate grievance procedures, and the denial of compensation rights from job-related injuries.[86] UMAS filed a thirty-six-page report to the UNM administration, Governor David Cargo and the federal Department of Health, Education, and Welfare (HEW), formally charging UNM with salary discrimination based on data showing gross differentials between Spanish- and English-surnamed employees.[87] A HEW contract compliance team failed to find deliberate discrimination, but criticized the university for its lack of enhancing promotion opportunities for minority group workers.[88] UMAS supported the physical plant workers until their issues were absorbed by a campaign to organize a union.

UMAS also took up student issues such as racism in the management of residence halls.[89] It fought to establish a presence in student government. Fiesta, the spring celebration funded by the Associated Students of UNM, was run by Anglo fraternity and sorority students for their entertainment largely. In dramatic protests at faculty senate meetings, UMAS succeeded in having some of its members involved in organizing the event. They went on to "Mexicanize" Fiesta with appropriately themed events, bringing in a band from Los Angeles to play in the newly constructed quad patio. It was called "liberating" the campus from Anglo control.[90] This was followed by what was called the Chicano Music Festival featuring "four of the best-known Chicano musicians in New Mexico." Workshops on Mexican American popular culture brought in guests to speak on the theme of "Chicano Music."[91] With funding from the Associated Students the Ballet Folklorico de la Universidad de Nuevo México put on popular performances.[92]

UMAS had an organizational rival in Estudiantes Mexicano Americanos Unidos (UMAS in Spanish). Established by Edward Benavidez and Albert Chávez, EMAU was ideologically moderate, choosing to go through institutional channels rather than protesting and working to improve conditions in the community.[93] With the assistance of university administrators, EMAU organized an important conference on the educational problems of Mexican Americans. Students from five of New Mexico's colleges and universities attended and formed a statewide council. One of the conference's resolutions maintained that UNM was a "racist institution because it does not pay physical plant workers a living wage, and because the University turned out teachers dedicated to 'keeping the Chicano ignorant.'" Attendees vented against *vendidos*, "sellout" Mexican Americans who "lost sight of the needs of the poverty-stricken barrios."[94] Graduate students got going with Mesa Chicana (for humanities students), the Mexican American Law Students Association, a chapter of the National Chicano Health Organization, and a Chicano Business Association even.

Chicana students in the CCM challenged sexism and discrimination against women in Chicano organizations, including their exclusion from leadership ranks.[95] Conferences addressed these issues, as did opinion pieces, testimonials, artistic productions, and a large body of feminist theory published in academic sources.[96] At UNM, Chicanas felt dissatisfied with male dominance in the campus movement. Jennie Chávez expressed these concerns in a national publication.[97] Chávez, Beverly Padilla, Laverne Armijo, Nancy Montaño, Kathy Gallegos, Mela Pino, Alicia Martínez, Margaret García, Vickie Rivera, and others established Las Chicanas. Padilla participated in the national debate concerning Mexican American women and their roles in the movement and in relation to societal issues such as abortion.[98]

Deeming UMAS outworn, a Chicano conference in California proposed Movimiento Estudiantil de Aztlán (MEChA) as a vanguard student organization. It caught on and soon MEChA coordinated with local protests and aligned itself with the spiritual goals of *El Plan Espiritual de Aztlán*, the manifesto of Corky Gonzales's Crusade for Justice's Youth Liberation Movement. California MEChistas highlighted *mestizaje* and their Indigenous legacy.[99] Students at UNM who supplanted UMAS with MEChA hosted a national MEChA conference. Other students established Estudiantes por la Cultura to highlight the New Mexican context of the CCM. It was a time of intense dialogue and debate on how to define Chicano/Chicana nationalism, "liberation," and "revolution."[100]

Other New Mexico universities witnessed the rise of Chicano Chicana student activism. At New Mexico Highlands University in Las Vegas, Vietnam veterans founded the Spanish American Student Organization, soon to become the Chicano Associated Student Organization (CASO) to reflect the spirit of the times and to reject "Spanish American" identity with its "Spanish ancestral fantasy."[101]

CASO promoted the boycotting of non-union grapes and lettuce by campus eateries, formed coalitions with white and Black students, called for the naming of buildings for historic nuevomexicano figures, and pushed for the preservation of culture and the Spanish language. CASO took over the student senate to demand an investigation of campus discrimination in such areas as faculty hiring. The American GI Forum, the district attorney, local, elected Democrats and Republicans supported this cause. Following the legislature's investigation, the Anglo president resigned.[102] Volatile protest affected the search for a successor, CASO demanding the hiring of a Chicano since nuevomexicanos made up most of the students by far. When the search committee selected an Anglo, CASO occupied the administration building for six days. Due largely to this action, the university hired Dr. Frank Ángel as president, the first Chicano university president in the country.[103]

At New Mexico State University in Las Cruces (NMSU), students founded Los Chicanos in 1969. By 1972, student leaders Larry Lucero, Oscar Vargas, Roberto Lavadie, Harvey Valenzuela, and J. Ventura García, addressed a host of issues including the problem of the high attrition rate of Chicano and Chicana students and the lack of Chicano Chicana representation on the administration and faculty. The group organized a Chicano Week; provided information to students on courses of interest and career opportunities;

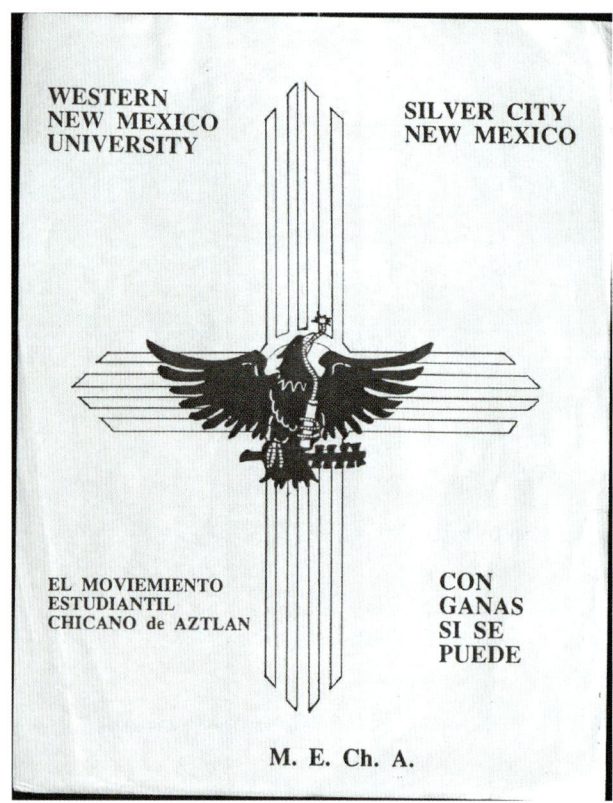

FIGURE 54. Logo, MECHA-Western New Mexico University, circa 1974. Artist unknown. Chicano Student Movement at Western New Mexico University Oral History Project, MSS-599, box 1, folder 3, Center for Southwest Research. Courtesy of the University of New Mexico.

worked with La Alianza Universitaria, a campus interest group; and supported El Teatro Chicano.[104] Los Chicanos found organizing in the conservative town difficult, especially when it came to criticizing capitalism, imperialism, and the Catholic Church for keeping the people docile. Nevertheless, student and community pressure resulted in the hiring of the first Chicano vice president at NMSU.[105]

At Western New Mexico University (WNMU) in Silver City, with its large Mexican American enrollment, two Vietnam War veterans, John Arzola and David Maestas, started Los Estudiantes Unidos, a name to reflect a politics "not too radical and not too conservative."[106] Estudiantes Unidos built an impressive work agenda.[107] Estudiantes Unidos became MEChA, going on to host a MEChA conference. Members collaborated with the American GI Forum and the League of United Latin American Citizens in support of a strike by public school staff over the unjust firing of thirteen janitors and the school district's refusal to recognize the staff union. MEChA ran into resistance from the board of regents and a series of presidents, including the Mexican American Rudolpho Gómez.[108]

CCM college students often used graphic design. The New Mexico terrain of the movement was represented on a WNMU MEChA logo that superimposed the Mexican eagle upon a Zia Pueblo configuration, representing the four sacred obligations, which New Mexico public relations had long appropriated to symbolize the state (fig. 5.4).

At Eastern New Mexico University in Anglo-dominant Portales, Mexican Americans (indicated by Spanish surnames) made up 10 percent of the student enrollment. In the late 1960s, a federally funded Upward Bound program recruited and enabled underrepresented minority students to enroll in college. The program enabled the emergence of a base for Chicano Chicana coyuntura. Students marched against the Vietnam War, contested police brutality, pointed to the problem of sexual harassment on campus, and decried racism on campus.[109] Juan Manuel Soliz and Frank Sánchez, who returned politically transformed from the Chicano National Youth Liberation Conference in Denver, cofounded A.H.O.R.A, the

Association to Help Our Raza Advance. The group set out "to better the communicative voice between Chicanos and non-Chicanos in civil and political affairs . . . preserve and promote our language, our culture and those areas considered of great importance and value to the Chicano . . . help in the advancement of Chicanos acquiring an education through means of recruiting, retaining and advising . . . [and] set up a scholarship fund . . . available to needy meritorious persons of Chicano descent."[110]

A.H.O.R.A. campaigned for Mexican American students to become the first elected student body senators. It defied the student body president who denied their request to designate a Chicano Day, on their own bringing in speakers and challenging the racialized pledging of the all-white fraternities and sororities. Student government funds were used to rent a building for a Chicano center. Members provided services to the North Portales barrio, sponsored Christmas parties, and mentored elementary school children.[111]

Chicano and Chicana students in New Mexico followed the lead of counterparts in California in advocating for Chicano studies. The philosophy and theory of Chicano studies were formulated by young intellectuals associated with the journal *El Grito* at the University of California Berkeley and *El Plan de Santa Bárbara*, which was a policy report authored by Chicano and Chicana students, faculty, and staff at a conference held at the University of California Santa Barbara.[112] Goals were defined to provide student services, increase Chicana and Chicano faculty, found Chicano studies departments, and link the academy to organizations in Mexican American communities.[113]

At the University of New Mexico (UNM), UMAS, the Black Student Union, and Kiva Club challenged the administration in 1969 to establish ethnic studies. That fall, President Ferrell Heady approved three programs, including Chicano Studies along with Black Studies and Native American Studies. As stipulated in "The Chicano and UNM," the UMAS proposal, the Chicano studies program would consist of courses in various disciplines, a student services center, a library, and community relations.[114] UMAS hired an interim director, Dr. Louis Bransford, followed by two others, Antonio Gómez (a former UMAS student), and math professor Ricardo Griego. In 1971, a student services director, Antonio Mondragón, and an academic director, Tobías Durán, were the first permanent administrators of UNM's Chicano Studies Program.[115]

Chicano Studies had offices in a former faculty home on campus. Students, clearly attuned to the key symbols of the *movimiento*, decked the walls of the meeting room with a mural that featured a militant Virgen de Guadalupe (fig. 5.5). Chicano Studies remained underfunded for decades, yet it was able to provide student services, offer a minor degree in the American Studies Department and coordinate the hiring of instructors in mainstream departments before finally becoming a department in 2015.[116] Chicano studies at other state universities had halting experiences.[117] At New Mexico Highlands University, President Ángel hired Pedro Rodríguez to head a Chicano studies initiative. When Rodríguez was denied tenure, students protested so vigorously they got arrested. The community came to

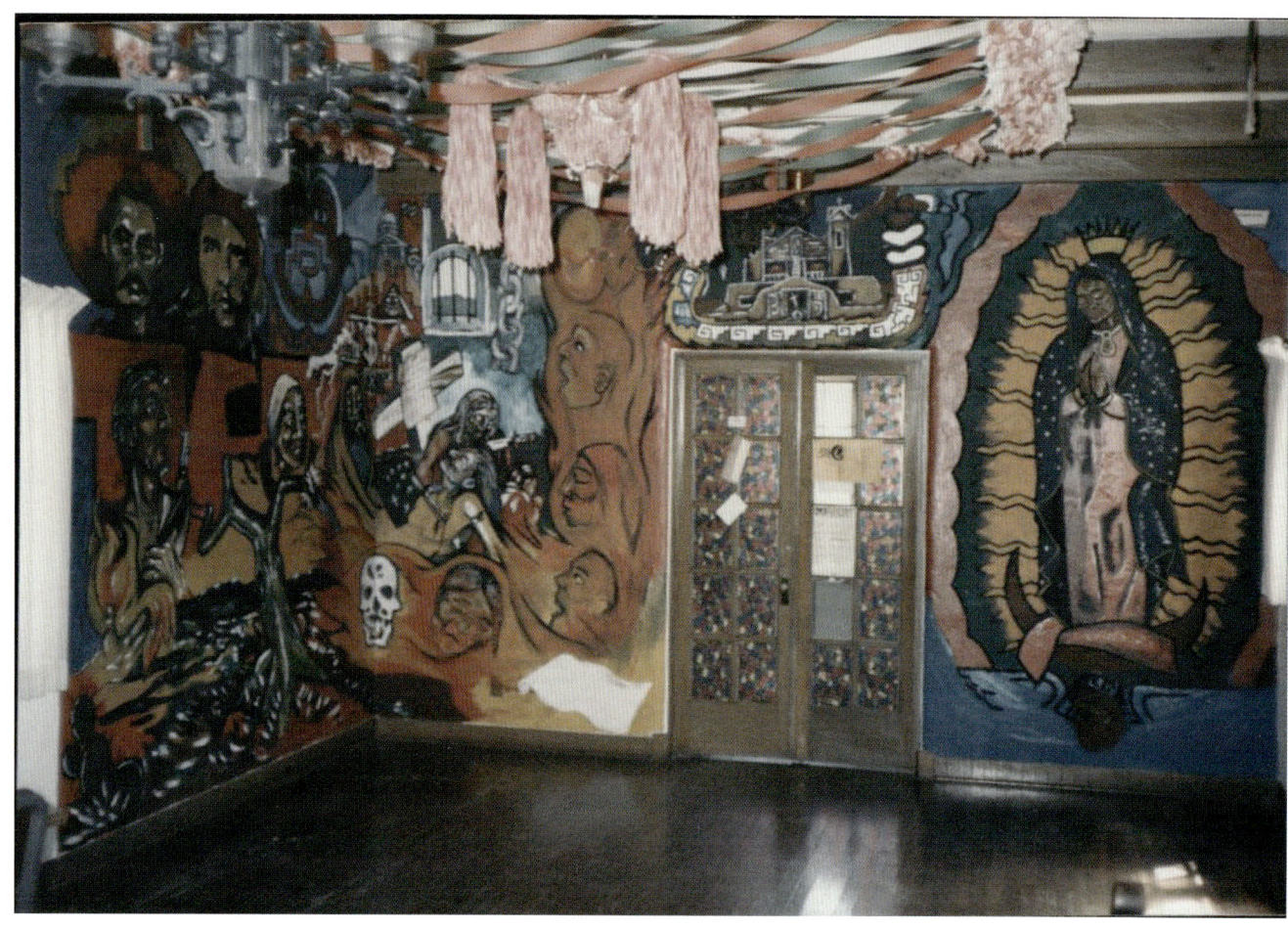

FIGURE 55. Interior of the Chicano Student Center, University of New Mexico, circa 1974. Photographer unknown. Gloria Montoya Chávez Papers, MSS-797–BC, box 1, folder 35, Center for Southwest Research. Courtesy of the University of New Mexico.

their support, however, as indicated by the $500,000 in property bonds that was provided for their release. In 1973, the Regents hired the Raza Unida Party veteran, Juan José Peña, to chair Chicano Studies. Peña fought for program expansion; however, Ángel retired and his replacement, Dr. John Aragón, opposed Chicano studies. Only the policy of hiring Chicano faculty in traditional departments was instituted.[118]

Los Chicanos at New Mexico State University used student government funds to hire two students, Barbara Barraza and Martín Quintana, to visit Chicano studies programs in the Southwest and report on best practices. They returned proposing courses (students to be involved in their design) and the hiring of a bilingual director. Their Chicano Studies Project sponsored a conference in which invited outside faculty presented the workings of their programs. President Gerald Thomas appointed a committee to review instruction for minority groups. It came away recommending directors of Chicano, African American, and Native American programs. The administration hired high school Spanish teacher Ray Paz to serve as director of Chicano Studies (changed to Chicano Affairs). However, Thomas denied Paz's request for resources to expand the program. Louis Sarabia was then hired as director of Chicano Affairs in 1975. Not a believer in comprehensive ethnic studies, he promoted a policy of existing departments offering courses and increasing Chicano and Chicana majors.[119] NMSU ended up designing "Chicano Programs" to support students "of ALL ethnic/racial backgrounds." "Chicano" here signified an intent to "also include students who identify as Hispanic, Mexican American, Latino, Puerto Rican, U.S. Cuban, etc."[120]

At Western New Mexico University, Los Estudiantes proposed Chicano studies to fill a gap in relevant cultural and political courses and the absence of Chicana and Chicano professors, but the administration failed to approve the proposal. One department offered "Psychological Aspects of Chicanos," taught by Bonnie Maldonado, a non-Chicana professor married to a Chicano who was the faculty sponsor of Los Estudiantes. As the university planned on dismissing Maldonado because her academic unit was being canceled, Los Estudiantes rallied to her support and she was eventually retained.[121] However, the president resisted student pleas to address numerous Chicano faculty disparities (three out of sixty-six and not one in the administration) as well as demands for a bachelor's degree in Chicano studies, a Chicano center, and increased Chicano representation on university committees. Seventy individuals, including students, community members, professors, and an administrator held a candlelight vigil. A press statement accused the university of the "systematic exclusion" of Chicanos and Chicanas.[122]

After the president left the university under charges of unethical behavior,[123] WNMU hired a Chicano, Rudolpho Gómez, as president (1986–1989) and Patricia Cano, a former Estudiantes Unidos member, as a Chicano studies professor. The Chicano Faculty Caucus worked with the administration to establish a Department of Chicano/Chicana and Hemispheric Studies. Dr. Felipe de Ortego y Gasca, a respected scholar on Chicano/Chicana and Latin American literature and recipient of *El Premio Estrella de*

Aztlán—Lifetime Achievement Award from the National Association for Chicana and Chicano Studies, was hired to direct the department. The program was phased out in 2015 for lack of enrollment in the major.[124]

At Eastern New Mexico University, ethnic studies proved very controversial. Two members of A.H.O.R.A., Albert Gonzales and Santiago Juárez, taught a noncredit course on Chicano history and culture based on a visit to Fresno State University's Chicano Study Center. Juárez submitted a proposal to make ethnic studies classes official and to invite the Chicano Studies coordinator at UNM come to explain the pedagogical basis and goal of Chicano studies. A.H.O.R.A. and African American students pressured the College of Liberal Arts to incorporate three ethnic studies courses, including Chicanos and the Humanities. Trouble ensued when the state Board of Educational Finance objected to funding ethnic studies, one conservative member calling it a "dangerous precedent" for states to provide such funding.[125]

At a sit-in protest at a regents meeting, A.H.O.R.A. demanded that the university pay for Chicano studies. Members stomped their feet and clapped their hands when President Charles Meister asked them to leave. Nine students were arrested on charges of interfering with university operations. All were convicted but the sentences were suspended. The Regents contributed $14,900 for a year's support of ethnic studies, promising to request $178,000 from the state legislature based on 284 students enrolled in 13 ethnic studies classes. Students again protested when Meister committed BEF funds to public television rather than ethnic studies. As historian Jamie Bronstein notes, "Ethnic Studies struggled on at ENMU, burdened with a messy curriculum of eight required and twenty-two optional classes, a poorly established chain of authority, a halfhearted university financial commitment, and a problem with faculty departures." When the urgency of curricular reform faded, the Chicano Affairs Office moved from emphasizing Chicano studies to providing academic assistance for Chicano and Chicana students.[126]

La Raza Unida Party and New Mexico

In the blazing Chicano imaginary, the building of a unified movement for the liberation of the whole Chicano/Chicana people appeared both necessary and possible. The attempt to centralize the wide-ranging *movimiento* concentrated on efforts to expand La Raza Unida Party (LRUP). LRUP had roots in the Mexican American Youth Organization (MAYO) in ethnically segregated south Texas. For three years, MAYO confronted the Anglo power structure over a score of issues, including institutional discrimination against high school students, the racist actions of whites, low-paying jobs, and political inequality.[127] In 1967,

MAYO leader José Ángel Gutiérrez proposed the idea of an independent political party conceived as a third-party alternative to the two main parties for Mexican Americans specifically.[128]

In 1970, a Chicano political party took shape at a meeting attended by 150 people in Zavala County, Texas. La Raza Unida Party (LRUP) was the name participants agreed to adopt. LRUP ran candidates for county offices and school boards in Crystal City, Hidalgo County, and four Winter Garden district counties. Facing the stiff opposition of white Texans, LRUP slates were elected in all of these places.[129] This success inspired the Chicana Chicano Movement outside of Texas to fight for empowerment on the ideal of self-determination. Gutiérrez reached out to Corky Gonzales in Denver, Reies López Tijerina in New Mexico, and activists in California to discuss organizing a third-party movement for the Chicano and Chicana people of *Aztlán*, the Prehispanic name projected by the Crusade for Justice for the Mexican American homeland in the Southwest.[130]

Building a statewide party, the Texas LRUP ambitiously nominated candidates for governor, lieutenant governor, state treasurer, the railroad commission, the land commission, both chambers of the state legislature, and local offices. After the Crusade for Justice endorsed LRUP, chapters sprung up in various states over the next two years. The California buildup centered in the Bay Area and Los Angeles. The model for the rest of the state chapters came out of the Berkeley founding document calling for rejection of the "existing political parties of our oppressor and to take it upon ourselves to form La Raza Unida, which will serve as a unifying force in our struggle for self-determination."[131]

LRUP agents took control of the First National Chicano Political Caucus held in San José, California, announcing the rejection of mainstream politics and calling for an independent political organization.[132] Among the participants was New Mexico's interesting Lieutenant Governor Roberto Mondragón. While serving as a high state official, Mondragón, a renowned cultural figure in northern New Mexico, was a friend of and participant in the CCM.[133] Along with Reies López Tijerina, Mondragón attended the San José LRUP event, hailing the importance of the Party for ending the Vietnam War and attacking Republicans and Democrats for feathering their nests with token Chicanos to make it look like they were responding to the people's needs.[134]

LRUP's first national convention in El Paso in 1972 generated what Ignacio García calls a "euphoria among Chicano activists never before known in the history of Mexican American people."[135] Delegations came from Colorado, Texas, Nebraska, Idaho, Wisconsin, Rhode Island, Maryland, Washington DC, as well as New Mexico.[136] Returning home, New Mexico delegates established El Partido de la Raza Unida de Nuevo México (NMLRUP).

The first organizational meeting of the NMLRUP occurred in Albuquerque on November 6, 1971.[137] The party's first State Central Committee consisted of Santiago Maestas, chair; Larry Candelaria, vice chair; Dan Armijo, treasurer; and Arlene Candelaria, secretary. Members included Randy Romero, Chris Eichwald Cebada, Ventura Chávez,

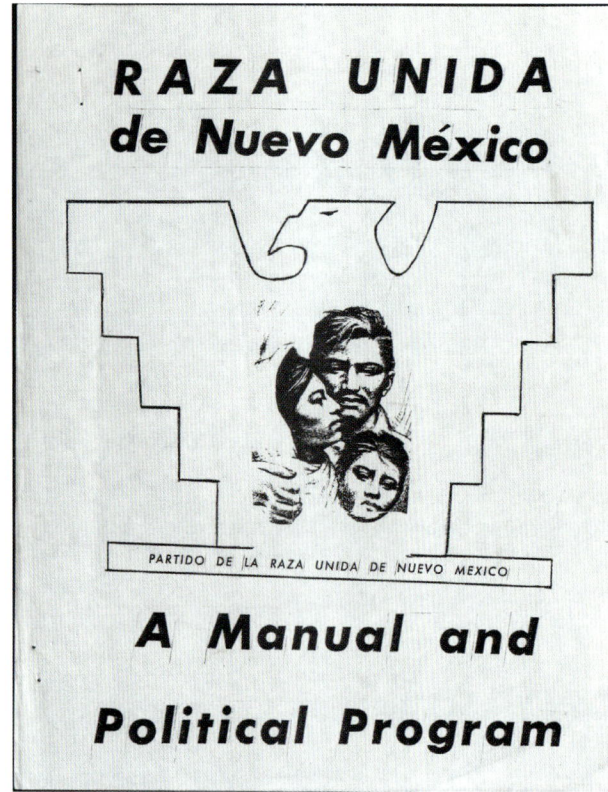

FIGURE 5.6. Cover, *New Mexico La Raza Unida Party Political Program,* no author, no date. Frank I. Sánchez Papers, MSS-612, box 28, folder 6, Center for Southwest Research. Courtesy of the University of New Mexico.

Daniel Casías, Ricardo Griego, Chris García, Crusita Chávez, and Ernesto Gómez.[138] NML-RUP followed the national party's purpose of offering an alternative to the two major political parties, which were criticized for having failed to "protect and defend our peoples' interests." NMLRUP would, as it pledged, provide a "political force to protect and further the human rights, education, and economic interests of our people."[139]

The NMLRUP developed a full-blown organizational structure with rules and regulations regarding the facets of a political party. The cover of its manual and political program featured a UFW style Mexican eagle offering protection for the prototypical Mexican family, which had been figuring centrally in conceptions of Chicano nationalism (fig. 5.6).

In one estimate, 1,500 people joined NMLRUP.[140] In Las Vegas, New Mexico Highlands University professor Pedro Rodríguez served as chair of the San Miguel County LRUP. He, Juan José Peña, and Manuel Archuleta put up LRUP candidates in San Miguel County elections and races for the East Las Vegas school board. Going up against the dominant Democratic Party was a tough test for the political aspirations of LRUP. Still, LRUP candidates won 25 percent of the San Miguel County vote in 1972. In 1974, Peña ran for Las Vegas mayor and five colleagues ran for four city council seats and for police magistrate, although under the banner of El Pueblo Unido, the name of a Progressive Era party that nuevomexicanos organized in the 1890s. Running against two other tickets, Peña received only 8 percent of the vote and the others fared likewise, yet the results helped defeat a slate of moderate Hispanos, serving an important LRUP goal of marginalizing "sell out" politicians from its ethnic group.[141]

The NMLRUP also entered candidates in Bernalillo County, which was important as it included Albuquerque, the largest population center in the state.[142] In Santa Fe, employees of the federal urban renewal Model Cities program who had returned from the Poor People's Campaign, organized a county Raza Unida Party. Running candidates for local offices, it was hampered by established Hispano leaders who called the Party radical and extreme.[143]

While regional LRUP organizations worked on the ground, the critical question of who to have as the national party chair turned contentious with José Angel Gutiérrez and Corky Gonzales vying for the position. Gutiérrez held to a pragmatic "balance of power" approach, working within the electoral system and negotiating with the powers that be to leverage on behalf of the Mexican American community. Gonzales aimed to take the party in the direction of cultural nationalism, expressed as revolutionary idealism in a (vague) separatist and direct confrontational stance toward the white power structure. The Colorado and Texas caucuses prepared for a battle between Gonzales and Gutiérrez for president of El Congreso de Aztlán, the supra LRUP authority.[144]

New Mexico's delegation was the third largest behind Texas and California and Reies López Tijerina rose as a third figurehead alongside Gonzales and Gutiérrez. Tijerina's main interest, having the federal government honor the New Mexico land grants, favored Gutiérrez's practical program. Nevertheless, in the Gonzales-Gutiérrez standoff, he played peacemaker.[145] Juan José Peña kept the New Mexico delegation relatively neutral, acting as mediator to ensure a fair selection of LRUP chairman. In contrast to the flamboyant Gonzales-Gutiérrez-Tijerina trio, Peña was a "soft-spoken intellectual" yet ready to debate "anyone anywhere." Eschewing scathing language, Peña skillfully restrained the hot-headed partisans who were ready to jump into a fight.[146]

Following fierce debate, Gutiérrez snatched the position of chair of El Congreso de Aztlán. At the climax of the conference, Tijerina joined him and Gonzales on stage. In a famous photo opportunity, the three posed with joined hands held in the air in a gesture of triumphant unity and harmony.[147] It was a false visual. If anything, the ideological split in the LRUP intensified further. Creating the Chicano National Congress for Land and Cultural Reform, Tijerina announced an October conference in Albuquerque. Proclaiming the need for unity above ideas, leaders, and organizations, he perceived his moment for ascending to top leader of the CCM based on consolidation of the land question. Its advantage, he argued, would stem from the support to be provided LRUP by the Black Civil Rights Movement as well as organized farm workers, while making for greater Mexican American participation in the electoral system.[148] Had Tijerina ascended, the center of the CCM would have possibly migrated to New Mexico. However, from the start, the Albuquerque meeting "became embroiled in controversy."[149] Gonzales, Tijerina's former brother in the fight for land justice, did not respect government bureaucrats, mainstream politicians, or middle-class liberals. Tijerina accused Gutiérrez of trying to take over his conference. The Texas leader denied it, but he and his delegation left in a huff. Turning to his other competitor, Gonzales pointed out that Gutiérrez was elected chair of LRUP Congreso not of the whole LRUP. He scheduled another conference; however, he, Gutiérrez, and Tijerina were hopelessly split. After walking out of the Gonzales event, Gutiérrez expended his energies in an effort to bring LRUP chapters in the Midwest together.[150]

Apart from the turmoil at the top of the national LRUP, the NMLRUP engaged in local electoral activity. In 1976 NMLRUP candidates were on statewide ballots including those for the US Senate and the state corporation commission.[151] In Rio Arriba County, LRUP chief Antonio "Ike" de Vargas entered eight candidates for county offices.[152] The Party ran campaigns for school boards, placing two members on the Jemez Mountain Independent School District. It recruited candidates for district administration offices and teacher jobs, city and county offices, and the US Senate.[153] Modest results were seen, but party spirit remained optimistic. State Committee Chair Juan José Peña predicted that with concentrated organizing, the party would control the state by the year 2000 as conditions for the people were getting worse under the Republican regime.[154]

In truth, the most significant role the NMLRUP played was that of social movement organization. While adhering to the general principles of the national party—working with the national office through El Congreso de Aztlán—its own policy framework gave state parties the autonomy to work on community issues.[155] The NMLRP thus went on to the support of the Chicano and Chicana students in the Las Vegas public schools and Highlands University. It provided leadership to take out a school superintendent who was recruited against the wishes of the Chicano students and the community. Police brutality in Clayton, Alamogordo, Rio Arriba County, Las Vegas, and Albuquerque formed a major issue. Support for strike efforts went to the Artesia municipal workers and the Las Vegas police association.[156]

NMLRUP and two other Chicano organizations fought tooth and nail to have Rio Arriba County Sheriff Emilio Naranjo removed from office. Naranjo was charged with intimidation and reprisals against critics, infringing on client-lawyer privilege, ordering county employees to harass, beat, extort, and arrest opponents on false charges, and other offenses.[157] NMLRUP leaders Juan José Peña, Ike de Vargas, and Larry Hill held a news conference to announce how law enforcement officers under Naranjo and elsewhere intimidated, harassed, and physically brutalized their party colleagues. Lawyer Larry Hill accused the police of, as he said, "trying to stifle our voice, our freedom of speech, guaranteed by the First Amendment."[158]

Conclusion

Clearly, New Mexico martialed a capacious share of the 1960s–1970s Chicano and Chicana Movement. Each of the organizational struggles referenced above went through more complex experiences than suggested. There were in addition many other Chicano Chicana mobilizations in New Mexico, for instance: a phase of the August 29th Movement, the national Marxist-Leninist organization that fought for a Chicano nationalist and communist revolution; high schoolers who "blew out" of classes to protest the shortcomings of their schooling; a widespread movement of community nonprofit organizations, which started in southern New Mexico; Los Padres and Las Hermanas, consisting of Catholic priests and nuns who committed their liberation theology to the cause; the *pinto* prisoners' rights movement; the *sin fronteras* Mexican immigrant rights movement; organizations within public institutions such as Chicanos Unidos de Sandia Labs, the Raza Medical Movement, and dedications within the legal profession.

Finally, of course, as other contributors to this volume have emphasized, there was the surge of art that both reflected and supported the Chicana Chicano Movement. It was a prodigious creativity expressed not only on canvases of various sorts for painting, drawing, posters, and murals, and by craft imaginaries; it was also inscribed in Chicano and Chicana poetry, novels, short stories, and literary propaganda. These too appeared in the New Mexican social landscape as they did wherever *el movimiento Chicana/Chicano* flowered. It all arose because of New Mexico's past experience as a charter member of the territorial expanse that the United States wrenched from Mexico in the mid-nineteenth century, making it integral to general Mexican American history.

By 1979, Chicano Chicana Movement activity ended or faded. Nevertheless, legacies endured. Movement *veteranos* and *veteranas* defined their life's work, vocations, and careers based on the ethos of Chicana-Chicano justice,[159] as in the continuing struggle for mercedes, the *acequia querencia* movement, the Black Beret makeover as the Southwest Organizing Project, the Southwest Network for Environmental and Economic Justice, and generations of students at the University of New Mexico and other higher education institutions. For those who stayed true to the struggle, the Movement was not over, just "transformed."[160]

Notes

1. Juan Gómez-Quiñones and Irene Vásquez, *Making Aztlán: Ideology and Culture of the Chicana and Chicano Movement, 1966–1977* (University of New Mexico Press, 2014), *coyuntura* 340–41, "ethos" 6.

2. On the CCM origins, see Armando Navarro, *Mexican American Youth Organization: Avant-Garde of the Chicano Movement in Texas* (University of Texas Press, 1995); and Gómez-Quiñones and Vásquez, *Making Áztlán*.

3. Susan Ferriss, Ricardo Sandoval, and Diana Hembree, *The Fight in the Fields: Cesar Chavez and the Farmworkers Movement* (Harcourt Brace, 1997), 102–104; Sam Kushner, *Long Road to Delano* (International Publishers, 1975), 137.

4. Kushner, *Long Road to Delano*, 135–38.

5. Richard Griswold del Castillo and Richard A. García, *César Chávez: A Triumph of Spirit* (University of Oklahoma Press, 1995), 52.

6. Randy Shaw, Beyond the Fields: Cesar Chavez, the UFW, and the Struggle for Justice in the 21st Century (University of California Press, 2008), quote 2, 51.

7. Katie Anastas, "Timeline of UFW strikes, boycotts, campaigns 1965-1975," *Mapping American Social Movements Project*, https://depts.washington.edu/moves/UFW_timeline.shtml.

8. Jamie Bronstein, "Big Trouble in Little Texas: The Chicano Movement in Southern New Mexico, 1968–1977," *New Mexico Historical Review* 95, no. 3 (Summer 2020): 283–321, 305.

9. Bronstein, "Big Trouble in Little Texas," 300.

10. Mario T. García and Ellen McCracken, *Roque's Corner: The Life and Times of Roque García and His Santa Fe* (Adelante Press, 2019), 119.

11. Margaret Garcia, letter to the editor, New Mexico *Lobo*, April 1, 1971, 5; also, Chris Reed, "Farmers' Market Target," New Mexico *Lobo*, February 4, 1972, 2.

12. Kushner, *Long Road to Delano*, 137.

13. Augustine (Gus) Romero was born and raised in Pueblo, Colorado, where he studied art and completed a BA in Graphic Design at the University of Southern Colorado. He continued his global education by traveling to Europe, Australia, Central America, the Dominican Republic, Cuba, and Mexico. In 1997 he received an MA in Sculpture from New York University. Before moving to Albuquerque, he taught at Parsons School of Design and participated in numerous New York exhibitions. He is the gallery curator for the City of Albuquerque, overseeing the South Broadway Cultural Center and KiMo Galleries. He serves on the advisory boards of 516 ARTS and SE-OC Right Brain Gallery. See, Albuquerque Art Business Association, "2014 Local Treasures, https://artscrawlabq.org/wp/2014-local-treasures-2/.

14. See, Augustine "Gus" Romero, "The Ghetto Curator and the Curandera," *Aztlan*, 46, no. 1 (Spring 2021): 195–201.

15. Richard Gardner, *¡Grito!: Reies Tijerina and the New Mexico Land Grant War of 1967* (Harper & Row, 1971), 49–53.

16. See, Phillip B. Gonzales, "Struggle for Survival: The Hispanic Land Grants of New Mexico, *Agricultural History* 77, no. 2 (Spring 2003): 293–324.

17. See, David Correia, *Properties of Violence: Law and Land Grant Struggle in Northern New Mexico* (University of Georgia Press, 2013).

18. Gonzales, "Struggle for Survival," 315.

19. Peter Nabokov, *Tijerina and the Courthouse Raid* (University of New Mexico Press, 1969), 17.

20. García and McCracken, *Roque's Corner*, 94–95, 100–105.

21. Nabokov, *Tijerina and the Courthouse Raid*, 254–55.

22. Muñoz, Jr. *Youth, Identity, Power*, 57–58.

23. Juan Martín Gallegos, "Reconstructing Identity/Revising Resistance: A History of Nuevomexicano/a Students at New Mexico Highlands

University, 1910–1973," PhD dissertation (The University of Arizona, 2014), 99.

24. Ernesto B. Vigil, *The Crusade for Justice: Chicano Militancy and the Government's War on Dissent* (University of Wisconsin Press, 1999), 30–31.

25. Griswold del Castillo and Garcia, *César Chávez* 83–84.

26. Carlos Muñoz, Jr.. *Youth, Identity, Power: The Chicano Movement* (New York & London: Verso, 1989), 58–59.

27. Vigil, *The Crusade for Justice*, 32–33; "Viva Tijerina," *El Gallo*, June 23, 1967, Elmer Martinez Collection, box 8, folder 8, Center for Southwest Research, University of New Mexico.

28. Mario T. García and Sal Castro, *Blowout!: Sal Castro and the Chicano Struggle for Educational Justice* (University of North Carolina Press, 2011), 135.

29. Navarro, *Mexican American Youth Organization*, 86.

30. Richard A. García, "The Origins of Chicano Cultural Thought: Visions and Paradigms—Roman's Culturalism, Alurista's Aesthetics, and Acuñas Communalism," *California History* 74, no. 3 (1995): 290–305, 297; Muñoz, *Youth, Identity, Power*, 58–59; Ernesto Chávez, *¡Mi Raza Primero!, My People First: Nationalism, Identity, and Insurgency in the Chicano Movement in Los Angeles, 1966–1978* (University of California Press, 2002), 45; Omar Valerio-Jiménez, "La Caravana de la Reconquista: The Brown Berets Contest Memories of Conquest," in Rewriting the Chicano Movement: New Histories of Mexican American Activism in the Civil Rights Era, Mario T. García and Ellen McCracken, eds. (University of Arizona Press, 2021: 71–91), 73.

31. García, "The Origins of Chicano Cultural Thought," 299; Rodolfo F. Acuña, *Occupied America: A History of Chicanos* (Canfield Press, first edition 1972).

32. Muñoz, *Youth, Identity, Power*, 85–86; Chávez, *¡Mi Raza Primero!*, 40, 43–46, 47, 49, 50, 59.

33. Valerio-Jiménez, "*La Caravana la Reconquista*," 72–88; Chávez, *¡Mi Raza Primero!*,

56; Navarro, *Mexican American Youth Organization*, 60–66.

34. Jerry Walz, "Berets Visit Western," *The Mustang* (Western New Mexico University), November 23, 1971, 1; Bronstein, "Big Trouble in Little Texas," 287.

35. Notes on the Brown Berets, Frank I. Sánchez Papers, MSS 612, Center for Southwest Research, University of New Mexico (hereafter Sánchez papers), box 27, folder 34; Bronstein, "Big Trouble in Little Texas," 298.

36. Gordon K. Mantler, *Power to the Poor: Black-Brown Coalition and the Fight for Economic Justice, 1960–1974* (University of North Carolina Press, 2013), 186. Mantler argues that the Poor Peoples Campaign's "most important, long-term legacy was its inadvertent strengthening of the Chicano movement and its unique form of identity politics" (185).

37. *El Papel*, May 1968, Martinez Collection, box 8, folder 8. Mantler, *Power to the Poor*, 187.

38. Patricia Bell Blawis, *Tijerina and the Land Grants: Mexican Americans in Struggle for Their Heritage* (New York: International, 1971), 175.

39. García and McCracken, *Roque's Corner*, 123–26.

40. Eric Mar, "Richard Moore," Key Wiki. https://keywiki.org/Richard_Moore.

41. Kent Paterson, "The Black Berets Live On," *Administrator*, New Mexico State University, October 10, 2012, https://fnsnews.nmsu.edu/the-black-berets-live-on/, 4/19/2019.

42. Kent Paterson, "The Black Berets Live On," *Administrator*, New Mexico State University, October 10, 2012, https://fnsnews.nmsu.edu/the-black-berets-live-on/, 4/19/2019.

43. Kent Paterson, "The Black Berets Live On."

44. "The Black Beret Organization 12 Point Program and Platform," mimeo copy in Sánchez papers, box 27, folder 27.

45. Paterson, "The Black Berets Live On"; "Minorities Press Demands to City," *Albuquerque Journal*, December 15, 1970, A-1.

46. Paterson, "The Black Berets Live On";
Eric Mar, "Richard Moore.

47. Paterson, "The Black Berets Live On";
Eric Mar, "Richard Moore." On COINTELPRO
and the Chicano Movement, see José Angel
Gutiérrez, *Tracking King Tiger: Reies Lopez Tijerina
and the FBI* (Michigan State University Press, 2019).

48. Black Berets Minister of Defense, "Black
Beret Organization: Why We Are Armed," circular,
Sánchez papers, box 27, folder 27.

49. Guillermo Rojas, "Chicano/Raza
Newspaper and Periodical Serials Listing," *Hispania*
58, no. 4 (December 1975): 851–63, 851.

50. Vigil, *Crusade for Justice*, 71, 396n8; Ignacio
García, *Chicanismo: The Forging of a Militant Ethos
among Mexican Americans* (University of Arizona
Press, 1997), 59–60. *La Raza Latina Press Association*,
pamphlet, copy in Sánchez papers, box 27, folder 42.

51. Ignacio M. García, *United We Win: The
Rise and Fall of La Raza Unida Party* (MASRC,
the University of Arizona, 1989), 77, 138, 139, 145,
146; Vigil, *The Crusade for Justice*, 187; Navarro, *The
Mexican American Youth Organization*, 113–14.

52. García, *Chicanismo*, 59–60.

53. For a comprehensive list of Chicano
newspapers, see, Rojas, "Chicano/Raza Newspaper
and Periodical Serials Listing." For *El Grito del Sur*
2, no. 3 (March 1973), see Ricardo Sánchez Papers,
1941–1995, Special Collections M652, Box 72,
Folder 9, 1973, Stanford University.

54. Soldatkenko, *Chicano Studies*, 77, 139. For
El Cuaderno 3, no. 2 (Spring, 1973), see Ricardo
Sánchez Special Collections M652, Box 72, Folder
9, 1973, Stanford University.

55. On how Martínez ended up in New
Mexico, see Elizabeth (Betita) Martínez, oral history interview by Loretta Ross, Voices of Feminism
Oral History Project, Smith College, March 3,
2006; and, Elizabeth Martinez, "*Social Justice* Salutes
Beverly Axelrod," *Social Justice*, January 1, 2002:
186–87, 186.

56. Elizabeth Martinez, "'Betita': A View from
New Mexico: Recollections of the Movimiento

Left," *Monthly Review* 54, no. 3 (July–August 2002);
García, *Chicanismo*, 59.

57. Lorena Oropeza, Introduction to Enri-
queta Longeaux y Vásquez, *Enriqueta Vasquez and the
Chicano Movement: Writings from El Grito del Norte*,
Lorena Oropeza and Dionne Espinoza, eds. (Arte
Público Press, 2006), xxxiii.

58. Lorena Oropeza, Introduction, xxxiv.

59. Dennis López, "'*El Grito del Norte*',
Chicana/o Print Culture, and the Politics of Anti-Imperialism," *Science & Society* 79, no. 4 (October
2015): 527–54, 541, 543, 547.

60. Longeaux y Vásquez, "¡Que Linda es Cuba:
Part I," *El Grito del Norte*, May 19, 1969, 178 in
Enriqueta Vasquez and the Chicano Movement: 178–181.

61. Dionne Espinoza, "Rethinking Cultural
Nationalism and La Familia through Women's
Communities: Enriqueta Vasquez and Chicana
Feminist Thought," 205–231 in *Enriqueta Vasquez
and the Chicano Movement*, 207; Oropreza, Introduc-
tion to Enriqueta Longeaux y Vásquez, *Enriqueta
Vasquez and the Chicano Movement*, xxxiii.

62. Tony Platt, "The Heart Just Insists: In
the Struggle with Elizabeth 'Betita' Sutherland
Martinez," *Social Justice*, June 22, 2021.

63. Martínez, "Betita."

64. Lee Bebout, *Mythohistorical Interventions:
The Chicano Movement and Its Legacies* (University
of Minnesota Press, 2011), 105.

65. Gomez-Quiñones and Vasquez, *Making
Aztlan*, 146.

66. Martinez, "'Betita': A View from New
Mexico: Recollections of the Movimiento Left."

67. Katharine Q. Seelye, "Elizabeth Martínez,
Voice of the Chicana Movement, Dies at 95," *New
York Times*, June 29, 2021.

68. Gómez-Quiñones and Vásquez, *Making
Aztlán*, 7. In 1991, the Southwest Organizing
Project updated *450 Years* as *500 Years of Chicano
History in Pictures*.

69. Tomás Atencio, *Resolana: A Chicano
Pathway to Knowledge* (Stanford Center for Chicano
Research, Stanford University, 1988), 5

70. Atencio, *Resolana*, 23.

71. Tomás Atencio, "El Oro del Barrio in the Cyber Age: Leapfrogging the Industrial Revolution," 9–68 in *Resolana: Emerging Chicano Dialogues on Community and Globalization*, Miguel Montiel, Tomás Atencio, and E. A Mares, eds. (Tucson: University of Arizona Press, 2009), 13, 53.

72. From the description of Academia de la Nueva Raza and the Rio Grande Institute records, 1965-1998, University of New Mexico. WorldCat record id: 454191249, box 1, folder 4.

73. Atencio, "El Oro del Barrio in the Cyber Age, 53–56, 13.

74. E.A. "Tony" Mares, "A Resolana on Networks: Chicanos, Connections, and Culture," 138–185 in Montiel, Atencio, and Mares, eds., *Resolana*, 138.

75. Atencio, *Resolana: A Chicano Pathway to Knowledge*, 1–2.

76. Mares, "A Resolana on Networks," 138.

77. Atencio, "El Oro del Barrio in the Cyber Age," 53–56, 13.

78. Fort the Ordemalas fable as told by Luz López, see Tomás Atencio, et al., eds., *Entre Verde Y Seco*, La Academia de la Nueva Raza, 1972, 73–78.

79. Miguel Montiel, Tomás Atencio, E. A. Mares, "Introduction," to *Resolana: Emerging Chicano Dialogues on Community and Globalization*, 5; Atencio, El Oro del Barrio in the Cyber Age," 32, 54; quote from Mares, "A Resolana on Networks," 173.

80. Atencio, "El Oro del Barrio in the Cyber Age," 41–42.

81. Muñoz, *Youth, Identity, Power,* 1. On the rise of Chicano Youth Movement, see Navarro, Mexican American Youth Organization, 45–56.

82. Navarro, *Mexican American Youth Organization*, 57–58.

83. Margaret Garcia to the editor, New Mexico *Lobo*, April 1, 1971, 5; Juan Abeyta, unpublished oral history interview conducted by Felipe Gonzales, June 28, 2022, Center for Southwest Research, University of New Mexico Libraries (hereafter Abeyta interview).

84. Gomez-Quiñones and Vasquez, *Making Aztlan*, 144.

85. Sandoval interview.

86. "Meier Says Workers Need New Affiliation," *Lobo*, October 6, 1969, 1.

87. "Discrimination at UNM," *The* [Santa Fe] *New Mexico Review and Legislative Journal* 1 (July 1969), 1; copy available in the Martínez papers, folder 13; "Senate Passes SOC Demands as Resolutions," (University of New Mexico) *Lobo*, October 1, 1969, 1.

88. "Committee Finds No Intended Racism," New Mexico *Lobo*, September 22, 1969, 1.

89. UMAS to editor ("Demand Apology"), New Mexico *Lobo*, October 20, 1969, 2.

90. Arturo Sandoval interview conducted by Felipe Gonzales, May 19, 2022, Center for Southwest Research, University of New Mexico Libraries (hereafter Sandoval Interview); Gonzales, "Birthing Chicano and Chicana Studies at the University of New Mexico: An Old Student's *Testimonio*, 8.

91. "Three-Day Festival Starts Today," New Mexico *Lobo*, April 15, 1971, 3.

92. "Ad hoc," New Mexico *Lobo* October 26, 1972, 2.

93. "Board Says UMAS Not Dissolved," New Mexico *Lobo*, February 11, 1970, 3.

94. "Will Hold Conference," New Mexico *Lobo*, December 10, 1969, 1; Conference Identifies Educational Problems-Of Mexican Americans," New Mexico *Lobo*, December 15, 1969, 1.

95. MAYO being one well-documented case; see, Navarro, *Mexican American Youth Organization*, 110–113.

96. Michael Soldatenko, *Chicano Studies: The Genesis of a Discipline* (University of Arizona Press, 2009), 132.

97. Jennie V. Chávez, "Women of the Mexican American Movement," 36–39, in *Chicana Feminist Thought: The Basic Historical Writings*, edited by Alma M. Garcia. Taylor & Francis Group, 1997, 36.

98. Beverly Padilla, "Chicanas and Abortion," New York: *The Militant*, February 18, 1972: 4.

99. For an analysis of the emergence of MEChA, see Muñoz, *Youth, Identity, Power*, 79–80.

100. Phillip B. (Felipe) Gonzales, "Birthing Chicano and Chicana Studies at the University of New Mexico: An Old Student's *Testimonio*," unpublished manuscript, 2023.

101. Eloy García, "The Chicano Student Movement at New Mexico Highlands: An Interpretive History," PhD dissertation (New Mexico Highlands University, 1997), 24; Julianna C. Wiggins, "Written and Oral Histories of the Chicano Movement at New Mexico Highlands University, 1968–1960," MA thesis (University of New Mexico, 2019), 26.

102. Gomez-Quiñones and Vasquez, *Making Aztlan*, 145–46.

103. García, "The Chicano Student Movement at New Mexico Highlands, 40; Wiggins, "Written and Oral Histories of the Chicano Movement," 39–41; Gomez-Quiñones and Vasquez, *Making Aztlan*, 146.

104. *El Grito del Sur*, March 1972, Sánchez papers, box 27, folder 30.

105. Bronstein, "Big Trouble in Little Texas," 288–290, 292, 294.

106. Initial Interview with Johnny Arzola notes, Chicano Student Movement at Western New Mexico University Oral History Project, CSWR, box 1, folder 5.

107. It included increasing Chicano enrollment; setting up a scholarship program for Chicano and Chicana students in education; developing minority representation on faculty, non-faculty and administrative positions; proposing social culture programs; enlarging its organization to qualify for federal funding; enhancing ethnic pride; forging links with the community; building a playground for the local Head Start program; screening *Salt of the Earth*, the pro-labor film made by Hollywood leftists; holding mariachi and *baile folklórico* events on *El Día de la Raza*; and bringing Reies López Tijerina in to speak. See, Danny Trujillo, "Los Estudiantes Unidos," *The Mustang*, Western New Mexico University, September 18, 1973, 2; Bronstein, "Big Trouble in Little Texas," 288, 289.

108. See, the Chicano Student Movement at Western New Mexico University Oral History Project, box 1, initial Interview with David Maestas; folder 8, and Notes taken from Interview with Luis Nolasco, folder 9.

109. Mía Angélica Sosa-Provencio and Rebecca Sánchez, "*Serna v. Portales*, 1974: Changing the Music and Asserting Language Rights for New Mexico's Children," in *The Shoulders we Stand On: A History of Bilingual Education in New Mexico*, edited by Rebecca Blum Martínez and Mary Jean Habermann López (Albuquerque: University of New Mexico Press, 2020): 138–61, 143.

110. "A.H.O.R.A.," *El Renacimiento*, September 1978, 20, Sánchez papers, box 27, folder 24.

111. Bronstein, "Big Trouble in Little Texas," 300.

112. Soldatenko, *Chicano Studies: The Genesis of a Discipline*, 12–31.

113. Muñoz, *Youth, Identity, Power*, 79–81; Navarro, *Mexican American Youth Organization*, 89; Armando, *Mexican American Youth Organization*, 60.

114. UMAS [Felipe Gonzales], "The Chicano and UNM," unpublished, 1969.

115. Phillip B. Gonzales, "Birthing Chicano and Chicana Studies at the University of New Mexico: An Old Student's *Testimonio*," unpublished manuscript.

116. Gomez-Quinoñes and Vasquez, *Making Aztlan*, 144–45.

117. As found in a press investigation; Casey Church, "Lobo survey shows 'studies' class void," New Mexico *Lobo*, April 8, 1970, 4.

118. Gómez-Quinoñes and Vasquez, *Making Aztlan*, 147.

119. Bronstein, "Big Trouble in Little Texas," 292–95.

120. Chicano Programs at New Mexico State University. https://nmsu.edu/academics/Chicano%20Programs%20.html.

121. Jim Peeler, "Maldonado Tenure Decision Delayed," *The Mustang*, Western New Mexico University, April 14, 1972, 1; Tom Hester, "Bonnie Buckley Maldonado: An Appreciation," September 27, 2023, Southwest Word Fiesta, https://swwordfiesta.org/bonnie-buckley-maldonado/.

122. Bronstein, "Big Trouble in Little Texas," 288–90.

123. "Former College Head Convicted of Fraud," *New York Times*, October 10, 1982, 28.

124. Bronstein, "Big Trouble in Little Texas," 289–90; "A Legacy Left: WNMU scholar-in-residence, Chicano studies pioneer dies at 92," *Silver City Daily Press*, January 5, 2019.

125. Bronstein, "Big Trouble in Little Texas," 300, 301, 302.

126. Bronstein, "Big Trouble in Little Texas," 303–4.

127. Navarro, *Mexican American Youth Organization*, 90; García, *United We Win*, 39–56.

128. Navarro, *Mexican American Youth Organization*, 42–43.

129. Navarro, *Mexican American Youth Organization*, 214–25.

130. Navarro, Mexican American Youth Organization, 225–29; Garcia, *United We Win*, 130, 223; Vigil, *La Raza Unida Party*, 186.

131. Navarro, *Mexican American Youth Organization*, 229–35; García, *United We Win*, 98.

132. Vigil, *The Crusade for Justice*, 184–85.

133. In Sánchez Papers, box 1, see Antonio Cordova to Querido Camarada (broadsheet), September 20, 1971, folder 11; "Chicano Group Asks Roswell Area Law Enforcement Probes," *Albuquerque Journal*, September 7, 1971, press clipping, folder 14; "Raza," broadside, folder 14; "Mondragon to Head Panel on Civil Rights," folder 14; "Mondragon Says 'Unite,'" Española *Sun-News*, n.d., folder 40. Vigil, *The Crusade for Justice*, 184.

134. Vigil, *The Crusade for Justice*, 184–85.

135. García, *United We Win*, 105.

136. Vigil, *The Crusade for Justice*, 187.

137. Ernesto Gómez, "La Raza Unida," New Mexico *Lobo*, November 15, 1971, 3, 4.

138. La Raza Unida de Nuevo México, *A Manual and Political Program*, 2, 10, a copy in Sánchez papers, box 28, folder 6.

139. "Constitution of La Raza Unida Party of New Mexico," pp. 9–18 in La Raza Unida de Nuevo México, *A Manual and Political Program*, 9.

140. García and McCracken, *Roque's Corner*, 118.

141. Garcia, *United We Win* 140–42; Gomez-Quiñones and Vasquez, *Making Aztlan*, 212.

142. Garcia, *United We Win* 140–42; Gomez-Quiñones and Vasquez, *Making Aztlan*, 212.

143. García and McCracken, *Roque's Corner*, 118–119.

144. Garcia, *United We Win*, 108; Vigil, *The Crusade for Justice*, 185–86, 190, 189.

145. Vigil, *The Crusade for Justice*, 192; Garcia, *United We Win*, 111–113, quote 142.

146. Garcia, *United We Win*, 143, 140.

147. See, e.g., the cover of Armando Navarro, *La Raza Unida Party: A Chicano Challenge to the U.S. Two-Party Dictatorship*. Philadelphia: Temple University Press, 2000.

148. Vigil, *The Crusade for Justice*, 189; Garcia, United We Win, 112, 136.

149. Garcia, *United We Win*, 135–37; Vigil, *The Crusade for Justice*, 192.

150. Vigil, *The Crusade for Justice*, 192; García, *United We Win*, 135–37, 138–40.

151. La Raza Unida de Nuevo México, *A Manual and Political Program*, 2.

152. Juan José Peña, "Partido de La Raza Unida de Nuevo México: Newsletter III," September 25, 1978, Sánchez papers, Box: 28, Folder: 6.

153. La Raza Unida de Nuevo México, *A Manual and Political Program*, ibid., 2.

154. Juan José Peña, "Partido de La Raza Unida de Nuevo México: Newsletter III," 3–4; also La Raza Unida de Nuevo México, *A Manual and Political Program*, 3.

155. La Raza Unida de Nuevo México, *A Manual and Political Program*, 3.

156. La Raza Unida de Nuevo México, *A Manual and Political Program*, 2.

157. "Naranjo answers charges," *Santa Fe New Mexican*, February 16, 1976; "Big group joins La Raza march," *Santa Fe New Mexican*, February 22, 1976; "RA probe is asked, *Santa Fe New Mexican*, March 4, 1976; Andres Valdez, "Press Release," and La Cooperación del Pueblo, "Terror in Tierra Amarilla, Sánchez papers, box 27, folder 24.

158. "La Raza Chiefs Claim Brutality," *Albuquerque Journal*, news clipping, no date, Albuquerque Urban Coalition Records, MSS-0049, box 12, folder 32, Albuquerque Special Collections Library.

159. Wiggins, "Written and Oral Histories of the Chicano Movement at New Mexico Highlands University, 43; Sandoval interview; Abeyta interview.

160. Dr. Tessa Cordova quoted in Paterson, "The Black Berets Live On."

Bibliography

ARCHIVAL SOURCES

Academia de la Nueva Raza and the Rio Grande Institute Records, 1965–1998, Center for Southwest Research, University of New Mexico (CSWR)

Albuquerque Urban Coalition Records, Albuquerque Special Collections Library

Gloria Montoya Chávez Papers, CSWR

Elmer Martínez Collection, CSWR

Reies López Tijerina Papers, CSWR

Ricardo Sánchez Papers, 1941–1995, Special Collections, Papers 1941–1995, Stanford University

Frank I. Sánchez Papers, CSWR

PUBLISHED BOOKS, ARTICLES, AND CHAPTERS

Acuña, Rodolfo F. *Occupied America: The Chicano's Struggle toward Liberation*. San Francisco: Canfield Press, first edition 1972.

Anastas, Katie. "Timeline of UFW strikes, boycotts, campaigns 1965–1975." *Mapping American Social Movements Project*. https://depts.washington.edu/moves/UFW_timeline.shtml.

Atencio, Tomás. *Resolana: A Chicano Pathway to Knowledge*. Stanford University, 1988.

Atencio, Tomás. "El Oro del Barrio in the Cyber Age: Leapfrogging the Industrial Revolution." *Resolana: Emerging Chicano Dialogues on Community and Globalization*, edited by Miguel Montiel, Tomás Atencio, and E. A Mares. University of Arizona Press, 2009.

Atencio, Tomás, Antonio Medina, Jerry López, Arturo Tenorio, Ruby Rodríguez, Vicente Martínez, eds. *Entre Verde Y Seco*. Academia de la Nueva Raza, 1972.

Bebout, Lee. *Mythohistorical Interventions: The Chicano Movement and Its Legacies*. University of Minnesota Press, 2011.

Blawis, Patricia Bell. *Tijerina and the Land Grants: Mexican Americans in Struggle for Their Heritage*. International, 1971.

Bronstein, Jamie. "Big Trouble in Little Texas: The Chicano Movement in Southern New Mexico, 1968–1977." *New Mexico Historical Review* 95, no. 3 (Summer 2020): 283–321.

Buelna, Enrique M. *Chicano Communists and the Struggle for Social Justice*. University of Arizona Press, 2019.

Chávez, Ernesto. ¡*Mi Raza Primero! My People First: Nationalism, Identity, and Insurgency in the*

Chicano Movement in Los Angeles, 1966–1978. University of California Press, 2002.

Chávez, Jennie V. "Women of the Mexican American Movement." In *Chicana Feminist Thought: The Basic Historical Writings*, edited by Alma M. Garcia. Taylor & Francis Group, 1997.

Chicano Communications Center. *450 años del pueblo Chicano / 450 years of Chicano history in Pictures.* 1976.

Correia, David. *Properties of Violence: Law and Land Grant Struggle in Northern New Mexico.* University of Georgia Press, 2013.

Espinoza, Dionne. "Rethinking Cultural Nationalism and La Familia through Women's Communities: Enriqueta Vasquez and Chicana Feminist Thought." In *Enriqueta Vasquez and the Chicano Movement.* Arte Público Press, 2006.

Ferriss, Susan, Ricardo Sandoval, and Diana Hembree. *The Fight in the Fields: Cesar Chavez and the Farmworkers Movement.* Harcourt Brace, 1997.

Gallegos, Juan Martín. "Reconstructing Identity/ Revising Resistance: A History of Nuevomexicano/a Students at New Mexico Highlands University, 1910–1973." PhD dissertation. The University of Arizona, 2014.

García, Eloy J. "The Chicano Student Movement at New Mexico Highlands: An Interpretive History." PhD dissertation, New Mexico Highlands University, 1997.

Gardner, Richard. *¡Grito!: Reies Tijerina and the New Mexico Land Grant War of 1967.* Harper & Row, 1971.

García, Ignacio M. *United We Win: The Rise and Fall of La Raza Unida Party.* University of Arizona, 1989.

García, Ignacio M. *Chicanismo: The Forging of a Militant Ethos among Mexican Americans.* University of Arizona Press, 1997.

García, Mario T., and Ellen McCracken. *Roque's Corner: The Life and Times of Roque García and His Santa Fe.* Adelante Press, 2019.

García, Mario T., and Sal Castro. *Blowout!: Sal Castro and the Chicano Struggle for Educational Justice.* University of North Carolina Press, 2011.

García, Richard A. "The Origins of Chicano Cultural Thought: Visions and Paradigms— Romano's Culturalism, Alurista's Aesthetics, and Acuñas Communalism." *California History* 74, no. 3 (1995): 290–305.

Gómez-Quiñones, Juan, and Irene Vásquez. *Making Áztlán: Ideology and Culture of the Chicana and Chicano Movement, 1966–1977.* University of New Mexico Press, 2014.

Gonzales, Phillip B. "Struggle for Survival: The Hispanic Land Grants of New Mexico," *Agricultural History* 77, no. 2 (Spring 2003): 293–324.

Gonzales, Phillip B. "Birthing Chicano and Chicana Studies at the University of New Mexico: An Old Student's *Testimonio.*" Unpublished manuscript.

Griswold del Castillo, Richard, and Richard A. García. *César Chávez: A Triumph of Spirit.* University of Oklahoma Press, 1995.

Gutiérrez, José Angel. *The Making of a Chicano Militant: Lessons from Cristal.* University of Wisconsin Press, 1998.

Gutiérrez, José Angel. *Tracking King Tiger: Reies Lopez Tijerina and the FBI.* Michigan State University Press, 2019.

Kushner, Sam. *Long Road to Delano.* International Publishers, 1975.

López, Dennis. "'*El Grito del Norte,*' Chicana/o Print Culture, and the Politics of Anti-Imperialism." *Science & Society* 79, no. 4 (October 2015): 527–54.

Mantler, Gordon K. *Power to the Poor: Black-Brown Coalition and the Fight for Economic Justice, 1960–1974.* University of North Carolina Press, 2013.

Mar, Eric. "Richard Moore," Key Wiki. https:// keywiki.org/Richard_Moore.

Mares, E. A. Tony. "A Resolana on Networks: Chicanos, Connections, and Culture," in Montiel, Atencio, and Mares, *Resolana,* 138–85.

Martinez, Elizabeth Sutherland. "*Social Justice* Salutes Beverly Axelrod." *Social Justice*, January 1, 2002: 186–87.

Martinez, Elizabeth Sutherland. "'Betita:' A View from New Mexico: Recollections of the Movimiento Left." *Monthly Review* 54, no. 3 (July–August 2002). https://monthlyreview.org/2002/07/01/a-view-from-new-mexico/.

Martinez, Elizabeth Sutherland. *500 years of Chicana women's history/ 500 años de historia de las chicanas*. Rutgers University Press, 2008.

Montiel, Miguel, Tomás Atencio, and E. A. Mares, "Introduction," to *Resolana: Emerging Chicano Dialogues on Community and Globalization*, edited by Miguel Montiel, Tomás Atencio, and E. A. Mares. Tucson: University of Arizona Press, 2009.

Muñoz, Carlos Jr. *Youth, Identity, Power: The Chicano Movement*. Verso, 1989.

Nabokov, Peter. *Tijerina and the Courthouse Raid*. University of New Mexico Press, 1969.

Navarro, Armando. *Mexican American Youth Organization: Avant-Garde of the Chicano Movement in Texas*. University of Texas Press, 1995.

Navarro, Armando. *La Raza Unida Party: A Chicano Challenge to the U.S. Two-Party Dictatorship*. Temple University Press, 2000.

Oropeza, Lorena. Introduction to Enriqueta Longeaux y Vásquez, *Enriqueta Vasquez and the Chicano Movement: Writings from El Grito del Norte*, edited by Lorena Oropeza and Dionne Espinoza. (Arte Público Press, 2006).

Padilla, Beverly. "Chicanas and Abortion." *The Militant*, February 18, 1972: 4.

Platt, Tony. "The Heart Just Insists: In the Struggle with Elizabeth 'Betita' Sutherland Martinez." *Social Justice*, June 22, 2021.

Rojas, Guillermo. "Chicano/Raza Newspaper and Periodical Serials Listing." *Hispania* 58, no. 4 (December 1975): 851–63.

Romero, Augustine (Gus). "The Ghetto Curator and the Curandera." *Aztlan*, 46, no. 1 (Spring 2021): 195–201.

Shaw, Randy. *Beyond the Fields: Cesar Chavez, the UFW, and the Struggle for Justice in the 21st Century*. University of California Press, 2008.

Soldatenko, Michael. *Chicano Studies: The Genesis of a Discipline*. University of Arizona Press, 2009.

Sorrell, Victor Alejandro. "The Persuasion of Art—The Art of Persuasion: Emanuel Martínez Creates a Pulpit for El Movimiento." In *Emanuel Martínez: A Retrospective*, edited by Teddy Dewalt. Denver: Museo de Las Américas, 1995, 26–28.

Sosa-Provencio, Mía Angélica, and Rebecca Sánchez. "*Serna v. Portales*, 1974: Changing the Music and Asserting Language Rights for New Mexico's Children." In *The Shoulders we Stand On: A History of Bilingual Education in New Mexico*, edited by Rebecca Blum Martínez and Mary Jean Habermann López. University of New Mexico Press, 2020, 138–61.

UMAS [Felipe Gonzales]. "The Chicano and UNM," unpublished manuscript, 1969.

Valerio-Jiménez, Omar. "*La Caravana de la Reconquista*: The Brown Berets Contest Memories of Conquest." In *Rewriting the Chicano Movement: New Histories of Mexican American Activism in the Civil Rights Era*, edited by Mario T. García and Ellen McCracken. University of Arizona Press, 2021), 71–91.

Vigil, Ernesto B. *The Crusade for Justice: Chicano Militancy and the Government's War on Dissent*. University of Wisconsin Press, 1999.

Voces del
Pueblo

Plates

IGNACIO "NACHO" JARAMILLO
(Born 1943, La Plaza de Arriba, NM;
current residence, Las Vegas, NM)

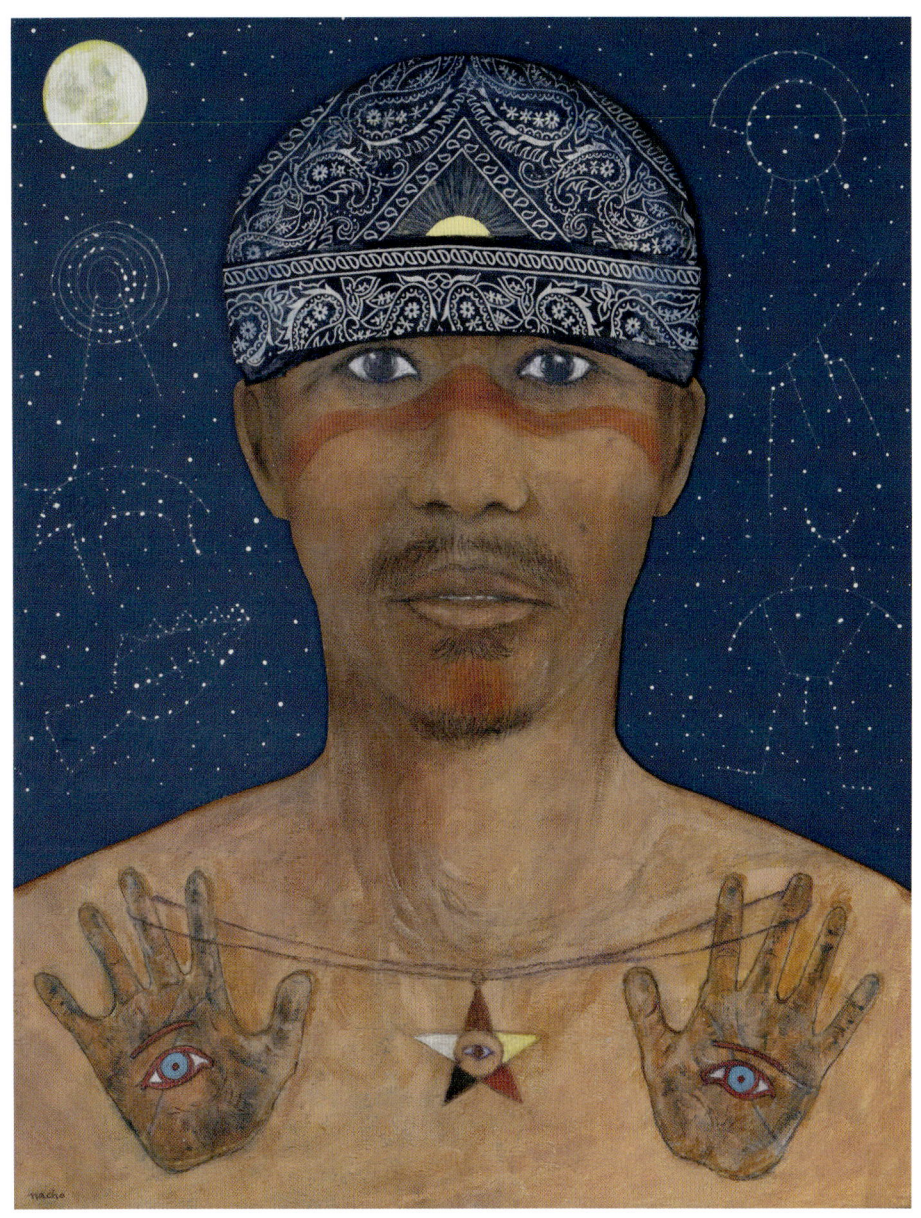

PLATE 1. *Raza cósmica*, 1970–1980. Water-based paints on illustration board fixed
on wood panel, cutout, 30″ × 22″. Collection of the artist.

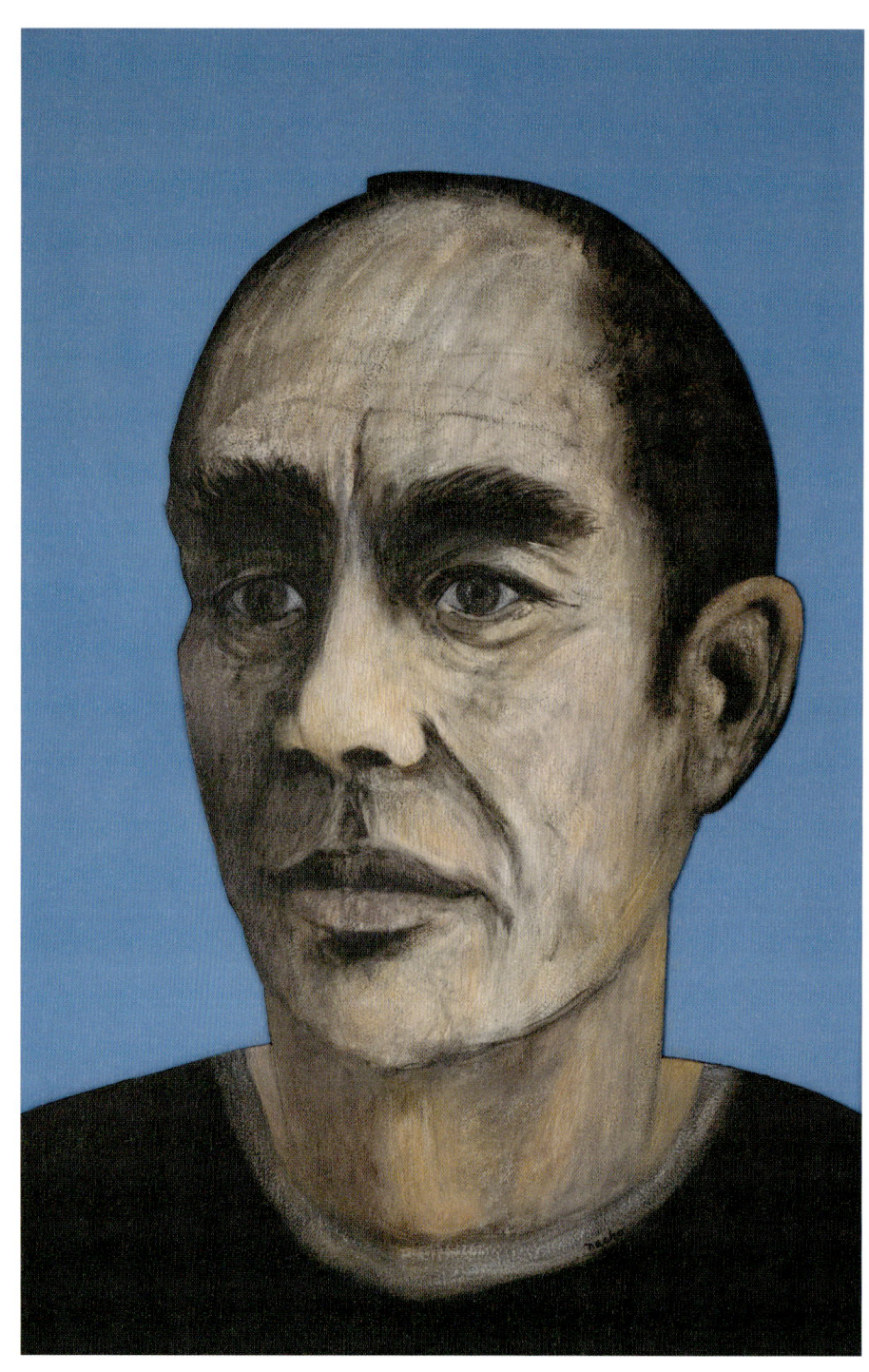

PLATE 2. *Jimmy Santiago Baca*, 1985–1986. Water-based paints on gessoed wood panel, cutout, 26″ × 24″. Collection of the artist.

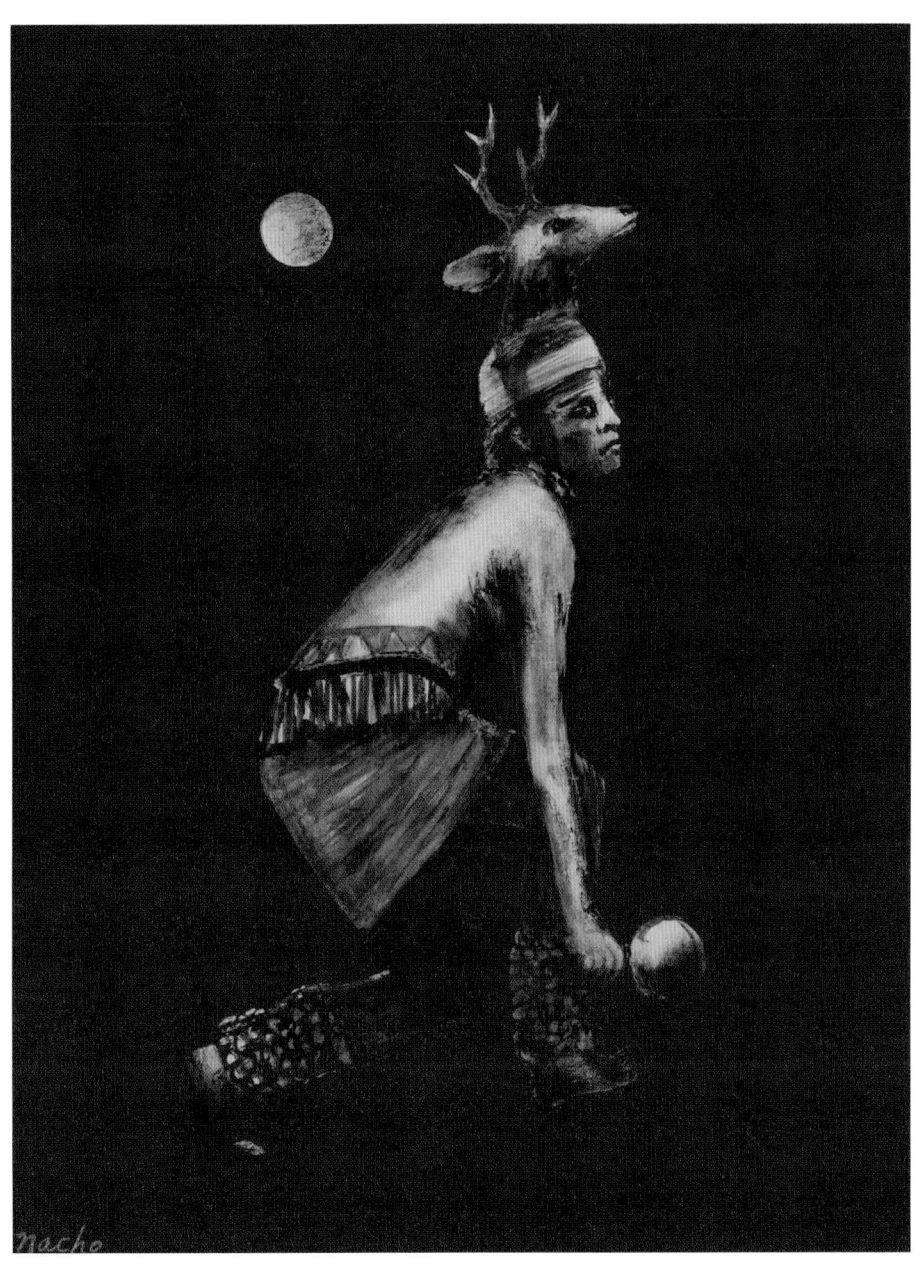

PLATE 3. *Yaquí Deer Dancer*, 1980. Water-based paints on illustration board, 17″ × 14″.
Collection of the artist.

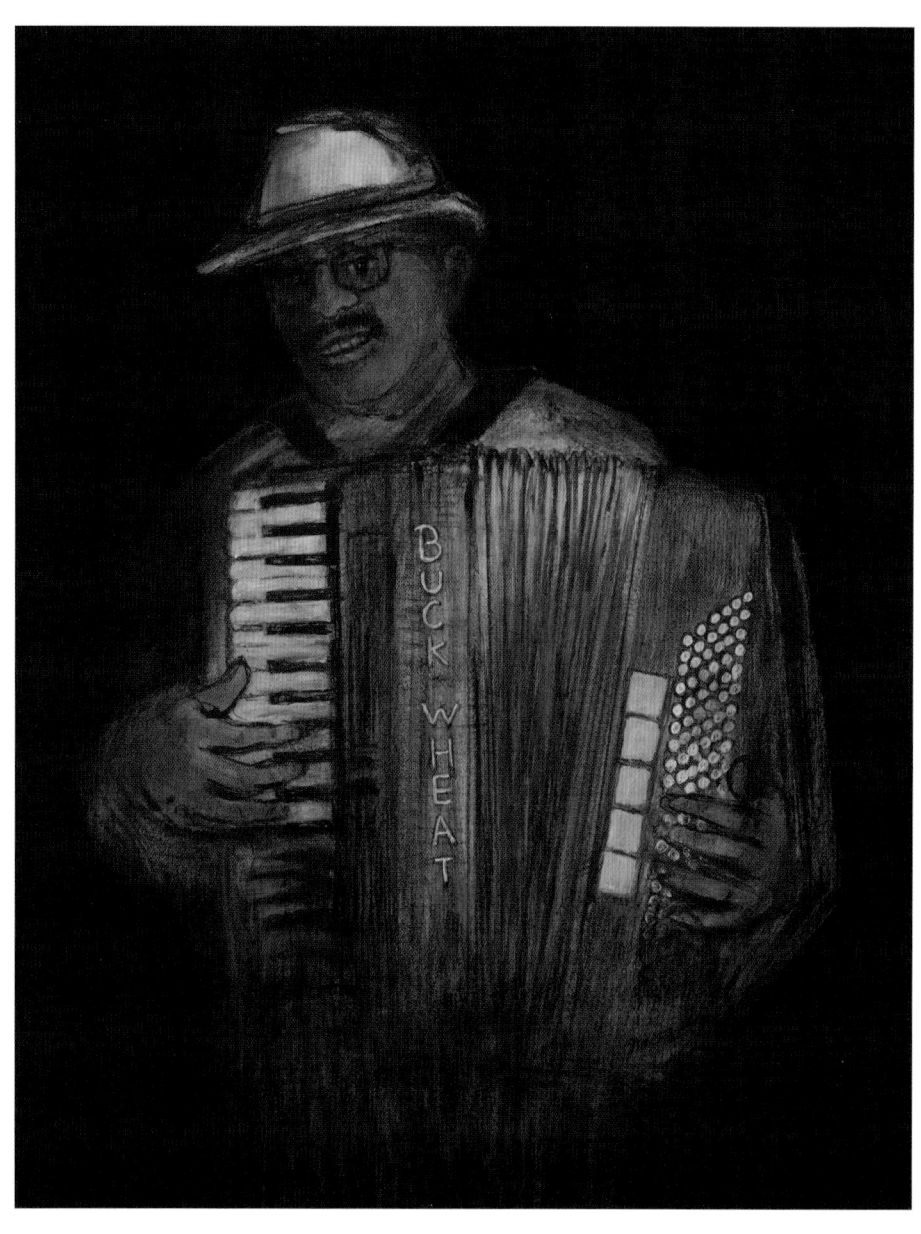

PLATE 4. *Buckwheat Zydeco*, 1994. Watercolor and tempera on paper, 20″ × 16″.
Collection of the artist.

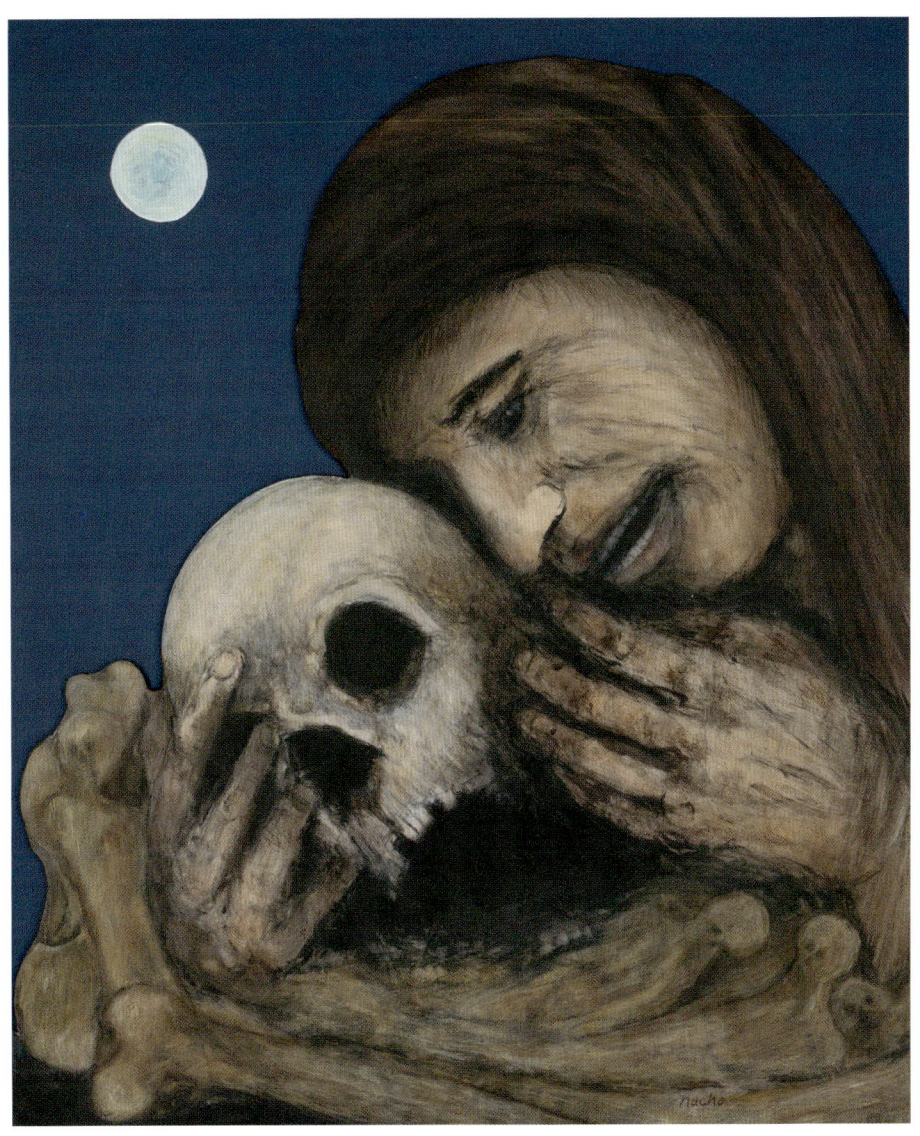

PLATE 5. *La Madre*, 1994. Water-based paints on illustration board fixed on wood
panel, cutout, 26″ × 22″. Collection of the artist.

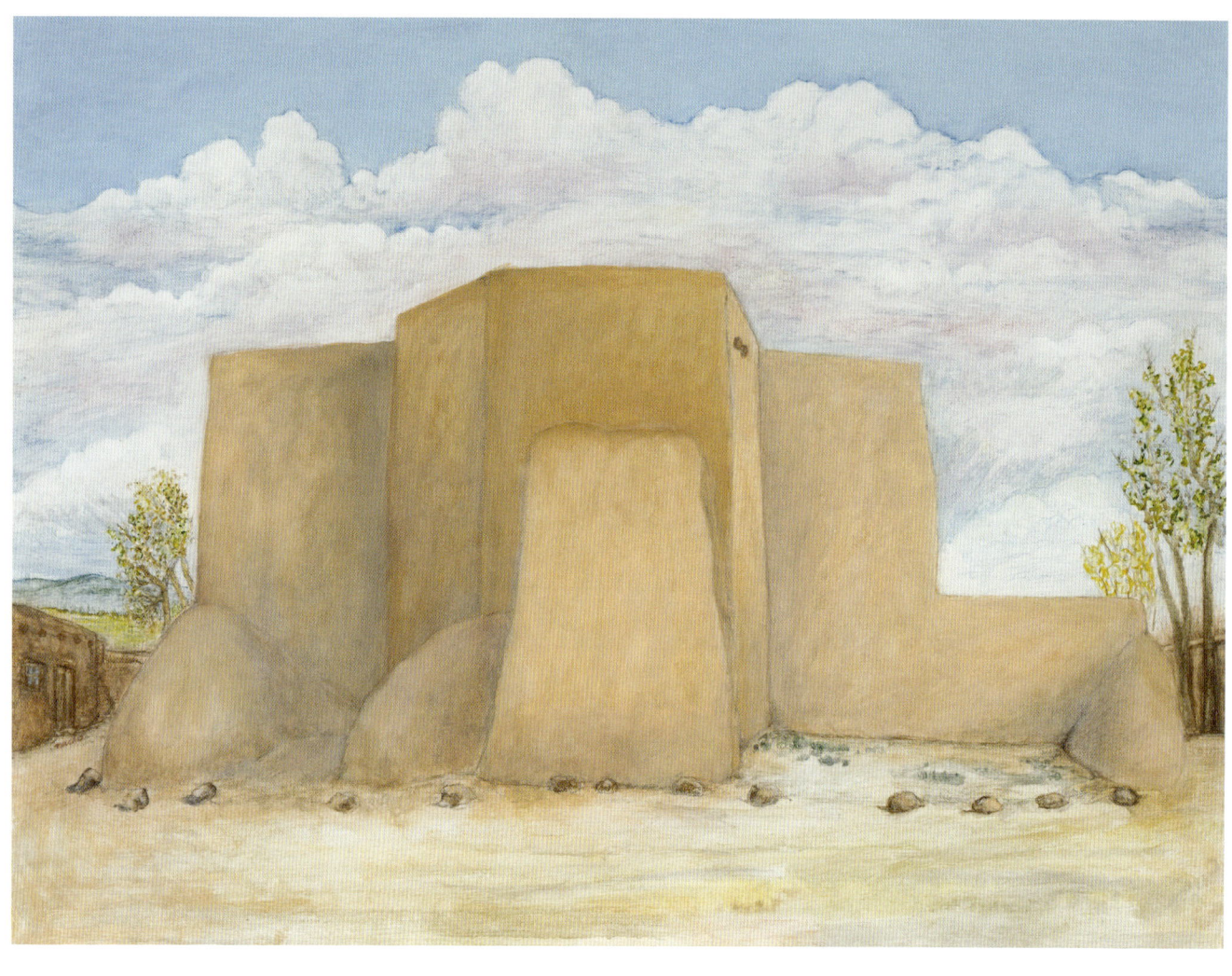

PLATE 6. *San Francisco de Asis*, 2002. Water-based paints on gessoed wood panel, 24″ × 36″. Collection of the artist.

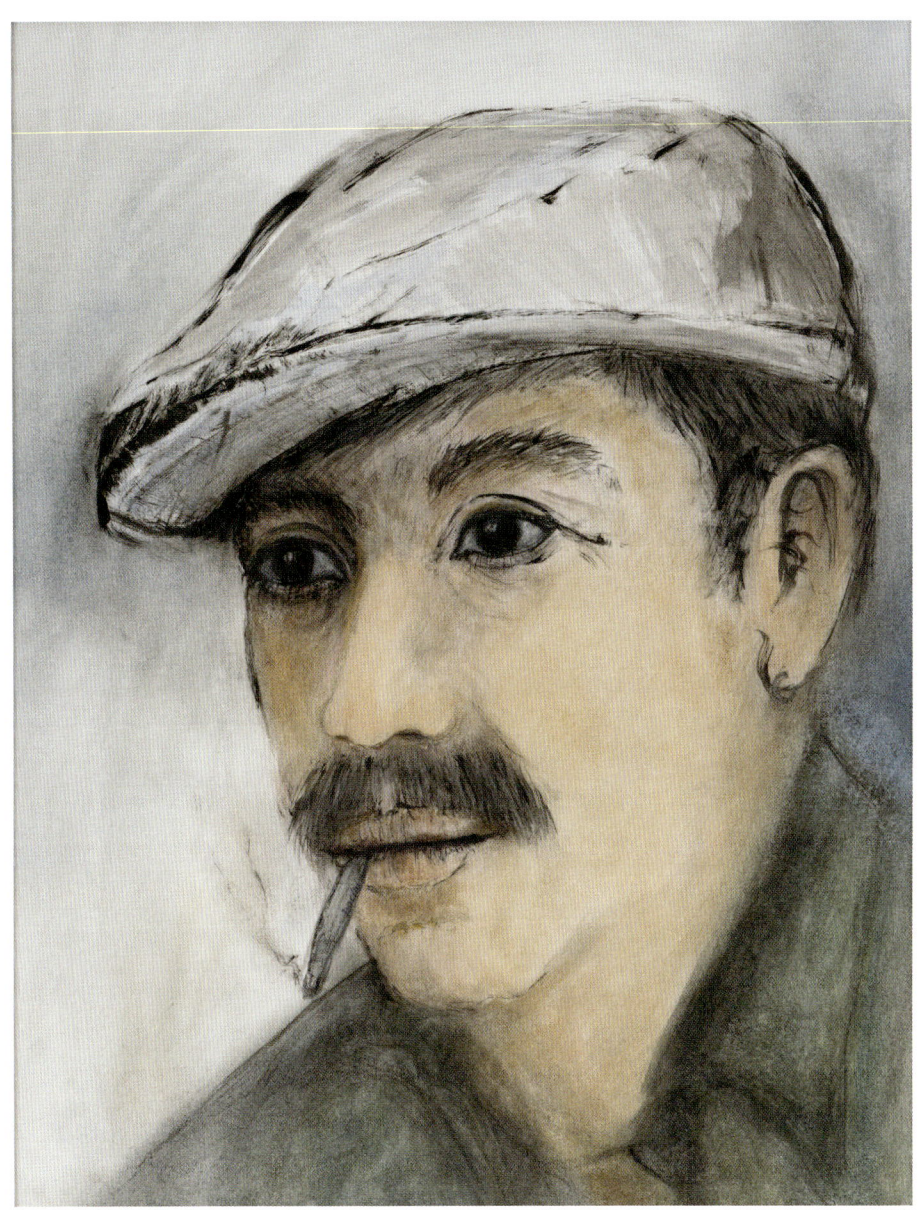

PLATE 7. *Self Portrait*, 2002. Water-based paints on illustration board, 28″ × 22″.
Collection of the artist.

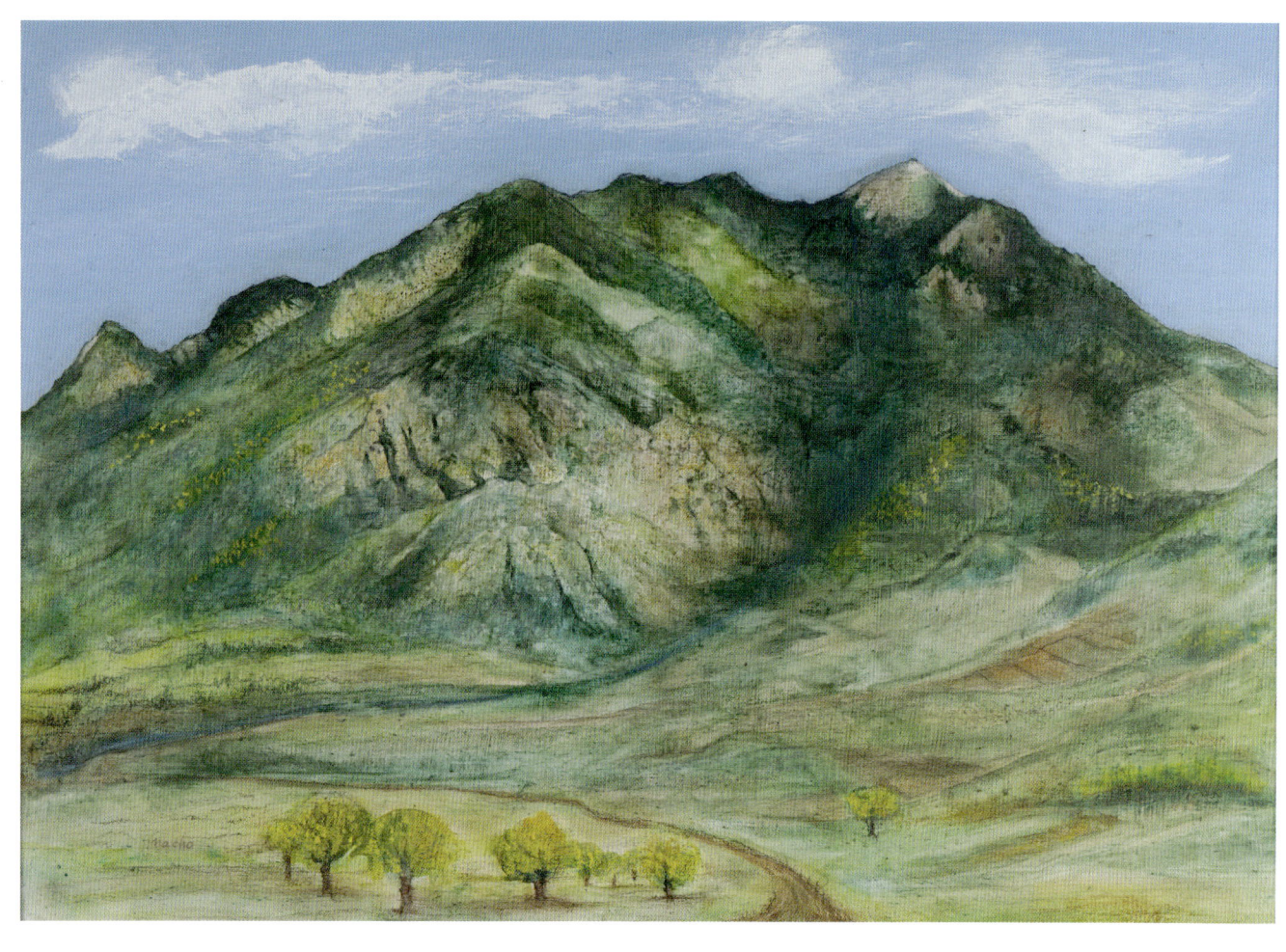

PLATE 8. *Taos Mountain*, 2002. Water-based paints on illustration board, 18″ × 24″.
Collection of the artist.

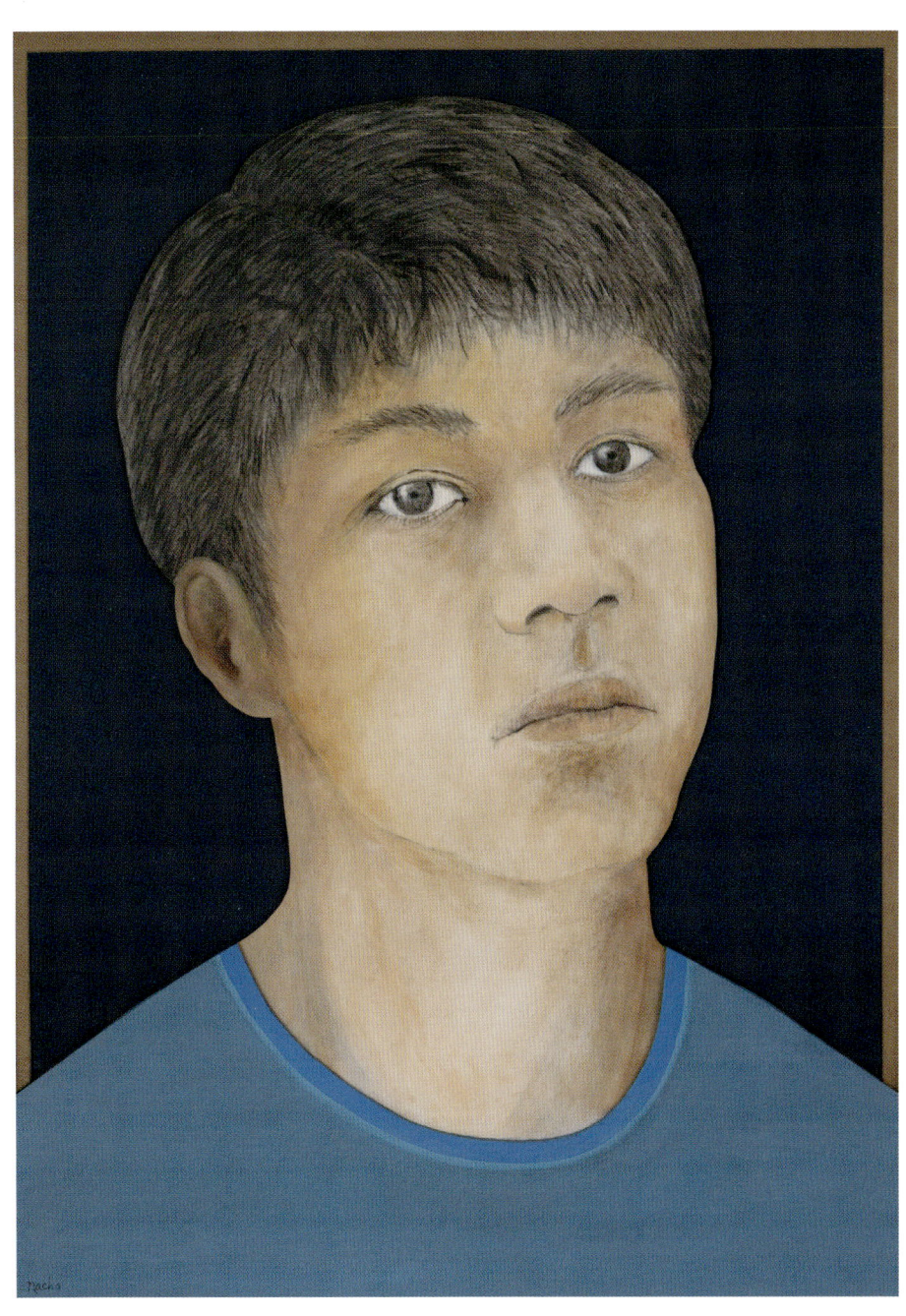

PLATE 9. *Sam*, 2003. Water-based paints on illustration board fixed on wood panel, cutout, 36″ × 24″. Collection of the artist.

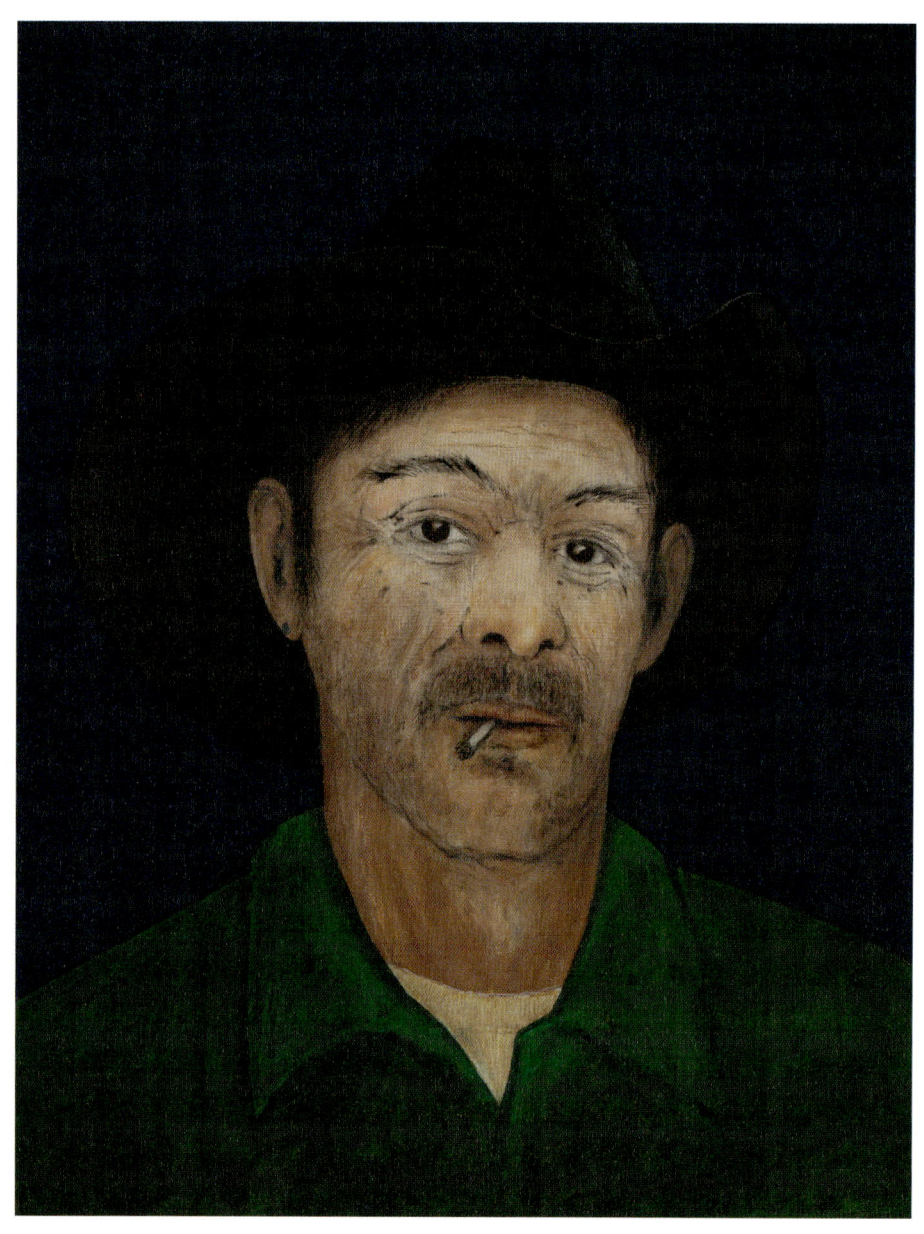

PLATE 10. *Vaquero,* 2007. Water-based paints on gessoed wood panel, cutout, 30″ × 24″. Collection of the artist.

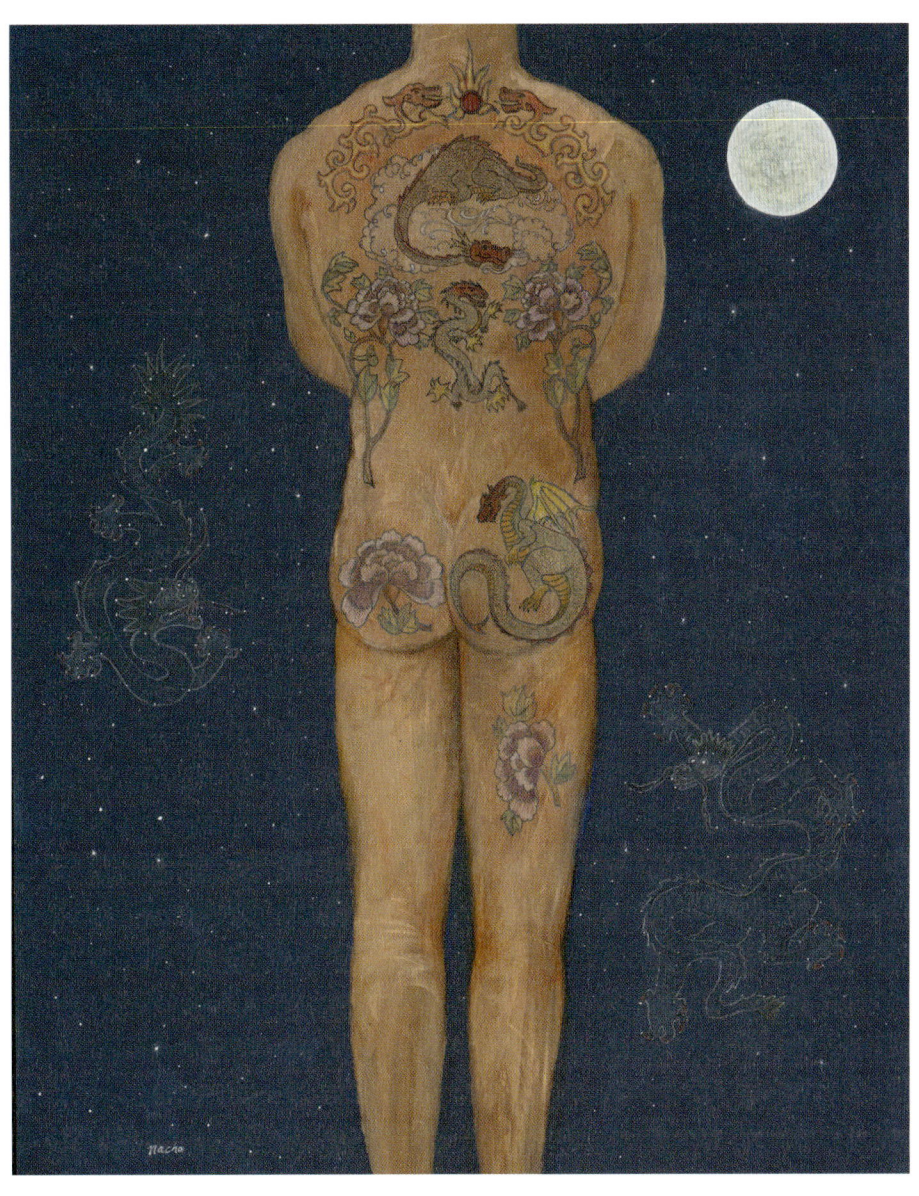

PLATE 11. *Piel de China*, 2010. Water-based paints on gessoed wood panel, 30″ × 24″.
Collection of the artist.

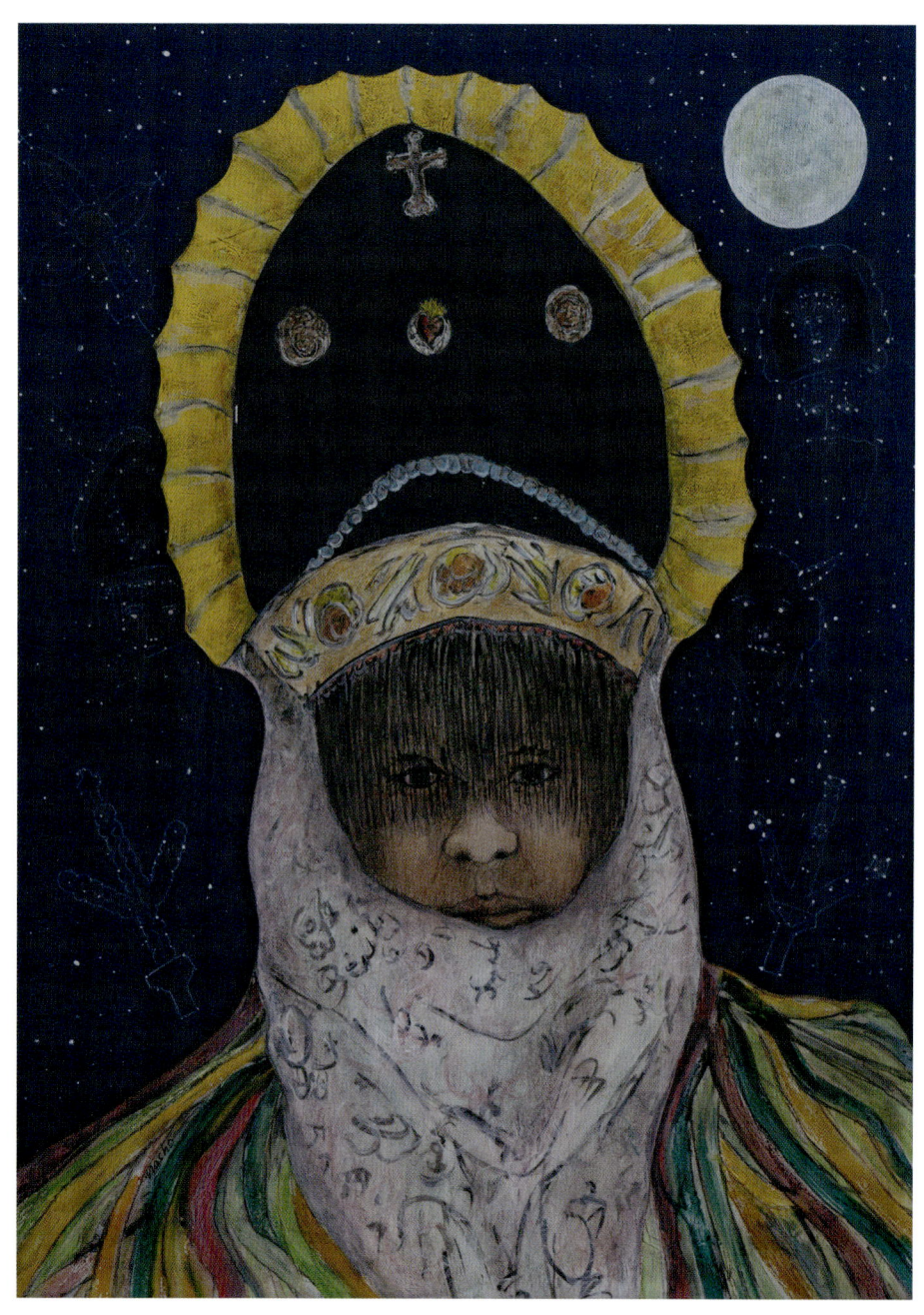

PLATE 12. *El matachín joven*, 2013. Water-based paints of illustration board fixed on wood panel, cutout, 24″ × 18″. Collection of the artist.

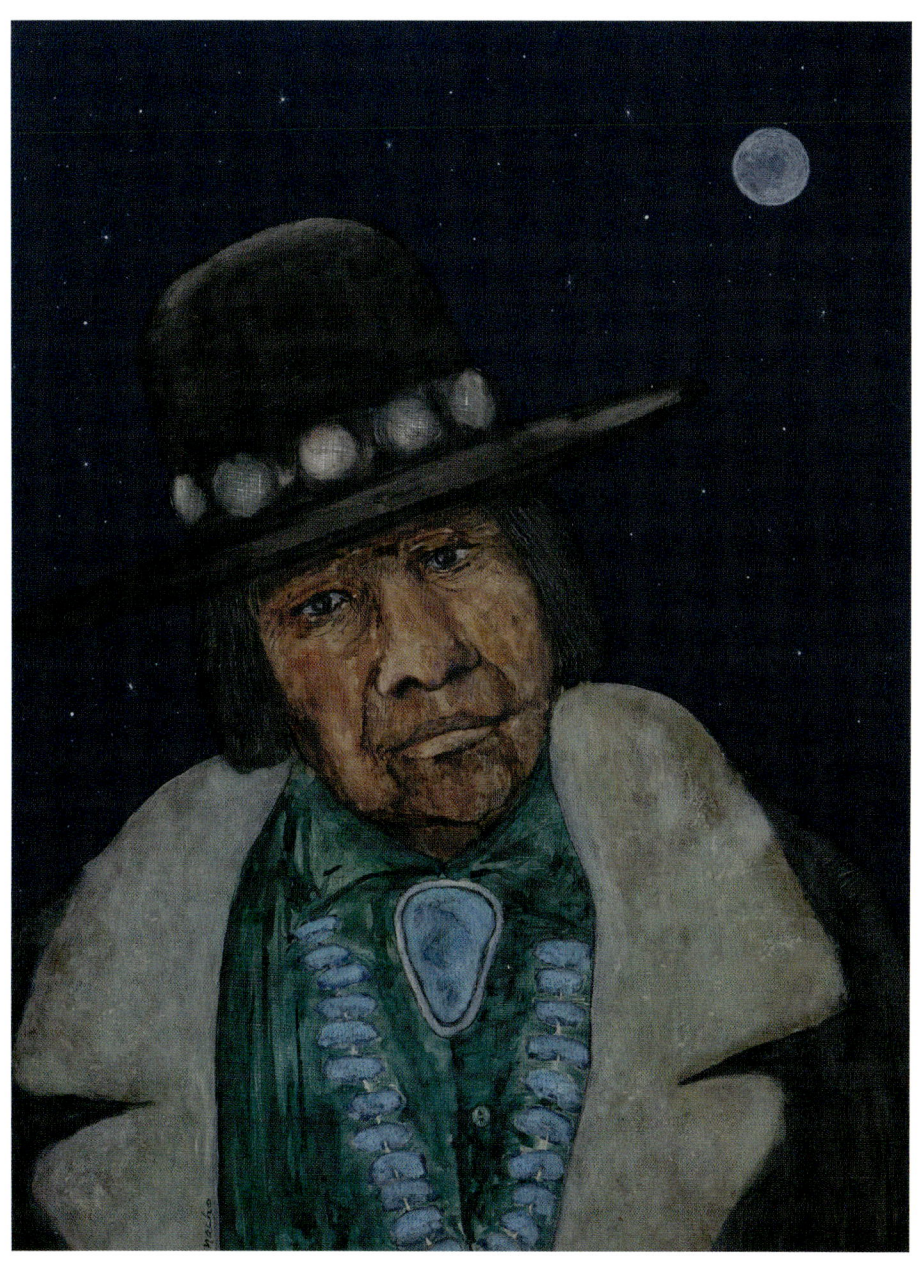

PLATE 13. *Elder*, 2016. Water-based paints on illustration board fixed on wood panel, cutout, 21″ × 16″. Collection of the artist.

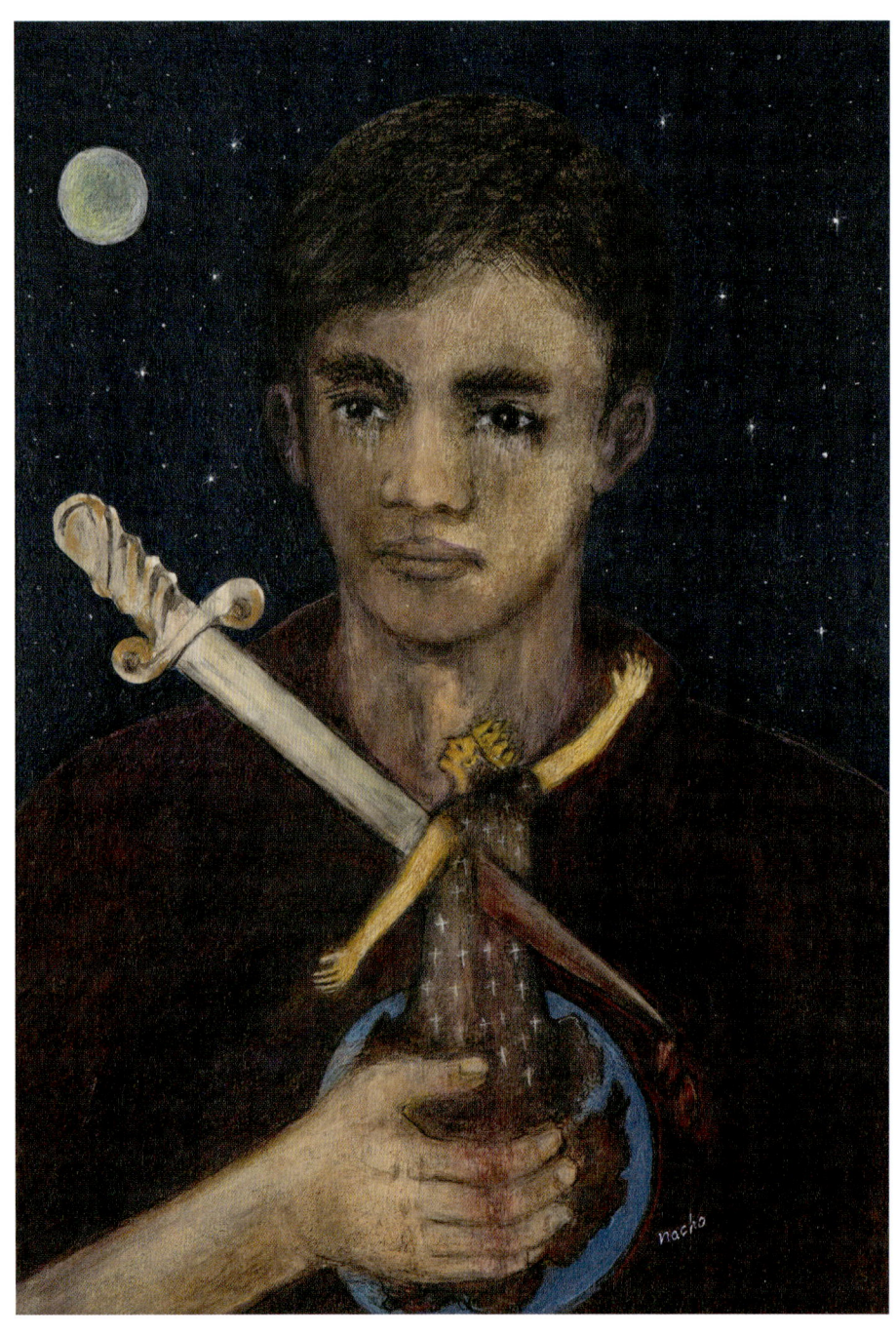

PLATE 14. *The Attempted Assassination de La Santa Madre/Mother Earth*, 2017.
Water-based paints on illustration board, 20″ × 14″. Collection of the artist.

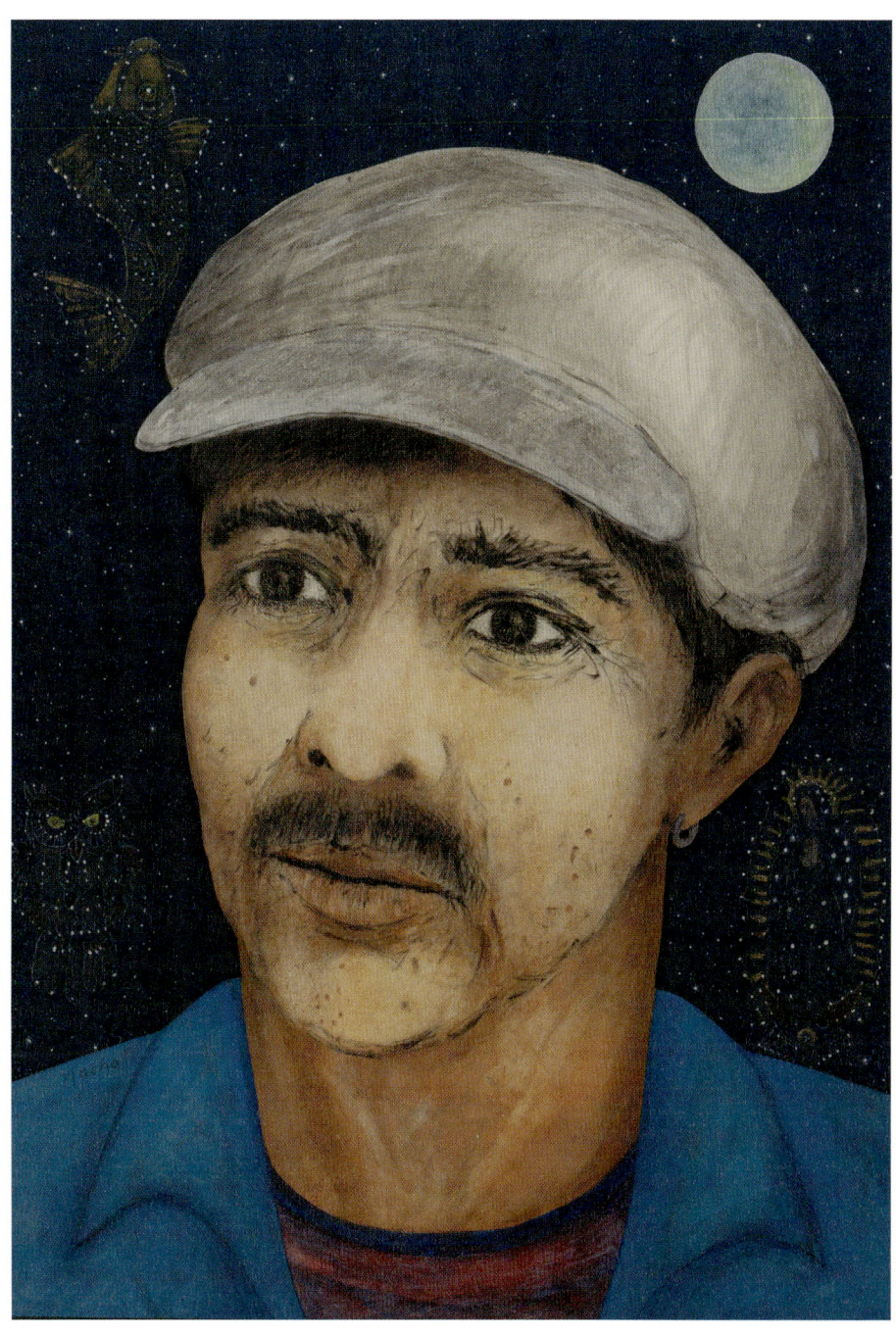

PLATE 15. *Hijo de la luna*, 2018. Water-based paints on illustration board fixed on
wood panel, cutout, 28″ × 20″. Collection of the artist.

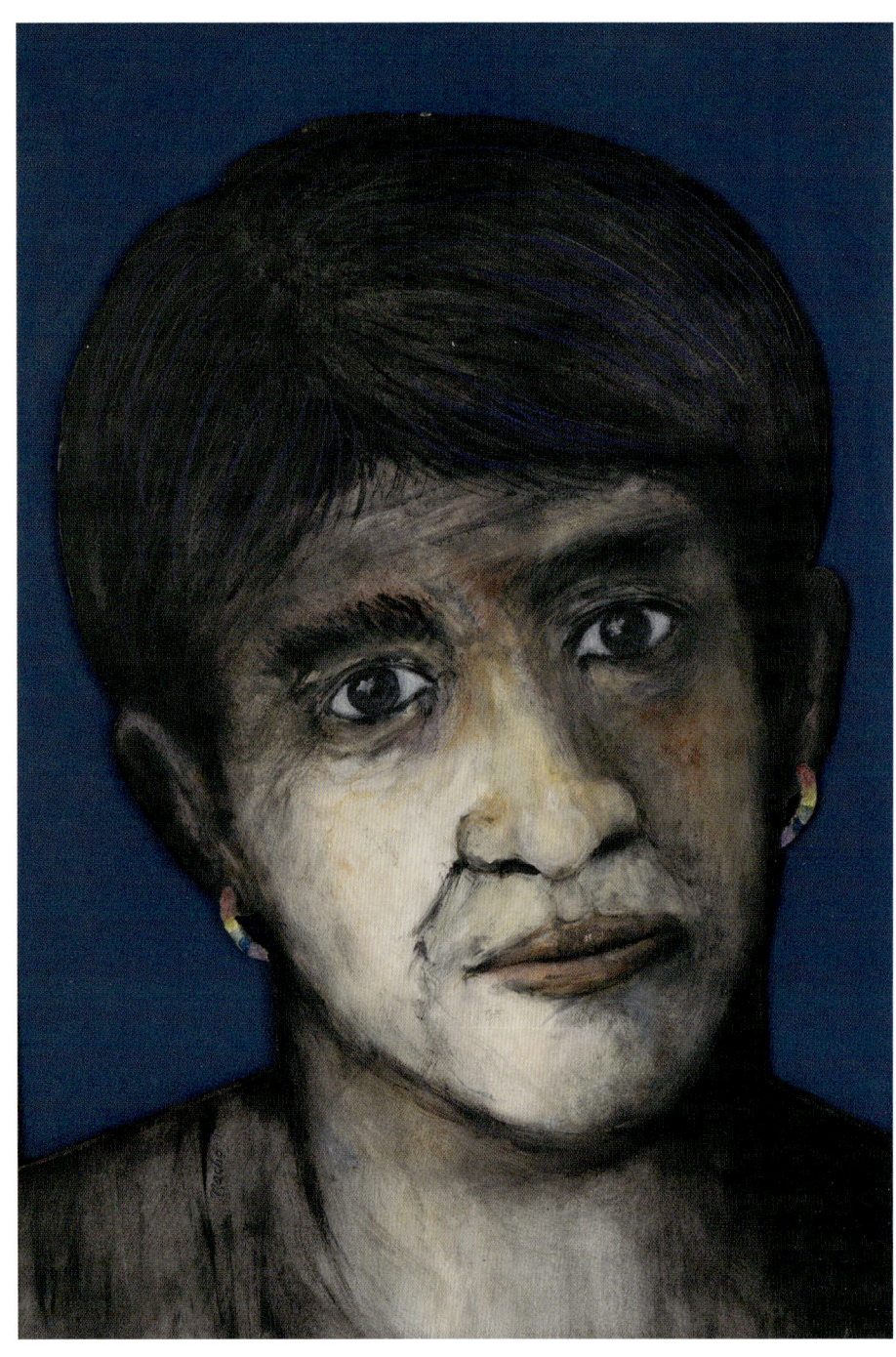

PLATE 16. *Anna*, 2021. Water-based paints on illustration board fixed on wood panel, cutout, 24″ × 18″. Collection of the artist.

PLATE 17. (*opposite*) *Through the Looking Glass*, 2022. Water-based paints on illustration board fixed on wood panel, cutout, 30″ × 18″. Collection of the artist.

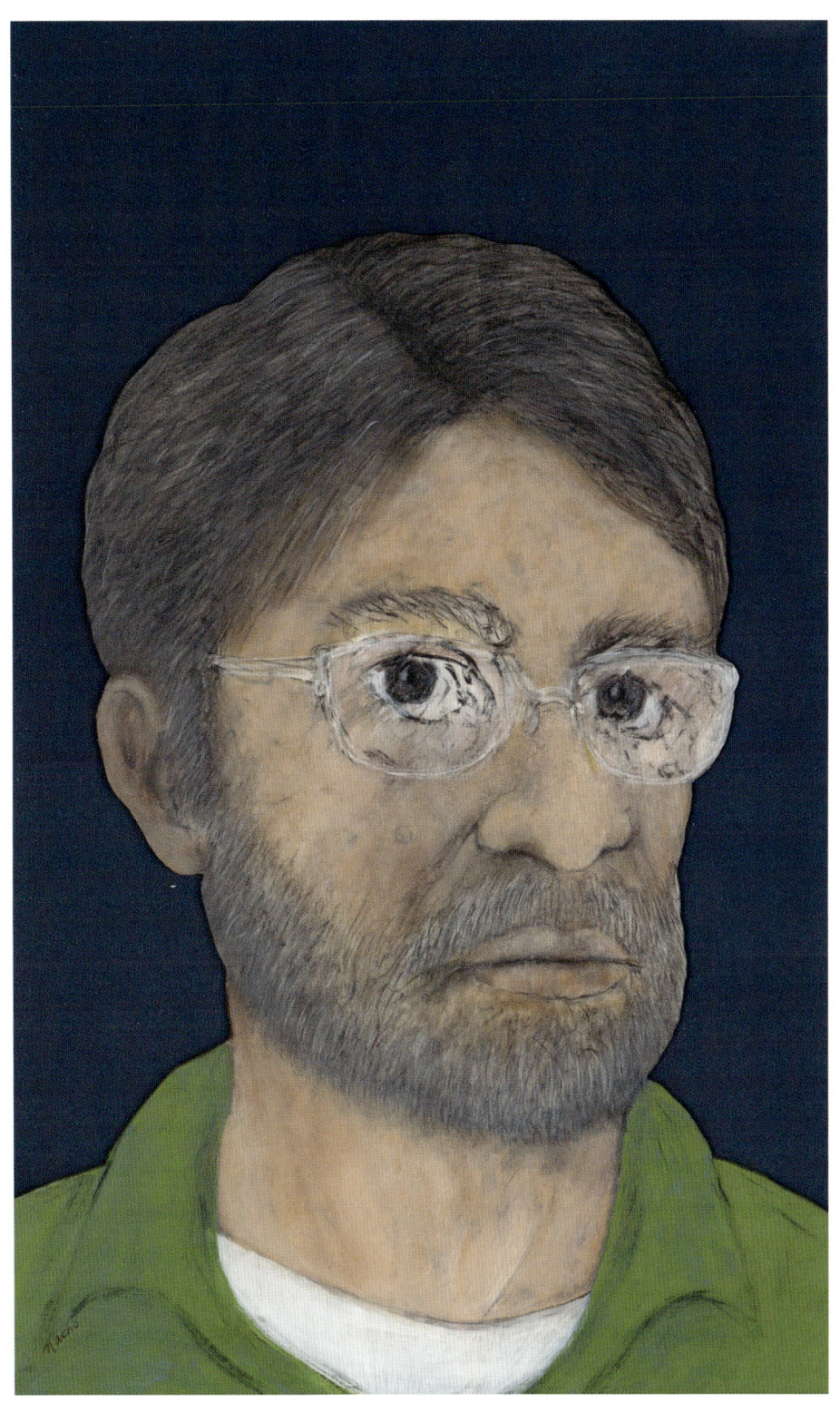

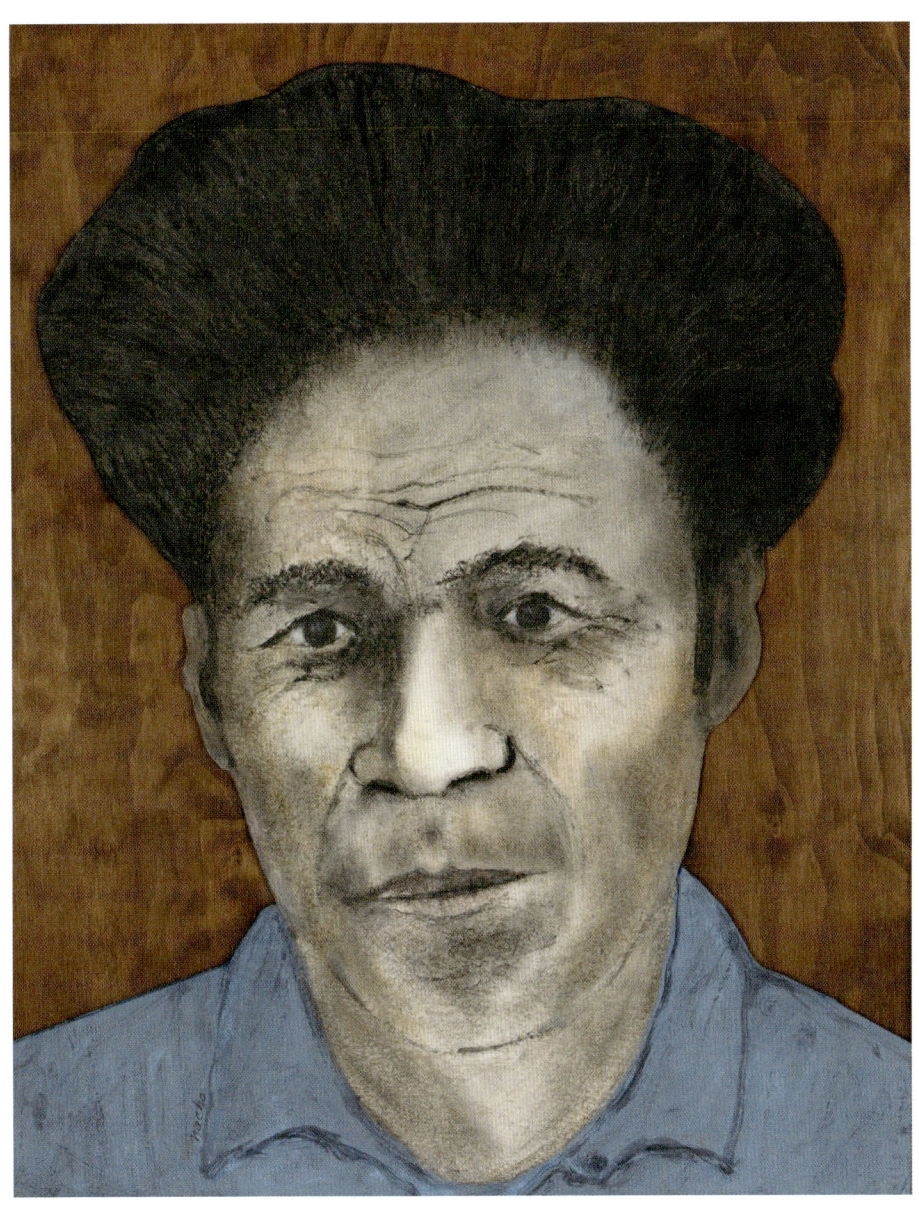

PLATE 18. *Patrocinio Barela, Carver*, 2024. Water-based paints on illustration board
fixed on wood panel, cutout, 32″ × 24″. Collection of the artist.

JUANITA J. LAVADIE
(Born 1949, Eugene, OR;
current residence, Taos, NM)

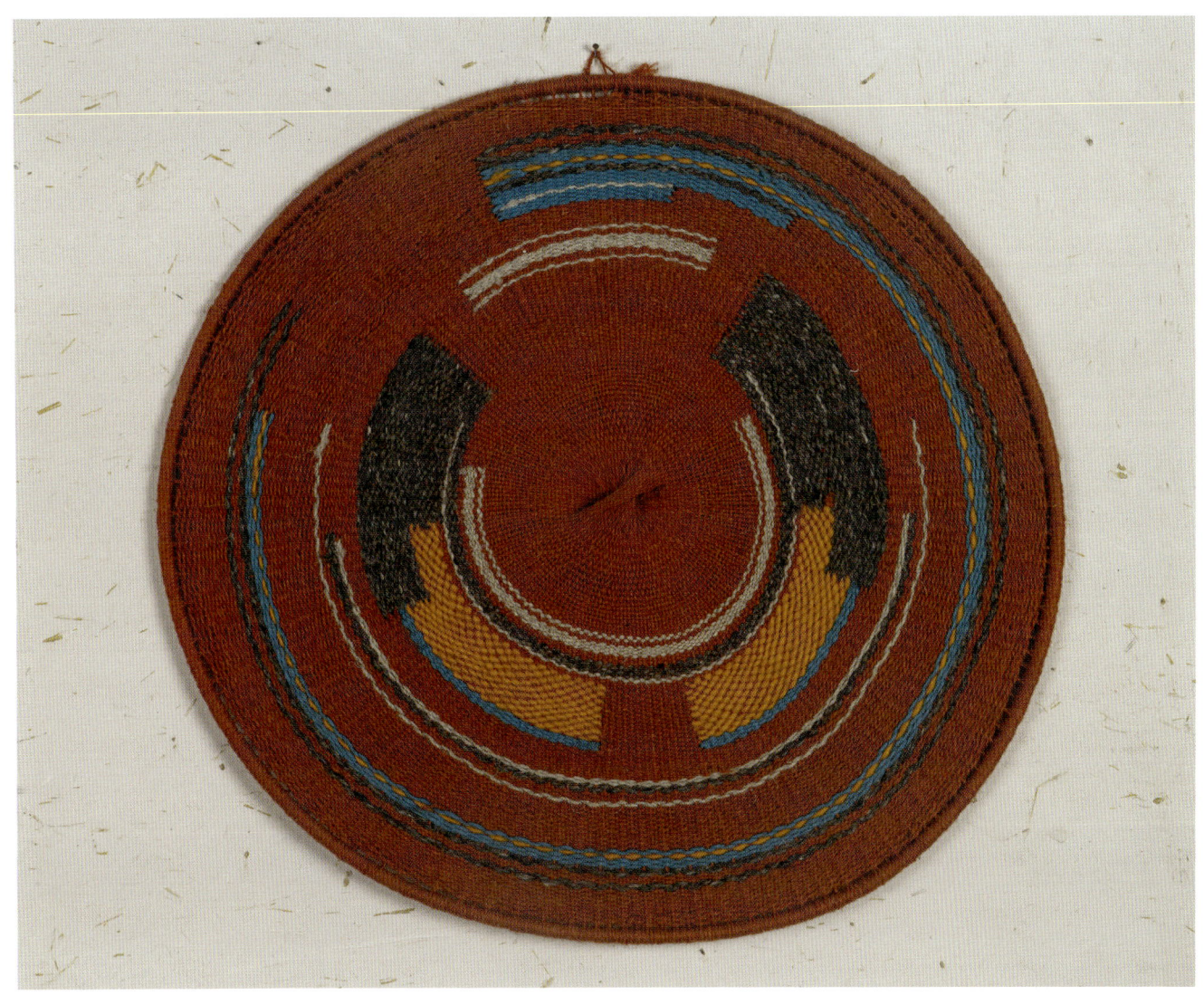

PLATE 19. *Round Tapestry*, 1974. Russet wool, 19″. Collection of the artist.

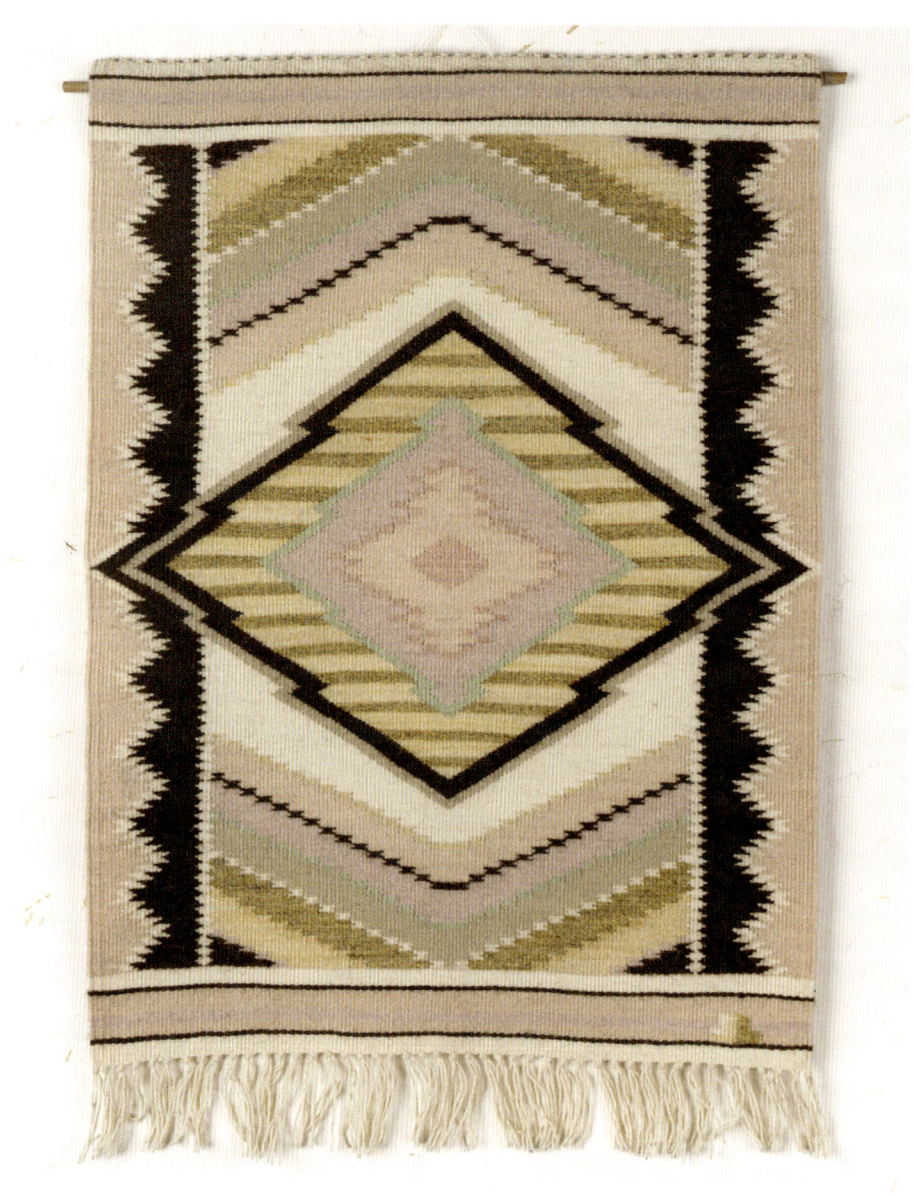

PLATE 20. *Amethyst Tiger Weaving*, ca. 1978–1983. Handspun wool and alpaca with vegetal dyes, 18″ × 32″. Collection of the artist.

278   —   Plates

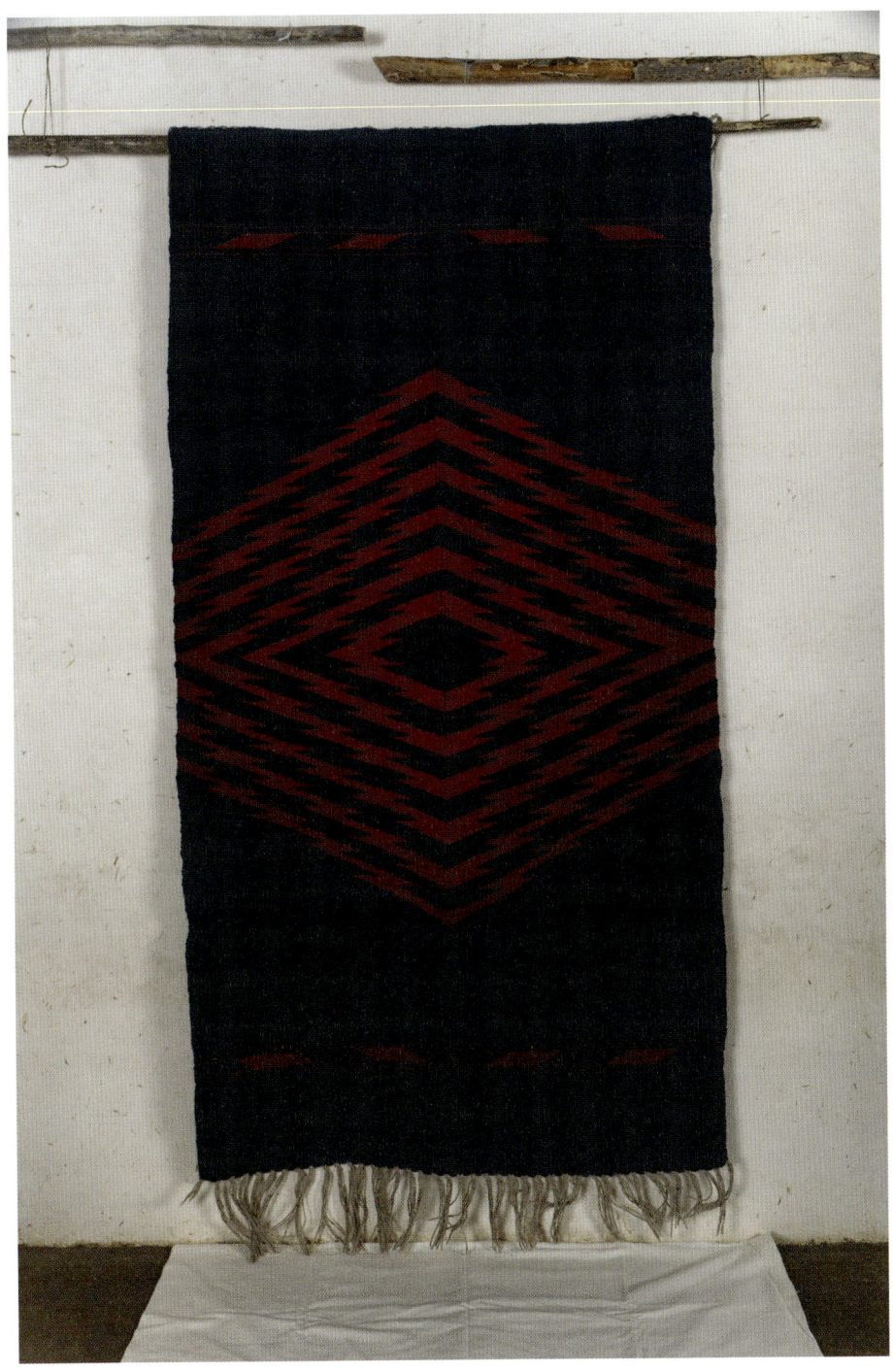

PLATE 21. *Red Saltillo Lightning Poncho/Camping Mat*, 1979. Commercial wool,
40″ × 76″. Collection of the artist.

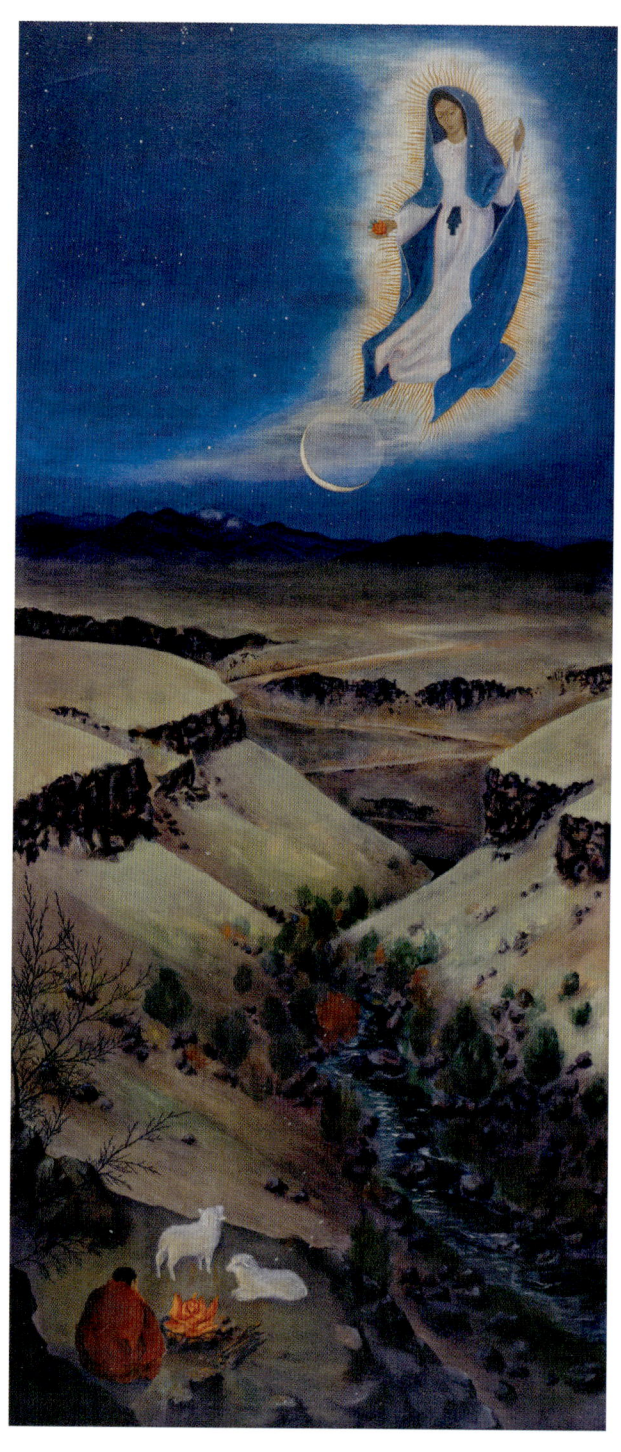

PLATE 22. *Nuestra Señora Guadalupe Norteña*, ca. 1980. Acrylic on canvas, 30″ × 80″.
Private collection of Robert "Corky" Frausto.

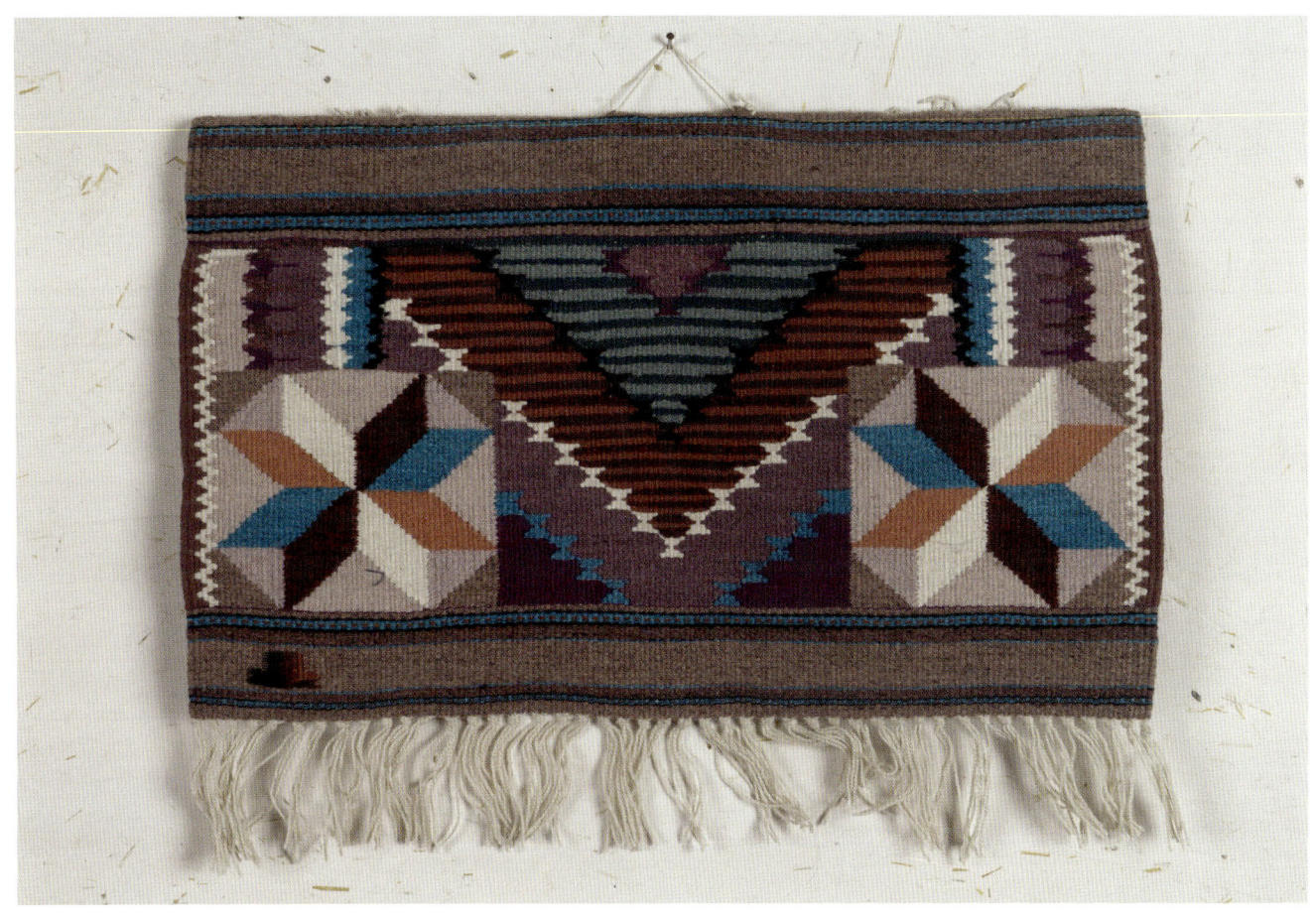

PLATE 23. *Vallero Tapestría Labrado* Sampler, 1983. Wool, 17″ × 12″. Collection of the artist.

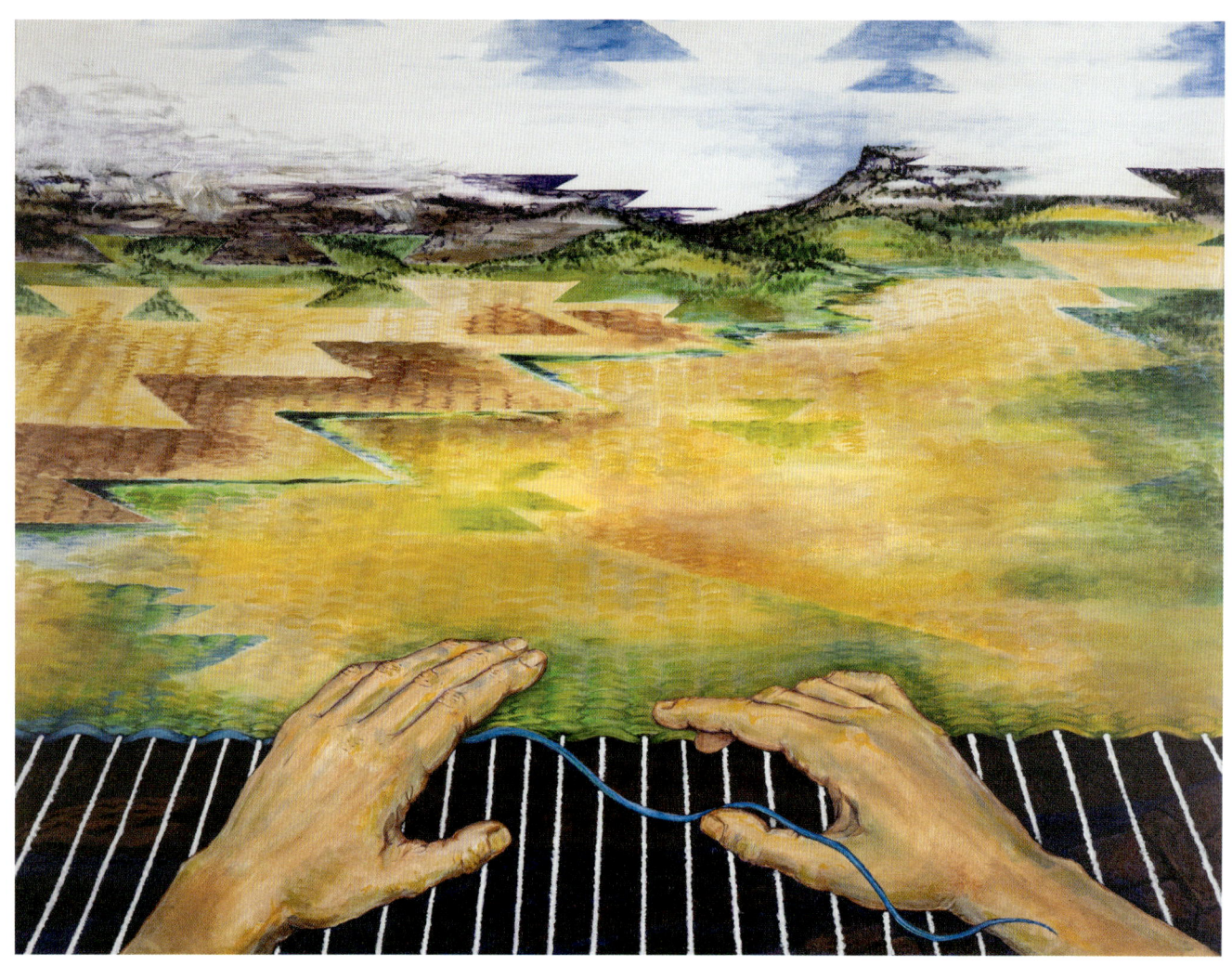

PLATE 24. *Tejiendo el Río Grande*, ca. 1990. Acrylic on canvas, 48″ × 36″. Collection of Taos Valley Acequia Association, Taos, New Mexico.

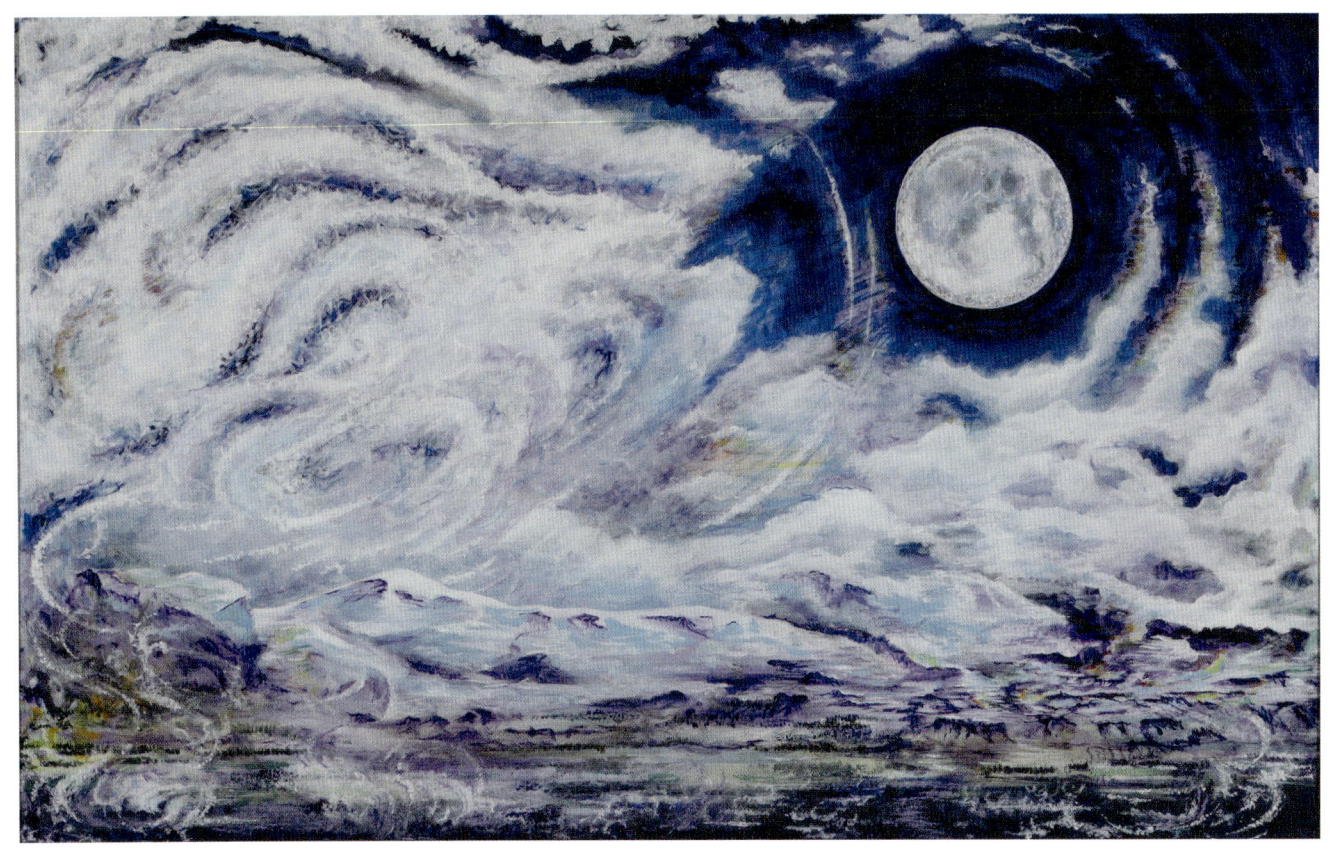

PLATE 25. *Full Moon at Perigee, Winter*, 1993. Acrylic on canvas, 48″ × 36″. Private
collection of Roberta Márquez.

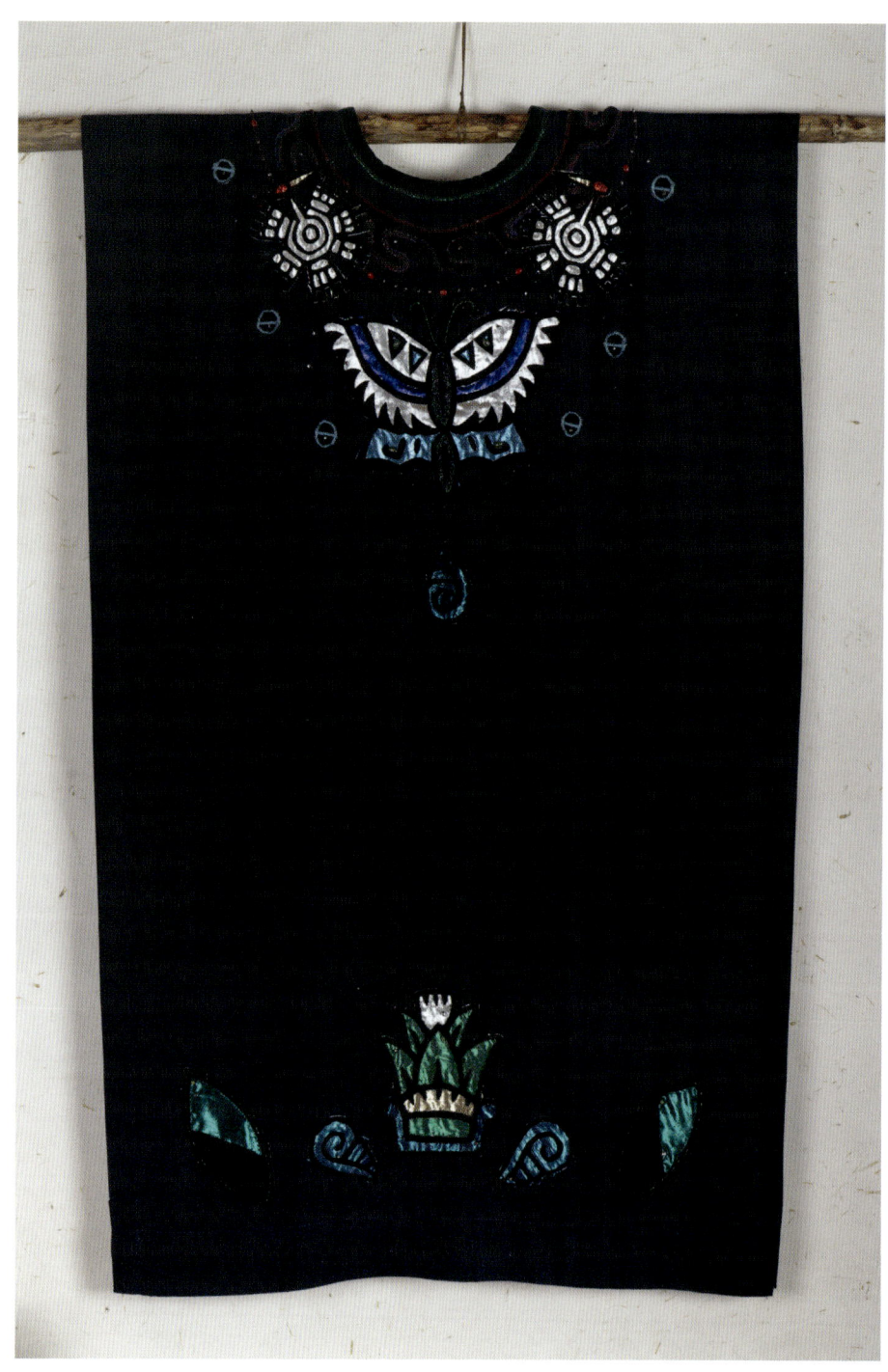

PLATE 26. *Huipil, Renacimiento,* ca. 1995–2015. Rayon, metallic tissue, coral, jade, and glass beads, 60″ × 36″. Collection of the artist.

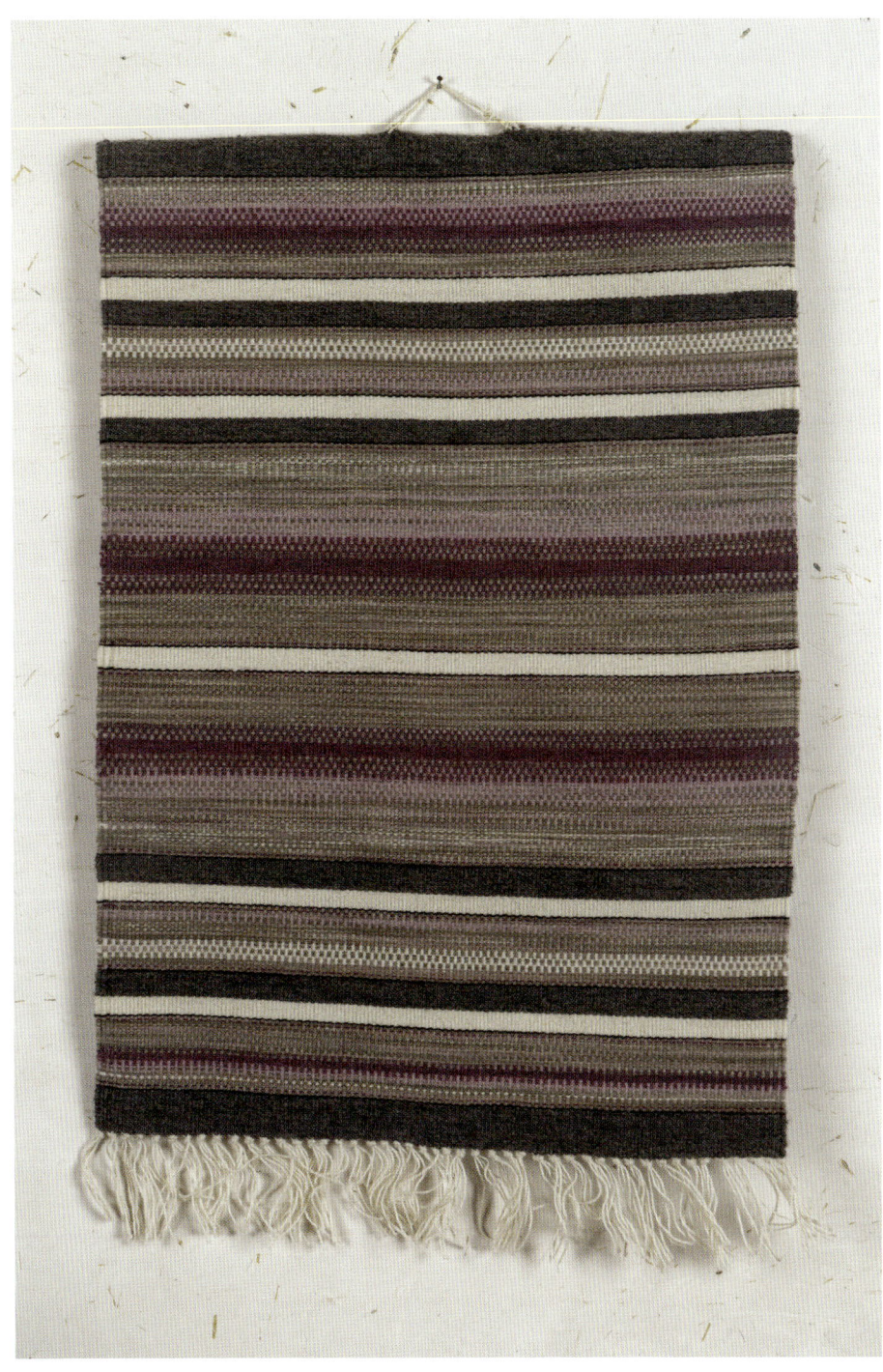

PLATE 27. *Colonias Style Bands and Stripes*, 2016. Gray and mauve vegetal dye, wool, 17" × 24". Collection of the artist.

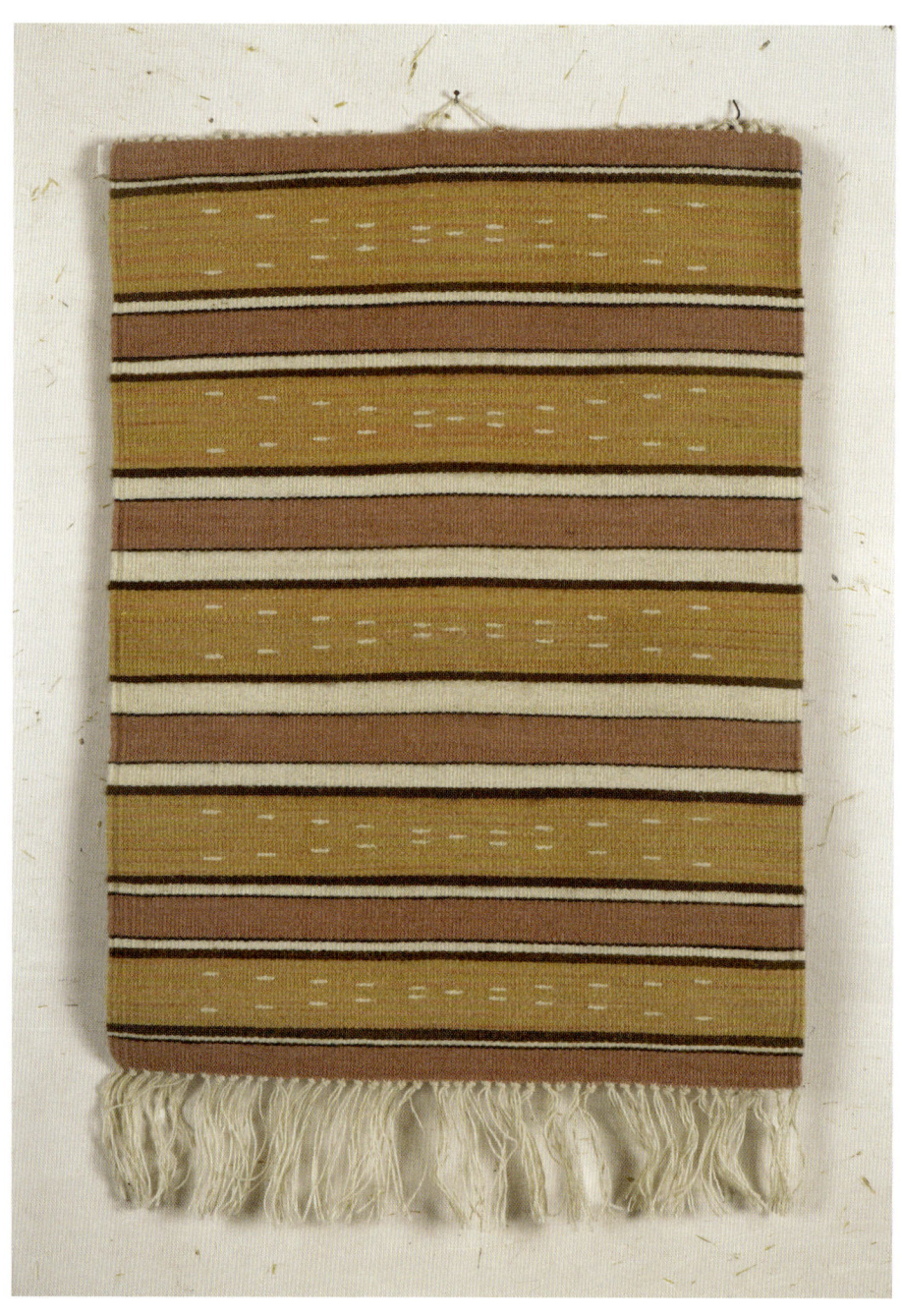

PLATE 28. *Colonias Style Bands and Stripes*, 2016. Rose and golden vegetal dye, wool, 17″ × 24″. Collection of the artist.

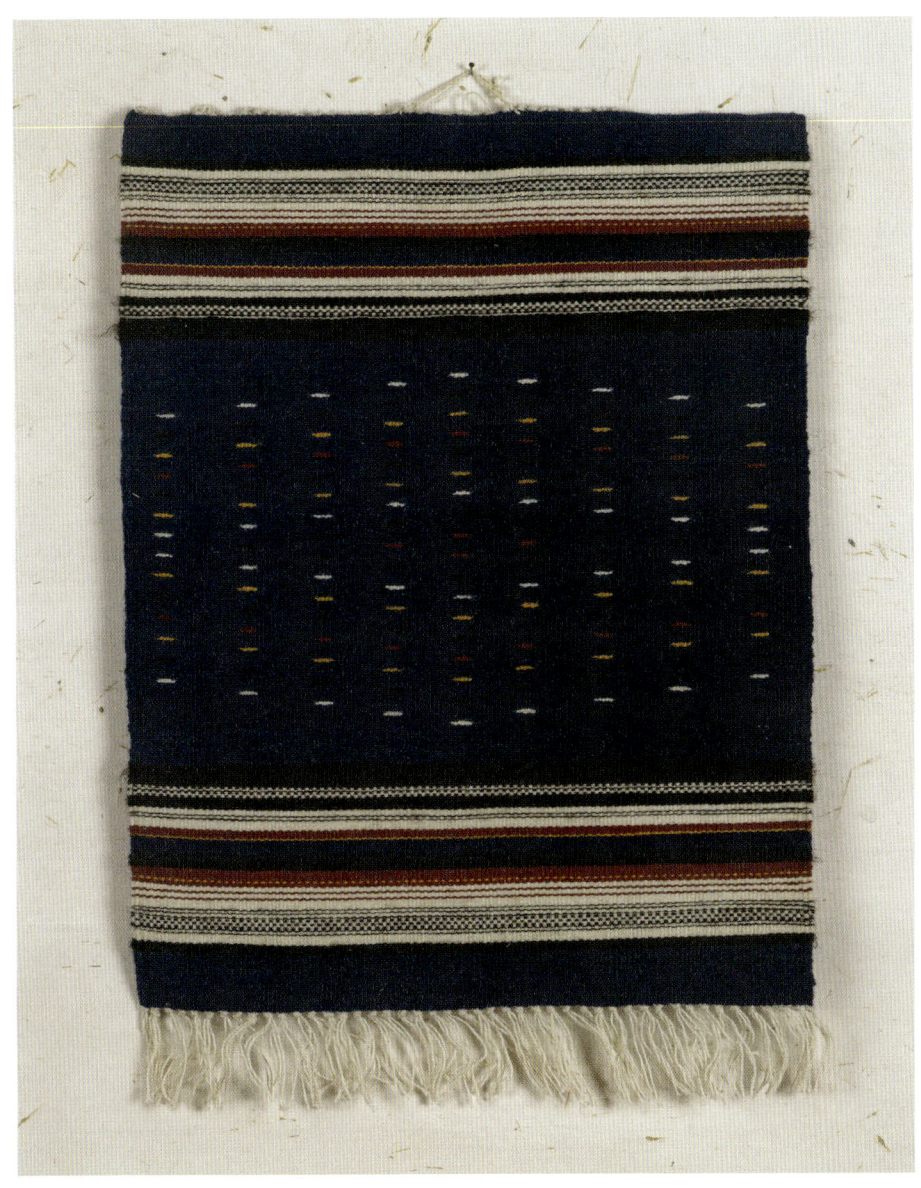

PLATE 29. *Colonias Style Bands and Stripes and Tapestry Dots*, 2016. Dark blue unplied
commercial wool, 17″ × 24″. Collection of the artist.

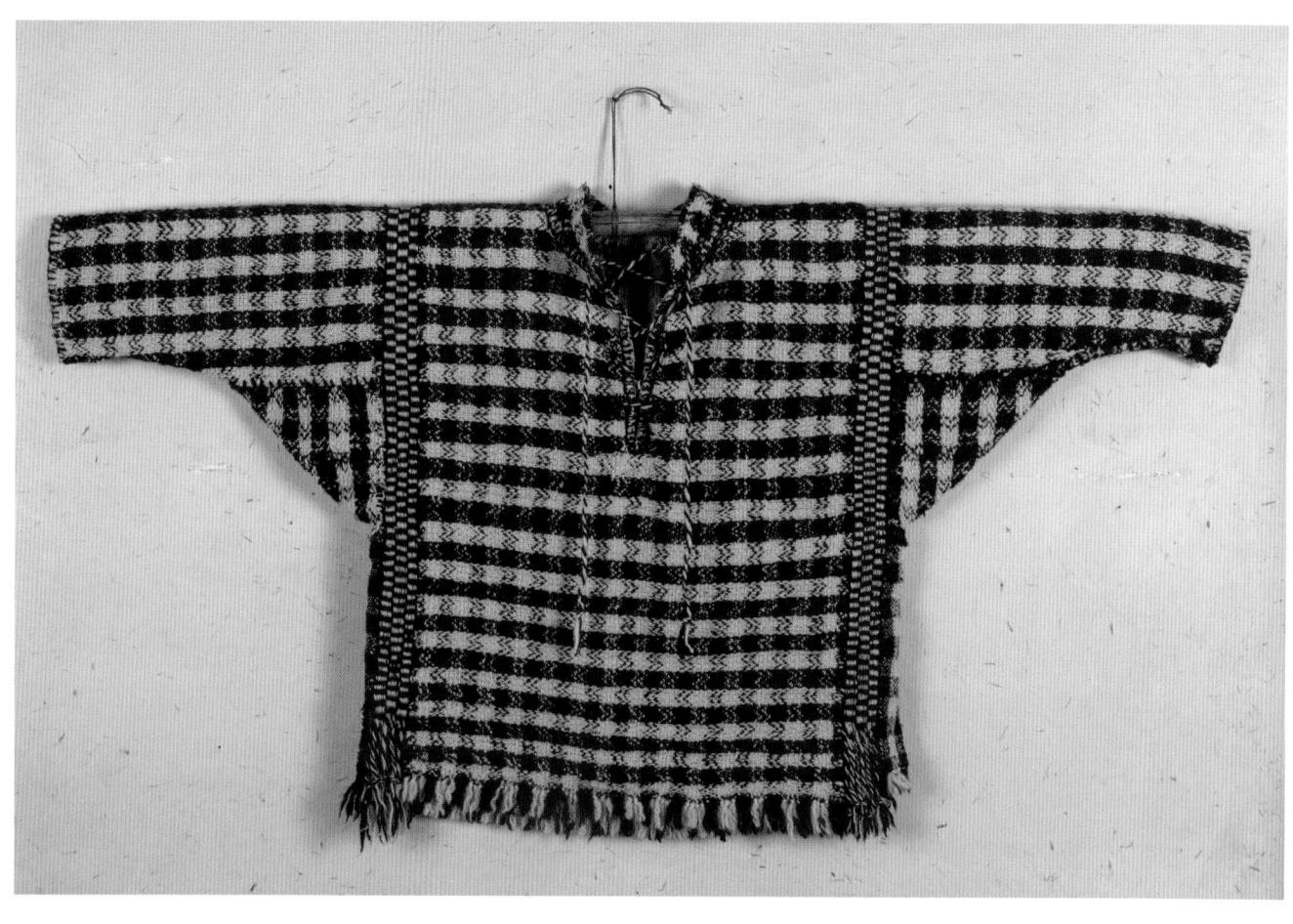

PLATE 30. *Cibolero Shirt, Jerga Cuadrada (Buffalo Plaid Work Shirt Prototype)*, 2016. Handspun and handwoven black and white raw wool, 70″. Collection of the artist.

288   ⌐   Plates

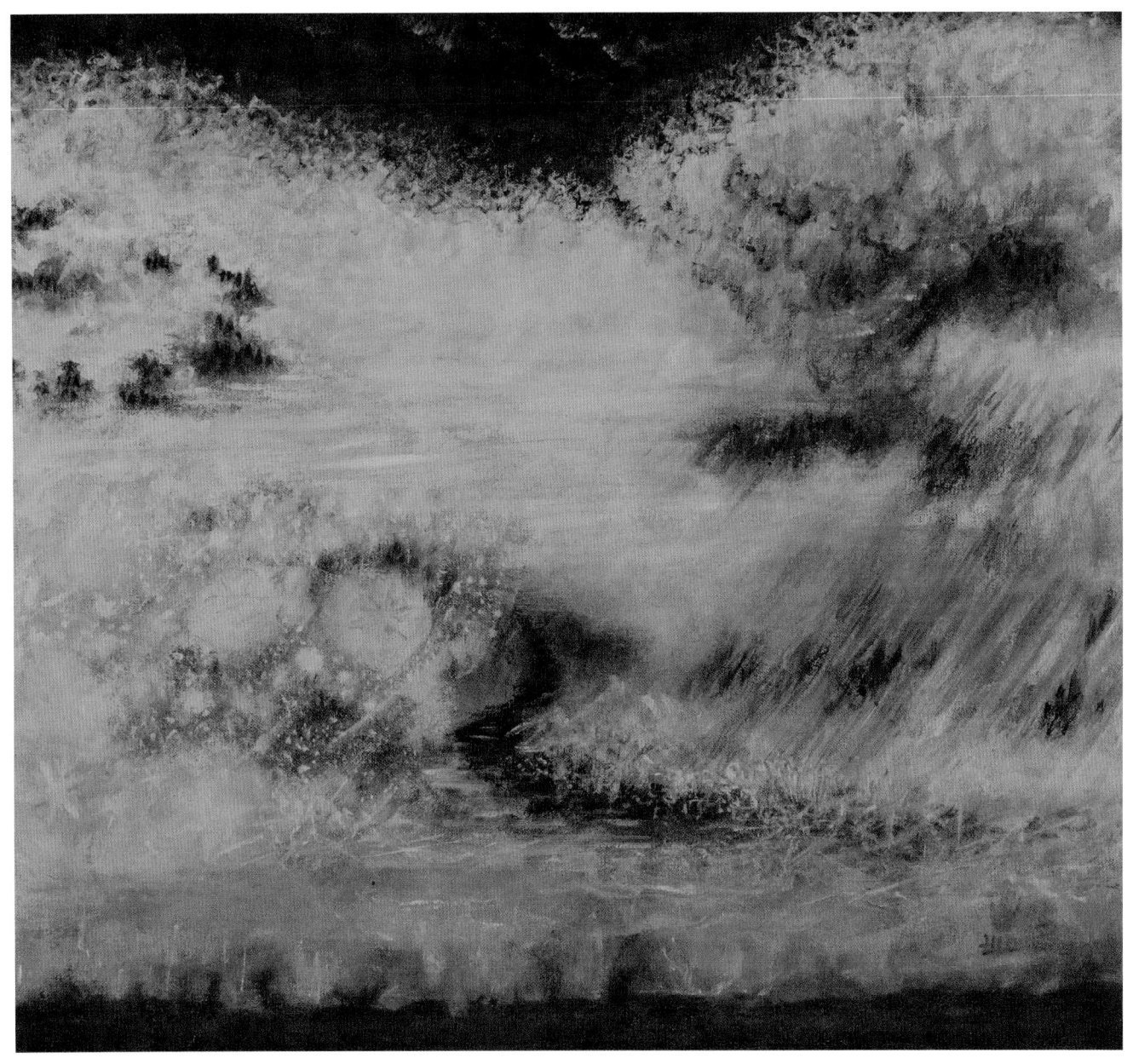

PLATE 31. *Agua: 4 Elementos*, 2017. Acrylic on canvas, 24″ × 18″. Collection of the artist.

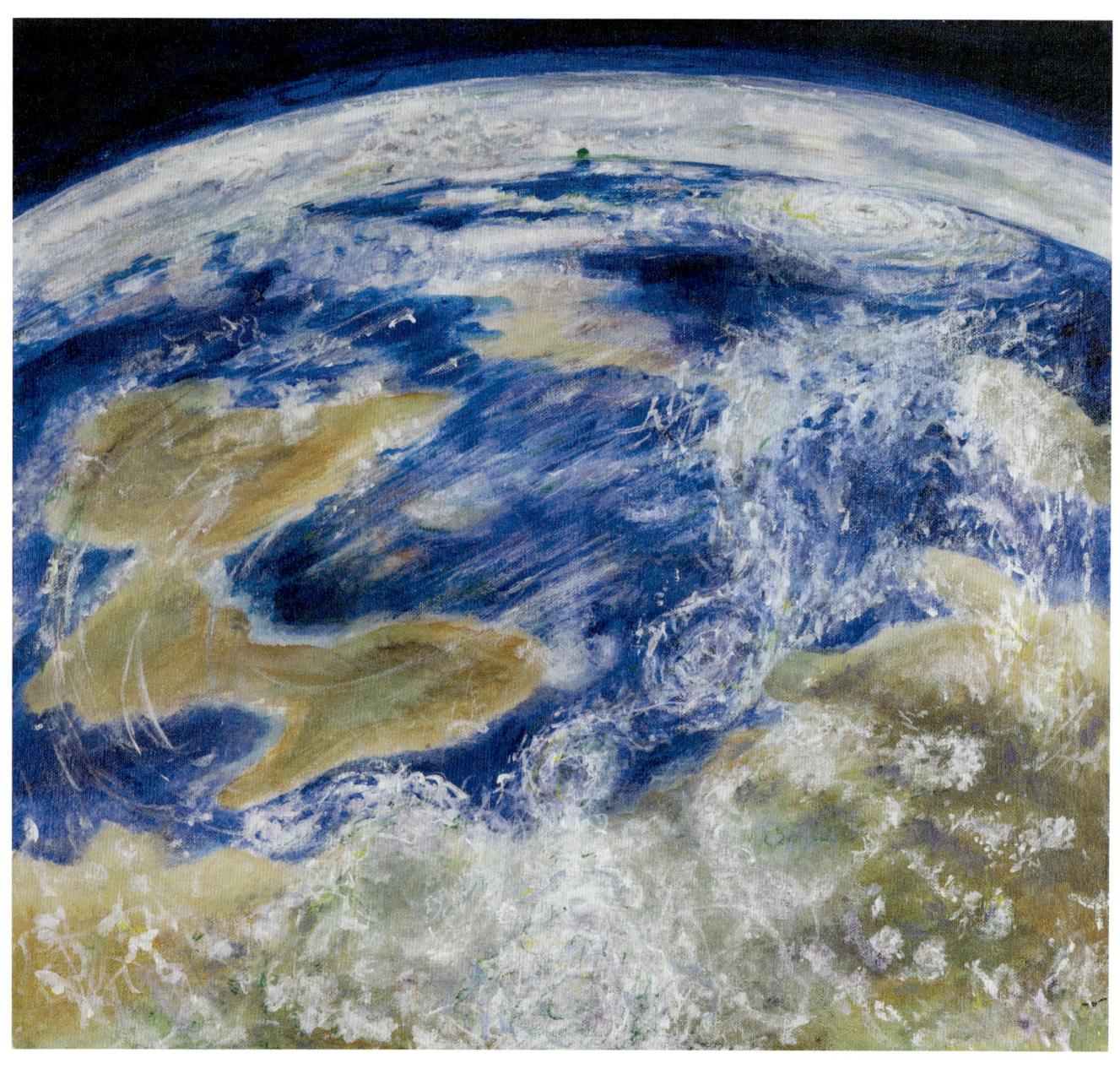

PLATE 32. *Aliento: 4 Elementos*, 2017. Acrylic on canvas, 24″ × 18″. Collection of the artist.

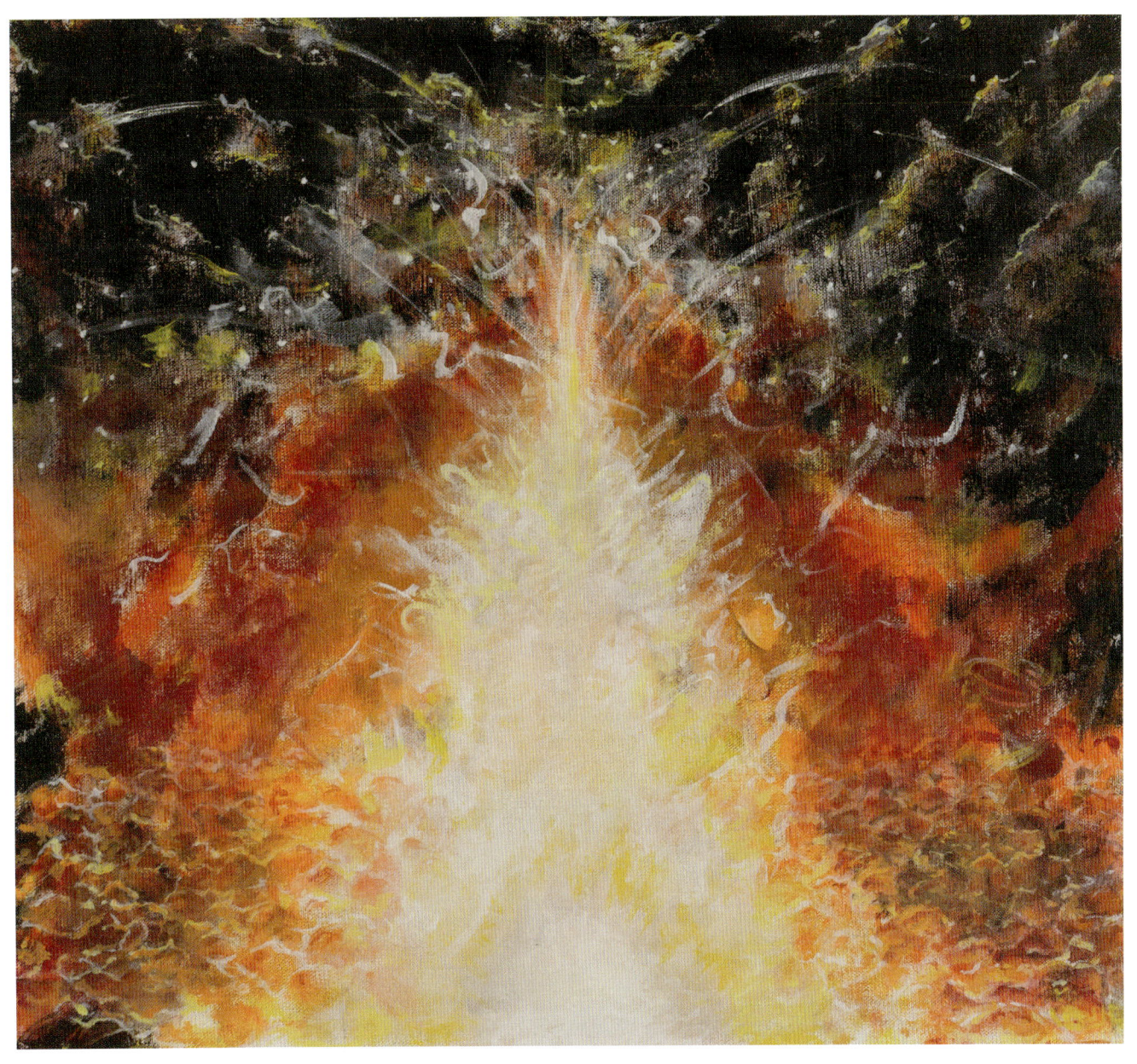

PLATE 33. *Fuego: 4 Elementos,* 2017. Acrylic on canvas, 24″ × 18″. Collection of the artist.

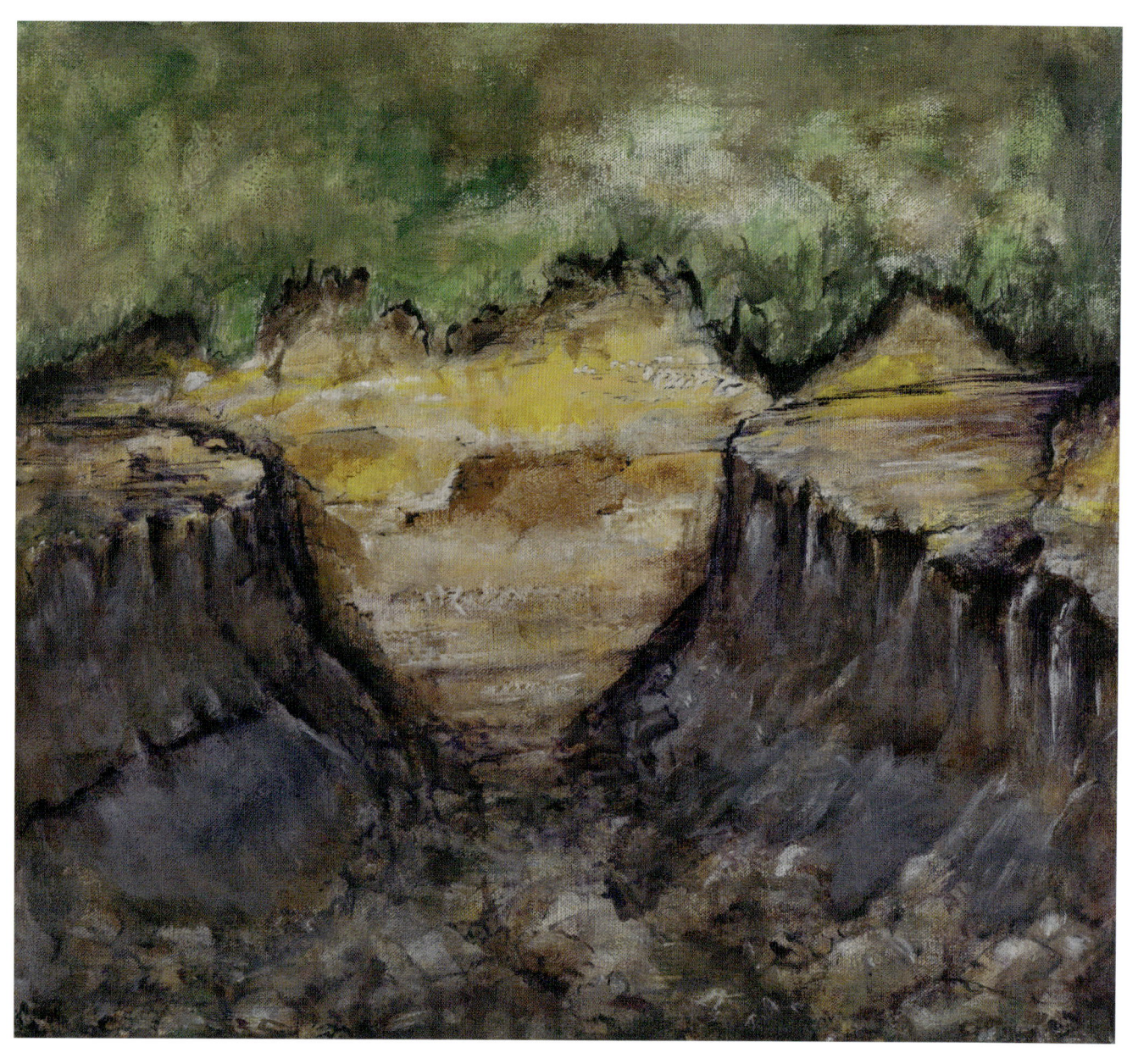

PLATE 34. *Tierra: 4 Elementos*, 2017. Acrylic on canvas, 24″ × 18″. Collection of the artist.

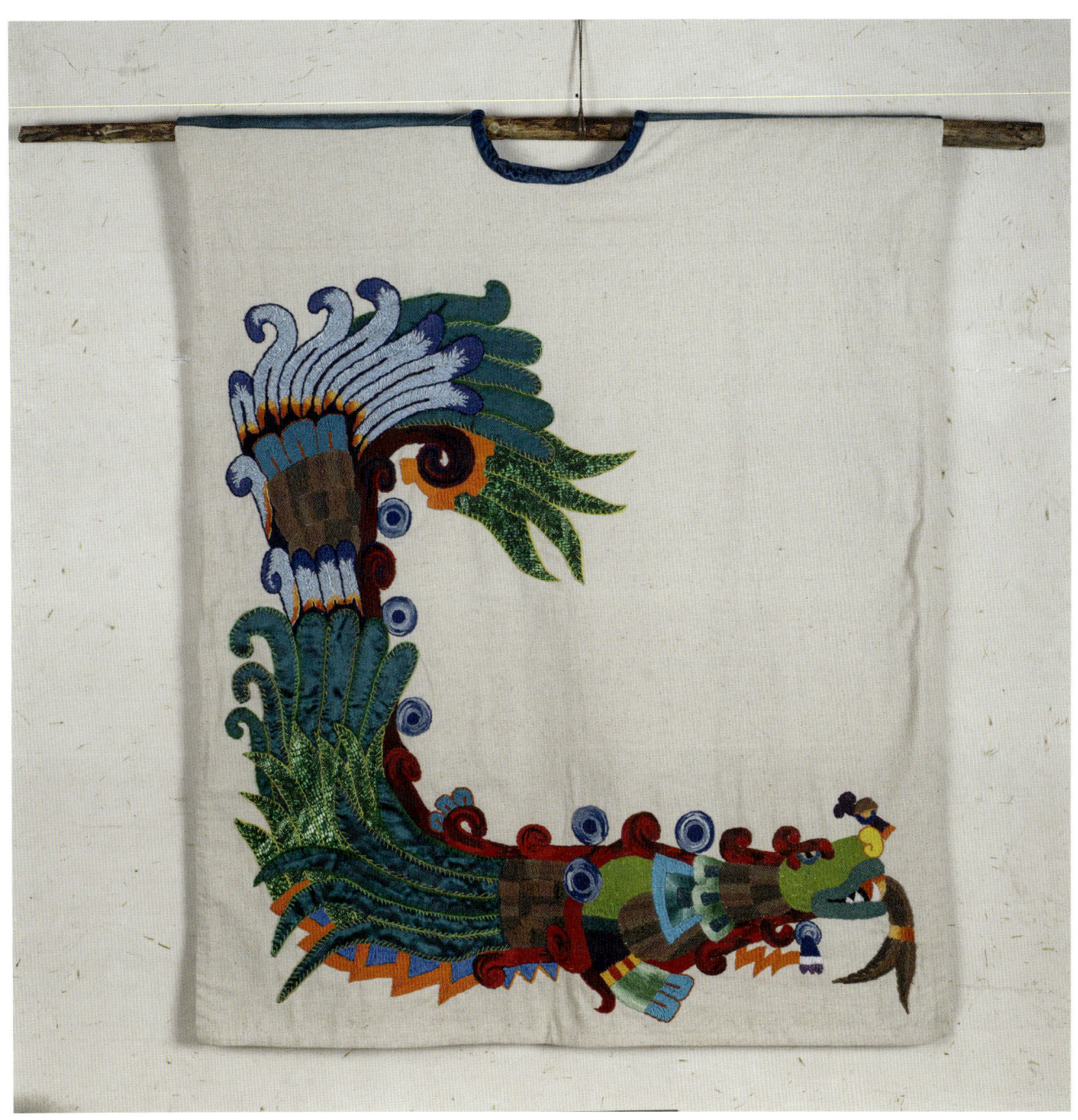

PLATE 35. *Huipil, Quetzalcóatl, Colcha Embroidery and Applique,* 2018. Manta, cotton, satin, and metallic cloth, 60″ × 40″. Collection of the artist.

FRANCISCO LEFEBRE
(Born 1947, Wagon Mound, NM; current
residence, Albuquerque, NM)

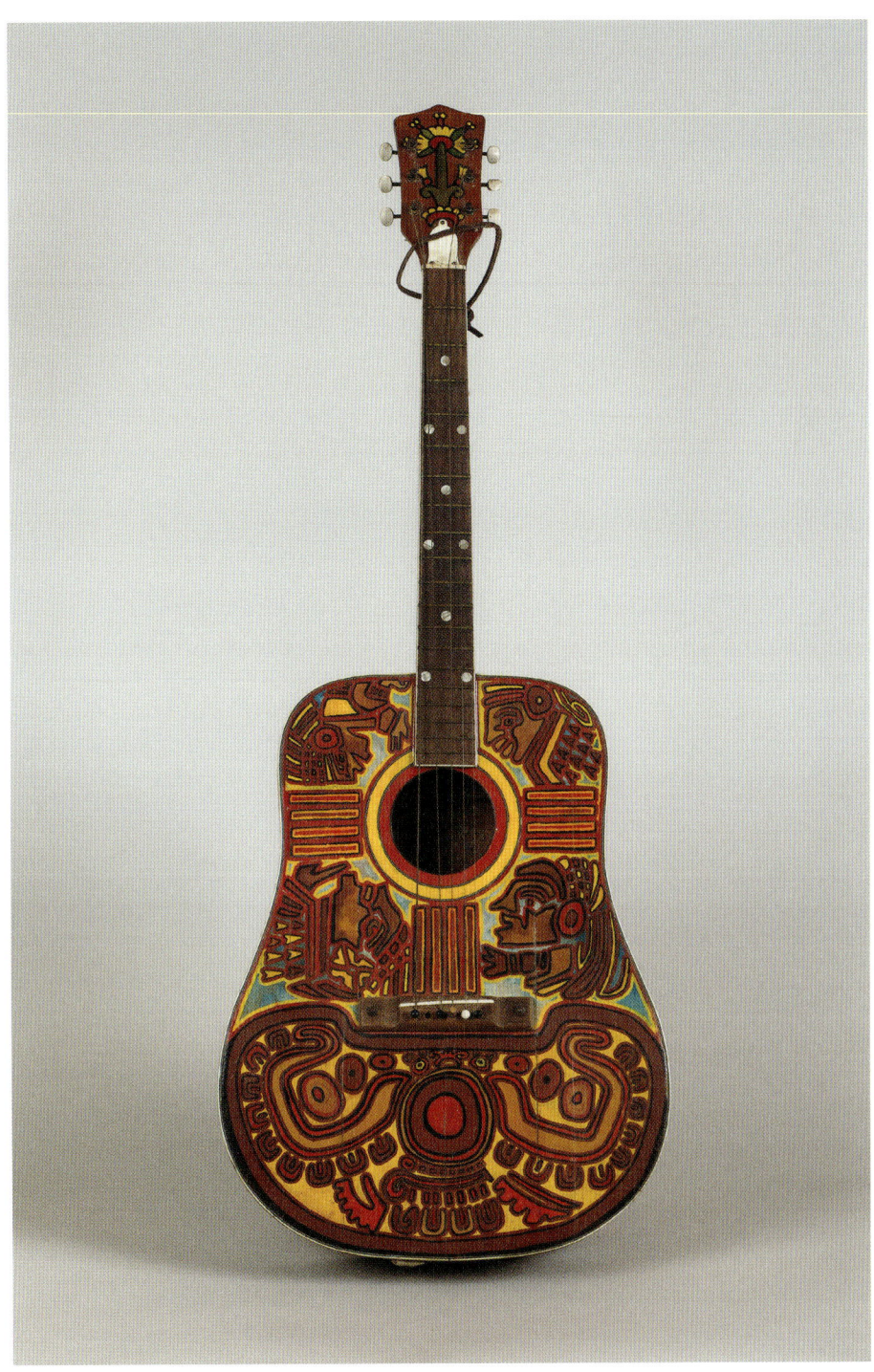

PLATE 36. *Guitarra Azteca*, 1972. Oil on wood, 18″ × 24″. Collection of the artist.

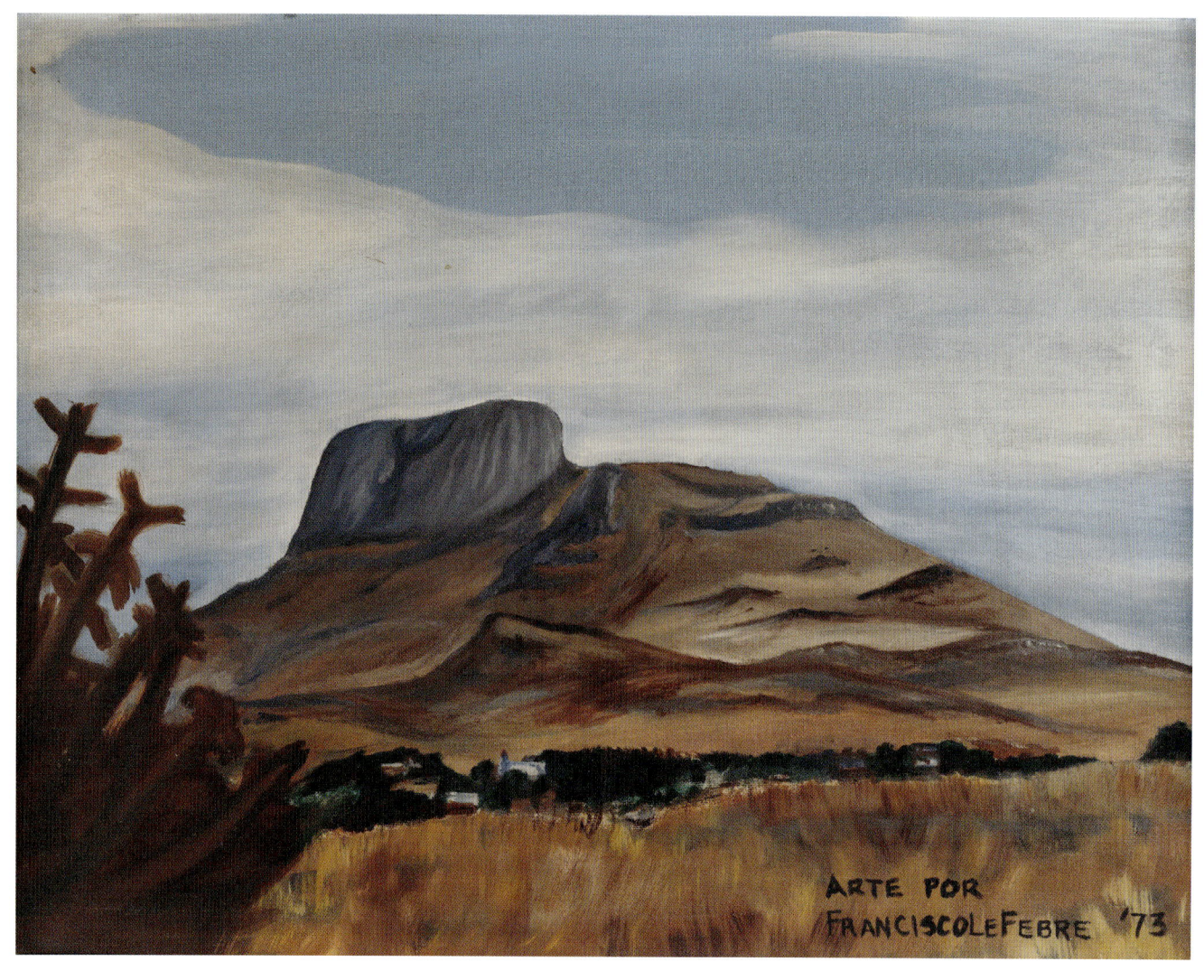

PLATE 37. *Wagon Mound*, 1973. Oil on canvas, 18″ × 14″. Collection of the artist.

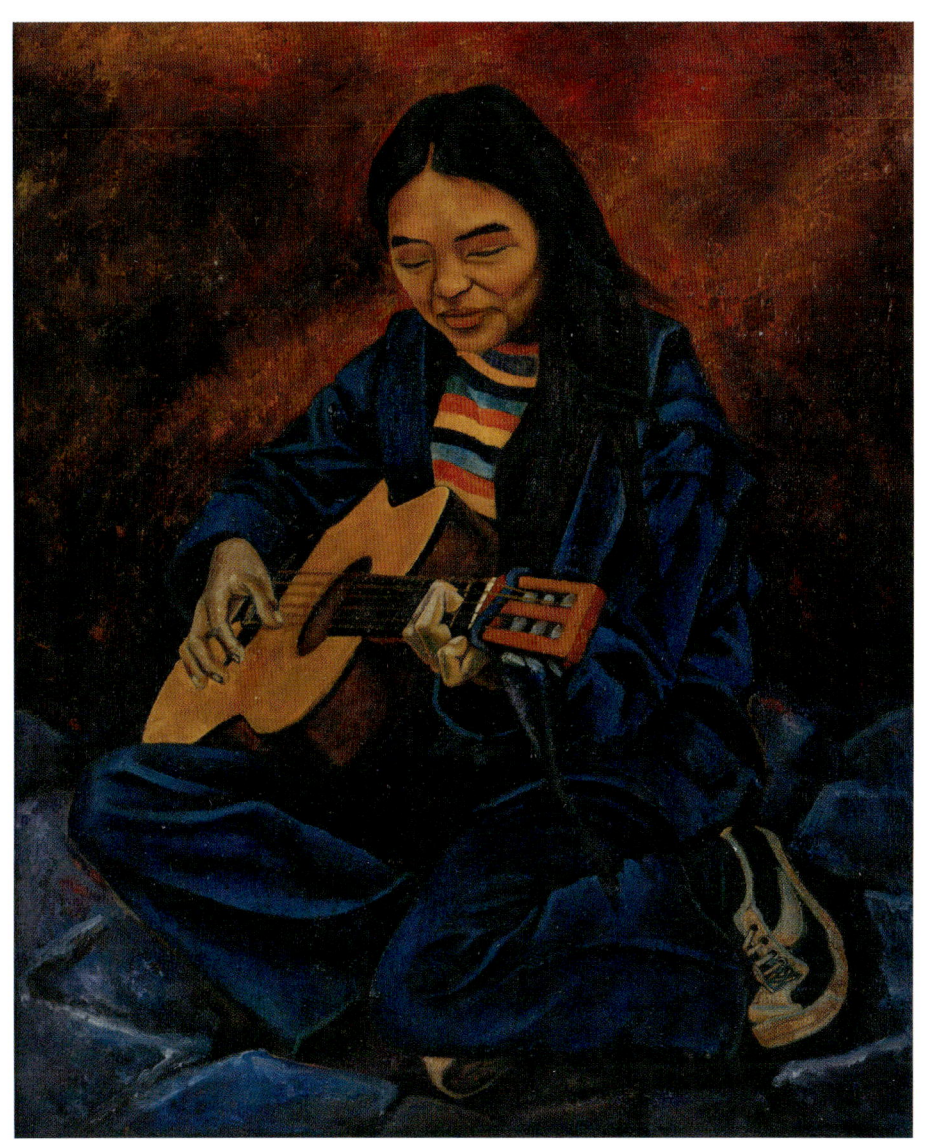

PLATE 38. *La niña y su guitarra*, 1974. Oil on canvas, 24" × 20". Collection of the artist.

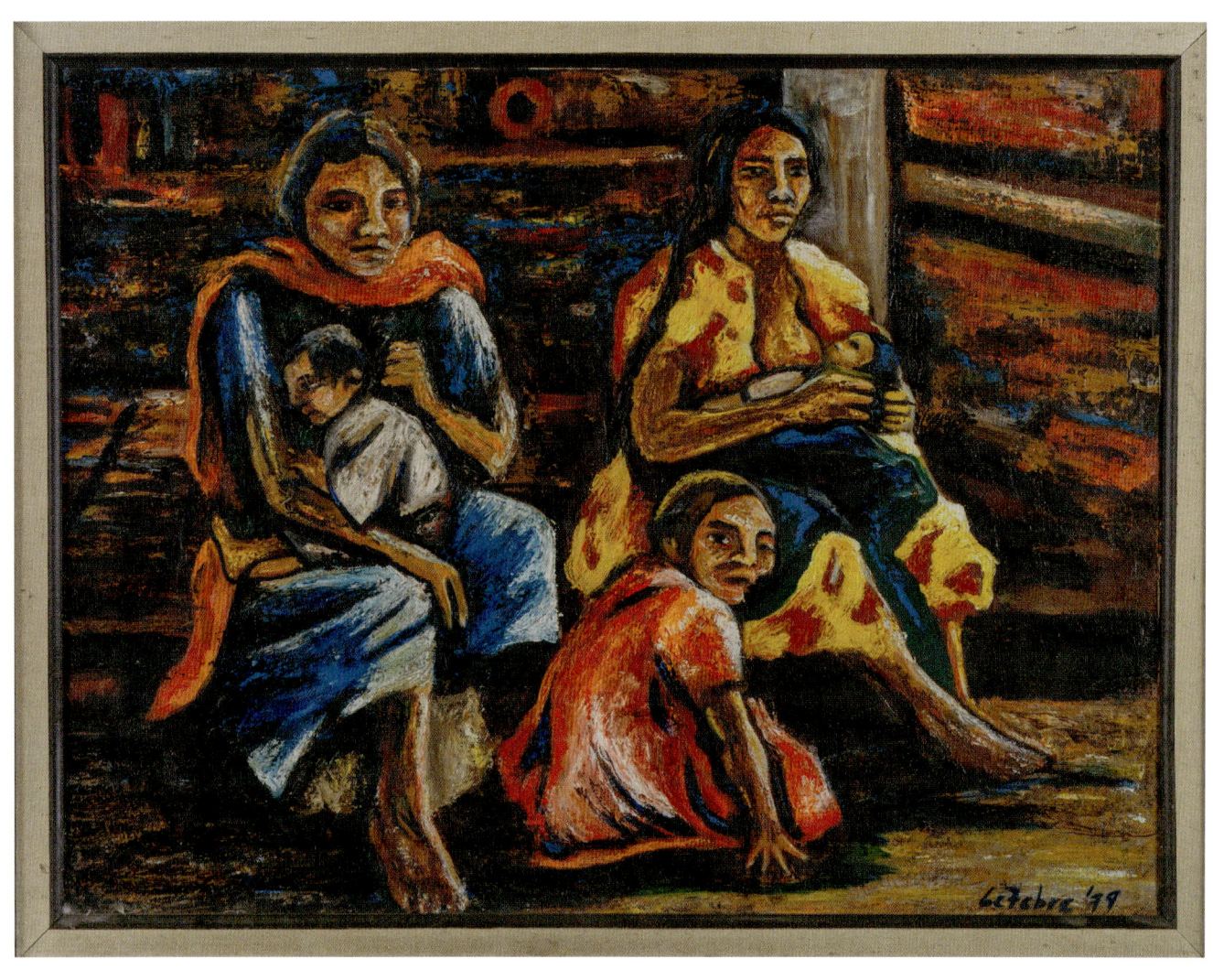

PLATE 39. *Madres con sus niños*, 1974. Oil on canvas, 24″ × 18″. Collection of the artist.

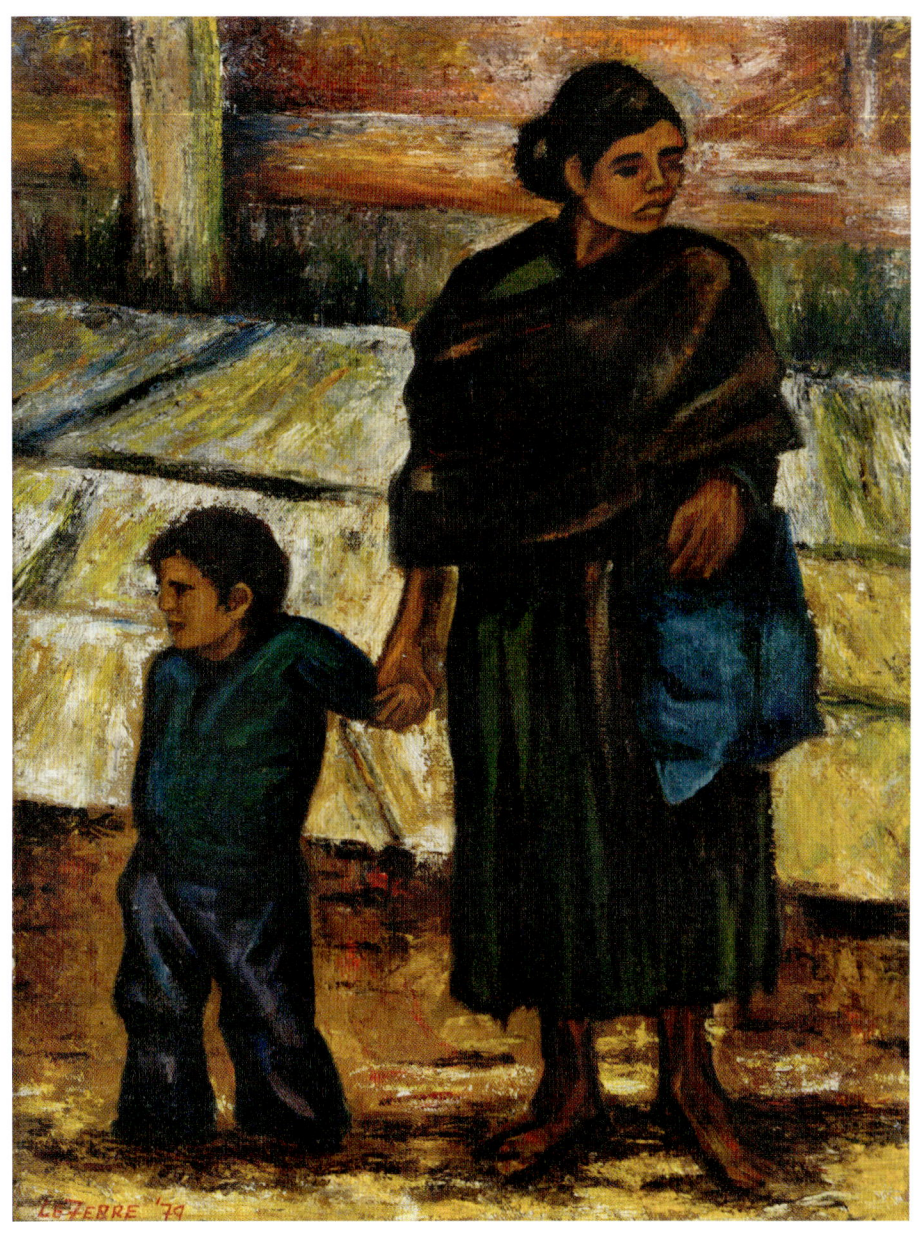

PLATE 40. *Madre y niño*, 1974. Oil on canvas, 20″ × 16″. Collection of the artist.

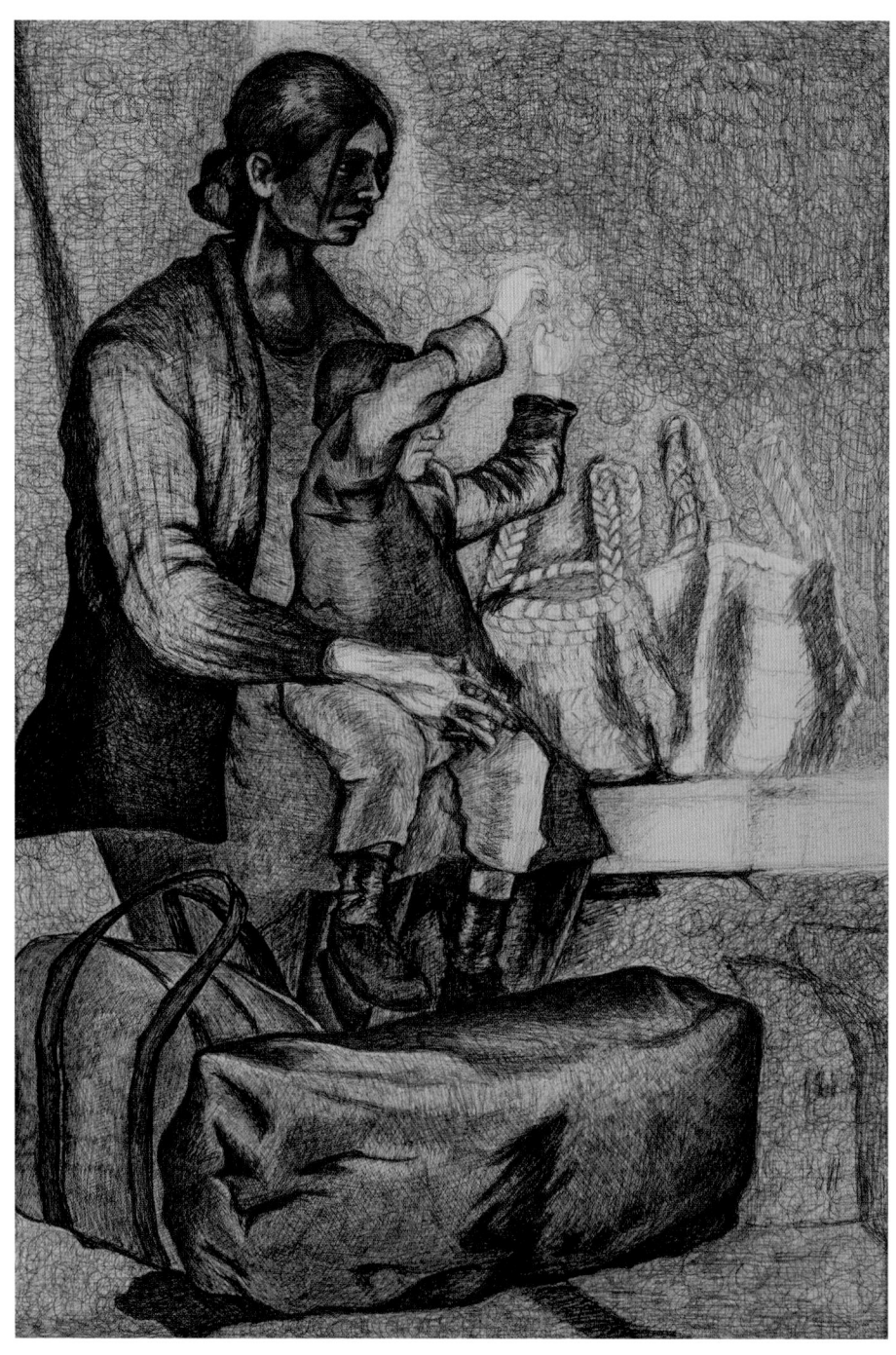

PLATE 41. *Señora con su hijo*, 1974. Graphite and ink on paper, 24″ × 16″. Collection of the artist.

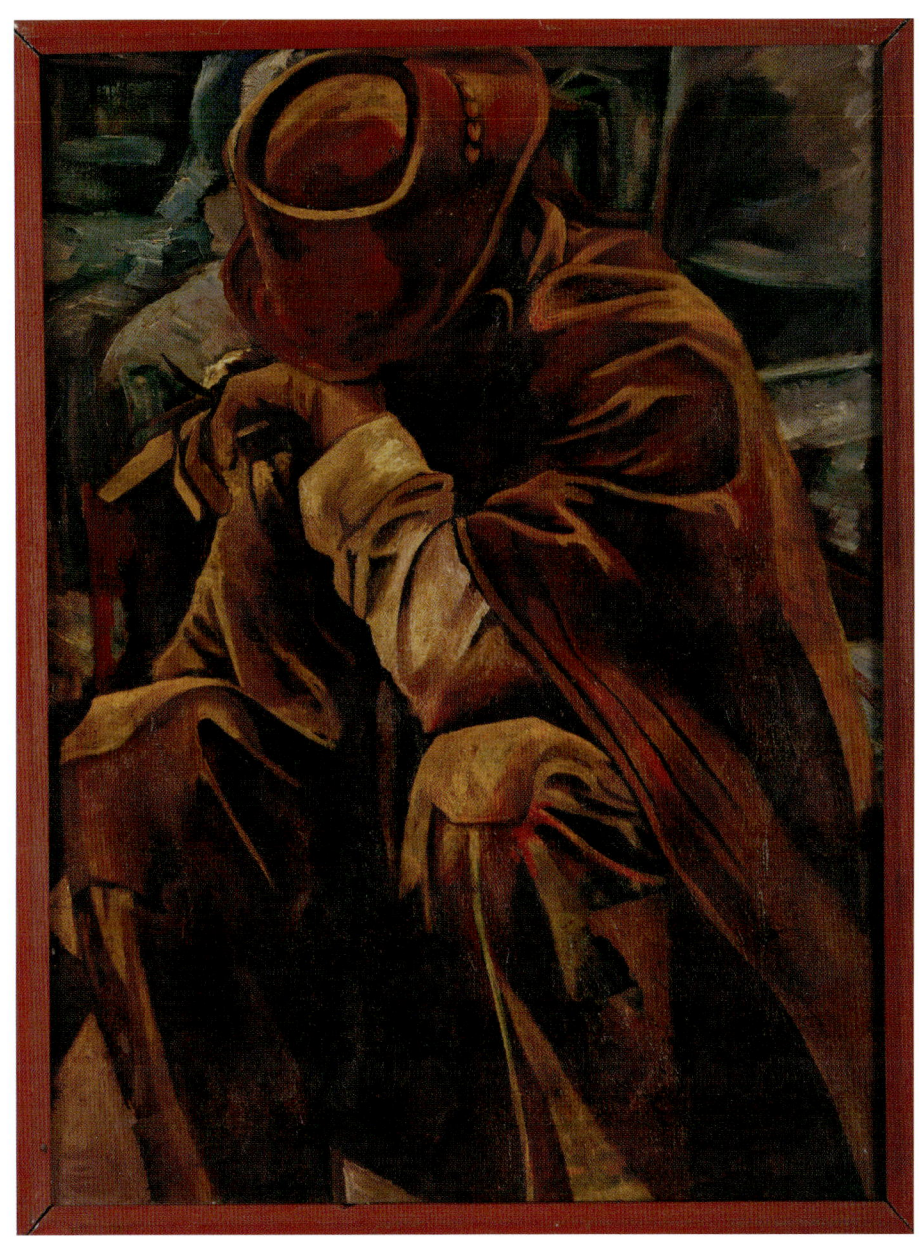

PLATE 42. *Señor pobre,* 1974. Oil on canvas, 24″ × 18″. Collection of the artist.

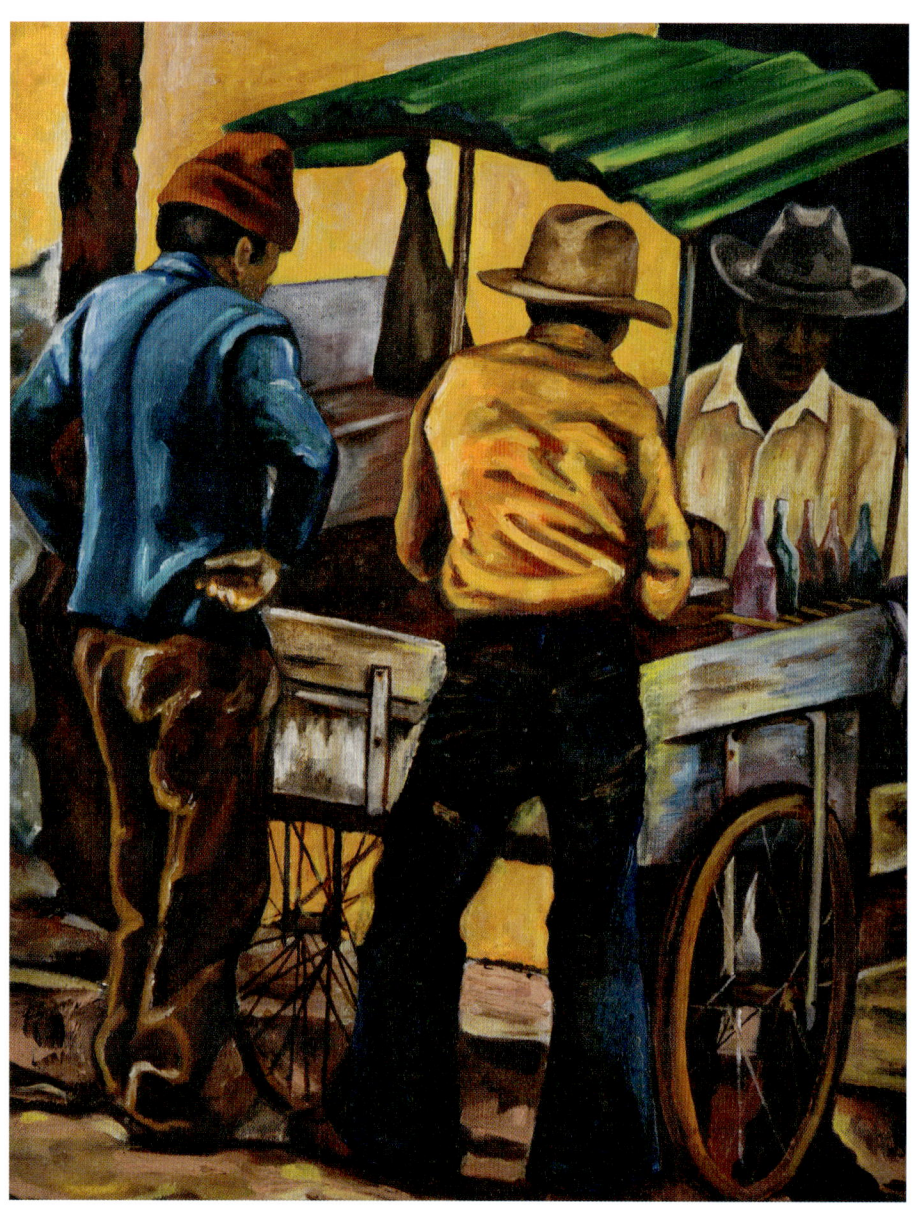

PLATE 43. *Trabajadores*, 1974. Oil on canvas, 20″ × 24″. Collection of the artist.

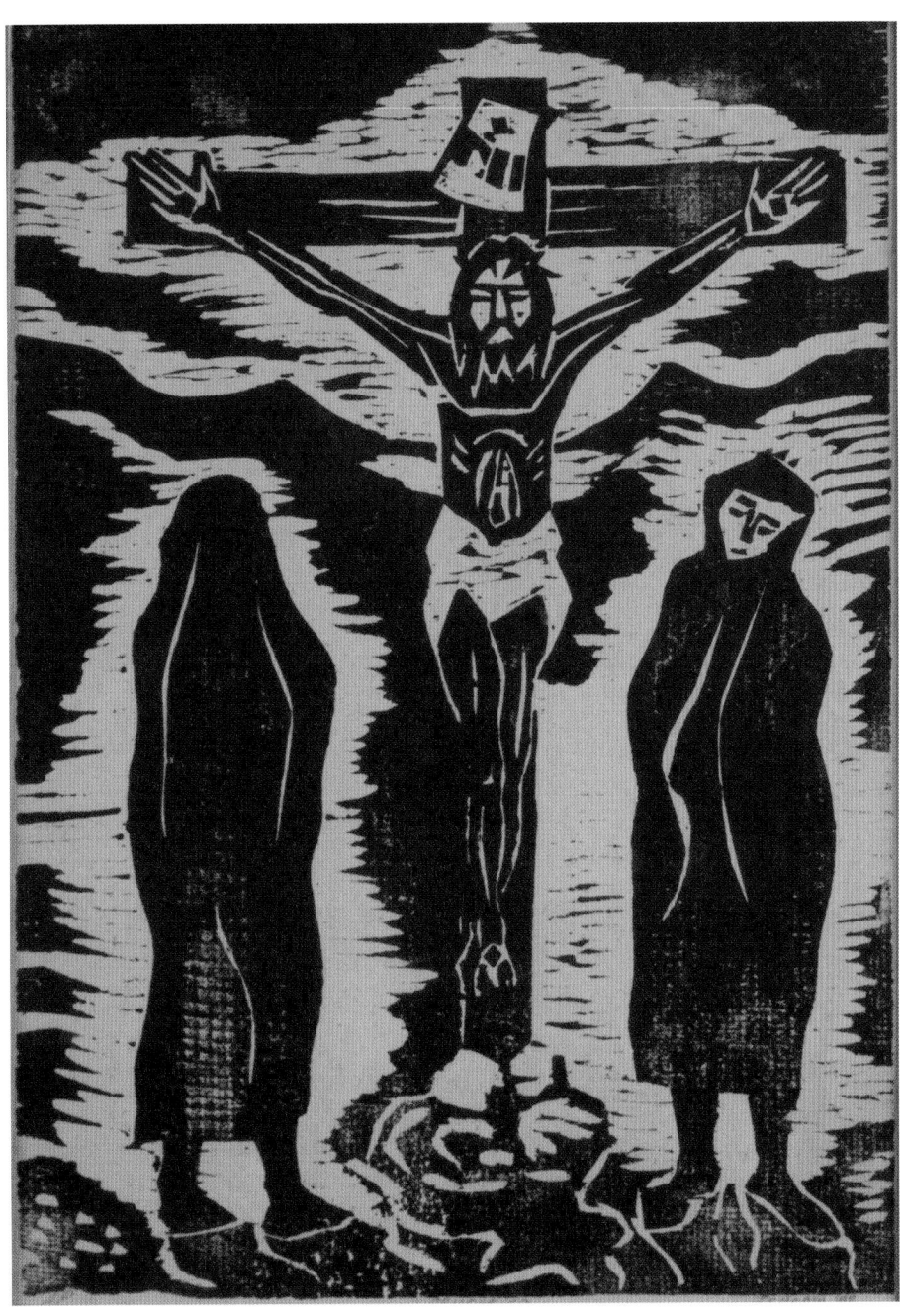

PLATE 44. *El penitente*, 1975, Linocut, 16″ × 14″. Collection of the artist.

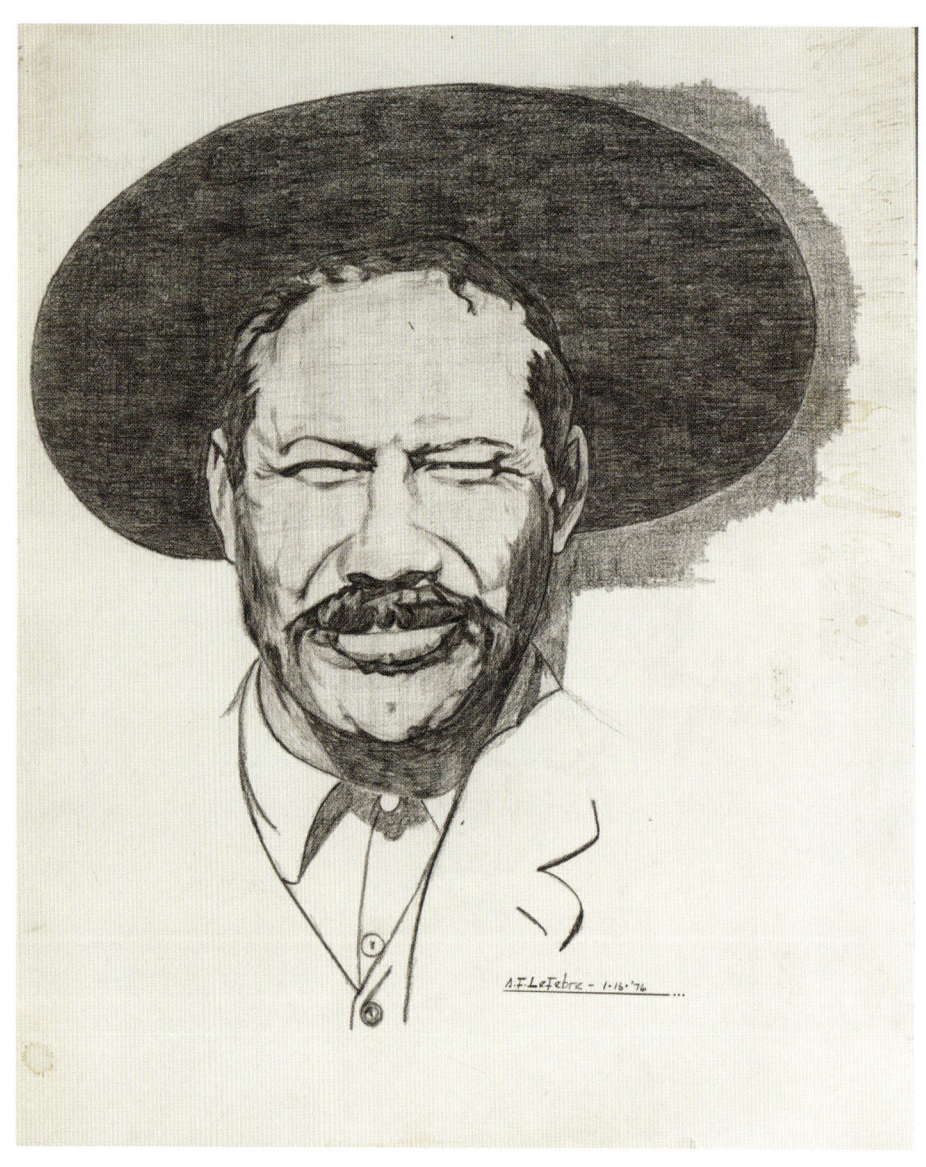

PLATE 45. *Francisco Villa*, 1976. Pen and ink on paper, 18″ × 22″. Collection of the artist.

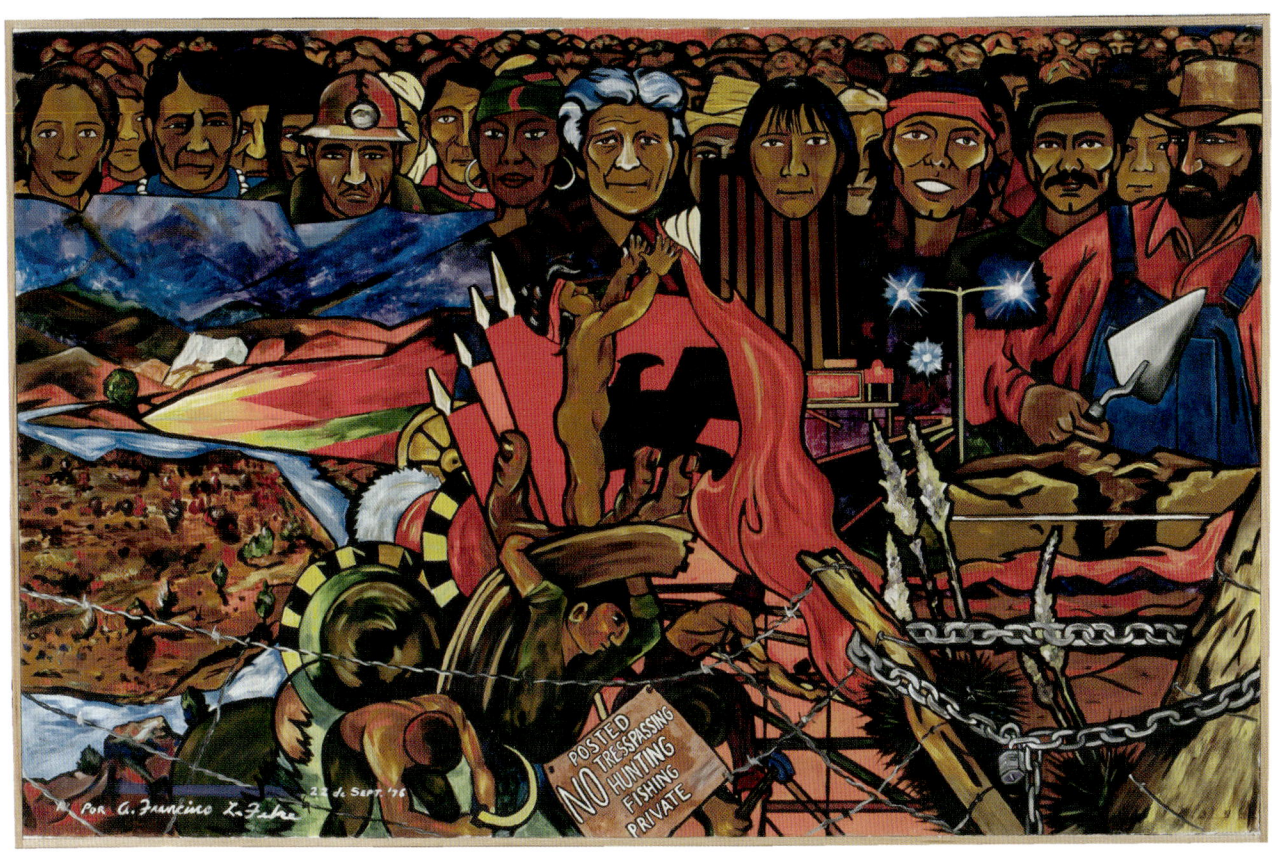

PLATE 46. *Realidades de Nuevo México*, 1976. Acrylic on canvas, 72″ × 96″. Collection
of Albuquerque Museum, museum purchase, 1985 General Obligation Bonds.

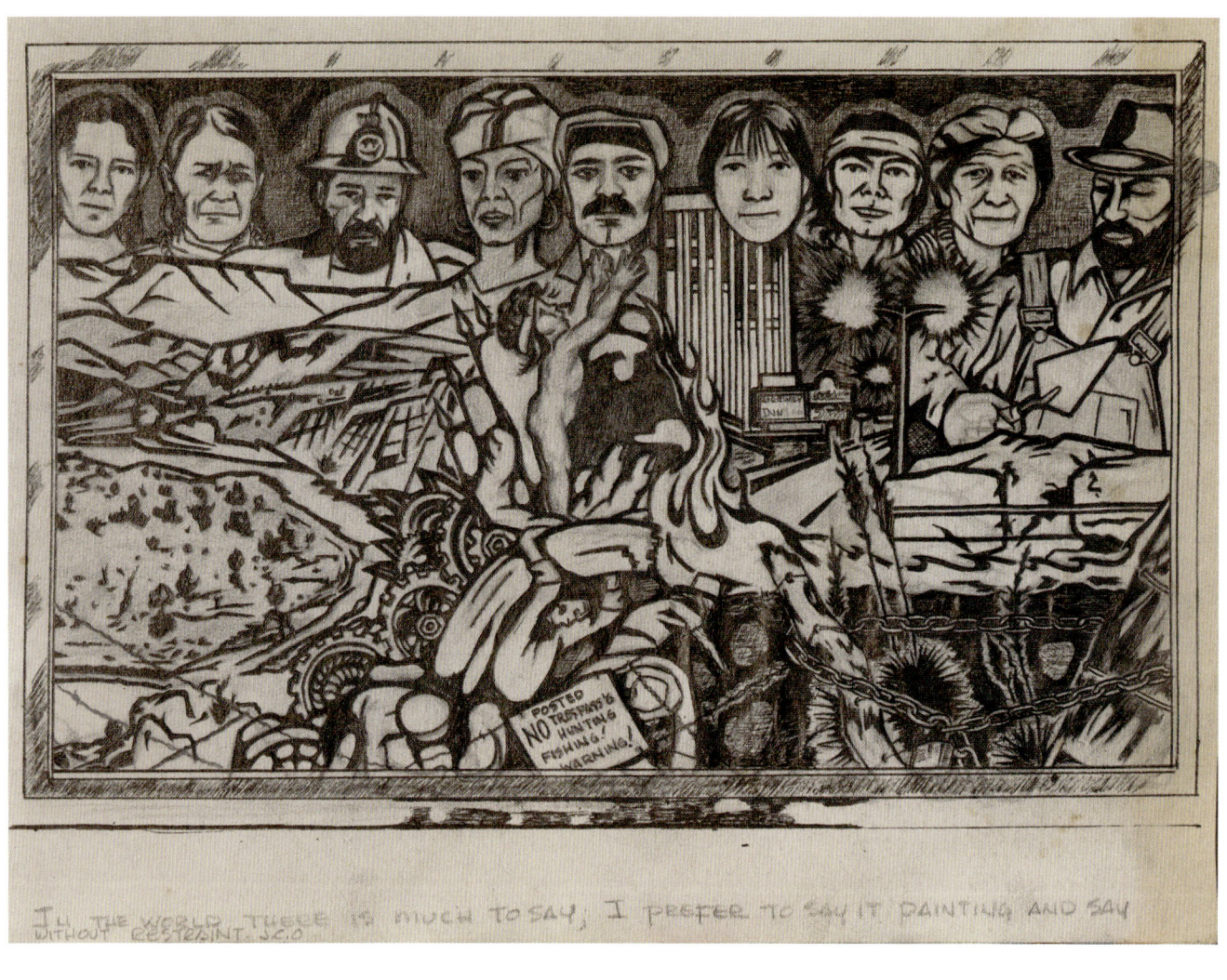

IN THE WORLD THERE IS MUCH TO SAY; I PREFER TO SAY IT PAINTING AND SAY WITHOUT RESTRAINT. J.C.O

PLATE 47. *Study: Realidades de Nuevo México*, 1976, Graphite on paper, 14″ × 8″. Collection of the artist.

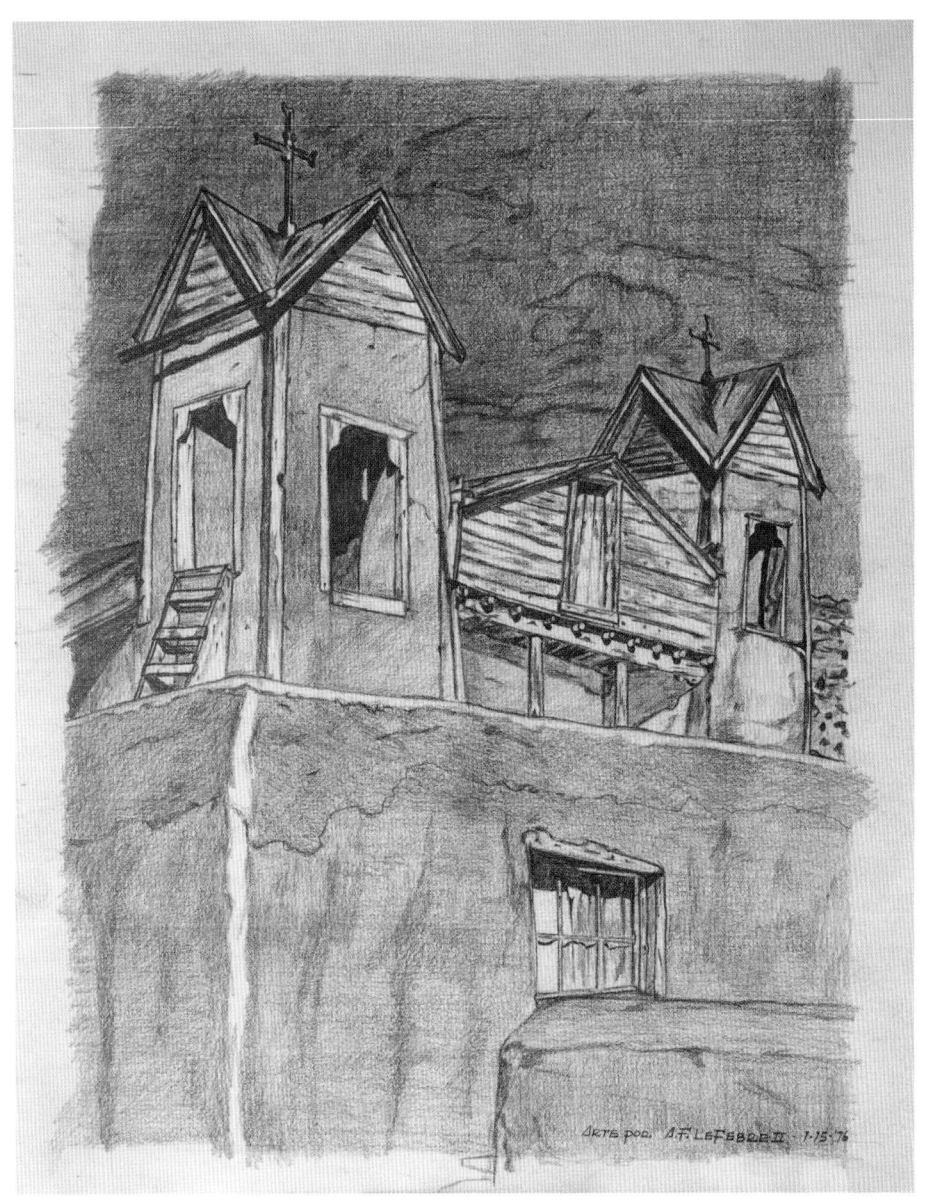

PLATE 48. *Santuario*, 1976. Graphite on paper, 24″ × 18″. Collection of the artist.

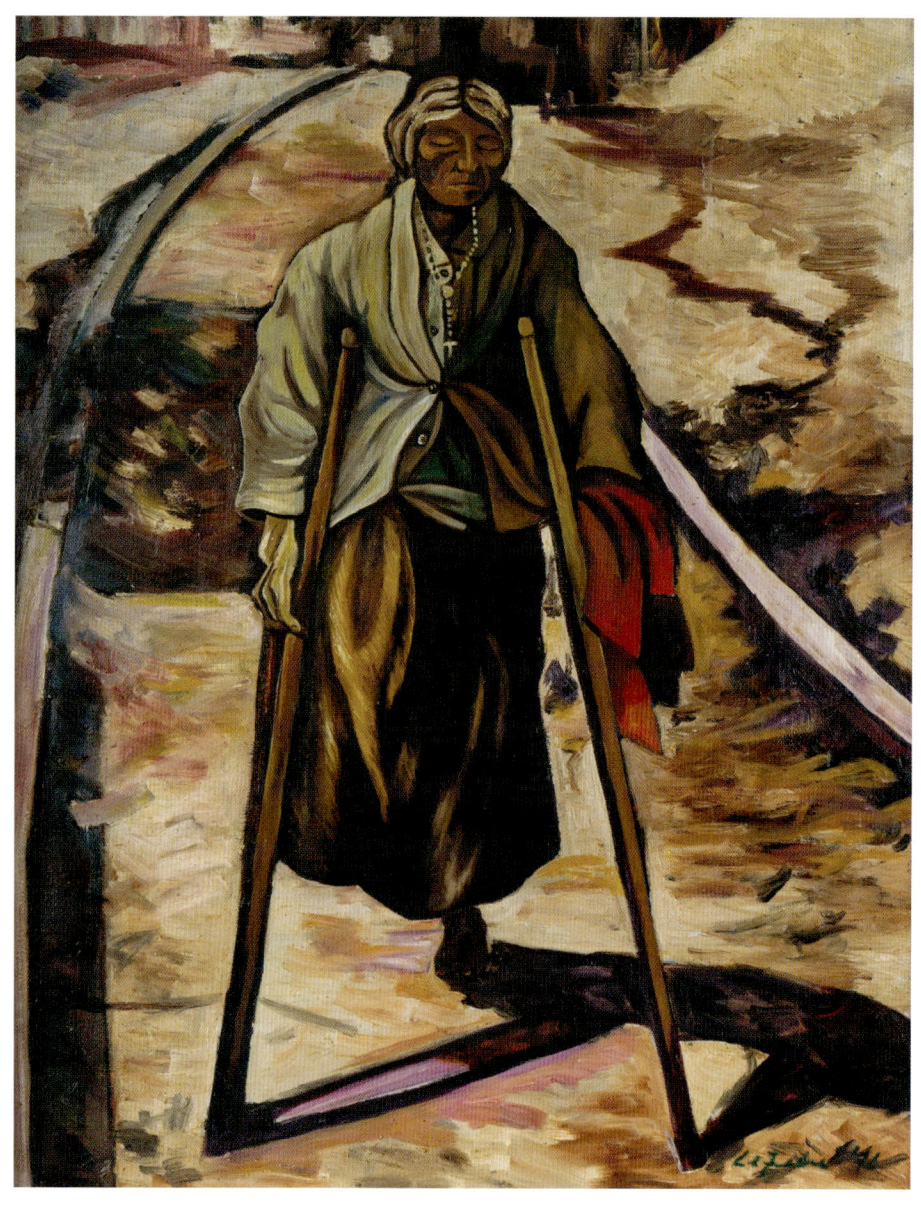

PLATE 49. *Señora en muletas*, 1976. Oil on canvas, 32″ × 26″. Collection of the artist.

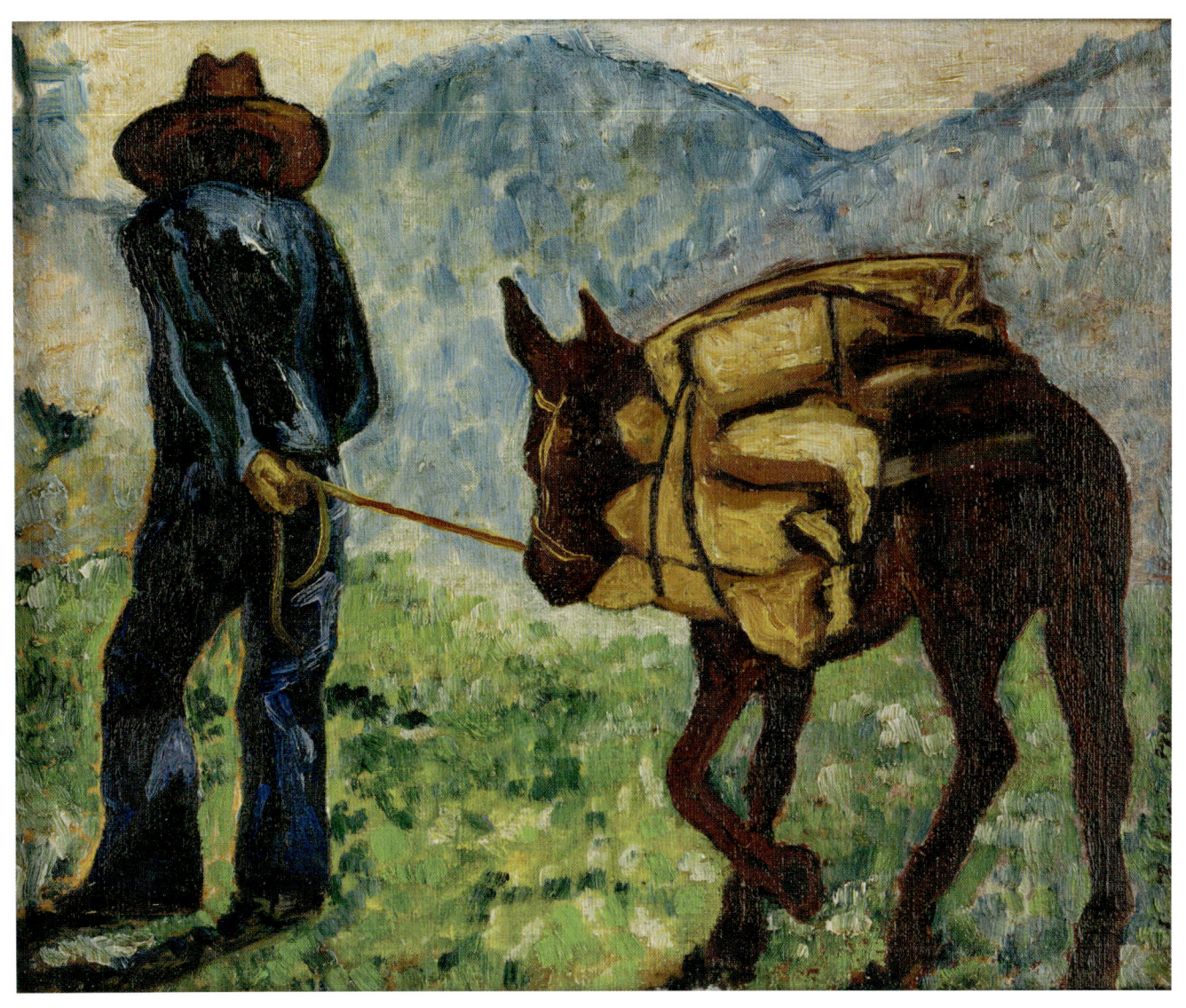

PLATE 50. *El arriero va*, 1977. Oil on canvas, 12″ × 18″. Collection of the artist.

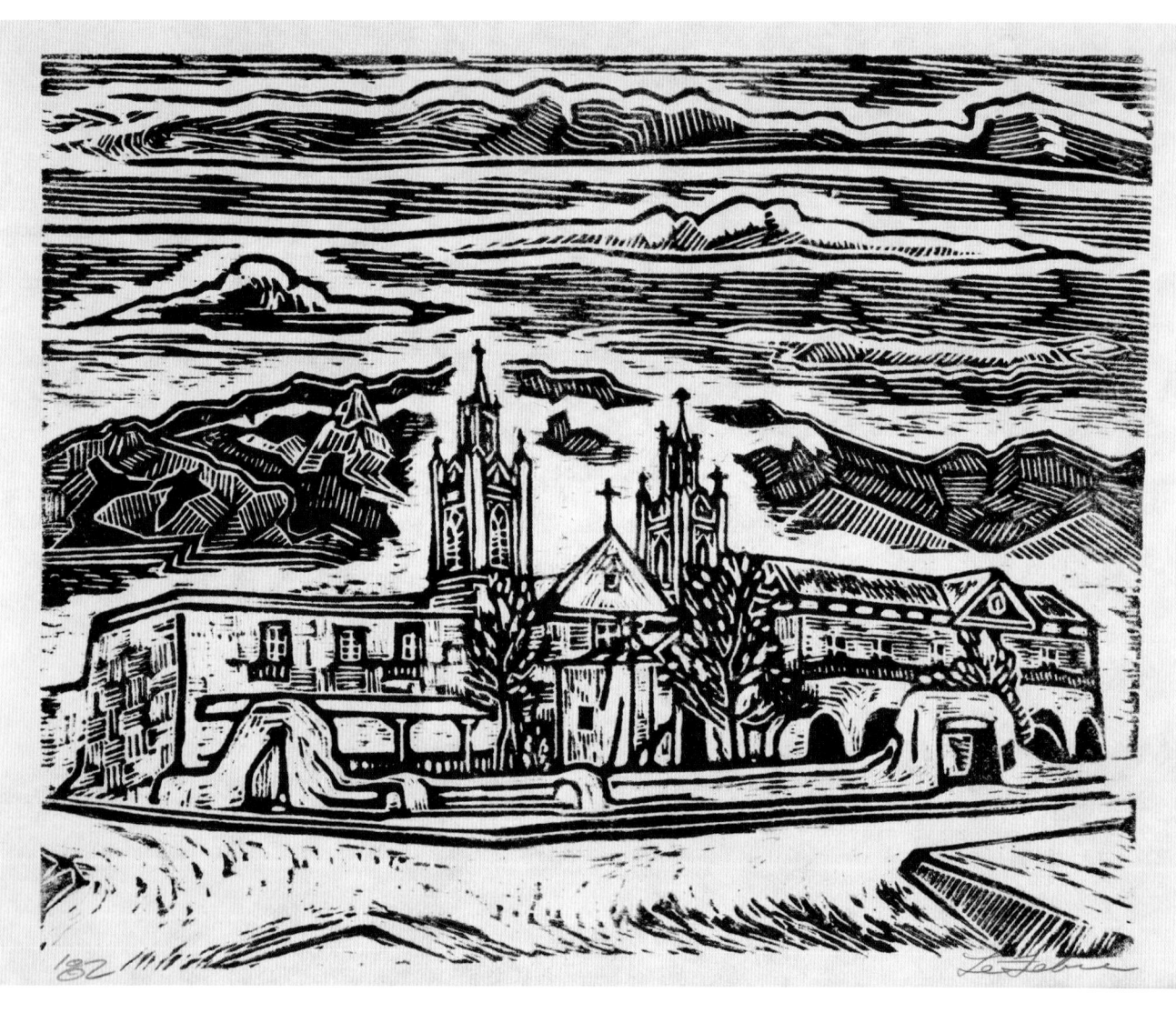

PLATE 51. *San Felipe*, 1977. Linocut, 8 ½″ × 11″. Collection of the artist.

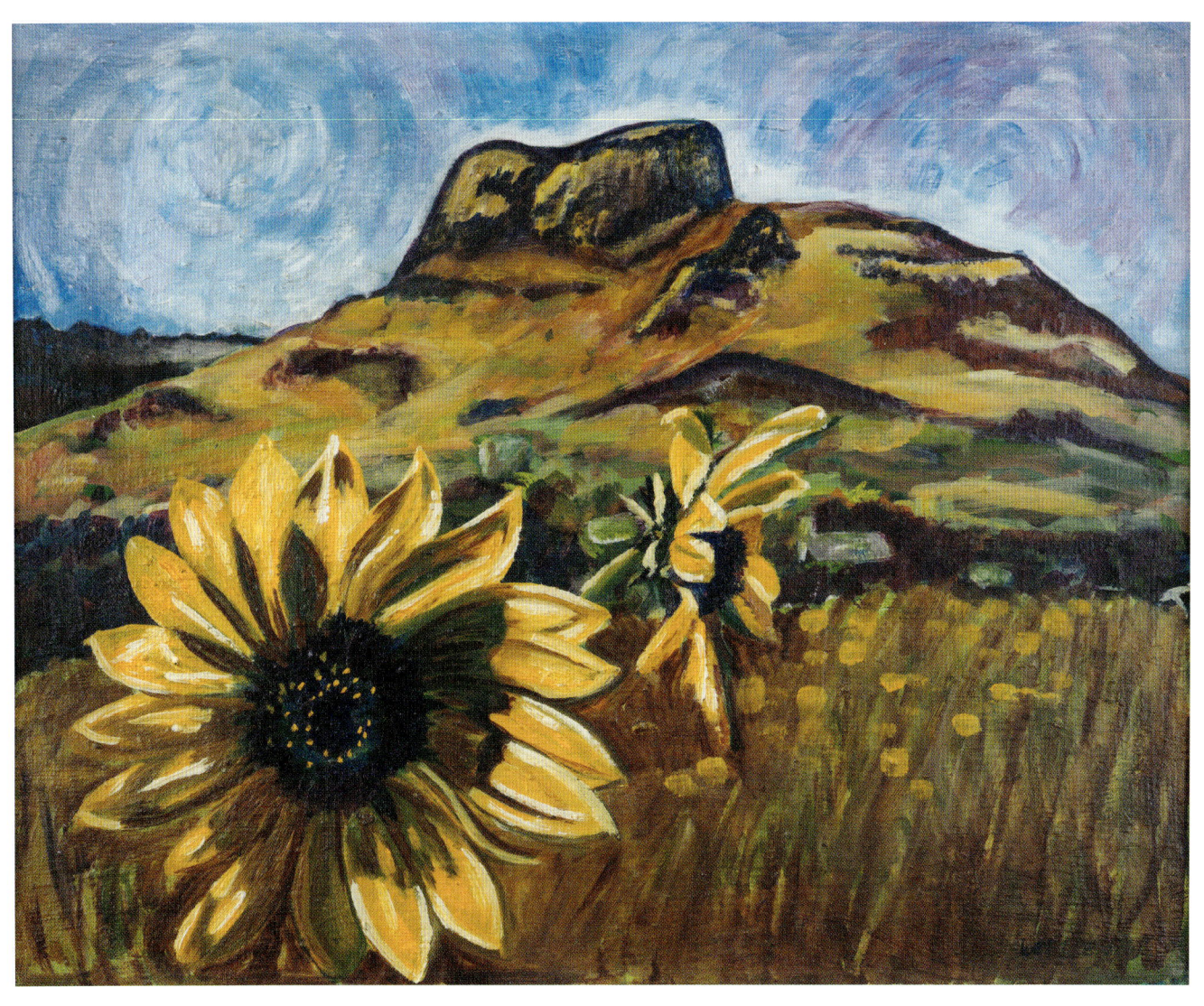

PLATE 52. *Añiles de mi tierra*, 1978. Oil on canvas, 23″ × 19″. Collection of the artist.

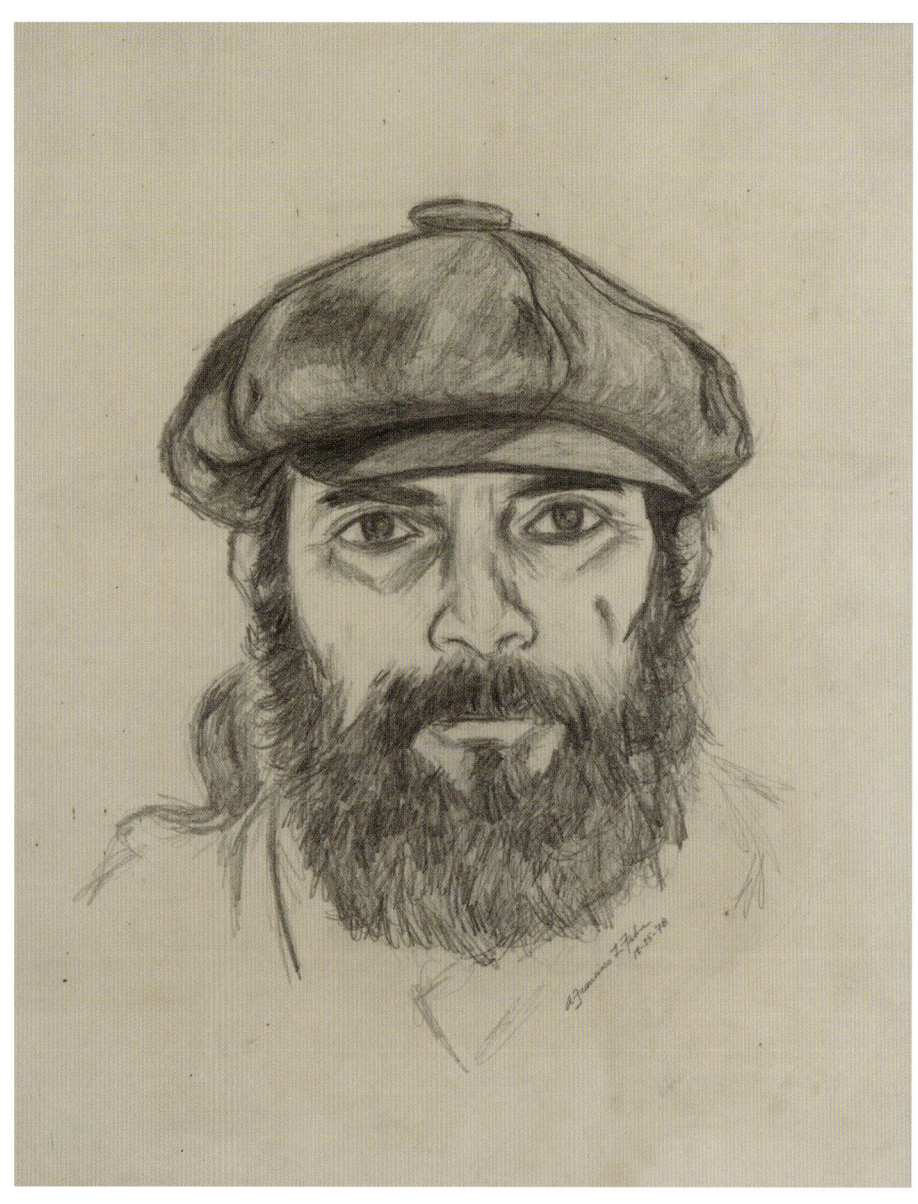

PLATE 53. *Autorretrato*, 1978. Graphite on paper, 22″ × 18″. Collection of the artist.

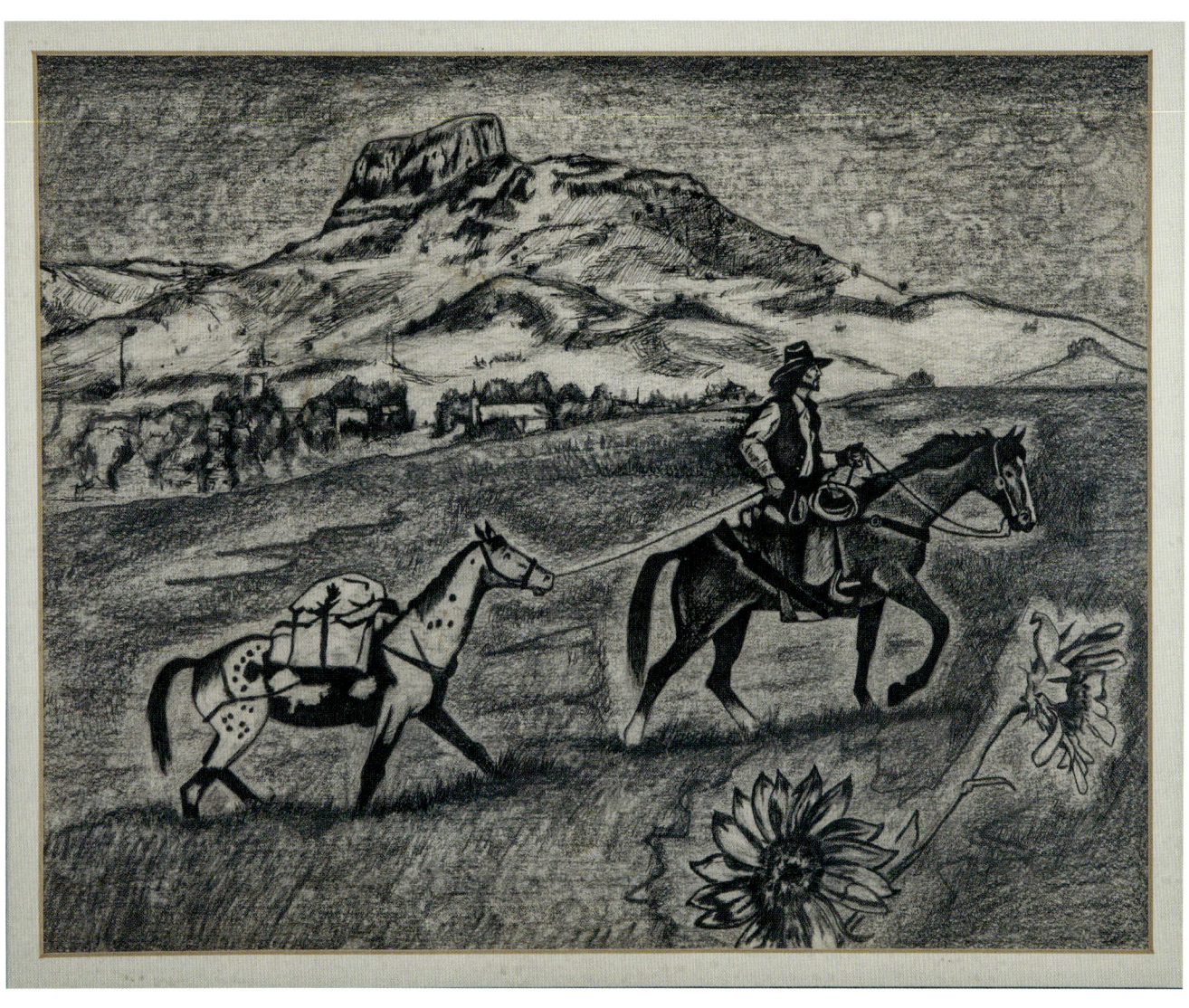

PLATE 54. *Vaquero norteño*, 1978. Graphite on paper, 12″ × 18″. Collection of the artist.

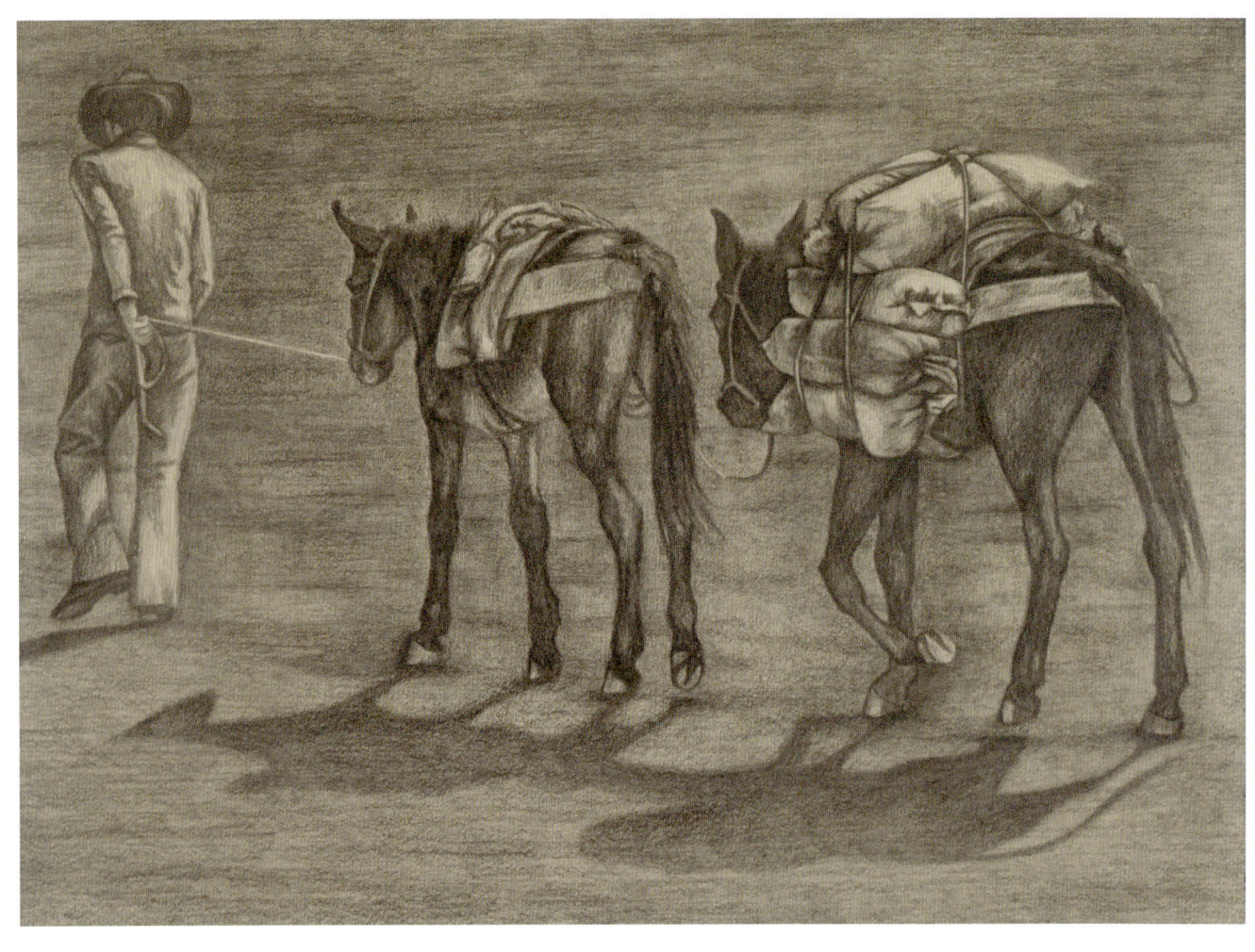

PLATE 55. *Arriero Number 1*, 1979. Graphite on paper, 19″ × 15″. Collection of the artist.

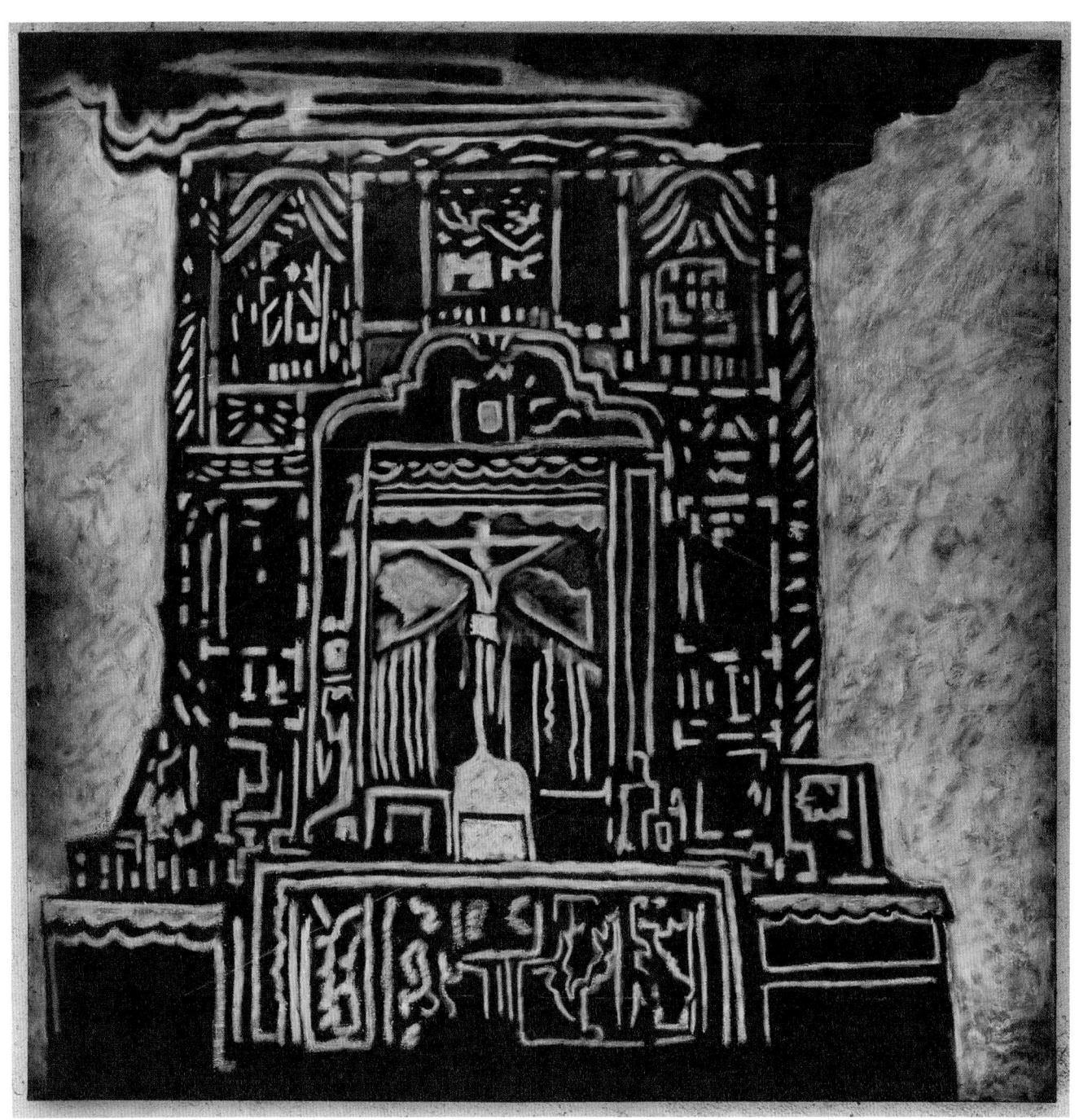

PLATE 56. *El altar del Santuario*, 1979. Oil on canvas, 59" × 59". Collection of the artist.

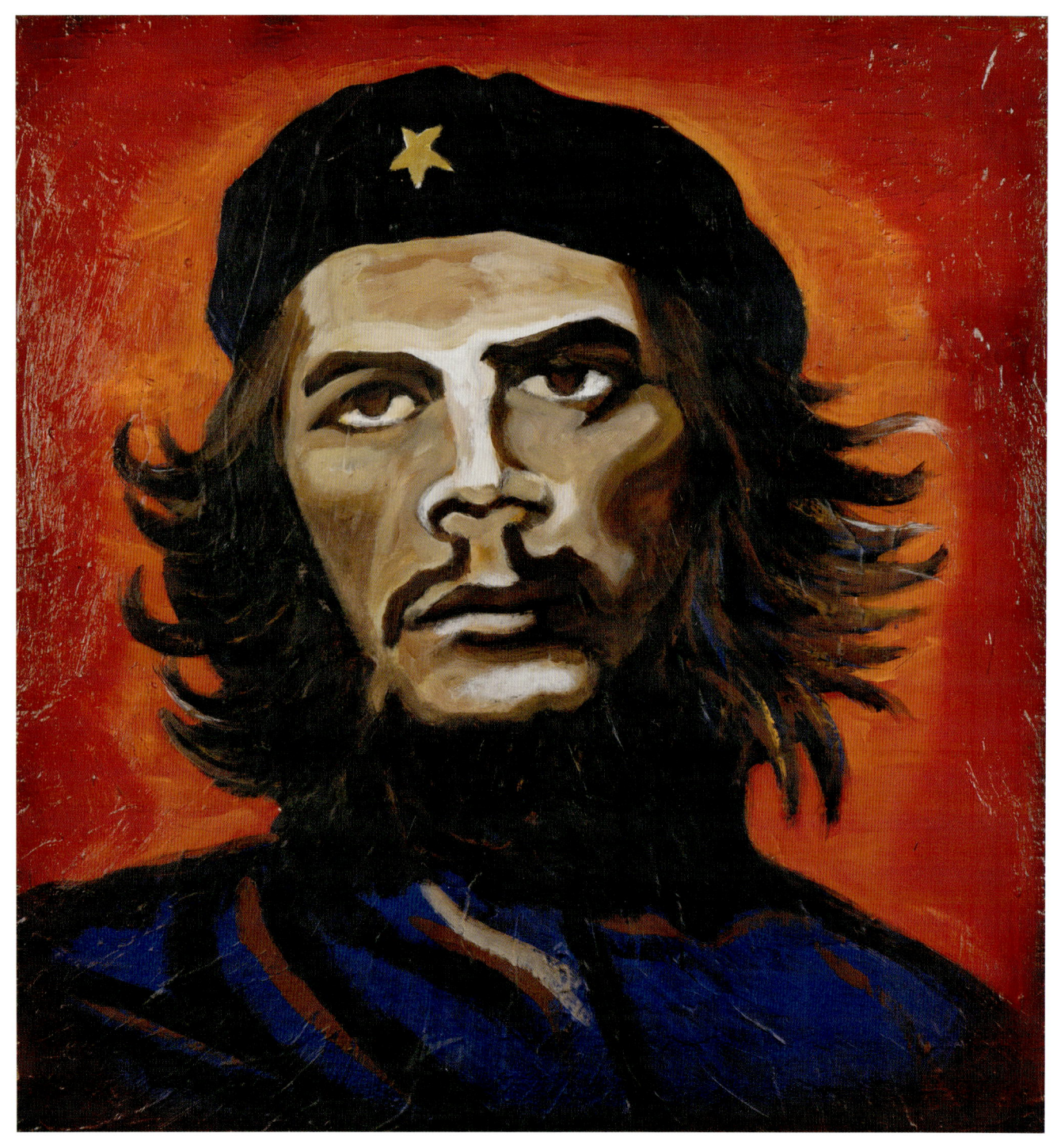

PLATE 57. *El comandante*, 1984. Acrylic on panel, 32″ × 34″. Collection of the artist.

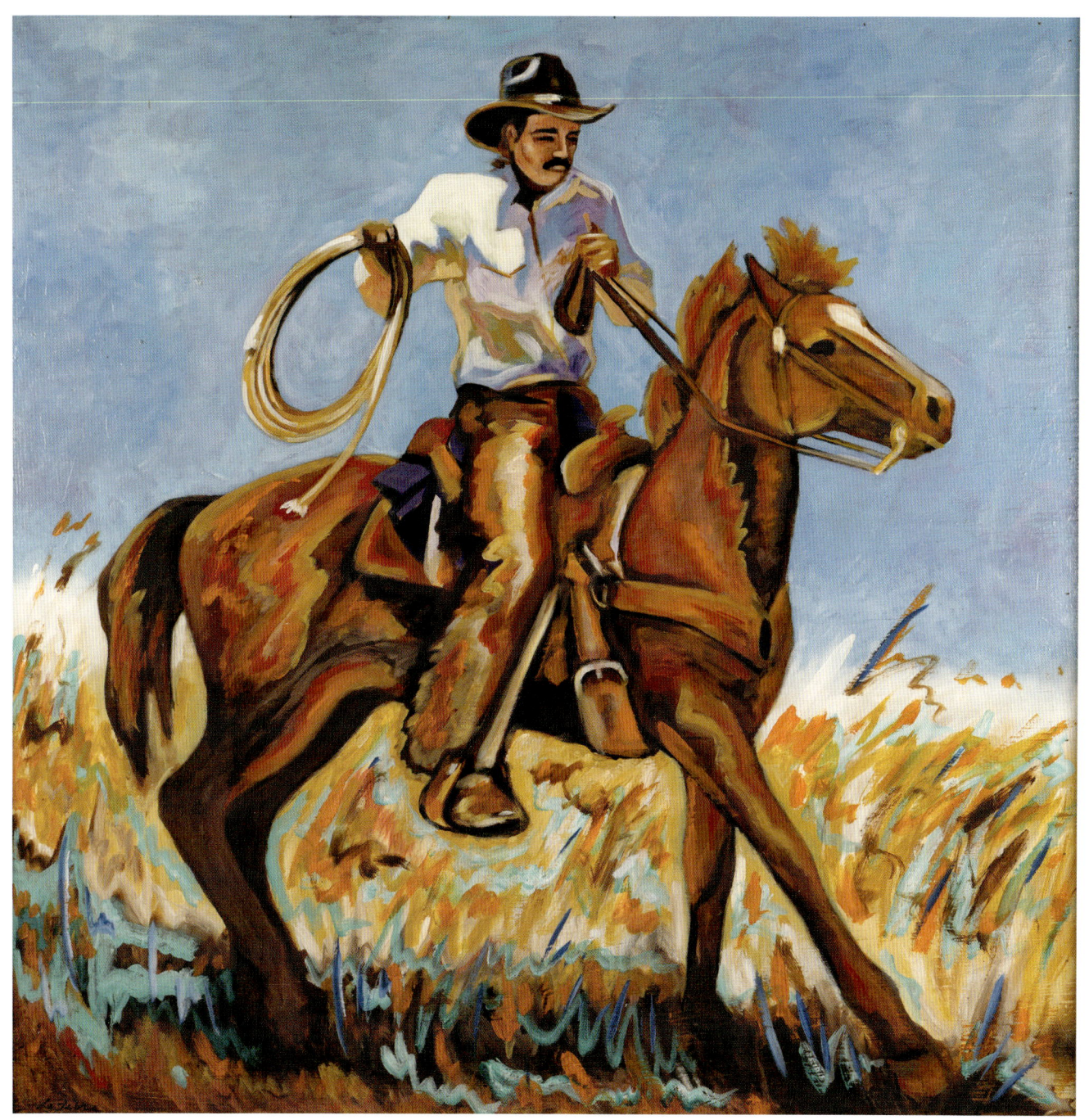

PLATE 58. *Mi primo Alfredo*, 1986. Acrylic on panel, 4′ × 4′. Collection of the artist.

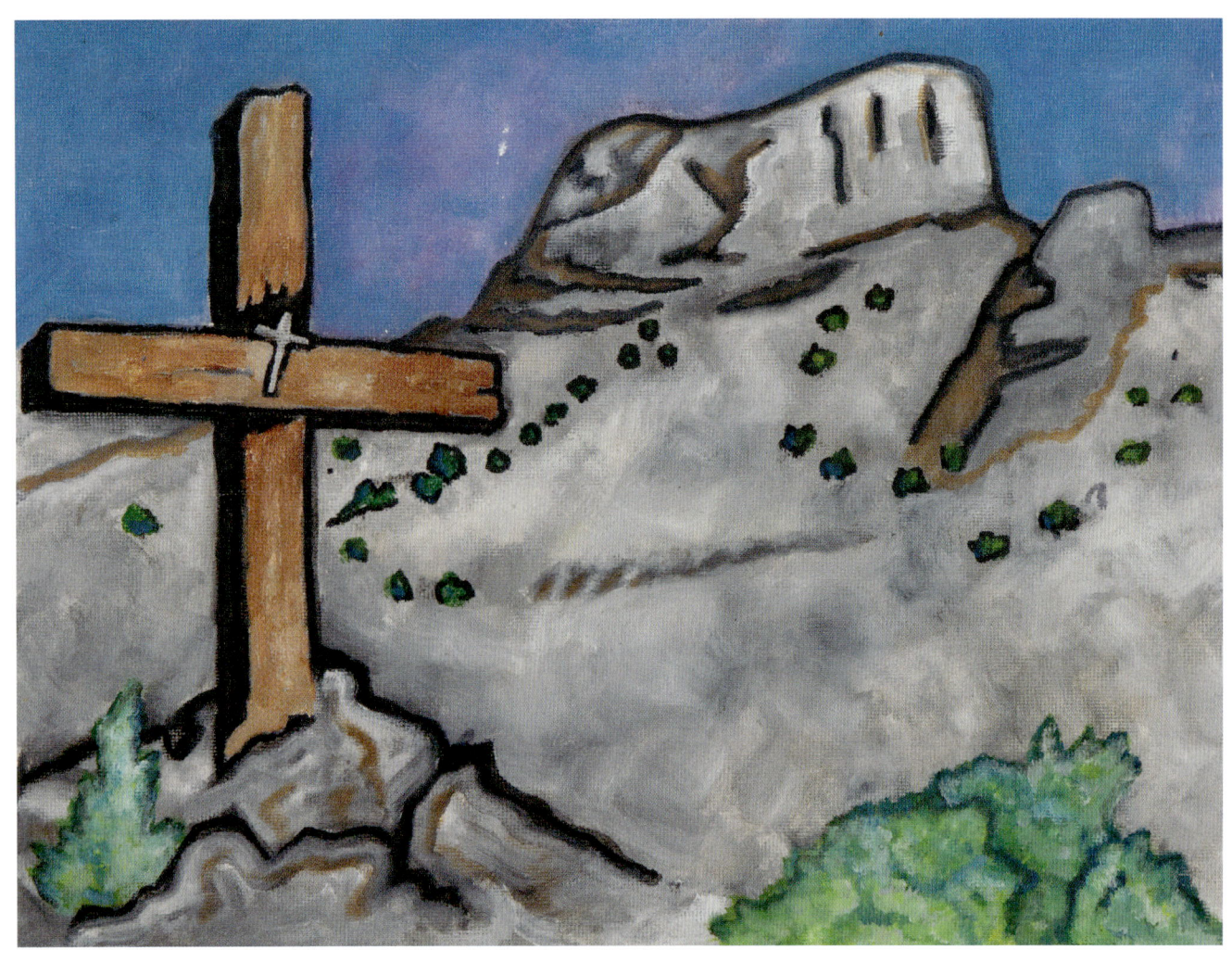

PLATE 59. *El calvario*, 1988. Oil on canvas, 12″ × 16″. Collection of the artist.

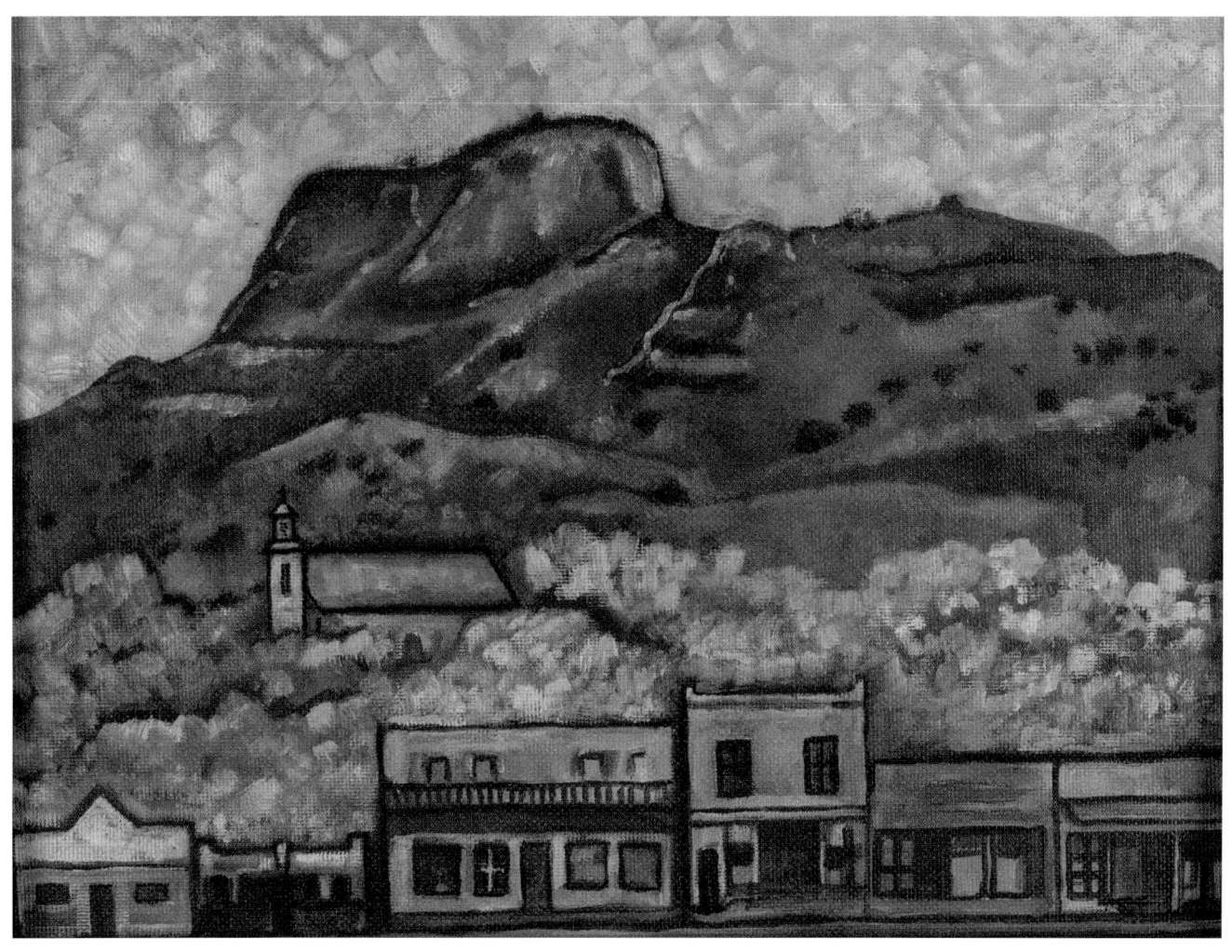

PLATE 60. *La plaza wagen*, 2016. Oil on canvas, 14″ × 10″. Collection of the artist.

NOEL MÁRQUEZ
(Born 1953, Artesia, NM; most recent
residence, Lake Arthur, NM; Died 2020)

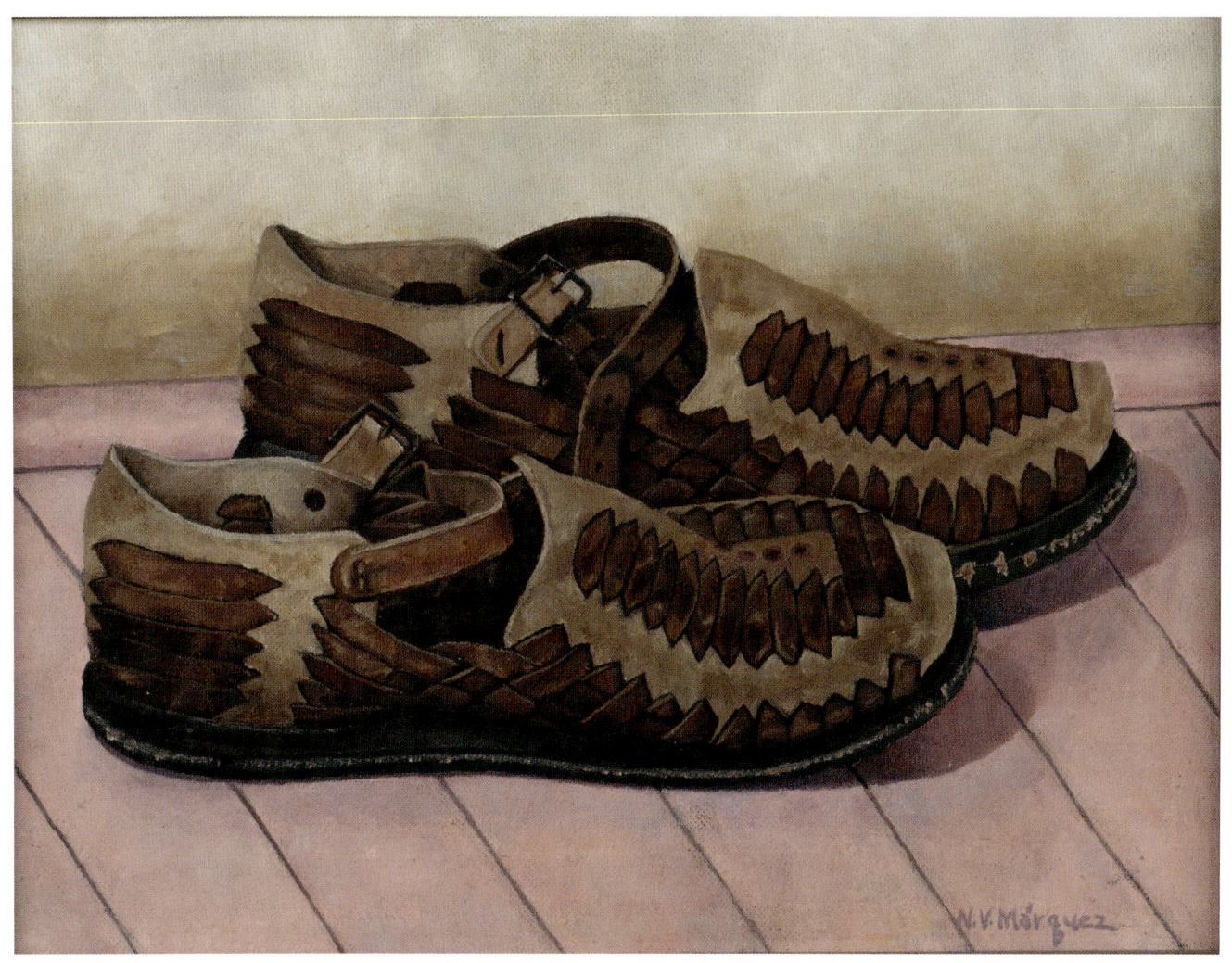

PLATE 61. *Huaraches, Mexico City*, 1974. Acrylic on board, 9″ × 12″. Collection of
the artist.

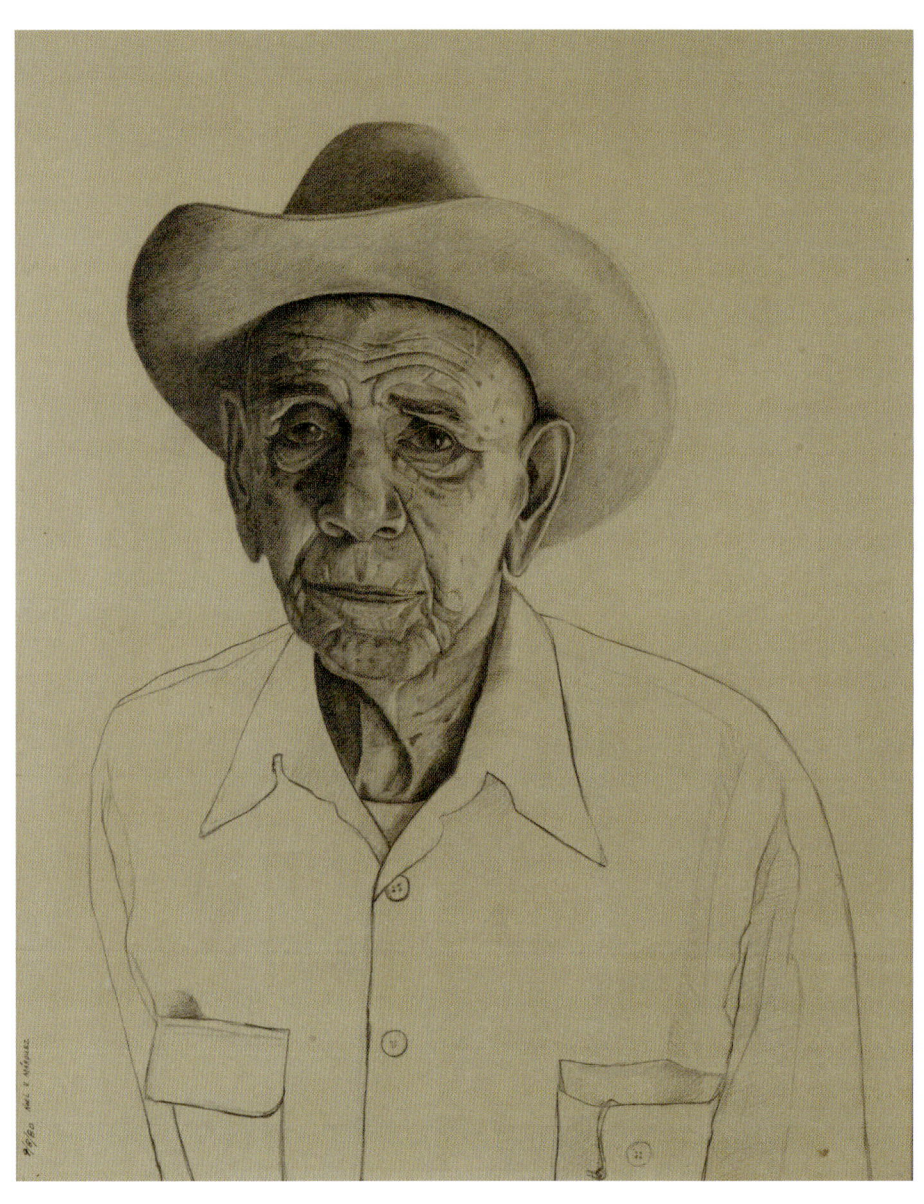

PLATE 62. *Mi abuelo*, 1980. Graphite on paper, 30″ × 26″. Collection of the artist.

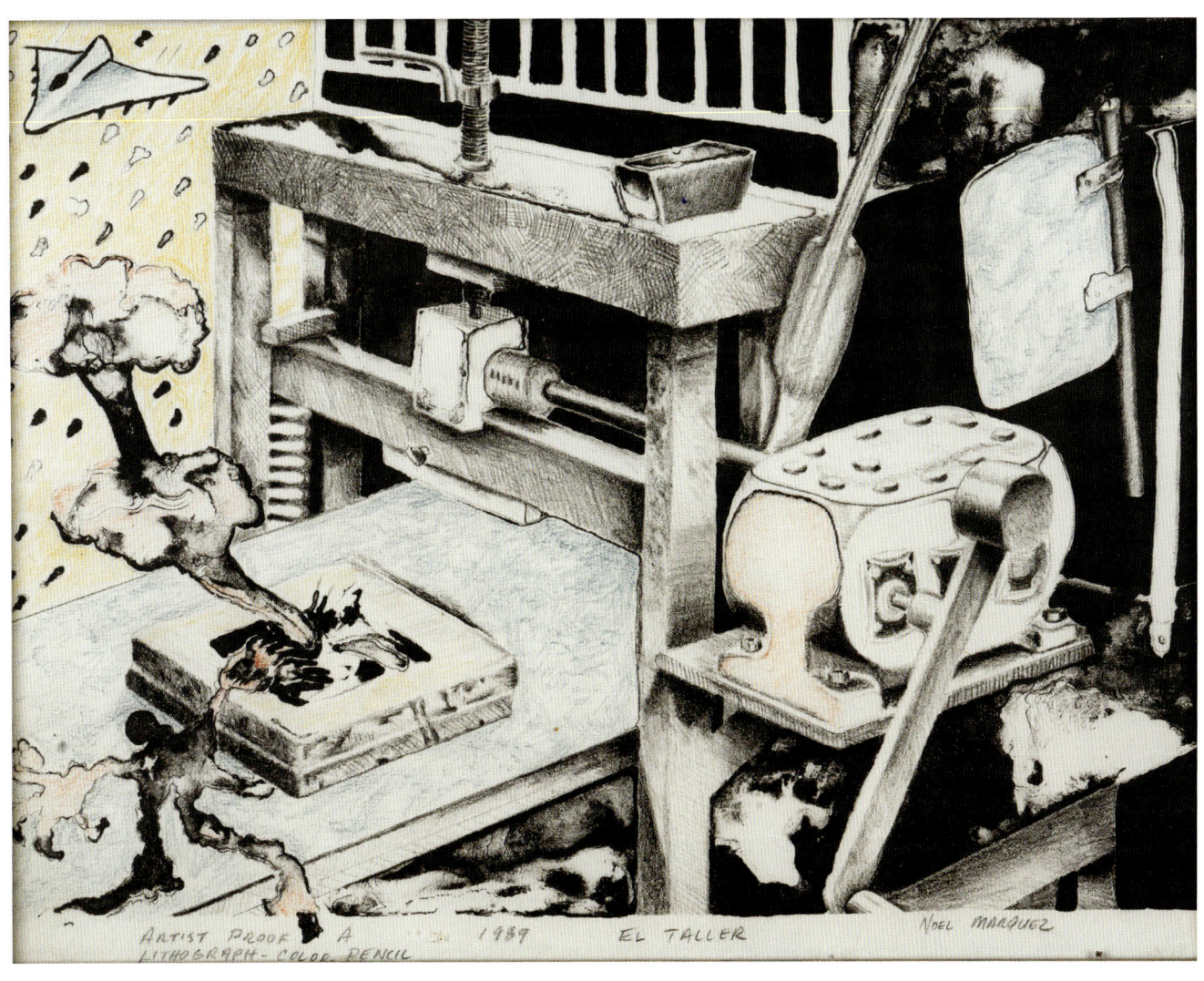

PLATE 63. *El taller*, 1989. Lithograph with color pencil: Artist Proof A, 10″ × 13″.
Collection of the artist.

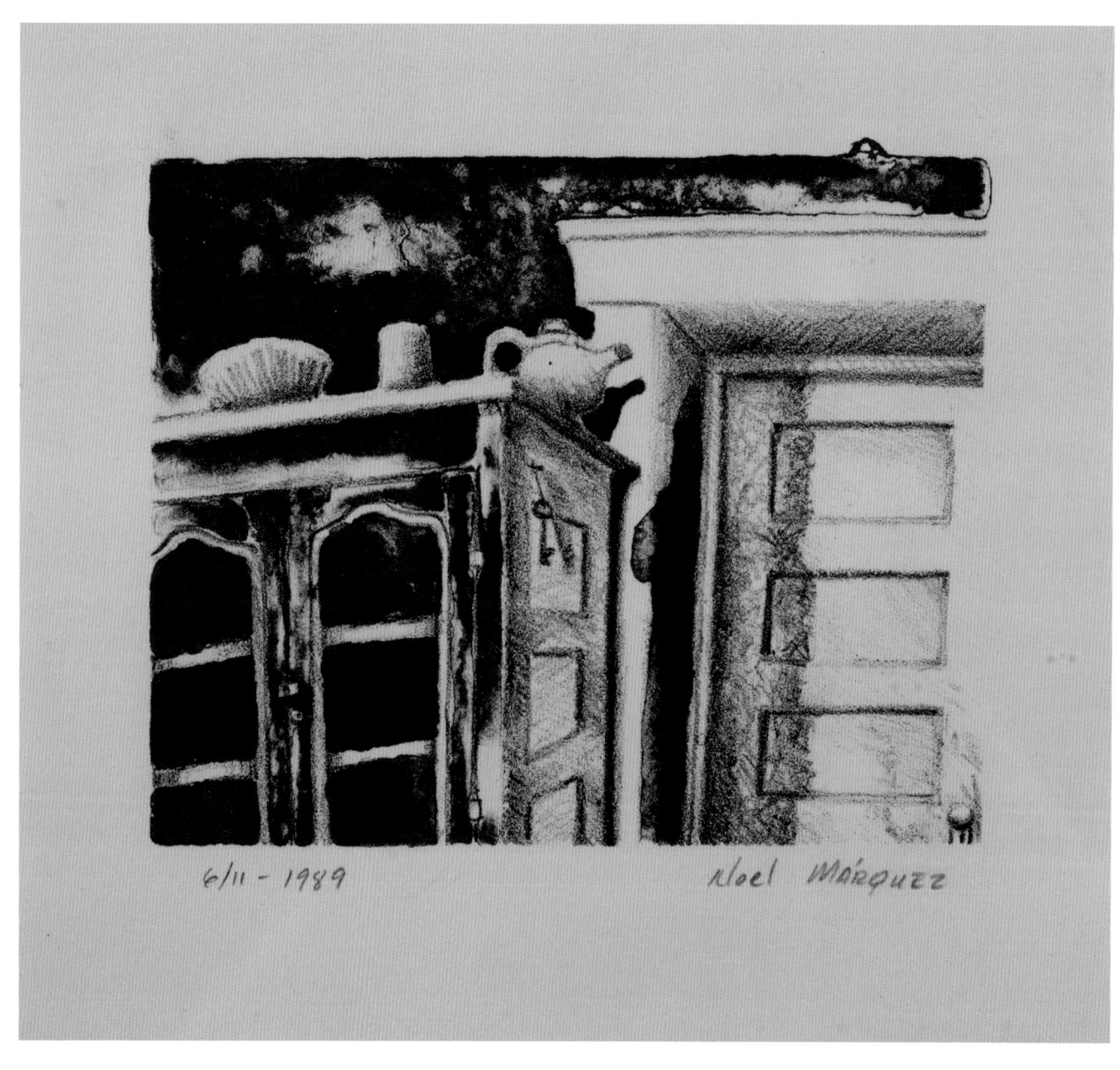

6/11 - 1989   Noel Márquez

PLATE 64. *Interior Scene: The Kitchen*, 1989. Lithograph, edition of 11, 6 ½″ × 7″.
Collection of the artist.

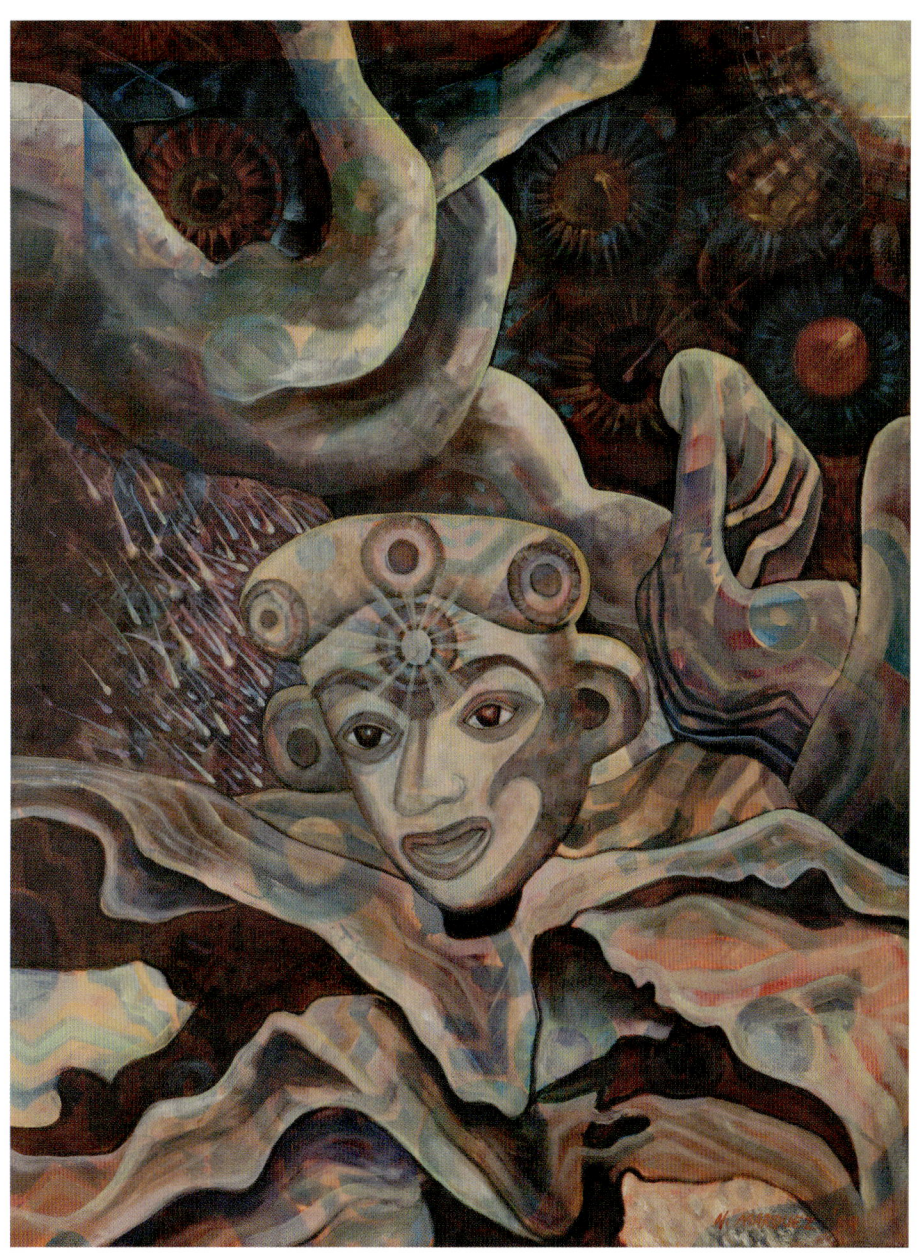

PLATE 65. *Painting III: Mask*, 1989. Oil on canvas, 42″ × 32″. Collection of the artist.

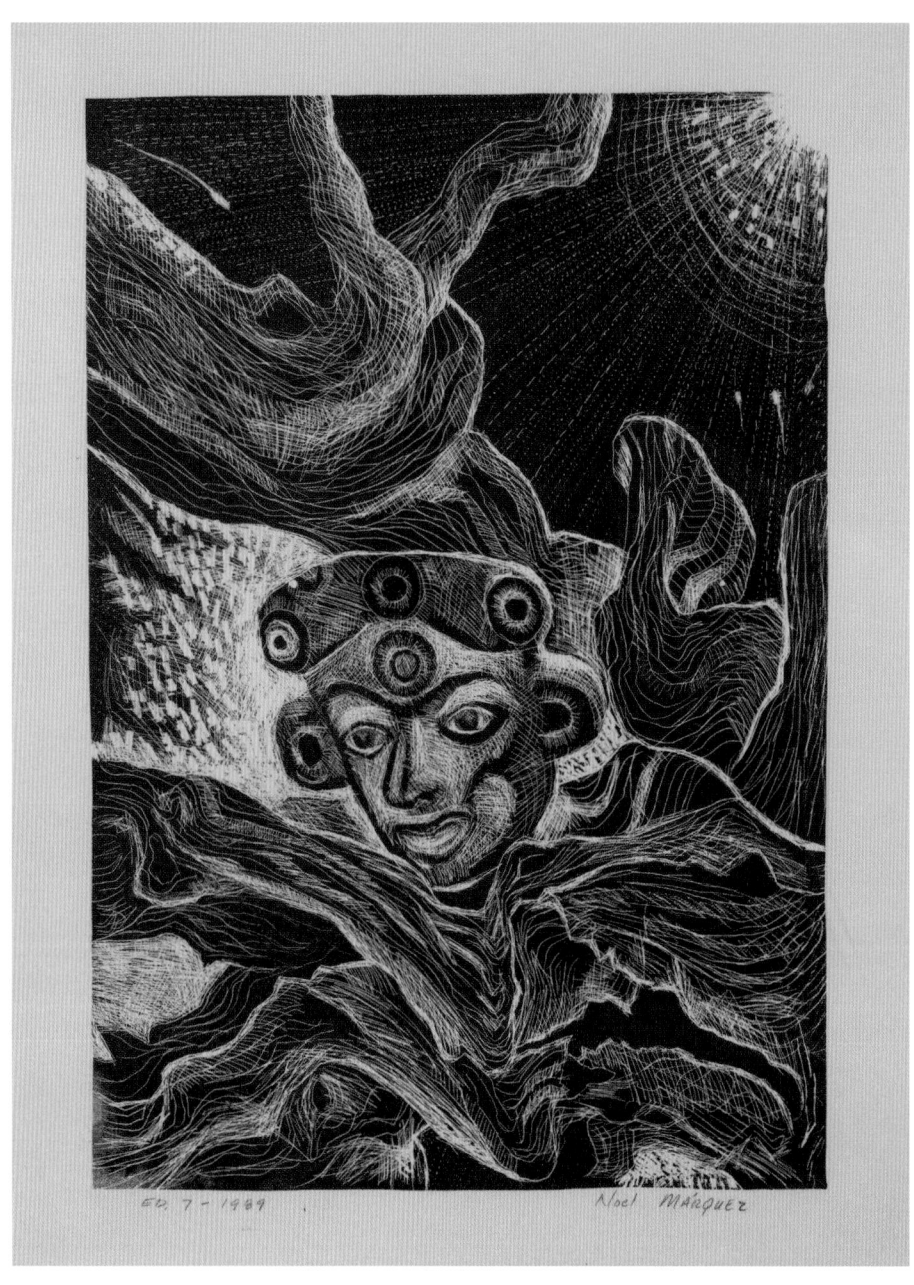

ED. 7 - 1989   Noel MARQUEZ

PLATE 66. *Print Variation: Mask,* 1989. Lithograph, edition of 7, 15″ × 11″. Collection of the artist.

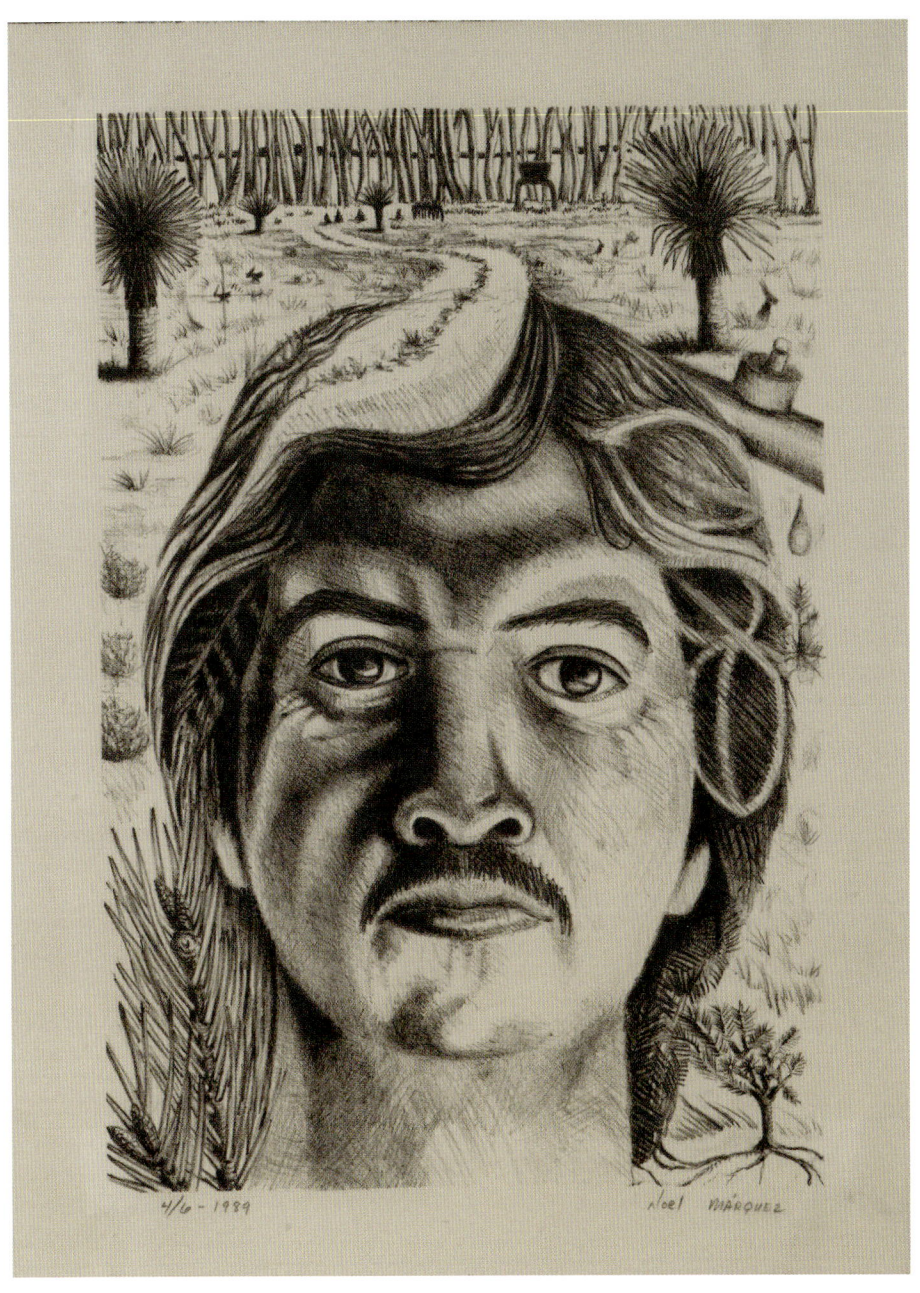

PLATE 67. *Self Portrait*, 1989. Lithograph, 11 ½″ × 15″. Collection of the artist.

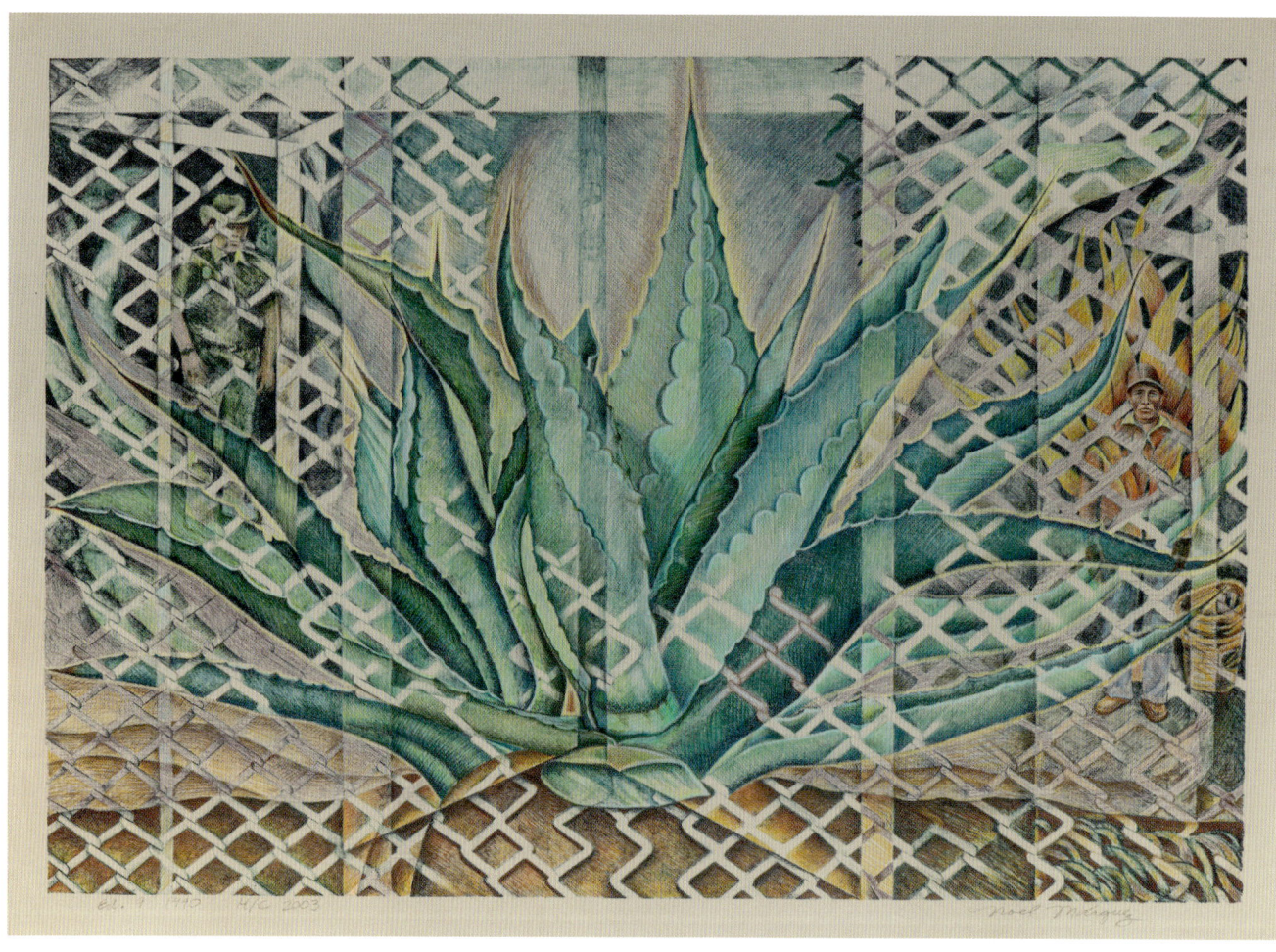

PLATE 68. *Agave: La frontera*, 1990. Lithograph, edition of 9, 30″ × 40″. Collection of the artist.

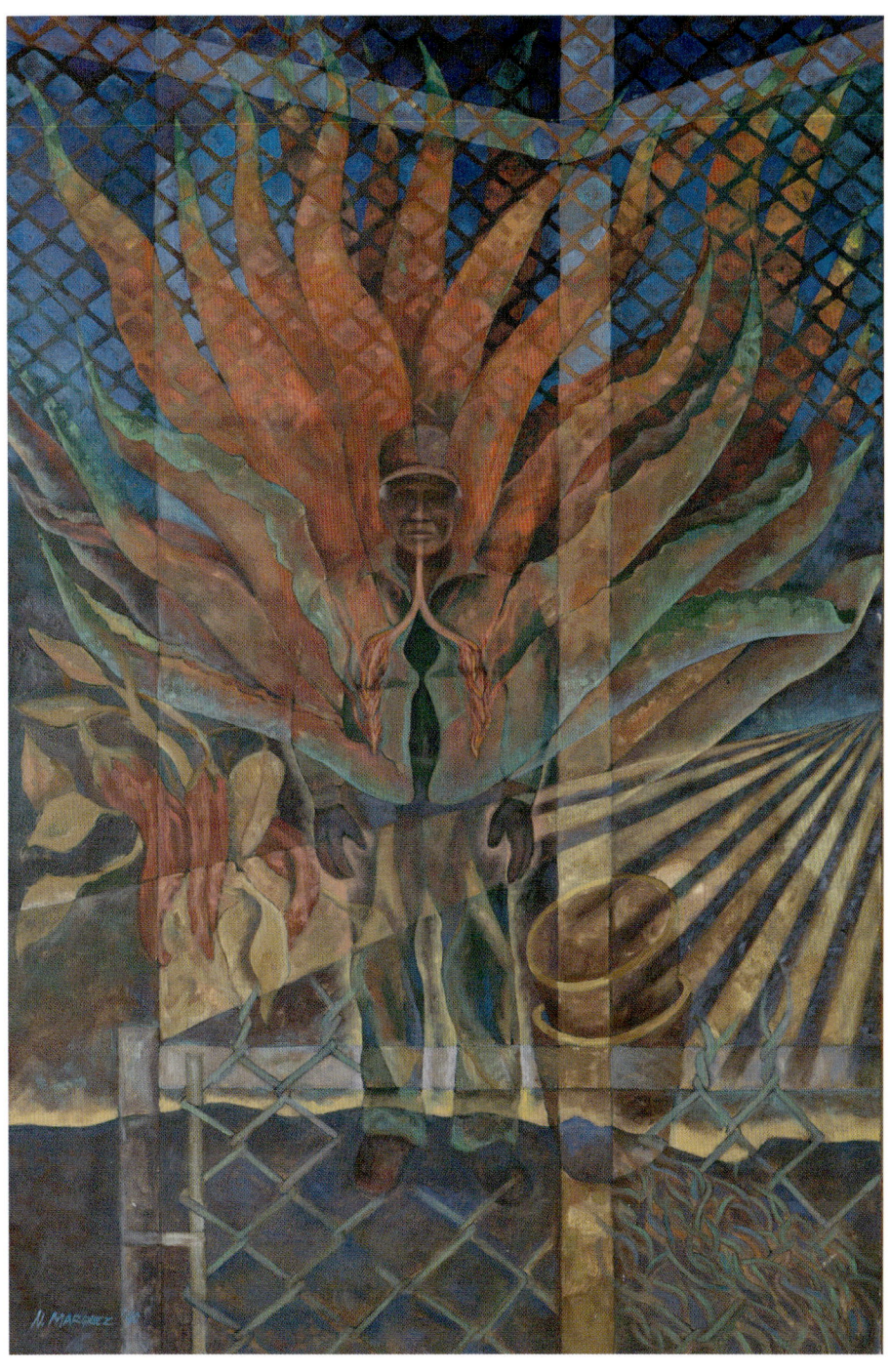

PLATE 69. *Agave #2*, 1990. Oil on canvas, 32″ × 44″. Collection of the artist.

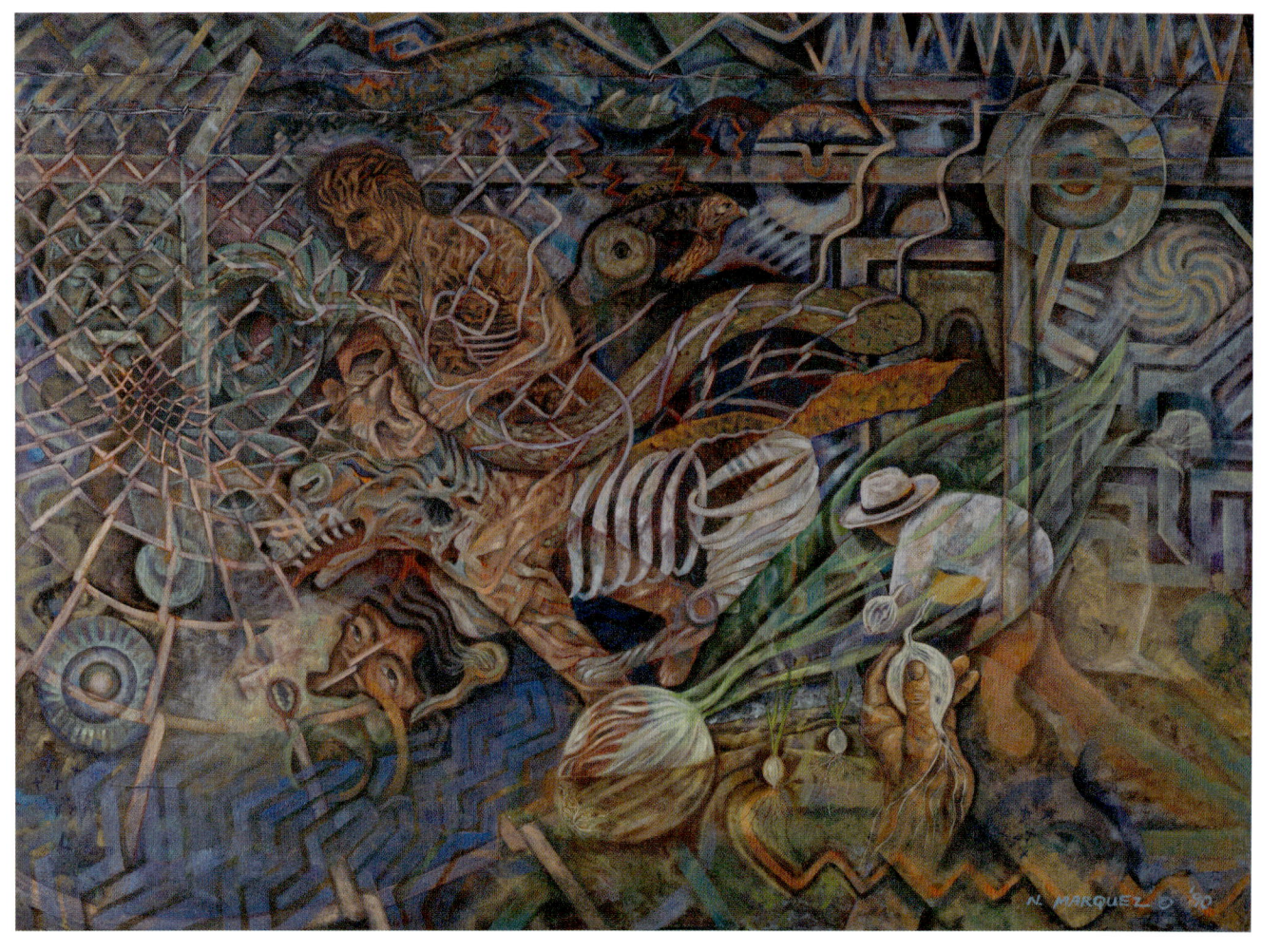

PLATE 70. *Nuestras raíces*, 1990. Oil on canvas, 50″ × 36″. Collection of the artist.

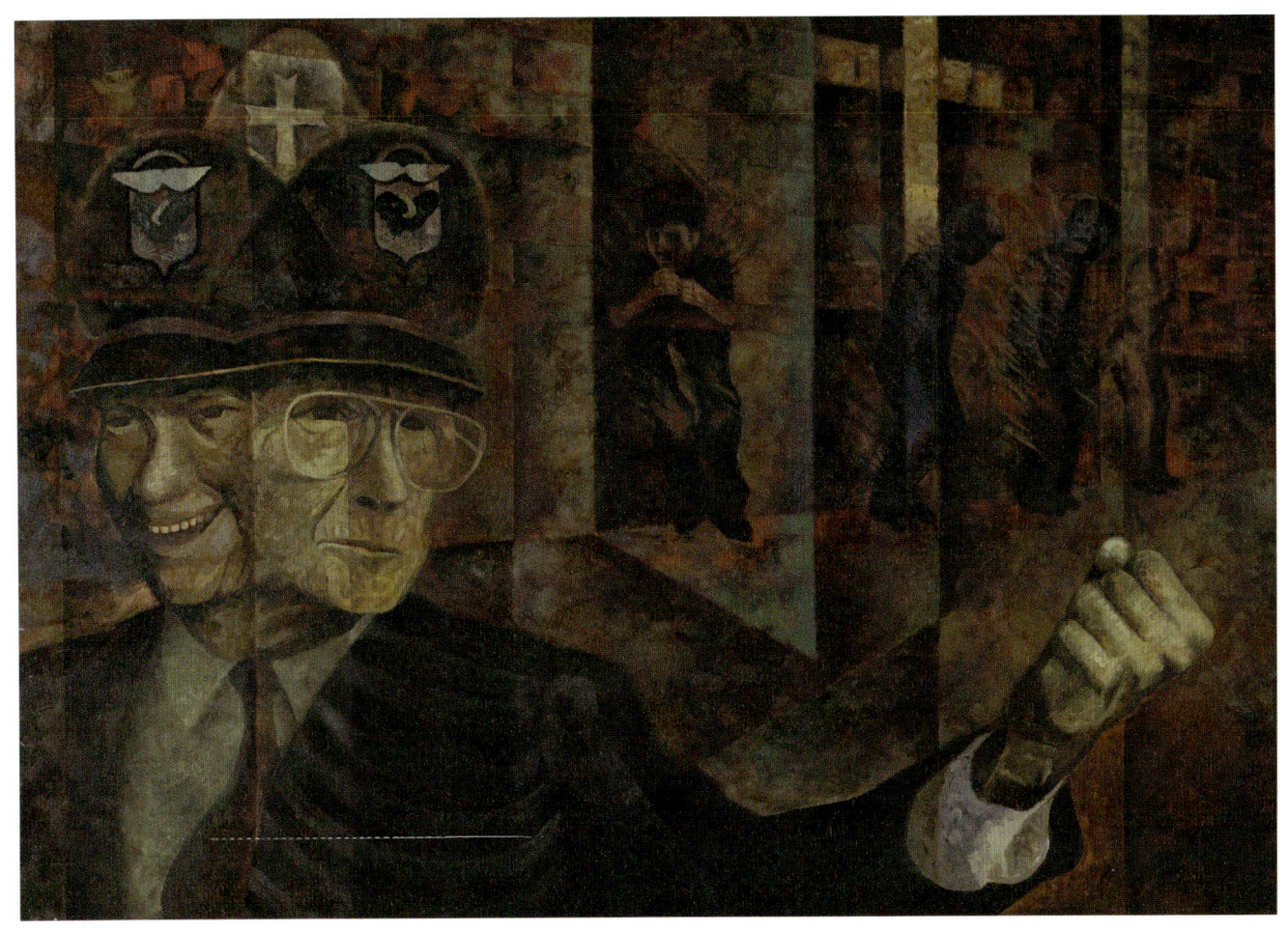

PLATE 71. *War*, 1990. Oil on canvas, 32" × 46". Collection of the artist.

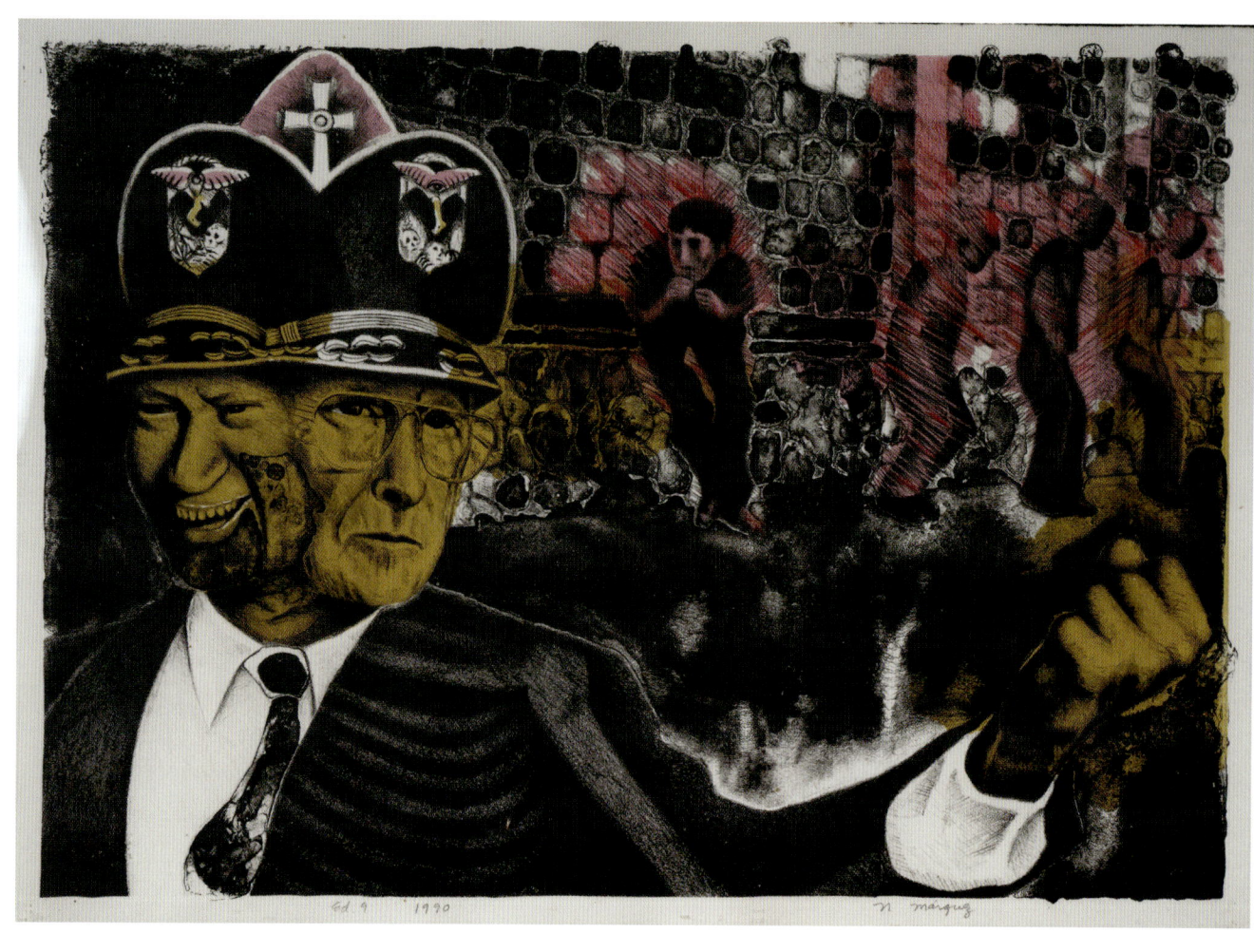

PLATE 72. *Print Variation: War*, 1990. Lithograph, edition of 9, 15″ × 21″. Collection of the artist.

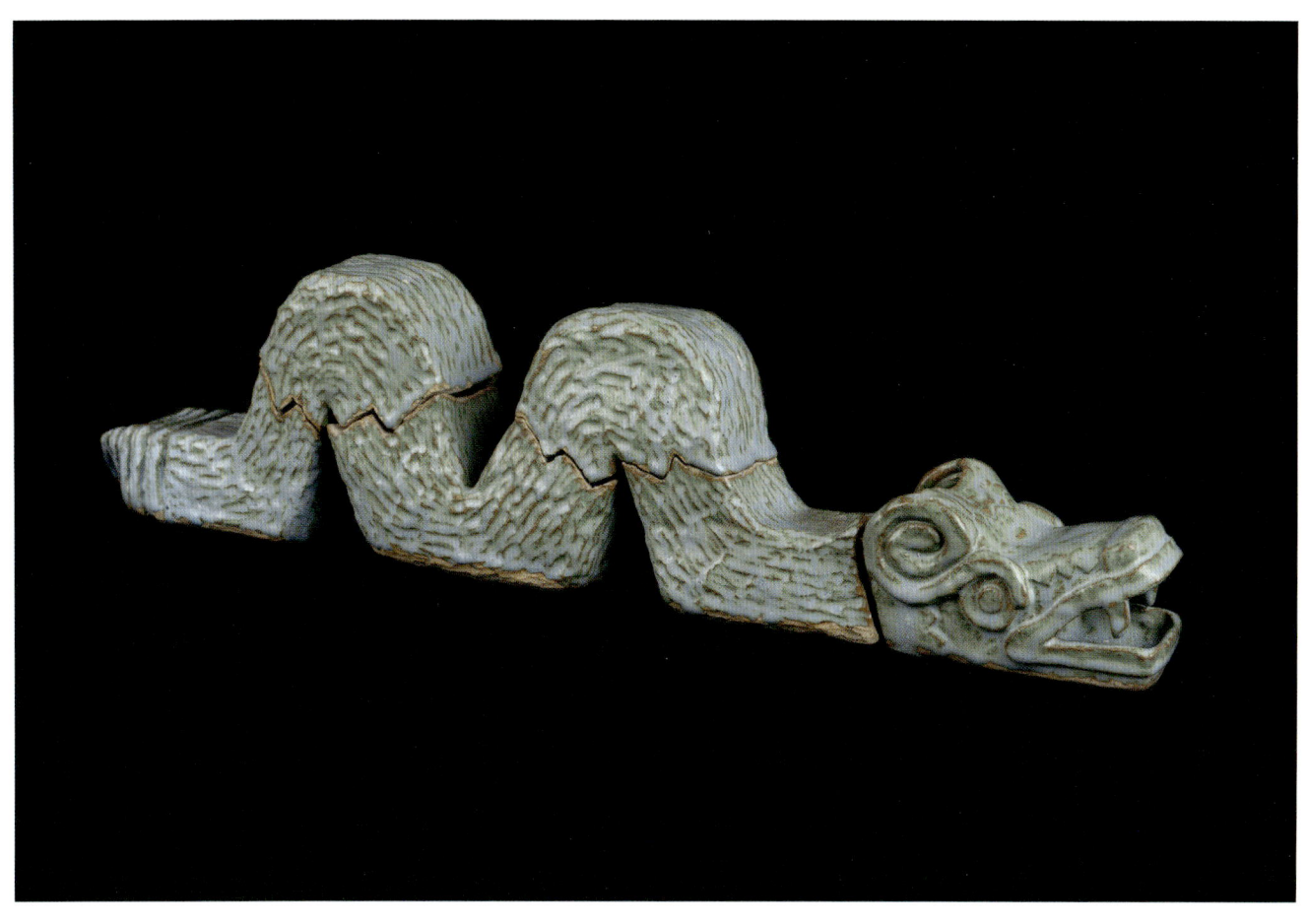

PLATE 73. *Quetzalcoatl*, 1990. Ceramic with colored glaze, 6″ × 27″ × 3″. Collection of the artist.

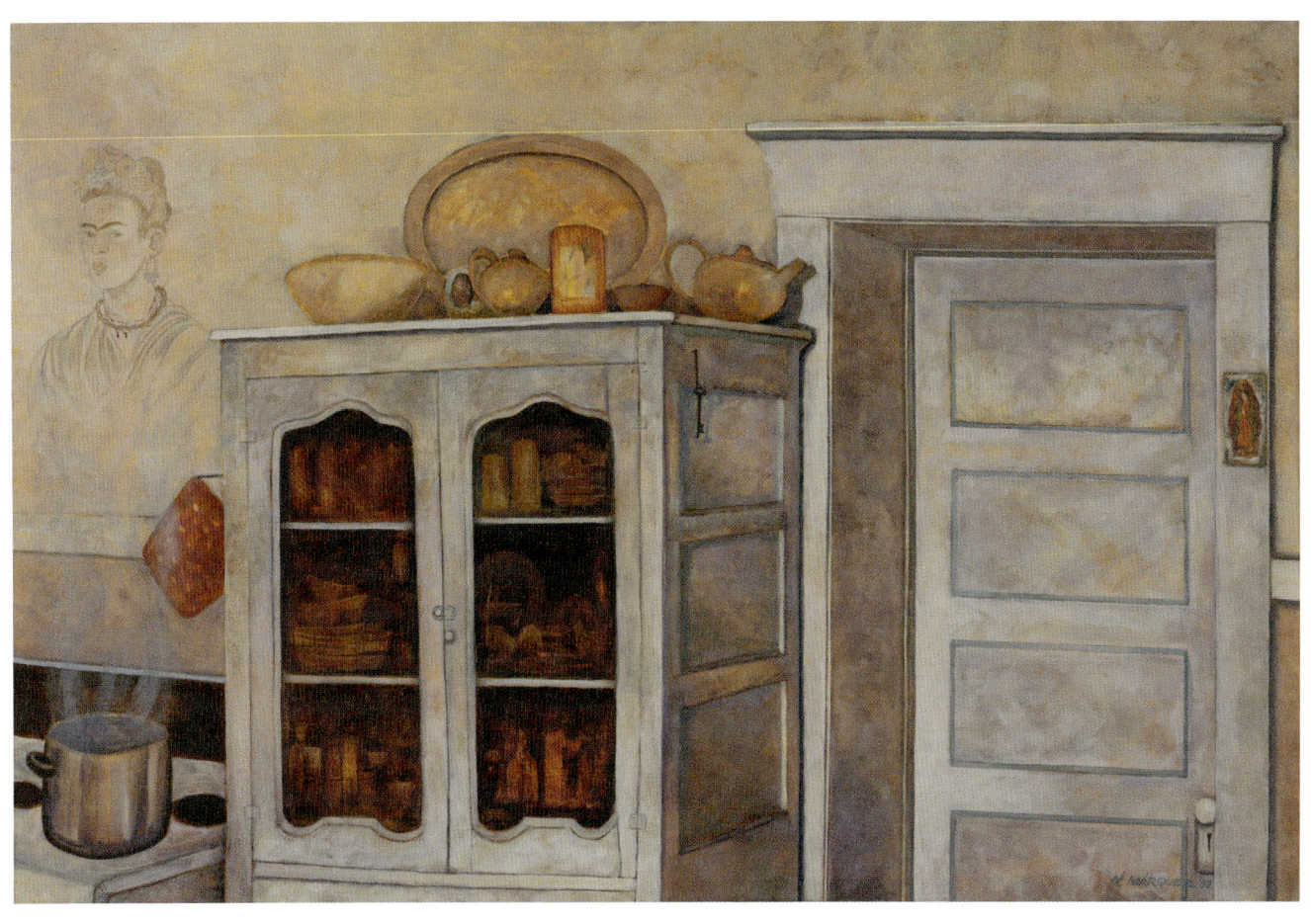

PLATE 74. *Painting III: Kitchen Interior*, 1992. Oil on canvas, 24″ × 36″. Collection of the artist.

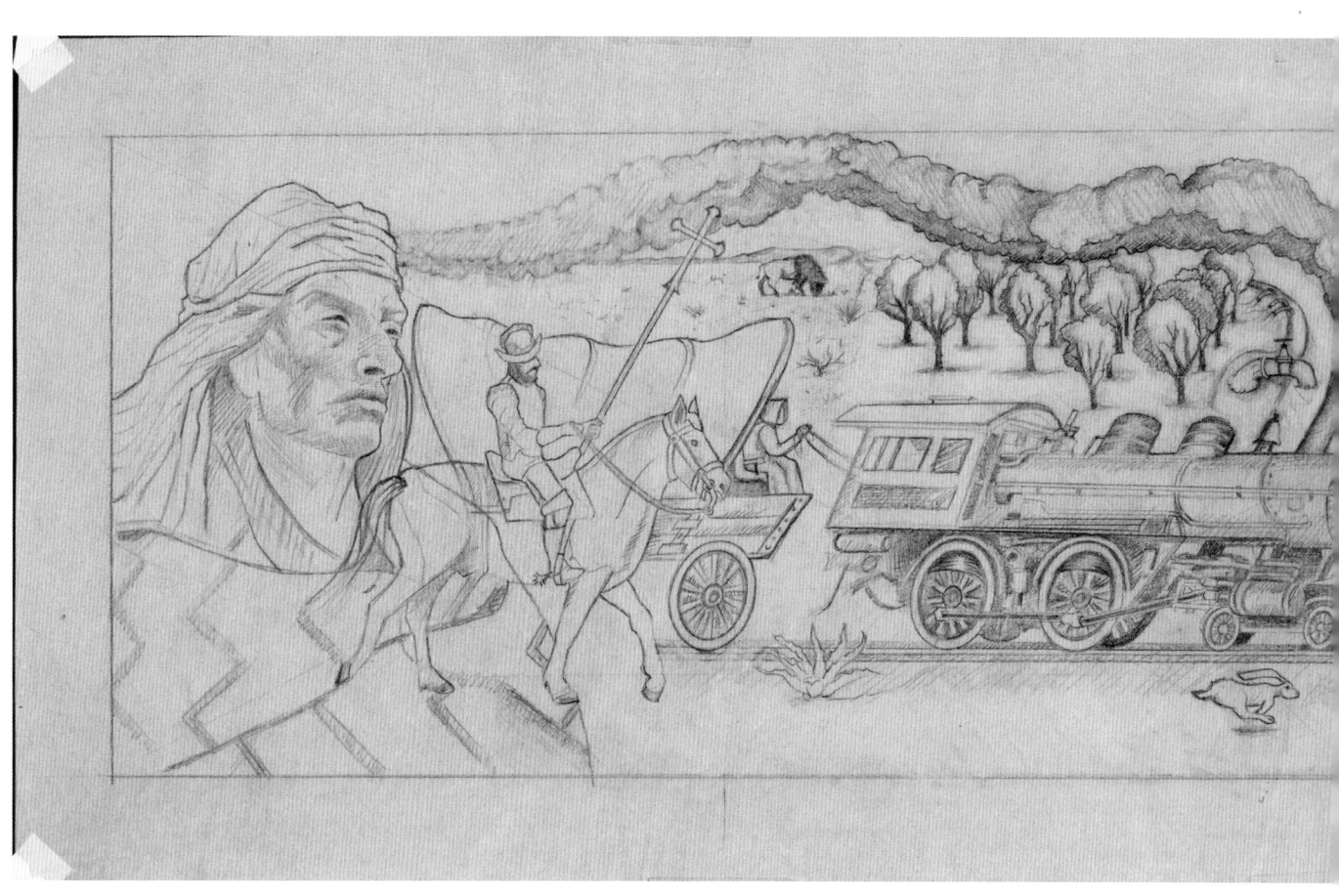

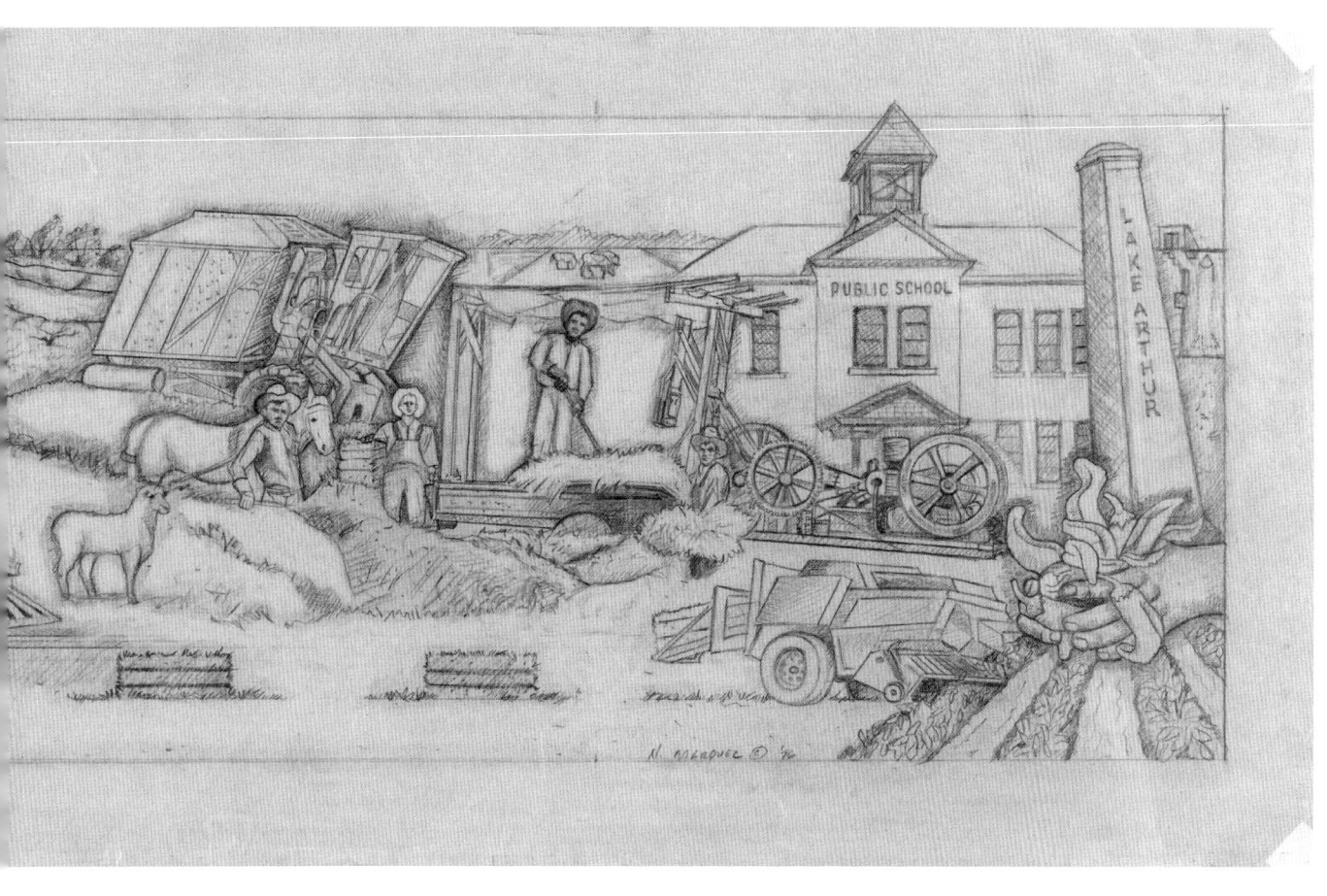

PLATE 75. *Mural Proposal: Lake Arthur,* 1996. Graphite on paper, 10″ × 34″. Collection
of the artist.

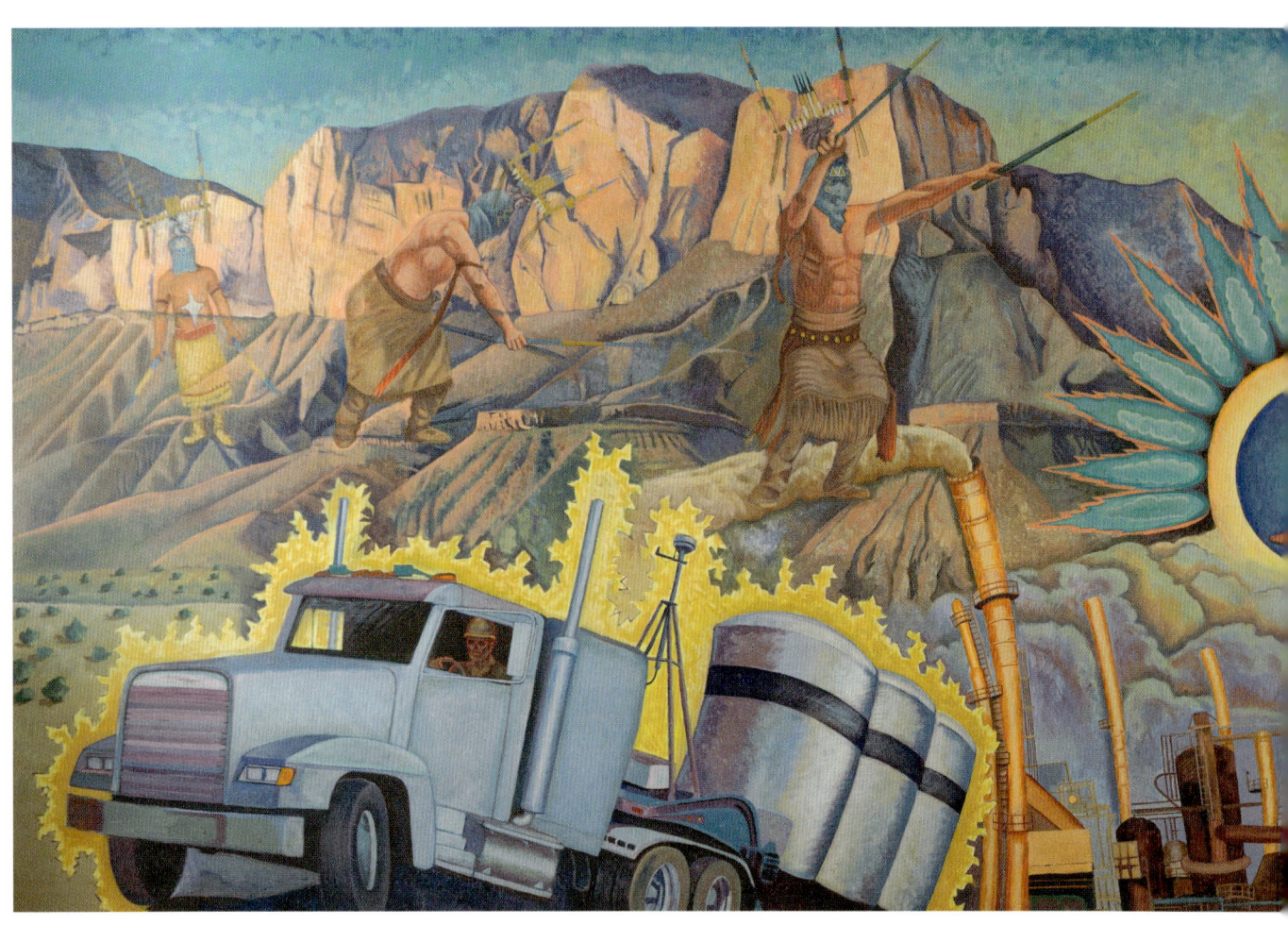

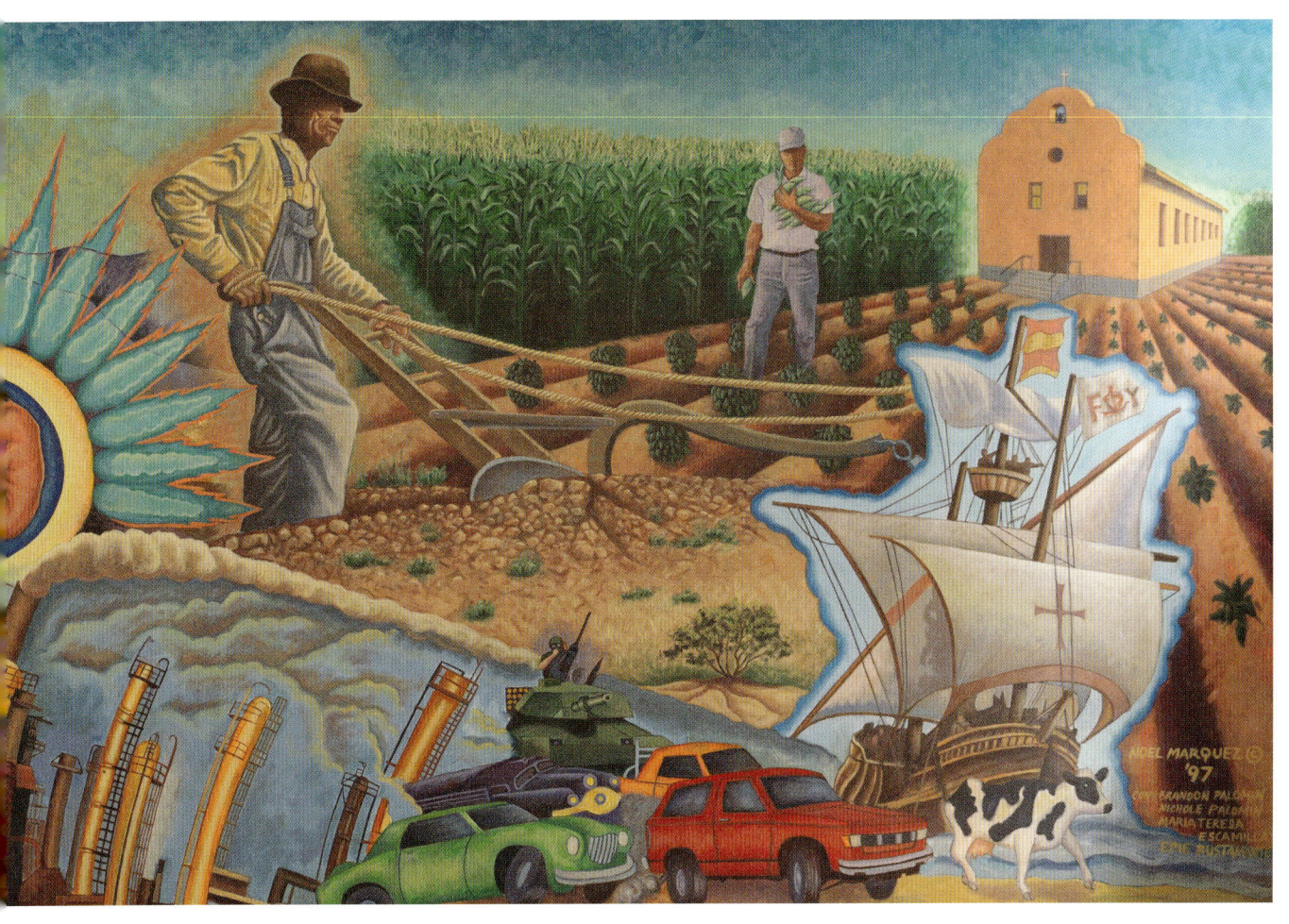

PLATE 76. *La Tierra,* 1997. Acrylic on canvas, 76″ × 19′. Collection of the artist.

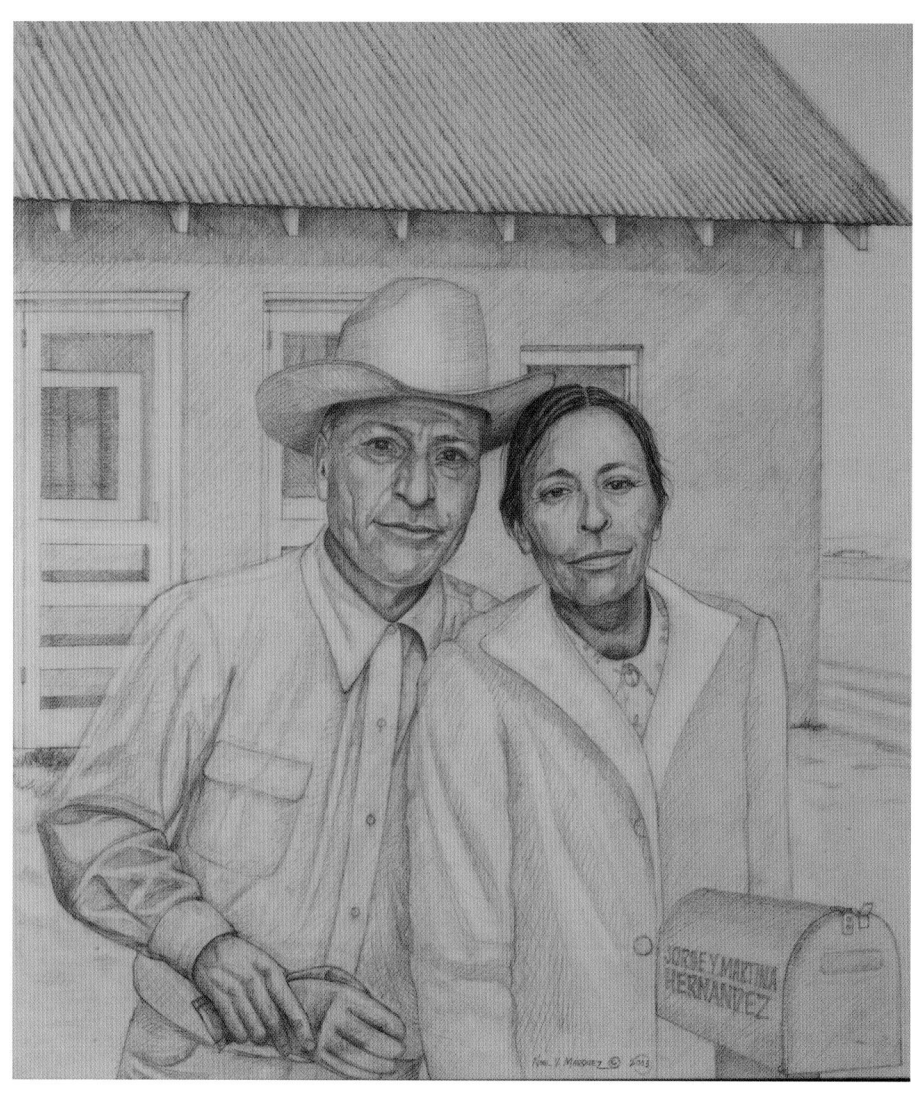

PLATE 77. *Jorge y Martina Hernández*, 2003. Graphite on paper, 36″ × 32 ½″.
Collection of the artist.

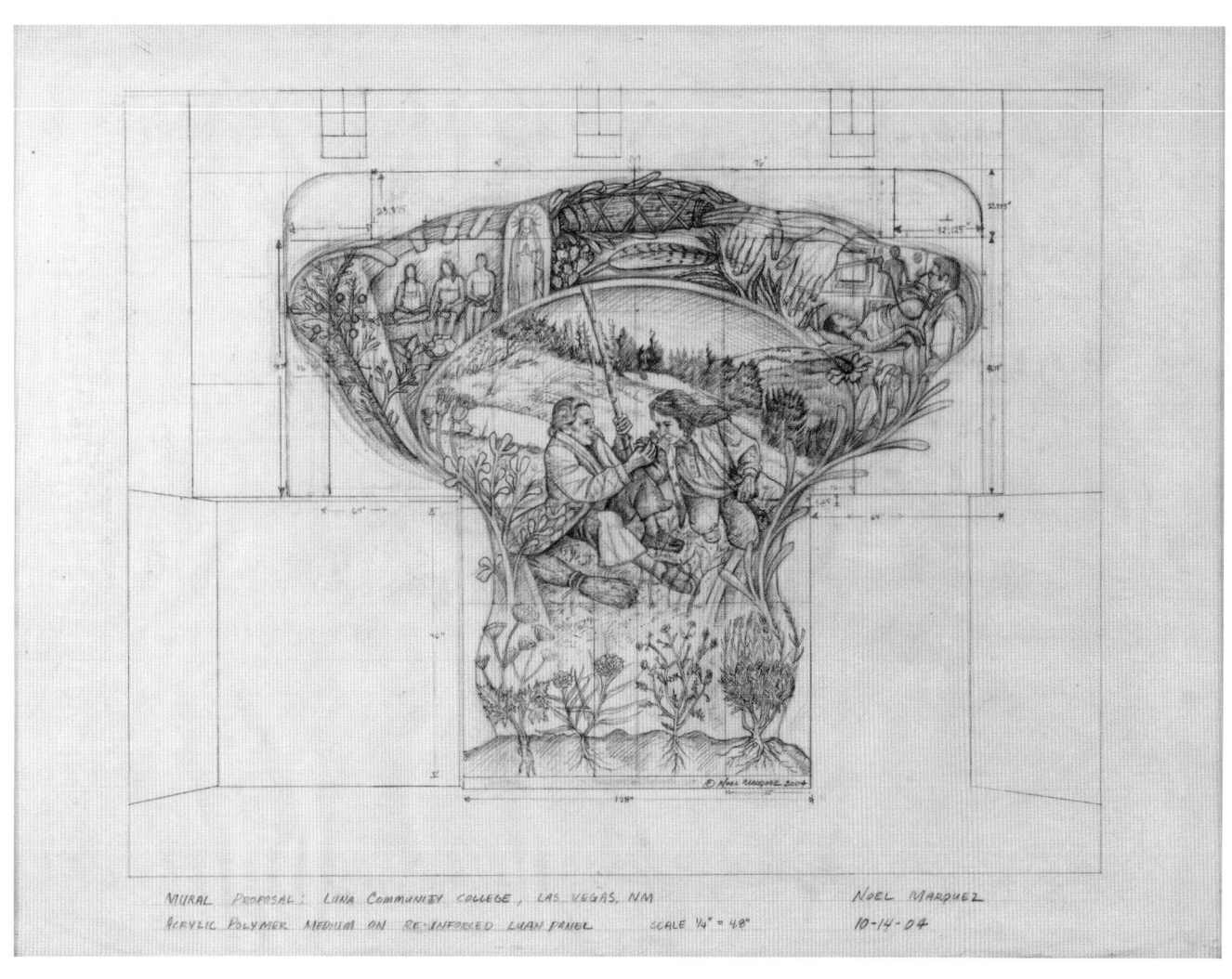

PLATE 78. *Mural Proposal: Luna Community College, Las Vegas, New Mexico*, 2004.
Graphite on paper, 20″ × 27″. Collection of the artist.

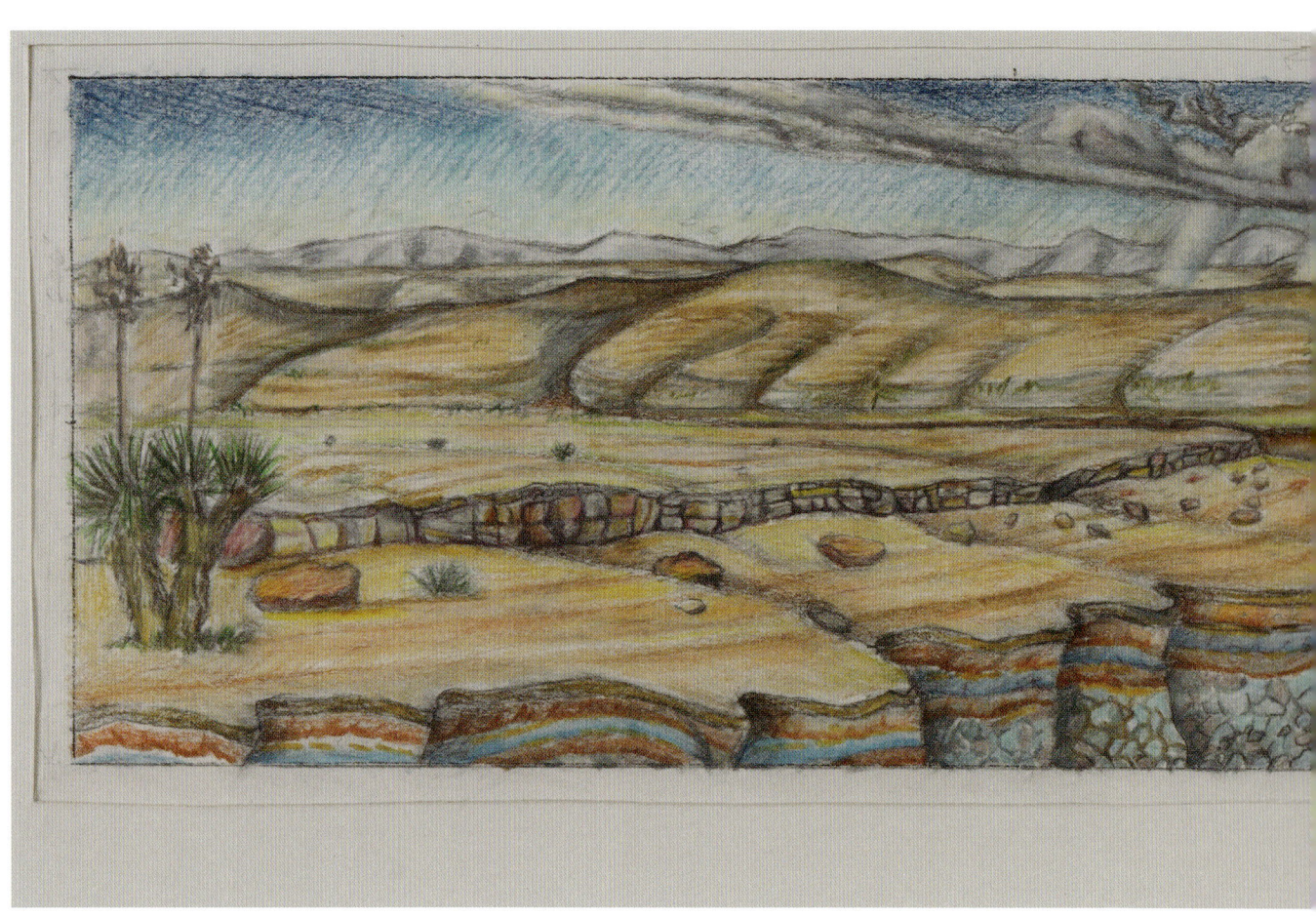

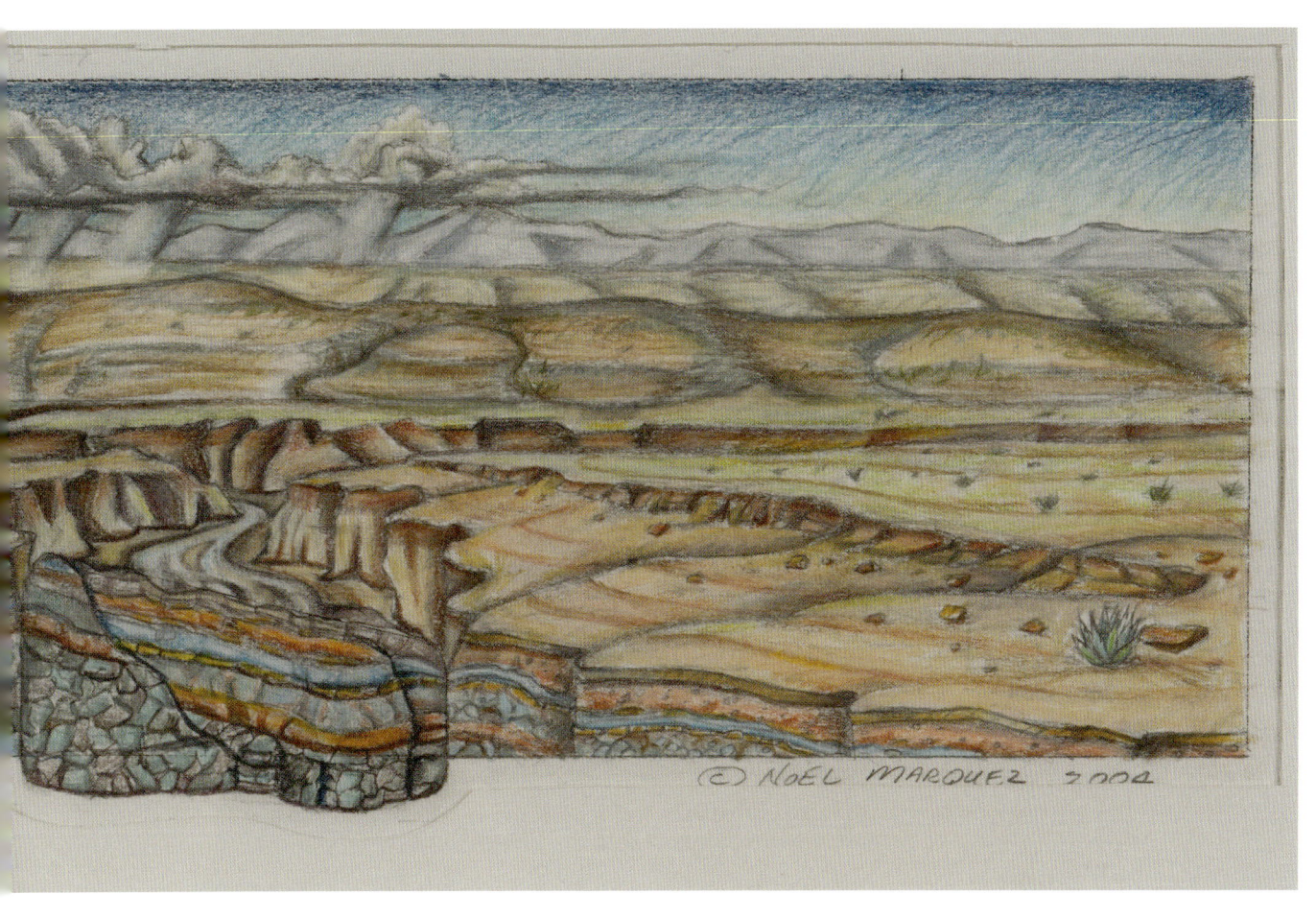

PLATE 79. *Mural Study: Landscape*, 2004. Graphite and color pencil, 4″ × 16 ½″.
   Collection of the artist.

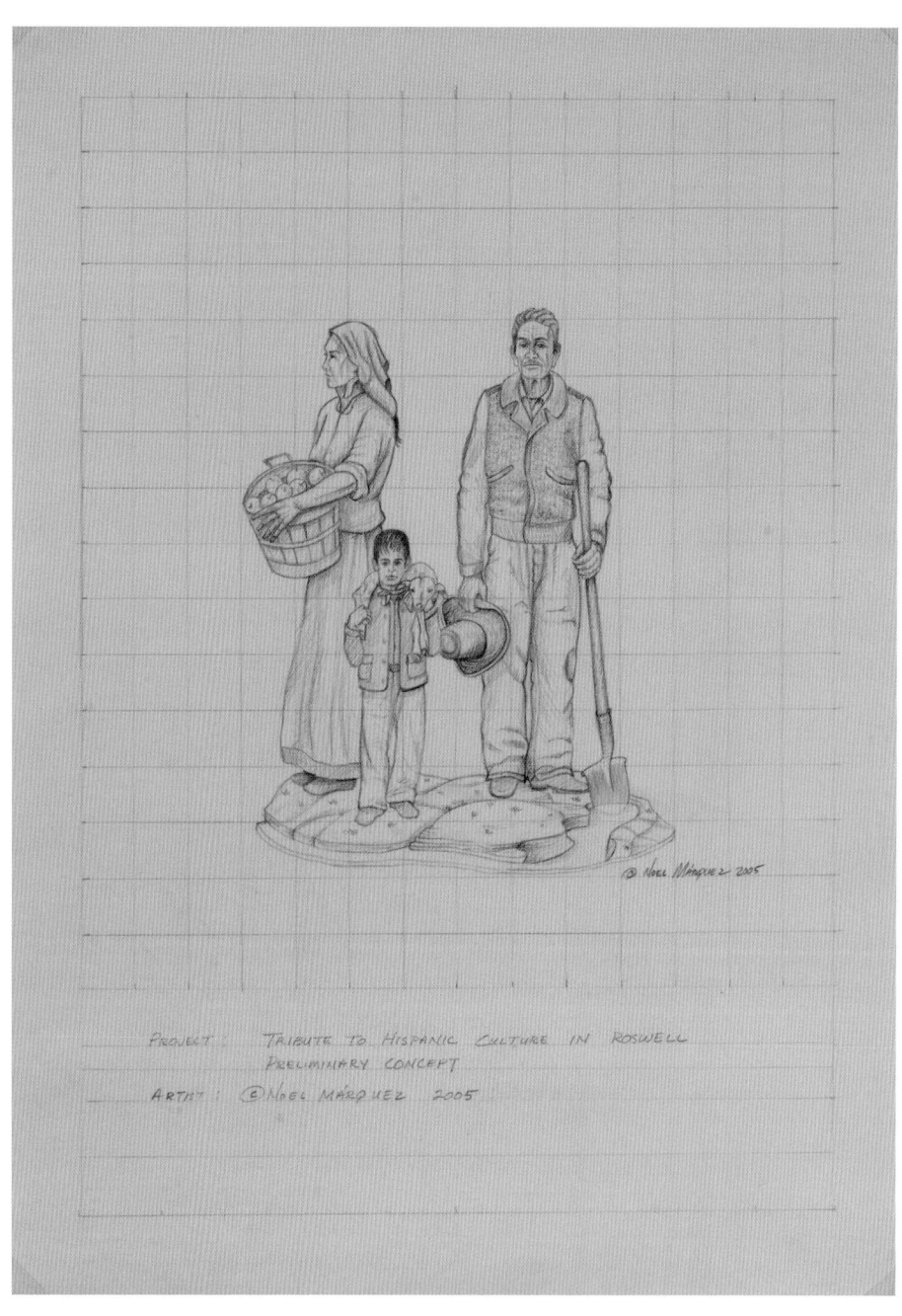

PLATE 80. *Tribute to Hispanic Culture in Roswell: Preliminary Concept*, 2005. Graphite on art board, 25″ × 18″. Collection of the artist.

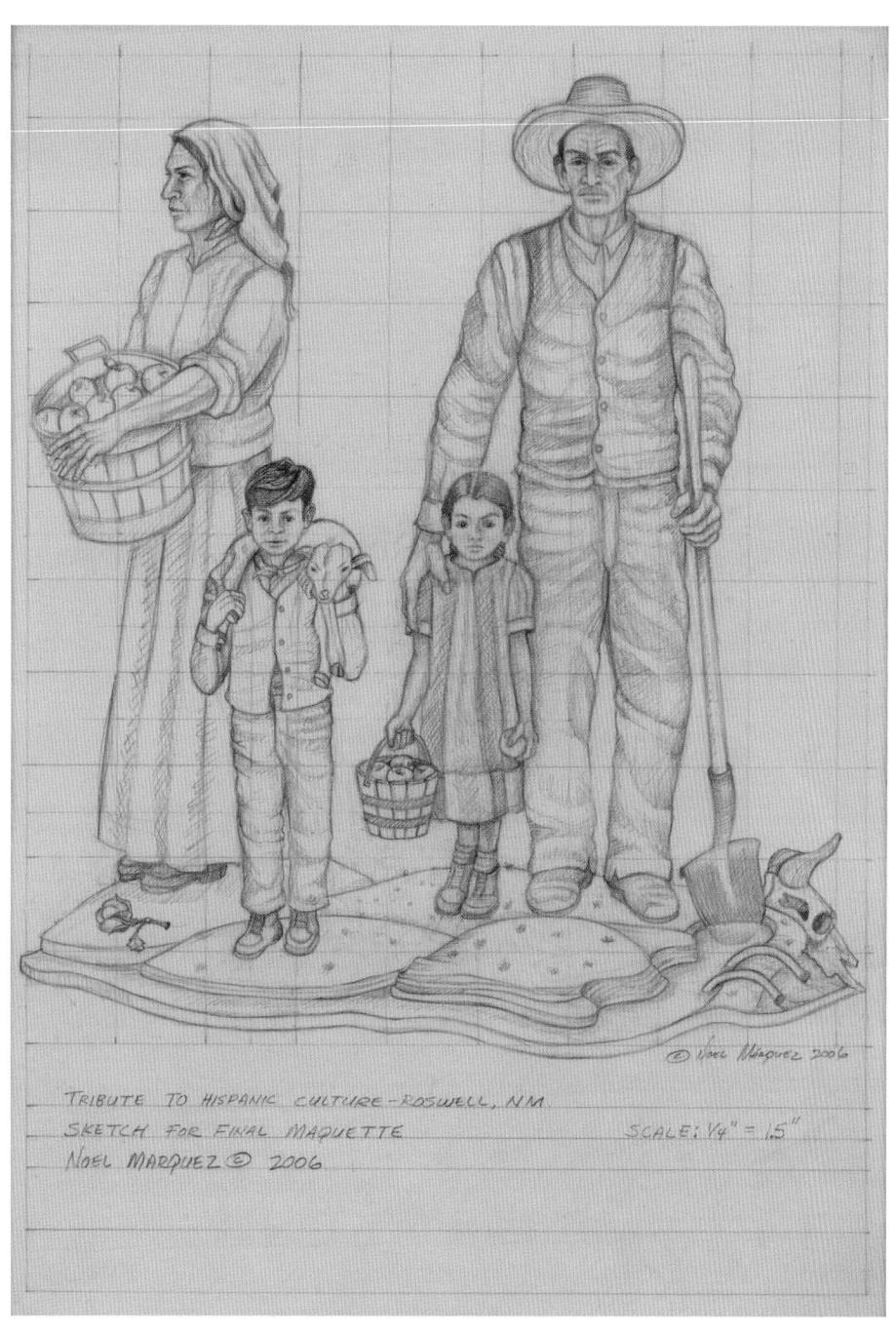

PLATE 81. *Sketch for Final Maquette: Tribute to Hispanic Culture*, 2006. Graphite on
paper, 21 ½″ × 15″. Collection of the artist.

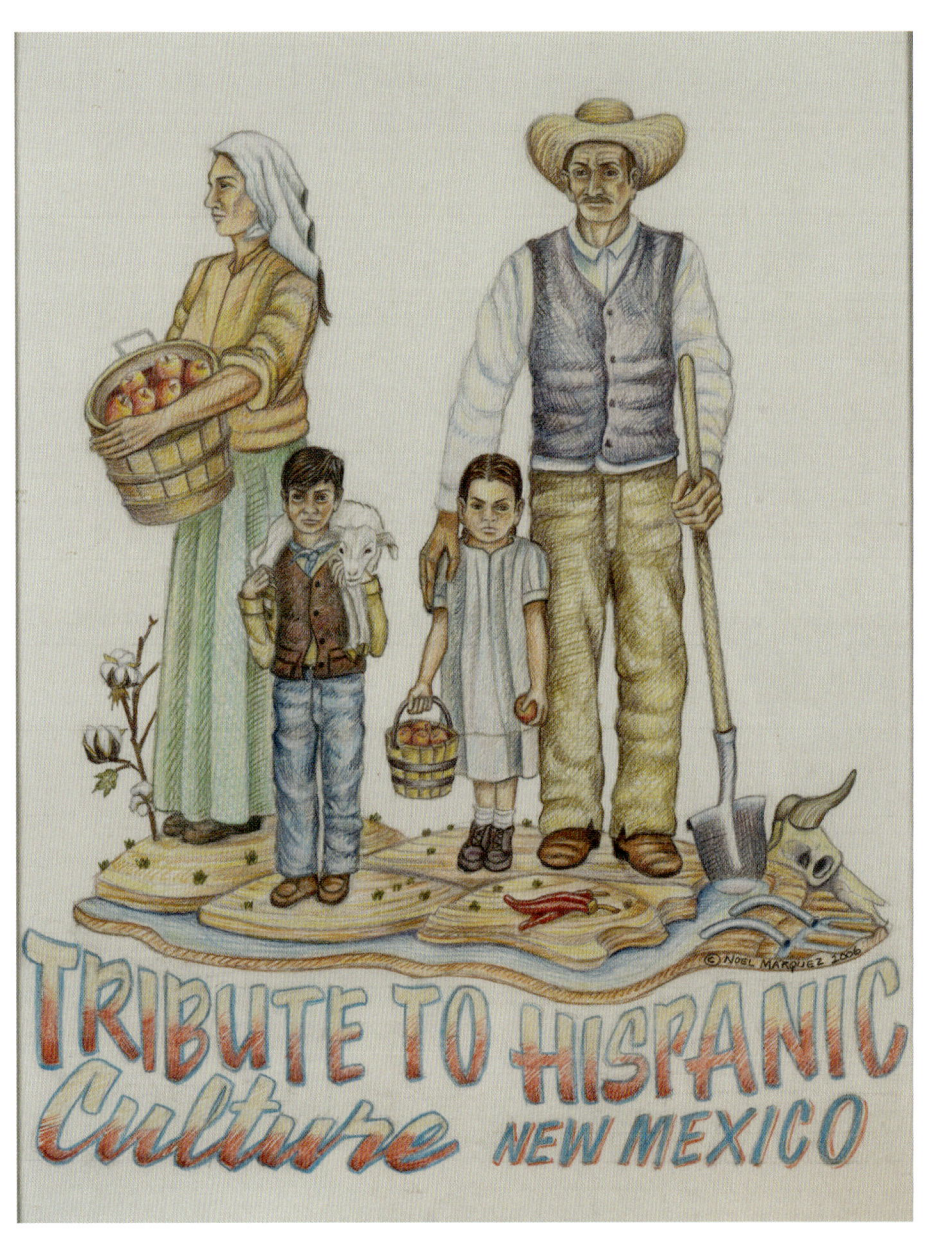

PLATE 82. *Tribute to Hispanic Culture, New Mexico*, 2006. Graphite and color pencil on art board, 18″ × 14″. Collection of the artist.

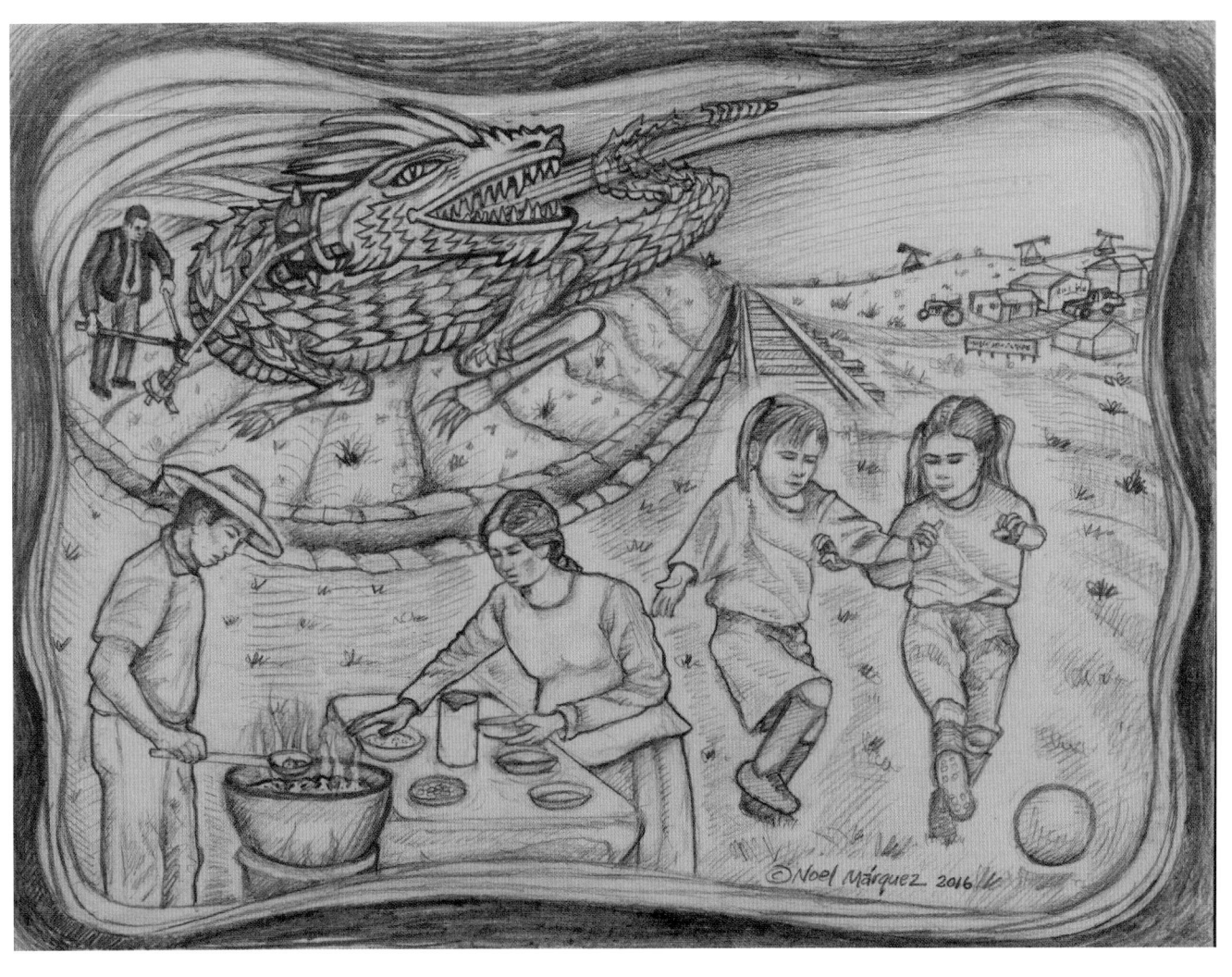

PLATE 83. *Smoking Dragon: The Refinery*, 2016. Graphite on paper, 9″ × 12″.
Collection of the artist.

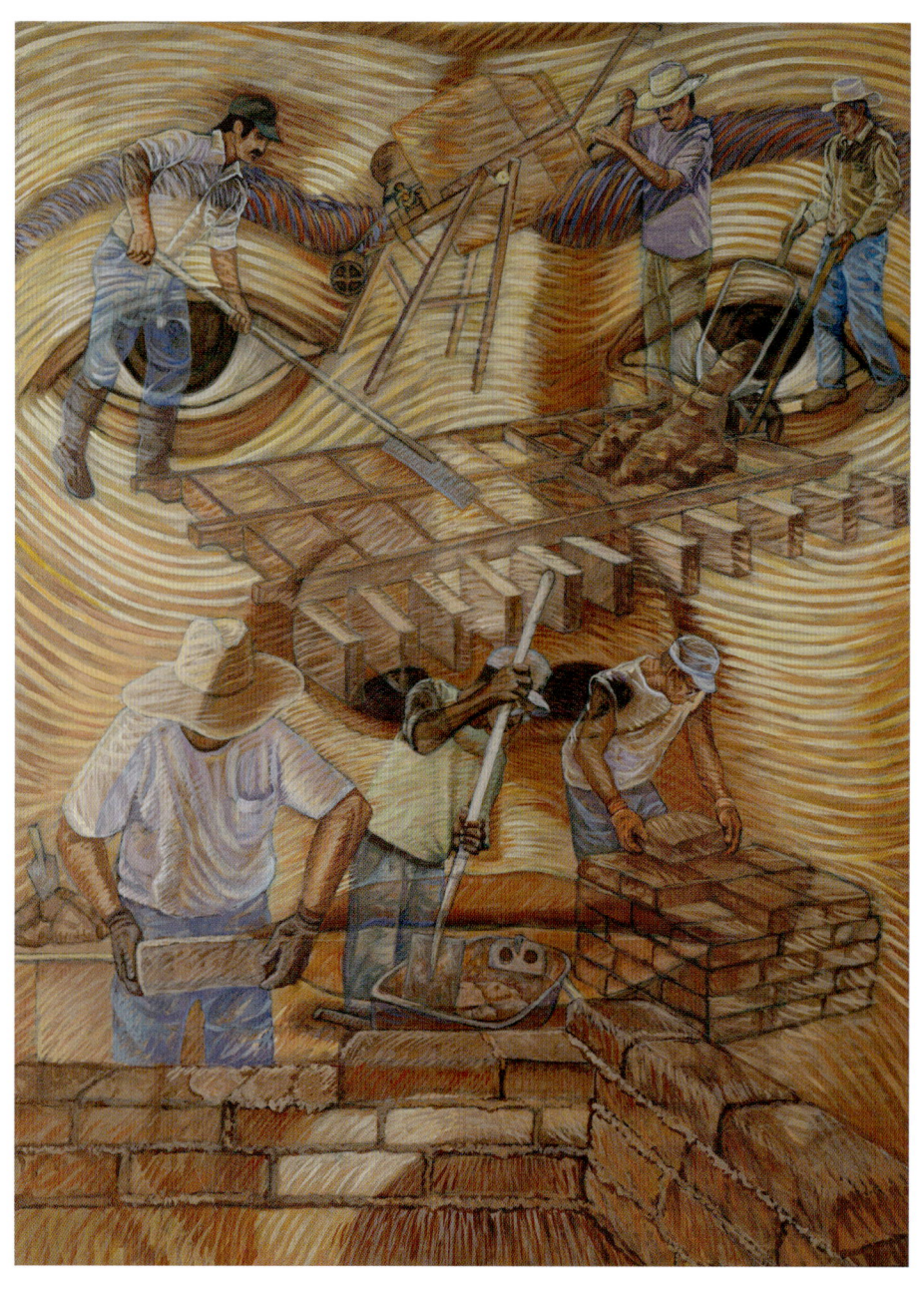

PLATE 84. *Rivera*, 2020. Oil on canvas, 32″ × 42 ⅜″. Collection of the artist.

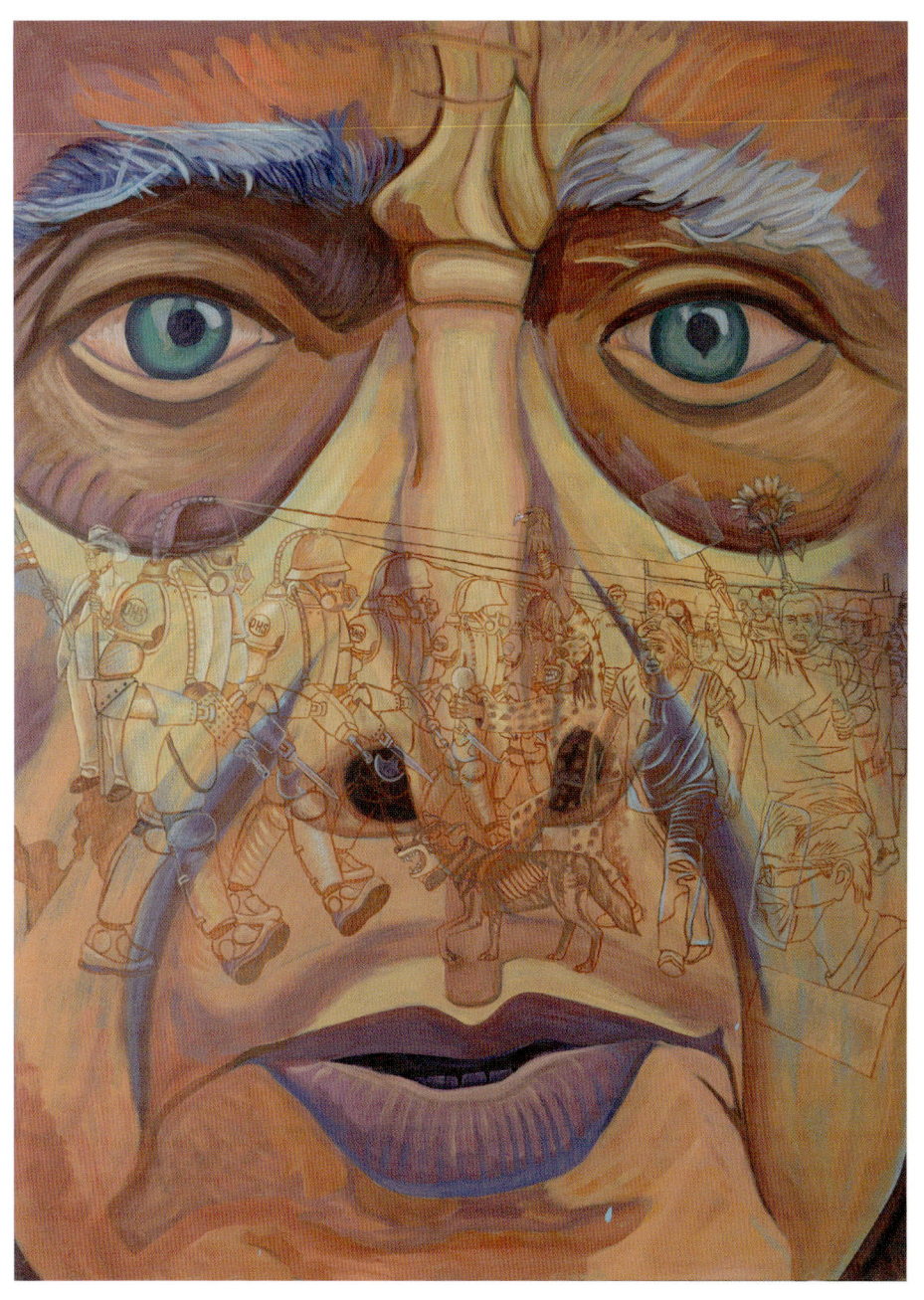

PLATE 85. *Siqueiros*, 2020. Oil on canvas, 32″ × 42 ⅜″. Collection of the artist.

ROBERTA MÁRQUEZ
(Born 1949, Tucumcari, NM; current
residence, Albuquerque, NM)

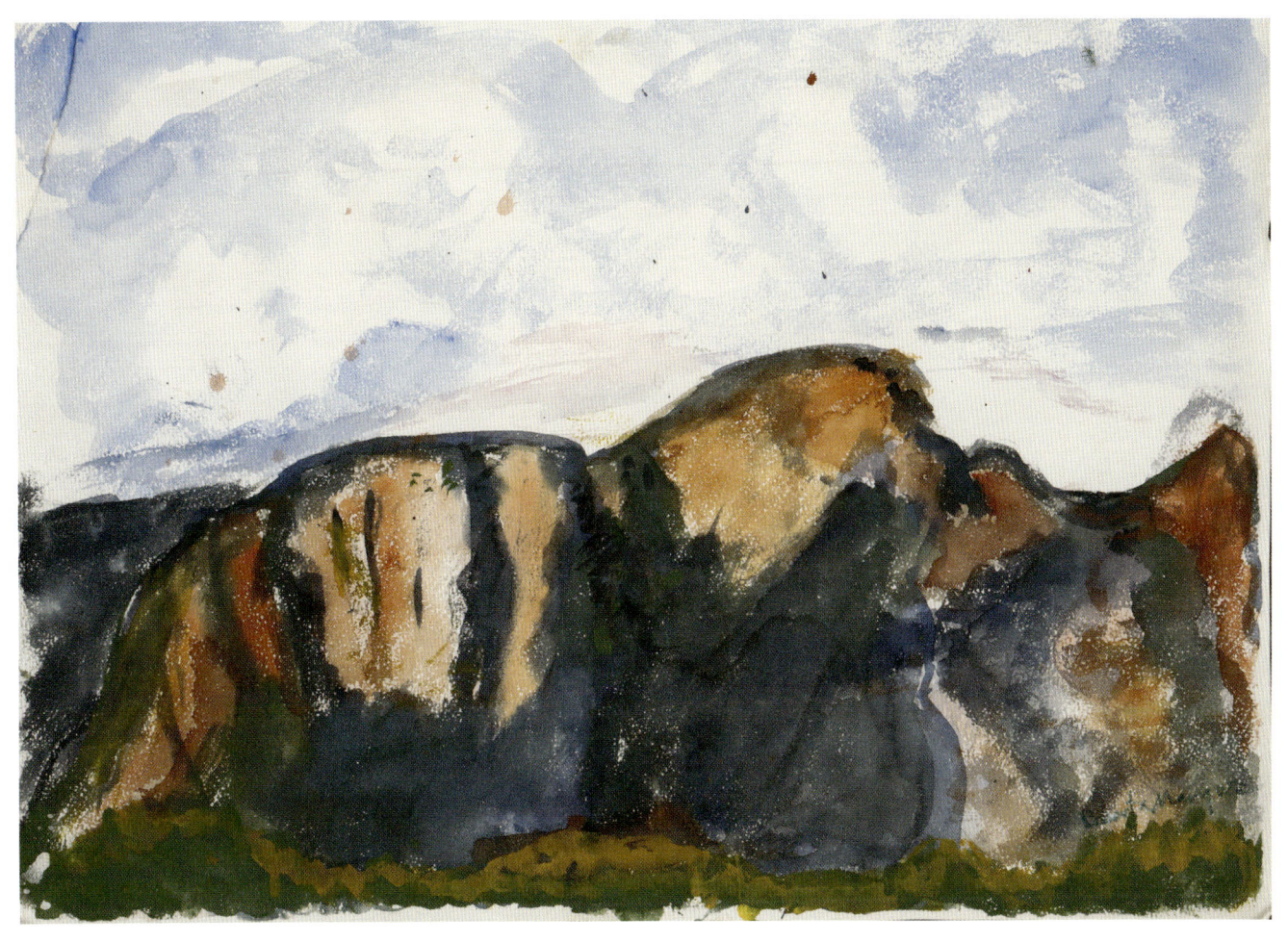

PLATE 86. *Hermit's Peak 1*, 1970. Watercolor on paper, 20″ × 14″. Collection of
the artist.

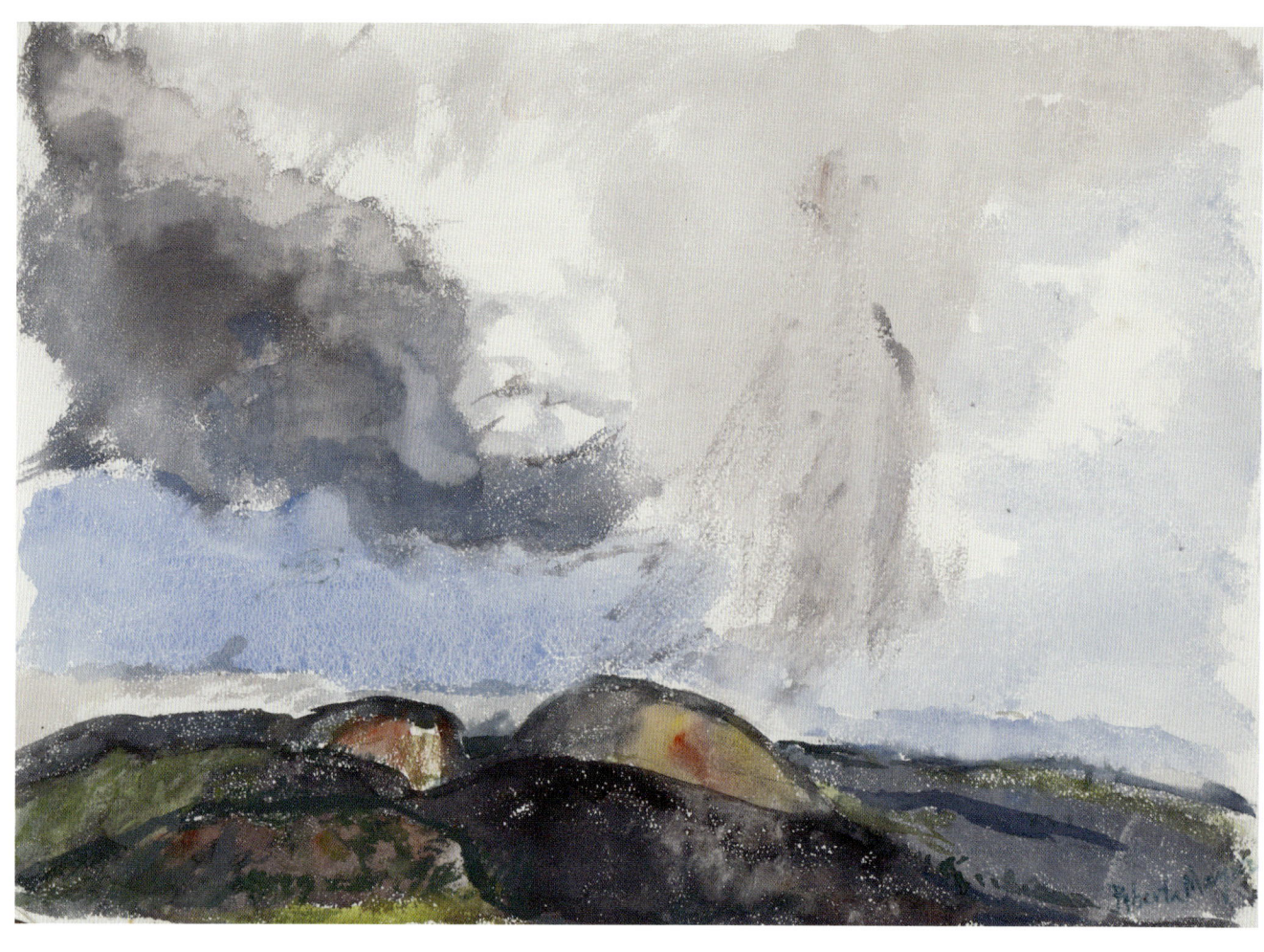

PLATE 87. *Hermit's Peak 2,* 1972. Watercolor on paper, 20″ × 14″. Collection of the artist.

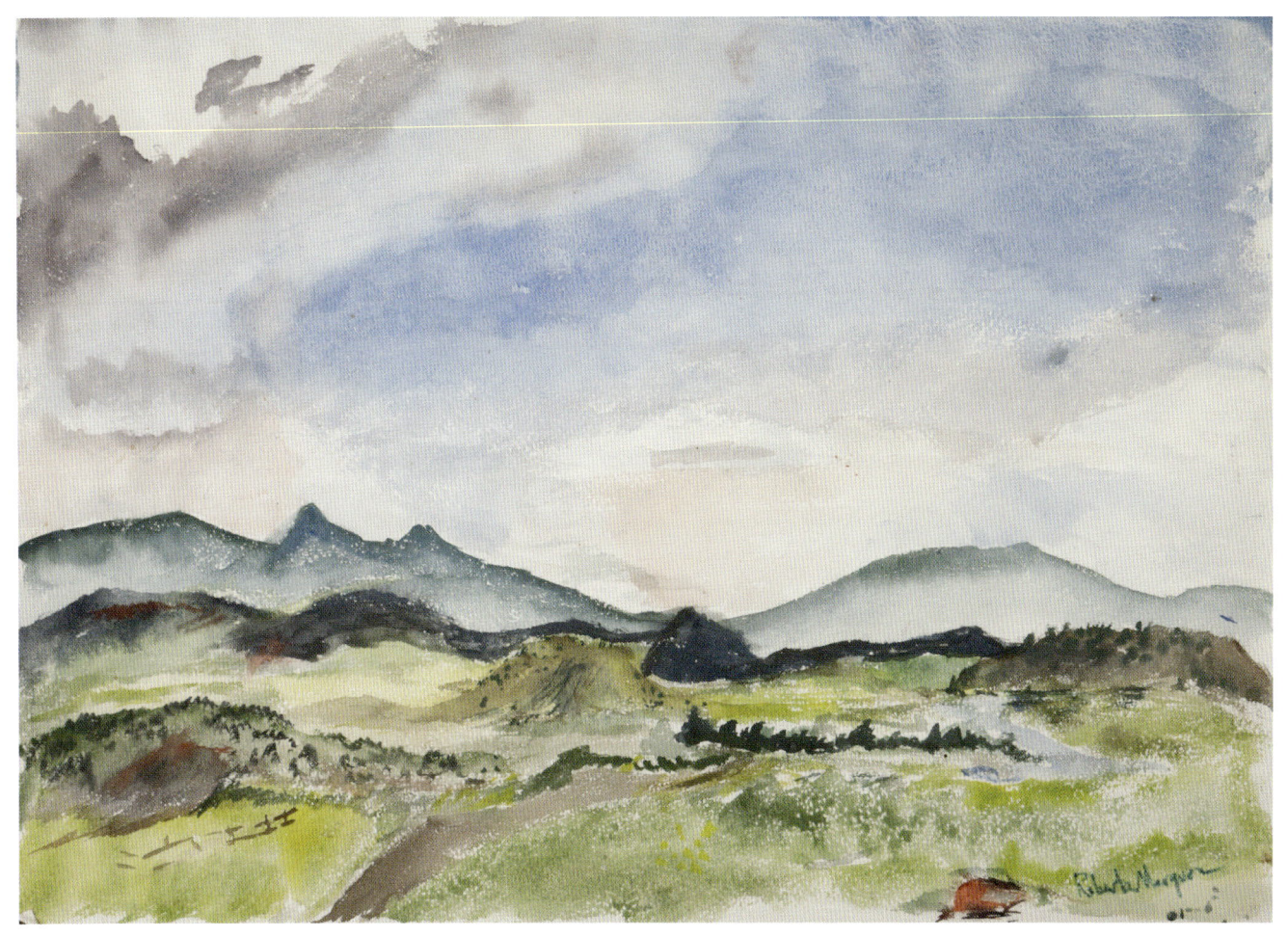

PLATE 88. *Las Vegas*, 1972. Watercolor on paper, 20″ × 14″. Collection of the artist.

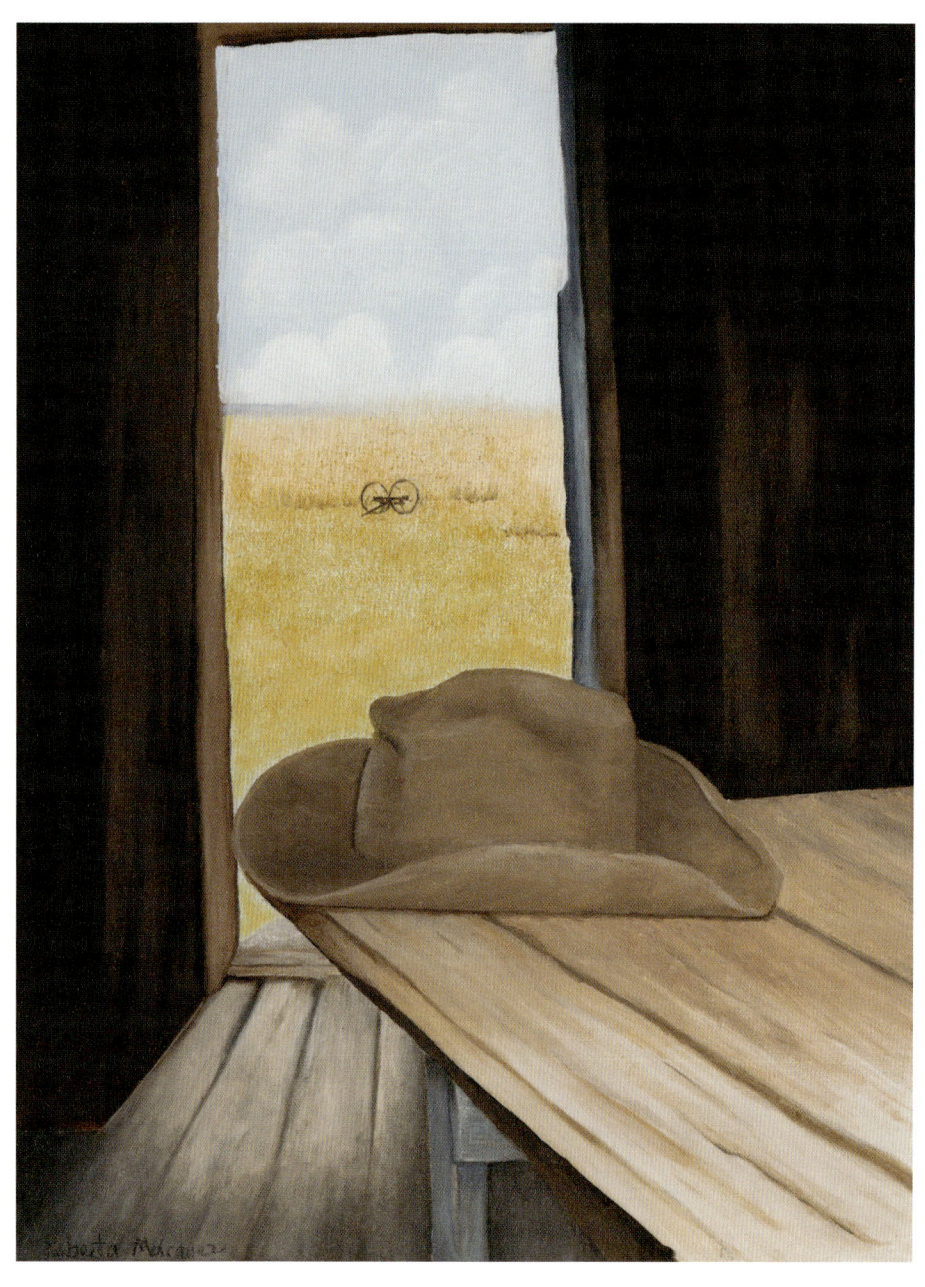

PLATE 89. *Florentino's Hat*, 1982. Oil on canvas, 14″ × 18″. Collection of the artist.

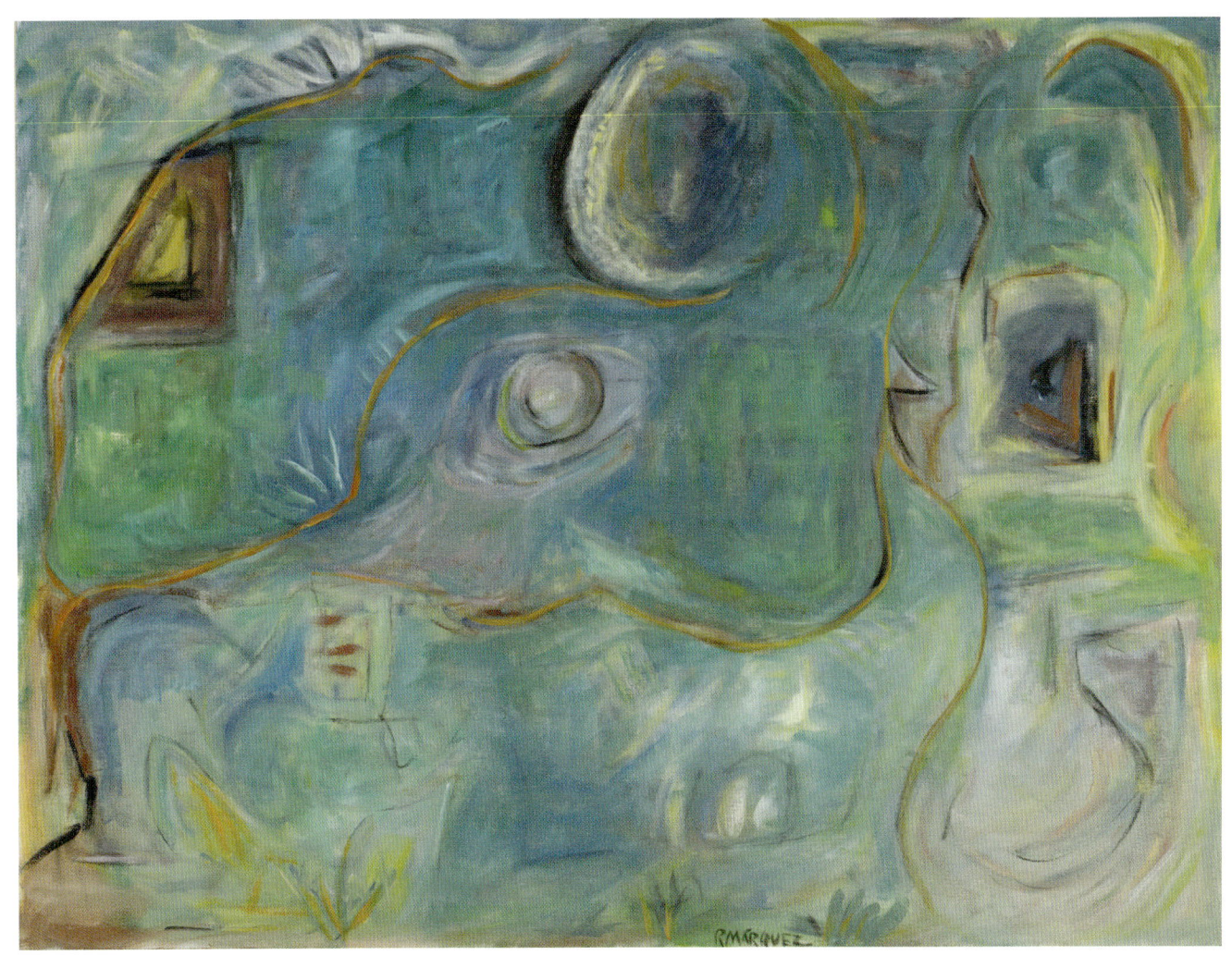

PLATE 90. *Abstraction,* 1994. Oil on canvas, 48″ × 36″. Collection of the artist.

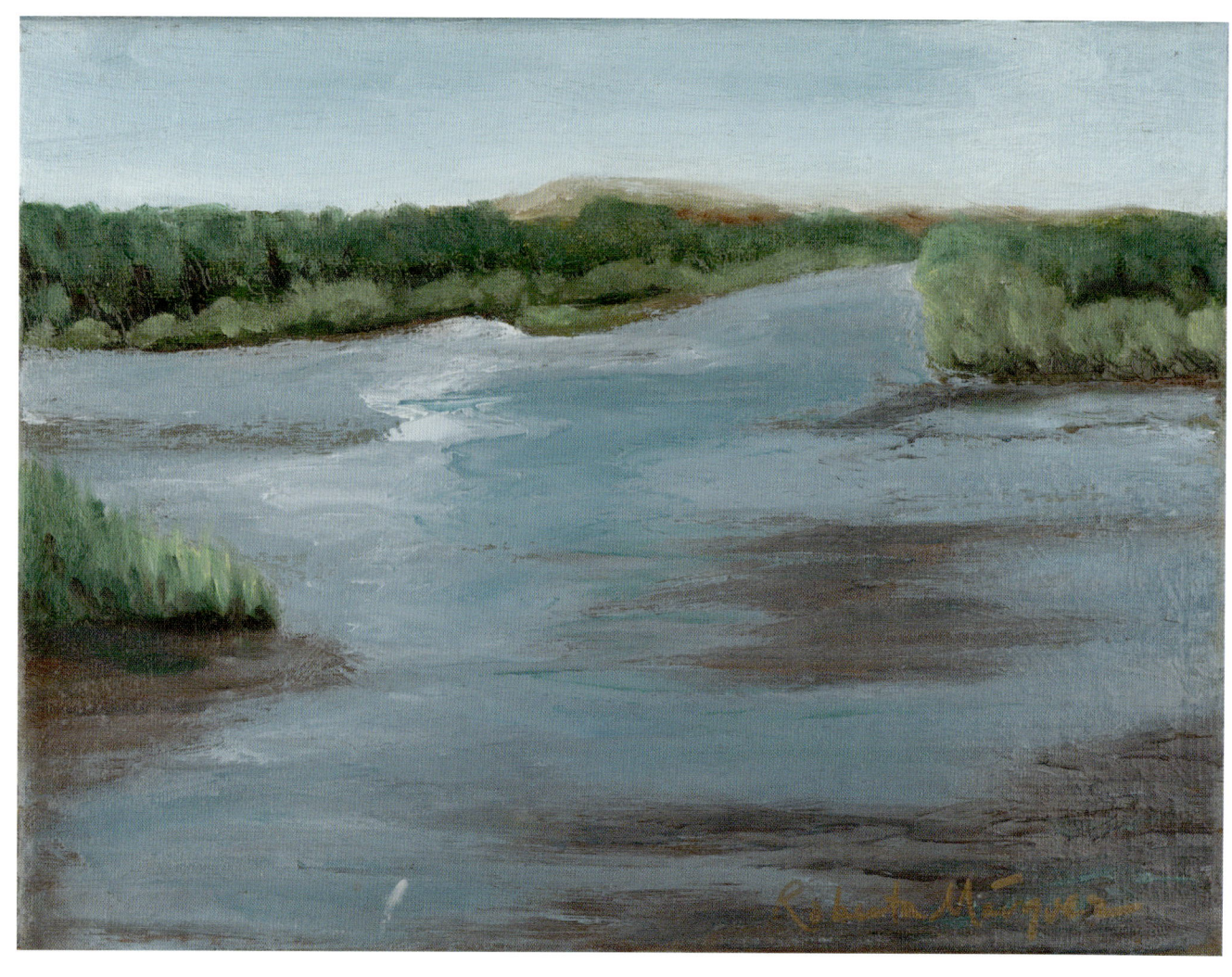

PLATE 91. *Along the Río Grande*, 2010. Oil on canvas, 11″ × 14″. Collection of the artist.

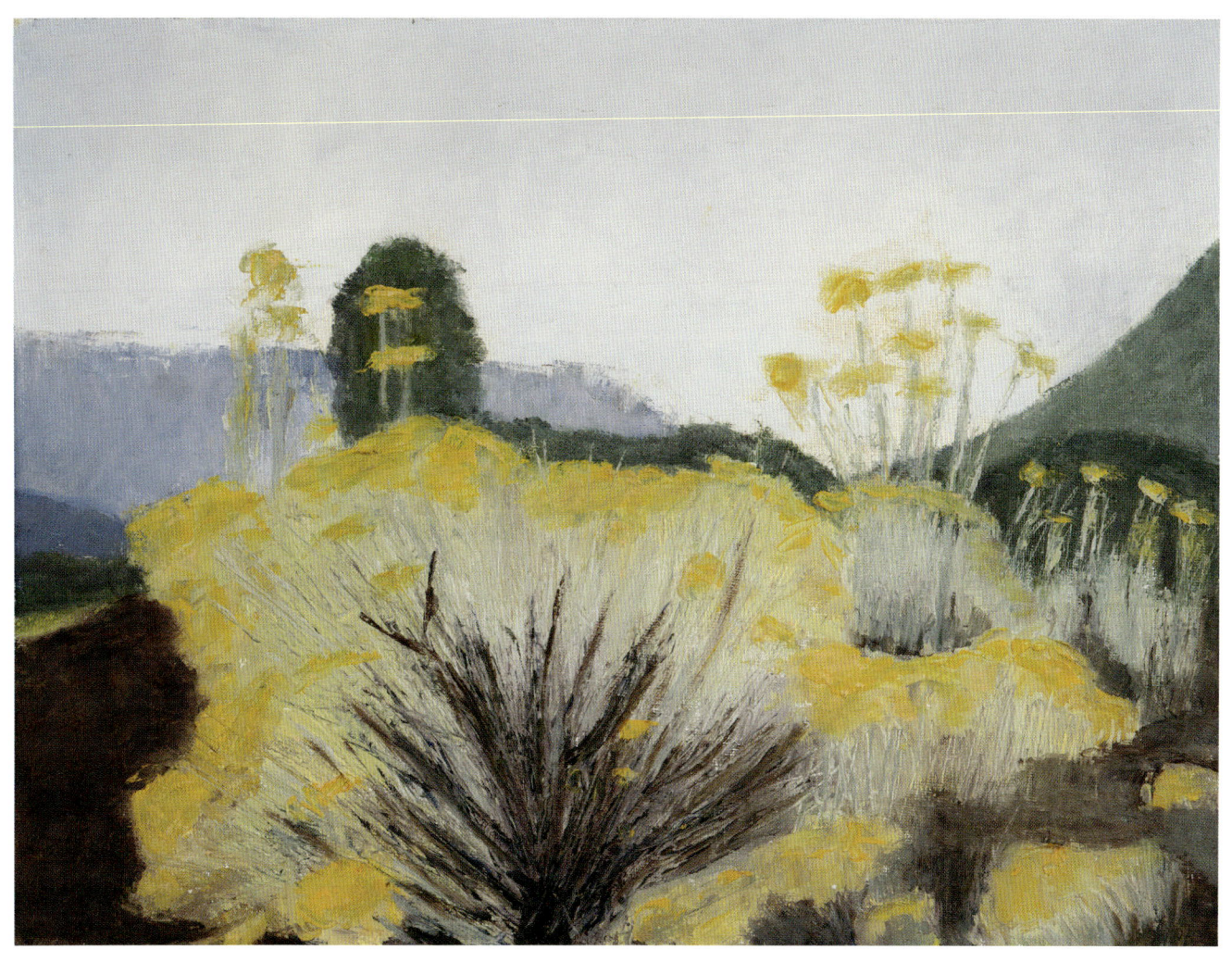

PLATE 92. *Chamisa at Magdalena Hills*, 2010. Oil on canvas, 11″ × 14″. Collection of the artist.

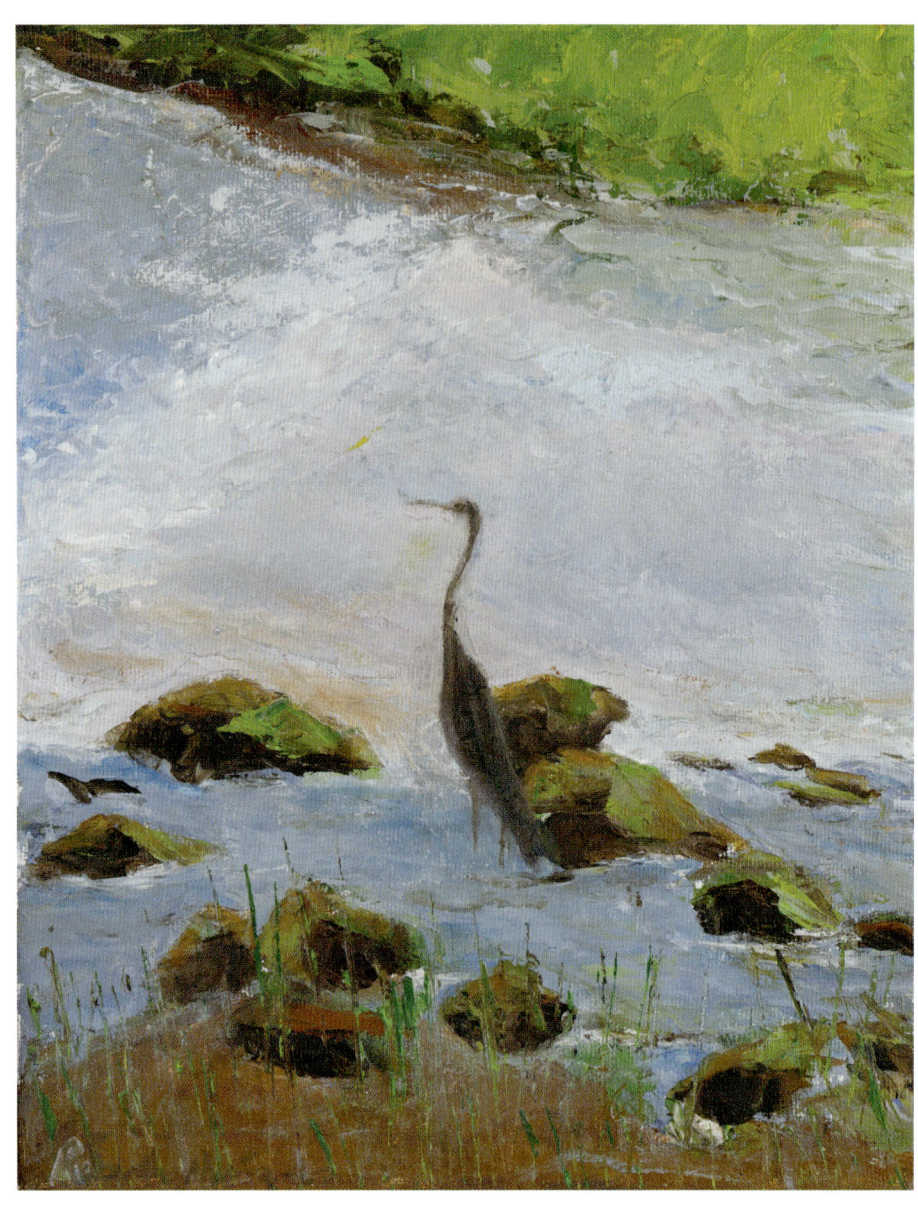

PLATE 93. *Cranes and Rushing Spring Waters*, 2010. Oil on canvas, 8″ × 10″. Collection of the artist.

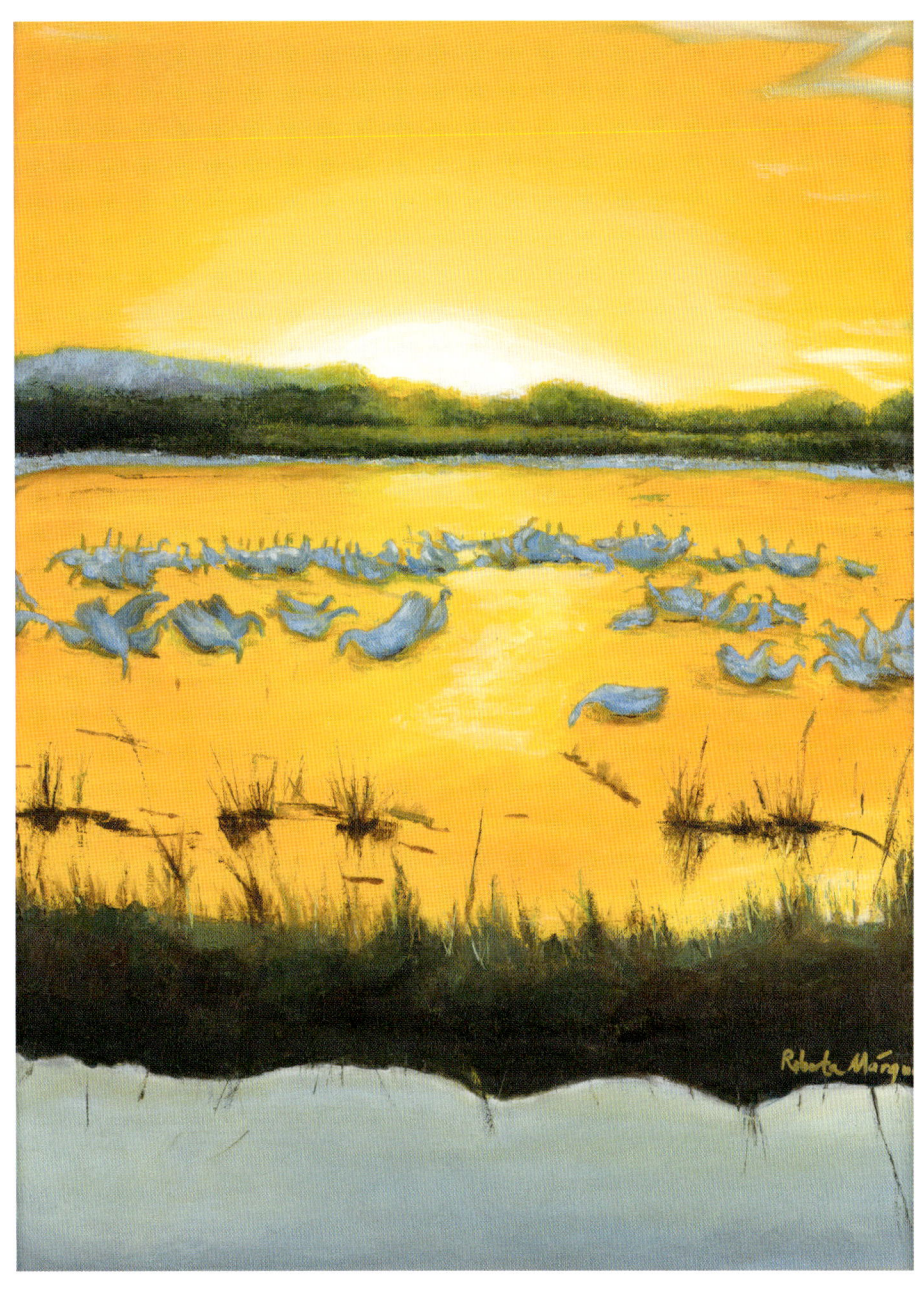

PLATE 94. *Dawn at Bosque del Apache*, 2010. Oil on wood panel, 16″ × 20″. Collection
of the artist.

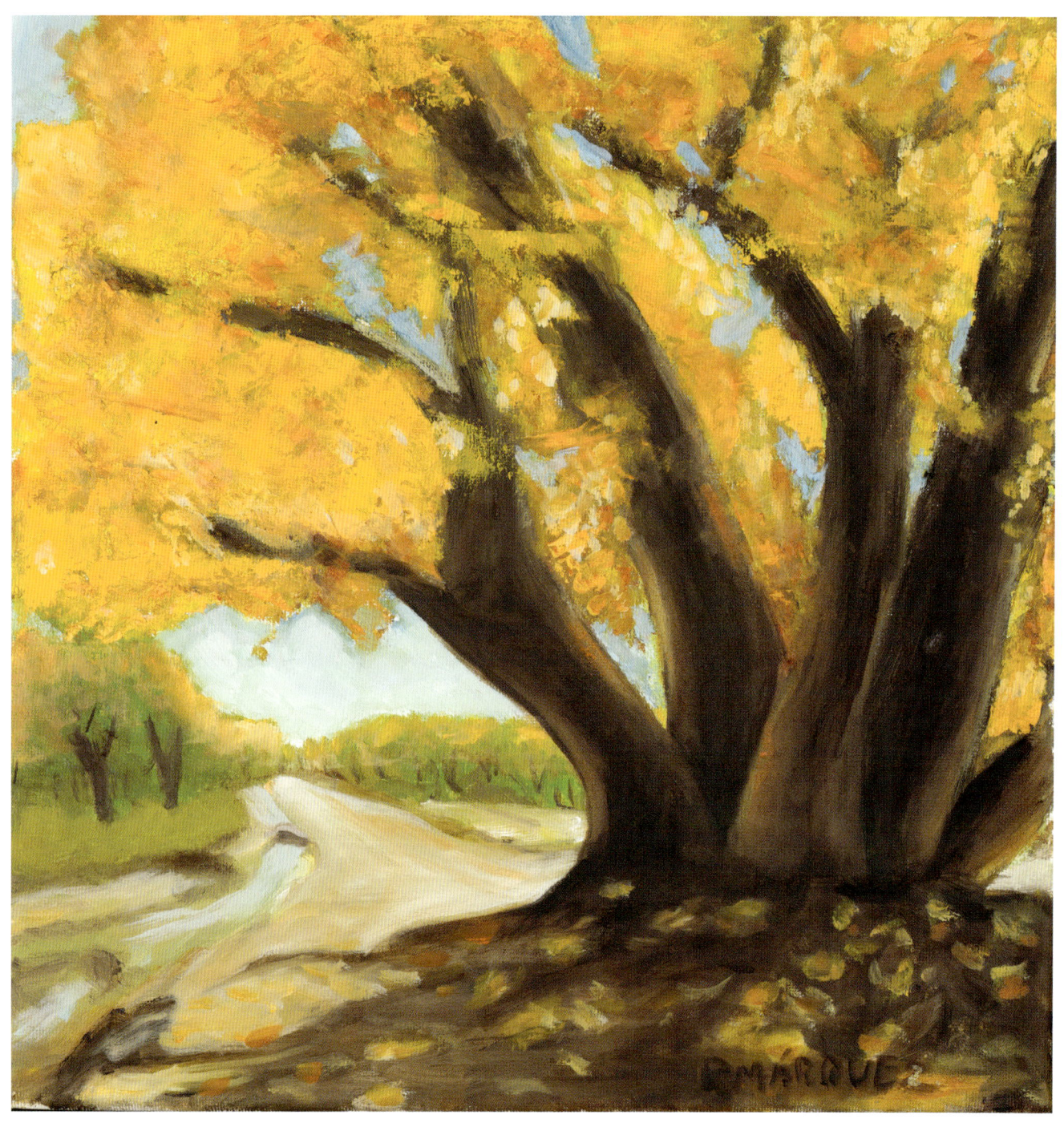

PLATE 95. *South Valley Acequia*, 2010. Oil on canvas, 11″ × 14″. Private collection of Virginia Sisneros.

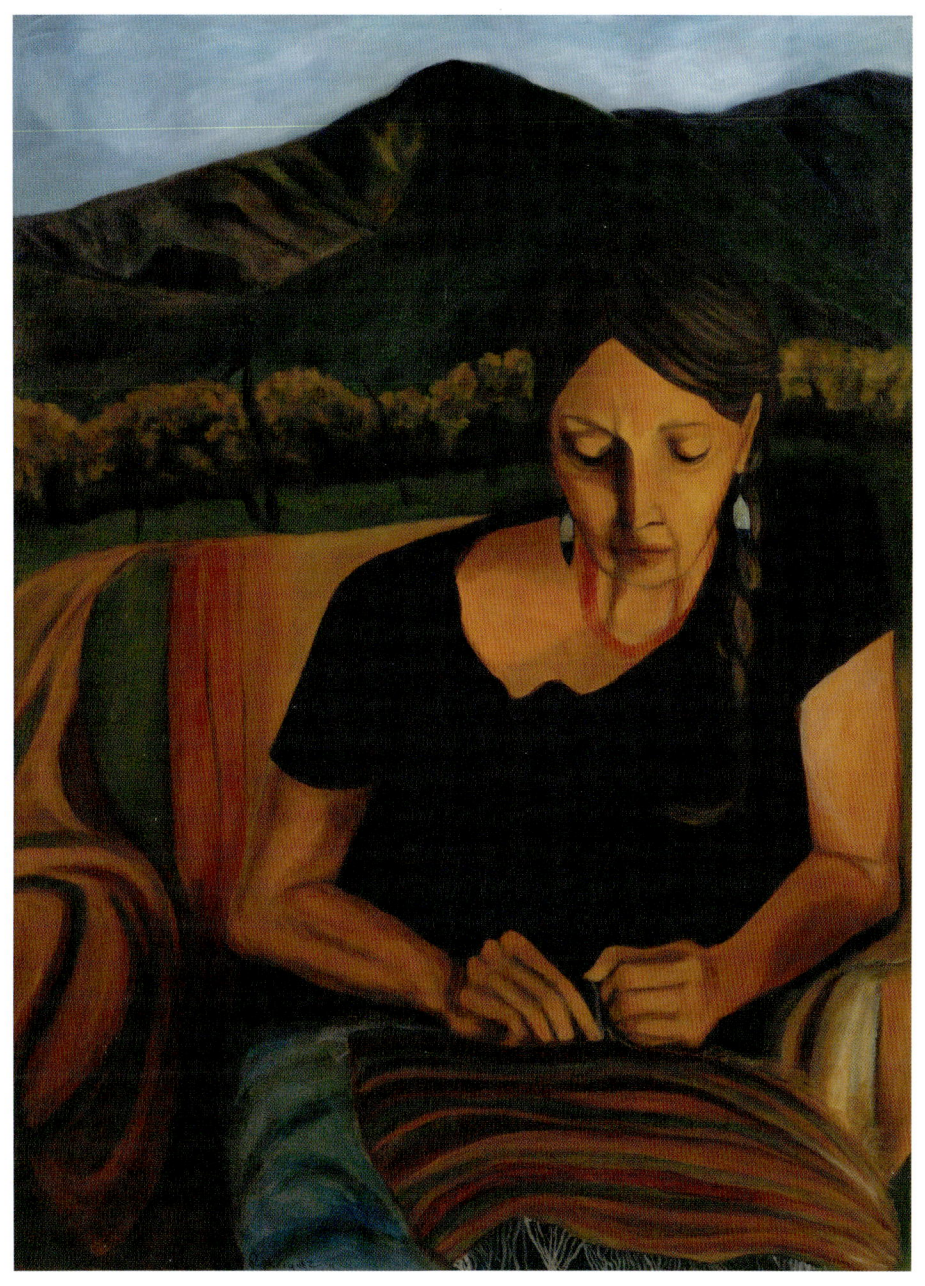

PLATE 96. *Juanita,* 2011. Oil on canvas, 32″ × 42″. Private collection of JoAnne
Márquez.

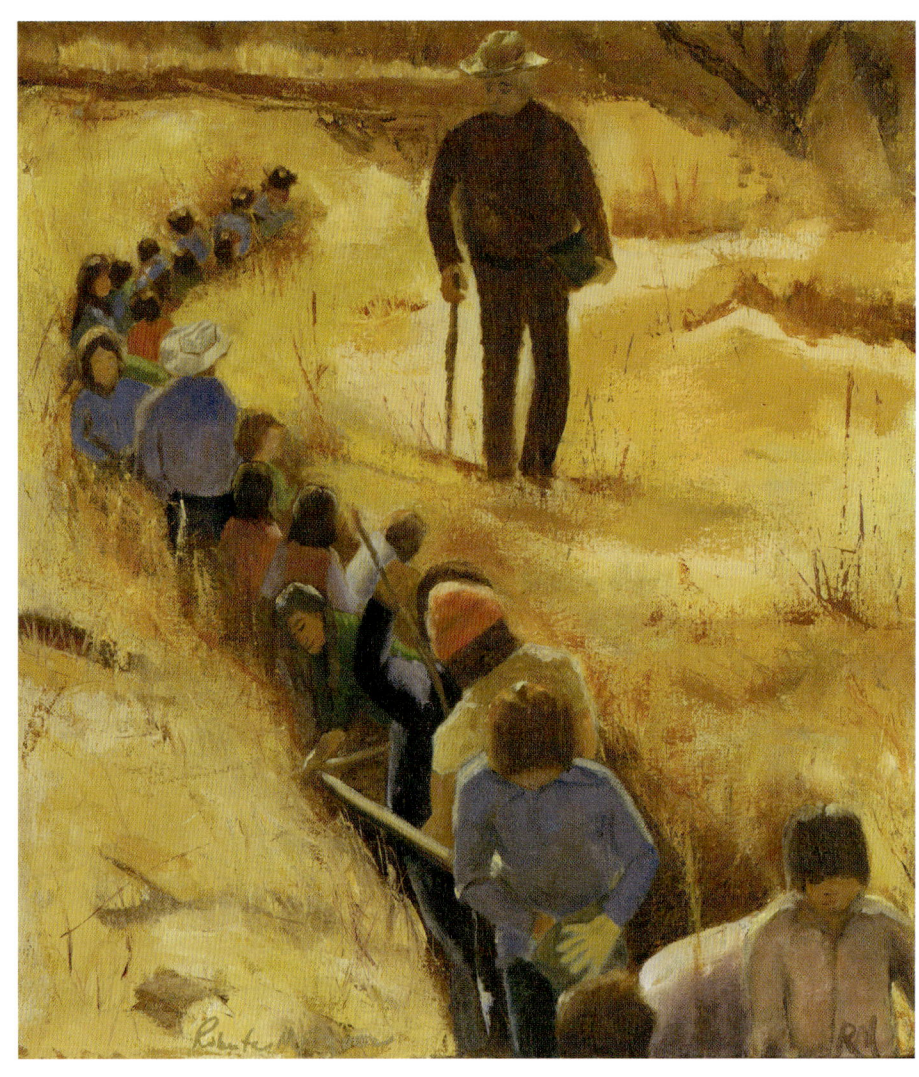

PLATE 97. *La acequia: Spring Cleaning*, 2013. Oil on canvas, 18″ × 18″. Private collection of Juanita J. Lavadie.

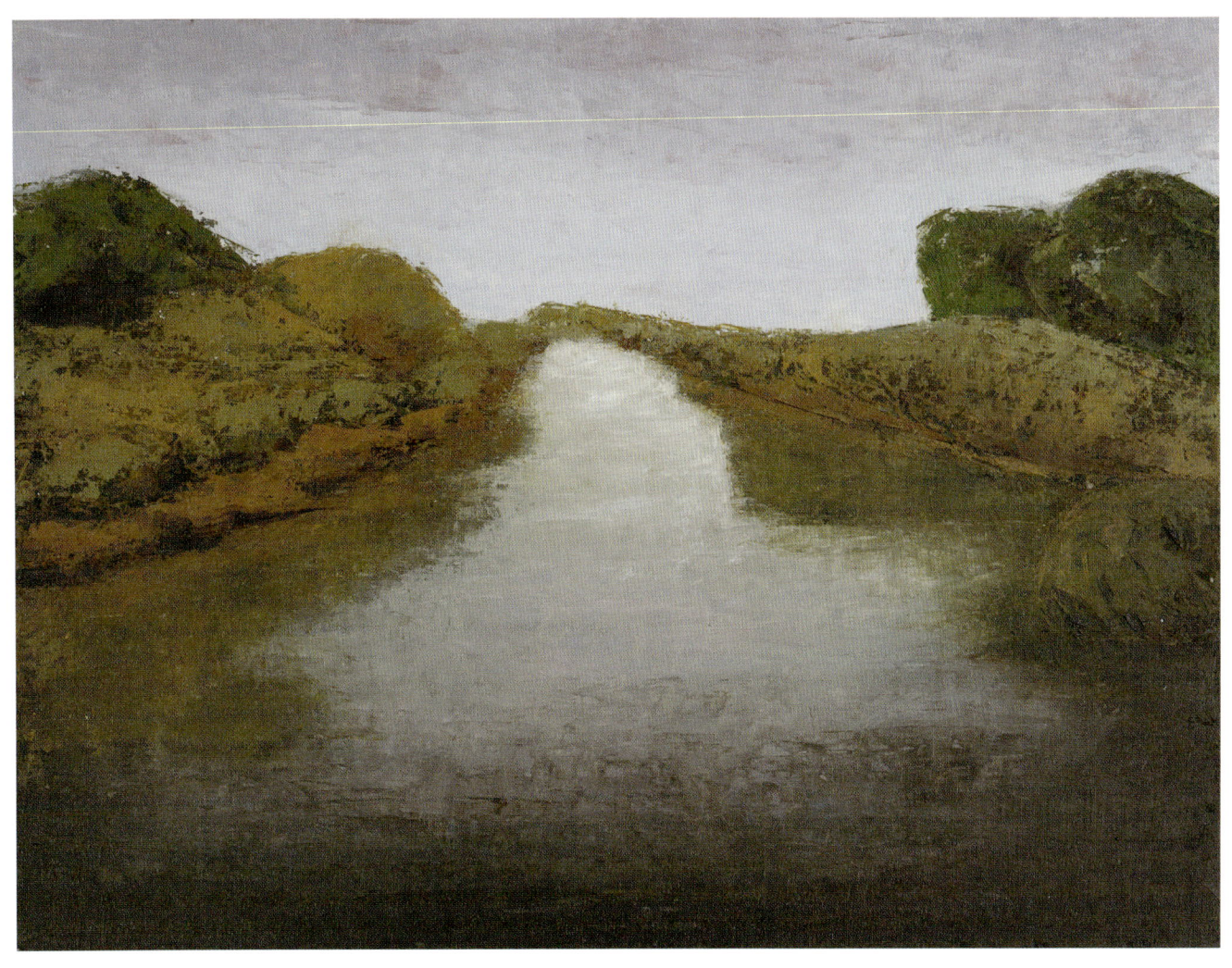

PLATE 98. *El Río Escondido*, 2014. Oil on canvas, 12″ × 16″. Collection of the artist.

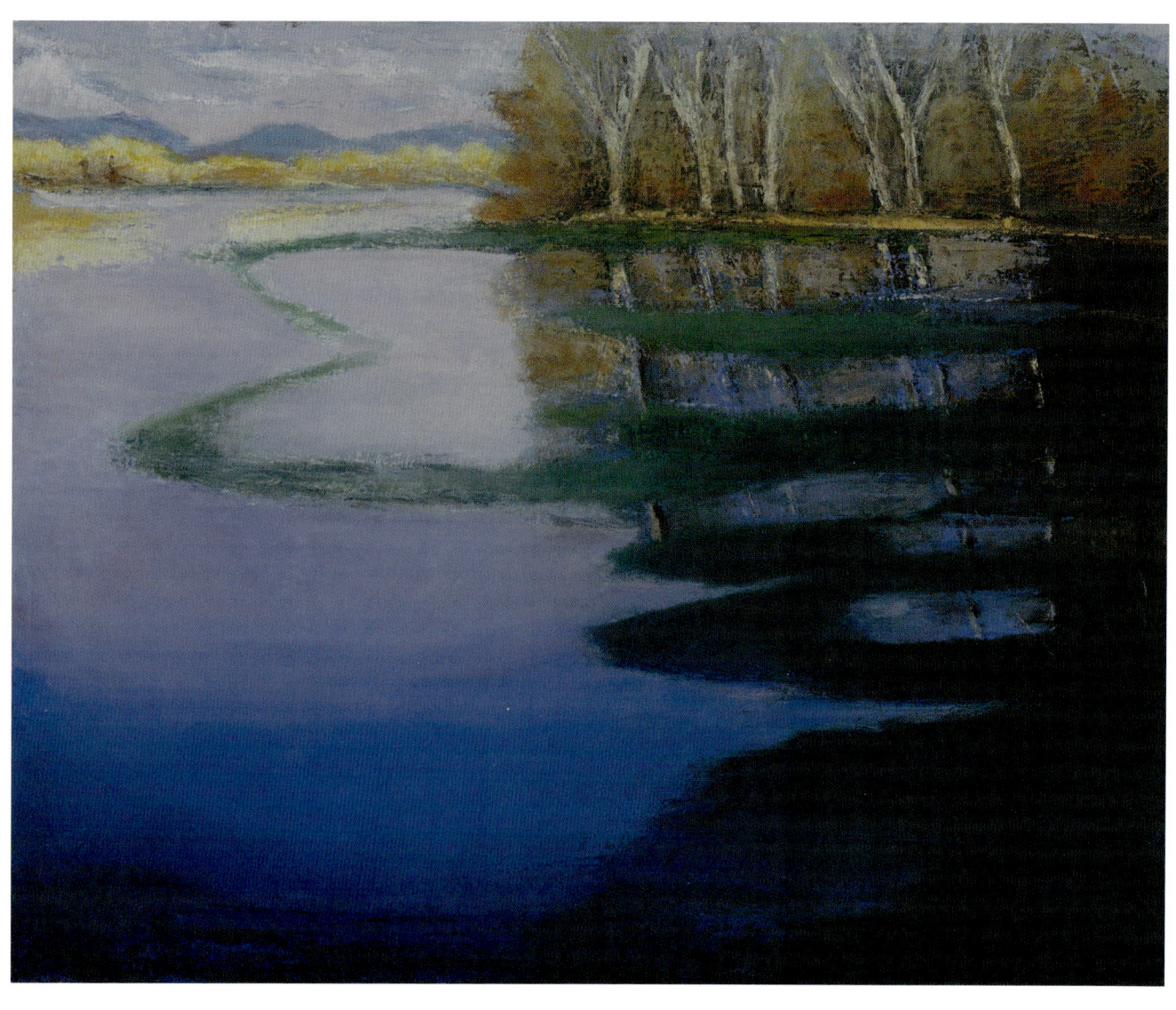

PLATE 99. *Sunset at Bosque del Apache*, 2014. Oil on canvas, 16″ × 20″. Private collection of Jeannie and Marcos González.

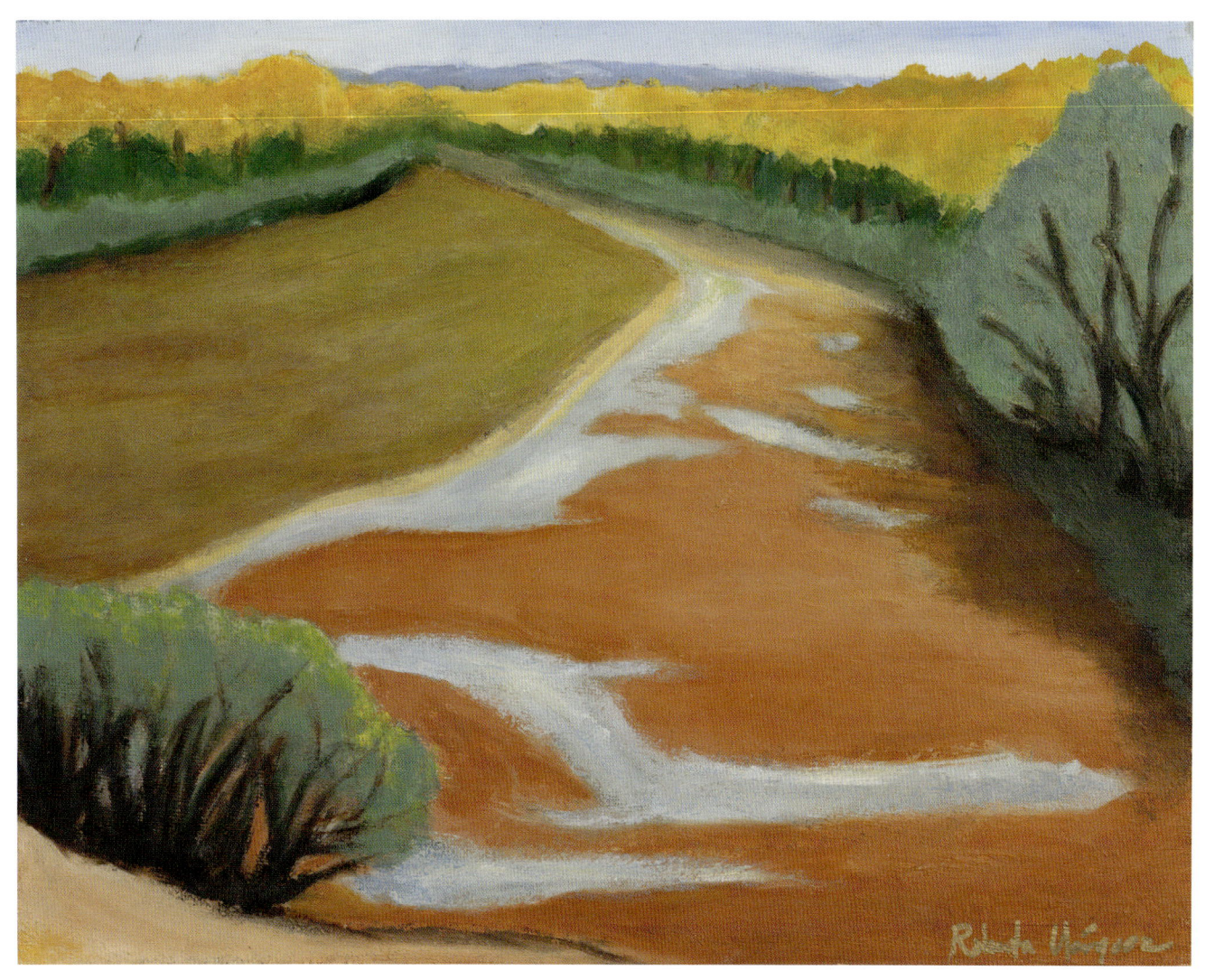

PLATE 100. *The End of the Season*, 2014. Oil on canvas, 12″ × 9″. Collection of the artist.

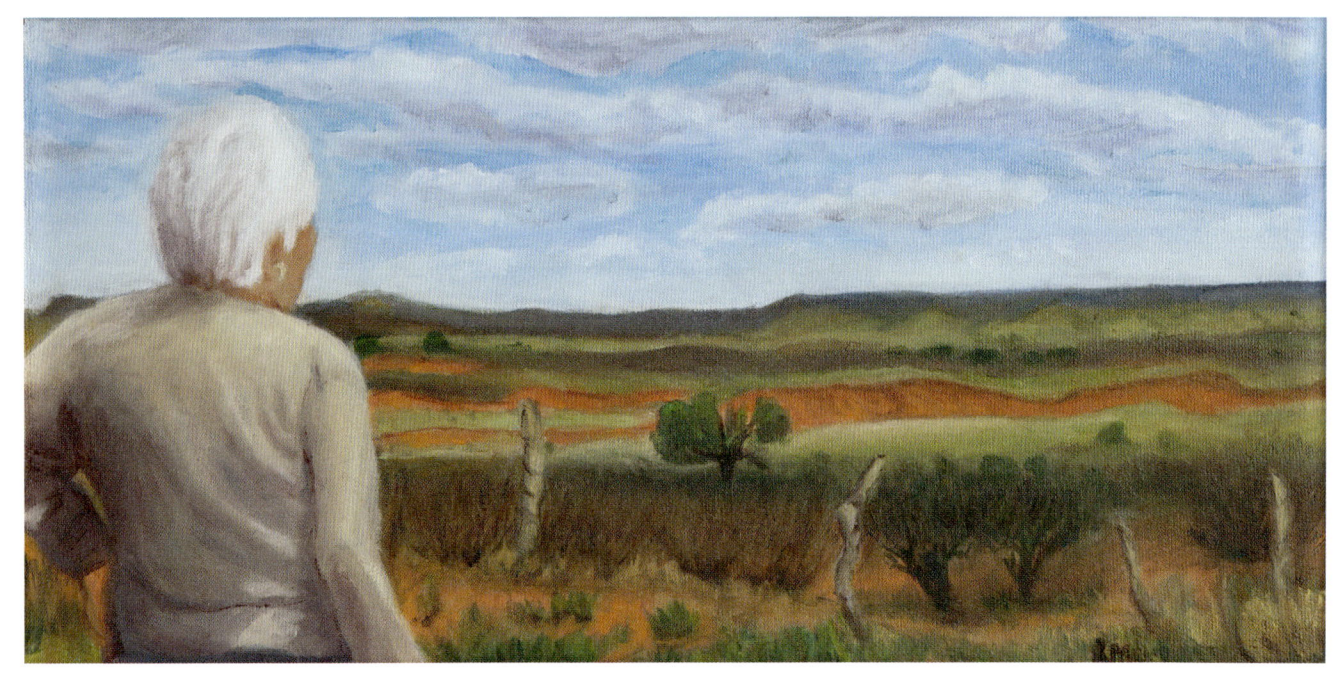

PLATE 101. *Lucy at Home*, 2015. Oil on canvas, 8″ × 16″. Private collection of Lucy Angel.

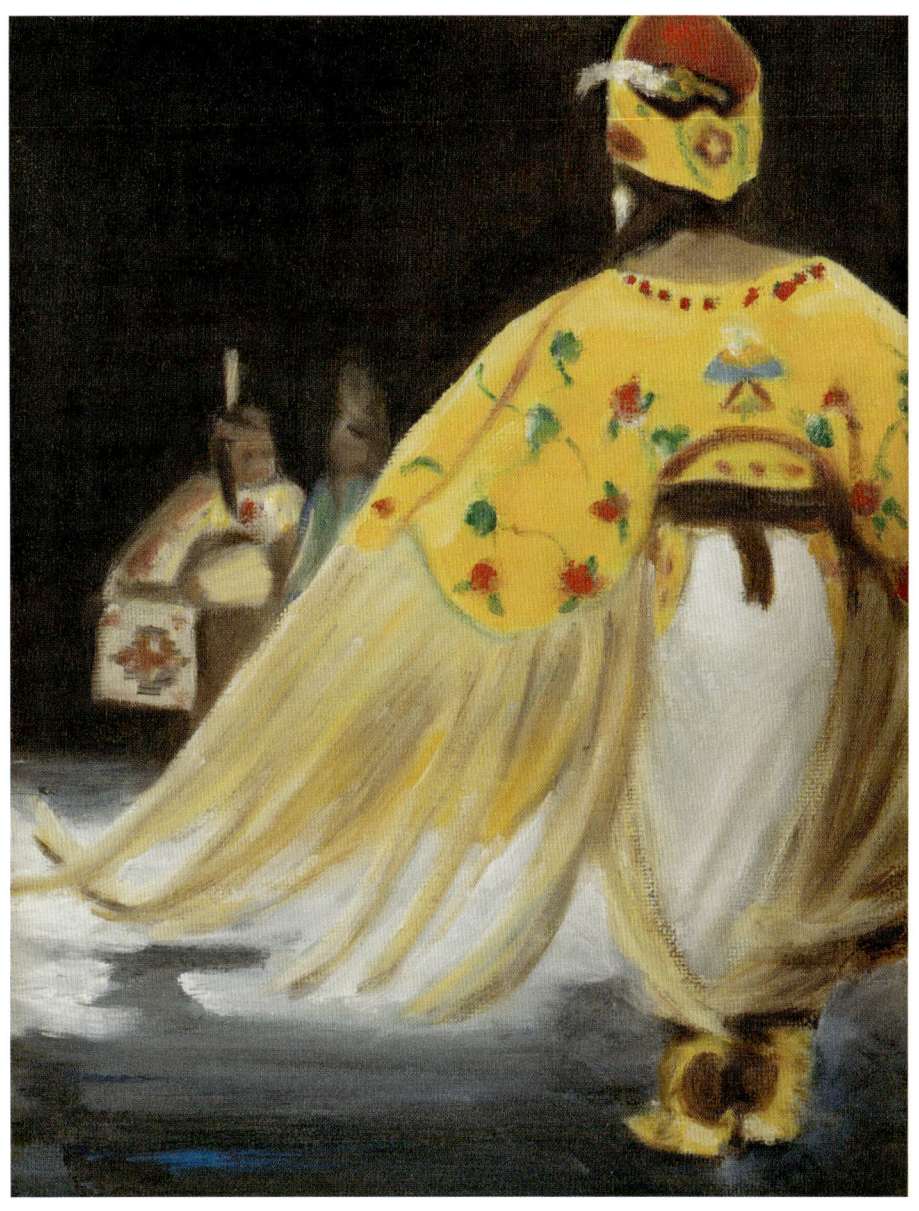

PLATE 102. *Pow Wow Dancer 1*, 2016. Oil on canvas, 8″ × 10″. Collection of the artist.

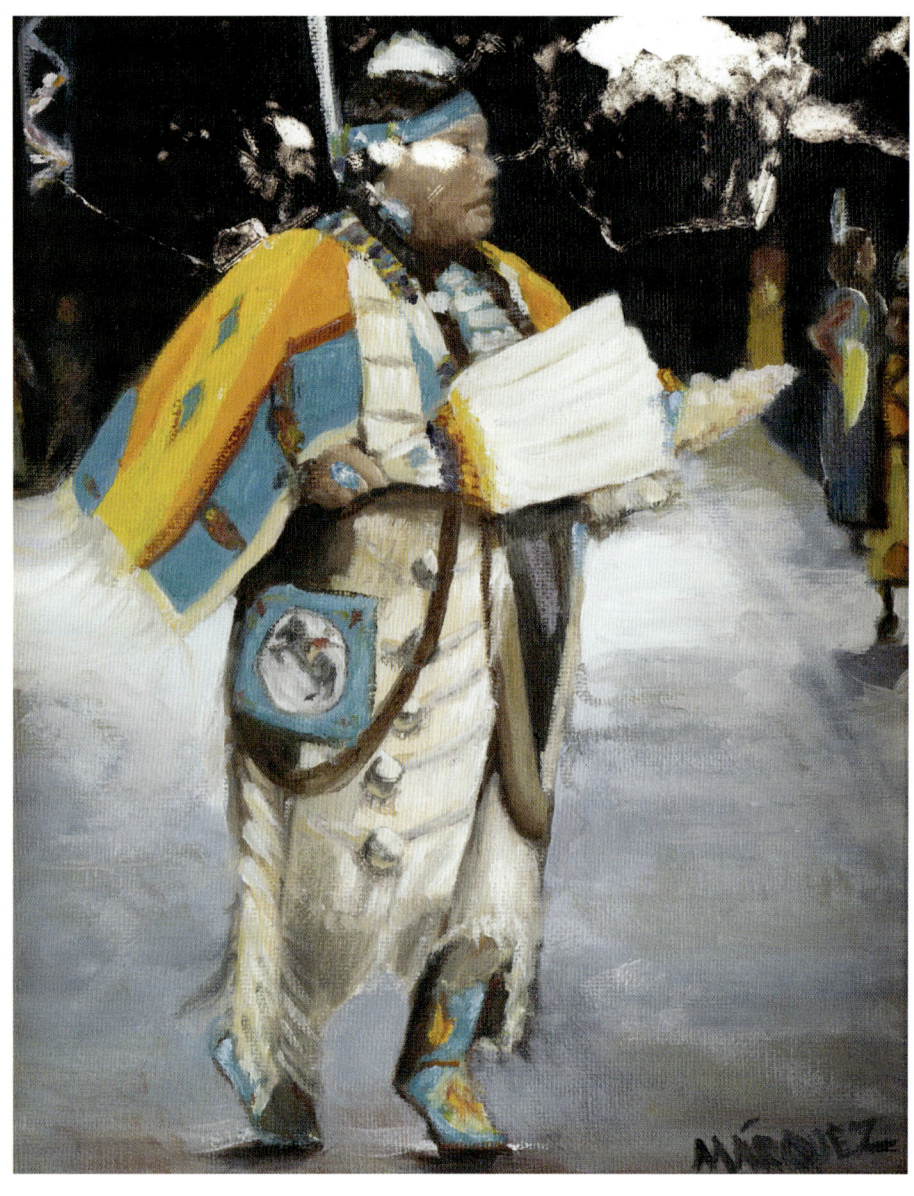

PLATE 103. *Pow Wow Dancer 2*, 2016. Oil on canvas, 8" × 10". Collection of the artist.

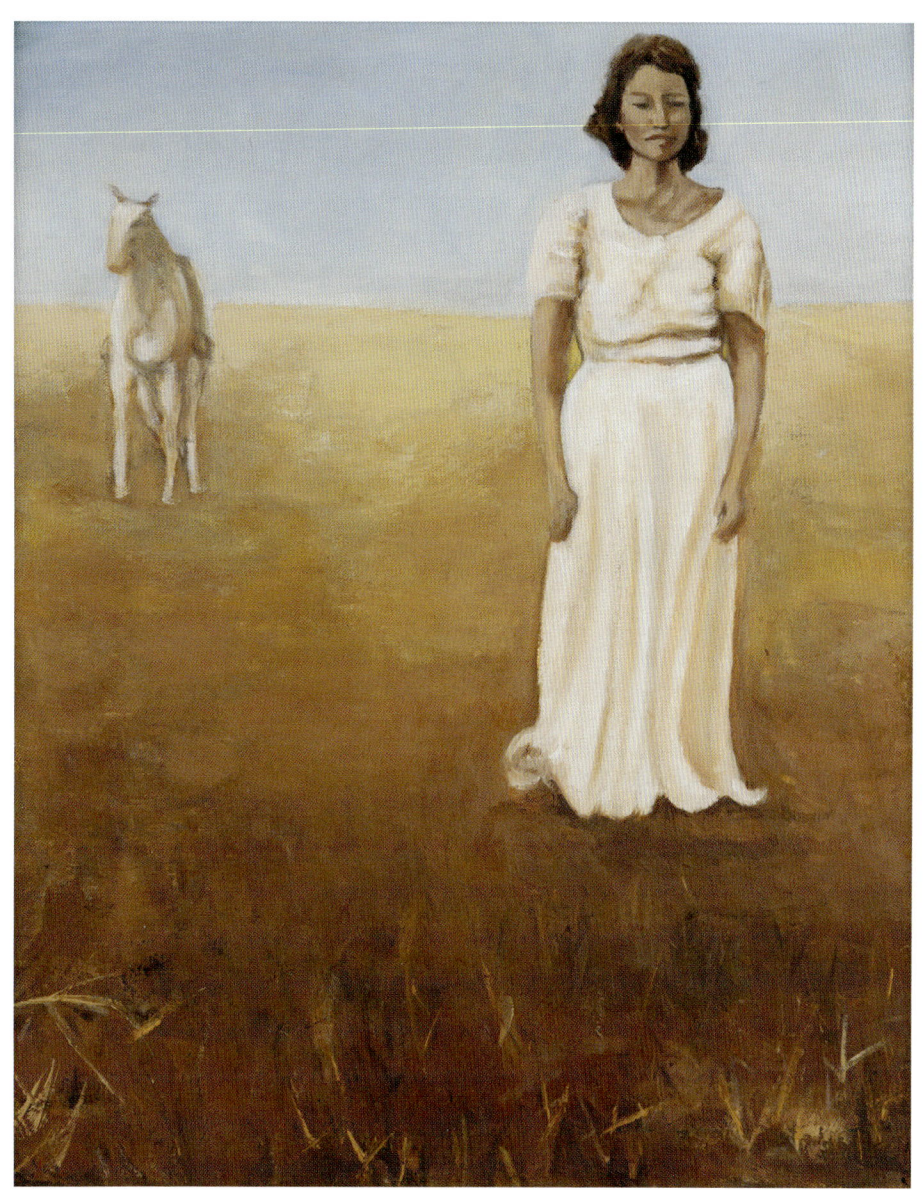

PLATE 104. *Senaida and Old Blue*, 2016. Oil on canvas, 16" × 20". Private collection
of Lucy Angel.

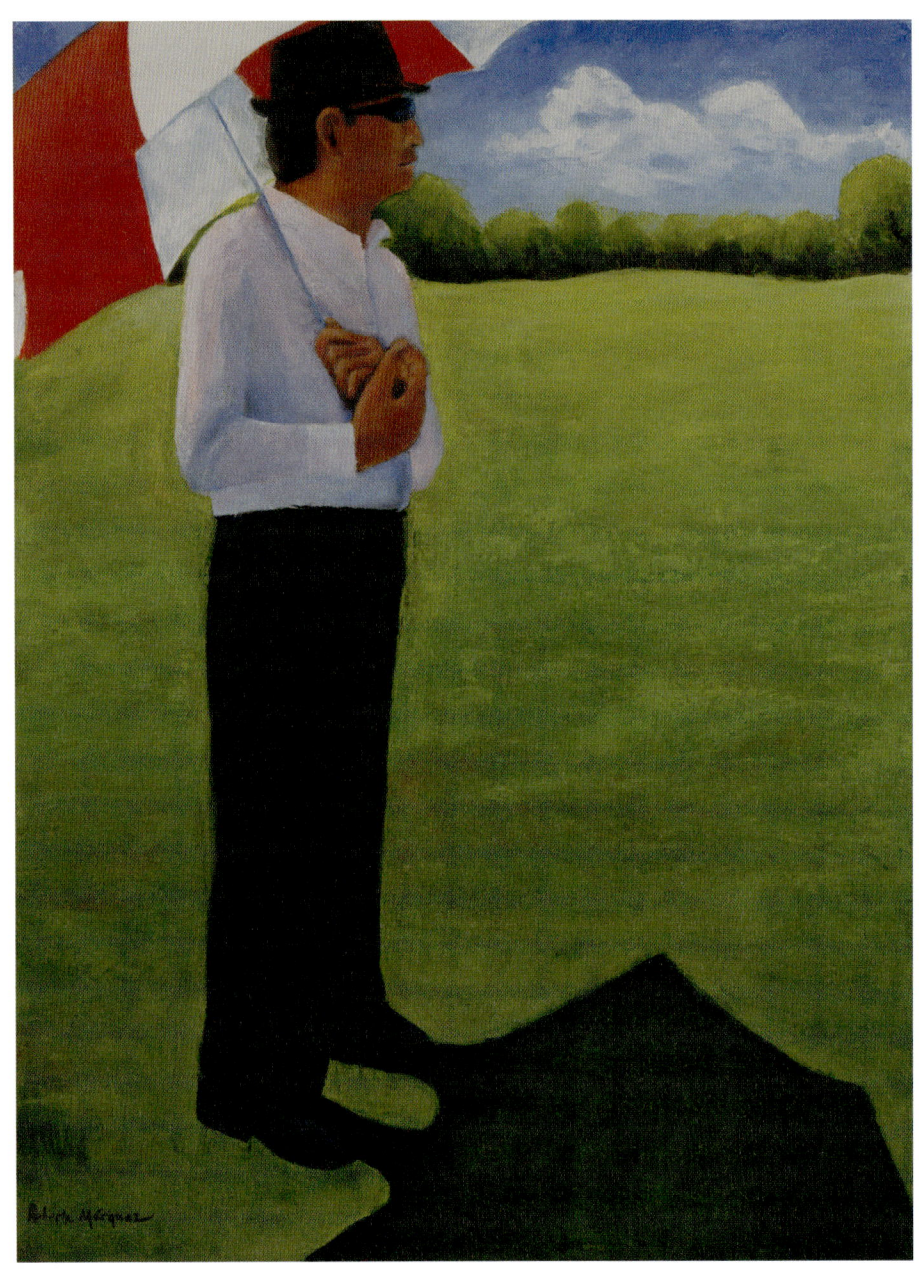

PLATE 105. *El entierro*, 2017. Oil on canvas, 30" × 40". Collection of the artist.

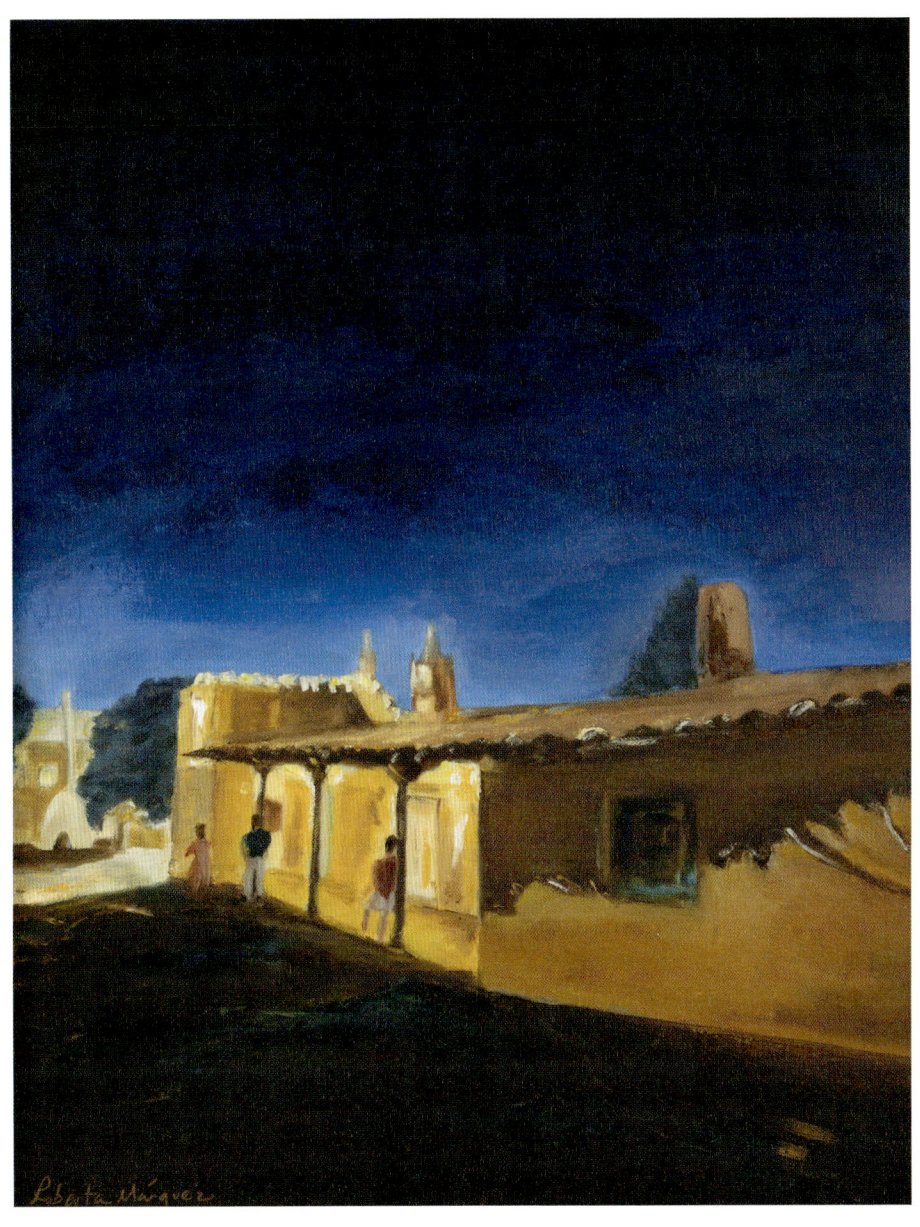

PLATE 106. *La plaza vieja*, 2017. Oil on canvas, 16″ × 20″. Private collection of
Mary Jean López.

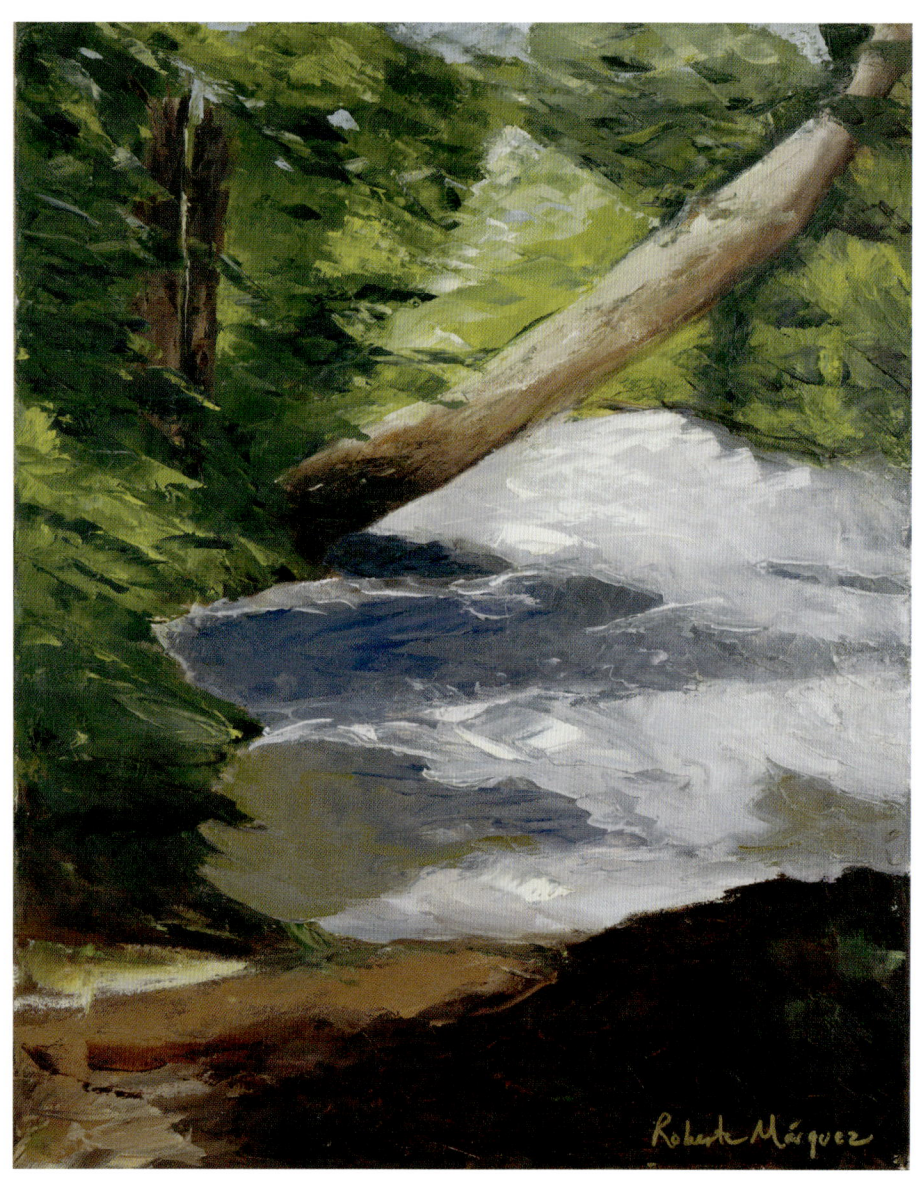

PLATE 107. *Spring Flow, Taos*, 2017. Oil on canvas, 16″ × 20″. Collection of the artist.

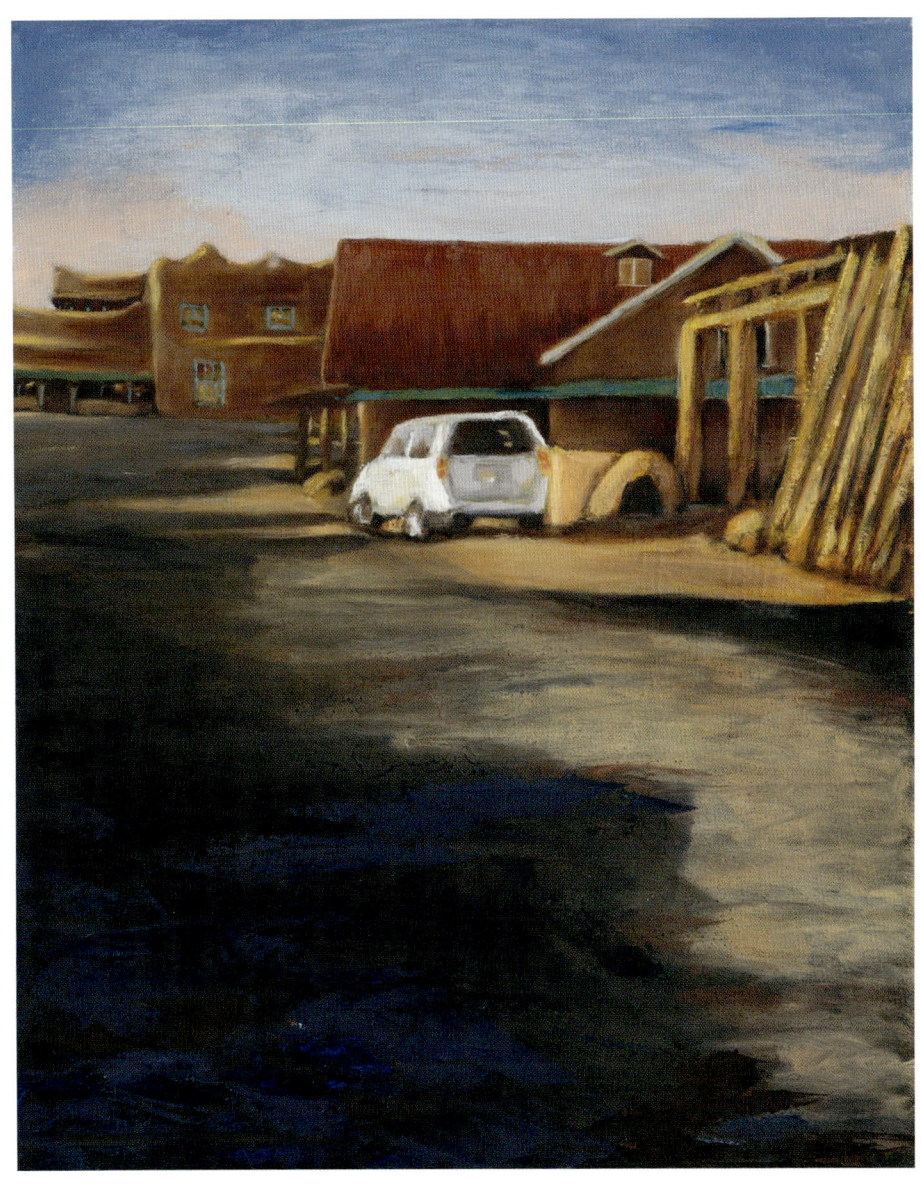

PLATE 108. *The Old and the New*, 2018. Oil on canvas, 16″ × 20″. Collection of
the artist.

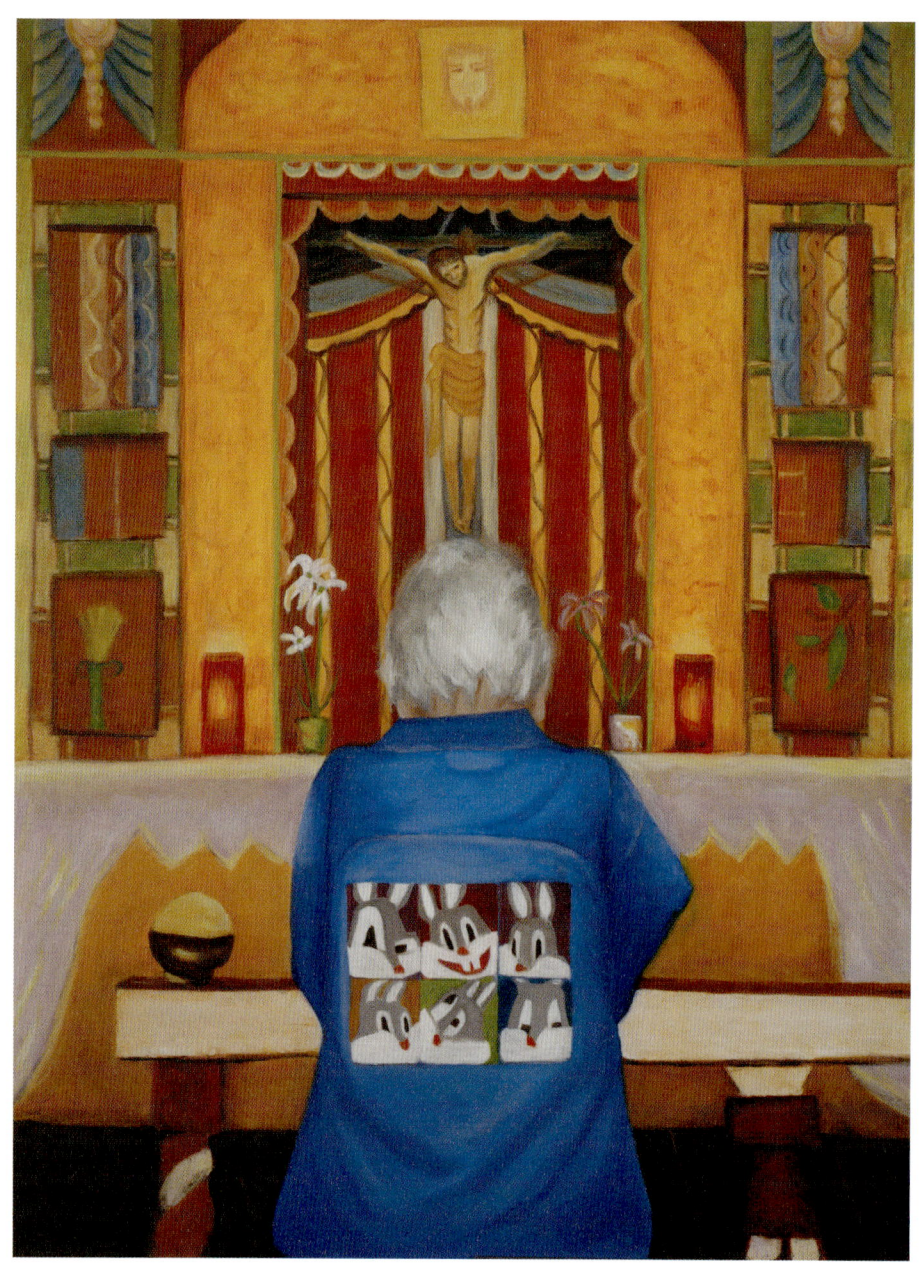

PLATE 109. *Devotion*, 2020, oil on canvas, 3″ × 4″. Collection of the artist.

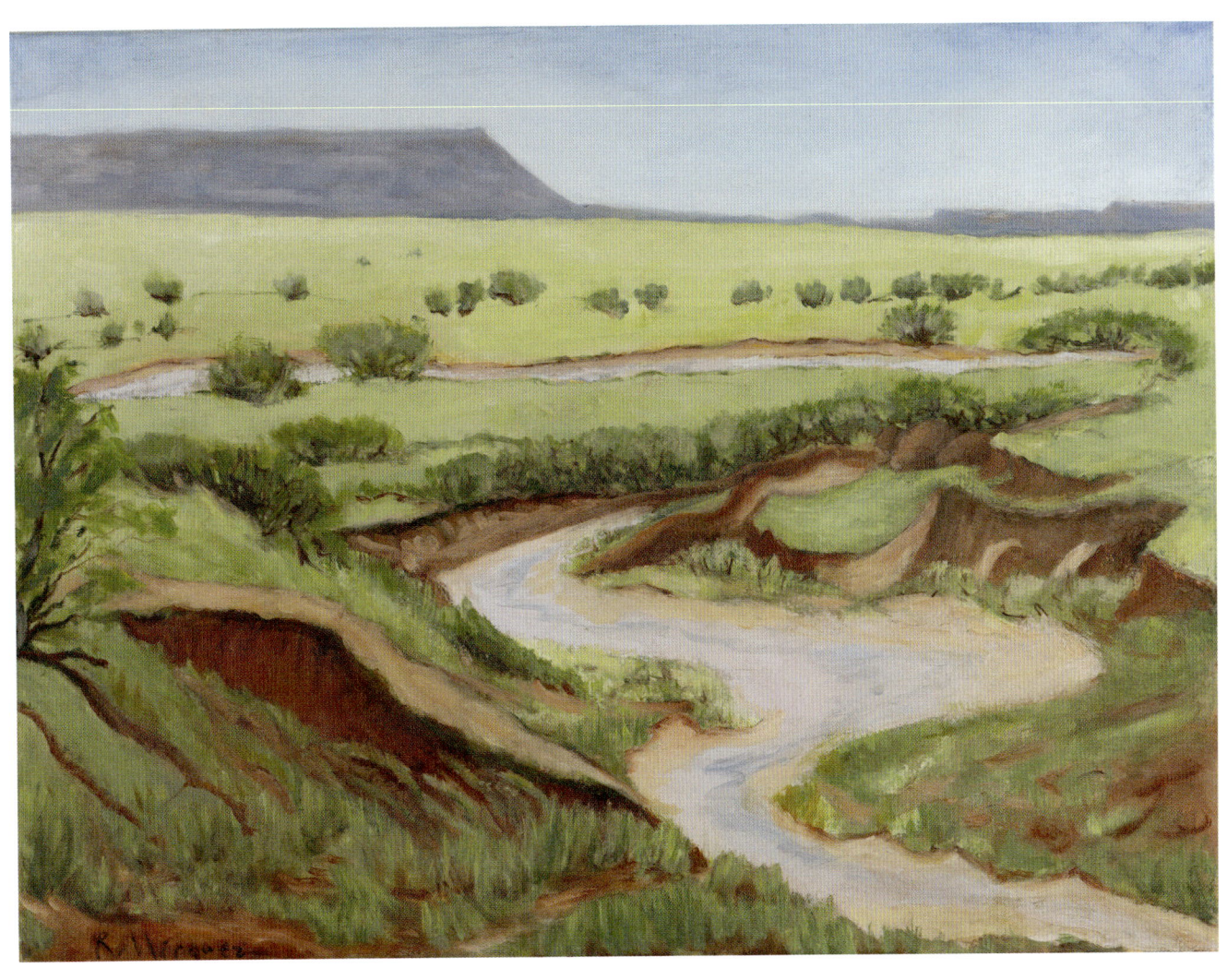

PLATE 110. *Mesas* and *Llanos, Eastern Plains*, 2021. Oil on canvas, 24″ × 18″.
Collection of the artist.

ADELITA M. MEDINA
(Born 1950, Española, NM; current
residence, Albuquerque, NM)

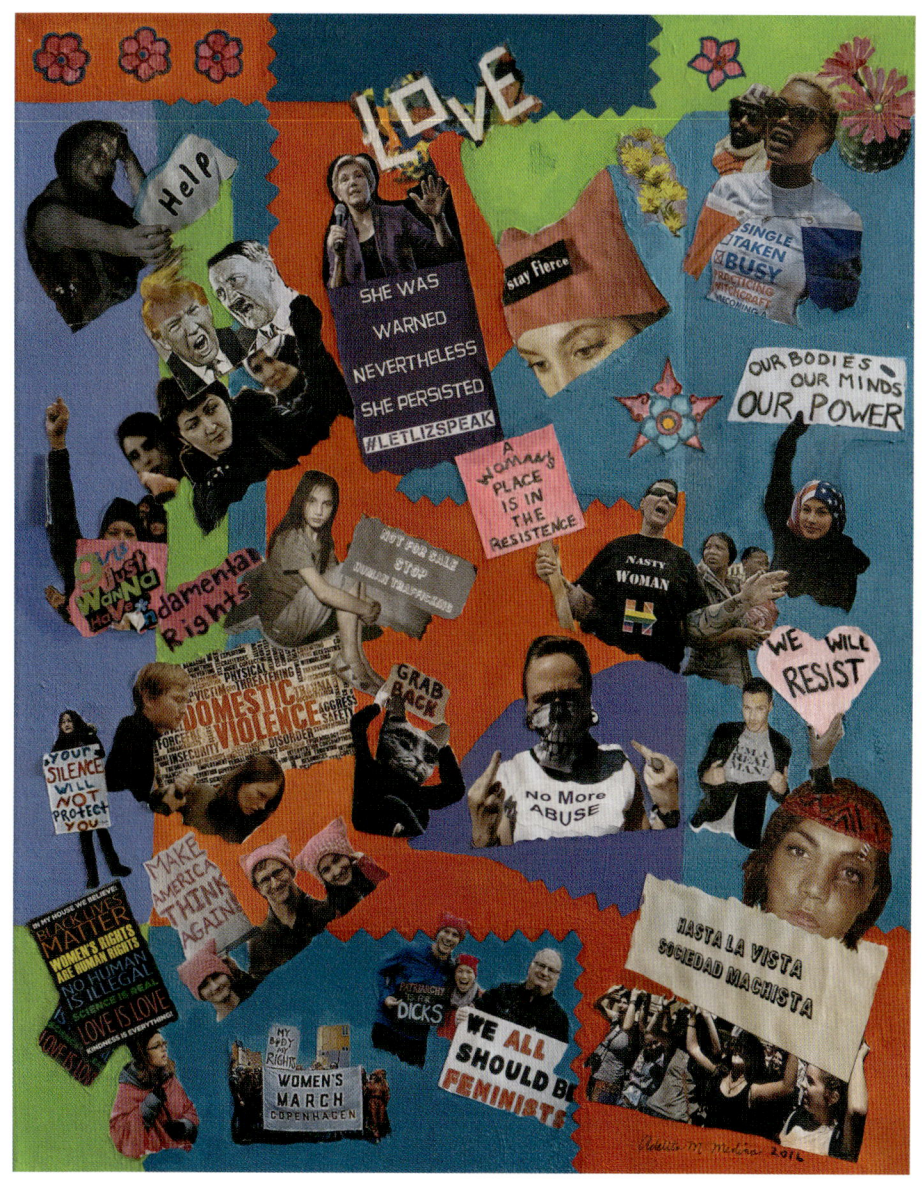

PLATE 111. *Poder Mujer*, 2016. Acrylic on canvas with collage, 15 ½″ × 20″. Collection of the artist.

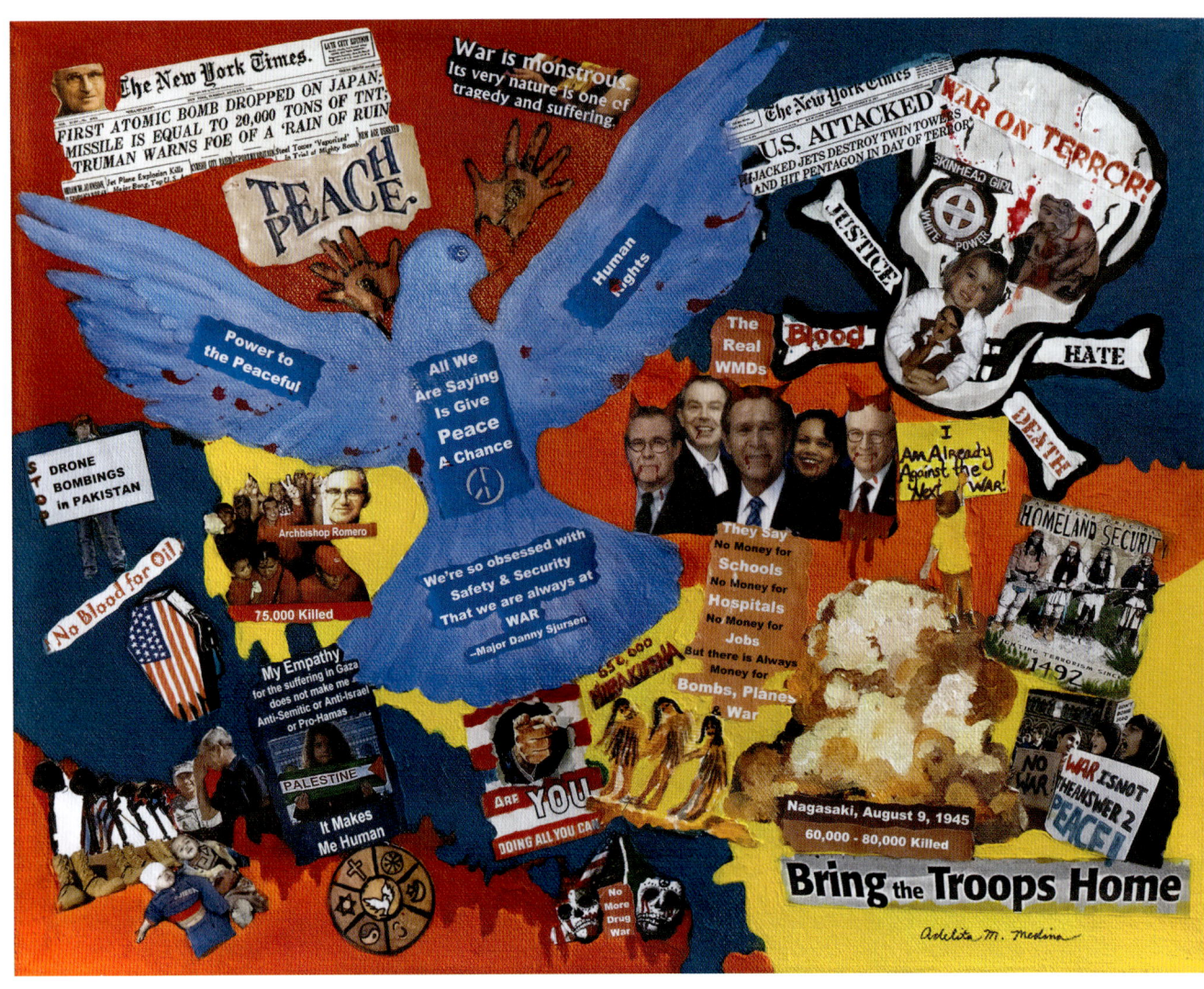

PLATE 112. *Teach Peace*, 2016. Acrylic on canvas with collage, 14 ½″ × 18″. Collection of the artist.

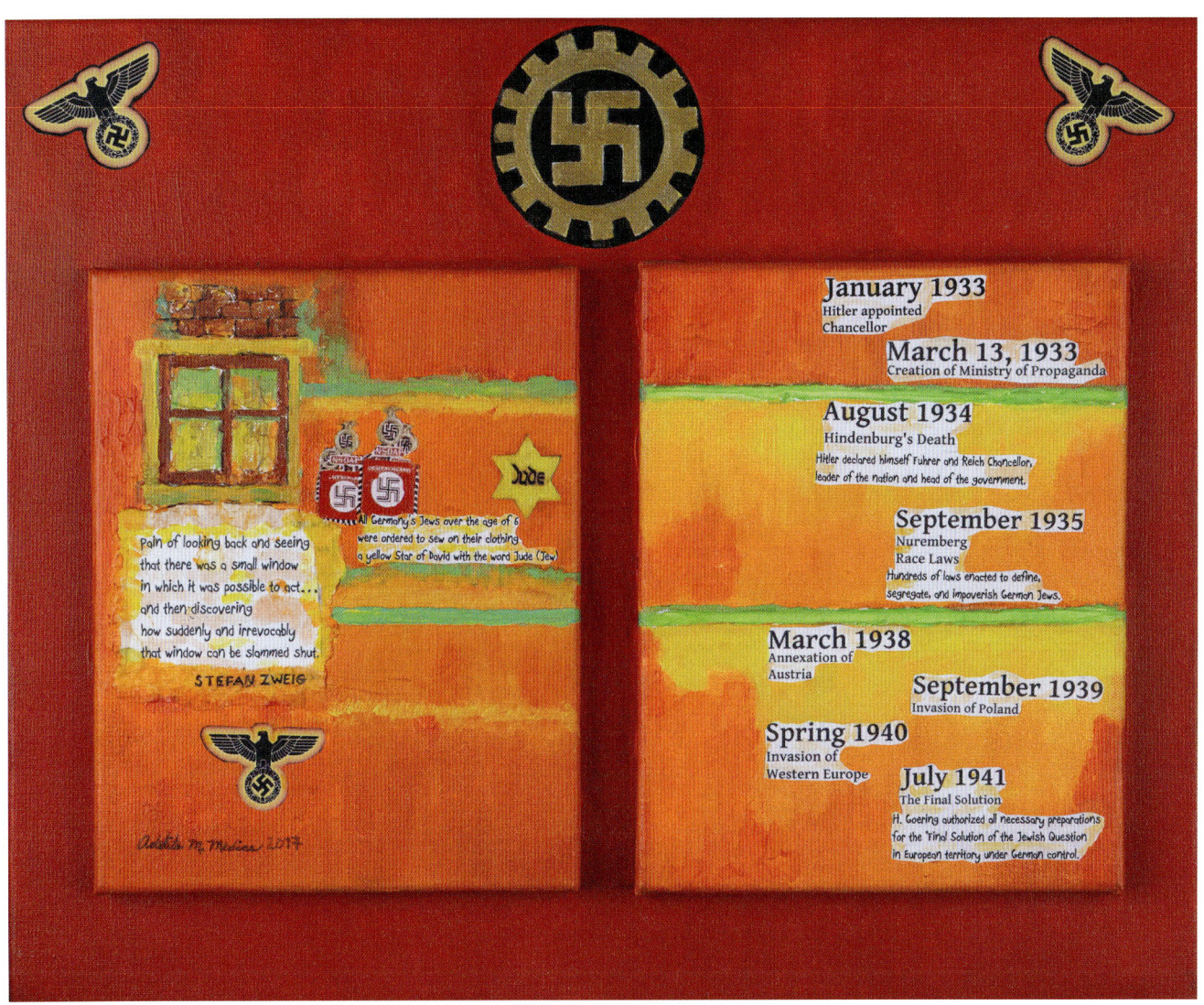

PLATE 113. *A Small Window*, 2017. Acrylic on canvas with collage, 15 ½″ × 20″. Collection of the artist.

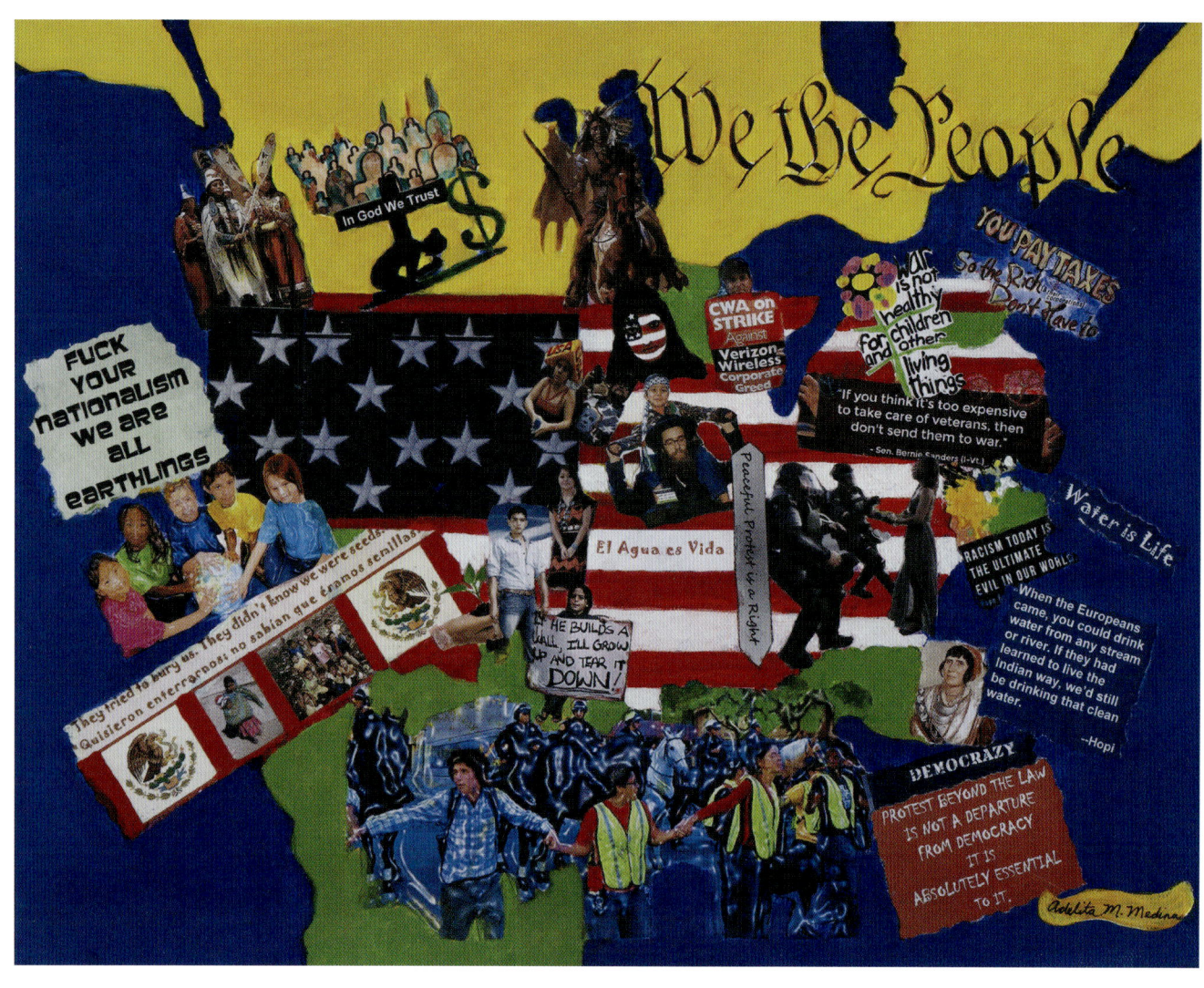

PLATE 114. *We the People–El pueblo unido*, 2017. Acrylic on canvas, paper collage, 14″ × 18″. Collection of the artist.

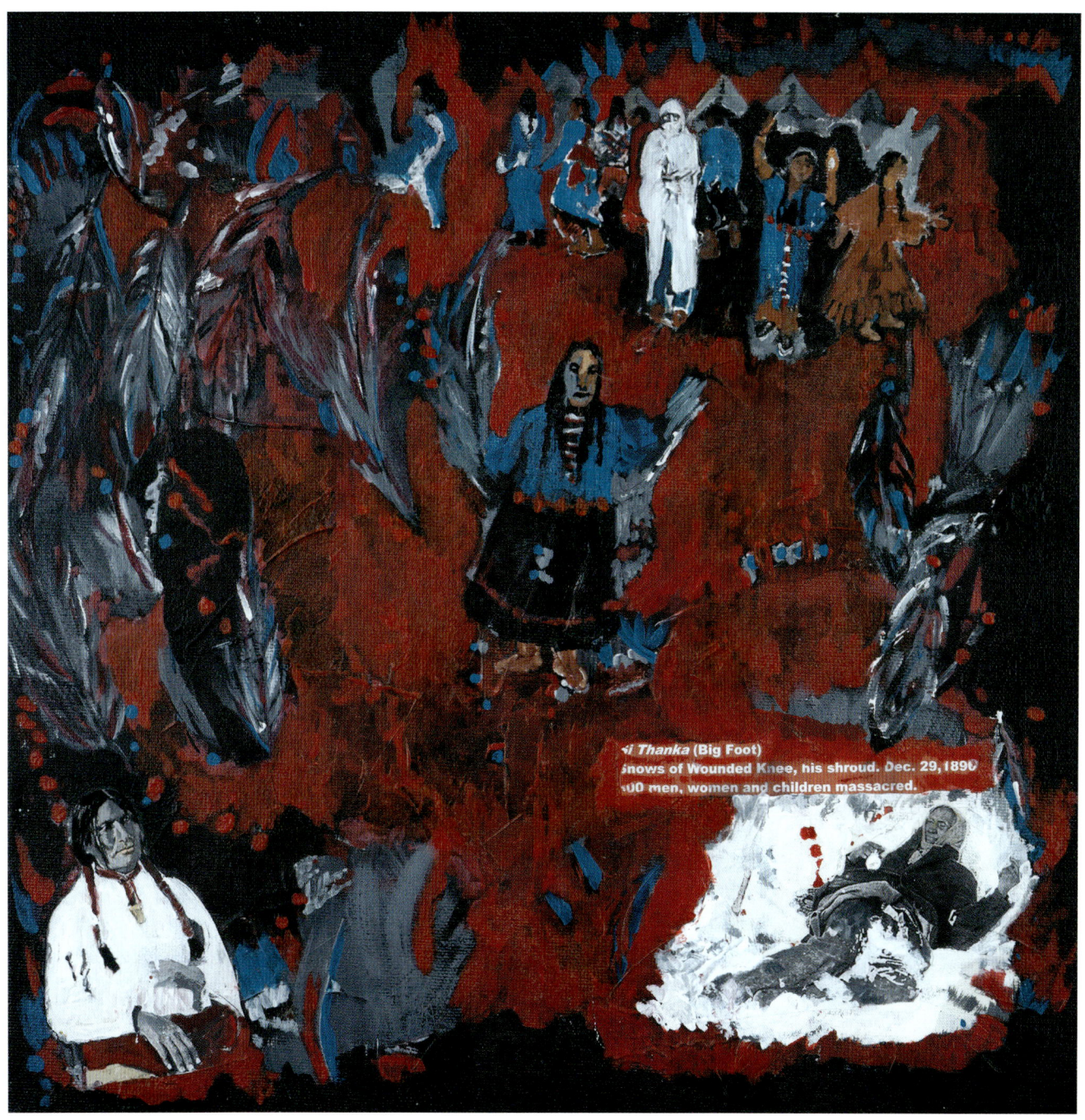

Text visible within the collage image:

...i Thanka (Big Foot)
...nows of Wounded Knee, his shroud. Dec. 29, 1890
...00 men, women and children massacred.

PLATE 115. *Ghost Dance*, 2017. Acrylic on canvas with collage, 14″ × 14″. Collection
of the artist.

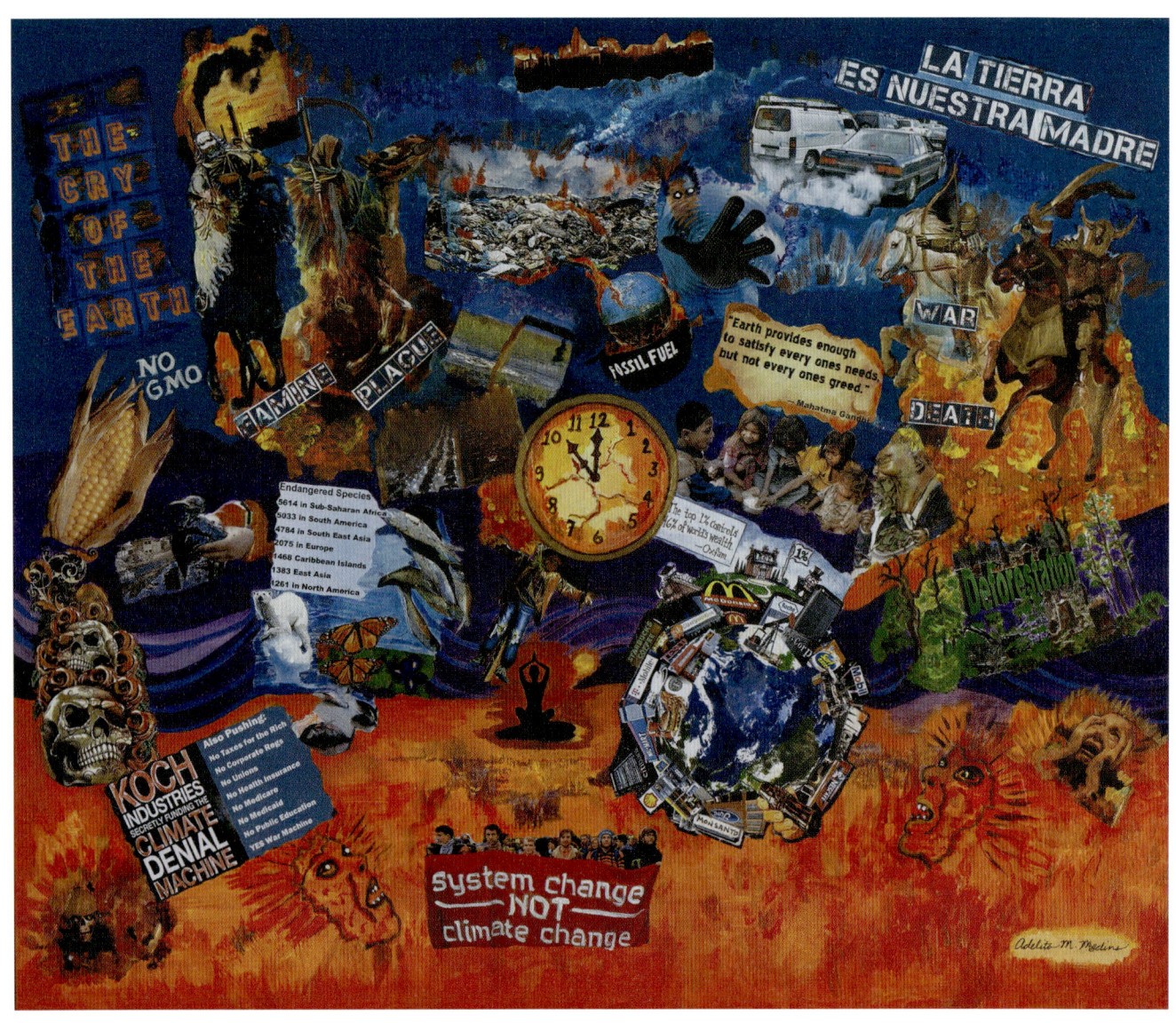

PLATE 116. *La tierra es nuestra madre–The Earth is Our Mother*, 2017. Acrylic on canvas, paper collage, 19″ × 24″. Collection of the artist.

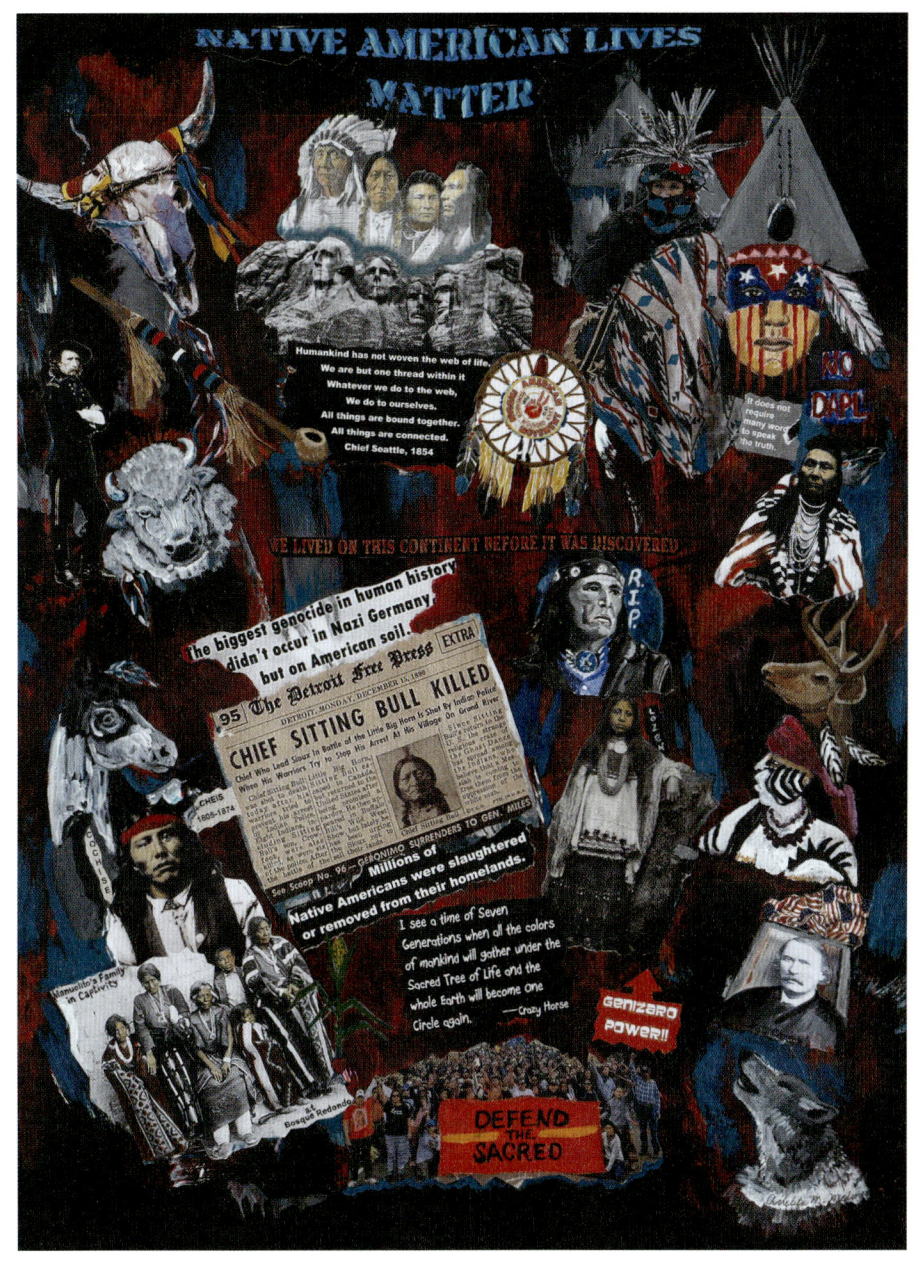

PLATE 117. *Native American Lives Matter*, 2017. Acrylic on canvas, paper collage,
24″ × 18″. Collection of the artist.

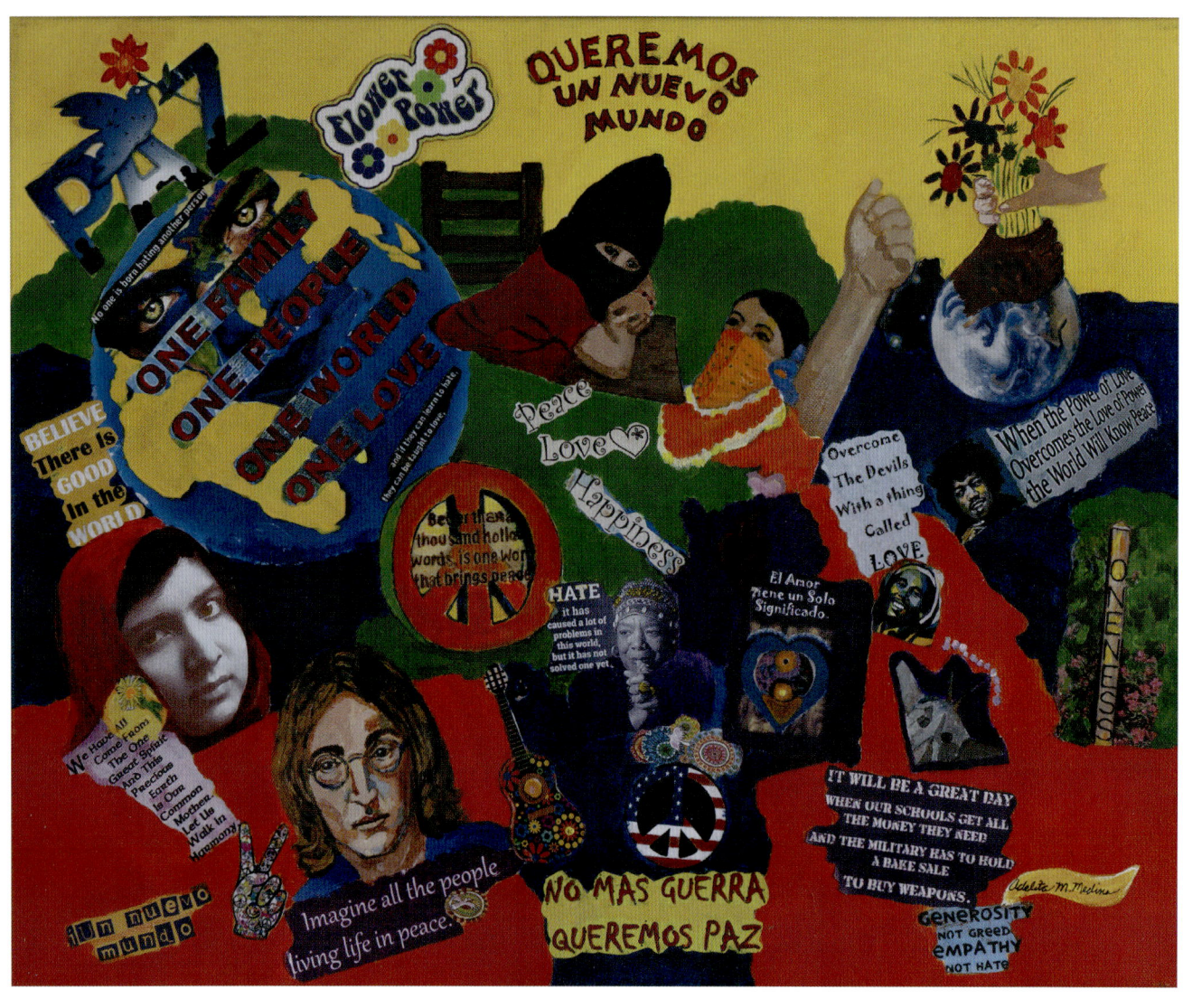

PLATE 118. *No más guerra–We Want Peace,* 2017. Acrylic on canvas, paper collage, 14″ × 18″. Collection of the artist.

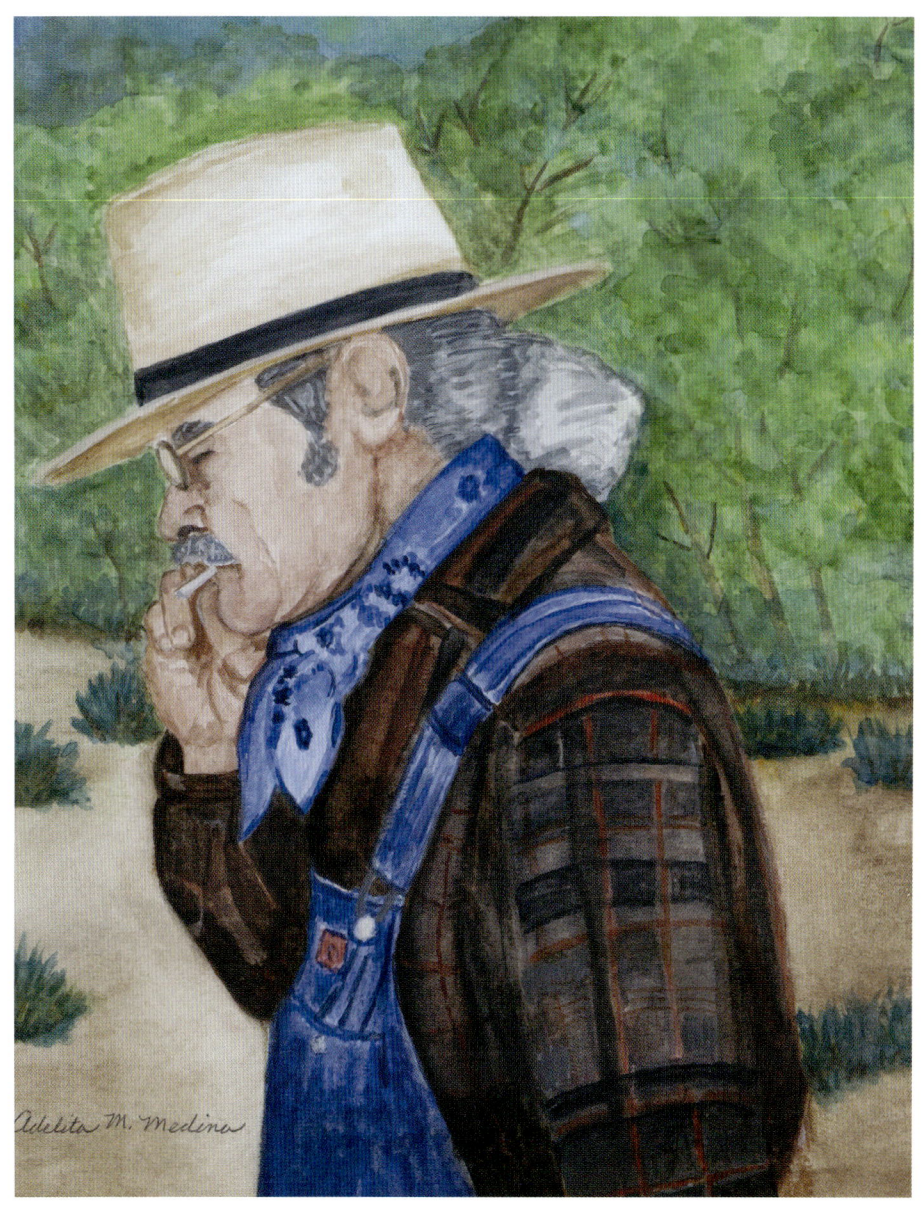

PLATE 119. *Lorenzo, hombre de la tierra*, 2018. Watercolor on paper, 14″ × 11″.
Collection of the artist.

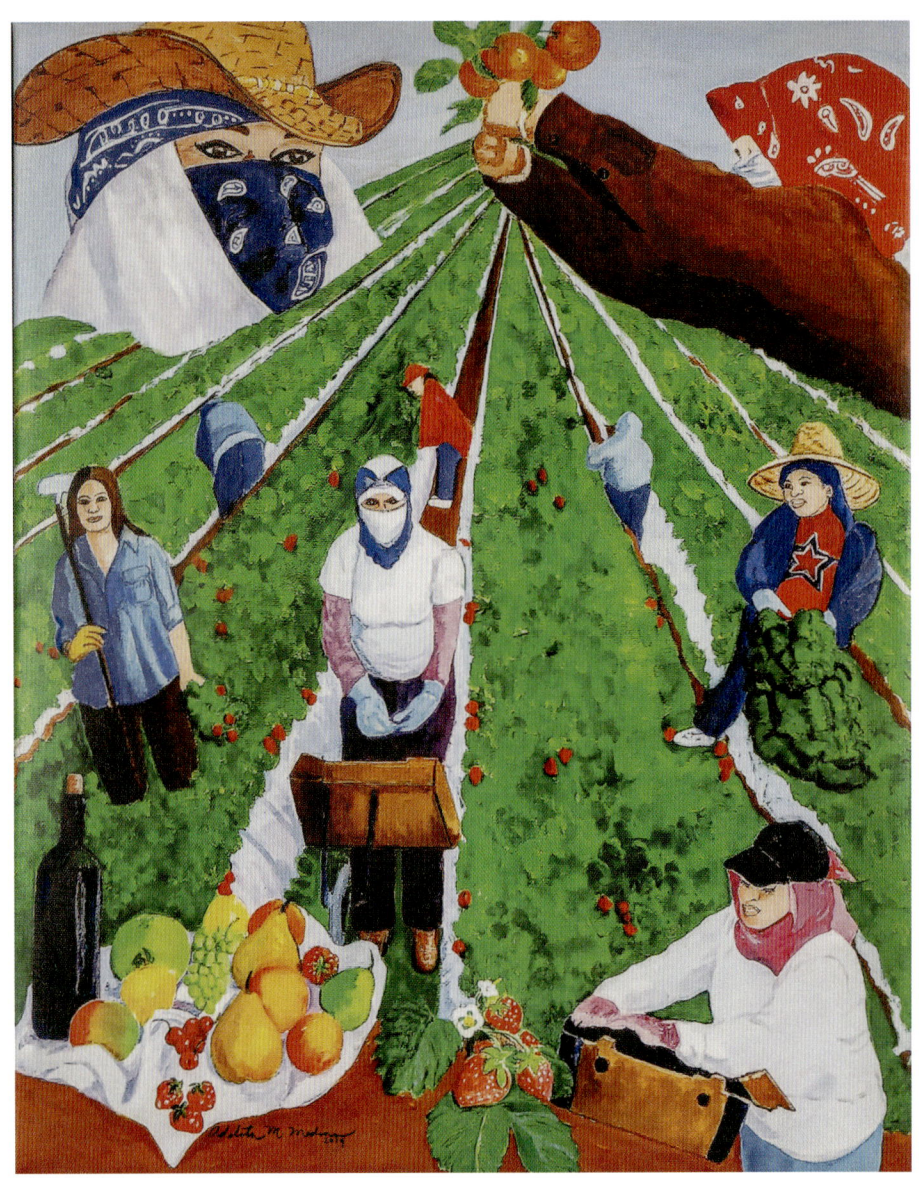

PLATE 120. *Campesinas*, 2019. Acrylic on canvas, 24″ × 18″. Collection of Alianza Nacional de Campesinas, Oxnard, California.

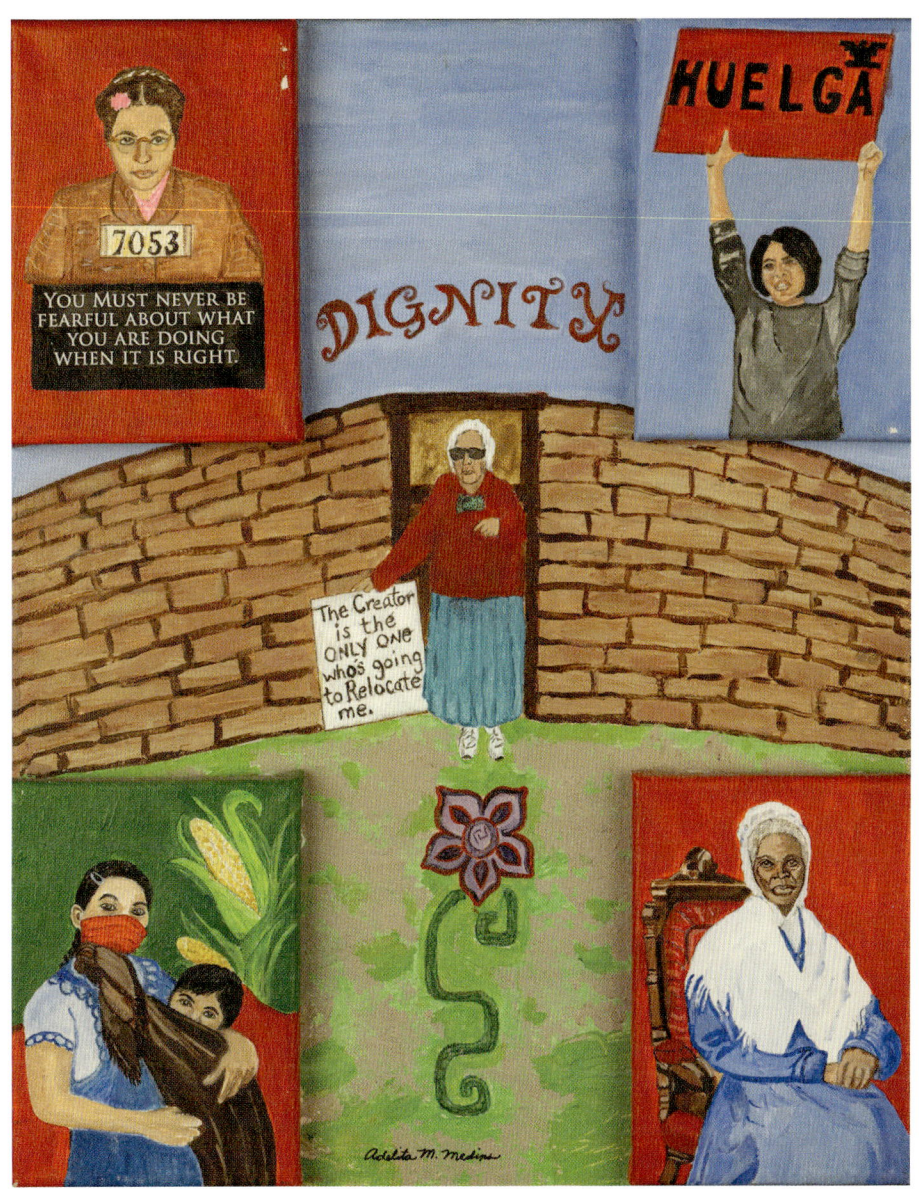

PLATE 121. *Dignity*, 2019. Acrylic on canvas, 15 ½″ × 20″. Collection of the artist.

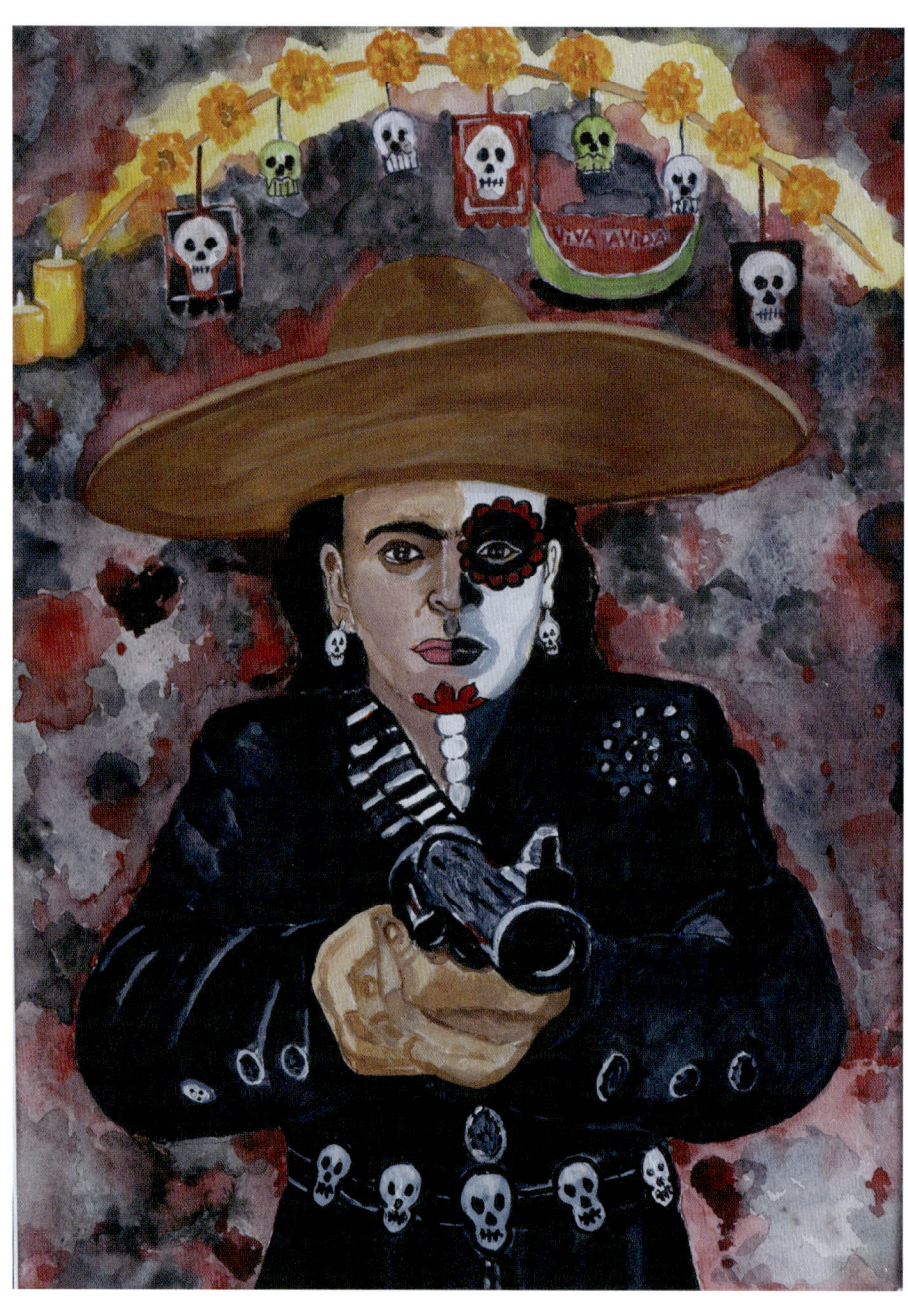

PLATE 122. *Frida Pistolera*, 2019. Watercolor and acrylic on paper, 20″ × 16″.
Collection of the artist.

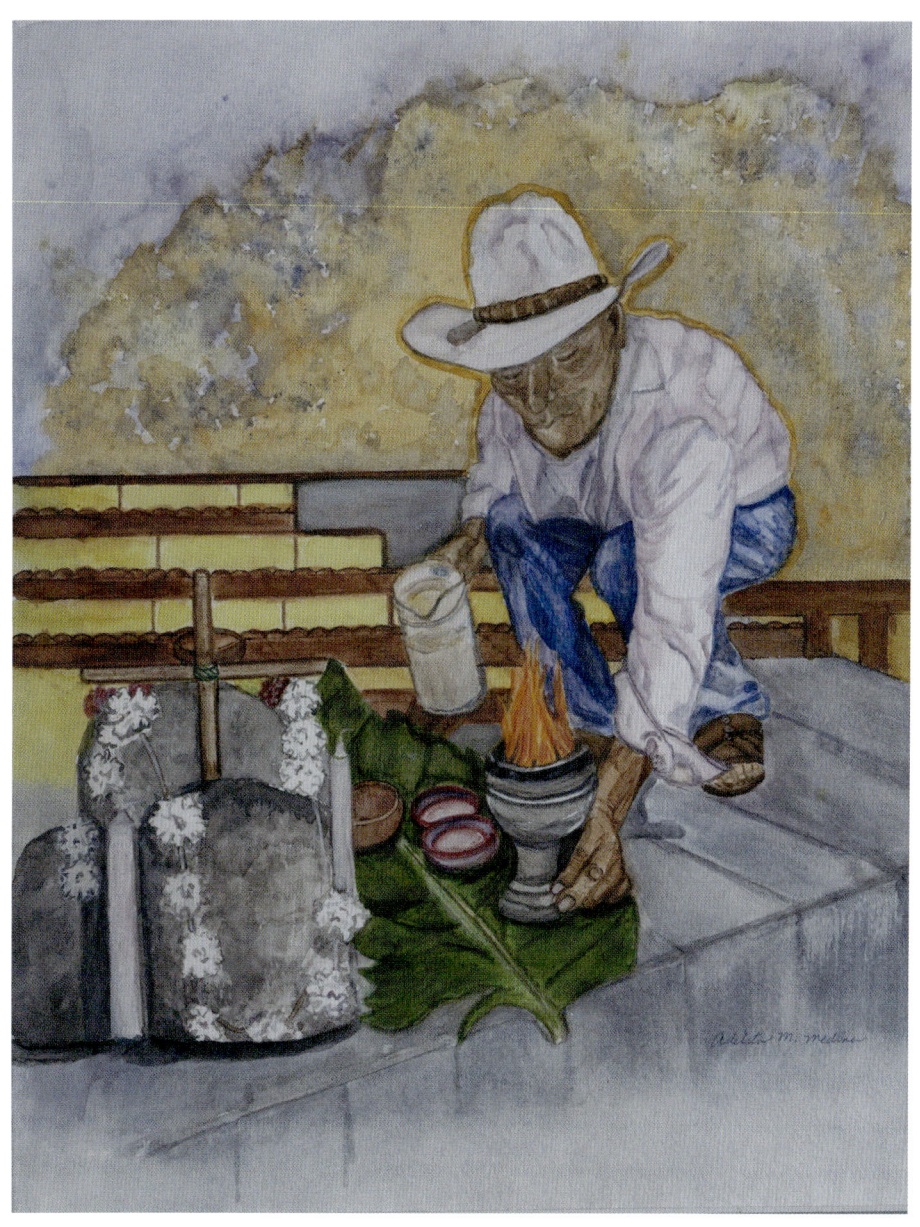

PLATE 123. *Pedrotzin, Keeper of the Stones*, 2019. Watercolor on paper, 20″ × 16″.
   Collection of the artist.

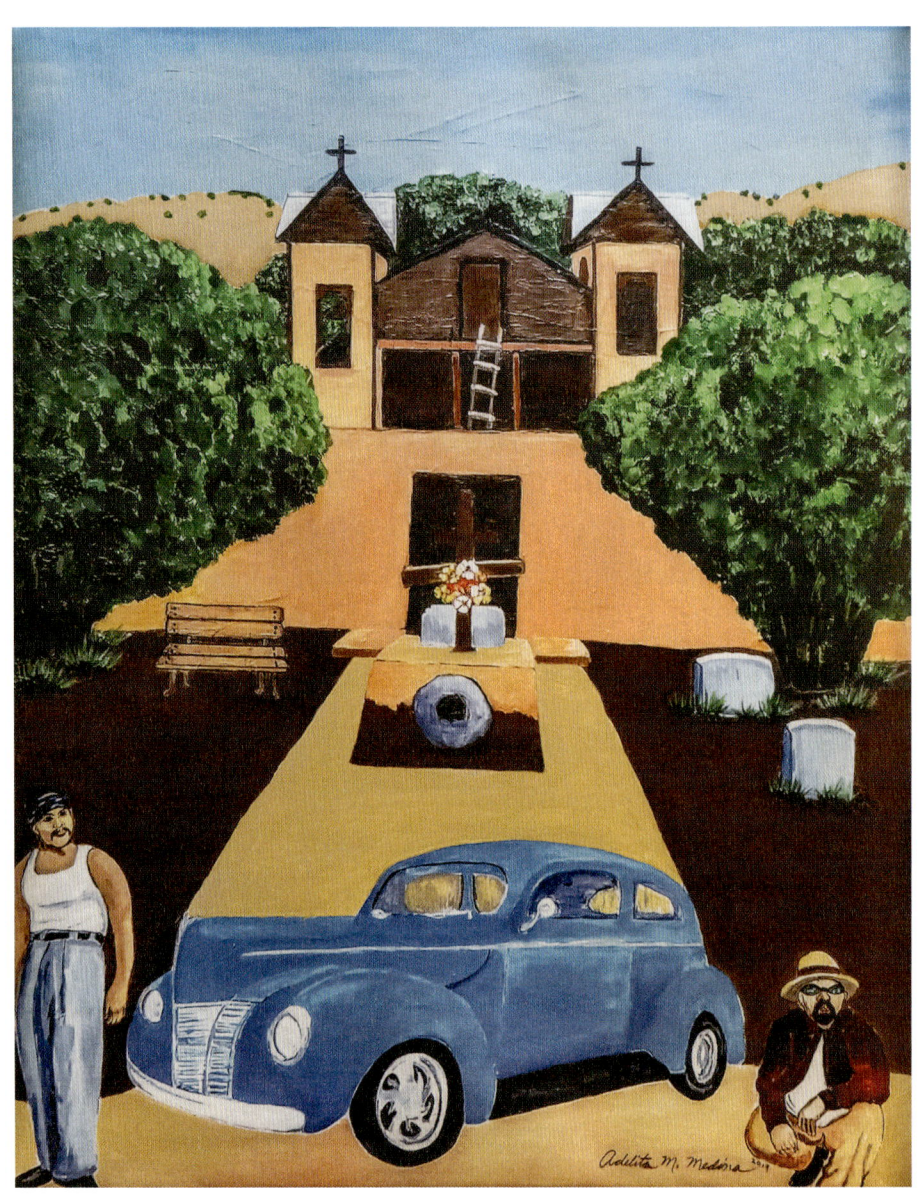

PLATE 124. *Vatos at the Santuario*, 2019. Acrylic on wood, 24″ × 18″. Private collection of Marvin Romero.

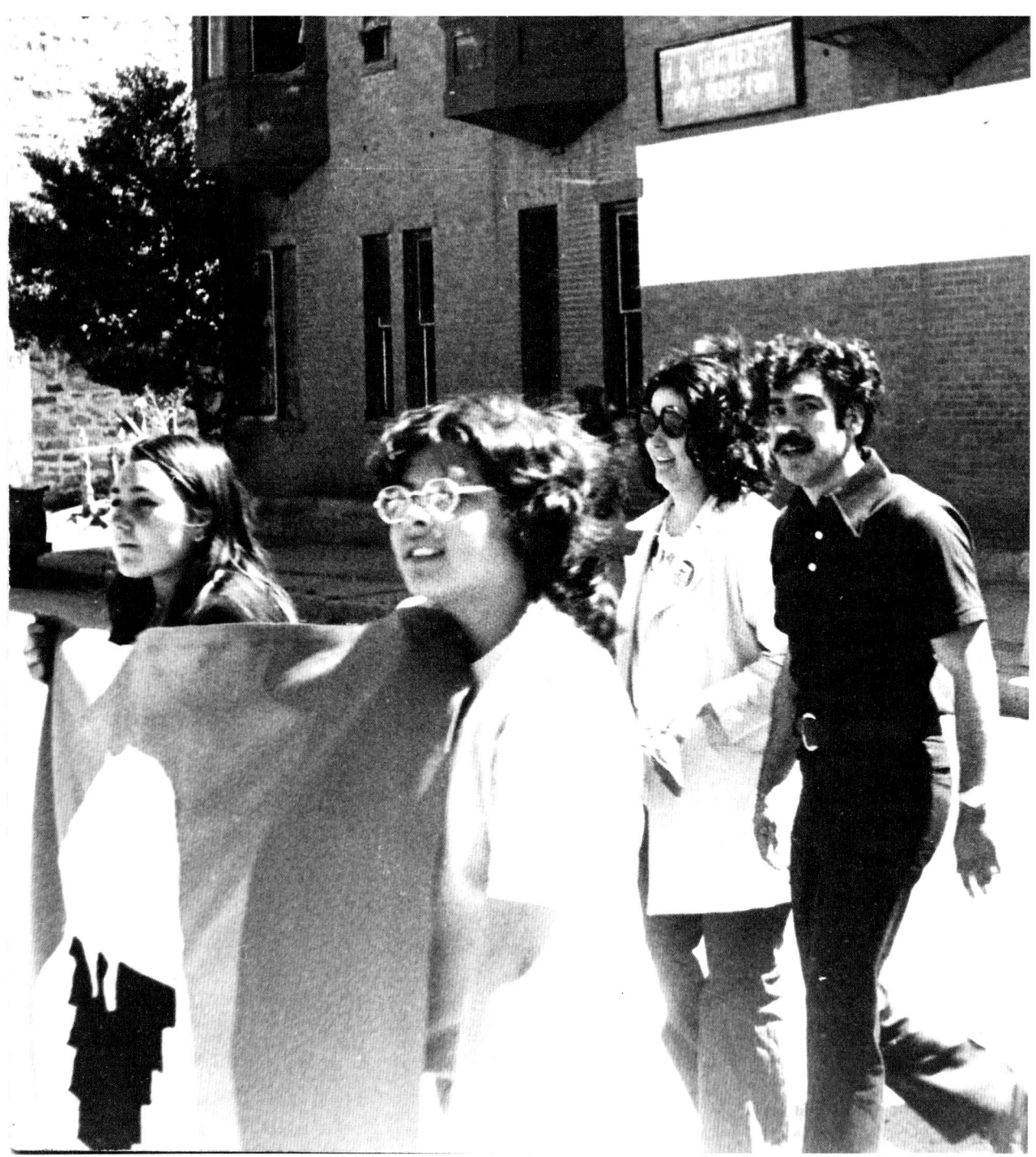

PLATE 125. *Barnie, Corky, and Geri*, 1973. Silver gelatin print, 9″ × 8″. Private
collection of David Montoya and Susan Seymour.

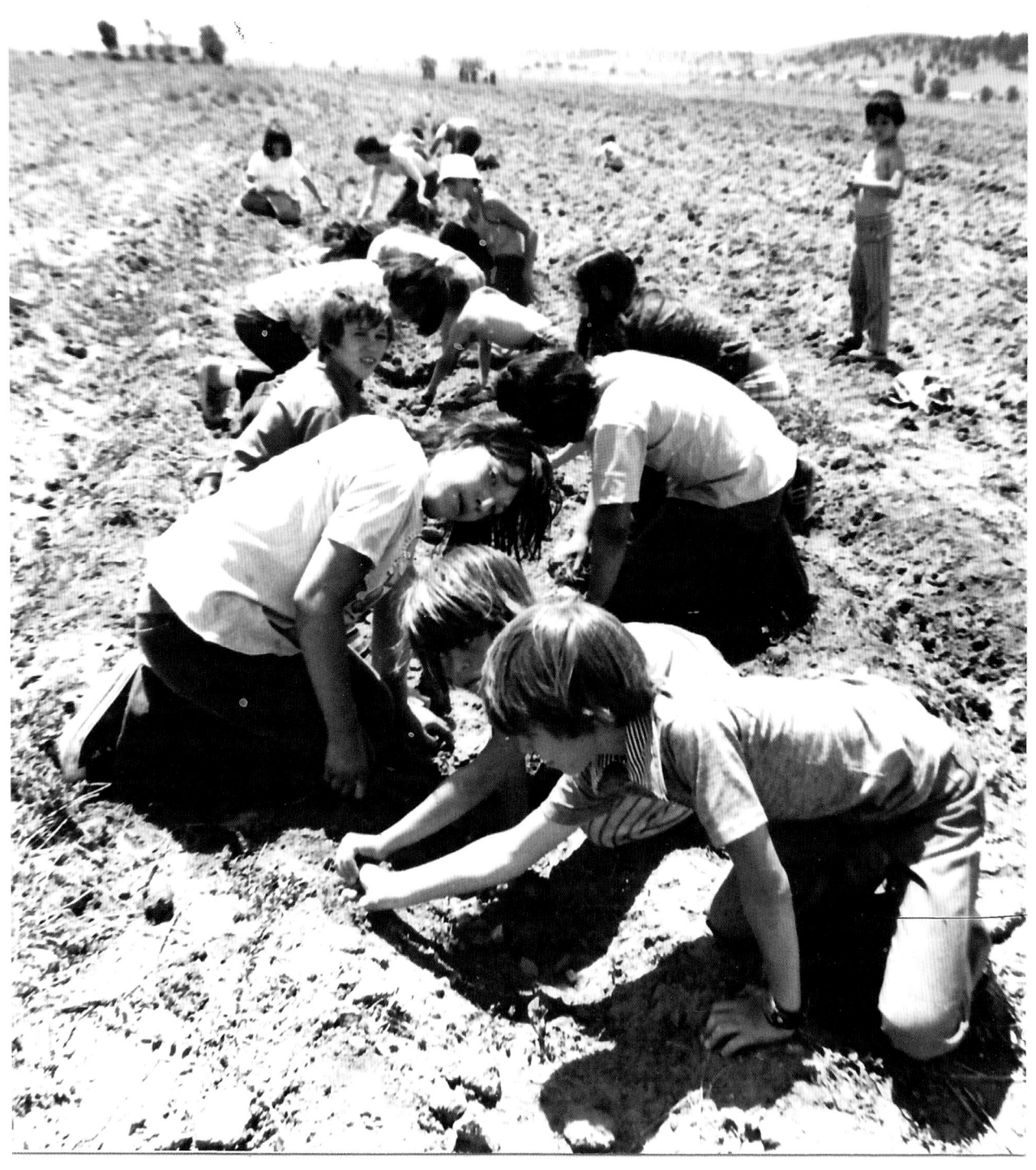

PLATE 126. *Niños sembrando en Moctezuma*, 1973. Silver gelatin print, 5″ × 4 ¼″.
Private collection of David Montoya and Susan Seymour.

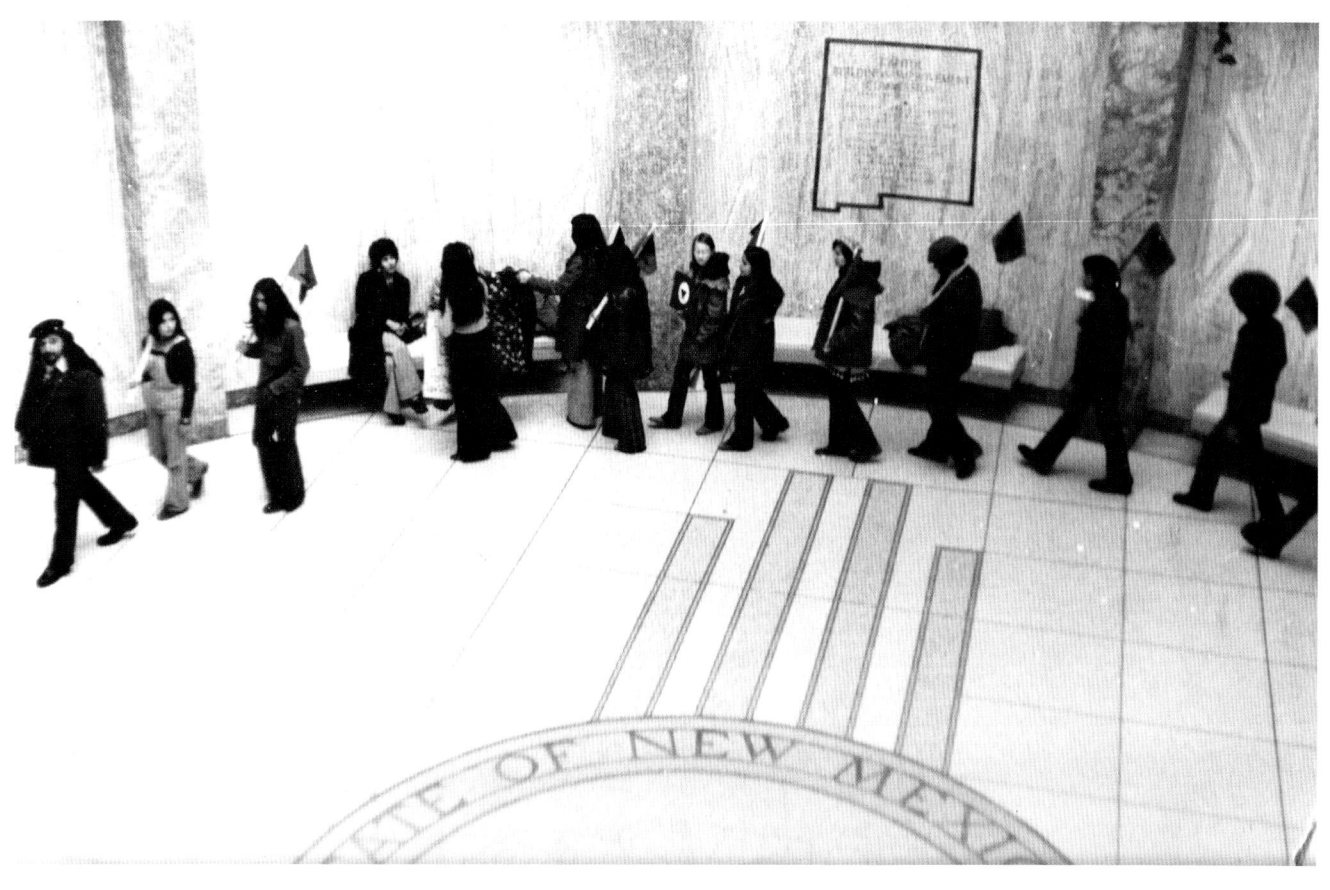

PLATE 127. *Protest at the Capitol*, 1973. Silver gelatin print, 9″ × 12″. Private collection
of David Montoya and Susan Seymour.

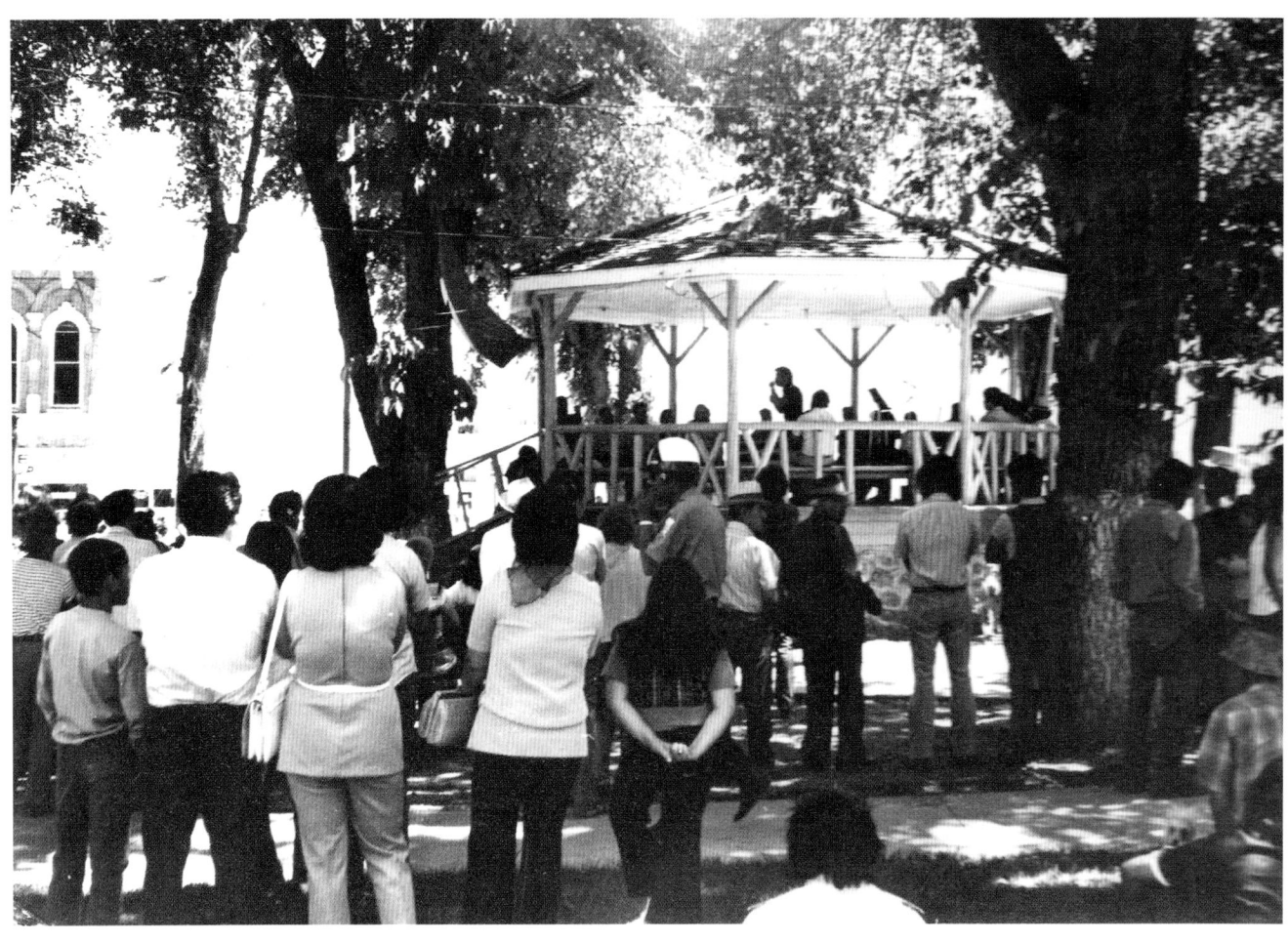

PLATE 128. *Corky Speaks in the Plaza*, 1973. Silver gelatin print, *6″ × 9″*. Private collection of David Montoya and Susan Seymour.

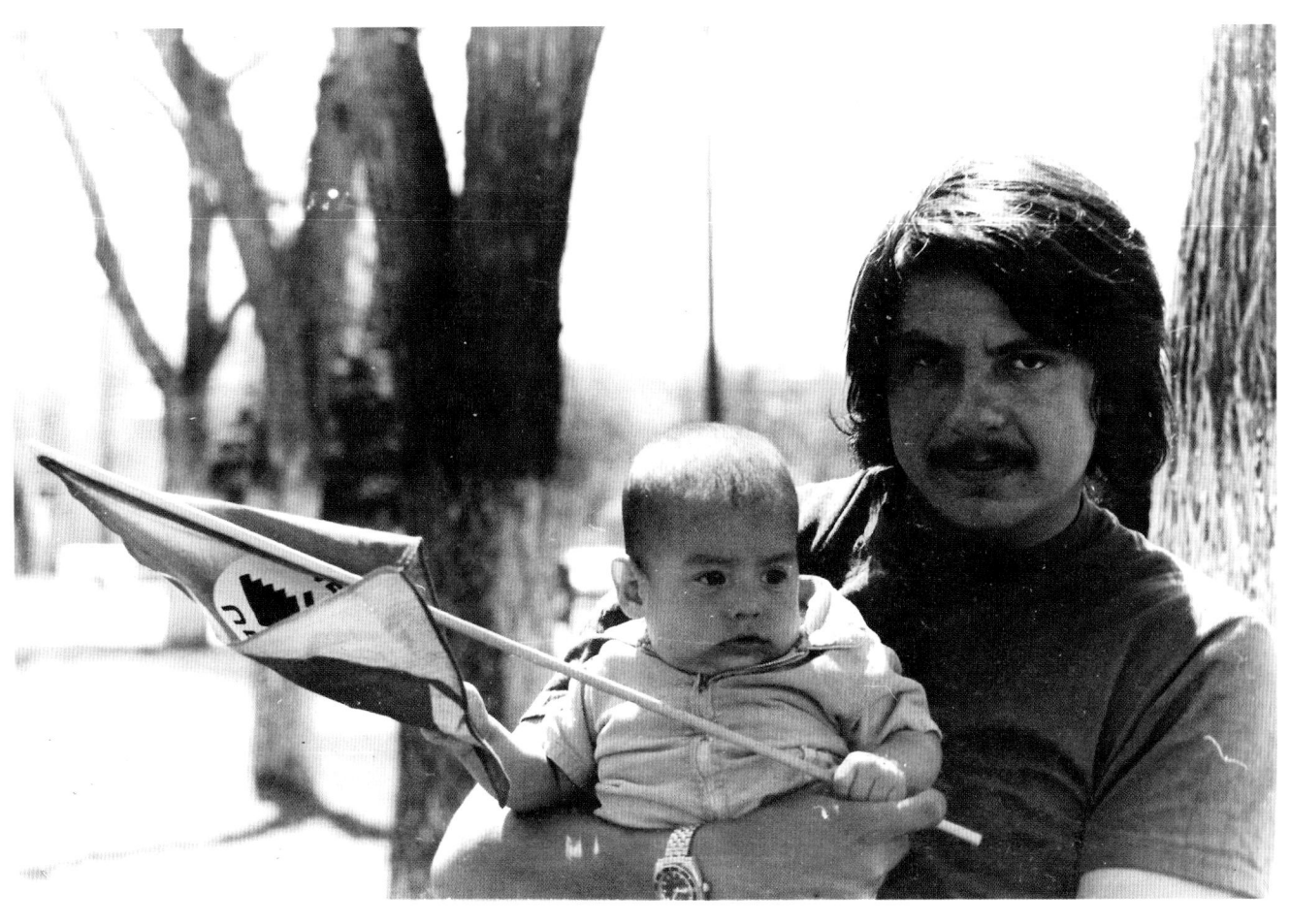

PLATE 129. *David and Joaquinito*, 1973. Silver gelatin print, 5″ × 8″. Private collection of David Montoya and Susan Seymour.

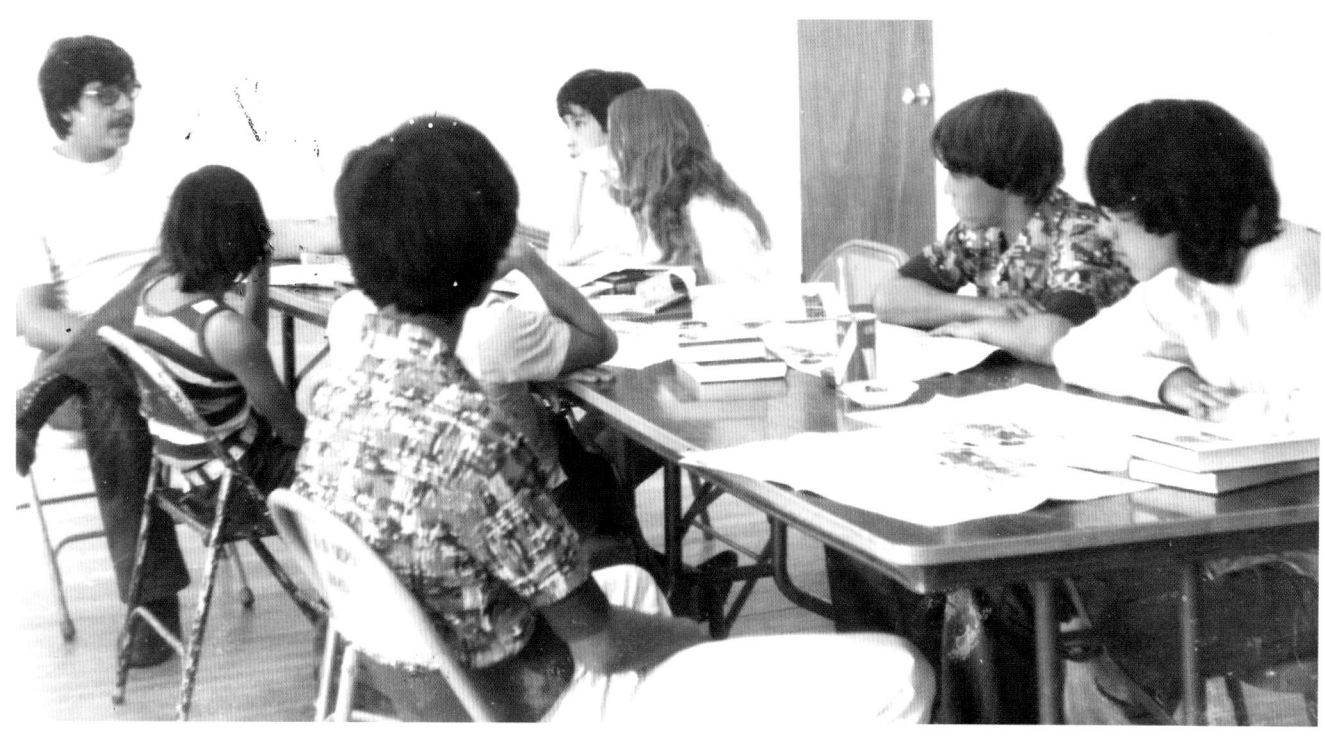

PLATE 130. *David with Students*, 1973. Silver gelatin print, 3″ × 6″. Private collection of David Montoya and Susan Seymour.

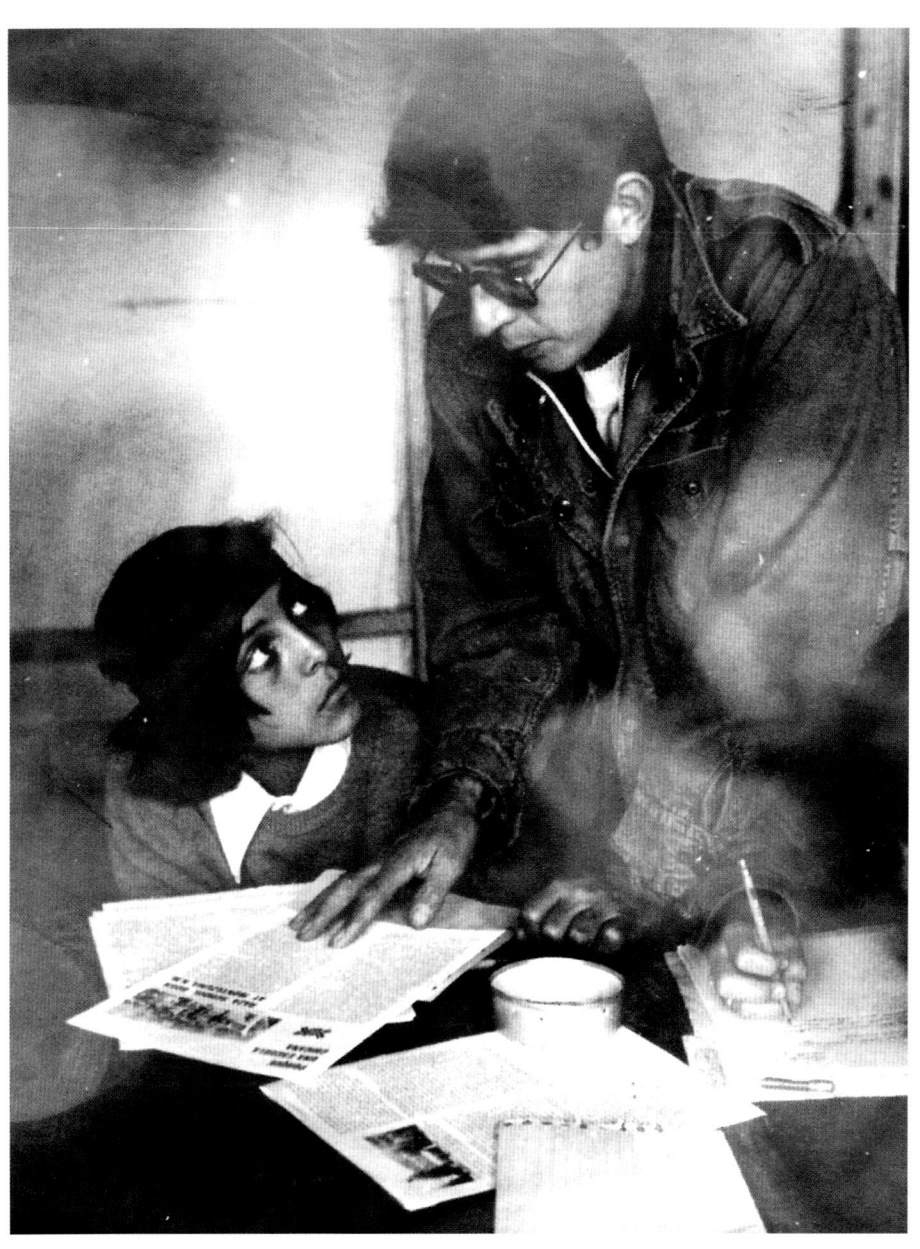

PLATE 131. *Fred with a Student*, 1973. Silver gelatin print, 8″ × 6″. Private collection
    of David Montoya and Susan Seymour.

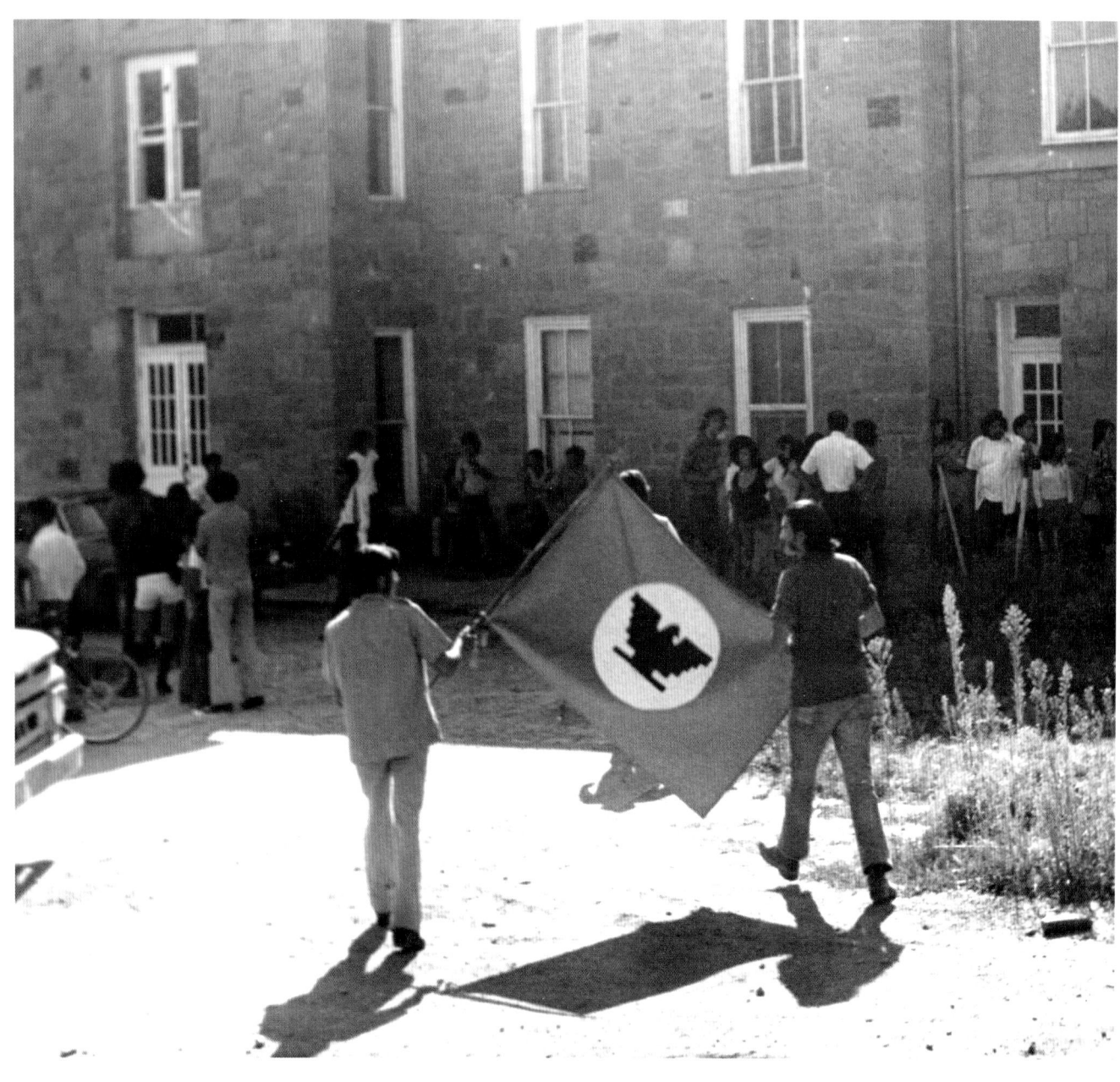

PLATE 132. *Pat Paiz and the Flag at Montezuma*, 1973. Silver gelatin print, 8″ × 10″.
Private collection of David Montoya and Susan Seymour.

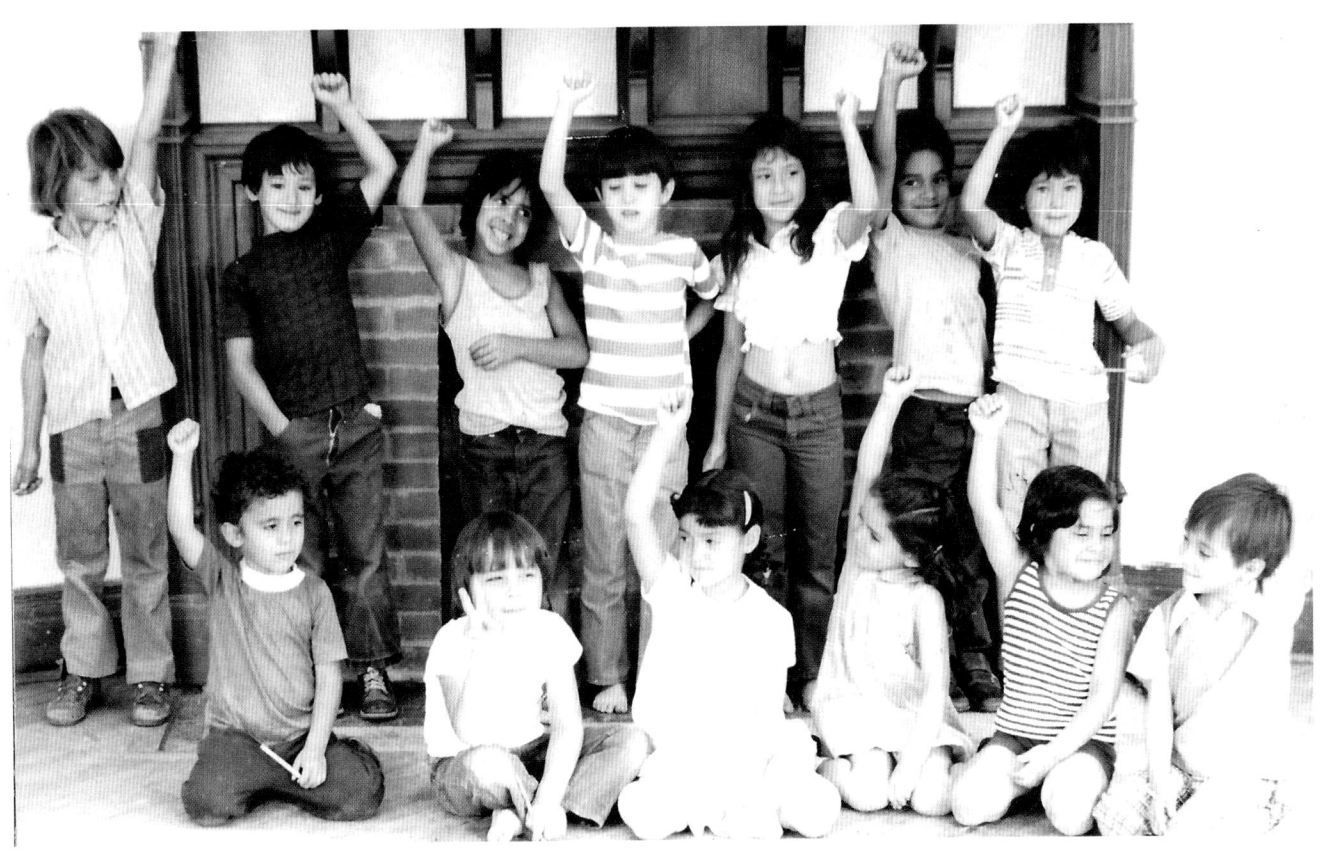

PLATE 133. *Chicanitos at the Escuela Antonio José Martínez*, 1973. Silver gelatin print,
4″ × 6″. Private collection of David Montoya and Susan Seymour.

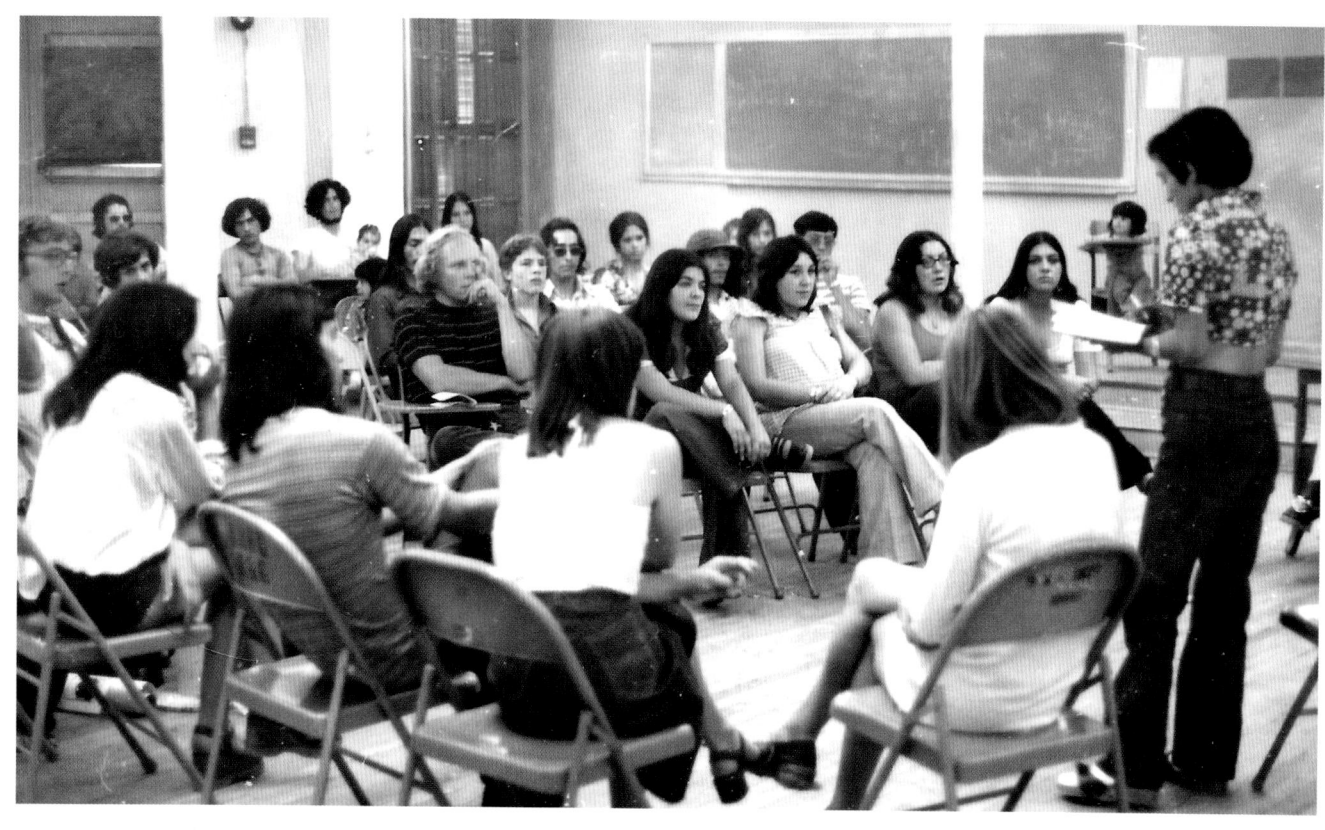

PLATE 134. *Lucila Ríos Teaching*, 1973. Silver gelatin print, 3 ½" × 5". Private collection of David Montoya and Susan Seymour.

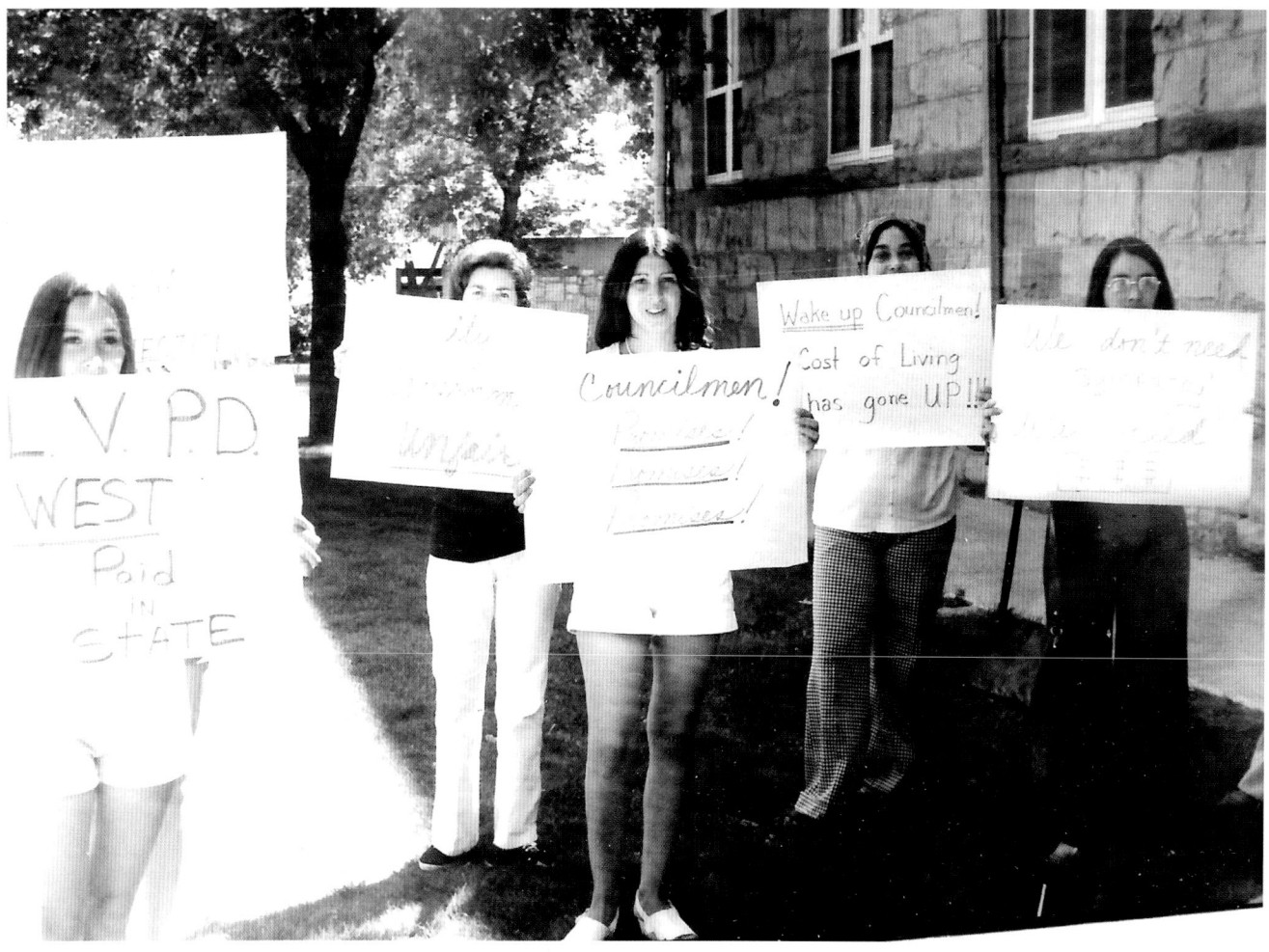

PLATE 135. *Las Vegas Police Department Protest*, 1973. Silver gelatin print, 5 ½″ × 9″.
   Private collection of David Montoya and Susan Seymour.

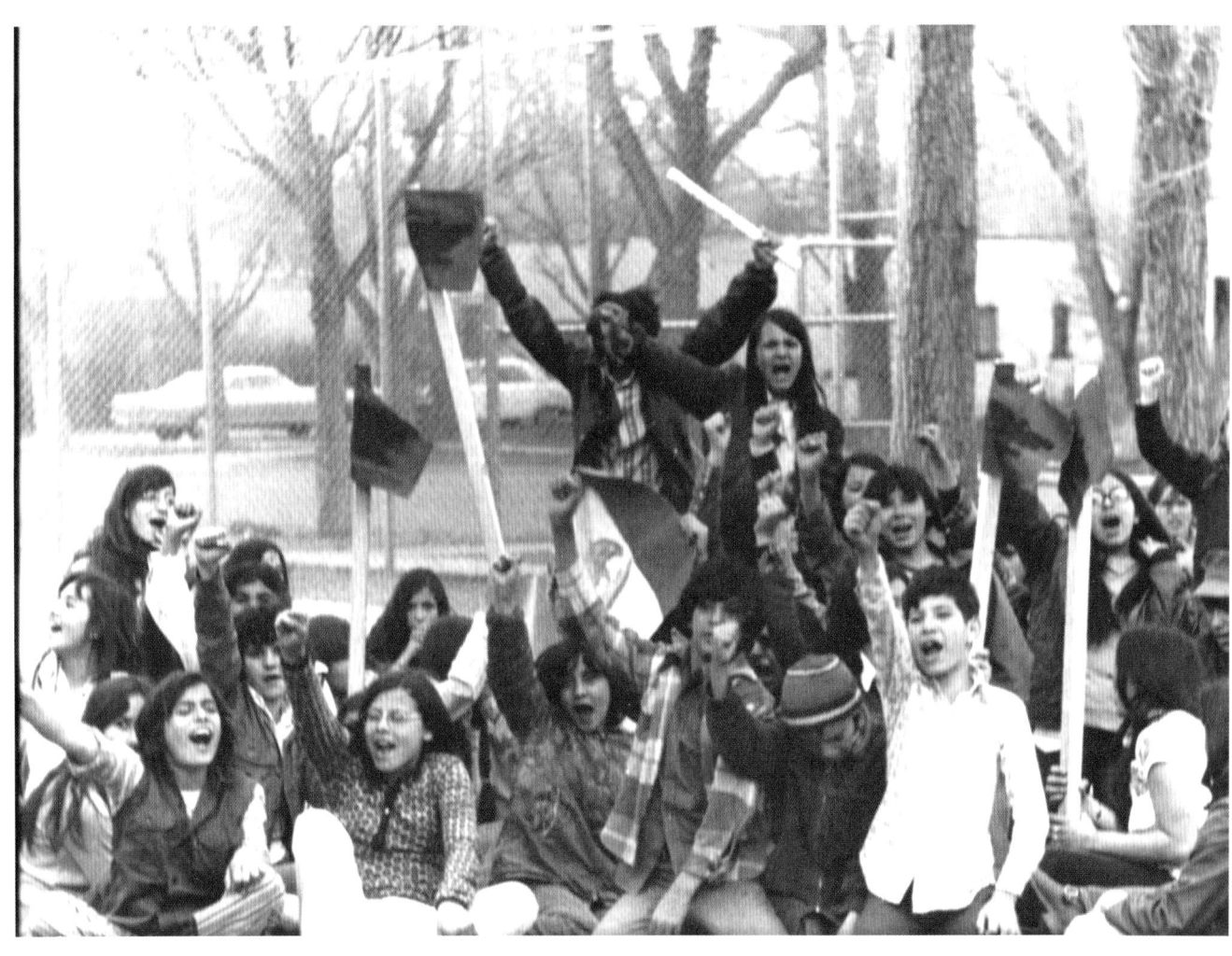

PLATE 136. *East Las Vegas Middle School Student Walkout*, 1973. Silver gelatin print, 11″ × 14″. Private collection of David Montoya and Susan Seymour.

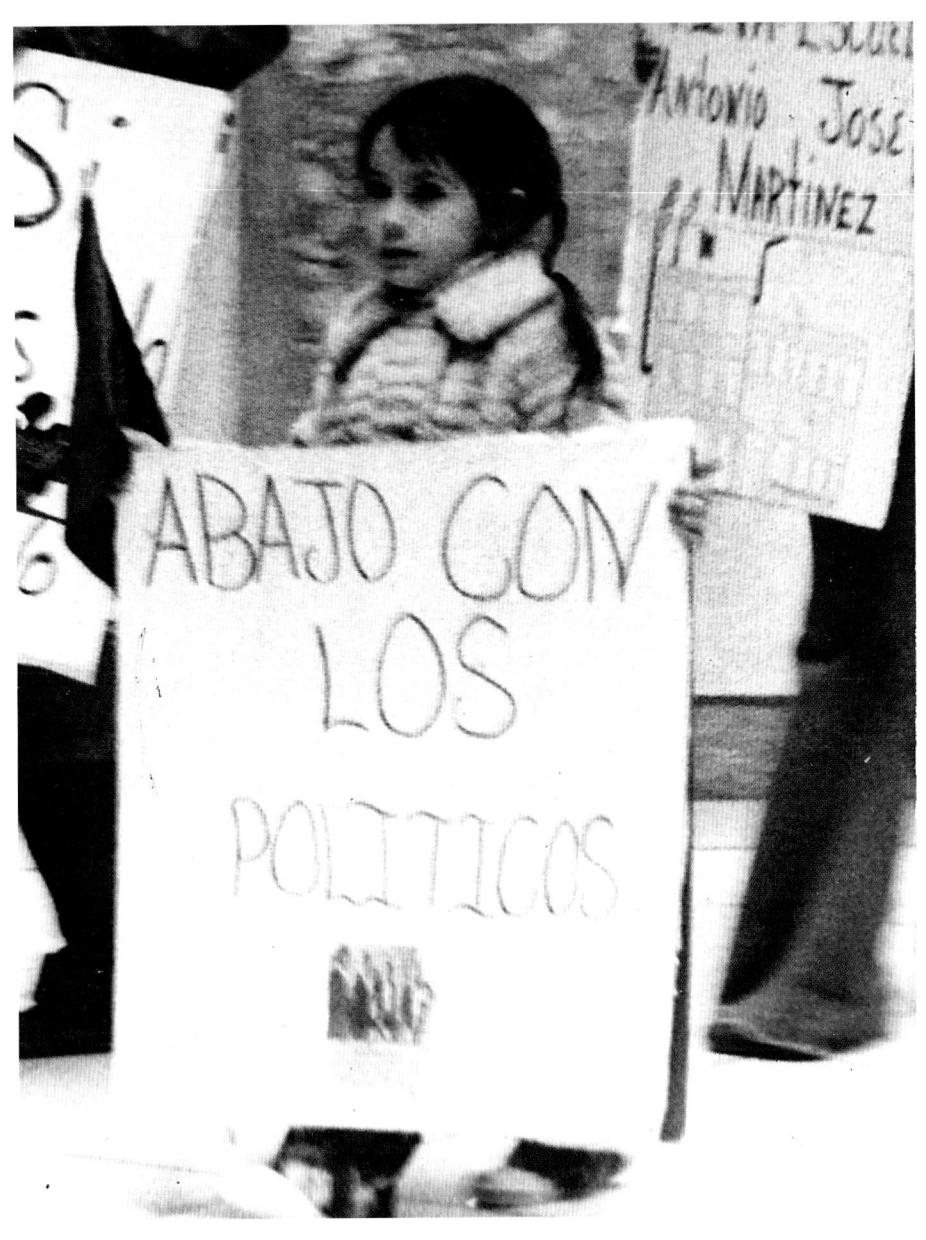

PLATE 137. *Mónica, Abajo con los Políticos*, 1973. Silver gelatin print, 6 ½" × 5". Private
    collection of David Montoya and Susan Seymour.

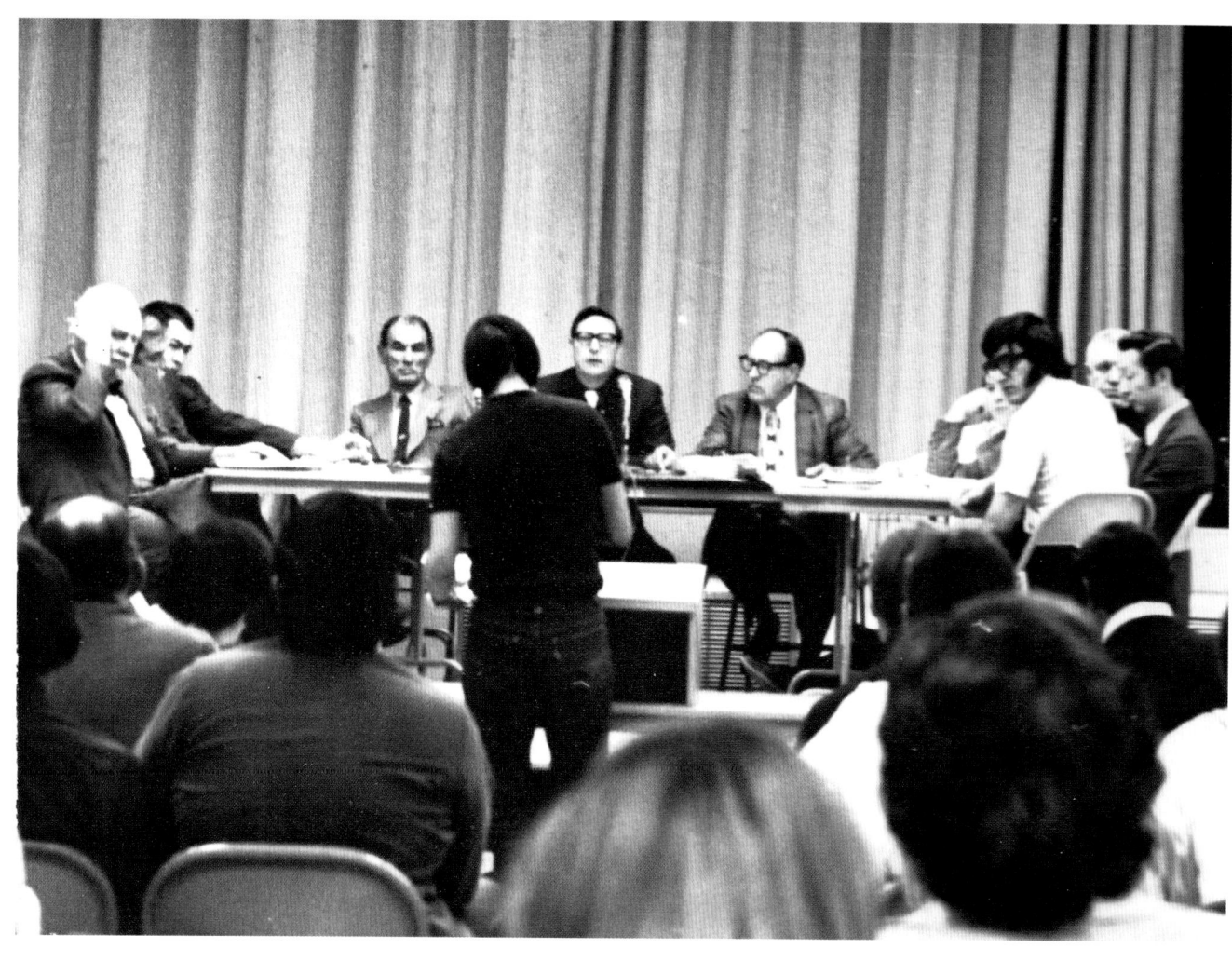

PLATE 138. *Meeting with Frank Ángel and the Board at NMHU*, 1973. Silver gelatin print, 6″ × 9″. Private collection of David Montoya and Susan Seymour.

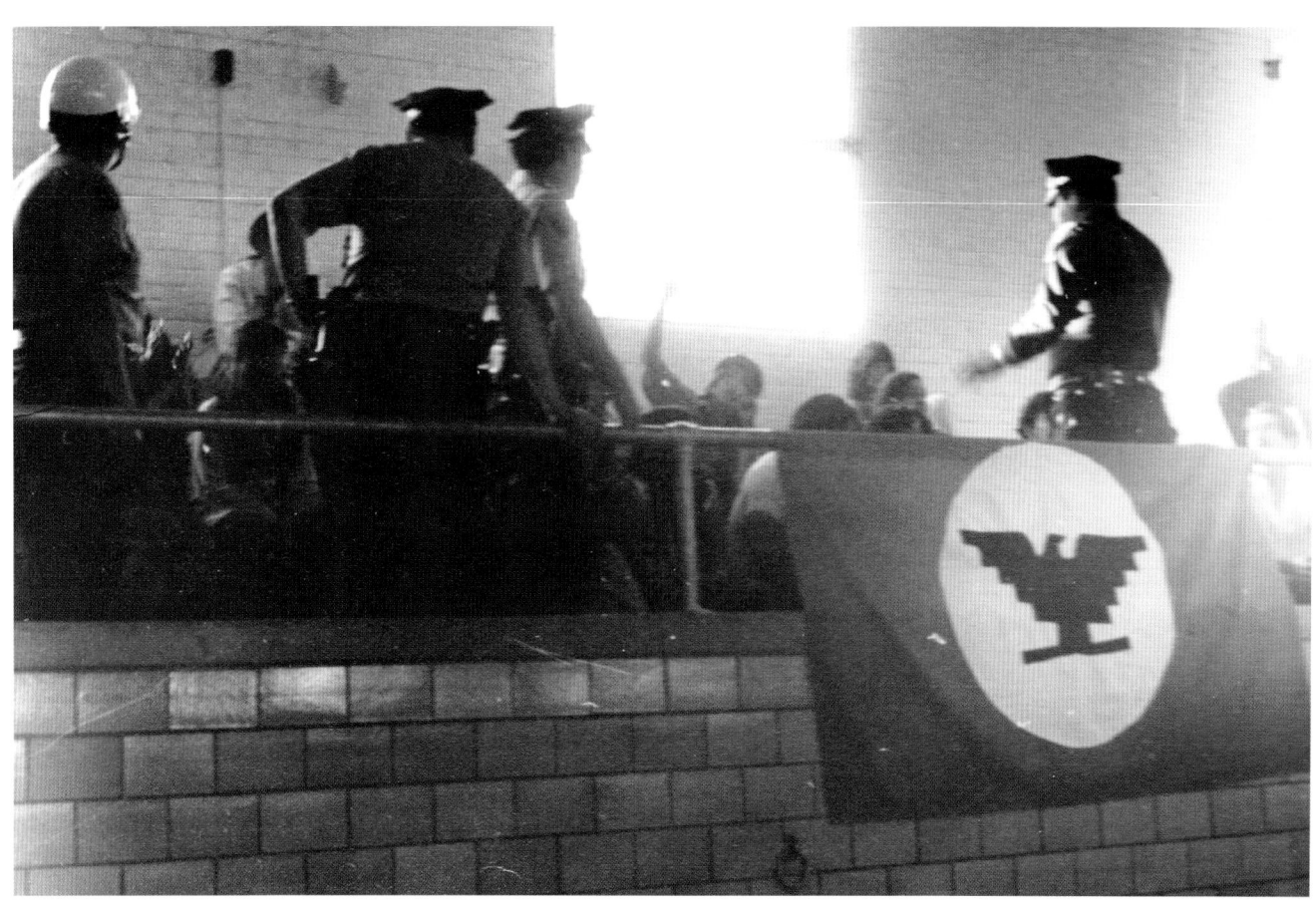

PLATE 139. *Police arrive at the East Las Vegas School Board Protest*, 1973. Silver gelatin
print, 6″ × 9″. Private collection of David Montoya and Susan Seymour.

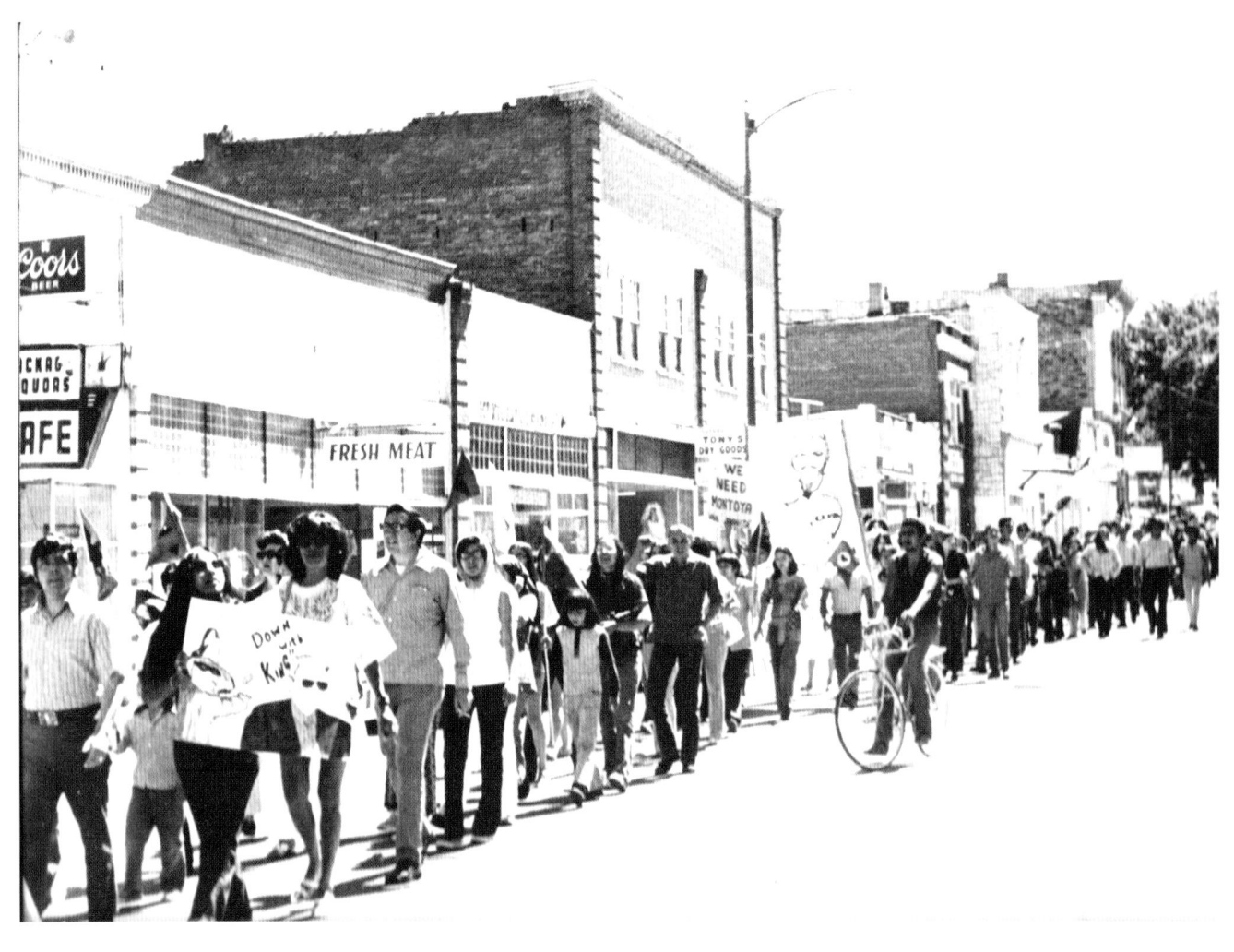

PLATE 140. *Sylvia and Betita March on Bridge Street, Down with King*, 1973. Silver gelatin print, 9″ × 14″. Private collection of David Montoya and Susan Seymour.

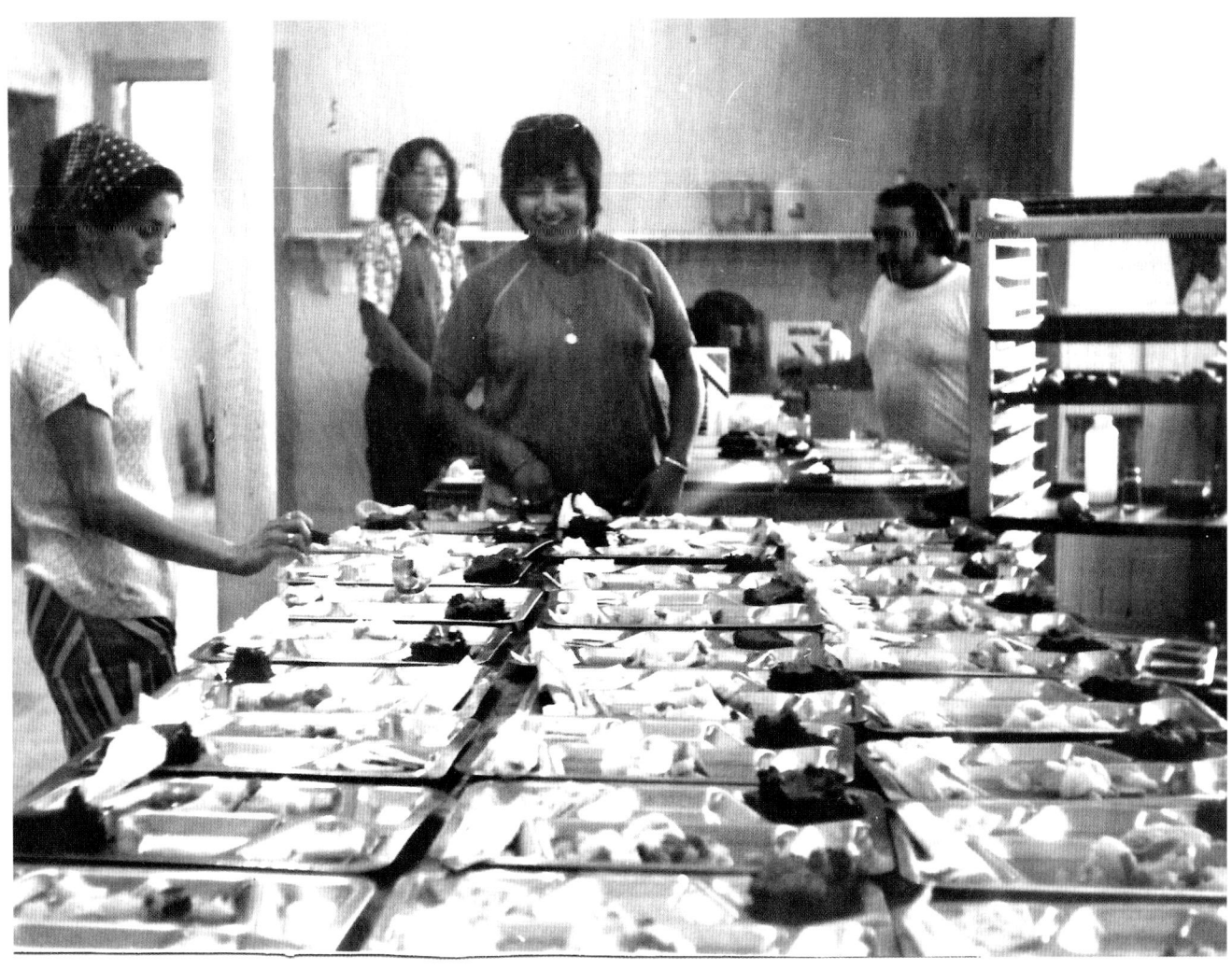

PLATE 141. *Sylvia and Pita in the Kitchen at the Castle*, 1973. Silver gelatin print,
4 ½" × 6". Private collection of David Montoya and Susan Seymour.

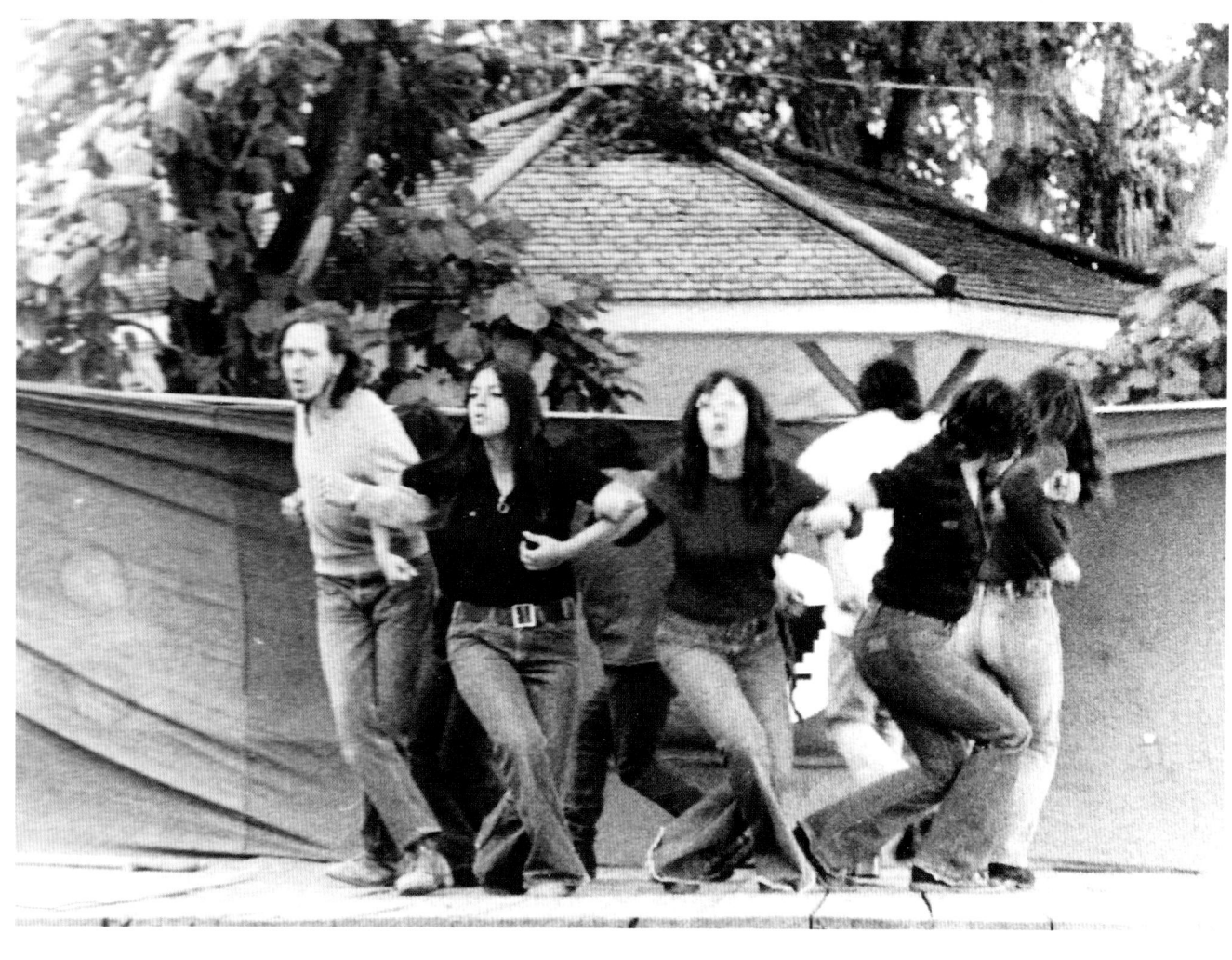

PLATE 142. *Teatro del Norte de Las Vegas*, 1973. Silver gelatin print, 6 ½″ × 9″. Private collection of David Montoya and Susan Seymour.

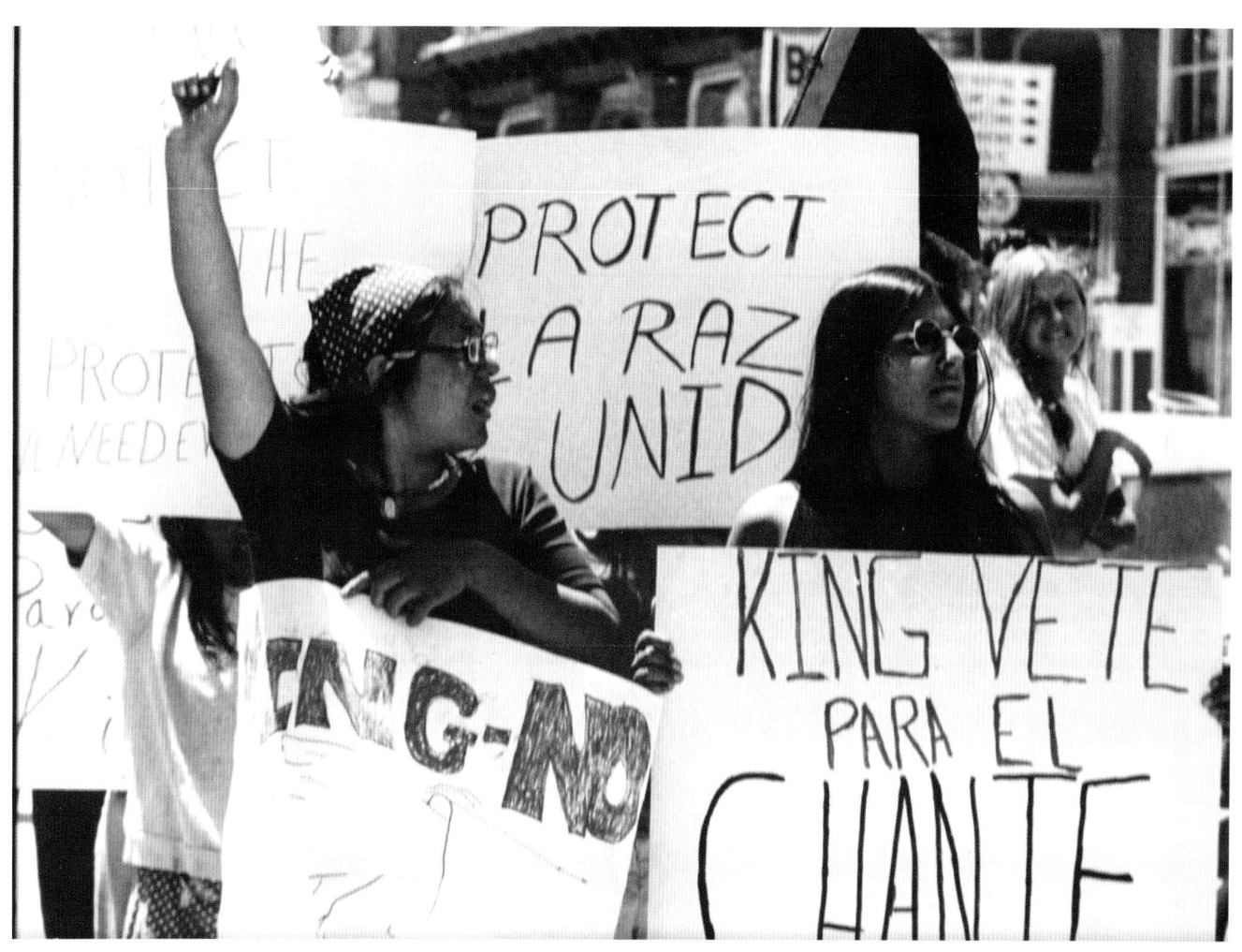

PLATE 143. *Trinnie and JoAnn (Racoon), Members of Chicanos Unidos Para Justicia,*
    1973. Silver gelatin print, 11" × 14". Private collection of David Montoya
    and Susan Seymour.

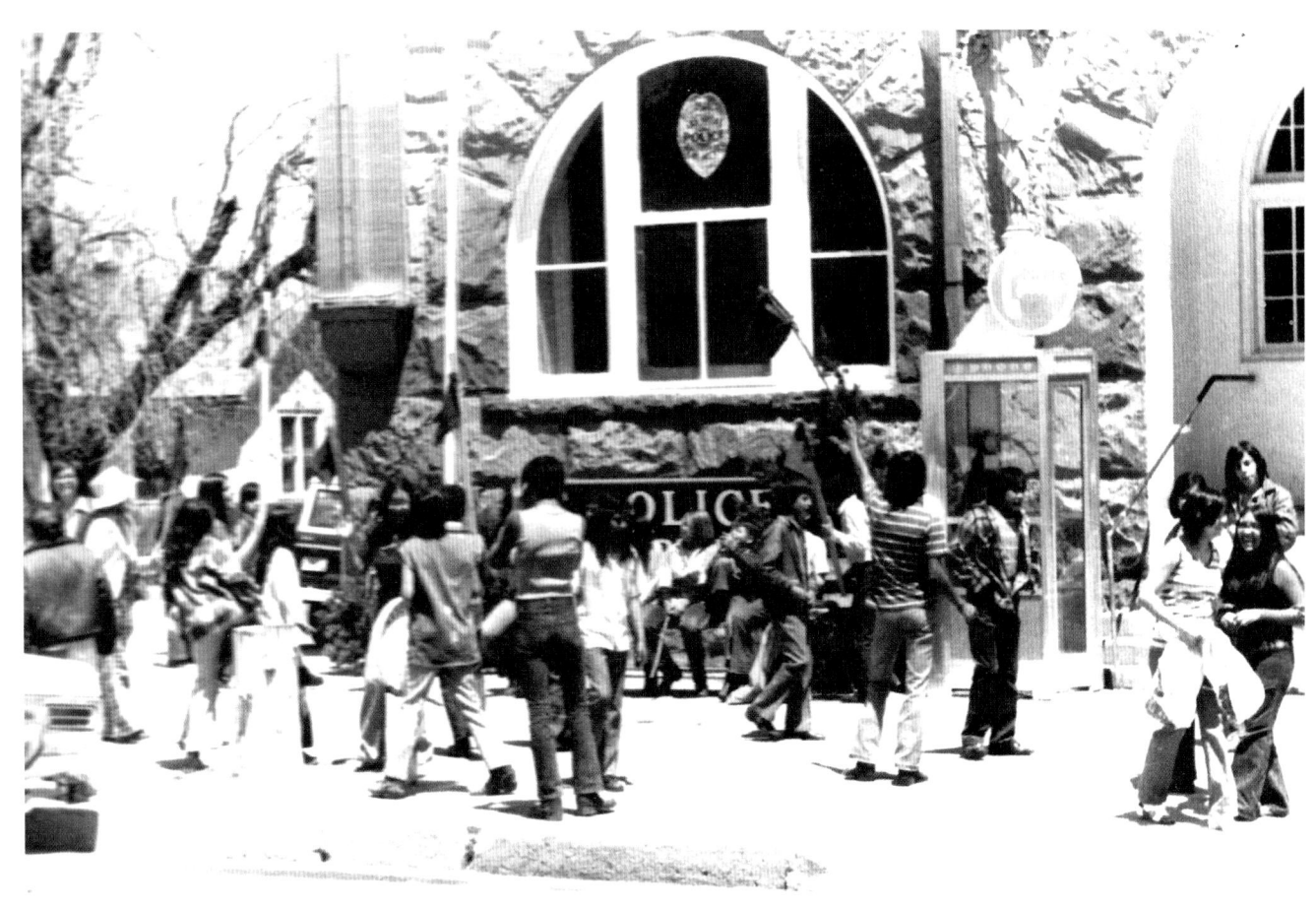

PLATE 144. *East Las Vegas Students Protest at the Police Station*, 1973. Silver gelatin print, 4 ½″ × 5 ½″. Private collection of David Montoya and Susan Seymour.

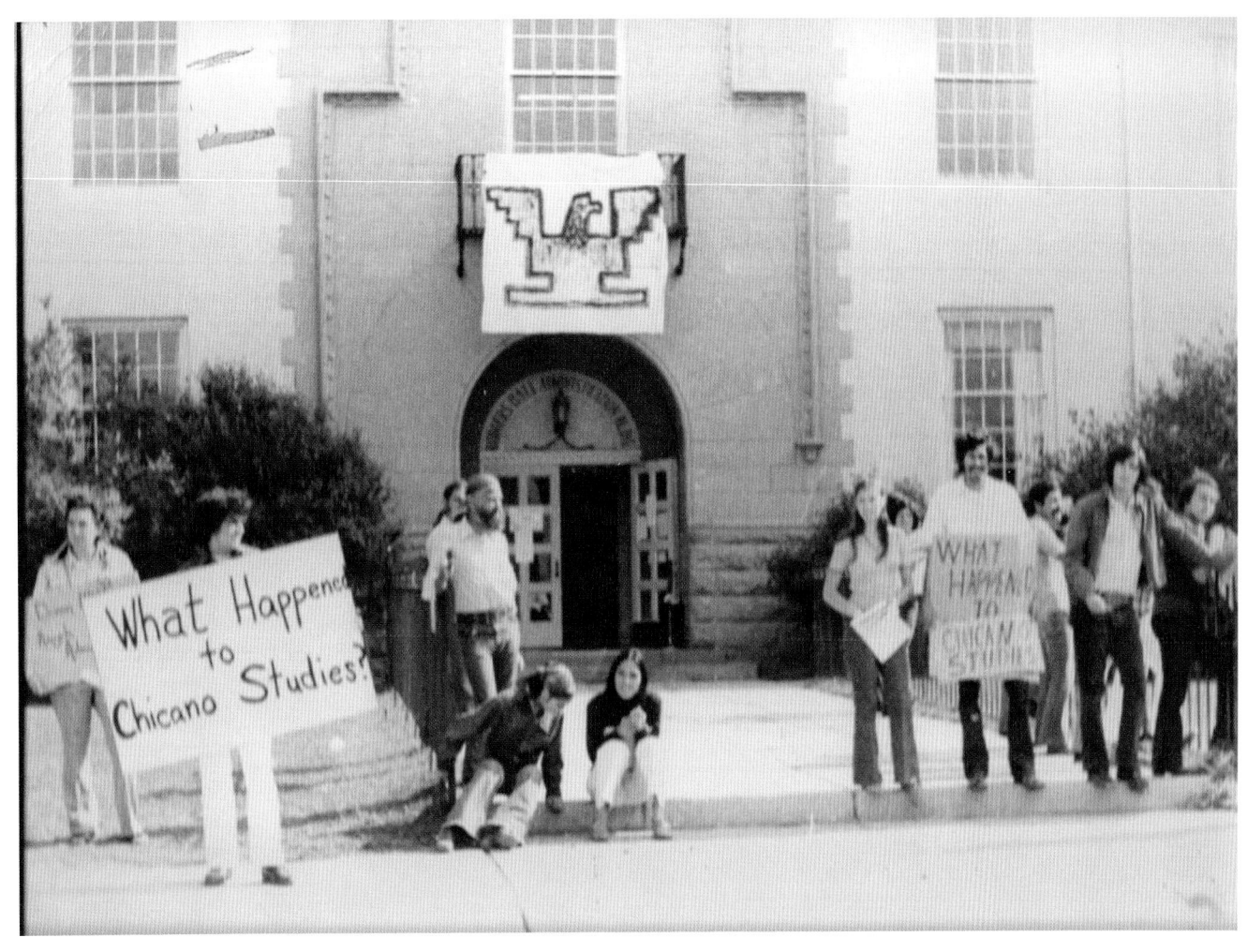

PLATE 145. *What Happened to Chicano Studies?* 1973. Silver gelatin print, 9″ × 13 ½″.
Private collection of David Montoya and Susan Seymour.

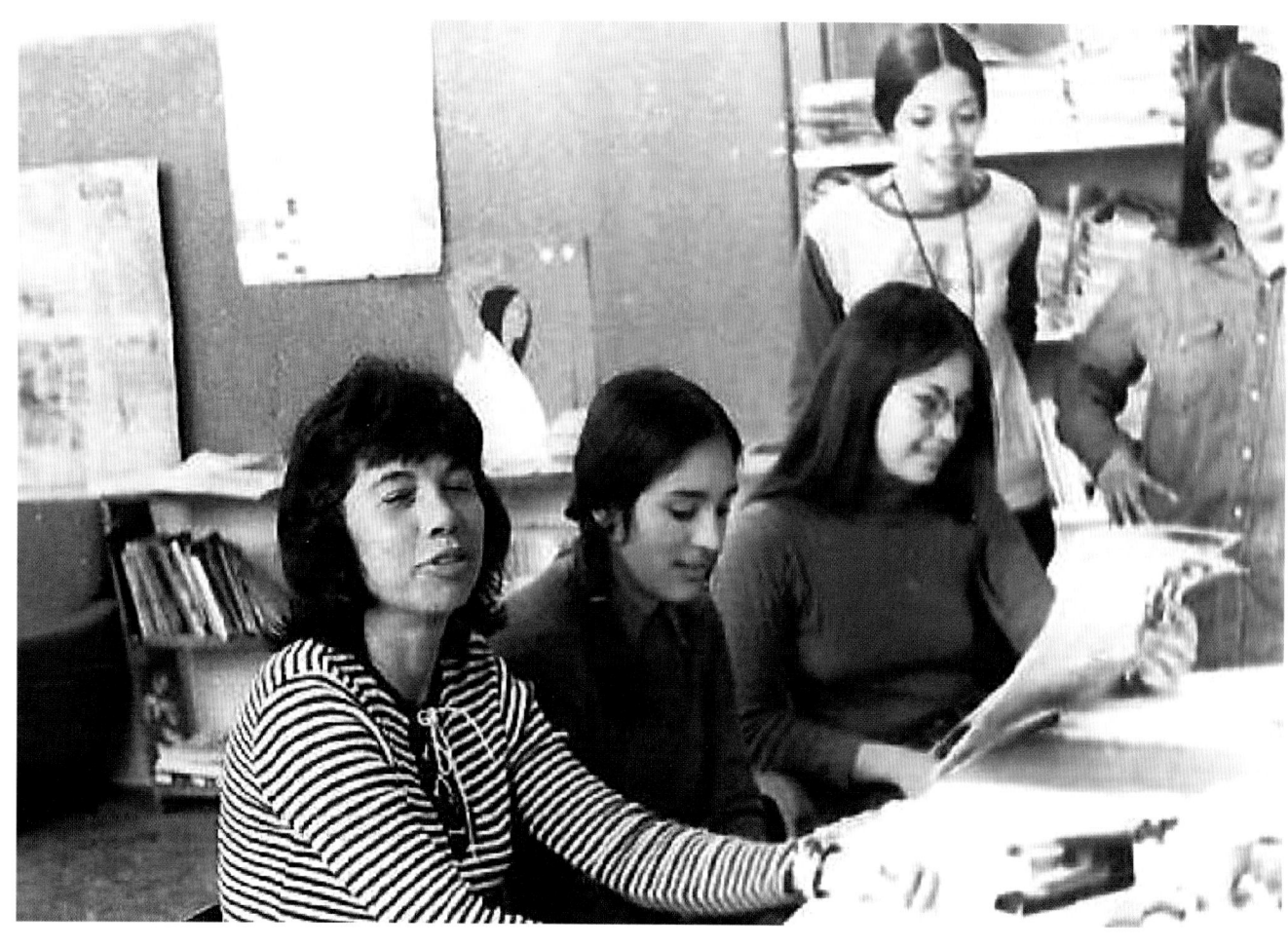

PLATE 146. Unidentified Photographer, *Betita with the Staff of El Grito*, 1973. Silver gelatin print, 4″ × 6″. Private collection of Adelita M. Medina.

Voces del Pueblo